D1710359

Hugh Gaine (1726-1807), publisher of the *New-York Mercury* and the *New-York Gazette and the Weekly Mercury*. (From a portrait attributed to Ralph Earl (1751-1801), privately owned. All rights of reproduction reserved by the owner.)

GENEALOGICAL DATA
FROM COLONIAL
NEW YORK NEWSPAPERS

A Consolidation of Articles
from The New York Genealogical
and Biographical Record

Compiled by
Kenneth Scott

GENEALOGICAL PUBLISHING CO., INC.
BALTIMORE   1977

Consolidated
from selected volumes of
*The New York Genealogical and
Biographical Record*
1964-1976

Reprinted with
A New Introduction and an Index
Genealogical Publishing Co., Inc.
Baltimore, 1977

Library of Congress Catalogue Card Number 77-79068
International Standard Book Number 0-8063-0777-3

Made in the United States of America

CONTENTS

Introduction vii

Genealogical Data from New York's First Newspaper, *from*
    NYG&BR, Vol. XCV (October 1964) 1

Genealogical Data from Zenger's New-York Weekly Journal,
    1733-1751, *from NYG&BR, Vol. XCVI (January 1965)* 14

Genealogical Data from the New-York Mercury, *from NYG&BR,*
    Vol. XCVI (April 1965)–Vol. XCIX (April 1968) 29

Genealogical Data from the New York Gazette and the Weekly
    Mercury, *from NYG&BR, Vol. XCIX (October 1968)–Vol.*
    CVII (October 1976) 129

Index 245

INTRODUCTION

It was not until November, 1725, when New York City had a population of approximately 7,500, that its first newspaper, *The New-York Gazette,* a weekly, was established by William Bradford (1663-1752), a printer from England. He came to Pennsylvania in 1685 and in 1693 removed to New York, where he held the position of Crown Printer from that date to 1742. At about that time Henry DeForeest, his former apprentice, went into partnership with Bradford and together they brought out the paper until its discontinuance in November, 1744.

The second newspaper in the city, the *New-York Weekly Journal,* was established on 5 November 1733 as an anti-administration publication. Its backers were Lewis Morris, James Alexander, and William Smith, and its editor was John Peter Zenger (1697-1746). (Zenger came from Germany at the age of 13, and, since his father died on shipboard, the governor of New York apprenticed the lad in 1711 to William Bradford.) In 1734 the Governor's Council had certain numbers of the *Journal* burned, while the editor was arrested and imprisoned. In April the courageous printer was tried, and the jury brought in a verdict of not guilty, a great victory for freedom of the press. After Zenger's death his widow, Anna Catharine, published the paper up to December, 1748. The Zengers' son continued the *Journal* until publication ceased in 1751.

The *New-York Weekly Post-Boy,* New York's third newspaper, appeared first on 3 January 1743, published by James Parker (*c.* 1714-1770), who was born in Woodbridge, New Jersey, was apprenticed to William Bradford, and, as a runaway, worked for Benjamin Franklin in Philadelphia. The paper continued under management of Parker and others until its termination in 1773.[1]

Hugh Gaine (1726/7-1807), who was born in Belfast, Ireland, and learned the printing business there, came to New York in 1745. There he worked with James Parker until 1752, when he founded the *New-York Mercury*—whose title was later changed to the *New-York Gazette and the Weekly Mercury*—which continued publication through 10 November 1783.

Another printer from abroad was James Rivington (1724-1802), who on 22 April 1773 established his *New-York Gazetteer.* The paper was well printed and edited and met with great success. Unhappily for the printer his Tory sympathies incurred the wrath of the Sons of Liberty, who on 27 November 1775 broke into his plant, wrecked his press and carried off the type. In 1777, however, Rivington returned triumphantly from England, to which he had fled in January, 1776, and as the King's Printer brought out a newspaper which he continued throughout the remainder of the war under various titles—*Rivington's New-York Loyal Gazette*, the *Royal Gazette*, and finally *Rivington's New-York Gazette and Universal Advertiser*.[2]

These were the leading newspapers of the Colonial and Revolutionary Periods, though there were a few others: Henry DeForeest's *New-York Evening Post*, 1744-1753, William Weyman's *New-York Gazette*, 1759-1767, and Robertson's *Royal American Gazette*, 1777-1783. The colonial newspapers (with the exception of Rivington's *Royal Gazette*, which appeared weekly and semi-weekly) were printed as weeklies, usually consisting of four pages, with occasional supplementary issues. Their contents included treatises on various subjects, essays, poetry, proceedings of Parliament and colonial assemblies, messages of governors and addresses to the governors, European and West Indian news, shipping news, incidents culled from the press of other colonies, and many advertisements. Clarence S. Brigham, in the introduction to his *History and Bibliography of American Newspapers, 1690-1820*, comments: "No history of a town or city can be written without recourse to its newspapers. In the eighteenth and early nineteenth centuries even the advertisements have unique value in social and economic study." He might well have added, "and for genealogical research *par excellence*."

In this volume may be found items yielding information concerning places of origin, marriages, births, deaths, ages, status, and residences—all abstracted from four New York newspapers, the two earliest (Bradford's and Zenger's) and the two published by Hugh Gaine, covering, in all, the years 1726 through most of 1783. The material, which appeared serially in *The New York Genealogical and Biographical Record* between 1964 and 1976, is here reprinted by kind permission of the Board of Trustees of the New York Genealogical and Biographical Society, with the addition of an index containing the names of some 10,000 persons. (The publisher is indebted to Mrs. Judy Teschke for typing this index.)

Coverage is not only of New York, for among individuals mentioned are those from all the other colonies, especially New Jersey, which had no newspaper in the Colonial Period, New England, Pennsylvania, and Maryland.

Notes

[1] See Kenneth Scott, *Genealogical Data from The New York Post-Boy, 1743-1777*, published in 1970 by the National Genealogical Society, Washington, D.C.

[2] See Kenneth Scott, *Rivington's New York Newspaper; Excerpts from a Loyalist Press*, published in 1973 by the New-York Historical Society.

GENEALOGICAL DATA FROM NEW YORK'S FIRST NEWSPAPER

The New-York Historical Society has assembled photostatic copies of all known numbers of William Bradford's *New-York Gazette*. From these have been abstracted all items 1726-1744, which throw light on places of origin, ages, marriages, deaths and family relationships of individuals in America. The material is by no means limited to New York, for it yields much information about other provinces, especially Pennsylvania, New Jersey and the New England colonies. In cases of runaway servants it is to be noted that detailed descriptions are to be found in the full accounts in the newspaper. In the following abstracts, the numbers in parentheses give the month, day and year of the issue of the newspaper in which each item appears.

Harrison, Col. John, dec'd.—estate of (4/11/26)
Willet, Widow Frances, NYC (6/20/26)
Byerly, Thomas (member of Council of N. Y.), dec'd.— (7/4/26)
Green, Capt. John—killed by mutineers aboard ship (7/11/26)
Fly, William (from Boston?)—executed July 9 for mutiny (7/18/26)
Cole, Samuel (from Boston?)—executed July 9 for mutiny (7/18/26)
Condick, George (from Boston?)—executed July 9 for mutiny (7/18/26)
Greenvil, Henry (from Boston?)—executed July 9 for mutiny (7/18/26)
Child, Cephas, six sons (eldest 14) of—burned to death July 17 at Wrights Town, Bucks Co., Pa. (8/1/26)
Drasdale, Major (Gov. of Va.)—died March 17 (8/22/26)
Lane, William—died Sept. 4 on board ship *Delasay*, John Williams master, bound for Jamaica (10/3/26)
Markham, Joanna, widow of Capt. Wm. Markham (former Lt.-Gov. of Pa.)—died in NYC Oct. 4 (10/10/26)
Waters, William (b. in Hartfordshire), age c. 35—runaway from Stephen Beaks of Chester Co., Pa. (10/31/26)
White, Peter, hatter, age c. 60—escaped from Amboy, N. J., jail (11/1/26)
Rudyard, John, late of Perth Amboy, dec'd.—estate of (4/17/27)
Dunster, Charles, late of Perth Amboy, dec'd.—estate (4/17/27)
Cranston, Samuel (for several yrs. Gov. of R. I.)—died Wed., Apr. 26 (5/15/27)
Leonard, John, of Perth Amboy—murdered by Indian King Wequalia (6/26/27)
Dulany, William (an Irishman), age c. 20—runaway from Walter Dongan of Staten Island (7/3/27)
Wequalia (Indian king)—executed at Perth Amboy, June 30, for murder (7/10/27)
Adams, John, of Boston, age. c. 30—died in well in Boston, Wed., July 19 (8/7/27)
Reardon, Thomas, of Boston, age. c. 20 (servant of John Adams)—died in well in Boston, Wed., July 19 (8/7/27)
Garland, Sylvester, dec'd. his plantation at head of Apoquinomie Creek in New Castle Co. for sale (8/14/27)
Conalley, William (an Irishman), weaver, age c. 24—runaway from Joseph Forman of Freehold, Monmouth Co., N. J. (9/18/27)
Hill, John, brasier, age c. 22—runaway from John Hyat of Philadelphia (10/16/27)
Waters, Sergt. James, late of NYC, dec'd—estate (11/6/27)

1

Gordon, Widow—her property 2 mi. above Amboy Ferry on Raritan River (3/18, 27-28)

Barberie, Peter, dec'd.—late partner of John Moore (3/18/ 27-28)

Hebon, Barnt, cooper, age c. 24—runaway from Joost Soye of Middlesex Co. N. J. (4/1/28)

Gordon, William (a Scotchman), age c. 26—runaway from William Cox of North East, Md. (5/13/28)

Jackson, Thomas, sadler, age c. 30—runaway from William Cox of North East, Md. (5/13/28)

Robinson, Samuel, age c. 20—runaway from William Cox of North East, Md. (5/13/28)

Classon, Nicholas, printer, age c. 21—runaway from Andrew Bradford of Philadelphia . (6/17/28)

Grimes, John, sailor—killed July 15 by David Simes, carpenter, on board brigantine *Rachel and Betty* of Whitehaven (8/5/28)

Cheney, Thomas (a Welshman), age c. 21—runaway from Stephen Onion of Principio Ironworks, Caecil Co., Md. (8/26/28)

Gibeons, David (an Irishman), age c. 25—runaway from Stephen Onion of Principio Ironworks, Caecil Co., Md. (8/26/28)

Evat, Ann, late of NYC, dec'd—estate (9/2/28)

Paxton, Andrew, late of Philadelphia—ref. to heir of (9/17/28)

Cooper, Elianor, late of NYC, dec'd.—estate (3/17/ 28-29)

Menzies, John (late Judge of Court of Vice Admiralty in Boston), dec'd.—successor appointed (4/28/29)

Smith, John (speaks like "a North Britain"), age c. 25—runaway from John Haskoll of NYC (4/28/29)

Yaff (a Negro, born in America), age c. 35—runaway from James Alexander of NYC (6/30/29)

Shennan, John (an Irishman), age c. 28—escaped July 2 from jail of New Castle Co. (7/7/29)

Smith, Thomas (a "young" man), stocking weaver, recently an usher—runaway from James Denune, master of the Free-school in Prince Georges Co. (7/7/29)

Weems, Capt. James, late of NYC, dec'd.—estate (7/7/ 29)

Johnston, James (late High Sheriff of Middlesex Co.), dec'd.—successor appointed (9/8/29)

Hill, Capt. Richard (late member of Council of Pa. and alderman of Phila.)—died Philadelphia of Sept. 5 (9/8/29)

Burnet, William (Gov. of Mass., born in The Hague in 1688, the son of the Rev. Gilbert Burnet, Bishop of Sarum)—died in Boston, 10:25 P.M. on Sunday, Sept. 8, age 42 (9/15/29 and 9/29/29)

Byrn, Edward (an Irishman), age c. 21—runaway from Michael Kearny of Perth Amboy (9/15/29)

Hues, Malaky (a servant "boy")—runaway from Alexander Mackaowell of Perth Amboy (9/15/29)

Janaway, William, dec'd.—land at the Fresh-Water, NYC, for sale (9/22/29)

Harris, Rev. Henry (one of ministers of Kings Chapel in Boston)—died in 42nd year about 10 P.M. on Monday, Oct. 11, in Boston (10/20/29)

Peter (an Indian), age c. 25—runaway from Capt. Andrew Meed living on Nancemund River, Va. (11/17/29)

Hayman, Charles Chasbar (a mulatto, born in Sweedland), age c. 20—runaway from Capt. Andrew Meed living on Nancemund River, Va. (11/17/29)

Ashley, John, late of Hempstead, L. I., dec'd.—estate (1/6/29-30)

Hammond, Joseph, age c. 20—runaway from brigantine *Frances* at NYC (3/23/29-30)

Orvis, David (prisoner for debt), age c. 36—escaped from jail of Westchester Co., N. Y. (4/27/30)

Chambers, Jame (prisoner for debt), age c. 30—escaped from jail of Westchester Co., N. Y. (4/27/30)

Lloyd, Elianor, new-born child of—the mother a servant of Thomas Inglis, of NYC, victualer (5/18/30)

Fincher, Henry (a West Country man), house-carpenter, mason and pump maker, age c. 26—runaway from Nicholas Matthisen of NYC, brewer (5/18/30)

Quash (a Negro), age c. 24—runaway from Cornelius De Peyster of NYC (5/18/30)

Clause (a Negro), age c. 27—runaway from Solomon Bates of Elizabeth Town (6/1/30)

Grimes, John, house-carpenter, age c. 21—runaway from William Parks, printer, of Annapolis, Md. (6/1/30)

Folks, Isaiah, age c. 30—escaped from jail of Burlington, N. J. (7/20/30)

Farrant, John, age. c. 19—runaway from Richard Bishop of NYC (8/17/30)

Dunn, John, tailor, late of NYC, dec'd. (widow named Mary)—estate (8/17/30)

De Peyster, Cornelia, dec'd.—estate (8/30/30)

Cockram (or Cockrem), Capt. Philip, late of NYC—killed by Spaniards (9/7/30)

Elrington, Widow Christina, of N. J.—act of N. J. Assembly naturalizing her (9/7/30)

Scipio (a Negro), cooper, age c. 22—for sale at house of Benjamin D'harriette' in NYC (9/21/30)

Cummins, Robert (a Scotchman), joiner, age c. 21—runaway from John Copson of North East (10/12/30)

Lyell, David, dec'd. (execs.: widow Catherine Lyell, David Lyell and Fenwick Lyell)— property for sale in N. J. at Middletown Point, Perth Amboy, Barngat and Crosswicks (11/9/30)

Sinclair, John, age c. 24 or 25—runaway from John Bell of NYC (11/9/30)

Jump, Capt., from Boston—killed by Negroes on board ship bound from Guinea Coast to Boston (12/7/30)

Stevens, James (Surveyor-General of H.M.'s Customs in North America)—died in Boston on Friday, Nov. 27 (12/7/30)

Long, John (servant of Jonathan Jones of Kingess, Pa.) while leading a horse over Cobb's Creek was thrown off bridge and drowned on Sunday, Nov. 29 (12/15/30)

Mitchell, Mr.—drowned at Newbury, Mass., Thursday, Dec. 1 (12/29/30)

Wentworth, John (Lt.-Gov. of N. H.) died Sat. morning, Dec. 12 (1/4/30-31)

Rescarricks, George, late of Perth Amboy, dec'd.—estate (1/4/30-31)

Reading, Capt., of ship *Katharine* of NYC—lost at sea (1/19/30-31)

Heathcote, George, late of N. Y., dec'd—estate (1/26/30-31)

Hoskins, Stephen (master of the brigantine *Keith*)—died on voyage from Jamaica to Philadelphia (3/22/30-31)

Price, Walter (formerly Collector and Naval Officer for ports of Salem, Marblehead, etc.), dec'd. (4/5/31)

Grislie, John (tailor by trade), drummer, age c. 40—deserted at Albany from Capt. William Dick's Independent Company of Fuziliers (4/5/31)

Lamb, Thomas, shoemaker, age c. 30—deserted at Albany from Capt. William Dick's Independent Company of Fuziliers (4/5/31)

Cranfurd, Joseph (born in Ireland), tailor, age c. 22—deserted at Albany from Capt. William Dick's Independent Company of Fuziliers (4/5/31)

Crondel, James (alias Samuel Cranson), shoemaker, age c. 24, from Musketo Cove, L. I.— deserter, supposed lurking on L. I., where father is a blacksmith (4/5/31)

Barberie, John, dec'd.—estate to be sold by his son John (4/5/31)

Penn, Springet—reported dead in Ireland in letters to Phila. (5/3/31)

Heldege, Peter ("young" man), tailor,—runaway from Andrew Peterson of New Castle Co. (5/10/31)

Walter, Capt. Robert, of NYC (member of Council and 2nd Judge of the Province of N. Y.)—died in NYC on Wed., June 16, age 67 (6/21/31)

Montgomerie, John (Gov. of N. Y.)—died at Fort George in NYC at 4 A.M. on Thursday, July 1; buried July 2 in King's Chapel (7/5/31)

Legrange, Johannes, age 106—lately died 26 miles above Albany, N. Y. (7/5/31)

How, Lt. Samuel, of Framingham, Mass. ,above 60—died in church on Sunday, July 18 (8/9/31)

Staats, Dr., dec'd.—ref. to land of (8/30/31)

Cousens, Barney—ref. to his son and heir, John Cousens (8/30/31)

Williams, Thomas, butcher, age c. 22—runaway from Richard Bishop of Amboy, N. J. (10/5/31)

Waters, Foster, of Jamaica, L. I.—died of smallpox (1/18/31-32)

Corey, David (of Southold, L. I.), little son of, killed by a horse on Feb. 27 (4/3/32)

Outman, Widow Samma (or Famma), late of NYC, dec'd.—estate (4/3/32)

Eirs, William, Esq., late of Woodbridge, N. J.—estate (4/3/32)

Poyer, Rev. Thomas (late rector of church at Jamaica, L. I., dec'd.—estate (5/8/32)

Hold, John, late of NYC, dec'd.—brew house and malt house for sale (5/8/32)

Claus (a Negro), age c. 28—runaway from Solomon Baites of Elizabeth Town, N. J. (5/8/32)

Eight, Widow Mary, of NYC—about 18 yrs. ago lent £100 to Dr. Jacob Moon (5/15/32)

Nicoll. William, late of NYC, dec'd.—land to be sold by his son William (5/22/32)

Levit, William, of Exeter (   ), age c. 13—accidentally shot by Sam Scribner, age c. 13 (6/26/32)

Andrew, John (formerly a servant of Alderman Stuyvesant of NYC), age c. 18 or 19— runaway from David McCamly of Orange Co., N. Y. (7/10/32)

Hood, Mrs., of Boston—died suddenly in Boston on June 9 (7/17/32)

Haber, Frederick, age c. 16—on July 17 ran away from his father, Christian Haber, of Queenbury, in the Camp in Albany Co., N. Y. (8/7/32)

Prout, Ebenezer (living near Trenton, N. J.), 9 year old son of,—killed Aug. 9 by light- ning (8/21/32)

Holton, two brothers, ages 5 and 7—died of an opiate in Charleston, S. C., on Wed., July 5 (9/11/32)

Moor, Capt. John (from N. H.)—murdered off Guinea Coast (9/11/32)

Rogers, Mr. (of Pembrook,   )—murdered Sept. 12 by an Indian (a runaway servant of Mr. Howard of Bridgewater (9/25/32)

Cook, Kathrine (of Newport, R. I.)—murdered by Thomas Hammett (10/23/32)

Ivey, John (born at Barnstaple in west of England), cooper, age c. 30—runaway from James Wallace of NYC (10/30/32)

Perkins, Capt. (of Newport, R. I.)—killed on sloop off Guinea Coast by Negroes (11/30/32)

Sarah (a mulatto), age c. 24—runaway from Joseph Reade of NYC (11/20/32)

Turner, Joshua, c. 15 year-old daughter of and also c. 12 year-old daughter of—perished in fire in Boston on Nov. 4 (11/27/32)

Moore, John (for upwards of 30 years Collector of Customs at Phila.), age 74—died in Philadelphia on Sat. A.M., Dec. 2 (12/26/32)

Middleton, Aaron, clockmaker, age c. 26—runaway from Isaac Pearson of Burlington, N. J. (12/26/32)

Vincent, Francis, sailmaker, late of NYC, dec'd.—estate (3/30/33)

Parker, James, printer, age c. 19—runaway from William Bradford of NYC (5/21/33)

Thurston, William, late of NYC—estate (6/11/33)

Campbell, Archanle, dec'd.—widow is Mary Campbell of NYC (6/11/33)

Scott, John, late of NYC, merchant, dec'd.—widow is Marianne (6/18/33)

Stoffil (or Stoffels), an Indian, cooper, carpenter, wheelwright, butcher, age c. 40—run- away from Judith Vincent of Mount Pleasant, Monmouth Co., N. J. (6/18/33 and 7/1/34)

Mills, Alexander, of NYC, dec'd.—estate (6/18/33)

Byfield, Nathaniel, late of Boston (Judge of Court of Vice Admiralty, First Judge of Court of General Sessions of the Peace and Inferior Court of Common Pleas of Suffolk Co, member of Council) died in Boston, age 80, about 12 P.M., Tue., June 5 (6/25/33)

Smith, William—stabbed to death on highway near Flushing, L. I., by a tinker named Edward King (6/25/33)

Holland, Thomas (an Irishman), age c. 18—runaway from Thomas Hall, of NYC, cordwainer (7/23/33)

Sullivan, John (an Irishman), age c. 18 runaway from Thomas Hall, of NYC, cordwainer (7/23/33)

Teer (an Indian), age c. 18 or 19—runaway from James Jackson of Flushing, L. I. (7/23/33)

Leyster, Jacob, late of NYC, dec'd.—estate (7/30/33)

Harding, Mrs. Amaziah, of Eastham on Cape Cod, Mass., murdered about middle of July, supposedly by her husband (8/13/33)

Frary, William (born in Suffolk, Eng.), smith, age c. 30—runaway from Bermuda on July 3 (9/13/33)

Hawkins, Thomas (born in Cambridgeshire, Eng.), age c. 21—runaway from Bermuda on July 3 (8/13/33)

Van Cliff (or Kliff), Widow Geetie—ref. to heirs of (9/10/33)

King, John, tinker—executed Sat., Sept. 15 at Jamaica, L. I. for murder of William Smith (9/17/33)

Mekay, Daniel, late of Penalopon in Freehold, N. J., dec'd.—estate (9/17/33)

Lander, Mr.—killed June 18 by Negroes on ship while coming down River Gambia (9/24/33)

Jack (a Negro), age c. 30—runaway from Robert Peirson of Nottingham, near Trentown, N. J. (10/1/33)

Marrow, Martin (a Frenchman), age c. 40—runaway from Robert Todd of NYC (10/15/33)

Thompson, John, late of Brunswick, N. J., dec'd.—estate (10/29/33)

Pittomee, John (an Indian), 3 year-old son of—died at Natick, Mass. (11/26/33)

Van Cortlandt, Widow Geertruydt (husband was Col. Stephanis Van Cortlandt), dec'd. —estate (12/10/33)

Goardon, Robert, late of Vallentown, R. I.—crushed to death by a tree on Wed., Dec. 5 (12/14/33)

Hunt, Jonathan—killed at Newtown, L. I., by William Petit, of Newtown, cordwainer, on Dec. 19 (12/24/33)

Joe (a Negro slave)—killed Dec. 19 at Newtown, L. I., by his master, William Petit (12/24/33)

Richman, William (born in Wiltshire, Eng.), shoemaker, age c. 22—runaway from Obediah Eldridge of Philadelphia (1/7/33-34)

Sanford, Benjamin, master of a sloop (from Newport, R. I. ?)—drowned at sea on Nov. 21 (1/14/33-34)

Munson, Mrs., of New London, Conn., age 74—drowned in well or spring on Dec. 7 (1/14/33-34)

Van Dyke, Mrs. (wife of the silversmith of NYC), died in NYC on Tuesday night, Jan. 8 (1/14/33-34)

Solem, Cornelius, late of New Brunswick, N. J., age c. 40—escaped Jan. 13 from jail of Perth Amboy (1/21/33-34)

Searle, Capt. John, dec'd.—estate (1/28/33-34)

Bell, Mr. (an "aged" man), prisoner in Boston jail, was killed on Sat., Jan. 22, by a fellow prisoner named Amesby (2/11/33-34)

Van Gelder, Mr., of NYC, on Sunday, Feb. 17 had a fit, fell into the fire and was burned to death (2/18/33-34)

Hedges, Stephen, late of Southampton, L. I., age c. 19—accidentally killed by his own gun (2/25/33-34)

Wood, Thomas, of N. J.—died in latter part of Jan. a few miles from New London, Conn. (2/25/33-34)

Rasper, John (born in Germany), age c. 24—runaway from John Copson of Caecil Co., Md. (4/22/34))

Thomas, Evan (a Welshman), age c. 22—runaway from Thomas Potts of Colebrook-Dale Ironworks, Phila. Co., Pa. (5/13/34)

Curfey, Jo (a Negro), born in Pa., age c. 20—runaway from Thomas Potts of Colebrook- Dale Ironworks, Phila. Co., Pa. (5/13/34)

Hole, John, late of NYC, dec'd.—brewhouse malthouse and lots for sale (6/3/34)

Palmer, Charles (a Quaker, son of William Palmer of Litchfield, Eng.), age between 20 and 30—sought as heir to an estate (6/10/34)

Pain, Edward, potter ,age c. 26—runaway from Samuel Hale of Phila., potter (6/10/34)

Plumer, Ensign Benjamin, of Rowley (   ), died Saturday eve., June 22, from kick of his horse (6/15/34)

Frasier, Mrs., of Phila.—died of the heat on Sat. night, July 7 (7/29/34)

Worthington, James, of Byberry, Pa., died of heat on Sunday, July 7 (7/29/34)

Lee, Jacob, gardner, died in or near Phila. of heat on Tues., July 9 (7/29/34)

Goforth, Aaron (of Phila.?), daughter of—died Tue. eve., July 9, of heat (7/29/34)

Davenport, Samuel, of Shrewsbury, Monmouth Co., N. J., age c. 25—accidentally killed by fellow soldier at training (7/29/34)

Pearce, Capt. Vincent, commander of H.M.S. *Winchelsea*—his wife a daughter of Col. Lewis Morris of Morrisania (7/29/34)

Norris, Capt. John, master of the pink *Tartar*—his wife a daughter of Col. Lewis Morris of Morrisania (7/29/34)

Parslow, Stephen (an Englishman), blacksmith, age c. 22—runaway from William Cox of New Brunswick, N. J. (7/29/34)

Dent, Abigail, of Portsmouth, N. H., age 17—murdered on Sat. eve., July 7, supposedly by two sailors, Thomas Pachal and Thomas Daniels (8/12/34)

Wells, Rev. Thomas (pastor of First Church of Amesbury, Mass.), age 88—died July 11 (8/12/34)

Trott, Benjamin, of Falmouth in Casco Bay, age c. 9—murdered July 9 by an Indian woman named Patience (8/14/34)

Pygan, Mrs. Lydia, of New London, Conn., age 90—died there Sat., July 20. She was born March 9, 1644, at Saybrook, Conn., the first female child born there (8/12/34)

Wheeton, Mr., of Newport, R. I.—died there on morning of Aug. 4 (8/26/34)

Moore, Deliverance—eloped from husband, James Moore of Woodbridge, N. J. (8/26/34)

Bell, Thomas (of Boston?)—murdered by John Ormesby (9/9/34)

Todd, Mr. (a brother of Capt. Todd, out of Phila.)—died in a wreck at sea (9/16/34)

M'Donel, —, tailor, age c. 35—runaway from John Fenton of Freehold, Monmouth Co., N. J. (10/7/34)

Garabrant, Francis, dec'd.—son-in-law is Cornelius Flamon (10/28/34)

Coffin, Ephraim (son of Jonathan Coffin of Nantucket), age c. 20—drowned at sea (12/30/34)

Clark, Mr. (from Nantucket), age c. 17 accidentally shot and killed at sea on board a Nantucket sloop (12/30/34)

Morphy, John (an Irishman), shoemaker, age c. 30—runaway from John Dunlap, of NYC, cordwainer (1/7/34-35)

Force, Benjamin, late of Woodbridge, N. J., dec'd.—estate (1/21/34-35)

Job (a Nantucket Indian), age c. 23—runaway from William Legget of Westchester, N. Y. (3/11/34-35)

Hezekiah (a Nantucket Indian), age c. 20—runaway from William Legget of Westchester, N. Y. (3/11/34-35)

Parmyter, Thomas—widow of, living at White Stone in Flushing, Queens Co., N. Y. (3/18/34-35)

Bowman, Mary (born in England), servant of John Williams (keeper of the jail of Monmouth Co. at Freehold, N. J.—she aided Eleanor White, convicted of murder, to escape (5/12/35)

Coggesholl, Joshua, of R. I.—killed April 30 as result of accident on horseback (5/12/35)

Nenegrare, Charles Augustus (chief sachem of the Narragansetts), age c. 25—died May 18 at Westerly, Mass., leaving a widow and a son of four months (5/26/35)

Hews, Malaciah, plasterer and painter, age c. 20—runaway from Morris Carill of Trent-Town, N. J. (5/26/35)

Eldrington, Francis, late of Somerset Co., N. J., dec'd.—estate (6/2/35)

Hunter, Samuel (born Dumfrieze, Scotland), tailor, age c. 50—runaway presumably from William Bradford of NYC (6/2/35)

Harding, James, apprentice carpenter, age. c. 19—runaway from John Bell, of NYC, carpenter (6/9/35)

Woodward, Joseph, age c. 19 or 20—runaway from John Butler, master of the ship *James and Joseph* at NYC (6/30/35)

Lurting, Col. Robert (Mayor of NYC)—died July 3 (7/14/35)

Bellarow, Widow (of NYC)—property for sale (7/14/35)

Symes, John (High Sheriff of NYC and NY County)—killed Wed., July 16, by a cannon that burst (7/21/35)

Courtlandt, Miss, only daughter of Hon. Col. Courtlandt (member of the Council of N. Y.)—killed Wed., July 16, by cannon that burst (7/21/35)

Romur, Alderman, son-in-law of—killed Wed., July 16, by a cannon that burst (7/21/35)

King, John, of Boston (a "young" man)—killed some 4 or 5 miles from Philadelphia on July 16 by an accident (8/4/35)

Redstrake, John, three year old son of—died at Pennsneck, West New Jersey, from eating poisonous mushrooms (8/4/35)

Johnson, Mrs. (of Woodbury, Conn.)—died from fire early in July (8/4/35)

Tork, John (of Boston), age c. 35—died in a well (8/18/35)

Williamson, William, late of Elizabeth Town, N. J., dec'd.—ref. to his widow Margaret; mills and lot for sale (8/18/35)

Hendricks, Abraham, shoemaker, age c. 19—runaway from John Ross of Elizabeth Town, N. J. (8/18/35)

Fitzroy, Hon. Charles(only son of Lord Augustus Fitzroy)—died in NYC, Aug. 10 (8/25/35)

Le Montet (or Le Montes?), John, dec'd.—estate (8/25/35)

Tappen, Aneke (late of Kingston, Ulster Co., N. Y.)—eloped from her husband Jurian (8/25/35)

Robinson, Capt. Robert (master of the *Oliver*)—drowned Monday night, Aug. 4, at the port of Charlestown, S. C. (9/8/35)

Bourdeaux, Thomas (director of the Royal Russian and Brandenboerg Co.)—died on Island of St. Thomas, July 2 (9/8/35)

Howell, Mathew, age c. 24—runaway from George Tilldine of Reading Town (9/8/35)

Dunn, Jacob, age 8—drowned at Phila. in river, Sat., Sept. 6 (9/22/35)

Vining, Benjamin (Collector of Customs at Salem, Mass.)—died at Salem, N. J., during week of Sept. 15-22 (9/22/35)

Gordon, Robert (Judge of the Courts of New-Castle and Probate of Wills)—died during week of Sept. 15-22 (9/22/35)

Tunis, Hannah—eloped from her husband Peter Tunis of Elizabeth Town, N. J. (9/29/35)

Boel, Thomas, late of Freehold, N. J., dec'd.—estate (10/27/35)

Tom (a Negro), age c. 35—runaway from Zebulon Stout of Sommerset Co., N. J. (10/27/35)

Lurting, William (son of late Col. Robert Lurting), age c. 13—drowned off NYC on Tuesday eve., Oct. 28 (11/3/35)

Hunter, Major General, dec'd.—real estate in N. Y. and N. J. for sale (12/15/35)

Macoy, William (an Irishman), age c. 25—runaway from John Lester of Hempstead, Queens Co., N. Y. (12/15/35)

Hatfield, Matthias (of Elizabeth Town, N. J.), young son of—accidentally killed by falling tree (1/13/ 35-36)

Tobey (a Negro), age 22—slave of Obadiah Hunt of NYC, tavernkeeper, for sale (1/13/ 35-36)

Wooster (a Negro), age 14 or 15—slave of Obadiah Hunt of NYC, tavernkeeper, for sale (1/13/35-36)

Beynton, Mr. (of Newberry, Mass.), 4 children of—died of the distemper, two on Sat., Dec. 28, and the other two on Sun., Dec. 29 (1/20/35-36)

Campbell, Archibald (late of NYC?), dec'd.—estate (2/10/35-36)

Christophers, Richard (Postmaster at New London, Conn.)—died there (2/17/35-36)

Knight, Mr. (of Newberry, Mass.), 3 children of—died in January of the distemper (2/17/35-36)

Brook, Henry (Collector of Customs at Lewis-Town on Delaware)—died Fri., Feb. 7, at Philadelphia (2/17/35-36)

Cook, Cornelius (of Caecil Co., Md.), two children of—burned to death in January (2/24/35-36)

Apty, Thomas, plasterer—died Feb. 2 at the Red Lyon Tavern in Elbow-Lane, Philadelphia, after drinking a gallon of "Cyder Royal" (2/24/35-36)

Bickford, Mr. (of Portsmouth, N. H.), 3 children of—died of the distemper (3/2/35-36)

Heard, Mrs. (wife of Capt. John Heard, of Kittery)—died of the distemper (3/2/35-36)

Fisher, Margaret, of Dedham, Mass., age 26—died of a "pulmonary pthisis" (3(2/35-36)

Boyntou, Mr., (of Newberry Falls) eight children of—died from the distemper (3/2/35-36)

Jeffers, John, of NYC,—died of apoplexy on Wed., Feb. 24 (3/2/35-36)

Jeffers, Mrs. John, of NYC—died Friday morning, Feb. 26 (3/2/35-36)

Smith, John (of Stamford, Conn.), 7 children of—died of the distemper (3/15/35-36)

Lawrance, Mrs. (wife of a glazier of Somerset Co., N. J.)—murdered by a lodger (3/22/ 35-36)

Cosby, William (Gov. of N. Y.)—died March 10 (4/5/36)

Anderson, John (for 18 days Pres. of Council and Commander in Chief of N. J.) died at Perth Amboy on Sunday, March 27, in 71st year of his age (4/5/36)

Cunningham, Col. (Gov. of Jamaica)—died there of the fever six weeks after his arrival there (4/12/36)

Parris, Alexander, age 74 wanting a few days—died at Charleston, S. C., on Wed., March 9 (his wife, to whom he had been married 41 years, had died about 2 years before) (4/19/36)

Hoff, Mrs. Rachel—eloped from her husband Peter of Somerset Co., N. J. (5/24/36)

Sonmans, Peter, late of Perth Amboy, dec'd.—ref. to widow Sarah (whose eldest brother is Samuel Nevill, of London, Eng.), to John Nevill of Perth Amboy and to Dr. Peter Sonmans of Philadelphia (7/5/36)

Thomas, John (a North Country man), ship carpenter or caulker—runaway from Patrick Creagh and William Medcalf of Annapolis, Md. (7/5/36)

Nevison, Peter (a North Country man), smith or cutler—runaway from Patrick Creagh of Annapolis, Md. (7/5/36)

Manning, Peter (born in New England), butcher or sailor—runaway from Patrick Creagh of Annapolis, Md. (7/5/36)

Voughton, Michel, dec'd.—estate (7/25/36)

White, Mary, late of Oysterbay, dec'd. (late Robert White was her husband see *Gazette* of 12/13/36)—estate (8/2/36)

Gordon, Patrick (Lt. Gov. of Pa. and Counties upon Delaware)—died at Philadelphia on morning of Aug. 5 (8/9/36)

James (a Negro slave)—sentenced to die for rape at Philadelphia on Sat., Aug. 7 (8/9/36)

Heathcote, Martha (widow of Caleb)—died in NYC on Wed., Aug. 18 (8/23/36)

Buckler, Andrew (of Barbados)—probably murdered on his ship on voyage from Dublin to Maryland (8/30/36)

Monroe, Lt., of NYC, dec'd. (9/20/36)

Shurmur, Samuel, late of NYC, merchant, dec'd.—estate; one of execs. is John Shurmur (11/1/36)

Moody, Henry, age c. 20—runaway from Ezekiel Smith of Windsor, Middlesex Co., N. J. (11/8/36)

Daily, Sam, apprentice "boy"—runaway from William Bradford, of NYC, printer (11/15/36)

Rowley, Edward (born in Worstershire, Eng.), a servant boy—runaway from on board the snow *Neptune* at NYC (11/22/36)

Cleeland, Mary—eloped from her husband, Andrew Cleeland of Burlington, N. J. (11/22/36)

Kennedy, Arthald (Collector of Customs at NYC) married Sat. eve., Dec. 4, at NYC, Mrs. Schuyler, widow of late Arent Schuyler (12/6/36)

Denne, Mrs. Elizabeth, late of NYC, dec'd—estate (1/11/ 36-37)

Smith, William, late of NYC, dec'd. (his widow was Susannah)—estate (2/3/36-37)

Maloan, Laughland—killed in Md. (2/17/ 36-37)

Grame, William (of Phila., Pa.)—frozen to death Tue. night, Jan. 18, on road to Frankford, Pa. (2/17/36-37)

Ayres, Joseph—frozen to death on Tue. night, Jan. 18, in Bucks Co., Pa. (2/17/ 36-37)

Sherrard, Francis, of Phila., attorney—drowned in upper part of Brandywine River on Sunday, Jan. 23 (2/17/36-37)

Percy, Alexander, of Phila., attorney—drowned in upper part of Brandywine River on Sunday, Jan. 23 (2/17/36-37)

Clark, Widow, of Boston, age c. 98—died in Boston on Thursday, Jan. 27 (2/17/36-37)

Chauncey, Rev. (minister of Hadley, Mass.), grown son of—died in fire in January (2/17/36-37)

Vanderspiegel, Widdow Anne—plans to turn over glazier's shop to her son John (2/22/36-37)

Harmon, Capt. (of York), wife of—died from burns (3/1/36-37)

Airs, Abraham (of Mass.), wife of—died from burns (3/1/36-37)

Rutgers, Capt. Harmanus (of NYC), wife of—died of a fit about 4 P.M. on Feb. 28 (3/1/36-37)

Faitout, Margarit—eloped from her husband Aaron Faitout of Amboy, N. J. (3/1/36-37); eloped a second time (8/29/37)

Richard, Stephen, late of NYC, dec'd.—estate (3/8/36-37)

Blair, Capt. James—died from exposure on Thursday, Feb. 10, near the harbor of Scituate, Mass (3/22/37)

Dobbs, Mary, age 104 yrs. and 9 mos.—died beginning of March at Barn Island, about 7 miles from NYC; she has a sister, age 102, living in NYC; they are sisters of Col. Wm. Merrit, dec'd., former Mayor of NYC (3/22/37)

Drummond, Evan, Esq., late of Bound Brook, N. J., dec'd.—estate (3/28/37)

We ein, Mary, of White Plains, Township of Rye, Westchester Co., N. Y.—eloped from her husband William (4/4/37)

Mestayer, Elias, late of Shrewsberry, Monmouth Co., N. J., dec'd.—estate (4/11/37)

Rumsey, Widow, of New Castle Co., and her grandaughter—burned to death about March 15 (4/25/37)

Mac Laughlin, James (an Irish boy), age c. 16 runaway from James Jones of Whitestone, L. I. (5/16/37)

Lawrance, Capt. Thomas, wife of, of Hackinsack, N. J., age 94, was buried there on June 2; her husband is aged 97 (6/6/37)

Rynders, Jacob, of NYC—found dead in bed on Thursday morning, June 2; his mother is described as "antient." (6/6/37)

Pitman, Capt. Caleb—killed at Salem, Mass., by lightning on Sat., June 4 (6/27/37)

Mifflin, John, of Philadelphia, married April 22 to Elizabeth Bagnall, daughter of Benjamin Bagnall, merchant (7/11/37)

Hamilton, Edward (an Irishman), forgeman, age c. 26—runaway from Thomas Mayburry of Poole, Philadelphia Co., Pa. (7/11/37)

Johnson, Ebenezer, late of Elizabeth Town, N. J., dec'd.; estate; widow named Sarah (7/11/37)

Van Horn, Capt. Garret (member of N. Y. General Assembly)—died in NYC of pneumonia, in 66th year, between 10 and 11 A.M. on Thursday, July 7 (7/11/37)

Wayne, Robert (an Englishman), age c. 30—runaway from Caledonia Copper Mines in Philadelphia Co., Pa. (7/18/37)

Harrison, William (an Englishman), age c. 28—runaway from Caledonia Copper Mines in Philadelphia Co., Pa. (7/18/37)

Smith, Samuel, of Lyme, Conn., miller—killed June 21 by being caught in machinery; leaves a widow and 10 small children (7/18/37)

Larby, Eliphalet—murdered on May 1 by runaway servants near Great Cape, Capon Creek, Orange Co., Va. (7/25/37)

Riddle, Thomas, of Orange Co., Va.—killed by a Negro slave (7/25/37)

Land, Richard—killed in Orange Co., Va., by a Negro slave (7/25/37)

Alexander, Robert—drowned in Pa. in the Schuylkil on Sunday, July 17 (7/25/37)

Carr, Anne (wife of Wm. Carr, of NYC)—bad behavior of; husband will not be responsible for her debts (8/1/37)

Jack (an Indian), age c. 40-runaway from Joshua Legget of Westchester Co., N. Y. (8/15/37)

Bagnall, Benjamin, Jr. (eldest son of Benjamin Bagnall, of Boston, merchant)—married on Thursday A.M., Aug. 4, in Boston, in old brick meeting house (with Quaker ceremony) to Anna Hawden, daughter of James Hawden of Boston, merchant (8/22/37)

Hambleton, Edward (an Irishman), age c. 26—runaway from Thomas Mayberry of Pool Forge, Pa. (8/22/37)

Patrick, William (who came as a convict from Bristol, Eng.; uses West Country speech), age c. 19—runaway from John Henderson of Freehold, Monmouth Co., N. J. (9/26/37)

French, Hugh—died at sea on way from London to Va. in same ship with Capt. Augustine Washington (10/3/37)

Cox, Dr. John and wife Rebecca—ref. to land in West Jersey purchased from them (10/17/37)

Rothwell, William, age c. 46—runaway from John Mather in Chester, near Philadelphia (10/31/ 37)

Bannister, Thomas—married in Rhode Island on Nov. 14 (12/5/37)

Basset, Thomas (a Bermudian Black-a-moore) married at Stratford to Nancy Cosby (an Irish washerwoman) (12/5/37)

Keir, Alexander (a Scotchman), age c. 24—runaway from Mr. J. Warrell of Trent Town, West New Jersey (12/12/37)

Buckhout, Darkas (alias Tabathy)—eloped from her husband, Peter Buckhout of Newtown, Queens Co., N. Y. (12/19/37)

Jenny (a Negro woman, born in N. Y.), age c. 14 or 15—runaway from John Bell of NYC, carpenter (12/19/37)

Dick, William (captain of one of H.M.'s Independent Companies)—died Dec. 11 in Albany (12/27/37)

Georges, John (Private Secretary to the Proprietors)—died in Phila. on Sunday morning, Dec. 18 (1/9/37-38)

Hutchinson, Col. Samuel (late one of the representatives for Suffolk Co., N. Y.—died Jan. 9 (1/16/37-38)

Vinton, Mr., (of Braintree, Mass.), a child of —— died of "pleuretick Fever and the sore Distemper of the Throat" (2/28/ 37-38)

Gott, John (of Wenham, Mass.), five children of—died of the throat distemper (2/28/37-38)

Cross, Nathan (of Ipswich Hamblets, Mass.), seven children of—died of throat distemper (2/28/37-38)

Stevens, John, late of Perth Amboy, dec'd.—real estate for sale; apply to Campbell Stevens at Rocky-hill or John Stevens at Amboy (3/7/37-38)

Preston, Joseph, blacksmith, age c. 17—runaway from Joseph Oldman of Philadelphia (3/27/38)

Ryon, Peter (an Irishman), age c. 20—runaway from Moses Vernon, of Providence, near Chester, in Chester Co., Pa. (6/12/38)

Adogan, Dennis (an Irishman), age c. 20—runaway from William Lindsay of Providence, near Chester, in Chester Co., Pa. (6/12/38)

Hauxhurt, Sampson, late of Oysterbay, dec'd.—estate; Hannah Hauxhurt is one of executors (6/19/38)

Dowell, William, age c. 23—runaway from Samuel Holmes of Middletown, Monmouth Co., N. J. (7/10/38)

Dean, Joshua (a London convict), age c. 40—runaway in June, 1737, from Alexander Spotswood, of Va., Post-Master General in America (7/17/38)

Coddrington, Capt. Thomas, late of Harlem, the Outward of NYC, dec'd.—estate (7/24/38)

Waldren, Peter (a Negro, born on L. I.), age c. 28—runaway from John Hunt, of Hopewell, Hunterdon Co., West New Jersey (7/31/38)

Wiggins, William, age c. 50—escaped from jail of Jamaica, L. I. (7/31/38)

Langdon, Amos, weaver, age c. 30—escaped from jail of Jamaica, L. I. (7/31/38)

Butterfield, William, age c. 19—runaway from Jonas Foster, of Hempstead, L. I. (8/14/38)

Aske, Capt. Benjamin, dec'd.—land in Dutchess, Queens, Ulster and Orange Counties, N. Y. for sale (8/21/38)

Johnson, Mary—eloped from her husband David, of Monmouth Co., N. J. (9/18/38)

Harry (a Negro slave), age c. 24—runaway from Charles Decker of Staten Island (10/9/38)

Perfect, John (a West Country man), age 36-40—runaway from Humphry Day at Cooper's Ferry, Gloucester Co., N. J., opposite to Phila. (11/20/38)

Putland, Heron, late of Perth Amboy, N. J., dec'd.—estate (11/20/38)

Still, Michael (born in Pa.), collier, age c. 30—runaway from John Burr of Burlington, N. J. (11/27/38)

Barnes, John (alias John Greenwood, alias John Thompson, alias George Brown, born in Lancashire, Eng.)—confession of; executed Nov. 17, 1738, at Newark, Essex Co., N. J. (12/4/38)

Mc Nachten, Neil (born in North Britain), shoemaker—came to Boston, where he lived 9 years; his brother Alexander, of the Island of Isla, has come to America and seeks his brother (12/4/38)

Wilson, John (of Andover, Mass.), 8 children of (eldest 16 or 18)—died of the throat distemper (12/25/38)

Long, Capt.—died on passage from Cowes to America and his ship was wrecked at Block Island (2/ 6 38-39)

Pero (an Indian), age c. 18—runaway from Moses Gombauld, merchant, of NYC (2/6/38-39)

Hooper, Robert Lettice (Chief Justice of N. J. and member of Council)—died at Perth Amboy on Thursday, Feb. 8 (2/13/ 38-39)

Burnet, John (of Perth Amboy, merchant)—died there Thursday eve., Feb. 8 (2/13/38-39)

Hickey, John (an Irishman), age c. 18—runaway from John Markham, living in the Highlands, near Goshen, N. Y. (2/27/38-39)

Lodwick, Col. late of NYC, dec'd.—estate (3/6/38-39)

Smith, Susannah, dec'd.—property at Flushing, L. I., and in NYC for sale (3/6/38-39)

Haszard, Mrs. Mary (widow of Robert Haszard of South Kingston, R. I. and grandmother of the dec'd. George Haszard, late Deputy Gov. of R. I.), age 100—died in R. I. on Jan. 28, 1738/39 (3/20/38-39)

Ingraham, Capt. John (of Boston)—died on Island of Jamaica of smallpox (4/9/39)

March, John, late of NYC—estate (5/14/39)

Smith, James (lately arrived from Cork)—died May 6 in Phila. (5/28/39)

Lasant, John (a Dutch Palatine), age c. 20—runaway from Harmon Richmon, of Piles Grove, Salem Co., N. J. (6/13/39)

Keriger, George Henry (a High Dutch servant), age c. 21—runaway from Anthony Engelbert of NYC, stone cutter (6/13/39)

Collis, Capt. (master of a sloop from Providence, R. I.)—killed about March 1 by Spaniards (6/18/39)

Williams, Joseph (probably from Providence, R. I)—killed about March 1 by Spaniards (6/18/39)

Barbour, William (probably from Providence, R I.)—killed about March 1 by Spaniards (6/18/39)

Royal, Col., age 67—died at Charleston, S. C., Thu., April 6 (6/18/39)

Balie, John, Jr., age 10—died at Warwick, Providence Co., R. I., about the middle of March (7/2/39)

Blake, Widow Jane—property in NYC for sale (7/9/39)

Rickets, Capt., dec'd.—property in NYC (7/30/39)

Howard, James, joiner, age c. 18—runaway from Joshua Delaplaine, of NYC, joiner (8/6/39)

Mackeffee, Daniel, age c. 20—runaway from the sloop *Venus*, Robert Bollard master, at NYC (9/2/39)

Coombs, Richard—to be executed on March 13 at Jamaica, Queens Co., N. Y., for burglary (10/8/39)

Hay, Andrew, late of Perth Amboy, N. J , innholder, dec'd.—property to be sold; widow is Agnes (10/21/39)

McIntaylor (or Makist), John (a Scotchman), tailor, age c. 22 or 23—brought to N. Y. about 13 or 14 months ago, now a runaway from Lt. Gov. George Clarke of N. Y. (10/29/39)

Greyless, James (an Irishman), age c. 19—runaway from John Stanley of Middle-Town, N. J. (10/29/39)

Tayler, Daniel (lately come from Highlands in Scotland), age c. 17 or 18—runaway from John Obrian of Eastchester, Westchester Co., N. Y. (10/29/39)

Mahane, James (an Indian, born on L. I.—formerly lived with Obadiah Smith in Smithstown), age c. 25—runaway from William Sims of NYC (11/5/39)

Sharpas, William (for about 46 years Town Clerk and Clerk of the Peace of the City and County of New York)—died in NYC in the 70th year of his age on Sunday A.M., Nov. 4 (11/12/39)

Hubbard, John, Jr. (son of John Hubbard of Conn.)—accidentally shot and killed by a younger brother, Benjamin, while hunting on Wed., Oct. 31 (11/19/39)

Bosch, Justus, late of NYC, dec'd.—real estate in NYC; widow named Anne (12/10/39)

Sarle, Capt. John, dec'd.—real estate in NYC for sale; execs. are: James Sarle, merchant in NYC; Samuel Pintard of Monmouth Co., N. J.; widow of Capt. Sarle, now wife of Robert Jenney (minister of Hempstead, Queens Co., L. I.) (1/15/39-40)

Braine, Dr. Thomas, late of NYC, dec'd.—estate; widow is Mary (1/22/39-40)

Towner, Deborah, late of Lyme—died Dec. 5 in 104th year of her age; she had four husbands: Jones (by whom she had seven children), Crane, Champion and Towner. She left 6 children, 42 grandchildren, 178 great-grandchildren and 26 great-great grandchildren (1/29/39-40)

Reade, John, dec'd.—real estate for sale in NYC; Joseph Reade is one of execs. (2/12/39-40)

George, Thomas, late of NYC, dec'd.—estate (2/26/39-40)

Wilder, Mrs Josiah, of Lancaster, Worcester Co.—perished, together with four children, in a fire in November, 1739 (3/4/39-40)

Conner, Barry, age c. 18 or 19—runaway from Robert Cuming of Bucks Co., Pa. (3/11, 39-40)

Dehart, Capt. (master of a sloop bound from NYC to R. I.)—drowned Tue., March 11, at Mt. Misery, about 60 mi. from NYC (3/18/39-40)

Sweet, Godf. (mate of sloop from NYC bound to R. I.)—drowned Tue., March 11, at Mt. Misery, about 60 mi. from NYC (3/18/39-40)

Hancock, ——— (foremast man of sloop from NYC bound to R. I)—drowned Tue., March 11, at Mt. Misery, about 60 mi. from NYC (3/18/39-40)

Seabrook, Capt. Tho. (passenger on sloop from NYC bound to R. I.)—drowned Tue., March 11, at Mt. Misery, about 60 mi. from NYC (3/18/39-40)

Mallone, Co— (passenger on sloop from NYC bound to R. I.)—drowned Tue., March 11, at Mt. Misery, about 60 mi. from NYC (3/18/39-40)

Stillwell, Dan (passenger on sloop from NYC bound to R. I.)—drowned Tue., March 11, at Mt. Misery, about 60 mi. from NYC (3/18/ 39-40)

Painter, John (master of the sloop *Huming Bird* from Lewis Town on Delaware) and his son—both suffocated in cabin of the ship (3/25/40)

Anderson, John, pedler—lately died in Conn.; his execs., Thomas and Matthew Benedict, live in Danbury, Fairfield Co., Conn. (3/31/40)

Keys, James (an Irishman), tailor, age c. 24—runaway from Charles Arding of NYC, tailor (3/31/40)

Bayeux, John—drowned (4/14/40)

Peyton, Capt.—drowned (4/14/40)

Clarke, Mrs. George (wife of Lt. Gov. of N. Y.), in 47th year of her age—died in NYC on Mon., May 19 (she was eldest daughter of Hon. Edward Hyde, Esq., of Hyde, Cheshire, Eng.) (5/26/40)

Pierce, Isaac (of Boston)—drowned near L. I. in June (7/2/44)

Tume, Lt. (of a sloop of war)—died in Boston, Thursday eve., July 5, from a fall (7/23/44)

Huey, Robert (late of Ulster Co., N. Y.), dec'd.—estate (8/23/44)

Smith, Geertruyd, late of NYC, dec'd. estate (8/20/44)

Porter, Thomas, Jr. (born in West Indies)—knowledge of whereabouts sought (9/24/44)

Ketletas, Abraham, late of NYC, dec'd. estate; execs.: Gerrit Ketletas of NYC and Samuel De Honneur of Sutakett, L. I. (9/24/44)

Davis, Thomas (a Welshman), age c. 20—runaway from Rice Williams of NYC (9/24/44)

Richards, Capt. Samuel (master of a sloop from NYC to Piscataqua)—killed off Cape Cod (10/1/44)

GENEALOGICAL DATA FROM ZENGER'S NEW-YORK WEEKLY JOURNAL, 1733-1751

The New York Weekly Journal was established by John Peter Zenger on Nov. 5, 1733, and printed by him until his death on July 28, 1746. It was continued by his widow, Catherine, and then by John Zenger, her step-son, until his death June 18, 1751.

Photostatic copies of all known numbers have been assembled by The New-York Historical Society. From these have been abstracted all items which throw light on places of origin, ages, marriages, deaths and family relationships of individuals in America. In these abstracts the numbers in parenthesis give the month and day of issue of the newspaper in which each item appears. Although the new year began in the period considered on March 25, for the sake of convenience the heading for each year is treated as beginning January 1.

1733

Ligget, William, late of Boston, mariner, age c. 22—affidavit of (12/17)

Gardner, John, of Boston, mariner, age c. 28—affidavit of (12/17)

Hill, Robert (a West Country man), brickmaker, age 18 or 19—runaway from Nathaniel Hazard of NYC (12/31)

1734

Kirton, William, late of NYC—estate of (1/14)

Bobin, Isack, dec'd—land of (1/14)

Cranell, Robert, Sr., overseer of the watch of NYC—died Jan. 18, 1734 (1/21)

Bradock, Capt. and son—killed on board ship by a free Indian (2/18)

Van Gelder, Johannes, of NYC, house carpenter—died Feb. 17, 1734 (2/18)

Elias, Benjamin—estate of (2/18)

Ratcliff, William, late of Albany—died from fracture of skull (3/18)

Scherp, Jacob, of Livingston's Manor, trader and farmer—drowned Feb. 16, 1734 (3/18)

Van Horn, Cornelius G., wife of—died March 16, 1734, in child bed (3/18)

Paxton, Capt. Roger—died on Island of Jamaica (3/25)

Morse, Capt. Edward, commander of sloop *Hopewel* of R. I.—died at sea Nov. 10, 1733 (3/25)

Merry, Sarah, born at Dartmouth—drowned March 18, 1734, while sailing from Stonington to Newport, and buried on Block Island (4/15)

Banks, James, dec'd—house and lot in Elizabeth Town for sale (4/22)

Bresteade, Peter, late of NYC, dec'd, blacksmith—estate of (4/29)

Cooper, Lena, dec'd—estate of (5/13)

Lagrange, Mrs. Anna, from Albany, in 86th year—died in NYC June 4, 1734; her husband had died about 1731 in his 104th year (6/10)

Mattysen, Cornelius, "of Hackingsack," age c. 35—runaway June 6, 1734, from Bergen County jail (6/10)

Powelse, Jacob, "of Hackingsack," mulatto, age c. 40—runaway June 6, 1734, from Bergen County jail (6/10)

Ball, Mr., child of—scalded to death in Boston June 15, 1734 (6/24)

Matthews, Isaac, Jr., son of Isaac Matthews, master of sloop *Friendship*—drowned at Philadelphia June 14, 1734 (6/24)

Hoy, Ralph—drowned at Philadelphia June 3, 1734 (6/24)

Pain, Edward, potter, age c. 26—runaway from Samuel Hale, potter, of Philadelphia (6/24)

Berogain, Mons. Peter, master of schooner *St. John* of Louisburg—lost on Isle of Sables (7/1)

Willson, Thomas, lately come from St. Christophers to Boston—died July 2, 1734 (7/15)

Worthington, James—died at Bybery from heat on July 6, 1734 (7/15)

Lee, Jacob, of Philadelphia, gardner—died there from heat July 9, 1734 (7/15)

Dent, Abigail, of Portsmouth, age 17—murdered July 6, 1734 (7/22)

Blake, John, late of NYC, dec'd—estate of; widow Jane (7/22)

Bisset, Capt., widow of—resides at corner of New-street and Valeten-berg in NY (8/5)

Peek, John, child of (Peek was overseer of "The Jonkers," estate of Fred. Philipse, Esq., in Westchester Co.)—drowned Aug. 10, 1734 (8/12)

Ryckman, John, late of NY County, dec'd—estate of (8/19)

Manchester, William, of Dartmouth (Mass.)—killed in quarrel by William Teber on Aug. 3, 1734 (8/26)

Stow, Jonathan (a Negro known as "Johnsey"), age c. 25—runaway from Johanna Kelsall of NYC (8/26)

Bell, Thomas, of Boston—murdered by John Ormsby (9/2)

Todd, ———— (brother of Capt. Todd from Philadelphia)—drowned (9/9)

Jansen, Johannes, Esq., of NYC, former high sheriff, alderman, assemblyman, mayor, in 70th year—died in NYC Sept. 11, 1734 (9/16)

Wendell, Abraham, of Boston (formerly of NYC), merchant—died in Boston Sept. 28, 1734 (10/7)

Gray, Adam, age c. 19—runaway from Hugh Waddell of NYC, merchant (10/14)

Howey, John (an Irishman), joiner, age c. 21—runaway from Thomas Rigby, of NYC, joiner (10/14)

Frasier, Mrs., of Albany—murdered Oct. 9, 1734, by husband (10/21)

Desbros, Widow—sells wine and oil in Hanover Sq., NYC (10/28)

Coffin, Ephraim (son of Jonathan Coffin), of Nantucket, age c. 20—drowned at sea on whaling voyage (11/11)

Clark, ————, age c. 17—accidentally killed off Cape Sable (11/11)

Brett, Catharine, widow—property in Dutchess Co. for sale (11/25)

Holt, ————, dec'd—property in NYC for sale (12/2)

1735

Reading, James, of the Old Slip Market, NYC, dec'd, puller of teeth—his successor and former pupil, James Mills (1/6)

Montgomerie, George, dec'd—estate of (1/20)

Gordon, Capt.—shot at Charleston, S. C., Oct. 30, 1734 (1/27)

Parker, Jacob, of Boston, "an ancient Man and noted Eastern-Coaster"—died Dec. 20, 1734 (1/27)

Bannister, Annesley, of Boston—died on Island of Jamaica (2/24)

Philipse, Catharina, dec'd—two of her houses in Bridge St., NYC, and other real estate to be sold (3/1)

Winkler, Herman (born in East Indies, served the States General in several considerable posts in "Suranam & Curacoa)—died in NYC March 21, 1735, in 46th year (3/24)

Miller, Jacob, "an eminent Sadler," of NYC—died April 14, 1735 (4/21)

Mesnard, Daniel (son of Daniel Mesnard, of NYC, tailor)—wounded in scuffle with William Cullen (5/19)

Norris, Isaac, esq., of Fairhill, Judge of County Court of Quarter Sessions and Common Pleas at Philadelphia, member of Council, Representative in the Legislature—died June 4, 1735, of an apoplectic fit in the Quaker Meeting House in Germantown (6/9)

Blyth, James (foremast man of the sloop *Three Friends*, John Rushton master, from Boston)—died May 25, 1735 (6/9)

Vaughan, Mrs. Henshman, of Marlborough, Mass.—delivered of three sons "last Sunday 7 night"; some years before gave birth to triplet daughters (6/16)

Jarrat, Capt. Alane, dec'd—real estate for sale; apply to his daughter, Mrs. Hannah Jarrat (6/30)

Johnson, Robert, Esq., Gov. of South Carolina—died May 3, 1735, in Charleston, in 59th year; his brother-in-law Thomas Broughton (7/7)

Twells, Rachel, of Philadelphia—died there June 15, 1735, from excessive drinking (7/7)

Symes, John Hendrick, Esq., Sheriff of NYC—killed by bursting of cannon in NYC, July 16, 1735 (7/21); his widow Catherine (11/24)

Courtland, Catharina (only daughter of Philip Courtland, Esq.), age c. 9—killed by bursting cannon in NYC, July 16, 1735 (7/21)

Vollweiller, Jacob Hendrick (the husband of daughter of Alderman William Rome of NYC)—killed by bursting cannon in NYC, July 16, 1735 (7/21)

Torke, John, of Boston, age between 30 and 40—drowned in well in Boston, Aug. 3, 1735 (8/18)

Mac-Nobb, John, sailor, age 22-23—drowned in well in Boston, Aug. 3, 1735 (8/25)

Le Mountes, John, late of NYC, dec'd—estate of (8/25)

Douthell, James—killed and scalped in Pa. about Aug. 1, 1735 (9/1)

Balden, William—probably killed in Pa. about Aug. 1, 1735 (9/1)

Winkler, Herman, gent., late of NYC, dec'd—his widow Gertruid plans to leave the province by April 1 (9/8)

Cuer, Mr., late of NYC, dec'd reference to houses and ground (9/23)

Van Gelder, John, late of NYC, dec'd—carpenter—property to be sold by John Van Gelder, near the Black Horse, or David Van Gelder, blacksmith, near the City Hall (9/23)

Sands, Nathaniel, of Long Island—wife Jane has eloped with William Davies in the sloop *Carolina*, John Blaer master, to North Carolina (9/23)

Reynolds, Capt., commander of a ship from England—perished in fire at a public house at Patapsco River, Md. Oct. 30, 1735 (11/10)

Tidmarsh, Mr.—perished in same fire (11/10)

Walton, William—perished in same fire (11/10)

Overy, Peter—perished in same fire (11/10)

Lees, John, of Md.—perished in same fire (11/10)

Earl, Jonathan (English servant), age c. 22—runaway March 23, 1735, from Joseph Earl of Portsmouth, R. I. (12/1)

Hunter, Major General, dec'd—real estate in N. J. and N. Y. for sale (12/15)

1736

Toby (slave of Obadiah Hunt, tavernkeeper, of NYC), age c. 22 for sale (1/5)

Wooster (slave of Obadiah Hunt), age 14 or 15—for sale (1/5)

Bisset, Mary, of NYC, widow—her Negro slave, George Goldin, runaway (1/19)

Boynton, Mr., four children of—died of distemper in Newbury, Mass. (1/26)

Berry, Col., two children of—died of distemper at Ipswich, Mass. (1/26)

Leighton, Samuel (son of John Leighton, Esq., dec'd)—died from an accident at Kittery, Dec. 25, 1735 (1/26)

Blake, widow—store of George Talbot in her house in the Smith Fly in NYC (2/9)

Sewall, Mrs. Margaret (only surviving child of Rev. Mr. Mitchel of Cambridge, Mass; in 1682 she married Major Stephen Sewall of Salem and lived with him 45 years, bearing him 17 children, of whom four sons and four daughters survive)—died at age 72 in Boston on Jan. 20, 1736 (2/16)

Cook, Mr., of Cecil County, two children of—perished in a fire, Jan. 26, 1736 (2/16)

Jeffers, Thomas, of NYC—died of a stroke, Feb. 24, 1736 (3/1)

Jeffers, Mrs. Thomas, of NYC—died there Feb. 26, 1736 (3/1)

Monro, Hugh (lieutenant in company posted in N. Y.; born in north of Scotland), age 63—died in NYC, March 5, 1736, leaving widow and three children (3/15)

Cosby, William, Gov. of N. Y.—died in NYC between 1 and 2 P.M., Wed., March 10, 1736 (3/15)

Smith, Mr., "of Stainford," Conn., five children of—died of distemper (3/15)

Lawrence, Mr., a glazier who kept an inn near the Somerset, N. J. courthouse, wife of—murdered in March, 1736 (3/22)

Hartshorne, Capt. Richard—drowned at mouth of Carendon River (3/29)

Smith, Richard (son of Capt. Smith of N. J.)—drowned at mouth of Carendon River (3/29)

Anderson, John, Esq. (President of the N. J. Council)—died March 28, 1736, at Perth Amboy (4/5)

Bisset, Capt. Andrew, late of NYC, dec'd estate of (4/5)

Whatnell, John (born County of Cheshire, Eng.), age 27—executed in Philadelphia, April 28, 1736 (5/10)

M'Deirmat, Michael (an Irishman), age c. 27—executed in Philadelphia, April 28, 1736 (5/10)

Watson, John (born near New-Castle on Delaware), age c. 40—runaway on May 2, 1736, from Cornelius Wynkoop and Elizabeth Antony, storekeepers (5/10)

Johnny (Negro), a cooper, age c. 35—runaway from Peter Valleau (5/10)

Cato (a Negro, native of Madagascar), age c. 22 runaway (5/10)

Anthony, Hendrick (postrider from NYC to Albany), son of—died in fall from a tree in Poughkeepsie (5/17)

York, James, of Stonington, Conn., mother and two of his children—burned to death on May 25, 1736 (6/7)

Hudson, Eleazer, of Newbury, Mass., shopkeeper—died there May 25, 1736 (6/7)

Rodman, James (an Irishman), age 20—runaway from William Finn, of Goshen, Orange Co., N. Y. (6/7)

Elsworth, Clement, late of NYC, dec'd—land for sale (6/14)

Thayer, David, Jr., daughter of, age c. 3—died June 20, 1736, at Mendon, Mass., from bite of rattlesnake (7/5)

Sonmans, Peter, late of Perth Amboy, N. J., dec'd—estate of; his late wife was Sarah Nevil; mention of Samuel Nevil of London, gent., John Nevil of Perth Amboy, and Dr. Peter Sonmans of Philadelphia (7/5)

Farrel, Roger—will not be responsible for debts of wife Elizabeth of NYC (7/19)

Bates, William and Ester—Bible containing dates of birth of three of their children

(William, Ester and Alexander) sold at vendue about fifteen years before; reward if brought to Zenger (8/9)

Walgrave, George, cooper (had wife and children)—killed by falling timber, Aug. 20, 1736, while assisting workmen in raising new addition to Trinity Church in NYC (8/23)

Visger, Johannes, dec'd—farm, settled by him sixteen years past in Maquase country about a mile from Fort Hunter, for sale (8/30)

Crackey, Sam (free mulatto)—fell Sept. 4, 1736, from the top of the new works of the English Church in NYC and died Sept. 15 (9/6)

Smith, Thomas—while driving cart along the street in Smiths Fly in NYC was injured when horse ran away; he died Dec. 19, 1736 (12/20)

1737

Williams, Capt., of Salem, Mass.—drowned in Dec., 1736, off Cape Ann (1/10)

Dewing, Nathanael, of south part of Boston, four children of—died of the distemper early in December, 1736 (1/10)

Matthews, James—convicted of horse stealing in Williamsburg, Va., and sentenced to death (1/10)

Greenley, Elizabeth—convicted of murder in Williamsburg, Va., and sentenced to death (1/10)

Graeme, William (who lived in the north liberties of Philadelphia)—frozen to death Jan. 18, 1737, about two miles from Philadelphia on the road to Frankford (2/14)

Ayres, Joseph—frozen to death Jan. 18, 1737, in Bucks Co., Pa. (2/14)

Williams, Mr., chimney sweeper—died in Boston in Jan., 1737, at south end of town, near the fortification (2/14)

Vanderspiegel, Anna, widow —will deliver her shop in NYC o son John (2/21)

Rutgers, Mrs. Catherine (wife of Capt. Hermanus Rutgers), of NYC—died there Feb. 28, 1737 (3/7)

Syms, Mrs. William, of Pinetree Creek, N. C.—killed by Indians Oct. 9, 1736 (3/14)

Died at Scituate harbor, Feb. 11, 1737, in wreck of the brig *Anne* from Edinburgh:

Banks, David, mate

Dalrymple, Patrick (son of Sir John Dalrymple of Craston, bart.)

Died Feb. 10, 1737, in the same wreck:

Fowler, David, carpenter

Muckle, Robert, boatswain

Beatson, Richard,   sailor

Campbell, William,   "

Olyphant, David,   "

Mcdonald, Alexander   "

Henderson, James,   "

Sutherland, John,   "

Sterland, James,   "

Mepherson, John, servant

Sharp, Henry, servant

Walker, Thomas, servant

Carsson, Archibald, servant (3/14)

Billinger, Capt., of Ashley Ferry, S. C., two sons of—drowned in mid-January, 1737 (3/21)

Van Dam, Sarah (wife of Rip Van Dam, of NYC)—buried in NYC March 20, 1737 (3/21)

Brian, Mrs. (her husband a carpenter of Charleston, S. C.) burnt to death Dec. 27, 1736 (3/28)

Drummond, Evan, late of Bound Brook, N. J., dec'd—property for sale (3/28)

Ackley, William, of NYC—will pay no debts of his wife Mary (4/4)

Allen, Alice (daughter of Ralph Allen, of Portsmouth, R. I.)—drowned in well in Newport, March 28, 1737 (4/11)

Codner, Capt. James of Boston—drowned upon wreck of his schooner on bar in N. C.; left widow and one child (5/9)

Wileman, Henry rec'd death sentence in Philadelphia upon conviction of breaking and entering at night (5/23) and executed July 2, 1737 (7/18)

Conner (alias Smith), Catharine—rec'd death sentence in Philadelphia on conviction of breaking at night into house of John Daily beyond Schuylkill and robbing (5/23) and executed July 2, 1737 (7/18)

Mac Laughlin, James (Irish servant), age c. 16—runaway from James Jones of Whitestone, L. I. (5/23)

Rynders, Jacob (a young gentleman), of NYC—found dead in his bed June 2, 1737 (6/6)

Tienhoven, Cornelius, late of NYC, dec'd—house and ground at Potbakers Hill in Smith St. for sale (6/6)

Harle, Capt. Ralph—died in Bay of Honduras (6/13)

Gorden, John (Irish servant of John Craig living on Ammonton River near Pippack), age c. 21—runaway June 1, 1737 from Schuylers Mines (6/13)

Van Horne, Capt. Garrit (had served in the Assembly)—died in NYC July 7, 1737, in 66th year (7/11)

Lane, John, apprentice, age c. 14—runaway from Cornelius Quackenbusch, of NYC, baker (7/11)

Beven, Thomas (born in England; transported to Md.)—executed July 2, 1737, at Chester, Pa., for firing and robbing a house (7/18)

Larby, Eliphalet, of Va.—murdered by runaway servants, William Marr (servant of Col. John Chiswell), Peter Heckie, Matthew and Brian Connor (servants of Capt. Avery and his son, of Prince William County) (7/25)

Roberts, Anthony (a West Country man), age c. 21 runaway from Samuel Hopson, of N. Y. ferry, butcher (7/25)

Mesnard, Daniel, of NYC, master tailor—buried in NYC Aug. 14, 1737 (8/15)

Hildereth, Benjamin, of NYC, master tailor—buried in NYC Aug. 14, 1737 (8/15)

Machon, Samuel, weaver, age c. 24—runaway from William Harrison, of New-Hanover, Burlington County (8/22)

Warren, Mr., miller—drowned Aug. 16, 1737, near Capt. Hill's wharf at south end of Boston (8/29)

Butts, Benjamin (of sloop *Mary*, Abraham Anthony commander, bound from Newport, R. I., to Jamaica)—drowned near Turks Island June 17, 1737 (8/29)

Phillips, Elisha—same as above (8/29)

Sheeff, James, cooper—same as above (8/29)

Mc'Cammel, Charles (Irish servant), age c. 25—runaway from the brigantine *Joanna*, Samuel Payton master (8/29)

Jack (a Negro), age c. 18—runaway from John Belden of Norwalk, Conn. (9/26)

Davison, John (alias William Mackgee, an Irishman), weaver, age c. 30—runaway from Samuel Belden of Norwalk, Conn. (9/26)

Sutton, Capt. (commander of ship of 300 tons from London)—drowned with wife and daughter in hurricane off St. Christophers (10/10)

Newlands, James (five or six years ago went as indentured servant, age c. 35, from Glasgow to one of plantations in America)—has succeeded to a considerable fortune; news of him desired by Alexander Newlands, skinner, of Edinburgh (10/24)

Owen, Charles, shoemaker, age c. 40—runaway from John Burr of Burlington County (11/28)

Meyer, Andrias (whose father was one of first settlers of NYC)—died in NYC Dec. 4, 1737, in 93rd year (12/5)

Dick, Sir William (captain of one of H.M.'s Independent Companies)—lately died in Albany (12/19); he came from Scotland (12/26)

1738

Broughton, Gov. (of South Carolina)—died lately in Charleston (1/2)

Johnson, Nathaniel (son of Gov. Johnson and nephew of Gov. Broughton), age c. 21—lately died in Charleston, S. C. (1/2)

Nutty, John, butcher, age c. 24—runaway from George Rice Jones, of Philadelphia, butcher (1/17)

Andrise, Elias—estate of, consisting of house, known as "the Union Flag," above Tortoise Bay (1/30)

Andrisen, Marytje—estate of (1/30)

Fiske, Mrs. Sarah, of Wenham, Mass., age 97—died there Jan. 26, 1738 (2/20)

Treadwell, John, of Ipswich, Mass., four children of—died of throat distemper in March, 1738 (4/17)

Denison, Timothy—to be executed in Burlington, N. J., June 2, 1738, for crime of burglary (6/5)

Turner, Enoch, of New Haven, Conn.—was 18 months old June 2, 1738, weighed 49½ lbs. and was 3 ft. 2in. in height (6/12)

Nickerson, Deborah (wife of Nehemiah Nickerson and granddaughter of John Scull, both of Absecom on Egg Harbor)—died on a small island during a storm May 7, 1738 (6/12)

Cary, Deacon Jonathan, of Charlestown—died June 4, 1738, in 92nd year (6/19)

Gwin, Elizabeth, single woman, of Boston, age c. 40—gave birth to a boy June 6, 1738 (6/19)

Plymton, Mrs. Priscilla, of Medfield, Mass.—died there May 24, 1738 (6/19)

Holbrook, Edward (mate of sloop *Mary*)—supposedly murdered on high seas by Nathaniel Darby in Sept. or Oct., 1736 (6/19); Darby acquitted July, 1738 (8/7)

Baker, ———— (son of Richard Baker, innkeeper, on Burnet's Key), age c. 8—died in NYC June 20, 1738 (6/26)

Whipple, Joseph, of Stow, Middlesex Co., Mass., infant child of—burnt to death June 12, 1738 (7/3)

Sellard, Mr. (a Frenchman), daughter of—accidentally shot and killed by two boys at Mottapoiset, a village in Rochester (7/3)

Pool, Anna Sophia, of Maxatawny, Pa.—accidentally shot and killed by her son Peter June 13, 1738 (7/3)

Dean, Joshua (a London convict), age c. 40—runaway from Alexander Spotswood, Postmaster General of America (7/3)

Parmyter, Thomas, dec'd.—ref. to house at Whitestone, Flushing, Queens Co., N. Y., of which he died seized (7/10)

Goelet, Catherina (wife of Jacob Goelet, of NYC)—died July 12, 1738, in New Rochelle and buried July 14 in NYC (7/17)

Coddrington, Capt. Thomas, dec'd—plantation in Harlem in Outward of NYC for sale (7/24)

Kersley, Samuel, age c. 32—runaway from James Hindes of Elizabethtown, N. J., (7/24)

Wiggins, William, age c. 50—broke out of Queens County Jail in Jamaica, L. I., night of July 29, 1738 (7/31)

Langdon, Amos, weaver, age c. 30—broke out of Queens County Jail in Jamaica, L. I., night of July 29, 1738 (7/31)

Lyde, Mary Belcher—born July 23, 1738, in Boston and baptized by Rev. Dr. Sewall; the mother is daughter of Governor Belcher of Mass. (8/7)

Jones, John—drowned off dock near Alderman Moor's in NYC, Aug. 3,1738 (8/7)

Ray, Richard, late of NYC, dec'd—estate of (8/14)

Lyell, Mrs. Catherin, widow, living in Perth Amboy—land and property in N. J. for sale (8/14)

Kantson (or Kanison), Philip—convicted of breaking and entering at night the house of James Hayes of Charlestown, Mass., and sentenced at Cambridge, Mass., to die Aug. 25, 1738 (8/21); reprieved until Sept. 15 (9/4)

Lackerman, Isaac, shoemaker, age c. 19—runaway from Stephen Wood of Staten Island (8/21)

Ask, Capt. Benjamin, dec'd—property for sale (8/21)

Bruit, Mr., late of Caroline Co., Va.—lately committed suicide (8/28)

Duram, Samuel, of Milton, Mass., leather dresser—injured while making repairs in his mill and died, Aug., 1738 (9/4)

Van Horne, Miss Helena (sister of wife of late Gov. Burnet)—died NYC, Sept. 2, 1738 (9/4)

Duykinck, Mrs. Mary—died in NYC Sept. 3, 1738 in 75th year (9/4)

Evans, Mr., coachmaker (once of Williamsburg, Va., but lately removed to Rappahanock)—murdered in Hanover Co. (9/25)

Decheseau, Adam (commander of sloop *Dolphin*)—killed at sea Sept. 3, 1738 (10/2)

Edward (an Englishman)—killed on board sloop *Dolphin* (10/2)

Decheseau, Stephen (nephew of Capt. Adam Decheseau), a boy—thrown overboard at Block Island (10/2)

Jack (a Negro), age c. 30—runaway from Frederick Zepperly of Reinbeek, Dutchess Co., blacksmith (10/2)

Brass, Gerrit—drowned Sept. 30, 1738, when boat of Johannes Beeck overturned in Newark Bay, (11/6)

Putland, Heron, lately dec'd—estate of (perhaps in Perth Amboy); ref. to widow (11/27)

Davis, Thomas (convicted of piracy)—hanged himself in jail at Newport, R. I., Oct. 5, 1738 (12/4)

Legrand, Peter—hanged at Bull's Point, Newport, R. I., Oct. 5, 1738 (12/4)

Bodoin, Francis—hanged at Bull's Point, Newport, R. I., Oct. 5, 1738 (12/4) 1739

1739

Marschalk, Andries—died in NYC, Dec. 26, 1738 (1/1); house in Broad St. in NYC in possession of Abraham Marschalk (12/13/1742)

Winslow, Hon. Isaac—died Dec. 14, 1738, at Marshfield in 68th year (1/22)

Payton, William, wife of—burnt to death in Wenham, Jan. 5, 1739 (1/22)

Weissenburg, Catherine (Palatine born), age c. 17—runaway from Capt. Langden of NYC (1/22)

Dittond, Anthony Francis—executed at Williamsburg, Va., Nov. 24, 1738, for murder of Mr. Evans, coachmaker (2/5)

Stelle, Col. Gabriel, late of Perth Amboy, dec'd—estate of (2/12)

Hooper, Hon. Robert Letice (late Chief Justice of N. J.)—buried Feb. 15, 1739, in NYC (2/19)

Gray, Joseph, late of Essex Co., N. J., dec'd—estate of; administratrix Ennice Gray (2/26)

Governeur, Nicholas, merchant—died March 21, 1739, in NYC from infection caused by pricking his finger with a pin (3/26)

Megoon, John—died March, 1739, at Pembrooke (4/9)

Carree, Lewis, Jr., of Allenstown, dec'd—lot, house and storehouse to be sold (4/9)

March, John, Esq., late of NYC, dec'd—house in Broadway near the Bowling Green and other property for sale (5/15)

Brower, Adolph, of Hackensack, daughter of—bitten in three places last week by rattlesnake and died within a few hours (6/4)

Bussey, ———, of NYC, carman—hanged himself June 3, 1739 (6/4)

Clarkson, Matthew—died in NYC and buried there June 8, 1739 (6/11)
Sharpas, William (Town Clerk and Clerk of the Peace of NYC)—died Nov. 11, 1739, in NYC, in 70th year (11/12)
Brown, Thomas, of south end of Boston, retailer—murdered Nov. 12, 1739 (12/10)
Knox, Peter (Irishman), age 20-30—murderer of Thomas Brown in Boston (12/10)
Cockrain, Samuel (Irishman), age 20-30—murderer of Thomas Brown (12/10)
Phipps, Thomas (son of Thomas Phipps), of Portsmouth, N. H., age c. 13—died there Nov. 24, 1739, from kick of a horse (12/10)
Towner, Mrs. Deborah, of Lyme, Conn.—died there Dec. 5, 1739, in 104th year; more than 500 persons descended from her (12/24); she had four hubsands (Jones, Crane, Champhion, Towner), by the first of whom she had seven children (1/1/1740)

1740

Pintard, Anthony, late of NYC, dec'd—house and lot for sale at N. W. corner of the new Dutch Church; apply to George Spencer, merchant, near the Fly Market, or John Pintard in NYC (1/7)
Jupitor (Negro), age c. 25—runaway from Gabriel Crooke of NYC (1/7)
Searle, Capt. John, dec'd—property in NYC for sale; apply to James Searle, merchant, in NYC, Samuel Pintard of Monmouth Co., N. J., or John Searle's widow, now wife of Rev. Robert Jenny, minister at Hempstead, Queens Co., L. I. (1/14)
Depeyster, Mrs. Anne (widow of Col. John Depeyster)—died Jan. 23, 1740, at New Brunswick, N. J., in 70th year from apoplexy (1/28)
Dunstar, Charles, late of N. J., dec'd—suit in Court of Chancery of N. J. regarding property (2/5)
Sarjant, Widow, of Perth Amboy, N. J.—vendue at her house (2/11)
Wilder, Mrs. Josiah, of Lancaster, County of Worcester, Mass.—perished, with four children, in fire on Jan. 23, 1740 (2/18)
Cockever (or Cochever), Charity (wife of John, of Queens Co., L. I.)—has eloped and husband will not be responsible for her debts (2/25)
Bullege, Andrew (eminent lawyer and adjutant of the New Regiment in Charleston, S.C.) —died there lately (3/10)
Seabrook, Capt.—died March 11, 1740, in wreck, at Mt. Misery on the north coast of L. I., of the *Johanna*, James De Hart master, belonging to New Brunswick, which sailed from NYC March 10 (3/17)
Painter, Capt. John (master of sloop *Humming Bird*, from Lewis Town on Delaware)— asphyxiated, together with his son (the mate) in the ship's cabin in the harbor of NYC (3/24)
Payton, Capt. (master of the *Johanna* from Madeira) perished in wreck of the ship on south side of L. I. near Hempstead April 4, 1740 (4/7)
Thompson, John, dec'd—house, storehouse and lot in New Brunswick for sale (4/7)
Clarke, Mrs. George (wife of Gov. of N. Y.; eldest daughter of Hon. Edward Hyde)— died May 19 in NYC in 47th year; interred May 22 in vault in Trinity Church (5/26)
Higgins (alias Eagon), John (Irishman), age c. 27—runaway from Mr. Wright on L. I. (7/7)
Wanton, John (Gov. of R. I.)—died July 5, 1740, in Newport and given Quaker burial there two days later (7/21)
Fresneau, Andrew, dec'd—inquire of his heir about land for sale (8/11)
Brookman, John—died in Cuba about Aug. 8, 1740 (10/20)
Plocknett, Andrew—died in Cuba about Aug. 8, 1740 (10/20)
Golloway, —— (Indian slave) leather dresser, age 21 (born in the fort at Albany)— runaway from John Breese, of NYC (10/20)
Van Nortshand, Casparus, late of Rariton, N. J., blacksmith—estate of (11/10)

Ringe, Capt. John, late of Portsmouth, N. H.—died there the first week in Nov. 1740 (11/24)

Defreest, Elizabeth (widow, living in Stone St., NYC)—intends to remove into the country (11/24)

Moses, Michael, late of Curacoa, dec'd—estate of (11/24)

1741

Smathers, William, carpenter (sailed from NYC in sloop *Ranger*, Samuel Bayard master) died at Antigoa (1/19)

Hyam, Uriah, late of NYC, dec'd—estate of (2/16)

Freeman, Robert, late of Flushing, L. I.—goods for sale (3/23)

M'Call, John (Irishman), tailor—runaway from John Sayre, of NYC, tailor (4/13)

Robin (Negro), age c. 40—runaway from John Jackson, of Whippeny Township, Morris Co., N. J. (5/18)

Caesar (half Spanish Indian, half Negro), age c. 20—runaway from John Jackson, of Whippeny (5/18)

Huson, John, of NYC—executed, together with his wife, last week (6/15)

Kerry, Margaret, of NYC—same

Hains, William (young servant)—runaway from Marten Ryerson, of Readingtown, Hunterdon Co. (6/15)

Becker, Conrad, of Albany, child of—carried into woods by a slave belonging to John Layer, Esq., and murdered May 31, 1741 (6/22)

Ray, Francis (Scotch apprentice), age c. 18—runaway from snow *Elizabeth* of Aberdeen, Patrick Hepburn master (6/29)

Hall, Thomas, age c. 25—committed suicide at Marlborough, Mass., April 22, 1741, by drinking laudanum (7/6)

Townley, George (English servant), age c. 24—runaway from William Maugridge, of NYC, ship joiner (7/6)

Jones, Francis (Welchman), tanner—runaway from Robert Hogg, of NYC (7/13)

Ury, John—executed in NYC Aug. 29 for implication in alleged Negro plot (8/31)

Claus (Negro), age c. 45—runaway from Philip French of New Brunswick, East Jersey (9/7)

Webb, Rev. Mr. (sometime minister at Newark)—drowned, together with son, in trying to cross the Connecticut River (11/2)

Schuyler, John (Mayor of Albany)—died (11/16)

De Lancey, Stephen, late of NYC, merchant—died in NYC on Nov. 18, 1741, in 78th year; descended from protestant family of Normandy; spent some time in Holland and England before coming to America (11/23)

Smith, John (formerly of NYC but now of Rochester, N. H.), trader—wife Elizabeth eloped in 1737; no one is to give her credit (11/30)

Koster, Joseph—killed on last night of the fair in Nov., 1741, in Philadelphia in a quarrel (12/21)

Dagg, John—fell overboard into river at Philadelphia Nov. 20, 1741, and died (12/21)

Durrem, William (Irish servant), age c. 30—runaway from Samuel Bayard, of NYC (12/21)

Coejemans, Andries, late of East New Jersey, dec'd—property in NYC and province for sale; apply, among others, to widow, Geertruid, of Rariton (12/28)

1742

Souther, James—killed Jan. 12, 1742, from blast in mine near Newark, N. J. (1/25)

Hunt, Thomas, of Westchester—drowned near Corlaer's Hook Jan. 19 (1/25)

Rochead, James and John—estate of; executrix Mrs. Elizabeth Home, of NYC (1/25)

Decker, Johannes, of Shawangonk—drowned while crossing Rosendal Creek about eight miles from Kingston (2/22)

Bullock, John (brother of William Bullock, of NYC, hatter)—executed some months ago for murder of his wife (3/1)

Tom (Negro slave of Widow Bratt, of NYC)—executed March 13 for having set fire to house of Baffie Van Dewater of NYC (3/8 and 15)

Cremmer, Timothy (Irish servant)—runaway from Samuel Brant, of Elizabethtown, N. J. (3/22)

De Marest, Guilliam—killed by fall of tree at Hackensack; left a wife (4/19)

De Grave, Garrit, late of Brunswick, East N. J., dec'd—estate of; apply to Dirck Van Aertsdalen or Garrit De Grave (4/26)

Challwell, Hannah, dec'd—goods from her estate to be sold in NYC (4/26)

Chambers, Williams, dec'd—plantation for sale on west side of Hudson (5/10)

Home, Charles, merchant, dec'd—estate of (5/10)

Magwigin, Patrick—accidentally killed in iron works in Douglass Township, Philadelphia County, May 7 (5/31)

Nutts, James, son of, age 12-14—drowned in river near Hellgate (6/14)

Byvanck, Anthony, late of NYC, dec'd—houses and lots for sale (6/28)

Brian, Dennis, age c. 21—runaway from Johannes Bratt, of Albany County (6/28)

Pike, Benjamin, of Newbury, Mass.—died June 12 from eating clams dug from sand in Plumbs Land River (7/5)

Nicols, Jonathan, of Almsbury, Mass., child of, age 2—died June 12 from eating clams from same place (7/5)

Clarkson, Matthew, late of NYC, dec'd—estate of (7/5)

Brower, Adolph, of Hackensack—killed July 8 by lightning (7/12)

Foster, Joseph (formerly schoolmaster in Newark, N. J.)—hanged himself at Newark July 27 (8/2)

Donaldson, Alexander (captain's clerk to H. M.'s ship *Gosport*)—died in NYC Aug. 6 and left widow (8/9)

Heaviland, Peter—drowned in the Sound during gale (8/16)

Sandwell, Capt.—shot by Spaniards near St. Simons (10/4)

English, Widow—house of, near Meal Market in NYC (11/15)

Denny, Daniel, of Liecester, Mass., child of—died from accidental scalding Nov. 17 (12/20)

Moen, Dr. Jacob, late of Curacoa, dec'd—estate of (12/27)

1743

Prince (Negro), age c. 20—runaway from Cornelius Van Rans, of NYC, sailmaker (1/10)

Hazard, Nathaniel, of NYC—has resigned over to his son Daniel his shop and business (European and West Indian goods) at Old Ship (1/31)

Weaver, Samuel, dec'd estate of (2/7)

Plunket, Anne—executed at Williamsburg, Va., Nov. 26 for murder of her bastard child (2/21)

Hayman, Mr., late of Dorchester, Mass.—died a few days ago; to be buried Feb. 3 (2/28)

Moore, Alexander, dec'd—house in New Brunswick for sale (3/7)

Vander Pool, Malgert (a miner)—fell nearly 114 ft. into mine in N. J. and died April 2 (4/4)

Bridgham, Joseph, of Plymton (formerly of Boston)—his wife was delivered of twins, which is the fourth time successively (5/30)

Stackey, Mrs., of NYC, widow—killed in an accident July 4 (7/11)

Sineau, Peter, of Elizabethtown, N. J.—kicked to death by a horse July 4 (7/11)

Garritson, Peter, of Hackensack, N. J.—run over by a wagon and killed July 4 (7/11)

Northover, Capt. Richard (master of pink *Hanover*, of Bristol)—married May 13 in Providence, R. I., Miss Elizabeth Barnard of Island of Jamaica (7/18)

Ellis, William (had been commander of H. M.'s ship *Gosport*)—died in NYC Aug. 12 in 46th year and was buried Aug. 13 under the altar piece of the English Church (8/15)

Stillwell, Richard, dec'd—estate of (9/12)

Nicolls, John, M.D. (born in North Britain; educated U. of Edinburgh)—died in NYC Oct; he survived his wife by only one day (10/3)

Vernon (alias Allman), Thomas (Irishman), age c. 36—in Jamaica had been comic actor, writer to an attorney and a tavernkeeper at Port Royal; about Nov. 10, 1742, he sailed for South Carolina; has forged three bills of exchange (10/17)

Isaacs, Abraham, late of NYC, merchant—estate of; ref. to widow Hanah (10/24)

McKeen, Adam, age c. 35—broke out of Bergen County Jail at Hackensack Oct. 16 (10/24)

Finch, John (Englishman by birth), age c. 35—runaway from John Nelson at Second River near Newark, N. J. (11/7)

Breese, John, late of NYC, leather dresser, dec'd—executrix his widow Flora (11/28)

Eyres, Phineas—Dec. 3 his pilot boat overturned at west bank below the Narrows and he was drowned (12/11)

Bowne, Robert, dec'd—real estate for sale; apply to widow Margaret (12/19)

1744

Bogart, William, of NYC, turner—died in NYC Jan. 10 of apoplexy (1/16)

Ford, Nathaniel—drowned in millpond at Pompton (2/6)

Peltreau, Abraham, boatman—injured by fall of tree at Stephen De Lancey's plantation, not far from NYC, and died Feb. 7 (2/13)

Martin, John (journeyman to Mr. Parkins, chairmaker, of Boston)—hanged himself in Boston March 21 (4/9)

Beekman, Gerard, dec'd—one of executors is Gerard Beekman (4/9)

Armstrong, John, an Indian trader—murdered while on way from Lancaster, Pa., to Allegheny (4/30)

Keney, Capt. (of a schooner from Marblehead, Mass.)—murdered at sea (9/3)

Isaacs, Joshua, late of NYC, shopkeeper, dec'd—his widow one of executors (9/3)

Antonides, Rev. Vincencius (late minister at Flatbush, Kings Co., L. I.)—estate of (10/15)

Fry, John (a Swiss)—runaway (with wife, a Palatine, and three children, of whom the eldest is c. 14) from Richwelly in Bucks Co., Pa.; reward offered by John George Koch, stocking weaver, at his lodgings in house of John Peter Zenger in NYC (12/17)

1745

Dyke, Thomas (born in England), age c. 25—runaway from Thomas Maybury of Green Lane Forge, Philadelphia Co., Pa. (1/28)

Shae, Francis (Irishman), age c. 26—runaway from same Thomas Maybury (1/28)

Mansfield, Capt. (master of the *King's Meadow*, from Jamaica to London)—murdered Oct. 10, 1744, on board ship (2/4)

Rounsevel, Widow—living in large corner house (formerly owned by Gilbert Van Imburg) near upper end of Long Bridge, NYC (2/25)

Cavenaugh, Thomas (Irishman), age c. 22—runaway from George Kelly, of Philadelphia, blacksmith (4/1)

Bryan, James (Irish apprentice), age c. 18—runaway from Nicholas Fenual, of Philadelphia, cordwainer (6/10)

Donahew, Capt.—killed by Indians at Gut of Canso (8/5)

Holland, Richard (English servant), shoemaker—runaway from Zachariah Robins, of Upper Freehold, N. J. (8/5)

Vanalen, Lyckas, of Kinderhook—wife Elizabeth has eloped and he will not pay her debts (8/27)

Pawling, Albert, Esq. (member of the Assembly for Ulster Co., N. Y.)—died in NYC Aug. 29 in 61st year (9/2)

Schuyler, Col., the younger—killed by Indians at "Saraghtogo" (12/16)

1746

Reilb, James (servant of Quintane Moore of Ridley Township, Pa.)—hanged himself there May 8 (5/19)

Primus (Negro), age c. 21—runaway from John Willett, Jr., of Flushing, L. I. (5/19)

Hunt, Eliakim—killed May 22 by Indians near Ft. St. George in eastern parts of Mass. (6/9)

Driscall, Dennis, late of Elizabeth Town, N. J., tailor—drowned June 11, apparently in NYC (6/9)

Skinner, Mr.—accidentally shot and killed at Hartford, Conn., May 26 (6/16)

Gorham, Capt. William (in a brig belonging to Boston)—accidentally burned and died May 8; he was third son of the late Hon. Col. Gorham (6/23)

Johnson, Richard—found floating dead in NY harbor June 17 (6/23)

Johnson, Capt. Jonathan (of privateer *Dolphin*)—killed in action at sea May 28 (6/23)

Wright, Joseph (of privateer *Dolphin*)—killed in action at sea May 28 (6/23)

Zenger, John Peter, dec'd—his widow will continue printing the *Weekly Journal* at the printing office in Stone St. (9/1)

1747

Southerland, Widow, of Rye, N. Y., son of, age c. 5—fell from horse and died Jan. 31 (2/2)

Price, Lady (wife of Col. Charles Price, Lt.-Gov. of Jamaica), age 27—died March 20 on board brig *Good Intent*, Capt. Jauncey master; she was married at age of 13; was mother of three children at age 16; she was buried in Trinity Church in NYC (3/30)

Coneen (or Graham), Catharine (came about seven years ago from Limirick, Ireland, to Philadelphia)—a handsome estate has been left her in England (3/30)

Vielie, Cornelius, of "Schenectady"—shot there by Indians and presumably was killed (5/25)

Storde (mulatto, born in Bermuda), carpenter, age c. 23—escaped from privateer *Pollux* (5/25)

York (Negro), age c. 23—runaway from Leonard Hoff, of Middletown, Monmouth Co., N. J. (7/6)

Prentice, Rev. Mr. (late minister in Grafton, Mass.), son of—killed in accident at Grafton Oct. 22 (11/9)

Coverly, Capt. (of brigantine bound from New Providence to Boston)—drowned at sea late in Nov. (12/7)

Harry (Negro), age c. 20—runaway from George Ryerson, Jr., of Pechqueneck, East New Jersey (12/7)

Kozyn, ———, of NYC, cartman, wife of—burned to death Dec. 19 (12/21)

1748

Lowder, Capt. Sanmuel, of Boston—killed in action near Jamaica (5/9)

Picksley, Noah—shot and killed by Indians at New Hampton, three miles west of Northampton, Mass. May 9 (5/30)

Weld, Edmond, of Roxbury, Mass.—killed by lightning May 28 (6/27)

Gunn, Samuel—killed June 23 in fight with Indians near Numb. 4 in Mass. (7/18)

Mitchell, Ebenezer—same as above.

Scot, Ely—same as above

Mack, Adam—killed by Indians June 23 near George Town on Arrowsick Island (7/25)

Bookins, Henry—same as above

Whitcom, Joseph, son of—same as above

Jenkins, ———, of NYC, leather dresser—shot and killed himself July 20 (7/25)

Yager, Henry—executed at Trenton, N. J., July 16, for having counterfeited money of N. J. (8/1)

Tol, Daniel, of Schenectady—killed by Indians July 18 at Popendahl, one mile north of Schenectady (8/1)

Van Slyck, Adrian—same as above

Fielen, Cornelius, Jr.—same as above

De Graf, Klas A.—same as above

Van Den Bogart, Frans, Jr.—same as above

Van Antwerpen, Daniel—same as above

Conde, Adam—same as above

Gelen, Jacob, Jr.—same as above

Van Antwerpen, Johannes Peter—same as above.

Merenes, Johannes—same as above

Brat, Abraham—same as above

Darling, John—killed (8/1)

Wyrick, Nicholas, of Hanover Township, Lancaster Co., Pa., age 20-30, daughter of, age c. 9 months—murdered by father May, 1748 (8/29)

Belcher, Gov.—married to a lady at Burlington (9/19)

Gunnison, Mr.—fell from stage of a new ship at Piscataqua and died about Sept. 15 (Boston item of Sept. 19) (9/26)

Thompson, Francis (of privateer *Hester*, Robert Troup master)—killed in action Aug. 30 (9/26)

Everts, Adam—same as above

Marduff, John—same as above

Paddy (the captain's boy)—same as above

Rivet, Tunis, pilot—drowned near Merrick Beach, L. I. (11/14)

Roome, William, Esq., of NYC (former justice of the peace and deputy mayor)—died Dec. 23 in NYC in 57th year and was buried Dec. 24 in Old Dutch Churchyard (12/26)

1749

Van Hoesen, Rynier, of Albany—run over by sled and killed (1/10)

Van Pelt, John, of Shooters Island, N. J., (a noted fisherman)—boat overturned Dec. 30, 1748, near Billop's Point and he was drowned (1/10)

Johnson, Capt. William, of NYC (master of sloop *Polly*, bound from NYC to Jamaica)— murdered on high seas in Nov., 1748 (1/23)

Nelson, John, of NYC (mate of sloop *Polly*)—same as above

Hall, Mr., of NYC, merchant—same as above

Scrol, Herman (or Carrol, Manus), of Albany—executed Jan. 27 in NYC for murder (1/23 and 30)

Crane, Joshua, late of NYC, carpenter and joiner, dec'd—debts to his estate to be paid to James Crane, of Newark, N. J. (1/30)

Munn, Jonathan, cabinetmaker—drowned toward end of Jan. trying to cross Gunpowder River in Md. on the ice (3/20)

Bond, Uriah, blacksmith—same as above

Deering, Mr., of Black Point, to eastward, in Mass.—killed wife (3/20)

Howard, Mrs., of Woodstock (Boston dispatch of Mar. 13)—March 4 gave birth to four daughters, all of whom soon died (4/3)

Marshall, John, Esq., of NYC (justice of the peace), wife of—died Tuesday last of apoplexy (5/22)

Kinnyman, Capt., of NYC—murdered at sea by three Portuguese sailors (6/26)

Stevens, Capt., son of—killed by Indians at No. 4 to westward last Tuesday P.M. (Boston dispatch of June 26 (7/3)

Bliss, Samuel (born Springfield, Mass., Sept. 7, 1647)—died there June 19 in 102nd year; leaves alive 6 children, 38 grandchildren, 114 great grandchildren, and 10 great-great grandchildren (7/24)

Palmer, Eliakim, Esq. (eldest son of late Thomas Palmer, Esq., agent for Colony of Conn.)—died May 19 in London, Eng., of fever (8/7)

Cohen, Samuel Meyer, late of NYC, dec'd, widow of—died in NYC Aug. 20 (8/21)

Taylor, James (living on northwest fork of Nanticike River, Dorchester Co.)—killed in June by a rattlesnake; left a wife (8/28)

Dodd, Widow, of Philadelphia (living next door to Capt. Dowers)—discovers man trying to come down chimney of her house (9/18)

York, Daniel (soldier of the NYC garrison), age 70-80—fell off wharf near the Exchange Sept. 24 and was drowned (9/25)

1750

Van Alstyne, Mrs. Cathrine, widow (living 2 miles above Albany), three of her sons (the eldest c. 14)—perished in fire (3/5)

Ridgely, Col. Henry (formerly chief justice of the county)—died early in Feb. at Elk Ridge, Md. (4/2)

Howard, Charles, a young man—killed Feb. 14 by fall of a tree near the fork of Patuxent, Md. (4/2)

Pugsley, John, staymaker (on north side of Severn, Md.)—perished in snow Feb. 20 (4/2)

Watts, Capt. (master of brigantine at Clark's Wharf in Boston)—struck by falling mast and killed Thursday last (Boston dispatch of March 10) (4/2)

Daugherty, Michael (Scotch-Irish servant), age c. 16—runaway from James McHugh (5/28)

Linch, Cornelius, of NYC, mathematical school master—his wife Rebecca eloped and he will not pay debts she make contract (6/4)

Cassey, John, age c. 40—runaway from Joseph Shippens Iron Works, formerly called Canby's Iron Works (8/6)

How, Capt. (according to letter dated at Chinecto, Oct. 4)—shot and killed by French and Indians (10/29)

Williams, Cathrine, of NYC, widow—claims she has been slandered (11/26)

1751

Canada, Mr., of Hartford East Precinct—smothered in well Dec. 11, 1750 (2/4)

Deming, Mr.—same as above

Cadwell, Katharine, of Hartford East Precinct (an only daughter), age c. 12—choked on piece of walnut shell and died Nov. 8, 1750 (2/4)

Gutrdige, Mr. of "Glassenbury," Conn.—about middle of Dec., 1750, fell down stairs and broke his neck (2/4)

Grimes, Hezekiah, of Rocky Hill, Conn., ferryman—fell down dead in ferry (2/4)

Richards, Stephens, of NYC, mariner (son of Widow Richards, of NYC, tavernkeeper)—had apoplectic fit, fell from ship near the New Dock, and drowned March 17; buried March 17 (3/18)

GENEALOGICAL DATA FROM THE NEW-YORK MERCURY

The New-York Mercury was established by Hugh Gaines in August 1752 and was continued until January 25, 1768. The New-York Historical Society has collected photostatic copies of all known issues of the newspaper, and from these have been compiled those items which yield vital statistics.

1752

Webber, John, and brother, Jonathan, from Wells, York Co.—convicted in Boston of passing counterfeit dollars (11/6)

M'Dermot, Philip, and wife, Margaret—committed to goal of Chester-Town on suspicion of being accessories to murder of John Thomas and Eleanor Davis; Phila. dispatch of Nov. 2 (11/6)

Smith, William, Jr.—married Friday night, Nov. 3, in NYC, to Jenney Livingston, daughter of James Livingston, alderman of the Dock Ward of NYC (11/6)

De Lancey, of NYC, merchant, brother of Lady Warren—sailed last week with Capt. Griffiths from NYC for London (11/6)

Carson, Hamilton—Oct. 26, at Lancaster, Pa., convicted of burglary and sentenced to death (11/13)

M'Connel, James, and wife, Esther—Oct. 26, at Lancaster, Pa., convicted of being accessories after the fact to burglary committed by John Webster and both burnt in the hand (11/13)

Matthews, Hugh—Oct. 30, in York Co., Pa., convicted of robbery on the highway, having taken a mare from John Carahan, and sentenced to death (11/13)

Diggs, Dudley, of Pa.—accused of his murder were Martin and Jacob Kitzmiller, of whom Martin was acquitted and Jacob found guilty of manslaughter (11/13)

Bradford, Cornelius—sells iron and pewter at his father's house in Hanover Square, NYC (11/13)

Vanhorne, Major Cornelius, dec'd—John Watts, merchant, of NYC, elected to serve in the assembly in place of Vanhorne (11/13)

Briton, Old (so called by the English), an old Pianguisha king—captured June 21 by French Indians called Tawaws and boiled and eaten by them; dispatch from Williamsburg, Va. (11/20)

Conner, Terence (born in Ireland)—executed at Annapolis, Md., Oct. 20, for murder of James Boyles in Frederick Co., in August, 1752 (11/27)

Crabb, John, seaman—died Nov. 13, in Boston, of a fractured skull, having been beaten that night between 8 and 9 P.M. by one Chubb, a sturdy white boy, and a Negro (11/27)

Lloyd, Nathaniel, young gentleman of Long Island, N. Y.—drowned Nov. 12 when his boat was overset by sudden gust of wind (11/27)

Hurley, Daniel—executed in Phila. Nov. 29 (12/4)

Kelly, Thomas—executed Dec. 16 for murder of John Thomas and Eleanor Davis (12/25)

Rice, James—executed Dec. 9 for murder of above Thomas and Davis (12/25)

Jillet, William—executed Oct. 16 at Newbern, N. C. for counterfeiting coin (12/18)

Johnson (*alias* Dixon), Daniel—same as above

Smith (*alias* Griffith), David—executed Oct. 16 at Newbern, N. C., for robbery of a store in Johnson Co. about four years before (12/8)

Valette, Peter, of NYC, merchant—died in NYC Dec. 9 in 75th year and buried Dec. 12 in family vault in Out Ward of NYC (12/18)

Doran, Bryan (one of murderers of John Thomas and Eleanor Davis), age c. 30—described; reward offered for his capture (12/25)

1753

Van Nest, Jacob—while returning home from Reading-Town, on Dec. 13, in Somerset Co., N. J., was killed with an axe by his Negro servant; the servant was burnt alive at Millstone on Dec. 27 (1/1)

Tucker, Capt. Stephen—while on schooner from NYC bound to Barbados died of smallpox (1/1)

Coey, Robert, seaman on sloop *Rhode Island* of port of NY—drowned Oct. 23 off Florida Keys (2/25)

Richardson, John, sailor on Liverpool ship, one Patrick master—drowned off Florida shore in Oct., 1752 (2/25)

Ogden, Jonathan, late of NYC, dec'd—his inn, "the Black Horse," near Alderman Benson's in NYC (and also his farm at North-Castle, Westchester Co.) for sale (2/25)

Haff, Lawrence, dec'd—his plantation in Nine Partners in Dutchess Co., for sale (2/25)

Burges, Capt. John, of NYC, merchant (who had been presented by merchants of NYC with two pieces of plate for his gallant action at sea against the French)—died in NYC March 9 in 28th year of smallpox and was buried March 11 in vault of family to which he was allied by marriage (3/12)

Coon, Capt., of brig *Shrewsbury* of port of NY—died of smallpox on Island of Jamaica (3/12)

Wickham, Samuel, Deputy Judge of Court of Vice-Admiralty for R. I., Chief Justice of Court of Common Pleas and General Sessions for Newport Co.—died in Newport night of Feb. 14 in 60th year (3/19)

Smith, Capt. John, of the sloop *Dragon* of Bermuda—died of smallpox about end of January while on way to St. Eustatia (3/26)

Brown, Thomas (Irish servant), age c. 28—runaway from Daniel Connar of Westchester Co, N. Y. (3/26)

Huxl(y), Capt.—lost with his brig (owned by Henry Collins) in bay near Newport, R. I., on March 14 (4/2)

Rice, Nathaniel, President and Commander-in chief of North Carolina—died Jan. 29, 1753, at Wilmington on Cape Fear (4/2)

(P)eterson, Walter (Irishman), age c. 28 or 30 (pretends to be a lawyer)—warning against this rogue (4/9)

Dubois, Miss Elizabeth, of NYC, daughter of the late Gualtherius Dubois—died in NYC in her 43rd year on morning of April 3 and was buried evening of April 5 in the Old Dutch Church (4/9)

Meares, Lewis (English servant), age 24 or 25, jeweller and engraver—runaway April 8 from Myer Myers of NYC (4/9)

Hylton, Capt. Ralph, of NYC, merchant—died night of April 11 in NYC after a short illness (4/16)

Thompson, James, of NYC, merchant—married night of April 21, in NYC, to Miss Catharine Walton, youngest daughter of late Jacob Walton of NYC (4/23)

Foerster, Jacob Christopher, dec'd—property in Orange Co., N. Y. (5/7)

Erwine, John (Irish servant), age c. 16 (who came to America with Capt. Woodlock)—runaway April 16 from Francis Wilson at Fish-Kills, N. Y. (5/7)

Doughty, Samuel, of Flushing—May 3 his horse stumbled and fell on him near Westchester, so that he died May 4 (5/7 and 14)

Swales (or Swait), John—executed June 2 at York Town, Pa., for murder of John Reily (or Relay) (5/14 and 6/11)

Reynolds, Catharine—sentenced at Lancaster, Pa., to die for murder of her bastard child (5/14)

Cox, James, sailor—when going on board ship *John* lying at the New Dock in NYC fell into water and was drowned night of May 7 (5/14)

Gouverneur, Mrs. Maria, dec'd—accounts of her estate to be settled (5/21)

Goodwin, ————, age c. 15—killed at Saco Falls when a log rolled onto his head and crushed his skull (5/28)

————, Hugh, of Springfield, Bucks Co., Pa.—killed May 8 by a falling tree (5/28)

Johnston, David, of NYC—married night of May 27, in NYC, Miss Helena Walton, daughter of late Jacob Walton, of NYC (5/28)

Stevens, George, age c. 15 on May 26, at NYC, while stepping from one vessel to another, fell in between them and was drowned (5/27)

Hogg, Rebecca, of NYC, dec'd—her lodging and boarding house is still being kept (5/27)

Campbell, Charles—executed May 16 at Annapolis, Md. for burglary (6/4)

Spinkle, Daniel—same as above

Brown, John—same as above

Hervey, Mr., mate of ship commanded by Capt. Falls—fell from foreyard and was drowned at sea (6/4)

Morse, Seth, of Medfield, Mass., and two eldest sons, one aged c. 10 and the other c. 7—drowned June 1 while trying to cross the Charles River from the Sherburn side (6/11)

Carpenter, John, age c. 16 or 17—same as above

Paine, Rev. John, of "Southole" on Long Island—accidentally shot and killed about three weeks ago by Richard Howell, who took the clergyman for a deer (6/11)

Cleveland, Capt., master of a sloop and brother of Rev. Mr. Cleveland—killed by Indians on Cape Breton (6/25)

Crew of sloop *Nancy*, William Shearer master, seized the ship in the River Gambia, April 1, 1753 (the sloop, built in Conn., was nine months old and was of seventy tons):

Read, William, born Paisley, near Glasgow, age c. 24, mate

Douglass, Robert, born Yorkshire, age c. 40, boatswain

Turner, Robert, born Aberdeenshire, age c. 24

Chicken, Cuthbert, born Newcastle on Tine, age c. 22

Ellis, John, from East Smithfield, London, age c. 22

Pheasant, James, from Fleetbridge, London, age c. 24

M'Muchan, Thomas, born in Ireland, age c. 18

The above mutineers, leaving their captain on the Guinea coast, got the ship to St. Thomas, where they were jailed. They escaped and fled to Puerto Rico (6/25)

Knowland, James (Irish servant), age c. 17—runaway from brig *Sea Nymph*, Henry Bethune master, at NYC (6/25)

Lewis, Rev. Daniel, of Pembroke—died there June 29 (7/23)

Fitz Morris, Richard (Irish servant who came to America about eight weeks ago with Capt. Brown, from Cork), tailor, age c. 23—runaway July 16 from Roger Magrah, of NYC, tailor (7/23)

Arrowsmith, Michael, born in Bristol, Eng., barber—runaway July 16 from Capt. Goodwin, of NYC (7/23)

Wall, Robert, born in Brunswick Co., Va., age c. 21—charged with stealing on night of July 25 about 1,400 pistoles from Edward Langford out of the house of Mrs. Mary Braddick in New London, Conn. (7/30)

Bryson, James, sailor on snow *Hawk*, Capt. Brown master, of Belfast—fell on July 8 from topmast of ship in NY harbor and was killed (8/13)

Priest, William (English servant), age c. 20—runaway from John Kingsland of Bergen Co., N. J. (8/13)

Malcolm, Mrs., of Brunswick (Boston dispatch)—her house burnt July 19 and she died the next day (8/27)

Jacobs, Henry, of Queen Anne's Co., Md., son of, age c. 30 mos.—fell into a well in August but survived (9/3)

Lavolet, Anthony (French servant), age c. 23—runaway Aug. 26 from John Griffin, of Mamoranack, Westchester Co. (9/3)

Storke, Samuel (noted N. E. merchant)—died in London (9/24)

Gainsberry, Elizabeth, hired servant of Mr. Suddler in Queen Anne's Co., Md.—child born to her first week in Sept., 1753 (10/1)

Nicholas, John (English servant), age c. 24, imported to America by Capt. Stephen Richard, who sold him to Alexander Sterling, who in turn sold him to William Kelly—runaway from Kelley in NYC (10/1)

Quigg, Charles, of Phila. age c. 15, murdered night of Sept. 28 in his parents' home by Thomas Ruth, a servant of Mr. Wall's, in Strawberry Alley, Phila. (10/8)

Elde, Mrs. Agnes, widow, of NYC, dec'd—debts to her estate to be paid to her executors, William Bryant, William Peartree Smith and Abraham Lodge (10/8)

Adams, Rev. Eliphalet, of New London, Conn.—died there at a very advanced age the first week in October (10/15)

Hill, Nathaniel, of Boston, apothecary—died there of apoplexy about 1 A.M. on Oct. 6 (10/15)

Osborn, Sir Danvers (just appointed Governor of NY)—died there suddenly on morning of Oct. 12 and was buried in a vault in chancel of Trinity Church (10/15)

Grant, Rev. John, of Westfield, N. J.—died there night of Sept. 16 (10/15)

Wright, Mary (English servant), age c. 23—runaway Oct. 11 from Carden Proctor, of NYC, watchmaker (10/15)

Cosby, Capt. Henry (late commander of H.M.S. *Centeaur*)—died Oct. 16 at New Brunswick, N.J., and his remains buried in vault in chancel of Trinity Church in NYC (10/22)

M'Neil, James, a pedlar—murdered Oct. 3 about ten miles south of Albany, N. Y., by John Turner (a Bristol man); Turner was pursued and taken at Kinderhook (10/22)

Rodgers, Mrs. William, of Middletown, N. J.—accidentally shot and killed by her husband Oct. 12 (10/22)

Wells, Obadiah, dec'd—real estate to be sold in NYC (10/22)

Ruth, Thomas—executed at Phila., Oct. 20, for murder of Charles Quigg (10/29)

M'Cormick, servant, age c. 28—runaway from Peter Gordon of Amboy Township (10/29)

Joe (or Joseph), (Negro slave), age c. 38 or 40—runaway Oct. 5 from Capt. Charles Ware of NYC (11/)

Rutgers, Hermanus, late of NYC, dec'd—demands on estate of (11/19)

Glentworth, John, late of NYC, tailor, dec'd.—demands on his estate to be brought to Elizabeth Glentworth, administratrix (11/19)

Tom (mulatto slave), age c. 30—runaway about Nov. 14 from Patrick Mott of Hempstead, L. I. (11/19)

Ross, Rev. George, of New Castle (on Delaware)—died there Sunday, Nov. 18, in 74th year (11/26)

Herin, Capt., of a ship belonging to Waterford and bound home from Cadiz—killed at sea by pirates (11/26)

Barrot, John—sentenced by Supreme Court held in Baltimore Co., Md., to die for murder of his wife (12/10)

O'Brian, Darby (an Irishman), butcher—died Nov. 20 in Boston from wound inflicted in a quarrel by George Kelly (*alias* William Welch), mariner (12/10)

Bramble, Sarah—executed Nov. 21 at New London, Conn., for murder of her bastard child (12/24)

Winslow, Edward, of Boston, formerly High Sheriff of Suffolk Co., Colonel of Militia,

Genealogical Data from The New York Mercury   33

Justice of the Peace and Quorum, Justice of the Inferior Court of Common Pleas for Suffolk Co., Treasurer of said county—died in Boston about 9 P.M., Dec. 1, in 85th year (12/24)

1754

Osborne, Hon. John—married Dec. 13 in Boston Miss Elizabeth Pierce, daughter of Hon. Joshua Pierce, dec'd, late of Portsmouth, N. H. (1/7)

Thair, Ephraim, of Braintree, Mass., age 85—married at noon, Dec. 18, in Weymouth, Mass., Mrs. Elizabeth Kingman, aged 78, of Weymouth; ceremony took place 15 months after burial of his former wife, with whom he lived 60 years, during which time he was father, grandfather, and great-grandfather of 66 male and 66 female children, since when there has been an increase of about 20 more (1/7)

Levy, Nathan, eminent merchant of Phila.—died there last Dec. 21 of an apoplectic fit (1/7)

Breton, John, late of Middletown, N. J.—frozen to death first week of January near Middletown Creek (1/7)

Rutgers, Petrus, dec'd.—house in possession of his widow, Mrs. Helena Rutgers of NYC, for sale, as also other real estate (1/14)

Frielinghuysen, Rev. Theodorus Jacobus, dec'd—his estate in Middlesex Co., N. J., for sale; apply to Joris Brinckerhoff, of NYC, merchant, or clergymen, Theodorus and Johannes Frielinghuysen in Albany and at Rariton (1/14)

Smith, Daniel, of Jamaica, L. I.—perished of extreme cold on Jan. 21 (1/28)

Leveredge, Samuel, married man of Newton—frozen to death in canoe Jan. 21 (1/28)

Roberts, Amos—same as above

Salier, William—same as above

Salier, Thomas, single man of Newton—same as above

Turner, John, late of NYC, dec'd—real estate for sale (1/28)

Pemberton, Israel, Sr., born in Pa. in 1684, merchant; for 19 years member of General Assembly—died evening of Jan. 19 in Phila. of apoplectic fit in 69th year (2/4)

Hylton, Mahetabel, widow, of NYC—India and European goods for sale at her house at the Old-Slip Market (2/11)

Burrough, William, late of NYC, dec'd—debtors to his estate (2/11)

Ross, Alexander, of NYC—his wife Anne has eloped and he will not be responsible for debts she may contract (2/11)

Thomas, Widow—lives in Maiden Lane, next door to Gerardus Beekman (2/11)

Bray, William, of NYC, a boy—drowned "last Saturday Sen'night" when pilot boat of Tunis Rivets, of Port of NY, was overset (2/18)

Burdine, Thomas, of NYC, a boy—same as above

Tenbrook, John, late of NYC, dec'd—demands on his estate to be brought to John Burnet, surviving executor (2/18)

Hyde, Mr., of Surrey Co., Va.—beheaded Jan. 14 by his Negro servant, who also killed Hyde's wife and three children; the murderer was taken and hanged (2/25)

Evans, Seth, a caulker—last Christmas eve crossed the Patuxent River in a canoe to fetch a midwife for his wife who was in labor; when returning, both Evans and midwife were frozen to death (Annapolis dispatch) (2/25)

Watts, Thomas, "a simple young man"—so abused for three days in a tippling house on Chester River in Queen Anne's Co., Md., in December, 1753, that he died (2/25)

Beasley, William, dec'd—trustees appointed to settle his estate to meet April 9 at house of John Yelverton of Goshen, NY (2/25)

Kenneway, Capt., from Phila.—died in Spanish jail in Port-Mahoo (3/4)

Swan, Capt.—same as above

Foyle, Robert, of Augusta Co., Va., living at head of the Memonangehalla River—killed Jan. 4, 1754, together with wife and five children (youngest aged 10), by Indians (3/18)

Warren, Sir Peter, dec'd—persons indebted to his estate to apply to Oliver De Lancey in NYC (3/18)

Riggs, Capt. Thomas, commander of H.M.S. *Jamaica*—died in Charleston, S. C., night of Feb. 11, 1754 (3/18)

Bresier, Mr., of NYC, child of, age c. 5—run over by team in NYC evening of March 23 and killed (3/25)

Groesbeck, Widow—her house and store in NYC, "opposite to The Gentleman's Coffee-House," to be let (3/25); Thomas Ross will teach languages and reading, writing and arithmetic in his house next door to that in which John Groosebeck, dec'd, lived and almost opposite the Merchant's Coffee House (9/16)

Drowned at sea Feb. 20, near Martha's Vineyard, in the wreck of a brigantine bound from South Carolina to Boston, Fortesque Vernon commander, were the following, all of Boston or neighborhood:
Erwin, Capt. Henry
Davis, Capt. Thomas
Herrington, George
Palmer, Isaac
Gordon, Nathaniel, a boy
Nasmus, William, a Negro
also, Mears, Francis, of Halifax
and Burges, James, a stranger (4/1)

Healey, Francis, mate of the brig *Fanny*, E. Kendrick master, bound from Bristol to NY—fell overboard and was drowned Feb. 21 (4/1)

Gabrielsund, Capt.—lost at sea on return to America from London (Annapolis dispatch) (4/8)

Melvin, Eleazer, of Carlisle, Middlesex Co., Mass, who for many years had held commissions against the Indian enemy—died there Oct. 18 and was buried Oct. 21 (11/11)

Steed, Smith, apprentice, son of Deborah Steed of Jamaica, L.I.—runaway from his master, John Forrest of NYC, tailor (11/11)

Newell, Mr., of Lynn, Mass.—killed by Indians about beginning of Nov. at Fort Halifax (11/18)

Mason, Capt. John, commander of ship *Neptune* of Rotterdam—died Nov. 14 in NYC (11/18)

Cornel, Giliam, late of Flatbush, Kings Co., NY, dec'd—house, land, etc. to be sold by executors, Cornelius Cornel, Dominicus Van Der Veer, and Christianus Lupardus (11/18)

King, Thomas, servant, age 40, worker in brass, copper, tin—runaway about two months ago from George Norris of Prince-Town, N.J., tinman (11/25)

Wieer, William—executed Nov. 21 in Boston for murder of William Chism (12/2)

Willing, Charles, Mayor of Phila.—died there Dec. 1 in 45th year (12/9)

Lightfoot, Michael, Treasurer of Pa.—died Dec. 3 in Phila. (12/9)

Kierstead, Benjamin, of NYC, dec'd—his dwelling near the poorhouse to be sold (12/9)

Warner, Edward, member of Pa. Assembly for Phila. Co., dec'd—James Pemberton elected assemblyman in his place (12/16 supplement)

Allison, John, of Haverstraw, dec'd—demands of his estate to be made to executors, John Johnson and John Peterson Smith (12/23)

Caesar, a mulatto, age c. 23—runaway Dec. 4 from Daniel Tuthill of Southold (12/23)

1755

Clough, Peter, of Hampton, N.H.—struck and killed there Dec. 12, 1754, by Eliphas Dow of Hampton (1/6)

Cunningham, John, servant, 30—runaway Jan. 3 from ship *Lydia*, Caldwell master (1/6)

Livingston, Philip, late of Coracoa, dec'd—his brother, Robert G. Livingston, has received from Philip's executors a sum of money for the account of Samuel Worth (1/13)

Benson, Robert, of NYC, dec'd—dwelling in Montgomerie Ward, once owned by him but now by Mr. Wood, for sale (1/13)

Sims, James, servant, "county born," pretends to be a cooper—runaway Dec. 19, 1754, from the castle sawmill in Burlington Co., N.J. (1/13)

Lawrence, Benjamin, of Elk Ridge, Md., planter—accidentally ran a pipe stem into the roof of his mouth and died Jan 4 (2/17)

Wild, William, Jr., of Braintree, Mass., two sons (ages 8 and 6)—drowned in pond Jan. 19 when they fell through ice (2/17)

Gibson, Joseph, a trader who formerly lived in Md., age c. 74—died Jan. 16 at Rehoboth (2/24)

Lawrence, Susannah, widow, of NYC, innholder—debts to her are to be paid to Ebenezer Grant, Daniel Styles or John Leake (2/24)

Beekman, Cornelius, of NYC, dec'd—Stephen Leach, tailor, has moved into house next to that of late Mr. Beekman opposite Burling's Slip (3/10)

Jeremy, a mulatto slave, age c. 21 and Anthony, age c. 18—runaways March 21 from Godfrey Mallbone and Robert Stoddard of Newport, R.I. (3/31)

Shilling, Barnet, German servant, age 21—runaway April 1 from John Van Zandt of NYC (4/7)

Mitchel, George, of Portsmouth, N.H., Master of Masonic Lodge—died there March 10 in 45th year, leaving wife and six children (4/14)

Teneyck, Coenrad, mate of sloop *Jenny* of NY, William Brown master—died from cold on board ship March 18 near Ocracock (4/14)

Harbard, John, drummer in the governor's regiment—drowned March 10 in Boston harbor (4/21)

Starr, Mrs., of Middletown, Conn.—March 23 gave birth to three boys (4/21)

Hames, George, Irish servant, mason by trade, age c. 24—runaway from Patrick Deaver of Scoharie, Albany Co., NY (4/21)

Moore, William, son of late Hon. John Moore of NYC, dec'd—William died in "Coracoa" (4/28)

M'Laughlin, William, Irish servant, age c. 14—runaway May 1 from John Torrans of NYC, merchant (5/5)

Race, William, living near Sheffield, Hampshire Co., Mass.—wounded and killed there April 15 by band of evil-minded persons (5/12)

Sparhawk, Rev. John, pastor of First Church of Salem, Mass.—died there about one o'clock April 30 (5/12)

Chambers, George, first week in May sentenced to death by court at Lancaster, Pa., for bestiality (5/12)

Davis, Hugh—same, but for crime of burglary

Smidt, Eve Mary—same, but for murder of her child

Lane, Capt., of Killingsworth, Conn.—April 21 accidentally shot and killed there while exercising militia under his command (5/19)

Moore, James, Irish servant "lad"—runaway May 20 from Edward Laight of NY, currier (5/26)

Kremer, Philip Barnet, German servant, age 18—runaway May 19 from Nicholas Bayard of NYC (5/26)

Vanalst, Andrew, late of Newtown, dec'd—Thomas Moone, of Flushing, L.I., on June 10 will divide among heirs money lodged with him as the acting executor, after the Hon. Rip Van Dam, dec'd (5/26)

Douglas, Thomas, age c. 25, soldier under Lt. Richard Bayly in regiment of Sir Peter Halkett—deserted April 29 and fled with stolen articles (6/2)

Stone, Mr., near North Yarmouth in Casco Bay—killed by Indians (6/9)

Torry, Rev., of North Kingston, R.I., son of, age c. 20—died there in mid-May when thrown from his horse (6/16)

Patterson, Mr., of Bedford on Merrimack River, N.H.—killed there by falling timber at raising of house (6/16)

Primmer, Johan Jury, of "Hossack," eldest son of—killed there June 2 by Indians (6/16)

Bokee, Mr., of NYC, son of, age c. 10—first week in June, while fishing for crabs in a pettiauger, was knocked overboard by the boom and drowned (6/16)

Derota, Maria, German servant, age 18—runaway June 20 from John Haydock of NYC (6/23)

Monsell, Joseph, mate of ship of Capt. Harden, which sailed about six weeks ago from Charlestown, Mass., bound for Newfoundland, on eighth day out fell from bowsprit and was drowned (6/30)

Mooney, John, an "apprentice lad"—runaway June 10 from Henry Hardcastle of NYC, carver (6/30)

Williams, Mr., living on north branch of Potowmack, about twelve miles above mouth of Will's Creek, Pa.—murdered, together with his wife and grandson, by Indians in latter part of June (7/7)

Grant, John, of NYC, dec'd—writ issued out of Mayor's Court at suit of William Wood against property of James Wilkes and wife Sarah, executors of Grant's estate (7/7)

Chase, Jeremiah, of Charles Co., Md.—murdered by poison (7/14)

Brown, Thomas, of NYC, ironmonger, wife of—night of July 9 killed by brick falling from house while she was sitting on stoop (7/14)

Low, Miss Margaret, daughter of Cornelius Low, merchant in Rariton—died July 8 and was buried in Old Dutch Church in NYC (7/14)

Davis, Henry, turner by trade, age c. 22—deserted from N.J. regiment of Col. Peter Schuyler and company of Capt. Nathaniel Rusco (7/21)

Murray, Mrs. Grace, wife of Hon. Joseph Murray (member of H.M.'s Council for NY)—died in NYC night of July 16 and buried next evening in the family vault in Trinity Church (7/21)

The following officers were killed July 9 in Braddock's defeat (7/28):

Halket, Sir Peter	Wideman, Lt.
Braddock, Gen. Edward	Hanfard, Lt.
Shirley, William	Brerton, Lt.
Allen, Lt.	Hart, Lt.
Tatton, Capt.	Smith, Capt. Lt.
Gethins, Capt.	Spendelow, Lt.
Townsend, Lt.	Talbot, Midsh.
Nartlow, Lt.	Stone, Capt.
Cholmsey, Capt.	
Crimble, Lt.	

Independent Companies of NY
  Soumain, Lt.
Virginia Troops
  Polson, Capt.
  Hamilton, Lt.
  Peronie, Capt.
  Hamilton, Lt.

Wright, Lt.

Splitdorff, Lt.

Waggoner, Lt.

Carnan, Rowland—same as above

Curtis, Capt. William, master of sloop belonging to Mr. Creagh of Annapolis, Md.—murdered by three of his crew who turned pirates (4/8)

Vessels, Widow, of Clements Bay in St. Mary's Co., Md., age c. 30 or 35—murdered March 1754 (4/15)

Clarkson, Matthew, dec'd—his house and land near upon Rariton River, opposite Rariton Landing and within a mile of New Brunswick, for sale (4/15)

Pomfret, Richard—drowned Jan. 21 while coming in a pettyauger to NYC from the oyster banks (4/15)

Liddel (or Leddle), Joseph, Jr., of NYC, pewterer—while fishing near Corlear's Hook on afternoon of April 13 died from violent bleeding of nose (4/15 and 6/24)

Butler, William, son of Thomas Butler, of Prince William's Parish, S. C.—shot and killed March 3 about one mile from Charleston by John Toomer, of Prince William's Parish, age c. 28 (4/22)

Welch, William (*alias* George Kelly)—executed April 11 at Boston for murder of Darby O'Brian (4/22)

Moreton, Mr., of Carlisle, Cumberland Co., Pa.—shot and killed there about beginning of April by John Hart, an Indian trader (4/22)

Temple, Robert, of Charlestown, Mass.—died there April 13 and was buried in Boston (4/29)

Lawrence, Thomas, of Phila., member of council, five times mayor, president of Court of Common Pleas for Phila. Co.—died in Phila. April 21 (4/29)

Cregier, Martinus, of NYC—between 9 and 10 P.M., April 25, during a quarrel, was struck on board his boat with a pole by Patrick Creamer, fell into the sea and died (4/29)

Poole, Thomas, of Charleston, S. C., pilot drowned March 20 near the swash bar (5/6)

Henderson, Widow, residing in Queen St., between Fly and Meal Markets in NYC—her house has been occupied by the store of Corne & Van Dam (5/6)

Crow, John—executed at Phila. May 25 (6/3)

Chester, ——— —same as above

Ludington, William, of North Branford, Conn., two infant children of—burned to death May 22 (6/3)

Jerry (Negro servant), age c. 26—runaway March 17 from Daniel Brewster of Brookhaven, Suffolk Co., NY (6/3)

Ratsey, Widow, who lately lived in Smith's St., near the Old Dutch Church in NYC—her house now occupied by James Ham, maker of mathematical instruments (6/3)

Loyde, Edward, of Queen Anne's Co., Md.,—killed by lightning bolt March 20 (6/10)

Howard, Beale, young man—drowned March 22 while going up Patapsco River, Md., in a sloop (6/10)

Cary, Henry, sailor on ship of Capt. Walters in Patapsco, Md.—killed March 23 by explosion of cannon on ship (6/10)

Sears, ———, —drowned off Robins Reef in NY Bay when boat from New Brunswick, owned by Derick Schuyler and commanded by Thomas Cholwell, overset June 4 (6/10)

White, ——— —same as above

Berry, ——— —same as above

Blank, Casparus, of NYC, dec'd—his houses and land in Broadway, the opposite corner to Widow Vangelder's, to be sold (6/17)

Fry, Col. Joshua, of Va., born in Somersetshire, Eng., educated at Oxford, first grammar master and then professor of mathematics at William and Mary College, commander of the forces gone to the Ohio—lately fell from his horse and died of injuries at Wills Creek (6/24 and 7/15)

Phillis (or Phillida), Negro slave, age c. 19—runaway June 18 from Robert Campbell of Tapan, Orange Co., NY (6/24)

Boel, Rev. Hendricus, of NYC—died afternoon of June 27 in NYC in 66th year (7/1)

Wilson, William, born in Yorkshire, Eng., age c. 20—runaway (taking his master's mare) June 24 from James Logan of Phila. (7/1)

Friend, John, Dutch servant, miller by trade, age c. 20—runaway May 19 from John Lesher's forge in Oley, Berks Co., Pa. (7/1)

Rouf, John, Dutch servant, age c. 24—same as above

Oxnard, Thomas, Grand Master of Masons in North America—died June 25 in Boston in 55th year and buried there June 28 (7/8)

Viscoup, Daniel, German servant, potbaker by trade, age c. 26—runaway July 5 from Adam States of Horse-Neck, Conn. (7/8)

Verplank, Gulian, dec'd—his store in Wall St., now occupied by Rudolphus Van Dyck (7/8)

Albee, Obadiah—in June while going down Sheepscut River in a canoe was wounded by a bear and drowned in the river (7/15)

Albee, ————, brother of the same—same as above.

Seymour, John, of York (now Maine)—July 7 drowned his infant in the river; he had a son thirteen years old (7/22)

Plymun, Margrietta, High Dutch servant, age c. 23—runaway June 2 from Charles Ware of NYC; she was formerly a servant of Edward Graham of NYC, merchant (7/22)

McEvers, John, of NYC, merchant, dec'd—his daughter, Miss Mary McEvers of NYC, wins £1,000 prize in NY lottery for benefit of college to be erected in the province (7/29)

Wright, William, of East Hartford, Conn., wife of—hanged herself on morning of July 13 (7/29)

Flanley, Patrick, Irish servant, leather britches maker and skinner, age c. 19—runaway July 27 from Samuel Farmar of NYC (7/29)

Duffet, ————sentenced to death by court at Dover (on Delaware) for murder of John Brown (8/12)

Dupuy, Mrs. Frances, widow of Dr. Dupuy—her house in King St., NYC, occupied by shop of Myer Myers, goldsmith (8/12); she sues John Perot for slander and wins case (2/3, 1755)

Allen, Joseph, English servant, founder by trade, age 38—runaway July 28 from James Smith of Phila., brass founder (8/12)

Williams, Lydia Mary Anne, servant from Lancashire, Eng., age c. 20—runaway July 27 from Stephen Leach of NYC, tailor (8/12)

Wright, John—executed Aug. 7 at Annapolis, Md., for murder of Capt. Curtis of sloop *Hopewell* March last (8/19)

Toney, a mulatto—same as above

Vatar, Thomas, of NYC, dec'd—all persons with demands on his estate to apply to Abraham Lynsen of NYC (8/19)

Dorlant, John, dec'd—his plantation in Somerset Co., N.J., at Nishenick for sale (9/19)

Smith, Hon. William, wife of—died Aug. 22 in NYC of a fever in 45th year (8/26)

Purry, Charles, of Beaufort, S.C., merchant—murdered there night of July 21 (9/2)

Call, Mrs. Philip, of Baker's Town (most northerly settlement on the Merimack River, N.H.), age c. 70—killed by Indians Aug. 15 (9/2)

Spullman, Hans, of Hoosack (about 25 miles N.E. of Albany)—killed by Indians Aug. 28 (9/2)

Barns, Samuel—same as above

Dwyer, John, Irish servant, age c. 20—runaway Sept. 1 from John Hance of Shrewsbury, mariner (9/2)

Martin, William Thomas, second son of Hon. Josiah Martin of NYC,—died Aug. 28 in Phila. in 16th year (9/9)

Pyra, Mary, English servant, age 22—runaway Sept. 4 from Mary Wright of NYC (9/9)

Welch, Nicholas, Irish servant, tailor, age 20—runaway from Daniel Campbell of Schenectady, Albany Co., NY (9/30)

Fowler, Michael—convicted of burglary and sentenced to death in Springfield, Mass., Sept. 24 (10/14)

Peter, French servant, age c. 28—runaway Oct. 3 from the snow *Charming Sally,* Thomas White commander (10/14)

Bursheau, French servant, age 30—same as above

Fonck, Cornelius, of NYC—accidentally shot and killed Oct. 15 by Jacob Cole of NYC and two others (10/21)

Hager (or Heger), Harmanus, who came from Germany to Pa. about five years ago—three of his children, Jacob, Anna Margerieta, and Valentine, have come to New York in the *Sarah-Galley,* Thomas Stap master, and Mr. Hager may find his children by enquiring of Philip Livingston, of NYC, merchant (10/21)

Lewis, Capt. (of a ship from Rhode Island) perished when ship was struck by lightning and buried at sea (11/4)

Parker, Jacob, of Boston, a deacon—died morning of Oct. 22 of apoplectic fit (11/4)

Tell, Richard, dec'd—his daughter, age c. 19, who at about age of 7 was carried off to Canada by Indians, has arrived in Phila, in search of her mother who has remarried and of an aunt named Lydia (11/4)

Furlong, Capt., master of the schooner *Catharine* of NYC—died on passage from Mahoo to Havannah (11/4)

Thompson, John, Jr., of Goshen, NY—died there about a month ago while working in the woods (11/4)

Hadley, Joseph, of Yonkers—died Oct. 30 on beach of the North River where he had been fishing (11/4)

Halembeck, Hans, of Albany Co., NY—dropped dead on board sloop in NY harbor night of Nov. 2 (11/4)

Howell, Capt. James, master of the snow *Beaumont* that sailed out of South River in Sept.—perished when ship foundered soon after it left the capes (11/11)

Conrad, Charlotte Maria, Hanoverian servant, about 7 months in America, age c. 22— runaway from Samuel Sansom in Front St., Phila. (8/4)

Hamanin, Maria Sharlotta, Dutch servant, age c. 20—runaway from William Bradford of Phila. (8/4)

Bayard, Mrs. Elizabeth, wife of Nicholas Bayard, of NYC, merchant—died in NYC Aug. 3 in 52nd year and buried in her family vault at her country seat (8/11)

Waters, Aeltye, (wife of John Waters of Smith-Town, L.I., formerly wife of Nicholas Carmer, dec'd, and daughter of Frederick Seabring of NYC)—has eloped from her husband (8/11)

Williams, Honor, wife of John Williams of NYC, mariner—has eloped from her husband (8/18)

Moore, Barbara (who has been in America three years)—seeks news of her brother Jacob, who left Holland and came to America three years before her (8/18)

Gouverneur, Nicholas, of NYC, merchant—"last Sunday Se'night" married Miss Sarah Cruger, daughter of late John Cruger of NYC, dec'd (8/18)

Patton, Col. James—killed July 31 at head branches of Roanoke by Indians (8/25)

Myrack, Mrs. John, of East Caln, Chester Co., Pa.—murdered by her husband, Aug. 19, as were also two of their children and a child of Mr. John Gilliland (8/25)

Myer, Margreta, German servant girl—runaway Aug. 17 from Benjamin Blage of NYC, distiller (8/25)

Aesop ("young" Negro)—broke out of Newark, N. J. jail, together with a "pretty old" white man named John Smith (8/25); age c. 25—runaway from Lawrence Janse Van Buskerk near Hackinsack (12/1)

Pitts, John, of Ashford, born in Glocester and came to New England when aged between 20 and 30—in Aug., 1752, was 85 when made an affidavit (9/1)

Myrack, John—Aug. 26 sentenced to death by court at Chester, Pa. (9/1)

Freidure, John Baptist, who came about 12 months ago from Brabant, Germany, leather dresser, age 28—runaway Aug. 24 from Thomas Dobson of NYC (9/1)

Sam, a mulatto, age c. 19 runaway Aug. 6 from William Stockton of Springfield Township, Burlington Co., N. J. (9/15)

Hazard, Jonathan, late of NYC, who died intestate—demands on his estate to be settled with James Sacket at his lodgings in King St (9/22)

Moore, James, Irish servant "lad"—runaway Sept. 21 from Edward Laight of NYC, currier (9/29)

General William Johnson in a letter from Lake George dated Sept. 9, 1755, listed the following officers killed in action on Sept. 8:
Williams, Col.
Ashley, Major
Ingersol, Capt.
Puter, Capt.
Ferrall, Capt. (brother-in-law of the general)
Stoddert, Capt.
McGin, Capt.
Stevens, Capt.
Titcomb, Col. (9/29)

Barker, Samuel, who lately lived at Peck's Slip in NYC, dec'd—persons are to pay debts due his estate to Joseph Haynes of NYC, merchant (10/6)

Christey, John, Undersheriff of NYC—died last Sunday Sen'night in NYC from sword thrust inflicted by James Wilkes of NYC, tavernkeeper (10/6)

Hansen, Henry, of NYC, "a considerable merchant"—died Oct. 5 in NYC of a fever (10/6)

Bunker, Capt. Peter, master of a whaling sloop of Nantucket bound home from Banks of Newfoundland—drowned Sept. 5 when ship foundered (10/13)

Hulse, Ebenezer, of NYC—his wife Anne has eloped and he will not be responsible for debts she may contract (10/20)

Burling, James, dec'd—property to be sold; apply to John Burling of NYC or Samuel Burling of Burlington, N. J. (10/20)

Sacket, Joseph, of Newton, lately dec'd—his dwelling at Newton Landing, three farms in the precinct of Goshen, and other property to be sold by Joseph, John, James, Samuel and William Sacket, executors (10/27)

Ketteltas, Abraham, of NYC—married night of Oct. 31 in NYC Miss Sarah Smith, daughter of Hon. William Smith (member of H.M.'s Council for NY (11/3)

Odwaller, Mr.—killed by Indians near first branch of Swetara on the road leading to Shamokin (11/10)

Kout, Elizabeth, German servant "girl" who has been in America about three years and speaks French, German and Dutch—runaway about three weeks ago from Hendrick Schinkle of Claverack, NY (11/17)

Galloway, Elizabeth—early in November killed by Indians at Great Cove near Conegochieg, Pa. (11/17)

Gilson, Henry—same as above

Pew, Robert,—same as above

Berryhill, William—same as above

M'Clellan, David—same as above

Hicks, Mr.—same as above

Anderson, James, son of Lt. Col. John Anderson, of Sussex Co., N. J., age c. 38—made deposition about his expedition against Indians and arrest of a German Indian trader named Miller who was apparently taking powder and lead to the Indians; he had also heard that Charles Broadhead, son of Daniel Broadhead, was transporting powder and lead to the Indians (11/17)

List of persons killed in Pa. in November by Indians:

Cola, Mr., and wife and three children

Philip, a shoemaker

Spring, Caspar

Wolf, Jacob, a child of

Leinberger, John

Candel, Rudolph

Beslinger, Mr.

Brosius, Sebastian (11/24)

Hunckler, Daniel, of Bethlehem, Northampton Co. Pa., age 36—made deposition (11/24 supplement)

Edmonds, of Bethlehem, age 33—same as above

Bartow, Thomas, of Bethlehem, age 18—same as above

Handlin, John, Irish servant, age 24—runaway Nov. 30 from James Jackson of New Windsor, boatman (12/1)

Persons killed by Indians Nov. 24 at Gnadenhutten on Mahony Creek, about 25 miles from Bethlehem:

Anders, Gotlieb, his wife and child aged 1

Nitchman, Martain, and wife

Senseman, Catharine (wife of Joachum Senseman)

Fabricius, Christian

Sweigart, George

Katermeyer, Leonard

Lesley, C. Frederick

Presser, C. E. (12/28)

Rutledge, Hon. Andrew, of Charleston, S. C., attorney and several times Speaker of the Assembly—died Charleston Nov. 19 (12/15)

Pearles, Uriah (runaway convict servant from one Oliver), age c. 17—arrested for attempted murder in Nov. of James Peck of Elk Ridge, Md. (12/15)

Leycock, Mrs., and son, living on Lizard Creek, Pa.—killed Dec. 2 by Indians (12/15)

Leonard, ————, of Baskinridge, N.J., age c. 8—accidentally shot and killed by another lad of eight names Ricky, probably son of Brice Ricky (12/15)

Colgan, Rev. Thomas—died at Jamaica, L.I. (12/15)

Heiss, George Caspar, of Northampton Co., Pa., blacksmith, age 36—gave affidavit Dec. 13, 1755 (12/22)

Persons killed by Indians in Northampton Co., Pa., Dec. 10:

Hoeth, Frederick, his wife and child of about 10 (12/22)

Bush, Hans, and wife (12/22)

Bush, Lambert (12/22)

Stahl, Daniel; left wife and six small children (12/22)

France, Henry (12/22)

Bennet, Capt. Richard, master of the snow *Jamaica Packet* of NYC, bound for Surenham—perished Dec. 16 in wreck of ship at Rockaway on south side of L.I. (12/22)

42

Halstead, Isaac, mate of *Jamaica Packet*—same as above
Gurney, Thomas, seaman—same as above
Couch, Original, seaman—same as above
Mersyer, Andrew, a boy—same as above
Harris, Capt. Newell, formerly of Brunswick, N.C., but late of NY, dec'd—debts to his estate to be paid to his attorneys in N.C. or to his executor in NYC, Sampson Simson (12/22)
Gaston, Robert, living at the head of Hunter's settlement on the forks of Delaware—killed by Indians on Dec. 14 (12/29)
Persons killed by Indians at the Minisinks in Dec. (excluding a few already mentioned):
  Rush, John, wife, son and daughter
  Brink, Lambert
  Tidd, Benjamin and family of 9
  Rue (or Roe), Matthew (killed near Broadhead's Fort) (12/22 and 29)
  Williams, Daniel, wife and five children
  Goulding, Piercewell
  Head, Mr. and ten of his family
  Vanaken, Cornelius and Vancamp, Guizebert and 15 of their families
  Vanfleara, Hans
  Snell, Adam and family (12/29)
Delanoy, James, late of NYC, dec'd—two-story house in Dye St. near the North River now occupied by Mrs. Jane Delanoy for sale (12/29)

GENEALOGICAL DATA FROM THE NEW YORK MERCURY

1756

Hand, John, Irish servant, age 24—runaway Nov. 30 from James Jackson of New Windsor, boatman (1/5)

Van Camp, Mrs. Gilbert, of Pa.—she and twelve children killed by Indians (1/5)

Dicker, Brewer, of Pa.—some of his family killed by Indians (1/5)

Worley, John, of Pa., and all of his large family—killed by Indians (1/5)

Van Gordey, Peter, of Pa., and three sons—killed by Indians (1/5)

Van Aken, Cornelius, of Pa., and family—killed by Indians (1/5)

Griffith, Capt. William, late of NYC, dec'd—debts to his estate to be paid to Rebecca Griffith (1/5)

Sipkins, Rebecca, late of NYC, dec'd—debts to her estate to be paid to Rebecca Griffith (1/5)

Brownsnord, John, English servant, age c. 25—runaway Dec. 27, 1755, from John Gilleylen of East Caten, Chester Co., Pa. (1/5)

Rouse, Robert, Irish servant, age c. 22—runaway from Roger Heffernan, at the Cocoatree, Front St., Phila., chocolate grinder (1/26)

Bowman, John, living near Nazareth, Northampton Co., Pa.—killed Jan. 1 by Indians (1/26)

Wilks, James—condemned to die for murder of John Christie, Undersheriff of NYC (1/26)

Quick, Thomas, of Northampton Co., Pa., age above 70—killed there Jan. 17 by Indians (2/2)

Bemper, Capt., of Northampton Co., Pa.—killed by Indians (2/2)

Franklin, John, Postmaster of Boston—died there morning of Jan. 29 from stone in the bladder (2/9)

Nicholson, Adam, of Patterson's Fort, on Juniata, and wife and son—killed there by Indians afternoon of Jan. 27 (2/9)

Willoc, William, of Patterson's Fort on Juniata, and wife—killed there by Indians Jan. 27 (2/9)

Mitcheltree, Mrs. Hugh, living near Patterson's Fort on Juniata—killed Jan. 27 by Indians (2/9)

Bowen, John—murdered by John Jenkins, of Vincent Township, Chester Co., Pa. (2/9)

Leaton, James—killed by Indians Jan. 28 at the Canalaways, Cumberland Co., Pa. (2/16)

Stillwell, Catharine (Mrs. Richard Stillwell) and one child—same as above; two other Stillwell children (one aged c.8 and the other 3) were carried off by Indians (2/16)

Sheridan, Mr. and wife—killed by Indians near Patterson's Fort on Juniata (2/16)

Mier, John, dec'd—debts to his estate to be paid to executors, John or Jacob Mier, living near Harlem (2/16)

Sisluf, John George, of Lynn Township, Northampton Co., Pa.—his brother and two sons killed there Feb. 14 by Indians (2/23)

Belchelsderfer, Frederick, of Albany Township, Berks Co., Pa.—one of his children killed Feb. 14 by Indians (2/23)

Livingston, Mrs. Catharine, widow of Hon. Philip Livingston, dec'd—died evening of Feb. 20 (2/23)

43

Cox, Matthew, of Cambridge, Mass.—fell from apple tree about sunset Feb. 16 and died of broken neck, leaving widow and eight children (3/1)

Lystrum, Johannes, of Middletown, N. J., age 66—died there about three weeks ago (3/1)

Christie, John, late of NYC, dec'd—debts due his estate to be paid to John Alsop (3/1)

Stevens, Capt. Phinehas (who in 1747 defended Fort No. 4 on the frontiers of Mass. and to whom Admiral Knowles presented a sword for his gallant behavior)—died recently (3/8)

Alexander, Lt., of the second battalion—died end of Feb. at Chiegnecto (3/8)

Judd, Ensign—same as above

Owen, Morgan, living near Goshen—killed by Indians Feb. 27 (3/8)

Lum, Capt. Samuel, late of Hanover, Morris Co., N. J., dec'd—his plantation for sale (3/8)

Van Wyck, Theodorus C., dec'd—his farm along the Fish Kills, about six miles from the landing (or Company store house) in Dutchess Co., NY, for sale (3/8)

Taylor, Widow Mary, late of Concord, Mass.—died there lately aged almost 94; she had 255 children and grandchildren, of whom 202 were still alive at the time of her death (3/15)

Neyson, Mrs. Balsar, of Berks Co., Pa.—killed by Indians March 6 (3/15)

Mulhaus, Mr.—killed March 1 by Indians at plantation of Philip Bussart in Northampton Co., Pa. (3/15)

Minser, George, son of—same as above

Bussart, Philip, son of—same as above

Alston, Capt., of Raway, N. J.—drowned March 11 when Staten Island ferry overset (3/15)

Moore, Mr., of Piscataway, N. J., and son—same as above

Van Tyle, Dennis, of Staten Island, boatman—same as above

Smallpiece, William, of General Shirley's regiment—same as above

Harison, Thomas, battoeman—same as above

Rose, Israel, battoeman—same as above

Fling, Daniel, battoeman—same as above

Jones, James, battoeman—same as above

Miller, John, of Setacut, L. I.—same as above

Miller, William (cousin of John), of Setacut, L. I.—same as above

Lawrance, William, of Raway, N. J., shipwright—same as above

Davis, David, father-in-law of, an old man—killed by Indians Feb. 29 at David's Fort in the Little Cove, Cumberland Co., Pa. (3/22)

Knowland, Mr., a soldier in Capt. Croghan's company—killed by Indians Feb. 29 near Peter's Township, Pa. (3/22)

Eliston, Robert, for many years Comptroller of H.M.' Customs in NY—died in NYC March 20 in 76th year (3/22)

Morrill, Levy, "well-known at Burlington," age c. 21, saddler by trade—deserted from Capt. Askwith's company (3/22)

Lynn, Mr., of Frederick Co., Md., age c. 22—killed there by Indians Feb. 27 (3/29)

Hayes, Mr.—killed by Indians about March 20 near Stoddert's Fort (3/29)

Lowther, Mr.—killed by Indians about March 20 near Little Toonaloways (3/29)

Taylor, Mr., belonging to Fort Shirley, Pa.—killed by Indians March 18 (4/5)

Krousher, Mrs. John, of Berks Co., Pa.—killed by Indians March 22 (4/5)

Yeth, William, of Berks Co., Pa.—killed by Indians March 22, and his son, aged 12, was carried off (4/5)

Zeislof, George, living near Allamingle, Berks Co., Pa., his wife, his sons aged 20 and 12, his daughter, aged 13—all killed by Indians March 24 (4/5)

Bielman, Mrs. David, of Lynn Township, Northampton Co., Pa., and two children—killed by Indians March 6 (4/5)

Alexander, Hon. James, member of H.M.'s Council for NY and N.J.—died April 2 in NYC in 65th year and buried April 5 in family vault (4/5)

Le Count, John, for some 36 years representative for Richmond Co. in the Assembly of NY—died Saturday Sen'night in 61st year; buried at his seat on Staten Island March 29 (4/5)

M'Dowell, Mr.—killed by Indians April 1 near M'Cord's Fort in Conecocheague, Cumberland Co., Pa. (4/12)

Catling, Lt., of Conn.—killed about March 18 near Ft. Edward (4/12)

Kidnee, John and Andries, residing in or near Albany—supposed killed by Indians in March (4/12)

Vanderheyden, John—same as above

Sickles, Jacobus—same as above

Dawson, Wolker—same as above

Brandt, Anthony—same as above

Giffins, Peter—same as above

Sprong, Cornelius—same as above

Cabot, Rev. Marston, of Thompson, Conn.—died there second week in April (4/26)

Killed in battle with Indians in March in Cumberland Co., Pa.:

> Culbertson, Capt. Alexander
> Reynolds, Ensign John
> Kerr, William
> Blair, James
> Layson, John
> Denny, William
> Scott, Francis
> Boyd, William
> Paynter, Jacob
> Jones, Jacob
> Kerr, Robert
> Chambers, William
> M'Coy, Daniel
> Robinson, James
> Peace, James
> Blair, John
> Jones, Henry
> M'Carty, John
> Kelly, John
> Lowder, James (4/26)

M'Cord, Mary—accidentally shot (and killed?) at M'Cord's Fort, Cumberland Co., Pa. (4/29)

Deronde, Nicholas, of NYC, brother of Rev. Lambertus Deronde—sells buckwheat at house where Mr. Rosevelt lately lived near the Fresh Water (4/26)

Bacon, Lt. John, of Capt. Dagworthy's company—killed by Indians about four or five miles from Cumberland Fort (5/3)

Lowe, Abraham—killed by Indians April 19 on the Minisink Road in Ulster Co., NY (5/3)

Dewint, Andries A.—killed by Indians April 23 at Rochester, Ulster Co., NY (5/3)

Mercer, Capt. John, of Va.—killed April 18 by Indians near Edward's Fort on Cape Capon, about 20 miles above Winchester (5/3)

Carter, Lt. Thomas, of Va.—same as above

Kelly, David—killed by Indians April 22 near Cunningham's Fort, Pa. (5/17)

Cressop, Thomas, son of Col. Cressop of Md., killed by Indians April 23 about 18 miles from Ft. Cumberland (3/17 and 24)

Sullivan, Owen, noted counterfeiter—executed NYC May 10 (3/17)

Franks, Abigail, wife of Jacob Franks, "eminent" merchant of NYC—died in NYC about 5 P.M. May 16 and buried May 17 (5/17 and 24)

Van Wyck, Abraham, Jr., late of NYC, dec'd—sale of iron and brass goods at his house near Coentie's Market; debts to his estate to be paid to executors, Theodorus Van Wyck and Dirck Brinkerhoff (5/17)

Beveridge, John, son of—killed by Indians about April 30 near North Yarmouth, Mass. (5/24)

Waldron, Cornelius, of Half Moon, Albany Co., NY—murdered last Saturday week by his German servant man (5/24)

Meaks, Mr., living near Merecocheague Neck, and child—killed by Indians May 9 (5/31)

The following were hanged May 24 as deserters at Albany:

> Penny, George
> Owen, David
> Collin, James
> Goldwin, Peter
> Magee, Brian
> Campbel (*alias* Hamilton, *alias* Johnson) (5/31)

Blair, Lt., age 18 or 19—killed in battle with Indians May 17 near Oswego, NY (5/31)

Livingston, Philip, late of NYC, dec'd, and his widow, Catharine, also dec'd—debts due their estates to be paid to John Livingston (5/31)

Swartwout, Mrs., near Paulin's Kills, 25 miles above Black River, in N.J.—killed about two weeks ago by Indians (6/7)

Wasson, John, of Peter's Township, Cumberland Co., Pa.—killed by Indians May 26 (6/14)

Evans, Lewis, author of the *Map of the Middle British Colonies in America*—died in NYC June 12 (6/14)

Banton, Edmond, of NY—killed by Indians about a month ago at Oswego (6/14)

Mitchell, John, of NY—same as above

Jackson, Henry, of NY—same as above

Jordan, John, of Brunswick—same as above

Mash, Samuel, of Brunswick—same as above

Murray, Michael—same as above

Grant, James, of Phila.—same as above

English, John, of Phila.—same as above

Wünsch, Felix, living at "The Hole," in Lancaster Co., Pa.—killed there by Indians June 8 (6/21)

Coltis, Sergt.—killed by Indians about June 10 near Stillwater (6/21)

Dyckman, George—same as above

Dally, Edward—same as above

Coletrust, Edward—same as above

McQuid, Barnably—same as above

Giles, Susannah—killed by Indians near Bigham's Fort, Pa. (6/28)

Cochran, Robert—same as above

M'Kinney, Thomas—same as above

Duppell, Lawrence, son of, age c. 4—killed by Indians (6/28)

Cox, Mr., "up Schuylkill"—killed June 22 by lightning (6/28)

Lightfoot, Alexander, of Albany, NY, innkeeper and victualler—died there June 17 of apoplectic fit (6/28)

Gulusha, Daniel, farmer, age c. 55—escaped June 5 from jail of Dutchess Co., NY (6/28)

Toms, Simeon, age c. 30—same as above

Smith, Abijah, age 28—same as above

Hubbel, Ichabod, "middle aged"—same as above

Licum, mulatto slave, age c. 24—runaway June 22 from Henry Allen of Great Neck, L.I. (7/5)

Coppeler, Martin, and wife, of Bethel Township, Lancaster Co., Pa.—killed there by Indians July 1 (7/12)

Lowe, Mr., a volunteer—killed by Indians June 23 at Oswego (7/12)

Bickers, Capt.—same as above

Crew, Capt. of NYC, child of, age c. 3—run over and killed by a cart in NYC July 8 (7/12)

Johnston, Abraham, soldier under Col. Cresap—killed July 7 by Indians (7/19)

Ashcraft, Jacob, soldier under Col. Cresap—same as above

Chapin, Elisha, formerly captain of the fort at West Hoosuck—killed July 11 by Indians (7/26)

Chidester, Sergt., son of—same as above

Ross, Charles, born in Stirlingshire, Scotland, age 34—deserted in July from Capt. Wetterstroom of the Royal Regiment of North Americans (7/26)

Smith, William, born in Pa., age 25—same as above

Vaux, Mr. and family—killed by Indians at fort on Holston's River in Augusta Co., Va., about July 1 (8/2)

Peeple, Mrs. Jacob—killed July 21 by Indians near M'Cluer's Gap, about 10 miles from Carlisle, Pa.; a son, age c. 13, and daughter, age c. 2, carried off (8/2)

Castle, Robert, age between 12 and 13—runaway July 31 from ship *Betsey* of London, Thomas Castleton master, at NYC (8/2)

Shadrack, Indian boy, age c. 16—runaway July 18 from Joseph Concklin of Southold, L.I. (8/9)

Joe, Negro slave, age c. 29 or 30—runaway Aug. 9 from William Mott of Great Neck, Hempstead Township, Queens Co., NY (8/16)

Lane, Henry and Lattouch, ———, dec'd—property once owned by them for sale (8/16)

Stevens, John, dec'd—reference to land once owned by him in Somerset Co., N.J. (8/16)

Shepherd, Capt., of New Hampshire—killed in skirmish with enemy between Ft. Edward and Ft. William Henry (8/16)

Dinwiddie, Mr.—killed Aug. 7 by Indians in Cumberland Co., Pa. (8/23)

Walter, Casper—killed Aug. 8 by Indians in Cumberland o., Pa. (8/23)

Dunscomb, Edward, master of brig *King George*—died a few days ago on voyage from Bay of Honduras to NYC (8/23)

Wezer, Mr. (father of Lenard Wezer)—killed Dec. 31, 1755, in Northampton Co., Pa. (9/6)

Moone, Thomas, late of Flushing, L. I., dec'd—estate for sale; demands on estate to be made to Elizabeth Moone, executrix, or Dr. Godard Van Solingen of NYC (9/6)

Philips, John, born at Effington, Devonshire, Eng., age 42—deserted Aug. 20 at Albany, NY, from regiment of Lt. General Otway and company of Capt. Bellew (9/6)

Jackson, Benjamin, born in England, butcher by trade, age c. 33—deserted Aug. 18 from transport *Mary* (9/6)

Scot, Thomas, born in Ireland, age 25—same as above

Patterson, John, born in Scotland, age 26—same as above

Monro, Hector Shirley, son of Hector Monro, Esq., of County Downe, Ireland—to learn something to his advantage he is to apply to Rev. Philip Hughes (chaplain to regiment of Major General Abercrombie) or to Messers Cunningham and Nesbitt of Phila. or to Hugh Wallace of NYC, merchant (9/6)

Mercer, Col.—killed at Oswego (9/13 and 10/4)

Philipse, Col. Frederick, of Philipsburg, NY—married Sept. 9 in NYC Mrs. Elizabeth Rutgers, widow of late Anthony Rutgers and daughter of Charles Williams, Esq. (Naval Officer for the Port of NY) (9/13)

Jarvis, Benjamin, late of NYC, hatter, dec'd—business is carried on by his son James Jarvis (9/13)

Woolsey, Rev. Benjamin, (formerly pastor of First Church in Southold)—died morning of Aug. 12 in his 69th year at his estate at Oysterbay, L.I. and was buried Aug. 14 (9/20)

Hogg, Lt. James—killed by Indians in Sept. near Kittanning on the Ohio (9/27)

Hope, Capt. Alexander—killed on board his sloop when Negro slaves rose against him (9/27)

Marston, Nathaniel (son of Nathaniel Marston, of NYC, merchant)—married night of Sept. 27 in NYC Miss Nancy Van Cortlandt, daughter of Frederick Van Cortlandt, dec'd (10/4)

Bird, Mr., of Augusta Co., Va.—killed by Indians close to Ft. Dinwiddie (10/11)

Brown, George, miller in Conecocheague Cumberland Co., Pa.—killed by Indians on Sept. 20 (10/11)

Hodges, Capt.—killed by Indians near Lake George (10/11)

Grant, Capt., of Conn.—said to have been killed by Indians near Lake George (10/11)

Bird (or Boyde), James, born in Ireland, age c. 26—deserted from 40th regiment of foot (10/11)

Pattison, John, residing on or near Duck Creek in Lower Counties on Delaware, age c. 32 —reward offered for his arrest by William Kelly (10/11)

Cook, Walter, servant, age 35—runaway (10/11)

Clark, David, apprentice, age c. 19—runaway Oct. 3 from Samuel Clizbe of Lyon's Farms, N.J. (10/11)

Jewell, Nathaniel, apprentice, age c. 17—runaway in Oct. from Ichabud Grommon of Lyon's Farms, N.J. (10/11)

Day, William, apprentice—runaway from James Still of Newark, N. J., to go privateering in brig *Johnson*, Grig master, of NYC (10/11)

Miller, Capt. Thomas, of NYC, merchant—married in NYC evening of Oct. 13 Miss Patty Willet (daughter of Thomas Willet of NYC, merchant (10/18)

Seabury, Rev. Samuel (son of Rev. Mr. Seabury of Hempstead, L. I.)—married in NYC night of Oct. 12 Miss Polly Hicks. daughter of Edward Hicks of NYC, merchant (10/18)

Frederick, Noah, of Hanover Township, Lancaster Co., Pa.—killed by Indians Oct. 12 (10/25)

Richard, Paul, former Mayor of NYC and representative in General Assembly, "eminent merchant"—died in NYC Oct. 22 in 59th year and was buried evening of Oct. 24 in Trinity Church (10/25)

Hector, Negro slave, age 13 or 14, formerly belonged to Mrs. Houtvat—runaway Aug. 20 from Anthony Sarly of NYC (10/25)

Dick, Negro slave, age c. 22—runaway Oct. 1 from James Brown of Westchester Co, NY (10/25)

Hughes, Joseph, late commander of schooner *Dove*—convicted by court at Providence, R.I., of murder on March 14 of Michael Clark, cooper, on board said schooner (11/1)

Saltonstall, Hon. Richard, Justice of Superior Court—died Oct. 21 at his seat at Haverhill, Mass (11/1)

Berryhill, Andrew—killed Oct. 21 at Hanover Township, Lancaster Co., Pa. (11/1)

Curtenius, Rev. Anthony, pastor of the five Dutch Reformed churches in Kings Co., L.I. —died Oct. 19 at Flatbush in 59th year and buried Oct. 21 in the church at Flatbush (11/1)

Fitz Randolph, Benjamin, "apprentice lad"—runaway Sept. 17 from William Stewart of Somerset Co., N.J., blacksmith (11/1)

Franck, Negro slave, age c. 20—runaway Oct. 25 from Evert Byvanck of NYC (11/8)

M'Donald, James, soldier—killed by Indians early in Nov. near M'Dowell's Mill, Pa. (11/15)

M'Donald, William, soldier—same as above

M'Cafferty, Bartholomew, soldier—same as above

M'Quoid, Anthony, soldier—same as above

Culbertson, John—same as above

Perry, Samuel—same as above

Kerrell, Hugh—same as above

Woods, John, and wife and mother-in-law—same as above

Archer, Elizabeth, wife of James Archer—same as above

Culmore, Mrs. Philip, her daughter, and Martin Fell (her son-in-law)—killed by Indians Nov. 3 near Ft. Lebanon, Berks Co., Pa. (11/15)

Holland, Hon. Edward, member of H.M.'s Council for NY and Mayor of NYC—died Nov. 10 in NYC and buried evening of Nov. 11 in Trinity Church (11/15)

Hews, Aaron, dec'd—his plantation in Somerset Co., N.J., between Kingstown and Princetown, for sale; apply to Samuel Worth at Stony Brook or James Hews, opposite to Black Horse Alley in Second St., Phila. (11/15)

Vau Cortlandt, Stephen, dec'd—creditors to send accounts to widow Mary Cortlandt (11/22)

Pearsall, Nathaniel, late of Queens Co., dec'd—reference to debts (11/22)

Ripenbergh, Adam—killed Nov. 25 by old Mr. John Van Gelder of Sheffield, Albany Co., NY (12/6)

Taylor, Job, apprentice—runaway from Thomas Longworth of Newark, N.J., cordwainer, to serve on privateer *Prince George* (12/6)

Eldert, Lucas, of Queens Co., NY, yeoman, dec'd—debts to his estate to be paid to Eldert Lucas or Hendrick Eldert, executors (12/6)

Christell, John (who arrived here from Newry a few days hence)—runaway from ship *Lord Dunluce*, Capt. Caldwell (12/6)

Steinbuchs, Jacob—killed by Indians evening of Nov. 28 at house of Balthazar Jager near Heidelberg in Northampton Co., Pa. (12/13)

Jager, Balthazar, daughter of, age c. 11—carried off by Indians (12/13)

Webb, John, private in Shirley's regiment—murdered in NYC Dec. 7 (12/13)

Fullerd, Thomas, mariner—his wife Margaret has eloped (12/13)

1757

Richard, Paul, late of NYC, dec'd—debts to his estate to be paid to Elizabeth, John and Stephen Richard or Theophilact Bache, execs. (1/3)

Hinson, John, age 29—runaway Dec. 17, 1756, from Stephen Tollman of Shrewsbury, East N.J. (1/3)

Jarvis, Benjamin, late of NYC, dec'd—debts to estate to be paid to Andrew Barclay, executor, at warehouse at upper end of Wall St., near the City Hall (1/3)

Quackenbush, Benjamin, late of NYC, dec'd—house in Broadway, opposite to Evert Pell's ropewalk, for sale (1/10)

Eldert, Lucas, late of Queens Co., yeoman, dec'd—debts due his estate to be paid to executors, Lucas and Hendrick Eldert (1/17)

Fullerd, Thomas, mariner—will not be responsible for debts of wife Margaret who has eloped (1/17)

Woodhull, Henry, of Brookhaven, L. I.—will not be responsible for debts of wife Martha who has eloped (1/17)

Thodey, Mrs. Elizabeth, relict of Michael Thodey, late of NYC, merchant—she died in NYC Jan. 27 in 62nd year and was buried Jan. 29 in Trinity churchyard (1/31)

Damsel, Andrew, Irish servant, weaver by trade—runaway Jan. 25 from Andrew Earle, of NYC, feltmaker (1/31)

M'Daniel, John—executed at NYC Feb. 4 (2/27)

Kilfoy, Simon—same as above

Spikeman, Capt.—killed Feb. 18 by French and Indians near Ticonderoga (2/7 and 2/21)

Kennedy, Lt.—same as above

Page, Ensign, of the Rangers—same as above

Ducket, Martin, dec'd—his house, farm and ferry on Staten Island to be let (2/14)

Duncan, Mrs., wife of Thomas Duncan, of NYC, merchant, and four children—burned to death in fire between four and five o'clock on Wed. morning, Feb. 16; her eldest daughter, age c. 18, was saved by jumping from burning house (2/21)

Bailey, Jane, wife of James Bailey of Montgomerie Ward, NYC, laborer—on Sunday, Feb. 13, when intoxicated, she fell into the fire and died (2/21)

Callichan, Mary, a noted lime seller, wife of Dennis Callichan of NYC, laborer—when intoxicated she fell into the water on evening of Feb. 17 and was drowned (2/21)

Gardiner, Mr., volunteer of 44th Regt. with Capt. Rogers—killed Feb. 17 by French and Indians (2/21)

Stinson, Thomas, of Robt. Rogers's company—same as above

Howard, Sergt. Jonathan, of Robt. Rogers's company—same as above

Cemp, Tinners, of Robt. Rogers's company—same as above

Edmonds, John, of Robt. Rogers's company—same as above

Farmer, Thomas, of Robt. Rogers's company—same as above

La Portuga, Emanual, of Robt. Rogers's company—same as above

Stevens, Joseph, of Richd. Rogers's company—same as above

Brown, Thomas, of Capt. Spikeman's company—same as above

Avery, Robert, of Capt. Spikeman's company—same as above

Fisk, Samuel, of Capt. Spikeman's company—same as above

Willet, Abraham, late of Flushing, L. I., dec'd—to purchase farm belonging to his estate apply to Abraham or Thomas Willet, executors (2/28)

Bayard, Samuel, late of NYC, dec'd—house and lot in Duke St, for sale (2/28)

Bedford, Catharine, late of Jamaica, L.I., dec'd—house and lot there for sale (3/7)

Moone, Thomas, late of Flushing, L.I., dec'd—house and land there for sale; demands on estate to be brought to Elizabeth Moone, executrix, or Dr. Godard Van Solingen in NYC (3/7)

M'Cutchin, Hugh, late of Fishkills, NY, dec'd—about two weeks ago, on a dark night, fell over the bridge there and was drowned; his wife died two days later (3/14)

Jurianse, Hermon, late of Aquenonka, upon Passaick-River, two miles from Second River, East N.J. dec'd—plantation there for sale (3/14)

M'Clean, William—killed Feb. 10 on board privateer brig *Prince of Orange*, of NY, in battle at sea with French ship (3/21)

Wilcox, Stillwell—same as above

Beekman, Cornelius, late of NYC, dec'd—furniture and Negro wench belonging to his estate to be sold at house of the widow of Abraham Van Horne (3/21)

Clarkson, David, dec'd—debts to his estate to be paid to executors, Freeman, David and Matthew Clarkson (3/21)

Wilcocks, Joseph, of Ringwood, Bergen Co., N.J.—his wife Nancy has eloped (3/21)

Gale, Col. Samuel, late of Goshen, Orange Co., NY, merchant, dec'd—house for sale; debts to estate to be paid to Elizabeth Gale, executrix (3/28)

Burger, Garret, late of NYC, dec'd—three houses belonging to his estate to be sold: one situated in Wyncoop St., next door to Adrian Bancker; another in Broad St., near the City Hall, in the tenure of Capt. Heysham; the third in Broad St., in the tenure of Mrs. Anne Verplank; apply to Johannah Man, executrix, or Thomas Oakes (3/28)

Gatefield, William, born at Bursit, Gloucestershire, Eng., age 26—deserted March 18 from Major Fletcher's company in General Charles Otway's regiment of foot (3/28)

Walsh, Walter, born at Cashell, County Tipperary, Ireland, age 27—same as above

Wright, William, born in Birmingham, Eng., button maker by trade, age 30—deserted from Captain Bellow's company (3/28)

Gray, Capt., of the ship *Mary* of London—shot himself in his cabin in NY harbor on morning of March 30 (3/28)

Connor, William, soldier of first battalion of Royal Americans—hanged at Phila. April 1 for desertion (4/11)

Bailey, Samuel, soldier of same battalion as above—same as above

Maginis, Paul, of NYC—his wife Isabella has eloped (4/11)

Phips, Spencer, Lt.-Gov. of Mass.—died at Cambridge, Mass., April 4 in 74th year (4/18)

Campbell, John, wife of—killed by Indians March 31 at Conecochieg in Cumberland Co., Pa. (4/18)

M'Kinley, William, and son—killed by Indians April 3 at Conecochieg (4/18)

Short, William, age c. 22—on April 7 in Phila. stole a horse owned by Richard Wagstaff of Phila. and fled to NYC (4/18)

Rick, Negro slave, age c. 23—runaway April 21 from Jacob Van Schaick, Jr. (4/25)

Glen, George, apprentice, silver buckle cutter by trade, age c. 18—runaway April 19 from his master, George Scot, mariner (4/25)

Murray, Joseph, attorney, member of Council for NY—died April 28 in NYC in his 63rd year (5/2)

Ellit, Francis, of Wallkill, Ulster Co., NY—his wife Nancy has eloped (5/2)

Van Kemp, Jacobus—killed by Indians May 4 at Minisink (5/9)

Brink, Petrus—same as above

Sprow, James, sailor and deserter—stabbed April 15 by grenadiers in tavern of John Waller in NYC and died of wound May 6 (5/9)

Taylor, Robert, of NYC—will not be responsible for debts of wife Elizabeth (5/9)

Green, Deacon Timothy, eldest printer on North American continent—died May 4 in New London, Conn. (5/16)

Hallet, Richard, Jr., of Newtown, L. I.—killed May 13 while felling a tree in the woods (5/16)

Jarvis, Benjamin, late of NYC, dec'd—house, now in tenure of James Jarvis, in French Church St. for sale (5/16)

Grant, Mrs. Elizabeth, late of NYC, dec'd—house in French Church St. for sale (5/16)

Hessee, Christophel, a grenadier of 4th battalion of Royal American Regt.—killed May 17 in NYC by Michael Fatt, a grenadier (5/23)

Tom, a Negro slave, age c. 40—runaway May 9 from Jacobus Kip of Kipsbay (5/23)

Walker, William—lately killed by Indians near M'Cormick's Fort, about six miles from Shippensburgh, Pa. (5/30)

Grig, Capt., of the brig *Johnson*—killed in May at sea in fight with the French (5/30)

Coils, William, of brig *Johnson*—same as above

M'Atee, Hugh, of brig *Johnson*—same as above

M'Collum, Duncan, of brig *Johnson*—same as above

Frank, a Negro slave, age c. 44—runaway May 25 from the sloop *Ranger*, Benjamin Bethel master (5/30)

Wan, an Indian slave, age c. 30—runaway from Frind Lucas at the mines near Second River, N.J. (5/30)

Allen, Sarah, apprentice, age c. 17—runaway March 8, 1756, from Richard Iverson of Maidenhead Twp., West N.J. (5/30)

Larrimore, Mr., of Somerset Co., child of—lately perished by accident near a fire in the house (Annapolis, Md., dispatch of May 19) (6/6)

Eckinrod, Mr., of Linn Twp., Northampton Co., Pa.—killed by Indians on May 28 (6/6)

Whitney, Capt., of Dunstable, Mass.—killed by Indians near Arseguntacook River on May 26 (6/13)

French, Lt., of Dunstable, Mass.—same as above

Pell, John, son of John Pell, Sr., late of Westchester Co., NY, dec'd—jailed May 13 in NYC for offering for sale several pieces of plate he had stolen from his uncle, John Pell, Esq., of the Manor of Pelham (6/13)

Lightfoot, Jean, a "strolling woman" from L.I.—on evening of June 7, when intoxicated, fell from the New Dock, near the ferry stairs, into the East River and was drowned (6/13)

Griffiths, Mr. ———, a child (age c. 7) of—on June 10 fell into a pond near the new battery and was drowned (6/13)

Murphy, Dominie—will no longer pay debts contracted by his wife Hannah (6/13)

Caesar, "young" Negro slave who had lived several years in Boston—runaway from John Humphreys of Island of St. Christophers (6/20)

Jackson, Edward, late of Boston, merchant—died there June 13 in 50th year (6/27)

Smith, John, at Broad Bay, and wife—killed there by Indians "last Tuesday was sev'night" (Boston dispatch of June 20) (6/27)

Holliday, Lt.—killed by Indians near Conecocheig, Pa., the first week in June (6/27)

Cicere, Dorothy, German servant, age c. 25—runaway from Judah Hayes of NYC (6/27)

Ashton, William, Irish servant, age c. 15—runaway June 25 from John Alexander of NYC (6/27)

Miller, Abraham, mother of, of Northampton Co., Pa.—killed by Indians about May 1 (7/4)

Snell, Hannah, of Northampton Co., Pa.—same as above

Trump, Mr.—killed by Indians June 22 at Allamingle, Pa. (7/4)

Tidd, John—killed by Indians June 23 near house of Mr. Broadhead in Northampton Co., Pa. (7/4)

Mc Allaster, James, of privateer snow *Hornet*, Capt. Spelling master—killed May 25 in battle at sea off Ft. Dauphin on Hispaniola (7/4)

Jones, Richard, of privateer snow *Hornet*—same as above

Meyer, Frederick, of Bern Twp., about 18 miles from Reading, Pa., and wife—killed by Indians June 28; son aged 10 escaped (7/11)

Thompson, William—killed about middle of April on board privateer sloop *Bleakney*, Capt. Horton master, in engagement with the French (7/11)

Moloy, William—same as above

Badger, Joseph—same as above

Lowrey, James, chief mate of privateer snow *Revenge*, Capt. Koffer master—killed July 1 in engagement with the French (7/11)

Van Wyck, Abraham, Jr., dec'd—debts due his estate to be paid (7/11)

Yager, Martin, of Lynn Twp., Northampton Co., Pa., and wife—killed by Indians July 9 (7/18)

Crowshore, John, of Lynn Twp., two children of—same as above

Secler, Abraham, of Lynn Twp., child of—same as above

Ashton, Philip, of Lynn Twp., child of—same as above

Miller, Alexander, of Antrim Twp., Cumberland Co., Pa.—killed by Indians about end of June (7/18)

Booth, Mingo, a mulatto, age c. 28—runaway July 14 from Jesse Hallock (7/18)

Luney (or Lewney), Peter, born in Phila. but now of Virginia, age c. 23—arrived in Phila. after having been a prisoner of the Indians (7/25 and 8/1)

Phalps, William, a young man, apprentice to Jones Wright of NYC (shipwright)—same as above

Dunning, Lewis, of N.J.—killed by Indians about May 11 (7/25)

Bristol, a Negro slave, age c. 30—runaway July 17 from Nathaniel Dalglish of Hanover, Morris Co., N.J. (7/25)

Vance, John, apprentice, age 20—runaway July 11 from John Dennis of Elizabeth, N.J., hatter (7/25)

Annow, John, apprentice, age c. 15—runaway July 23 from Francis Van Dyck of NYC, cutler (8/1)

Brown, Arthur, dec'd—plantation at Middletown Point, Monmouth Co., N.J. for sale; apply to executors, John Anderson and Peter Bowne (8/1)

Kirkpatrick, John—killed by Indians July 8 in John Cosney's field in Cumberland Co., Pa., about 7 miles from Shippensburgh (8/8)

Oneidon, Dennis—same as above

Mitchell, Joseph—same as above

Mitchell, James—same as above

Mitchell, William—same as above

Finley, John—same as above

Steenson, Robert—same as above

Enslow, Andrew—same as above

Wiley, John—same as above

Henderson, Allen—same as above

Gibson, William—same as above

Wilson, Samuel, age c. 17—killed about middle of July near house of George Pow, not far from Anti-Eatam, Md. (8/22)

Ashton, John, Irish servant, age 35—runaway Aug. 9 from William Newbold of Chesterfield Twp., Burlington Co., West N.J. (8/22)

Winklepleigh, John, of Bethel Twp., Lancaster Co., Pa., two sons of—killed by Indians Aug. 9 (8/22)

Long, Leonard, son of—killed Aug. 9 by Indians in middle of Hanover Twp., four miles from the mountain (8/22)

Williams, Isaac, wife of—killed Aug. 10 by Indians near Benjamin Clark's house, four miles from the hill, in Lancaster Co., Pa. (8/22)

Cleveland, Rev. Mr., lately appointed to the mission at New Castle by the Society for Propagating the Gospel—died at New Castle Aug. 12 (8/22)

Ross, William, apprentice, age c. 14—runaway from master, Hugh Gaine of NYC and supposed hidden by his mother, Catharine Montgomery, living in town of Bound Brook, N.J. (8/22)

Dudley, Jonathan, a New Englander by his speech, age c. 40—escaped Wed. night last from jail of Somerset Co., N.J.; reward for his capture offered by Sheriff Robert Stockton (8/22)

Craig, Widow, late of NYC, dec'd—house in Beaver Lane for sale (8/29)

Beatty, Mr.—killed by Indians Aug. 17 at Paxton, Lancaster Co., Pa. (9/5)

Mackey, James—killed by Indians Aug. 18 in Hanover, Lancaster Co., Pa. (9/5)

Belcher, Jonathan, Gov. of N.J.—died Aug. 31 in Elizabeth Town, N.J. (9/5)

Hyat, Abraham, apprentice, cordwainer by trade, age 18—runaway from master Daniel Tooker of Greenwich, Conn. (9/5)

Dusseau, Col. Joseph, of H. M.'s 62nd Regt.—died Sept 10 at Brunswick, N.J. (9/12)

Watson, James—scalped by Indians near Paxton, Pa., about Sept. 1 (9/19)

Rust, Robert—killed by Indians Sept. 19 near Conecocheague in Pa. (10/3)

Mackron, Mr.—same as above

Burr, Rev. Aaron, President of New-Jersey College—died Sept. 24 in 41st year and was buried Sept. 26 (10/3 and 10/10)

Simmons, William, of the privateer snow *Royal Hester*, Solomon David commander—killed Sept. 12 at sea in fight with the French (10/3)

Thorp, Peter, of the *Royal Hester*—same as above

Vanderhoff, ————, of the *Royal Hester*—same as above

Cuff, Negro slave, age 20—runaway Aug. 14 from his master, Capt. Peter Bourn, of the sloop *Bilboa*, then in the harbor of Halifax (10/3)

Frazier, Thomas, postrider—killed Sept. 15 in a tavern brawl at Fredericksburg, Va., by an officer of the Va. regiment (10/10)

White, Benjamin, of Md.—killed some time past by Richard Clark (10/10)

Wilson, Mrs. Samuel—killed by Indians Sept. 24 at M'Cluer's Gap, about 7 miles from Carlisle, Pa. (10/10)

Walton, William, Jr., of NYC, merchant—married in Sept. in NYC Miss De Lancey, daughter of Lt. Gov. James De Lancey (10/10)

Cunningham, Widow, daughter of Christopher Kilby, Esq.—married in NYC week before last Capt. McAdam, aide de camp to John, Earl of London (10/10)

Kar, Patrick—"last Sunday Se'ennight" killed by Indians at Minisink Bridge, about 18 miles from Hudson River (10/10 and 10/17)

Mercer, Capt. James, of 48th Regt., oldest captain in H.M.'s service in North America—died first week in October in Albany, NY (10/10)

Cowan, Samuel, apprentice (hence young)—runaway from ship *Lydia*, Capt. M'Kinze master, at Phila. (10/10)

Duffey, Cornelius, apprentice—same as above

Richardson, William, soldier in Capt. Crookshank's Independent Company of "Fuzaleers" —shot Oct. 17 on Nutten Island for desertion (10/24)

White, Capt.—killed in September by bursting of a cohorn on board privateeer brig *King of Prussia* from Rhode Island (10/?)

Watt, Alexander—killed Oct. 17 by Indians near Hunter's Fort in Lancaster Co., Pa. (10/30)

M'Kennet, John—same as above

Taylor, Joab, of the snow *Mary Anne*, Capt. John Shoals master—killed Sept. 23 at sea in engagement with French off Cape Francois (10/30)

Porter, John, of snow *Mary Anne*—same as above

Penny, James, born at Grannarn, County of Antrim, Ireland, shoemaker by trade, age 20; had enlisted in 35th regt. of foot at York Town, Pa.—deserted Oct. 12 (10/30)

O'Brien, John, born in Kilkenny, Ireland, shoemaker by trade, age 32, enlisted in 35th regt. of foot at Carlisle, Pa.—same as above

Colquhoon, Hugh, born at Strabane, Ireland, age 30, enlisted at Lancaster, Pa.—same as above

Alagon, Richard, born in England, by trade a pettiauger man, age 36—same as above

Brown, Arthur, dec'd—plantation at Middletown Point, Monmouth Co., N.J. for sale (11/7)

Croxton, Capt., of Warburton's Regt.—drowned at sea near Louisbourg (11/14)

Bainsley, Capt., of marines—same as above

Mutts, Johannes, late of Orange Co., NY, farmer, dec'd—debts due estate to be paid (11/14)

Ellit, James, of privateer sloop *George*, Capt. Haly master—killed Oct. 17 in engagement with French at sea (11/21)

Holms, John, of sloop *George*—same as above

Burling, John, of sloop *George*—same as above

M'Farling, Richard, of sloop *George*—same as above

Horne, Joseph, of sloop *George*—same as above

M'Illroy, William, of sloop *George*—same as above

Haynes, Samuel, age c. 17—runaway Nov. 19 from sloop *Swan* in NY harbor; reward for his capture offered by Jacob Van Wagenen (11/28)

Foine, Thomas, born at Maidstone, Kent, Eng., matross in Capt. Godwin's company of the royal regt. of artillery—deserted Sept. 27 from the ship *Morning Star* on way from NYC to Albany (11/28)

Ayres, Charles, born at Reading in Berkshire, matross in above company—deserted at NYC (11/28)

Bear, John, born in Germany, carpenter by trade, matross—deserted in NYC (11/28)

Graham, Edward, late of NYC, dec'd—debts to estate to be paid (12/5)

Belcher, Jonathan, late Gov. of N.J.—remains brought last week to Cambridge, Mass. and deposited in tomb (12/19)

Anderson, John, cooper by trade—last week fell from canoe and drowned in Hackinsack River (12/19)

Bigelow, Isaac, carpenter's mate—died in Oct. of smallpox on board privateer ship *Hercules* of NYC (12/19)

Haffy, Francis, a mulatto—same as above

Tony (Mr. M'Ever's Negro)—same as above

Burling, Samuel, late of NYC, dec'd—goods to be sold; debts to estate to be paid to John Burling (12/26)

Welch, Richard, a tanner by trade, age c. 45—runaway servant, 7th or 8th Dec. from Robert Alexander (12/26)

Douglas, John, a wheelwright by trade, age 23—same as above.

Justee, John, Negro servant, born among the Spaniards and served his time with Mr. Lawrence in Middlesex Co., N.J.—runaway Dec. 5 from John Reid, Jr., of Cranberry, Middlesex Co., N.J. (12/26).

Ralph, Negro slave, age c. 28—runaway Dec. 23 from sloop *Walter*, William Price, master, lying in Rotten Row; reward if brought to Waddel Cunningham, of NYC, merchant, or to Alexander Hamilton, of Phila., merchant (12/26)

Arding, Charles, late of NYC, dec'd—debts to be paid estate and demands also to be brought in (12/26)

GENEALOGICAL DATA FROM THE NEW YORK MERCURY

1758

Ramsen, Jacob, late of Brooklyn, dec'd—goods belonging to estate to be sold (1/2)

Davis, Sarah, wife of Thomas Davis of NYC, mariner—she has eloped and husband will pay no debts of her contracting (1/2)

Hannibal (*alias* Sandy), "young" Negro, born at Barbados—runaway about five weeks ago from Cornelius Tiebout of NYC (1/2)

Kinloch, James, some forty years member of H.M.'s Council of South Carolina—died in Charleston, S.C., Nov. 6, 1757, in 85th year (1/9)

Supple, Catharine, daughter of Garrit Supple of Limerick, Ireland—seeks information about her brother Daniel who arrived in America some years before (1/9)

Bussing, John, of the privateer snow *Mary Anne*, John Shoals commander—killed Oct. 10, 1757, in engagement with French ship not far from Monto Christo (1/16)

Hayter, Catharine, late of NYC, dec'd—accounts with estate to be settled with Donald Morison at his store on the wharf between the ferry stairs and Burlings Slip (1/23)

Ramsey, Capt. Thomas, late of NYC, dec'd—accounts with estate to be settled (2/6)

Williams, Rice, late of NYC, merchant, dec'd—accounts with estate to be settled with John Troup or Dorothy Williams, executrix (2/6)

Haviland, Ebenezer, dec'd—his farm in Westchester now occupied by Daniel Quinby to be sold by executors, Thomas Haviland and Richard Cornell (2/13)

Harris, John, late of the Oblong, Dutchess Co., NY, dec'd—his lot, no. 73, for sale (2/13)

Odiorne, Mr., late of Piscataqua, passenger on ship of Capt. Hooker, bound from Piscataqua to West Indies—died from fatigue and cold a few days after shipwreck and was buried about Jan. 26 from Col. Winslow's house in Marshfield, Mass. (2/20)

Hamilton, Lt., of the privateer brigantine *Earl of Loudoun* of NYC, John Wallace commander—killed Jan. 4 in engagement with French ship off east end of Puerto Rico (2/20)

Titus, Edward, of Newtown, L. I., son of, age 8 to 10—fell through ice and was drowned Feb. 21 (2/27)

Craig, Widow, late of NYC, dec'd—demands on estate to be brought to Daniel Dunscomb (2/27)

Berrien, Cornelius, late of Newtown, L. I., dec'd—plantation and other effects for sale; demands on estate to be brought to executors, Jonathan Fish or Cornelius Berrien (3/6)

Wilson, James, late of NYC, dec'd—his dying business in John St. is carried on by Joseph Northup near house of late Alderman Van Courtlandt, dec'd (3/13)

Arding, Charles, late of NYC, dec'd—accounts with estate to be settled (3/13)

Brown, Arthur, dec'd—plantation on N.W. side of Mattawan Creek at Middletown Point, Monmouth Co., N.J., for sale (3/13)

Green, William, Gov. of R.I.—died in R.I. the last week in Feb. (3/20)

Durjee, Jacob, late of Brooklyn, dec'd—his plantation at Bushwick for sale (3/20)

Lawrance, Daniel, late of Flushing, L. I., dec'd—house and other items for sale; accounts with estate to be settled with Abraham Lawrence (3/27)

Wentworth, Hugh, late of Flushing, L.I., dec'd—mills, house and land for sale; enquire of widow (3/27)

Van Zandt, Wynant, late of NYC, dec'd—his house on Golden Hill and furnishings for sale; accounts to be settled with Catharine Van Zandt, executrix, and Jacobus, Wynant and Tobias Van Zandt, executors (3/27)

Buckley (or Bulkley), Capt., of the Rangers—killed by French and Indians March 13 near Ticonderoga (3/27 and 4/3)

More (or Moore), Lt., of the Rangers—same as above

Pottinger, Lt., of the Rangers—same as above

Ross, Ensign, of the Rangers—same as above

McDaniel (or M'Donald), Ensign, of the Rangers—same as above

Campbell, Lt. (or Ensign?), of the Rangers—same as above

White, Ensign, of the Rangers—same as above

Belford (or Belfore), Ensign, of the Rangers—same as above

Gaffe, Thomas, smith by trade, age c. 25—deserted from the NY Provincial Force commanded by Francis Moore of NYC (3/27)

Kent, Mr., of the Rangers—killed March 13 near Ticonderoga (4/3)

Pannil, Sergt., of the Rangers—same as above

Edwards, Rev. Jonathan, President of the College of New Jersey—died March 22 at Nassau Hall (4/3); was son of Rev. Mr. Edwards of Windsor, Conn. (who, together with his wife, was living about two months ago) and grandson of "the famous Mr. Stoddard" at Northampton (4/10)

Lodge, Abrahan, attorney, of NYC—died morning of March 27 at NYC in 51st year (4/3)

Van Horne, Cornelius G., late of NYC, merchant, dec'd—accounts with estate to be brought to Gerrit Van Horne (4/3)

Thurman, Francis, late of NYC, dec'd—house (opposite Christopher Banker's) in Wall St. for sale; administrator of estate is John Thurmond, Jr. (4/10)

Nickels, Mr., mate of schooner commanded by Capt. Woodward—killed by French March 30 near Chignecto (4/17)

Woodward, Capt.—same as above

Buck, Robert—killed by Indians April 5 at Robert Jamieson's near Marsh Creek, York Co., Pa. (4/17)

Schaterly, two brothers—killed April 8 by Indians at Swetara, Pa. (4/17)

Souder, Michael—same as above

Hart, William—same as above

Levergood, Mr. and Mrs.—killed April 8 by Indians at Tulpehocken, Pa. (4/17)

Gieger, Mrs. Nicholas and two children—killed April 8 by Indians at Northkill, Pa. (4/17)

Titlefer, Mrs. Michael—same as above

Lane, Jacob—killed near Winshester by Ensign Colby Chew and his men (5/1)

Cox, James—same as above

Farmer, Jasper, late of NYC, merchant—died in 51st year on night of April 24 at NYC and was buried April 26 in Trinity Church (5/1); Mary Farmer, executrix (6/5)

Saltur, Dr., of privateer snow *Cicero*, of NYC, Capt. Smith master—blown up in engagement with French March 13 (5/1)

Mitchell, Alexander, of privateer *Cicero*—same as above

King, Thomas, of privateer *Cicero*—wounded March 13 in engagement with French and has since died of wounds (5/1)

Mauritze, Mrs., wife of a farmer of Hackinsack—injured March 26 in collision of two boats in the North River and not expected to live (5/1)

Narbury, Peter, captain of marines on privateer *King of Prussia* of NYC, Capt. Seymour commander—killed off Cape Francois in engagement with seven sugar ships (5/1)

Purcel, Michael, born at Kilkenny, Ireland, house carpenter by trade, age 22—deserted from H.M.'s sloop *Hunter*, Capt. John Laforey commander (5/8)

Belcher, John, born in N. J., age 22—deserted from Capt. Moore's company of the NY Provincial Regiments (5/8)

Fitzgerald, John, born in Ireland, age 26—same as above

Wiel, Thomas, born in London, age 24—same as above

Watens, William, born in Liverpool, age 19—same as above

Connely, Roger, born in Ireland, age 27—same as above

Murphey, Edmund, born in England, age 20—same as above

Stinson, James, born in Ireland, laborer, married to a humpbacked woman called Margery Curry; he enlisted at New Castle on Delaware—deserted May 2 from Capt. Joseph Jaquet's company of battoemen at Albany (5/2)

M'Gill, Michael, born in Ireland, enlisted at New Castle on Delaware—same as above

Durham, Widow—at her house in NYC John Alvay sells Jamaica rum, sugar and black giner (5/8)

Potter, Thomas—killed April 27 by Indians in Pa. (5/15)

Baird, Thomas, child of—same as above

Hunter, Samuel—killed by Indians in April in Pa. (5/15)

Paul, John, apprentice, age 21—runaway May 18 from transport ship *Duke of Cumberland*, Thomas Hurry master, in NYC (5/22)

Polly, Samuel, apprentice, age 19—same as above

York, Negro slave, age 28—runaway May 16 from William Keese of Flushing, L.I. (5/22)

Thodey, Capt. Michael, and wife Elizabeth, of NYC, both dec'd—sale of their effects (5/22)

Van Cortlandt, Stephen, dec'd—farms in Manor of Cortlandt to be sold (5/22)

Sisirey, Dorothy, German servant, age c. 30—runaway March 23 from Judah Hays of NYC, merchant (5/29)

England, Mr., second lieutenant of privateer *Blakeney* of Barbados—recently killed at St. Christophers by bursting of swivel gun (6/5)

Tolon, Barnabas—killed May 22 by Indians at Hanover Twp. in Lancaster Co., Pa. (6/5)

Cole, Nicholas, of Minisink, Sussex Co., four children of—killed May 16 by Indians; wife and son Jacob, age 10, escaped (6/5)

Clarkson, Matthew (son of David Clarkson of NYC, merchant)—married night of June 1, in NYC, Miss Betsey De Peyster, daughter of Abraham De Peyster of NYC (6/5)

Stockton, John, of Princeton, N.J., Judge of Court of Common Pleas—died May 20 in 57th year at Princeton (6/5)

Remsen, Jacob, dec'd—lands in Orange Co., NY, for sale (6/5)

Gould, William, of Mass.—his wife bore twins three times in past six years, first two boys, then two more, and last week a son and a daughter (6/12)

Bradford, Mr. and Mrs.—killed May 22 by Indians at Maduncook (6/12)

Mills, Mrs., and child—same as above

Croker, Joseph, a young man—killed March 20 by Indians near Wyoming, Pa. (6/12)

Livingston, Peter Robert, son of Robert Livingston of the Manor of Livingston—married night of June 6 in NYC Miss Peggy Livingston, daughter of James Livingston of NYC, merchant (6/12)

Kate, an Indian servant, age c. 15—runaway May 20 from Aaron Forman, Jr., of North Castle, Westchester Co., NY (6/12)

Roseman, James, born at Killishandria in north of Ireland, age c. 24—deserted June 6 from company of Capt. Ormsby of the 35th Regt. (6/12)

Fauconier, Peter, dec'd—farm once belonging to him on west side of Hackinsack River, in Bergen Co., N.J., for sale (6/12)

Smith, Henry, of Ulster Co., NY, farmer—his wife Juliana has eloped (6/19)

Westbrook, Lt., and another Westbrook—killed about the first week in June by Indians in Pa. (6/19)

Braning, John, of privateer snow *Hornet* of NY, Capt. Spelling commander—killed Oct. 14, 1757, in engagement with French (6/19)

Jones, John, of the *Hornet*—died in France (6/19)

Jones, Thomas, of the *Hornet*—same as above

Jump, Valantine, of the *Hornet*—same as above

Drinkwater, John, of the *Hornet*—same as above

Taylor, Joseph, of the *Hornet*—same as above

Williams, John, of the *Hornet*—same as above

Wilson, Thomas, of the *Hornet*—same as above

Trickey, William, of the *Hornet*—same as above

Hamilton, John, of the *Hornet*—same as above

Black, Michael, of the *Hornet*—same as above

Gunner, George, of the *Hornet*—same as above

Drummond, Joshua, of the *Hornet*—same as above

Milwater, John, of the *Hornet*—same as above

Shannon, Hugh, of the *Hornet*—same as above

Giles, Charles, of the *Hornet*—same as above

Charles, William, of the *Hornet*—same as above

Stevens, Charles, of the *Hornet*—same as above

Brown, John, indented servant, shoemaker by trade, age c. 19—runaway June 23 from snow *Prince of Wales* in NY harbor (6/26)

Cuba, a Negro woman, born in West Indies, age c. 25—runaway June 23, along with child Peggy, age c. 22 mos., from William Albrespy of NYC, living next door to Mr. Livingston's sugar house (6/26)

Hammond, James, age c. 20—drowned June 2 in Parish of Westbury after falling into the west branch of the Waterbury River in Conn. (6/26)

Atkins, John, age c. 11—same as above

Galliday, Joseph—killed by Indians about three weeks ago at Conecocheague, Pa. (6/26)

Frantz, Mrs. John, of Berks Co., Pa.—killed by Indians about middle of June (7/3)

Snabely, Jacob, son of—killed by Indians about middle of June in Berks Co., Pa. (7/3)

Robinson, Samuel, of Swetara, Lancaster Co., Pa.—killed by Indians in June (7/3)

Arding, Charles, late of NYC, dec'd—those with claims against his estate to apply to Dr. Charles Arding (7/10)

Vetch, Margaret, dec'd—those with claims on her estate to apply to William Bayard (7/10)

Bayley, Capt., of the Highlanders—killed in expedition against Cape Breton (7/10)

Ward, William—killed by Indians June 13 on frontier of N.J. and Pa. (7/10)

Van Kamp, Jacob—killed by Indians May 2, 1757, in N.J. (7/10)

Brink, Peter—same as above

Doty, John—killed by Indians Nov. 9, 1757, in N.J. (7/10)

M'Hurin, Otho—same as above

Westbrook, Gideon—killed by Indians Nov. 10, 1757, near Brink's Fort in N.J. (7/10)

Pressler, John—killed by Indians Nov. 11, 1757, in N.J. (7/10)

Cole, Nicholas, four children of—killed by Indians May 15, 1758, in N.J. (7/10)

Willing, Mary—killed by Indians May 25, 1758, near Fort Gardiner, N.J. (7/10)

Westbrook, Cornelius—killed by Indians June 3 in N.J. (7/10)

Westbrook, Abraham—same as above

Courtract, Bastian—killed by Indians June 13 in N.J. (7/10)

Kirkindale, Mary—same as above

Eustace, Catharine—has eloped from husband Charles Eustace (7/17)

Sheels, Timothy, born at Larne, Ireland, a servant lad—runaway from Stephen Leach of NYC, tailor (7/17)

Morrison, James, a Scotch servant lad—same as above

Rassett, John, of NYC, boat builder—hanged himself July 12 near the Whitehall in NYC (7/17)

Smith, Capt. Richard R., late commander of the privateer *Cicero*, dec'd—claims on his estate to be brought to Joanna Smith, exec. (7/24)

Howe, Genl. Lord—killed in July at Lake George (7/24)

Clarke, Lt., of 27th Regt.—same as above

Campbell, Capt. Lt., of 42nd Regt.—same as above

Farquarson, Lt., of 42nd Regt.—same as above

M'Pherson, Lt., of 42nd Regt.—same as above

Bailie, Lt., of 42nd Regt.—same as above

Sutherland, Lt., of 42nd Regt.—same as above

Stewart, Ensign, of 42nd Regt.—same as above

Rattery, Ensign, of 42nd Regt.—same as aboev

Needham, Capt., of 46th Regt.—same as above

Wynne, Capt., of 46th Regt.—same as above

Lallhie, Lt., of 46th Regt.—same as above

Lloyd, Lt., of 46th Regt.—same as above

Croston, Ensign, of 46th Regt.—same as above

Carbonelle, Ensign, of 46th Regt.—same as above

Donaldson, Col., of 46th Regt.—same as above

Proby, Major, of 46th Regt.—same as above

Murray, Capt. Lt., of 46th Regt.—same as above

Stewart, Lt., of 46th Regt.—same as above

Rutherford, Major, of the Royal Americans—same as above

Forbes, Capt. Lt., of the Royal Americans—same as above

Hazellwood, Lt., of the Royal Americans—same as above

Davis, Lt., of the Royal Americans—same as above

Lyman, Elihu, Commissary of the Conn. Provincial Regts.—died July 18 at Albany, NY (7/24)

Fleet, Thomas, of Boston, printer—died there July 21 in 73rd year (7/31)

Burlingham, Thomas, of Cranston—died last week aged 94; his sister and her husband, both aged upwards of 90, live at Warwick; they have been wed nearly 70 years—Boston dispatch dated July 24 (7/31)

Robin, Negro slave, age c. 36—runaway July 30 from Hobuck; his master, Samuel Bayard, lives near the Old English Church in NYC (7/31)

Hoff, Jacob, Jr., dec'd—412 acres of land and house and orchard, belonging to his estate, situated some 3 miles from landing place of Jacobus Stoutenburg, in the Crum Elbow Precinct, Dutchess Co., NY, for sale; apply to Joris Storm of said precinct (7/31)

Lawrence, Capt.—recently killed on way from Lake George to Ft. Edward (8/7)

Jones, Capt.—same as above

Fales, Capt.—same as above

Smith, John, for some time confined for debt in City Hall of NYC—Aug. 6 jumped from "cupalo" to street and was killed (8/7)

Williams, Rice, dec'd—his Negroes and shares in sloop *Williams* and ship *Sturdy Beggar* for sale (8/7)

Farmer, Jasper, dec'd—his goods for sale at store of James De Peyster in NYC (8/7)

Lyons, Samuel, of NYC, mariner—will pay no debts henceforth contracted by wife Mary (8/7)

Cannon, John, late of NYC, dec'd—three of his houses in Queen St., near Beekman Slip, (one in tenure of Mrs. Jane Goelet, one of Capt. John Schermerhorne, the third of Arthur McNeal) for sale (8/7)

Withers, John, indentured servant, born in Belfast, Ireland, age c. 18, shoemaker by trade —runaway Aug. 6 from *Tartar Frigate* in NY harbor, Hugh M'Quoid master (8/7)

Concklin, Edmond, dec'd—farm at Dance-chamber, Ulster Co., NY, for sale (8/7)

Campbell, Major, of the Highlanders—died of wounds July 17 at Ft. Edward (8/14)

Clerk, Mr., chief engineer of army—died of wounds July 18 at the camp near Ft. Edward (8/14)

Daken, Capt. Samuel, of Sudbury—killed July 19 in skirmish with French near Half-Way Brook (8/14)

Jones, Capt. Eben, of Wilmington—same as above

Lawrence, Capt. Thomas, of Groton—same as above

Curtis, Lt. Samuel of Sudbury—same as above

Godfrey, Lt. Simon, of Billerica—same as above

Davis, Ensign Daniel, of Methuen—same as above

Russel, Sergt., of Concord—same as above

Wright, Sergt., of Westford—same as above

Cold, Corp., of No. One—same as above

Satel, Abel, of Groton—same as above

Harden, Abraham, of Pembrook—same as above

Foster, Stephen, of Groton—same as above

Eames, Eben, of Groton—same as above

Wheeler, Simon, of Westford—same as above

Hagge, Moses, of Andover—same as above

Fry, Daniel, late of NYC, dec'd—accounts to be settled with widow Elizabeth at her house in French Church St. (8/21)

Skaats, Bartholomew, dec'd—his house in Hanover Square, now in possession of Hugh Gaine, for sale; apply to Jacoba Skaats, exec., at her house near the Whitehall (8/21)

Van Horne, Garrit, late of NYC, dec'd—accounts with his estate to be settled with Garrit, Augustus and Cornelius Van Horne (8/21)

Web, Samuel—killed by Indians Aug. 14 at Goshen, NY (8/28)

Cooley, Isaac, wife of—killed by Indians Aug. 18 one half mile from Blockhouse No. 1 near Goshen, NY (8/28)

Middah, Jacobus, and son—killed by Indians Aug. 11 near Cole's Fort on frontiers of N.J. (8/28)

Whelpley, Joseph, late lieut. of privateer *Duke of Marlborough* of NYC, Capt. Richardson commander—drowned Aug. 9 near the Watering Place (8/28)

Leech, Stephen, late of NYC, tailor—died Aug. 23 of wound inflicted Aug. 11 during a quarrel by one Norwood, a blockmaker of NYC (8/28)

Connel, William (*alias* William Weaver), age c. 45, who had served on privateer sloop *Fox*, Capt. Crew, and brig *Prince of Orange*, Capt. Dixon—fled Aug. 11 from NYC with money belonging to George Remer of Somerset Co., N.J. (8/28)

Stewart, Mr.—killed by Indians about Aug. 5 near Culberton's Fort in Pa. (9/4)

Gallacher, Mr.—killed by Indians in August near Shippenburgh, Pa. (9/4)

(Note: A list of officers killed, June 8 to July 26 incl., at Island of Cape Breton is given; apparently all British—9/4)

Hall, Mr., of NYC, dec'd—William Elphinstone has removed his school from John Bell's in Queen St. to the house in the Sloat where the late Mr. Hall lived (9/4)

Shannon, Robert, foremast man on privateer *New-Grace*, Capt. Carr, from Phila.—killed at Charleston, S. C. on Aug. 7 (9/11)

Burr, President, late of Princeton, N.J., dec'd—his library for sale (9/11)

Smith, Patrick, of NYC, mariner—will not pay debts henceforth contracted by wife Mary (9/11)

Stewart, James, apprentice, age c. 14—runaway from Stephen Fitzpatrick of NYC, tailor (9/11)

Stebbins, Mr., of New Haven, Conn.—killed there by Indians on Aug. 26 (9/25)

Simson, Joseph, born in N.J., age c. 30, carpenter by trade; has a wife in Poughkeepsie—broke out of NYC jail on Sept. 22 (9/25)

Titfort, ————, age c. 17—voted 20 silver dollars and a silver medal by N.J. Assembly for bravery against the enemy (9/25)

Riddle, John, apprentice, age 23—runaway Sept. 23 from ship *Nancy*, Ralph Foster commander, lying at Crommeline's Wharf in NYC (9/25)

Bell, Walter, and son—killed by Indians about Sept. 10 in Hanover Twp., Lancaster Co., Pa. (10/9)

Bristol, Negro slave, age c. 26—runaway Oct. 2 from Benjamin Williams of Newark, N.J. (10/9)

Sergt. Israel Calkins of the 13th Company of the Conn. Regt. commanded by Col. Lyman was taken prisoner Aug. 5, 1757, between Ft. Edward and Ft. William Henry and was carried to France last fall. He compiled the following list of prisoners who died in Quebec or France up to Feb. 16, 1758:

Adams, Deacon Thomas—died in Quebec Oct. 27, 1757

Spafford, Asa—died in Quebec Aug. 28, 1757

Webb, Joseph—died on board ship in passage to France

Ames, Jacob, a ranger—same as above

Woodward, Caleb—same as above

Warner, Elihu—same as above

Preston, Joseph—same as above

Bush, John—same as above

Putnam, John—died in France

Keys, Cornelius—same as above

Sileway, John—same as above

Washborn, Thomas—same as above

Langaster, Christopher—same as above

Prescot, Jonathan—same as above

Preston, Jonathan—same as above

Young, John—same as above

Randall, Peter—same as above

Saunders, William—same as above

Stimson, Abraham—same as above

Narran, Thomas—same as above

Goodwin, Joseph—same as above

Baker, James—same as above

Hilyard, Joseph—same as above

Parker, Jesse—same as above

Kidder, Benjamin—same as above

Manning, Sergt. Thomas—same as above

Wald, John—same as above

Woodcock, Ebenezer—same as above

Samson, George—same as above

Flingert, George—same as above

Franois, Daniel—same as above

Fausy, John—same as above

Wood, John—same as above

Swan, Timothy—same as above
Rogers, William—same as above
Stewart, Henry—same as above
Morrison, Jonathan, same as above
Sheldon, Elisha—same as above
Mitchel, Sergt. John, of Roger's company—same as above
Rows, James—same as above
Pierce, John—same as above
Miller, Samuel—same as above
Belknap, Caleb—same as above
Prescot, Solomon—same as above
Belding, Jonathan—same as above
Marshal, Joseph—same as above
Qualls, John—same as above
Knight, Thomas—same as above
Root, Seth—same as above
Loyd, Joseph—same as above
Hall, William—same as above
Atkinson, Benjamin—same as above
Cluff, William—same as above
Green, Godfrey—same as above
Farrington, John—same as above
Bunnil, David—same as above
Morgan, Lawrence—same as above
Capen, Edward—same as above
Carey, Thomas—same as above
Boar, Christopher—same as above (10/16)

Warring, Jacobus, lately from Holland, dec'd—house and lot, belonging to his estate, situated behind the Lutheran Church, near the North River, adjoining the stable of Simon Johnson, Esq., for sale; apply to executors, John Godfried Miller and Cornelius Kuiper (10/23)

Duncason, Lt. James, of the Va. Regt.—killed Oct. 15 at Loyalhanning in engagement with French (10/30)

Pratter, Lt., of the Marylanders—same as above

Mathew, Lt., of the Marylanders—same as above

Graham, Edward, dec'd—dividend from his estate to be paid by James Sackett, assignee (10/30)

Haff, Lawrence, late of Rumbout Precinct, Dutchess Co., NY, dec'd—plantation for sale (11/6)

Dekey, Helena, widow, dec'd—accounts with estate to be settled (11/13)

Apthorp Charles, Esq., of Boston, merchant—died there yesterday sen'night in 61st year (11/20)

Proctor, John, lately of Halifax, master of schooner laden with salt and bound from West Indies to Boston—drowned yesterday sen'night in wreck of ship on Ipswich Beach (11/20)

Van Renslear, Elizabeth, dec'd—accounts with estate to be settled with Abraham Ten Brook, admin. (11/20)

Smith, Thomas (son of Hon. William Smith), of NYC—married last week Miss Elizabeth Lynsen, daughter of Abraham Lynsen of NYC, merchant (11/27)

GENEALOGICAL DATA FROM THE NEW-YORK MERCURY

1758

Orser, Johannis, born in NY, dec'd—children or heirs, at or near Egg Harbour, to apply to Daniel Dunscomb of NYC to learn something to their advantage (12/11)

Pearsall, Nathaniel, dec'd—land in Hempstead, Queens Co., at head of Cow-Neck, for sale; apply to executors, Thomas and Israel Pearsall and Samuel Latham (12/11)

Emory, John, dec'd—house and goods to be sold by executor, Henry Cuyler (12/11)

Connor, Michael, late of Orange Co., NY, dec'd—house and goods for sale (12/11)

Rand, Robert, late commander of *Earl of Halifax Packet*—died in NYC Dec. 15 (12/18)

Ralph, Negro slave, born in Maryland, age c. 22—runaway Dec. 23, 1757, from sloop *Walter* of Maryland, then at Hunters-Quay in NYC (12/18)

Carpenter, Capt. Nathaniel, of North Castle, Westchester Co., NY, dec'd—accounts with estate to be settled (12/18)

Whichcotton, Lt., of the South Carolina Regt.—attacked by ruffians on Nov. 3 at Mr. Alexander Shaw's cow-pen, about 25 miles from Ft. Moore; he died of wounds Sunday se'nnight (12/23)

De Lo, John Hendrick, late clerk of Dutch ship *Clara Magdalena*, Elias Van Houten master—drowned Nov. 20 in NY harbor (12/23)

Ryckman, Jacobus, of NYC—attacked Dec. 9 in the Bowery by a soldier belonging to the Royal Americans and died Dec. 17 (12/23)

Renaudet, James, dec'd—property in NYC for sale; apply to Andrew Renaudet at the Widow Rutgers's near the Fly Market (12/23)

Ward, Jonas, apprentice, age 19—runaway Nov. 19 from Walter Erwin of Ringwood, Bergen Co., N.J. (12/4)

1759

Duane, Anthony, late of NYC, dec'd, merchant—real estate in NYC of his devisees, Abraham, James and Cornelius Duane, to be sold at auction (1/1)

Thurman, Francis, late of NYC, dec'd—accounts with estate to be settled with admin., John Thurman, Jr., living in Wall St., opposite to Nathaniel Marston's (1/1)

Smith, John, age c. 21—deserted from H.M.'s 44th Regt. at Hempstead; speaks English with a German accent (1/1)

Amory, John and Mary, late of NYC, dec'd—accounts with estates to be settled with Henry Cuyler, admin. (1/1)

Carpenter, Capt. Nathaniel, late of North Castle, Westchester Co., dec'd., carpenter—accounts with estate to be settled with execs., Caleb Fowler and Caleb Green (1/1)

Ralph, Negro slave, Maryland born, age c. 22—runaway Dec. 23, 1757, from sloop *Walter* of Md., then at Hunter's Quay, NYC, owner James Campbell of Charles Co., Md. (1/1)

Pearsall, Nathaniel, of Cow Neck, Hempstead, dec'd.—farm for sale; apply to execs., Thomas and Israel Pearsall and Samuel Latham (1/1)

Ward, Jonas, apprentice, age c. 19—runaway Nov. 19, 1758, from Walter Erwin of Ringwood, Bergen Co., N.J. (1/1)

Dunbar, Lt. Patrick, of General Amherst's Regt.—died Dec. 20, 1758, in Boston, in 28th year and buried Dec. 22 in vault of Kings Chappel (1/8)

Bloodgood, William, late of Flushing, dec'd.—farm for sale by exec., Susanna Bloodgood (1/8)

Webbers, Wolfart—offers for sale farm where his son Arnout now lives, joining Bloomingdale Road, about four miles from NYC (1/8)

Chetwood, widow, dec'd—tavern, Sign of the Hogshead, once kept by her in Elizabeth Town, N.J., for sale (1/8)

Hoff, Jacob, Jr., dec'd.—farm in Crum Elbow Precinct, Dutchess Co., for sale (1/8)

Renaudet, James, dec'd.—real estate in NYC for sale; apply to Adrian Renaudet at the widow Rutgers's near the Fly Market (1/8)

Lispenard, Anthony, dec'd.—real estate in NYC for sale; apply to execs., Leonard and David Lispenard (1/15)

Tom, Negro slave, age c. 30—runaway Jan. 4 from Richard Harris of Staten Island (1/15)

Harry, Negro boy, age 14; speaks good English—same as above

Thody, Capt. Michael, dec'd—house on west side of John Van Horne's, near the Long Bridge, for sale at auction (1/15)

Tom, Negro slave, Bermuda born, age c. 23—runaway Jan. 12 from the snow *Mary-Anne*, at Burling's Slip, NYC (1/15)

Holland, Mr., dec'd—house and lot near Coenties Market in NYC for sale; apply to widow, Frances Holland, or to Henry Holland or Benjamin Nicoll (1/22)

Trubey, Andrew, late of Fairfield, Conn., dec'd—accounts with his estate to be settled with the execs., David Burr., Esq., of Fairfield, and Ralph Isaacs, of Norwalk (1/22)

Peck, Benjamin, late of NYC, dec'd—houses belonging to his estate for sale (1/22)

Dwight, Thomas, late of NYC, dec'd—accounts with estate to be settled with execs., Catharine and Stephen Dwight (1/22)

Haughwout, Joseph Arrowsmith, dec'd—accounts with estate to be settled with Benjamin Townsend at Oyster Bay (1/29)

Angel, Jeremiah, mariner, dec'd—heir to apply to Capt. Quill in NYC (1/29)

Young (or Smith), John, age 22—runaway Jan. 25 from privateer ship *St. George*, James Devereux commander (1/29)

Cheasman, William, Jr., dec'd—real estate in Perth Amboy for sale (2/5)

M'Michell, John, late trader from Albany and Schenectady to the Mohawk River, dec'd—accounts with estate to be settled with Kennedy and Lyle, merchants, in Albany, or Andrew M'Farsen, in Schenectady (2/5)

Bridges, Timothy, dec'd—dwelling in Jamaica, L.I., opposite the English Church, to be let (2/5)

Richard, Paul, late of NYC, dec'd—on application of exec., Theophilact Bache, of NYC, merchant, goods of Nathaniel Robins, Jr., seized for debts due estate of the deceased (2/12)

Clarkson, Mrs. Anne Margaret (widow of David Clarkson, of NYC, merchant)—died Jan. 26 in NYC and buried in family vault at Trinity Church (2/12)

Marston, Thomas (son of Nathaniel Marston, of NYC, merchant)—married Feb. 7 Miss Ketty Lispenard (dau. of Leonard Lispenard, Esq., of NYC, merchant) (2/12)

Wilson, James—executed at NYC on Feb. 9 for robbery (2/12)

Smith, Benjamin, late of Hunterdon, West Jersey, dec'd—trustees on behalf of his brother, Robert Smith, have sold that part of Robert's estate which he held by virtue of Benjamin's will (2/19)

Hunt, Jacob, late of Borough of Westchester, dec'd—his plantation, Grove Farm, adjoining the Sound and Westchester Creek, for sale; apply to execs., James Graham, of Morrissania, James Tucker, of NYC, merchant, Thomas Willet, John Hunt and Anthony Bartow, all of the Borough of Westchester, gentlemen (2/19)

Colgan, Rev. Mr., dec'd—house near the Beaver Pond in Jamaica, Queens Co., for sale; apply to exec., Mary Colgan (2/26)

Warne, Joshua, dec'd—fulling mill at Perth Amboy, N.J., for sale; apply to execs., Elizabeth, Thomas and Joshua Warne (3/5)

Simon, mulatto slave, age c. 24—runaway about three months ago from George Norton of Huntington, L.I. (3/5)

Horton, Samuel, born in New England, age 23—deserted Jan. 31 from recruiting party of the 45th Regt. at Hartford, Conn., commanded by Lt. Dugdale (3/5)

Nealan, Bridget, servant, age c. 20—runaway March 3 from Arthur M'Neel (3/5)

Watson, John, born at Dalranck, Shire of Inverness, North Britain, laborer, age 21—deserted from H.M.'s 55th Regt. of Foot (3/12)

Otterson, William, born at Newtown, County Down, Ireland, laborer, age 22—same as above

Forbes, Brigadier General John, from Petincrief, Shire of Fife, Scotland—died in Phila. March 11 in 49th year and buried March 14 in the chancel of Christ Church, Phila. (3/19)

Farquhar, Dr., of NYC—married last week in NYC Miss Colden, daughter of the Hon. Cadwallader Colden of Coldensburgh (3/19)

Murray, Joseph, Esq., dec'd—accounts with his estate to be settled with his execs., Charles Williams and Thomas Jones (3/19)

Williams, Mark, born in Norwich, New England, laborer, age 30—deserted from H.M.'s 48th Regt. of Foot (3/19)

Fry, David, dec'd—vendue to be held at his house in French Church St. (3/26)

Robinson, Joseph, dec'd—house and lot, now in tenure of Balshazer Van Kleck, fronting the Old Slip Market, for sale; apply to execs., Leonard Lispenard and Andrew Abramse (4/2)

Pinkny, Elizabeth—has eloped from husband Israel Pinkny of Eastchester, currier and tanner (4/2)

Sergeant, Martha, of Morris Co.—has eloped from husband David (4/2)

Fisher, John, born in Prussia, butcher by trade, age 28—deserted from recruiting party of 46th Regt. from on board sloop bound to Albany (4/2)

Bet, Negro slave, born at Jamaica, L.I., age c. 20—runaway March 18 from John Leake of NYC (4/2)

Van Cortlandt, Philip, Esq.—last Assembly passed an act enabling his surviving execs. to sell items from estate to pay debts; since passage of the act Stephen Van Cortlandt has died, leaving Pierre Van Cortlandt as surviving exec. (4/2)

Remsen, widow—plantation where she resides at Brookland, L.I., adjoining the East River and between property of Isaac Seabring and that of Jacobus Debvoises, for sale; apply to Hendrick and Peter Remsen (4/9)

Amery, Jane—has eloped from husband, Joseph Amery, of NYC, mariner (4/9)

Williams, Rice, dec'd—Isaac Man intends to remove in May from Williams's house to that where Thomas Doughty now lives, near the Meal Market (4/9)

Clarkson, David, dec'd—accounts with estate to be settled with execs., Freeman, David and Mathew Clarkson (4/16)

Fisher, Dr. Archibald—died in NYC April 13 and was buried April 16 (4/16)

Cunningham, Samuel, born in Pa., age 22—deserted from H.M.'s 80th Regt. of Foot (4/16)

Cunningham, John, born in Pa., age 25—same as above

Pardy, John, born in Ireland, age 21—same as above

Dooly, Michael, born in Ireland, age 25—same as above

Mac Manus, Daniel, born in Ireland—same as above

Hopkins, Mathew, born in north of Ireland, age c. 30—same as above

Norman, Edward, born in north of Ireland, age c. 23—same as above

Lawrance, John, of NYC, merchant—married Sat. night, April 21, Miss Catharine Livingston, daughter of the Hon. Philip Livingston, Esq., late of NYC, dec'd (4/23)

Manchester, Capt. Joseph, of the sloop *Dolphin*, bound from NYC to Albany—knocked overboard April 14 by the boom near the Highlands, about 50 miles from NYC, and drowned; reward offered for discovery of his body by his father-in-law, Joseph Shelden, of Providence, R.I. (4/30)

Dyer, Mr., of Stafford, Conn.—murdered his wife and then killed himself on either April 8 or 9 (4/30)

Clayton, Capt.—killed by Indians March 28 near Venango (4/30)

Van Horne, Major, dec'd—Elias Desbrosses has removed to the late major's house in NYC (5/7)

Pemberton, Rev. Mr., of NYC, dec'd—Philip Doughty has removed from Mrs. Steel's to the house of the late Mr. Pemberton in Beaver St., near the Bowling Green (5/7)

Otlay, Anthony, indentured servant, age 25—runaway "a few days ago" from ship *Hopewell*, George Masterman captain (5/7)

Stringer, Robert, age 18—same as above

Markeshin, John, a servant "boy"—runaway April 28 from John Duryee, of NYC, baker (5/7)

Allen, James, late overseer on plantations about Ashley River, S.C.—after attacking members of the Peters family he was wounded and died in jail on April 15 (5/14)

Smith, William, born in England, age 26—deserted May 8 in Albany Co. from Major Whiting's company of the Rhode Island Regt. (5/14)

M'Neal, Samuel, apprentice, age c. 20—runaway from William Riddle of Bound Brook, Somerset Co., N.J. (5/14)

Larking, Moses, born in Ireland, age c. 50—deserted April 8 from H.M.'s service (5/14)

Johnston, John, of the privateer *Britannia* of Phila.—killed in action (5/14)

Jones, William, of the privateer *Britannia*—same as above

M'Evers, John, son of the late Patrick M'Evers, of NYC, merchant, dec'd—died in NYC on May 7 (5/14)

Tiebout, John, son of Bartholomew Tiebout of NYC—killed a few days ago by the enemy in sight of Ft. Edward (5/14)

Tappa, Mrs., of Esopus, Orange Co., noted trader—perished in fire at her house on May 11 (5/21)

Blackwood, John, cooper by trade, age 29—deserted from a N.Y. Provincial regt. (5/21)

Williams, Charles, laborer, age 18—same as above

Arnold, Benedict, weaver by trade, age 18—same as above

Smith, Hannah Elizabeth (*alias* Doliane)— her husband, Christian Smith, will no longer be responsible for her debts (5/21)

Rowland, Elijah, apprentice, age 18—runaway May 20 from Samuel Bowne, of Somerset Co., N.J. (5/28)

Holland, Mr., a battoeman—drowned May 6 between Albany and Half Moon (5/28)

Watts, Lt., of late Brigadier General Forbes's Regt.—killed by Indians in May between Stillwater and Scorticoke (6/4)

Duffee, Duncan, late of NYC, carpenter, dec'd—accounts with estate to be settled with Ennis Graham, acting executor (6/4)

Coons, Adam, German servant, age c. 35-40—runaway from Aaron Louzada of Bridge Water, Somerset Co., N.J., shopkeeper (6/4)

M'Neelage, Donald, born in Shire of Argyle, Scotland, house carpenter, age 23—deserted from H.M.'s First Highland Battalion (6/4)

Cyrus, Negro servant, a good butcher, age c. 28-30—runaway May 26 from John Lloyd of Stanford, Conn. (6/4)

Waldo, Brigadier General—died May 23 in apoplectic fit just above the first falls while on Penobscot expedition with governor of Mass. (6/11)

London, Negro slave, age c. 30—runaway June 4 from Gabriel Ligget of Westchester (6/11)

Morris, Richard, Esq., son of Lewis Morris, Esq., of Morrissania—since our last married Miss Sally Ludlow, daughter of Henry Ludlow of NYC, merchant (6/18)

Shannon, James, born in Ireland, age c. 18—runaway June 7 from Benjamin Jackson of Laetitia Court, Philadelphia (6/18)

Dyer, Christopher, of Casco Bay, skipper of a fishing schooner—killed by Indians June 10 (7/2)

Pomp, Negro slave, age c. 27—runaway June 23 from Edmund Leavenworth of Stratford (7/2)

Deffoe, Daniel, late of NYC, dec'd—accounts with estate to be settled with execs., David Van Horne and David Clarkson (7/9)

Van Wye, Lawrence, of NYC, house carpenter—died July 3 in a well in Montgomery Ward in NYC (7/9)

Bennet, Peter, of NYC—same as above

Skaats, Bartholomew, late of NYC, dec'd—accounts with estate to be settled with Jacoba Skaats, executrix (7/16)

Pepperrell, Sir William—died July 6 at Kittery in 63rd year (7/16)

M'Michael, John, a suttler—murdered by an Indian in January between Ft. Stanwix and Harkiman's (7/16)

Jones, Capt., of the Pa. Regt.—killed by enemy July 6 at Ft. Ligonier (7/23)

Sowers, Capt., an engineer—killed by enemy July 5 or 6 at Oswego (7/23)

Otter, Lt., of the Royal American Regt.—same as above

Walters, John—died July 8 in NYC in 72nd year and buried in his family vault at Trinity Church (7/23)

Kemp, William, Esq., for six years past Attorney General of Province of NY—died July 19 in NYC and was buried July 21 at Trinity Church (7/23)

Wraxwall, Peter, Esq., Secretary of Indian Affairs and lately captain of an Independent Company posted in NY—died July 10 in NYC and was buried July 12 in Trinity Churchyard (7/23)

Jacob, a Negro, age 25-30—jailed in Goshen, Orange Co. (7/23)

Dick, (sometimes called "Martin"), Negro slave, age c. 33—runaway May 18 from James I. Ross of the Nine Partners, Dutchess Co. (7/30)

Hamilton, William, of Prince George's Co., Md.—accidentally killed July 5 near Patuxent Bridge by musket shot (7/30)

Harrison, Ensign, of General Forbes's Regt.—killed about July 23 near Ticonderoga (7/30)

Prideaux, General—killed in July near Niagara by bursting of a cohorn (7/30)

Johnston, Col., of the NY Regt.—killed in July near Niagara (7/30)

Townsend, Col.—killed by a cannonball near Niagara; body interred July 20 at Albany (7/30)

Thurman, Francis, late of NYC, dec'd—brother was John Thurman (8/6)

Tone (or Anthony), Negro slave, bred in Madagascar, age 25—runaway early July from Johannes Roorbach of NYC (8/6)

Primus, Negro slave, age c. 30—runaway July 25 from Nicholas Stike, of Battoe St., NYC (8/6)

Wolfe, Elizabeth—her husband, Patrick Wolfe, of NYC, schoolmaster, will pay no debts henceforth contracted by her (8/13)

Flora, Negro slave, age 30 (lived several years with Elias Ellis near Oswego Market in NYC)—runaway July 24 from Capt. Samuel Bayard of NYC (8/13)

Prince, Negro slave, age c. 30—runaway Aug. 3 from Joshua Levy, of Batteau St., NYC (8/13)

Flierboom, Ser Vas, dec'd—for sale: two of his houses, one in Queen St. (now occupied by Robert Griffith) and the other opposite the Moravian Meeting House, fronting Fair St. (8/20)

Morris, Nicholas, born County of Kilkeny, Ireland, age c. 30—deserted Aug. 8 from Royal American Regt. at Oswego (8/27)

Campbell, William, born County of Donnegal, Ireland, age c. 28—same as above

Danolson, Archibald, born in Ireland, age c. 30—same as above

Kanpschneider, John, born in Germany, age c. 28—same as above

Ryan, John, born in Pa., drummer, age c. 20—same as above

Lutz, Simon, born in Germany, age c. 22—same as above

Reese, Robert, born in Wales, age c. 26—same as above

Barry, David, age 60 (for 14 years prisoner of the French)—released at Niagara (8/27)

Grant, Ebenezer, of NYC, merchant—died Aug. 23 in NYC in 60th year and was buried evening of Aug. 24 in his family vault in Trinity Churchyard (8/27)

Emory, Capt., late of NYC, dec'd—David Shaw has opened his store in the house of the late Capt. Emory, opposite the Fly Market (8/27)

Cochran, James, pedlar, dec'd—accounts with his estate to be settled with administrators, Isaac Hodge and James Wilson, both of New Windsor, Ulster Co. (9/3)

Bellamy, John, born in London, mariner, age c. 22—runaway from his bail; reward for his capture offered by Lawrence Sweeny, living in Bayard St., NYC (9/3)

Weatherly, Benjamin, age c. 19—runaway Tuesday last in NYC from Thomas Crookshanks, pilot (9/10)

Kannief, Jeremiah, of Dutchess Co.—died there a few months ago at age of 96; his wife died about three years ago; they were married 71 years and 9 months (9/10)

Delaplain, Joshua, late of NYC, dec'd—John Halsted has opened a store at the house of William Weaver, next door to house in which Delaplain lived, between Burling's Slip and the Fly Market (9/10)

Jarvis, Benjamin, late of NYC, dec'd—house and lot belonging to his estate in Montgomery Ward (now in tenure of George Mesurvey) for sale (9/24)

Brown, Lawrance, sailor—stabbed to death Sept. 30 in NYC by Henry Cobb (9/24)

Wood, William, late of Six Mile Run, Somerset Co., N. J., dec'd—accounts with estate to be settled with administrator, W. Wood (10/1)

Quick, Jacobus, late of NYC, dec'd—house and lot, fronting Queen St., near the Fly Market (now in tenure of Francis Basset, pewterer, and next door to John Robbins, currier) for sale (10/1)

Read, Thomas (*alias* Cuthbert), a convict servant, jeweller and motto-ring engraver by trade, age 25 to 30—runaway in June from John Inch of Annapolis, Md. (10/1)

Hunt, Jacob, late of Borough of Westchester, dec'd—accounts with estate to be settled with James Tucker, of NYC, or Thomas Willett and James Hunt on Frog's Neck, Westchester Co. (10/1)

Ramond, Joshua, of privateer sloop *Bellisle*, Capt. Sears commander—killed in action near Newfoundland (10/8)

Moorehouse, John, of the *Bellisle*—same as above

Cable, Ebenezer, of the *Bellisle*—same as above

Moorehouse, Stephen, of the *Bellisle*—same as above

Batterson, Joseph, of the *Bellisle*—same as above

Lockwood, Joshua, of the *Bellisle*—same as above

Springer, Gideon, of the *Bellisle*—same as above

Welch, John, of the *Bellisle*—same as above

Oreer, John, of the *Bellisle*—same as above

Jerrey, a Negro, age 30 to 40—runaway Sept. 23 from John Pugsley, John Hunt and Arabella Hedy, all of the town of Westchester (10/8)

Bohenah, a Negro, age c. 35—same as above

Eastwick, Thomas, born in Boston, married in Phila., captured by the French in a sloop from Va., one Outerbridge commander—now in French prison in Bordeaux (10/22)

Tom, a Negro, age c. 22—runaway Oct. 14 from Jacob Van Wagenen of NYC (10/22)

M'Daniel, Cornelius, an Irishman—runaway from his bail about three months ago in Phila. (10/22)

Marston, Nathaniel, son of Nathaniel Marston, of NYC, merchant—died Oct. 26 at his house in NYC and was buried there Oct. 27 (10/29)

Miller, John Christophel, a German, cooper by trade—runaway Oct. 30 from Jacob Reader, of Newtown, L. I. (11/5)

Reynolds, John, of privateer *Duke of Cumberland*, James Lilley captain—drowned on last cruise (11/5)

Stillwell, Major Thomas, late of Kings Co., dec'd—accounts with estate to be settled (11/5)

Woolsey, Col. Melancthon Taylor, dec'd—estate near Musqueto Cove, Oyster Bay, L. I., for sale (11/5)

Gilmore, John, of Ker's Creek, Augusta Co., Va., and wife and son—killed there by Indians on Oct. 17 (11/5)

Gilmore, Mrs. William—same as above

Burnham, Elisha, of the sloop *Patty*, Capt. Highly master, of Middletown, Conn.—drowned at sea Oct. 24 (11/5)

Sage, Ebenezer, of sloop *Patty*—same as above

Roberts, Stephen, of sloop *Patty*—same as above

Duane, James, Esq., attorney at law, of NYC—married about a fortnight since Miss Polly Livingston, daughter of Robert Livingston, Esq., of the Manor of Livingston (11/5)

Sharpas, Mrs. Elizabeth, of NYC, dec'd—real estate for sale; apply to execs., Charles Crook and Theophilact Bache (11/5)

Hinds, Abraham, born in Bristol, matross in Capt. Martin's company of the Royal Regt. of Artillery, age c. 20—deserted Nov. 11 (11/19)

Fisher, Dr. Archibald, dec'd., and Fisher, Garrit V. H., merchant, dec'd—accounts with estates to be settled with Cornelius Fisher of NYC (11/19)

Lynsen, Abraham, of NYC, "eminent" merchant—died Nov. 17 at his house in Wall St., NYC, in 60th year (11/19)

Lauder, Robert, indentured servant from Scotland, age c. 18 or 19—runaway Nov. 17 from ship *Prince Ferdinand* of Liverpool (11/26)

Edward, William, apprentice, born in Bristol, age c. 18—runaway Nov. 21 from William Smith of NYC, blockmaker (11/26)

Kemptie, Lt., of Major General Anstruther's Regt.—died in Boston Nov. 29 and was buried there Nov. 30 (12/10)

Price, John, apprentice, age c. 13—runaway Nov. 25 from Capt. Isaac Sheldon of NYC (12/10)

M'Hugh, James, apprentice, age c. 14—runaway Nov. 25 from Capt. Hait of NYC (12/10)

Gill, Samuel, a Guernsey man, age c. 23—he is suspected of having lured the two apprentices mentioned above to Phila. (12/10)

M'Clean, Mary, servant, born in Scotland, age c. 25—runaway Dec. 2 from Jacob Eage, of Campbell Hall, Ulster Co. (12/17)

Rutherford, Major, late of NYC, dec'd—furniture of his estate for sale (12/24)

Jacklin, Robert, of NYC, dec'd—goods, including shoemaker's tools, for sale (12/24)

Kelly, Nugent, schoolmaster at Woodbridge, N. J.—drowned when boat upset outside NY harbor Dec. 27 (12/31)

GENEALOGICAL DATA FROM THE NEW-YORK MERCURY

1760

Rutherford, Major, dec'd—a vendue to be held at the house where he lived in the Broad-Way (1/7)

Jacklin, Robert, dec'd—a vendue to be held at his house in NYC (1/7)

Basset, Josiah, of Judea, Conn.—accidentally shot and killed Dec. 11, 1759, by Jesse Baker (1/7)

Baker, Mr., a brother of Jesse Baker—accidentally shot and killed while hunting, about 20 years ago, by Cornelius Holabord (1/7)

Groenendeyk, Samuel, of NYC, dec'd—two houses belonging to his estate for sale (1/7)

M'Clean, Mary, servant, born in Scotland, age c. 25—runaway Dec. 2, 1759, from Jacob Eage of Campbell Hall in Ulster Co. (1/7)

Giraud, Peter, dec'd—house and lot belonging to his estate in upper end of French Church Street (now in tenure of Dr. Abram Van Vleck) for sale; execs. are Anne Giraud and Francis Child (1/14)

Goddard, Nicholas, an English servant, tinman by trade, age c. 30—runaway Jan. 7 from William Puntiner (1/14)

Hubbell, Catharine, widow, late of NYC, innholder, dec'd—accounts with estate to be settled with administrator, Benjamin Stout (1/14)

Lynsen, Abraham, dec'd—accounts with his estate to be settled with execs, Catharine and Abraham Lynsen and Elizabeth Smith (1/14)

Stiles, Capt., of Phila., commander of a privateer—lately murdered by his crew (1/21)

Johnson, Anthony, late of Albany, dec'd—accounts with his estate to be settled with administrators, Messers Benson and Turner of Albany, merchants (1/21)

Tucker, James, of NYC, dec'd—accounts with his estate to be settled with execs, Mary Tucker and John and Bazel Bartwo (1/21)

Marsden, Capt., of *The Brothers*—drowned at sea (1/28)

Ryder, Robert, late of NYC, dec'd—accounts with estate to be settled with Amos Dodge (1/28)

Moore, Col., dec'd—house near the Whitehall to let; apply to Mrs. Frances Moore, opposite the fort (2/4)

Long, George, of Capt. Delancey's Company, born in Queens County, Ireland, woolcomber by trade, age 21—deserted from H.M.'s 46th Regt. at Schenectady (2/4)

Washington, William, corporal in Capt. Forbes's Company, born in Lancaster, England, weaver by trade—same as above

Kelsy, James, of Capt. Osborn's Company, born in Sheffield, England, cutler by trade, age 27—same as above

Right, Hendrick (who formerly went by the name of Henry Miller), servant, age c. 25—runaway Tuesday last from John Vought of NYC (2/4)

Adriance, Joris, dec'd—farm in Rumbout Precinct, Dutchess Co., for sale; apply to execs, Abraham Adriance, Richard Van Wyck and Cornelius Van Wyck, Jr. (2/18)

Chapple, William, dec'd—house, lot and stable in Queens St., NYC, for sale by execs, William Dyckman and Michael Turner (2/18)

Bowne, Joseph, of Flushing, dec'd—farm for sale; apply to William Lawrence at Musqueto Cove, or Joseph Bowne at Flushing (2/18)

Elliot, Mr., an Indian trader—killed Feb. 1, together with his family, by Indians at Ft. Prince George in South Carolina (2/25)

Wolf, Catharine, widow of Matthew Wolf, dec'd—accounts with her estate to be settled with administrators, Renier Skaats and William Vredenburgh (2/25)

Verplank, Mrs., of NYC, dec'd—furniture for sale near Ellis's Dock (2/25)

McIntosh, John, born at Inverness, Scotland, silversmith by trade, age 23—deserted from H.M.'s 17th Regt of Foot at Ticonderoga (3/3)

Findley William, born at Killebeg, County of Westmeath, Ireland, weaver by trade, age 24—same as above

Carril, Bryant (called by acquaintances "Gilderoy"), servant, age c. 16—runaway March 8 from ship *Two Friends*, James Spellen master (3/10)

Cockchick, Anthony, Indian servant, age c. 15—runaway from Stephen Ward of East-chester (3/10)

Tobler, Capt. Ulric—killed by Indians Feb. 15 near Ft. Moore in South Carolina (3/17)

Woolven, John, captain of schooner of Boston—drowned at sea end of Feb. (3/17)

Walton, Jacob, of NYC, merchant—married night of March 11, in NYC, Miss Polly Cruger, daughter of Henry Cruger, Esq., "eminent" merchant of NYC (3/17)

Farquhar, Mrs., wife of Dr. Farquahar of NYC, and daughter of Hon. Cadwallader Colden, President of Council of NY—died in NYC night of March 10 (3/17)

Glasgow, Negro slave, age c. 18—runaway March 15 from the snow *Sadler*, William Fitz-herbert captain, lying at New Dock in NYC (3/17)

Jones, Dr. Evan, late of Ulster Co., dec'd—his farm on Hudson River, about one mile from New Windsor, for sale; apply to Dr. John Jones in NYC or Thomas Jones on the premises (3/17)

Lambert, Valentine, of NYC, dec'd—accounts with estate to be settled with execs, George Petterson and Lawrence Eman (3/24)

Cobham, James of NYC, dec'd—accounts with estate to be settled with execs, Waddel Cunningham and Hugh Gaine (3/24)

Standard, Rev. Thomas, of Eastchester, dec'd—accounts with estate to be settled with execs, James Barnard and Andrew Clements (3/24)

Colgan, Rev. Thomas, of Jamaica, Queens Co.—plantation where he once lived for sale (3/31)

Tom, Negro slave, age c. 27—runaway "about ten days since;" apply to printer for reward if runaway is captured (3/31)

Collins, Giles, of the artillery—killed by Indians in March near Pittsburgh (3/31)

Auboyneau, Mrs. Frances, of NYC, dec'd—accounts with estate to be settled with Elias Desbrosses, exec. (4/7)

Sharpas, Mrs. Elizabeth, of NYC, dec'd—goods will be sold at her house in the Broadway (4/7)

Gomez, Mordecay, of NYC, dec'd—lots belonging to estate in the Outward to be let; apply to Daniel Gomez (4/7)

Caesar, Negro slave, born in America, age c. 25—runaway March 30 from Barnardus Ryder of Flushing (4/14)

Nicol, Benjamin, Esq., of NYC, eminent lawyer—died in NYC April 15 (4/21)

Cruger, Mrs., wife of Henry Cruger of NYC, merchant—died in NYC third week of April (4/21)

Alexander, Mary, widow of Hon. James Alexander, dec'd, and mother of present Earl of Sterling—died in NYC third week of April (4/21)

Bradford, William, of NYC, pewterer, dec'd—accounts with estate to be settled with William Mercier; vendue to be held at house of dec'd in Hanover Square (4/21)

Long, John, of Rowan Co., North Carolina—killed by Indians about middle of March some 7 miles from Ft. Dobbs and 20 miles from Salisbury (4/28)

Gillespie, Robert, of Rowan Co., N.C.—same as above

Van Wyck, Abraham, Jr., dec'd—accounts with estate to be settled with execs, Mary Van Wyck, Theodorus Van Wyck and Dirck Brinkerfoff (5/5)

Windsor (*alias* Jammy), Negro slave, born in West Indies, age c. 20—runaway April 27 from John Clopper, in Stone St., NYC (5/5)

Cochran, Hugh, born in Scotland or North of Ireland—deserted from the Newport, R.I., Regt. (5/5)

The following, on board the snow *Britannia* of NYC, Lambert Garrison captain, were drowned off County of Devon, Eng., when the long boat overset: Matthew Carter, Thomas Craig, Lewis Woolcock, John Catness, Timothy Roach, Hugh Duff (the above all taken up and buried in Hotham Parish Churchyard), Robert Welsh (a pasenger), James Forbis, John Clark, William Fisher, William Cronick (5/12)

Wallace, Hugh, of NYC, merchant—married last week to Miss Sally Low, daughter of Cornelius Low, of Rariton, N.J. (5/12)

Forbush, John, Jr., dec'd—goods to be auctioned at his house near Success on Long Island (5/12)

Mc Bride, Rose, "young" woman servant, born in Ireland—runaway from John Thompson, of Jamaica, L. I. (5/12)

Ashton, Hester, servant, born at Ashton under Line, Lancashire, age c. 19—runaway May 8 from Erasmus Williams of NYC (5/12)

Allen, Mrs. Margaret, wife of Chief Justice William Allen of Pa., and sister of the Hon. James Hamilton, Gov. of Pa.—died May 12 in Phila. and was buried there May 14 in the family vault (5/19)

Rutgers, Cornelia, of NYC, dec'd—goods to be auctioned at her house; accounts with estates of Cornelia and Anthony Rutgers to be settled with execs, Rev. Henry Barclay and Leonard Lispenard (5/19)

Foy, family of, who arrived from Ireland about 40 years ago and settled in Boston—members asked to write to near relative, Dennis Mahony, mariner, at house of Capt. William Dobs, back of the English Church in NYC (5/19)

Sarah (*alias* Jenny), mulatto slave, born at New Rochelle, Westchester Co.—runaway May 16 from Hendrick Rutgers, brewer (5/19)

Gregg, Robert, dec'd—accounts with estate to be settled with James Beekman, administrator, in Queen St., NYC (5/26)

Francis, ———, son of Capt. Francis—killed by Indians about April 17 near Ft. Ninety Six (5/26)

Ayscough, Dr. Richard, eminent surgeon and apothecary of NYC—died May 29 at his house in Hanover Square (6/2)

Wetmore, Rev. James, rector at Rye—died of smallpox May 13 in his 65th year (6/2)

Somerindick, Tunis, late of Greenwich, in the OUTWARD of NYC—accounts with estate to be settled with William Burnham, admin. (6/9)

Van Ivere, Myndert, dec'd—farm at Bloomendal, adjoining farm of Oliver De Lancey, Esq., for sale; apply to execs, Sarah Van Ivere, widow, Abraham Parsell and Ide Van Ivere (6/16)

Ratsey, Mrs. Alice, of NYC, shopkeeper, dec'd—accounts with estate to be settled with Peter Goelet, exec., or Alice Ratsey, executrix; goods being sold at her late dwelling in Smith St. (6/16)

Johnston Capt., of the Rangers—killed June 4 by enemy near Nutten Island (6/16)

Wood, Ensign, of General Monkton's—same as above

Vanhall, mulatto slave, age 31—runaway June 4 from Abraham Davenport of Stanford, Conn. (6/16)

Tom, Negro slave, born in NY, age 15 or 16—runaway June 6 from Roger Barnes, of Staten Island (6/16)

Rae, William, trader—killed by Indians about May 16 in Georgia (6/23)

Robertson, William, a pack-horseman—same as above

Ross, John—same as above

Cesar, mulatto slave, born in America, age c. 26—runaway in October, 1759, from Joseph Hall of Wallingford, Conn. (6/23)

Bromlow, Negro slave, age c. 24—runaway June 15 from Henry Richardson (6/23)

Prior, Hannah, wife of Stephen Prior, of White Plains—has eloped and her husband will not pay future debts (6/30)

Morrill, Amos, dec'd—land owned by him on Oak Neck, Oysterbay, L.I., for sale (6/30)

Donnolly, Mr—killed by Indians early in June near Enoree, 30 to 40 miles N.E. of Fort Ninety Six (7/6)

Rickets, Miss Polly, daughter of Col. William Rickets of Elizabeth Town, N.J.—died July 5 in her 16th year (7/14)

Bryan, Isabellah, wife of John Bryan, schoolmaster on Golden-Hill—has eloped and husband will not pay future debts (7/21)

Denormandie, Mr.—drowned in July on passage from Oswego to Niagara (7/21)

Thodey, Col. Michael, late of the NY Provincials—married July 10 in NYC to Miss Betsey Jones, only daughter of Humphry Jones, of NYC, merchant (7/21)

Williams, Capt., of the Royal Light Infantry—killed by enemy last week in June (7/28)

Morrison, Capt. killed June 27 in engagement with Cherokees (7/28)

Simeson, Rem, of Staten Island, dec'd—ferry in possession of his widow to be sold or let (7/28)

Collins, Mrs. Margaret, of Albany, dec'd—accounts with estate to be settled with John R. Bleeker, exec. (7/28)

Will, Negro slave, born on Island of Curacao, age c. 17—runaway July 26 from John Johnson of NYC (7/28)

Horsmanden, Mrs. Mary, of NYC, late wife of the Hon. Daniel Horsmanden, Esq., and formerly wife of the Rev. William Vesey, Rector of Trinity Church in NYC—died in NYC July 21 and was buried July 23 in family vault (7/28)

White, Timothy, of Orange Co., dec'd—reference to a bond by which White was indebted to Samuel Hazard, late of Phila., merchant, dec'd (7/28)

Van Horne, Cornelius G., dec'd—house and blacksmith's shop in Kins St., NYC, formerly belonging to estate, for sale at auction; apply to Garrit Van Horne (7/28)

Princess, Negro slave, age c. 20—runaway July 29 from Thomas Hill of NYC (8/4)

Parks, Samuel, mate of schooner *Francis*—sentenced, in Newport, R.I., to die on Aug. 1 for piracy; (8/4); executed (9/1)

Hawkins, Benjamin, of schooner *Francis*—same as above

De Lancey, James, Lt.-Gov. of NY—died July 30 at his seat in the Bowery, near NYC, in his 57th year (8/4)

Ward, ———, 10 year-old son of Thomas Ward of Bergen Co., N.J.—died June 21 from wounds inflicted on him six weeks before by a wildcat (8/4)

Robin, Negro slave, born in America, age c. 25—runaway July 30 from George Codimants of Bergen, N.J. (8/4)

Cathern, Arthur, master of a brigantine from NYC—died of starvation in a boat (8/11)

Campbell, Duncan, of NYC—drowned Aug. 8 when a pettiauger overset in a gust of rain and wind on way from the Narrows to NYC (8/11)

M'Alpine, Daniel, son-in-law of the abovementioned Duncan Campbell—same as above

Wilson, James, dec'd—property adjoining Rariton River, opposite Perth Amboy, for sale (8/11)

Primus, Negro slave, age c. 20—runaway Saturday night last from Henderick Onderdonk of Cow Neck, L.I. (8/18)

Thorp, Michael, sailor—drowned in the North River while trying to escape from H.M.'s ship *Winchester*; he had a sister married to John Mitchell, stationer, in Southampton Buildings, Greys Inn, London (8/18)

De Groote, ———, lad aged c. 20—fell afternoon of Aug. 20 from scaffold where he was shingling house of Judah Hays, merchant, in Broad St., NYC; his life is despaired of (8/25)

Duncan, Thomas, of NYC, merchant—died morning of Aug. 24 at his house in Broadway (8/25)

Fisher, Dr. Archibald, dec'd—accounts with his estate to be settled with Cornelius Fisher, exec (8/25)

Fisher, Garrit Van Horn, dec'd—same as above

Woodhouse, Anthony, of North Castle, Westchester Co., dec'd—accounts with estate to be settled with Benjamin Kip, exec., living at Philipsburgh (8/25)

Lewis, John—indicted Aug. 25 at court in Chester, Pa., for murder of his wife (9/1)

Glegg, Capt. of the Artillery—killed in an engagement about Aug. 15 (9/1)

Clowns, Samuel, Esq., of Jamaica, L.I., a noted lawyer—died there in his 87th year (9/1)

Dawson, Jonas—killed as result of a blow in a boxing match with William Rodwell near Magothy River, Md.; left wife and five small children (9/8)

Waldron, Daniel, of Tewksbury, Hunterdon Co., dec'd—accounts with estate to be settled with execs, Johanna Waldron and John Van Sickle, Jr. (9/8)

Kinsale, Negro slave, age c. 22—runaway from John Long (9/8)

Ludlow, Gabriel, Jr., of NYC, merchant—married Thursday night last to Miss Nancy Verplanck, daughter of the late Gulian Verplanck of NYC (9/8)

Scull, Robert, of Phila.—shot July 27, while playing billiards at the Center House in Phila., by Mr. Brulumman, late an officer in the Royal American Regt.; he died July 30 (9/8)

Johnston, Mrs. Elizabeth, of Perth Amboy—died a few days ago (9/8)

Cebbe, the widow, dec'd—accounts with estate to be settled with John Hastier, goldsmith, in Hanover Square, or Edward Laight (9/15)

Kiersted, Luke Benjamin, dec'd—accounts with estate to be settled with the widow, Martha Kiersted, exec.; dwelling house on Golden Hill for sale (9/15)

Hill, Anthony, dec'd—farm near Foster's Meadows in Westchester Co., for sale (9/22)

Kelly, Henry, dec'd—house, lot no. 234, fronting Murray's St. . in the Fields, near Mr. Benjamin Keats, fit for a shop or tavern, for sale (9/29)

Cox, Daniel, the "late"—his farm called "Bellemont," where he lived, situated on the Delaware, 12 miles from Trenton, for sale; apply to William Pidgeon or Moore Furnam, Esqs., at Trenton, William Coxe at Phila., or Daniel Coxe at Amboy (10/6)

Van Varck, Andrew, of NYC, hatter—accounts with estate to be settled with Else Van Varck, exec., and James Van Varck, exec.; James carries on the hatter's business (10/6)

Frank, Negro slave, age c. 30—runaway Sept. 12 from Thomas Morley (10/6)

Hamersly, Lucretia, dec'd—accounts with estate to be settled (10/13)

M'Cleve, Capt. John. dec'd—accounts with estate to be settled with Elizabeth M'Cleve, admin. (10/13)

Wheelwright, Hon. John, Esq., member of H.M.'s Council for Mass., principal officer for managing Indian affairs, and Commissary General—died Oct. 5 in Boston in 71st year (10/13)

Bruleman, John—executed Oct. 8 in Phila. for murder of Robert Scull (10/13)

Charles, Negro slave, born in America, formerly belonging to Col. Moore, age c. 24— runaway Oct. 6 from John Waddell (10/13)

Bache, Theophilact, of NYC, merchant—married night of Oct. 16 in NYC to Miss Nancy Barclay, daughter of Andrew Barclay of NYC, merchant (10/20)

Kennedy, Capt. Archibald, son of Hon. Archibald Kennedy of NYC—appointed to command of H.M.'s frigate *The Quebec* (10/20)

Peters, Sergt. George, born in Phila., blacksmith by trade—deserted from Capt. Ogilvie's Independent Company at Stillwater (10/20)

Greenland, James, born in London, glazier by trade—same as above

GENEALOGICAL DATA FROM THE NEW-YORK MERCURY

1760

Carver, William, of Marshfield, Plymouth Co., Mass., brother's son to Gov. Carver of the Plymouth Colony—died in Marshfield Oct. 2, aged 102; has left the fifth generation of male issue, in all, children, grandchildren, great-grandchildren, and great-great-grandchildren 96 (10/27)

Peet, Deacon Thomas, employed the last 32 years of his life as a post-rider between New York and Saybrook—died lately of a fever at Stratford in hs 62nd year (10/27)

Wigg, John, born at Villverton in Norfolk, age c. 21—deserted Oct. 7 from H.M.'s 27th Regt. of Foot at Crown Point (10/27)

Marshal, James, born in London, printer by trade, age 28—same as above

Ganter, Helena, late Helena Wall, now wife of John Henry Ganter of NYC—has eloped from her husband (10/27)

Frost, George, of Oysterbay, dec'd—farm for sale; apply to Benjamin Townsend in Jericho or John Underhill at Metenicock (11/4)

De Visme, Philip, dec'd—account with estate to be settled with Anne De Visme, admin. (11/4)

Reed, Thomas, born at Warsall (Warslow?), County of Stafford, England, bucklemaker by trade, age 24—deserted from H.M.'s 17th Regt. of Foot at Ft. Stanwix (11/10)

M'Intosh, John born near Ft. George in Scotland, silversmith by trade, age 25—same as above

Guest, John, born at Shifnall, County of Salop, England, laborer, age 28—same as above

Minors, Norton, Negro slave, caulker and ship carpenter by trade, once owned by Mark Quane of Newbury in New England, who sold him to Mr. Craddock of Nevis, who in turn sold him to Messers Bodkin and Ferrall of the Island of St. Croix—runaway July 1 from his masters (11/10)

Bayeux, Thomas, of Staten Island, dec'd—accounts with estate to be settled with Anne Groesbeck, admin. (11/10)

Murray, Joseph, dec'd—accounts with estate to be settled with execs, Charles Williams and Thomas June (11/17)

Murray, John, born in Ireland, laborer, age 23—deserted Oct. 20 from H.M.'s 17th Regt. of Foot at Schenectady (11/17)

Senior, William, born in England, tailor by trade, age 27—same as above

Griffiths, Paul, born in England, barber by trade age 40—same as above

Allen William, shoemaker by trade, age 27—same as above

Reece, John, laborer, age 47—same as above

Cavendish, Joseph, tailor by trade, age 27—same as above

M'Evers, Charles, of NYC, merchant—married night of Oct. 12 in NYC to Miss Johnston, only daughter of Simon Johnston, Esq., Recorder of NYC (11/17)

Huffpouer, Catharine, wife of Christean Huffpouer of Elizabeth Town, N.J.—husband will not pay debts contracted by her in future (11/24)

Bishop, Robert, apprentice, age c. 13—runaway Sept. 11 from James Spellen (11/24)

Hughes, William, an "old" man—killed by Indians about middle of October on the Enoree River, about 5 miles from Capt. Isaac Pennington's fort (12/1)

Newling, Mr., an "old" man—same as above

Harris, Phebe, wife of Nathaniel Harris of NYC, mariner—has eloped from her husband (12/1)

Jack, (calls himself John Johnson), mulatto slave, age c. 23—runaway Nov. 12 from Joseph Burr of Northampton Township, Burlington Co. (12/1)

Kiersted, Mrs. Elizabeth, of NYC, shopkeeper—died Nov. 26 at her house in Smith St. in her 81st year (12/1)

Forbes, John, Jr., dec'd—administrators will make settlement of estate at house of John Combs on Dec. 18 (12/1)

Elbersen, John, dec'd—house and lot in Bayard St., now occupied by James Mc Cartney, for sale; apply to Abraham Elbersen in Wynkoop St. (12/8)

Robinson, Margaret, servant girl, born in Cheshire, England, age c. 22—runaway Friday night last about 10 o'clock from Thomas Steel at the King's Arms Tavern in NYC (12/8)

Reeve, William, of Ridgfield (formerly of Southold, L.I.), dec'd—accounts with estate to be settled with Obadiah Plat of Ridgfield, admin. (12/22)

Robinson, John, born at Manchester, England, worsted weaver by trade, age 23—deserted Dec. 10 from H.M.'s 17th Regt. of Foot (12/22)

Menagh, William, born in North of Ireland, tailor by trade, age 22—same as above

Hull, Dr., of Bethlem, Conn.—died, together with wife and two children, in Nov. of a malignant pleurisy; 34 persons in that town died of this malady in Nov. (12/22)

Capt. Hayer, late master of a snow of NYC, reported that early in October his ship lost its masts, and the following members of the crew died of starvation and lack of water: William Barton, mate; John Cobley, boatswain; William Beasley; Francis Mud; Scot Handy; ———— Doran; Thomas Park; Joseph Park; William Kelly; William Hutchins (12/22)

Bush, Justice, of Greenwich, Conn., dec'd—accounts with estate to be settled with Justice and Henry Bush, admins. (12/22)

Taggart, James, dec'd—accounts with estate to be settled with Isaac Lattouch, admin. (12/22)

Jacob, mulatto slave, age 28—runaway Nov. 17 from James Sharp of Salsbury, Chester Co., Pa. (12/29)

Robin, Negro slave, born in America, age 28—runaway about two months ago from David Fowler of Eastchester, Westchester Co., NY (12/29)

1761

Jacob, mulatto slave, age c. 28—runaway Nov. 17, 1760, from James Sharp of Salsbury Township, Chester Co., Pa. (1/5)

Dean, Samuel, dec'd—farm at Jamaica, L. I., for sale; apply to Capt. Amos Smith at Jamaica (1/12)

Hamilton, James, Irish servant, age c. 27—runaway Dec. 28, 1760, from John Hill of Bucks Co., Pa. (1/12)

Birdsall, Samuel, of Norwalk, Conn., dec'd—surviving partner of his, William Hawxhurst, living in Queen St., Burlings Slip, NYC, will sell goods belonging to the partnership (1/12)

Hutchenson, Sally, white servant girl, born in NYC, age 13—runaway Dec. 30, 1760, from William Bedlow of NYC (1/12)

Wall, Negro slave, born at Oysterbay, L. I., age c. 40—runaway Dec. 26, 1760, from John Leake of NYC (1/12)

Man, Elizabeth, widow, dec'd—house and lot in Broad St., NYC, next door to Dr. Eustace, near the Watch House, for sale; apply to the execs, Isaac Man and Ennis Graham (1/9); accounts with estate to be settled with Isaac Man or Sarah Graham (2/2)

Tom, a Negro slave, formerly property of R. R. Livingston, Esq., age c. 22—runaway Jan. 5 from Henry White of NYC (1/19)

Pearse, Thomas, staymaker, dec'd, late a partner of William Clark, who will carry on the business—accounts with estate to be settled with execs, William Taylor, James Swan and Catharine Hons (1/26)

Squire, Anabella, wife of Zophar Squire, of Newark, Essex Co., N. J.—has run her husband into debt and he will pay no debts contracted by her in the future (2/2)

Hermensen, Nanneng and Holland, Henry, dec'd—land patented to them and others Sept. 23, 1708, called Shepondehowah, *alias* Clifton Park, adjoining bounds of Nestiguone, for sale (2/2)

Eyre, George, dec'd—his note, dated Dec. 30, 1760, obtained by fraud; all are forbidden by execs, Samuel, Manuel, and Jehu Eyre, to take assignment of it (2/2); above note said to have been obtained from the dec'd by Isaac Conro in presence of James Mills, Thomas Shreve, and Aaron Stockholm (2/9)

Caesar, Negro slave belonging to Widow Furman at Colt's Neck, Monmouth Co., N. J.—apparently murdered a few days before Christmas, 1760 (2/2)

Catharine, German servant "girl"—runaway Feb. 4 from John Taylor of NYC (2/9)

Gin, Negro slave, age c. 20—same as above

Suck, mulatto slave, formerly belonging to the Buskirks—runaway Feb. 1 from Anthony Hunter of NYC (2/16)

Davies, Rev. Samuel, President of the College of New Jersey—died about 2 P.M., Feb. 5, at his house in Princeton in his 38th year (2/16); furniture and library for sale; accounts with estate to be settled with Richard Stockton, admin. (3/23)

Bowne, Joseph, of Flushing, dec'd—farm near the town landing of Flushing for sale; apply to William Lawrence at Musqueto Cove or Joseph Bowne at Flushing (2/23)

O'Hara, John, of Middletown, N. J., dec'd—accounts with estate to be settled with execs, Samuel and Lewis Forman (2/23)

Elrington, Ensign, of company of Capt. John Campbell in H.M.'s 22nd Regt.—died Sunday last in Charleston, S. C. (3/2)

Brown (*alias* Edwards), Mary, born in Pa., indentured servant, age 26 to 30—runaway from James Crofton of Albany (3/2)

Wilson, James, dec'd—tract of 380 acres belonging to estate and adjoining Rariton River, opposite Perth Amboy, for sale (3/2)

Bearman, Catharine, wife of Johannis Bearman of Burnets Field—warning not to trust her or buy from her; husband will not pay future debts (3/2)

Chrytie, George, bound servant, born at Aberdeen, Scotland, age c. 26—runaway Feb. 26 from George Burns at the King's Head, NYC, tavernkeeper (3/2)

Jeffery, John, apprentice, age c. 20—runaway from *General Wall Packett* (3/2)

Blaau, Uriah, of Kings Co., dec'd—plantation of 200 acres in Brookland, 2 miles from ferry, adjoining the water, for sale; apply to Cornelia Blaau on the premises or Richard Waldron in NYC (3/9)

Gilmore, Phaebe, wife of Robert Gilmore, long since separated from her husband—warning by John Farrall not to grant her credit (3/9)

Hadden, Thomas, dec'd—farm belonging to his estate in Manor of Scarsdale to be sold at auction by order of execs, Jonathan Griffin and Caleb Hyatt (3/9)

Van Horne, James, dec'd—farm at Dover, near Cheesequaks, Middlesex Co., East New Jersey, four farms at Rockey Hill, Somerset Co., N. J., several farms in Manor of Cortland for sale; apply to James M'Evers or William Cockcraft of NYC or John Berrian of Rockey Hill (3/9)

Bassett, John, of NYC, dec'd—accounts with estate to be settled with widow, Efey Bassett, or Francis Bassett (3/16)

Power, Mary, wife of Bernhard Power, of Albany, baker—she has gone off with George Gaub, taking along her child, Catharine, aged 8; he will not be responsible for debts she contracts in the future (3/16)

Stuart, William, of Bound Brook, East New Jersey—accounts with estate to be settled with Elizabeth Stuart, executrix, or John De Groot, exec. (3/30)

Willet, John, servant, age -8—runaway March 28 (3/30)

Proctor, Mrs., and son—supposed to have been murdered by Creek Indians (4/6)

Munro, Pardon—during voyage on a sloop from Sagg Harbor, L. I., to NYC was drowned March 13 near Setaquet (4/6)

Woodruff, Jehiel—same as above

Foster, Samuel—same as above

Barrington, Eunice, wife of Nicholas Barrington—husband will not be responsible for debts she may contract (4/6)

Warrel, Joseph, dec'd—land at Cranberry, adjoining Mill-Stone River, for sale; conditions of auction will be published by execs, Andrew Reed, John Berrian, Joseph Warrell and Francis Hollingshead (3/13)

Du Bois, Miss Helena, come from NYC to Boston to visit—died April 8 of consumption in Boston and buried there April 11 (4/20)

Hubbard, Joseph, of Boston—died afternoon of April 9 in Boston in 85th year; remains to be interred April 14 from his son's house in Summer St. (4/20)

Webb, Joseph, of Wethersfield, Conn., dec'd—accounts with estate to be settled with trustees, John Alsop, James Jauncey, Theophilact Bache and John Ernest (4/20)

Allen, Joseph, of Hebron, Conn.—died in fall from his horse on April 7 (4/27)

Taylor, Mr., recently deceased in the West Indies—letter addressed to his wife Margaret at Mr. William Digges's on Potomack River in Md. was lost (4/27)

Hay, David, dec'd—accounts with estate to be settled with widow, Mary Hay, admin., who carries on the shop (5/4); name of widow changed to Sarah in next issue of newspaper (5/11); estate on the Paltz River in Ulster Co. for sale (5/1)

Nelson, James, apprentice, born at Trenton, N. J., shoemaker, age 19—runaway April 26 from master, Samuel Large of Maiden Head, N. J., while at New Utrecht, L. I., on business (5/4)

Morrell, Phebe, wife of Samuel Morrell—has left her husband, who will not pay debts contracted by her in future (5/4)

Deserted from H.M.'s 22nd Regt. of Foot at NYC between March 30 and April 27 (5/11):
Craddock, Joseph, born at Durham, Eng., weaver, age 23
Wood, David, born in Yorkshire, laborer, age 24
Price, William, born in Brecknochshire, tailor, age 24
Stewart, Robert, born at Donaghmore, weaver, age 22
Carson, James, born in County of Fermanagh, laborer, age 25
Gallagher, James, born in County of Tyrone, weaver, age 22
Griffin, John, born at Inniskilling, laborer, age 24
Wright, John, born at Carlow, laborer, age 29
Herron, David, born on County of Down, laborer, age 23
Rogers, Peter, born in Flintshire, laborer, age 27
Smith, Robert, born in County of Tyrone, laborer, age 23
Civil, Charles, born in Cheshire, laborer, age 24
Shelly, William, born at West-Chester, shoemaker, age 26
Faxon, William, born in Warwickshire, laborer, age 26
Frazer, James, born at Inverness, laborer, age 22
Randell, Edward, born in County of Caven, shoemaker, age 26
Chandler, Thomas, born in Warwickshire, laborer, age 29
Carr, Mark, born in Middlesex, laborer, age 23

Alsop, John, attorney, dec'd—accounts with estate to be settled with John Alsop, admin. (5/11)

Lutwidge, Capt., master of the *General Wall Packet*—wounded March 4 in an engagement with a French privateer and died 40 hours later; was buried March 25 at Falmouth (5/18)

Hawkins, Edward, born in England, baker, age 24—deserted May 10 at Schenectady from Capt. Barnaby Burns's company of the 1st NY Regt. (5/25)

Herbert, David, born in Ireland, tailor, age 46—same as above

Chambers, Edward, born in Wales, mariner, age 38—same as above

Bryant, Ebenezer, of Elizabeth Town, N. J., dec'd—law books for sale (5/25)

Clague, Robert, mate of ship *Manchester*, Capt. Chambers master—presumably drowned near Charleston, S. C., about beginning of May (6/1)

Polhill, Nathaniel, of Georgia, passenger in the *Polly and Betsey*, Capt. Muir master— drowned when waterspout struck ship in road at Charleston, S. C. (6/1)

Kay, Robert, nephew of Capt. Muir of the *Polly and Betsey*—same as above

Rothenbuhler, Rev. Frederick, native of Bern, Switzerland, minister of the Reformed German Church in NYC, lodging at house of Mr. Ryckman, shoemaker, in Broad St., near the City Hall—will give French lessons (6/1)

Hunt, Sampson, of Ervingshire—drowned May 21 on fishing trip when canoe overset just above the rapid water near Deerfield (6/8)

Osgood, Silas, of Ervingshire—same as above

Rowe, John, born in Shropshire, Eng., porter, age 26—deserted May 14 from 27th Regt. at Crown Point (6/8)

Howey, Robert, born in Buckingham [!] Co., West N. J., carpenter, age 22—same as above

Savage, John, born at Great Markham in Nottinghamshire, Eng., age 23—deserted from H.M.'s 43rd Regt. (6/8)

Fish, Joseph, born at Andover, Mass., carpenter, age 26—deserted May 26 from H.M.'s Inniskilling Regt. of Foot at Crown Point (6/8)

Roberts, George, born in town of Glinward, County of Cork, Ireland, cabinetmaker, age 24—same as above

Rypel, John, of NYC, baker, dec'd—accounts with estate to be settled with Catharine Rypel, executrix (66/15)

Lena, mulatto slave, age 17—runaway June 9 from David Devore at Turtle Bay (6/15)

Johnson, Rev. Dr., President of King's College, NYC—married last week in Stratford, Conn., Mrs. Beach, widow of a merchant of Stratford (6/29)

Deserted from NY Regt. (6/29):

Miller, John, age 37

Briggs, Isaac, age 21

Warren, Stephen, age 22

Price, John, age 18

Dean, Jonathan, age 18

Golding, Justis, age 19

Thompson, John, age 28

Jones, John, age 43

Diver, Edward, age 25

Cash, David, age 18

Wanser, Thomas, age 22

McGrisor, Alexander, age 24

Meanderson, Joseph, age 23

Keys, George, age 26

Farren, Riging, age 26

Colskin, Nicholas, age 32

Sullivan, Owen, age 27

Clark, Cornelius, age 23

Storey, Joseph, age 25

Donean, John, age 27

Rogers, Hugh, age 30

Shedman, John, age 21

Harrington, Dennis, age 41

Forguson, James, age 29

Holland, Capt. William, dec'd—Henry Holland, Esq., of NYC, seeks information concerning Agnes Holland, late of NYC, mother of the dec'd, or concerning her daughter, Elizabeth Holland (6/29)

Liddle, Dr., "late of Passaick"—medicines and shop furniture for sale (6/29)

Dunforth, John, born in "Bellacray in the Province of New-England," shoemaker, age 29—deserted May 17 from the Inniskilling Regt. of Foot at Crown Point (7/13)

Rogers, Major Robert—married Tuesday, June 30, at Portsmouth, N. H., to Miss Betsy Brown, daughter of Rev. Arthur Brown of Portsmouth (7/13)

Hamilton, Mr., silversmith—jailed at Poughkeepsie for counterfeiting, he hangs himself early in July (7/13)

Jack (or Selem), Negro slave, born in New England, age c. 20—runaway July 8; apply to printer for reward in case of capture of slave (7/13)

Consiglio, Francis, apprentice, age c. 20—runaway July 2 from Joseph Jenkins of Phila. (7/13)

Dunlap, James, of Stratford, dec'd—accounts with estate to be settled with Samuel Jones of Stratford, admin. (7/13)

Joe, mulatto "boy"—runaway July 6 from Joh Gill of NYC (7/13)

Anthony, mulatto, age 28—runaway July 6 from Hendrick Hoeghtelen at Kocksackie (7/20)

Fifield, Joseph, of Kingston, N. H.—died there June 7 in his 85th year, leaving wife and four children; one daughter deceased (7/27)

Shephard, Micheal, of Boston, gunsmith—drowned at Boston July 15 (7/27)

Cregier, John, dec'd—house and lot at upper end of Chapel St., near the Commons; enquire of Capt. Thomas Cregier near the premises (8/3)

Cornell, Ebenezer, of Middletown, Conn.—jumped overboard July 14 from a sloop in the Sound on way to NYC and was drowned (8/3)

Jordan, Negro slave, born at Lyme, Conn., age c. 27—runaway July 1 from Roger Gibson of New London, Conn. (8/3)

McInvin, John, soldier in 1st Battalion of Royal Highland Regt. at Staten Island, age c. 27—deserted July 31 (8/3)

Graydon, Alexander, of plantation "Fairview," near Bristol in Bucks Co., Pa., about 20 miles from Phila., dec'd—plantation for sale; apply to Rachel Graydon, executrix, on the premises, or James Biddle, exec., or Joseph Marks, merchant, at Phila. (8/10)

Dunn, Phineas, of Piscataqua, N. J.—evening of Aug. 3 fell from a gang of hay at Rariton River and was drowned (8/17)

Deserted Aug. 2 from H.M.'s 35th Regt. between Stillwater and Albany (8/17):

  Sheerby, Thomas, born at Warwick, England, age c. 30

  Thompson, James, born in County of Derry, Ireland, age c. 21

  Answorth, Lawrence, born in London, age c. 22

  Oglevie, James, born in Scotland, age c. 32

  Fryar, John, born in England, age c. 30

  Douglass, John, born at Redding, Berkshire, England, age c. 32

  Peggs, Richard, born in England, age c. 27

Watson, Wallace, born near Hexham, Northumberland, England, shoemaker, age c. 26—deserted from Staten Island (8/17)

Taylor, Edward, born near Hassington, Lancashire, England, weaver, age c. 27—same as above

Smith, John, "a yellow Fellow," age c. 50—runaway Aug. 17 from Cornelius Tebout, living in the Bowery Lane, NYC (8/24)

Castalio, Negro slave, age c. 18—runaway Aug. 19 from Thomas Truxton of Jamaica, L. I. (8/24)

M'Neal, Thomas, late Lt. in the NY Provincials, having a wife and children at the Fishkills in NY—on morning of Aug. 17 cast himself from the Battery into the North River and was drowned (8/24)

Watson, John, indentured servant, age 19—runaway from the *Industry Transport*, Richard Killet master, lying in the North River; reward for capture will be paid by John Abeel (8/24)

Good, Dorothy, "transient vagrant"—found dead Aug. 7 in a desolate bog meadow in the North Parish of New London, Conn. (8/31)

Vaughan, Catharine, dec'd—lots near the swamp or New Goal and house and lots in Chappell St. for sale; apply to Mauritz De Haert on Hunter's Quay (9/7)

Will, Negro slave, "with grey Beard and Hair"—runaway from George Townshend of Norridge in Oysterbay (9/7)

Hunter, William, Esq., one of H.M.'s Deputy Postmasters of North America and printer to the General Assembly of Virginia—died Aug. 5 at his house in Williamsburg, Va. (9/7)

Pierse, Thon.as, staymaker, dec'd—accounts with estate to be settled with execs, Catharine Hones in Bayard St., NYC, or James Swan on Golden Hill (9/7)

Prince, Negro slave, brought up in New England, age 30—runaway Sept. 14 from Gale Yelverton of Poughkeepsie (9/21)

Livingston, Philip, of NYC, dec'd—suit of Peter Van Brugh Livingston and other execs against Joh Lawrence and Alida Hanson, admins. of Leonard Lewis, dec'd (9/21)

Clowes, Samuel, of Jamaica, L. I., dec'd—house and lot in main street of Jamaica for sale; apply to Thomas Truxtun on premises or Joseph Griswold in NYC (9/21)

Hervey, Thomas, late of Bermuda, dec'd—accounts with estate to be settled with John Hervey, admin. (9/28)

Rogers, Richard, dec'd—lot on North River granted to dec'd by Dirick Ryerson to be leased; accounts with estate to be settled with execs, Joseph Delaplane or John Lawrence (10/12)

Ascough, Richard, of NYC, apothecary and surgeon, dec'd—house on south side of Hanover Square for sale; apply to Thomas William Moore and wife Anne in King's St. (10/12)

Cyrus, Negro servant, butcher by trade, age c. 30 or 32—runaway Oct. 5 from John Lloyd of Stamford, Conn. (10/12)

Appy, John, Esq., Judge Advocate and principal secretary to Sir Jeffery Amherst—died Thursday A.M., Oct. 15, in NYC and was buried Oct. 16 in Trinity Church (10/19)

Connor, Hannah, who sold limes in NYC—found murdered Oct. 15 near the college in NYC (10/19)

Griffith, James, servant, formerly drummer in Capt. Cruckshank's independent company —runaway Aug. 20 from John Farrel of Stone-hook, near Albany (10/19)

Pollydore, Negro slave, coming from North Carolina and belonging to Mr. Mabson, age c. 24—runaway Oct. 4; reward for his capture will be paid by Samuel Cornell at Flushing (10/26)

Robert, Negro slave, born in Jamaica, W. I.—runaway Oct. 15 from Andrew Hunter of Newport, R. I. (10/26)

Budd, the widow, of Marineck—dark sorrel horse stolen Oct. 16 from her stable; reward will be paid by John Bartram of Fairfield, Conn. (11/2)

Amelia, "young" Negro slave, Creole born—runaway Oct. 1 from Edward Price of NYC (11/2)

Holly, Charles, a mulatto—convicted at Lancaster, Pa., of the murder of Darby Loobey, and sentenced to die (11/16)

Armstrong, Nehemiah—convicted at Lancaster, Pa., of bestiality and sentenced to die (11/16)

Loo, Negro slave, age c. 30—runaway Nov. 5 from John Gosline of Newtown, L. I. (11/16)

De Lancey, James, Esq., dec'd—accounts with estate to be settled with Mrs. Anne De Lancey, admin. (11/23)

Sylvester, Negro slave, age c. 30—runaway Nov. 21 from Edward Agar in Beaver St., NYC (11/23)

Holman, Stephen, of Sutton—Nov. 17 thrown from wagon in south part of Boston and run over by wheel; died Nov. 19, leaving a widow and four children (11/30)

Davidson, Lawrence, a Swede, servant, age c. 17 or 18—runaway Nov. 25 from the *Masquerade Transport*,Christopher Moon commander (11/30)

Rigar, John, a German indentured servant, age c. 26—runaway from Lt. Shute of the New Jersey Regt., living at Greenwich, Salem Co., West Jersey (11/30)

Harry, Negro slave, baker, age c. 32—runaway Nov. 28 from Teunis Rapalye (12/7)

Peter, Negro slave, born in Jamaica, W. I.—runaway Dec. 3 from James M'Cartney (12/7)

Bancker, Christopher, Jr., dec'd—accounts with estate to be settled with Anne Bancker (12/7)

Pratt, Mrs. Sarah, of Hingham, Mass.—died there Nov. 22 in her 101st year, leaving children, grandchildren, great-grandchildren to the fifth generation to number of 182 (12/14)

Van Inburgh, Gilbert, dec'd—house and lot in Broad St., at corner of Wynkoop St., in NYC, for sale; enquire of John Steuart at house where Wessel Wessels lives in Broad St. (12/14)

Jones, Rebecca, wife of John Jones of NYC—has eloped from her husband (12/14)

York, Negro slave, age 30—runaway Dec. 12 from John Comes of Jamaica, L. I. (12/14)

Garden, Mrs., wife of Benjamin Garden—drowned in S.C. when schooner belonging to Mr. Wilkie from Indian-Land bound to Charleston was lost on the breakers on Edisto (12/21)

Butler, Miss—same as above

Macpherson, James, Jr.—same as above

Gidney, Mr., with wife and child—drowned about a month ago when pettyauger, crossing from Depeyster's Ferry to New Windsor on the North River, was overset (12/21)

Gorton, Mr., from "Lebannon" in New England—same as above

Whitmore, Brigadier General, Governor of Louisbourg and Colonel of the 22nd Regt. of Foot—drowned Dec. 11 near Plymouth, Mass., when he fell from deck of Capt. Church's ship (12/28)

Obrien, Mary—her dead body found Dec. 14 near Fresh Water in NYC; when "in Liquor" she was dragged from house of Mary Lyhin (*alias* Moll White) by said Lyhin and two men; Mary Obrien, after being beaten and abused, perished because of the severity of the weather (12/28)

GENEALOGICAL DATA FROM THE NEW-YORK MERCURY

Livingston, Cornelius, captain of a ship of NYC—died some time ago on way from Africa to Jamaica (1/4)

Babrien, Margaret Barbery, male infant of—found dead behind wood in a garret (1/11)

Barkley, Robert, apprentice, age 14—runaway from ship *King of Prussia*, Thomas M'Glathay master (1/11)

Williams, William, late of Fairfield, Conn., dec'd—accounts with estate to be settled with admins., Ephraim Jackson and Eleazer Williams (1/11)

Alexander, Mary, dec'd—accounts with estate to be settled with Evert Bancker (1/11)

Fish, Henry, dec'd—house and lot in Broad St., near the Watch House in NYC, for sale (1/18)

London, Negro slave, age c. 30—runaway from Gabriel Leggett of Westchester (1/18)

Jem, Negro slave, age 28—runaway Jan. 4 from David Anderson of North Castle, Westchester Co. (1/18)

Van Pelt, John dec'd—farm on north side of Staten Island, now occupied by Simon Symonsen, between lands of Col. Thomas Dongan and Joseph Rolph, Esq.; apply to execs., Evert Byvanck and Dirck Lefferts (1/18)

Baker, Joseph, master of schooner belonging to Salem—drowned Jan. 6 when schooner, en route from Phila., was wrecked at Montook at eastern end of Long Island (1/18)

Tucker, John, mate of the above schooner—same as above

Colden, Mrs., wife of Lt. Gov. Cadwallader Colden of NY—died night of Jan. 16 in NYC in 73rd year (1/18)

Matthews, Moses, of NYC, mariner, dec'd—accounts with estate to be settled with Mary Van Gezan and David Dickson (1/25)

Montayne, Jacobus, dec'd—house in Little Queen St., now in possession of Dr. Van Vleck, for sale; apply to Benjamin Payne, exec. (1/25)

Johnson, widow, dec'd—furniture to be sold at her house in Maiden Lane, "a little higher up than Alderman Lispenards" (2/1)

Janney, Rev. Robert, rector of Christ Church in Phila.—sermon was preached at his funeral Jan. 10, 1762, by William Smith (2/1)

Higgins, John, born at Alexandria, Va., age c. 30—convicted in NYC of counterfeiting and hanged Feb. 12 (2/1 and 2/22)

Anderson, John, born in NYC, age c. 24—convicted in NYC of burglary and hanged Feb. 12 (2/1 and 2/22)

Huber, Martin, native of Basel, Switzerland, who 10 or 12 years ago came to America as soldier and was discharged; news of him desired by Wm. Bayard & Co. in NYC (2/22)

Seaman, David, late of Oyster Bay, Queens Co., dec'd—farm in Oyster Bay, about 2 miles from Jericho, for sale; apply to execs., Richard Willets and William, David and Zebulon Seaman (2/22)

Likens, John, together with wife Mary and Elizabeth Ridgeway—committed to jail in NYC for attempting to rob a man near the Fresh Water (3/1)

Sims, John, servant, born in Yorkshire, England—a runaway Feb. 8 from Ellis Lewis of Phila., in company of Eleanor Debutcher (alias Catherine Colton), said to have been born in Boston (3/1)

Schuyler, Peter—died morning of March 7 at his house in the Jerseys in his 52nd year (3/8)

Hogeboom, Annatie, wife of Jeremiah Hogeboom of Claverack—has eloped from her husband (3/8)

Gatehouse, Richard, of Wallkill, Ulster Co., dec'd—his heir, John Gatehouse of Here-fordshire, Great Britain, exec. power of attorney to David Beckman and David Cox, who have administered the estate (3/8)

M'Laughlan, John, indentured Irish servant, age c. 30—runaway about middle of Feb-ruary from Malcolm Campbell of NYC, merchant (3/8)

Becker, Michael, master of brig on voyage from Antigua to Portsmouth—drowned Jan. 24 in wreck of ship on rocks of La Have, about 15 leagues west of Halifax (3/15)

Gillet, Mr., "an elderly man", who kept house alone at Harrington, Conn.—found Feb. 24, naked and burnt to death at back of chimney in his house (3/15)

Heyanan, Catharine, dec'd—goods to be sold at her house in Wall St., NYC, next door to Mr. Lentot's; accounts to be settled with John Thurman, Jr. (3/15)

Griffiths, Thomas, age c. 25—escaped from jail in NYC night of March 15 (3/22)

Sedon, Henry, native of South Carolina—died there Feb. 21 in his 67th year; a brother, age 74 died there four years ago (2/29)

Lucy, Negro slave, age c. 26—runaway March 7 from Caleb Morgan of Eastchester, NY (3/29)

Lycorn, Mrs., St. Luke—died a few days ago in Montreal after drinking coffee (4/5)

Shate, Sergt., of NYC, of 3rd Battalion of Royal Americans in Col. Haviland's regt.—killed in action at Martinico (4/5)

Treehill, Mrs. Martha, wife of Dr. Treehill of Eastchester, NY—died there Feb. 18 in her 97th year (4/5)

Lafyear, Mr., of Hacklasack, N.J.—shot and killed himself after quarrel with his wife (4/5)

Hopson, Samuel, Sr., of Brookland Ferry—on April 10 warns against buying from his son, Samuel Hopson, Jr., papers relating to water lot (4/18)

Wall, Negro slave, born at Oysterbay, age c. 40—runaway April 4 from John Leake of NYC (4/12)

Dina, Negro slave, age c. 34, and her child of 18 months—for sale; apply to Amos Smith at Jamaica, L.I., or John Burnet in NYC (4/12)

M'Evers, Mrs. Margaret, wife of Charles M'Evers of NYC, merchant, and daughter of Simon Johnson, Recorder of NYC—died Wed. morning, April 7, in her 47th year and was buried next evening in family vault in Trinity Church Yard (4/12)

Rue, Rev. Lewis, dec'd—house and lot adjoining his house for sale (4/12)

Runaway April 16 from the snow *Cape Breton*, Robert Wilson master (4/19):
   Stewart, John, apprentice, age 18
   Allan, Robert, apprentice, age 16
   Wilson, John, apprentice, age 16

Martin, John, laborer under contract, age c. 27—runaway from Sterling Iron Works in Bergen Co., N.J.; reward for his capture offered by William Hawxhurst (4/19)

Roberts (or German), Charles, mulatto servant, age 28 or 30—runaway April 12 from John Holt of NYC (4/19)

Bayard, Nicholas, Jr., of NYC, merchant—married Tuesday night, April 20, in NYC, to Miss Livingston, daughter of Peter Van Brough Livingston of NYC, merchant (4/26)

Franklin, James, of Newport, R.I., printer—died there April 20 (5/3)

Jewell, James, "West-Country" born, age 16—runaway April 24 from the transport ship *Three Sisters*, John Maltby master (5/3)

Brabner, Robert, apprentice, age c. 19—runaway from Joseph Darlinton of West Nant-mill Township, Chester Co., Pa., tanner (5/10)

Williams, Nicholas, age 37 or 38, committed on suspicion of bigamy—escaped April 25 from Phila. jail (5/10)

M'Daniel, John, a "young" fellow, gardener—same as above

Hawkins, Thomas, age c. 25—same as above; Jane Jones, an Englishwoman, is supposed to have gone with him.

Tomlinson, Nathaniel, of "back Country" in Maryland—killed by Indians in April (5/17)

Ames, Mrs. John, of Bridgewater, Mass.—safely delivered April 24 of three girls (5/17)

Colden, Miss Catharine, daughter of Lt.-Gov. Colden of NY—died May 19 in NYC (5/24)

Taylor, Kitty, wife of John Taylor of Middletown, N.J.—has eloped from her husband (5/31)

Waddell, Capt. John, of NYC, merchant—died May 29 in NYC (5/31); accounts with his estate to be settled with his widow, Anne Waddell, at her store in Dock St. (7/5)

Alsop, John, attorney, dec'd—accounts with his estate to be settled with John Alsop, admin. (5/31)

Juba, Negro slave, age c. 25—runaway May 16 from Benjamin Cole of Killingsworth, (Conn.) (5/31)

Caesar, Negro slave, age c. 19—runaway May 23 from William Williams of Pittsfield, Mass. (5/31)

Nero, Negro slave, age c. 28—runaway May 23 from Charles Goodrick of Pittsfield, Mass. (5/31)

Charles, Negro slave, born in Jamaica, age 20—runaway from the printer (5/31)

Miller, Henry, late of NYC, dec'd—accounts with estate to be settled with William Robinson at William Ireland's on Golden Hill, NYC (5/31)

Mayfield, Joseph, of 46th Regt.—fell June 5 from deck of Ship *Amherst Frigate* in NYC and was drowned (6/14)

Mulharon (or M'Caron), Richard, servant "boy," born in Ireland—runaway June 5 from James Wallace of Phila. (6/14)

Crawford, Alexander, of Marcus Hook, Pa., age c. 28—went away about March 24, supposedly to defraud his creditors (6/14)

Smyth, John, Esq., of Perth Amboy—married Friday evening, June 18, in NYC, to Miss Susanna Moore, of NYC, daugther of late Col. Moore (6/21)

Vincent, William, only surviving son of Abraham Vincent of Dublin, woolen draper, who left England as Steward of a man of war and is now supposed to reside in Virginia —news of him is sought (6/21)

M'Mahan, Dennis, born in Ireland, blacksmith by trade, age c. 28—runaway about June 8 from his bail; reward for his capture offered by George Johnson of Perth Amboy (6/21)

Smith, Margaret, servant, born in Erwin, Scotland, age c. 26—runaway June 22 from Gilbert Shearer (7/5)

Ayscough, Dr. Richard, dec'd—accounts with estate to be settled with Thomas William Moore at request of execs., Charles Williams and Anne Moore (7/5)

Walker, Thomas, dec'd—land in Spring Garden, adjoining Phila. for sale; accounts with estate to be settled with Cunningham & Nesbit, Moses Heyman or James Eddy (7/5)

Burr, Jonathan, of Hingham, Mass.—run over by wheel of his ox cart on June 28 and died, leaving wife and eight children (7/5)

Merrick, Noah, son of Rev. Mr. Merrick of Springfield, student at Harvard, age c. 19— drowned June 24 in river at Cambridge (7/5)

Woodbridge, Mrs., of Portsmouth, N.H., age upwards of 70—tapped May 28 for dropsy by Mr. Jackson of Portsmouth, and nine gallons of water came from her (7/5)

Cushing, Col., of Hanover—dropped dead in Boston July 3 (7/5)

Brown, Obadiah, Esq., of Providence, R.I.—died June 17 at his seat in the country in his 50th year (7/5)

Westgate, Earl—killed by lightning June 25 at Portsmouth, R.I. (7/5)

Murphy, Reynolds, a "lad"—same as above.

Johnston, Hon. Andrew, Esq., member of N.J. Council and Treasurer of East New Jersey—died "last Thursday Se'nnight" at advanced age (7/5)

Morris, Col. Lewis, Esq., Judge of Court of Vice-Admiralty of NY—died July 3 at Morrissania, Westchester Co., NY, at advanced age (7/5)

Fish, Mr., of Portsmouth, R.I.—killed there by lightning June 25 (7/12)

Bolles, Ebenezer, of New London, Conn., trader, member of sect called Rogerenes—died in New London "Thursday se'nnight," leaving daughter aged 17; he was poisoned from cutting what was apparently poison ivy and refused medication because of his religious convictions (7/12)

Gansey, Benjamin, English servant, who says he was born in Stanford, Conn., age c. 23 or 24—runaway from Michael Hopkins of Dutchess Co., NY (7/12)

Vandeursen, Abraham, dec'd—house and lot in Duke St., NYC, now in possession of John Ten Broeck, for sale; apply to execs., Abraham, Annaka and Hester Vandeursen; lot extends back into Synagogue Alley (7/12)

Graydon, Alexander, dec'd—estate called "Fairview," near Bristol, Bucks Co., 20 miles from Phila., for sale (7/12)

Robbin, Negro, born in West-Chester, age c. 28—runaway from care of constable in East-Chester; reward for his capture offered by Dr. Thomas Wright (7/12)

Hureen, Matthias, Swedish sailor—runaway July 20 from ship *Mary*, lying at the New Dock in NYC; reward for his capture offered by William Deverson, master of the *Mary* (7/26)

Tankard, George, mulatto servant, age c. 26 or 27—runaway July 19 from Caleb Humastun of Waterbury, [Conn.] (7/26)

Sleght, Matthew, dec'd—accounts with estate to be settled with Elizabeth Sleght, executrix, and execs, Francis and Isaac Marschalk and Evert Bancker (8/2)

Kelly, William, apprentice, tailor by trade, age 18—runaway from Elias Van Court of Bound Brook, Somerset Co., N.J. (8/9)

Harris, Jacob, apprentice, tailor by trade, age 18—same as above.

Juel, Samuel, apprentice "boy"—runaway from Jacob Baker, shoemaker (8/9)

Hendrick, Sarah, servant, age c. 13—runaway Aug. 6 from Elizabeth Dogworth; she was taken away by her mother, Sarah Summers, and John Jones, born in England (8/16)

Deserted July 6 from Col. Oughton's company of 55th Regt. of Foot at Fort George (8/23):

Hardie, John, born in Phila., shoemaker, age 22

Kieff, Daniel, born at Casco Bay, "bred up to the Sea," age 21

Patter, John, born at Stoneystratford, Buckinghamshire, England, brazier, age 24

Deserted from Capt. Hargrave's company of the 55th Regt. of Foot, at Albany (8/23):

Taylor, Solomon, born at Groton, New London Co., laborer, age 29

Price, William, born at Newport, Pagnell, Buckinghamshire, England, butcher, age 24

Chamberlain, Ensign, of Douglass, "County of Worchester," Mass., ten-year-old daughter of—accidentally killed when a child struck her with a pair of shears (8/23)

Deserted from Capt. Cochran's company of the Royal American Regt. in NYC (8/23):

Fronheyser, Andrew, a German

Brannan, Christopher, born near York-Town, Pa., age 16

Deserted July 19 from Capt. Lehunt's company of H.M.'s 80th Regt. at Fort William Augustus (8/30):

Ledby, John, born in Pa., age 25

Sample, Henry, born in Ireland, age 20

Stork, Edward, born at Bristol, Pa.—deserted from Major Wilkins's company of the 80th Regt. at Fort William Augustus (8/30)

Eltinge, Jan, late of Kingston, Ulster Co., dec'd—accounts with estate to be settled with William or Petrus Eltinge, two of the execs., at Kingston (9/6)

Quackinbush, John, late of New Brunswick, N.J., cooper—has eloped from his wife Mary (9/6)

De Visme, Philip, dec'd—accounts with estate to be settled with Anne De Visme, admin. (9/13)

Barcklay, John, born in Ireland, clothier, age c. 50, who lived many years at Basking Ridge and lately at Elizabeth Town, N.J.—escaped from Sheriff of Essex Co., N.J., (9/20)

Hamilton, William, butcher, age c. 50, who has lived at Basking Ridge—same as above

Bryant, Roger, an Irishman, painter, age c. 28—runaway from Barnabas Hughes of Baltimore, Md. (9/20)

Jacobs, Mrs. Sarah, wife of Ralph Jacobs, of NYC, merchant, and daughter of Joseph Simpson, merchant—died Sept. 20 in NYC in her 35th year (9/27)

Dubois, Peter, of NYC, merchant—married evening of Sept. 23 in NYC to Miss Catharine Depeyster, eldest daughter of Pierre Depeyster, Esq. (9/27)

Woodruff, Joseph, painter, dec'd—accounts with estate to be settled with Flores Bancker, living in Bridge St. (commonly called Wynkoop St.) near the Exchange (8/16)

Johnston, Andrew, Esq., of Perth-Amboy, N.J.—accounts with estate to be settled with execs, John Barberie, John Johnston and Stephen Skinner (10/4)

Wright, Elizabeth, wife of Jonathan Wright, Jr., of Fish-Kills—husband will pay no debts she may contract (10/4)

Harry, Negro slave, age c. 26—runaway twelve days ago from Long Island; reward if captured and brought to William Cobhan at the Golden Hand in Hanover Square, NYC (10/11)

Morris, Capt., formerly master of a packet in the American service—died lately in England (10/18)

Quin, Francis, servant, age c. 20—runaway early in October from Dennis M'Peak living near Coldenham in Ulster Co. (10/18)

Baldrige, Daniel, indented servant, born in Scotland, age c. 50;—has a wife, a son aged c. 13 and a daughter aged c. 5—runaway Oct. 3 from John King, living at John Frazer's on Society Hill, Phila. (11/1)

Hude, Col. James, Esq., member of Council of N.J. and Mayor of Corporation of New Brunswick—died Nov. 1 in New Brunswick at an advanced age, leaving a wife and children (11/8)

Somerset, Negro slave, formerly property of Theodorus Van Wyck, age c. 30—runaway Oct. 25 from Manuel Josephson, living in Smith St., near the Old Dutch Church in NYC (11/8)

Hay, Dr. David, dec'd—accounts with estate to be settled with Sarah Hay, admin. (11/8)

Cooper, Mary, wife of Hugh Cooper of Baskinridge, Somerset Co., N.J.—husband will pay no debts she may contract (11/8)

Van Ranst, Cornelius, dec'd—property in NYC for sale; apply to execs, Luke Van Ranst & Lawrence Kortwright (11/15)

Runaway Oct. 31 from Moses Ogden (11/15):

Anderson, James, apprentice, tanner, age 19

Woodruff, Uzal, apprentice, cordwainer, age 18

Beeck, Epenetus, apprentice "lad," cordwainer

Franklin, William, newly-appointed Governor of N.J.—married Sept. 5 in St. George's Church, Hanover Square, NYC, to Miss Downes of St. James's St. (11/22)

GENEALOGICAL DATA FROM THE NEW-YORK MERCURY

Bowley, Richard and Cornelia, late of NYC, dec'd—effects to be sold at auction; accounts with estates to be settled with Verdine Elsworth, admin. (11/22)

Lawrence, Daniel, dec'd—accounts with estate to be settled with execs, Abraham Lawrence and John Willet (11/29)

Erwin, Rachel, supposed to be widow of Amos Erwin of Pa., mariner—she died in childbed at Currituck, North Carolina, leaving three daughters, Susannah, Sarah and Mary (11/29)

Newkirck, William—murdered Nov. 14 by Indians about half way between Niagara and Albany (11/29)

Mines, Joshua—same as above

Ross, James Isaiah, late of Dutchess Co., dec'd—accounts with estate to be settled with execs, Margaret Ross, Bartholomew Crannel and William Kennedy (11/29)

Ross, David, apprentice, born at Edinburgh, Scotland, age c. 18—runaway from John Jump, master of the transport *Hercules*, lying at Degrushe's Wharf in NYC (11/29)

Cruger, John, son of Henry Cruger, Esq., of NYC, merchant—married Nov. 30 in NYC to Miss Delancy, daughter of the Hon. Oliver Delancy, Esq., of NYC (12/6)

Schuyler, John and Cornelia, late of Albany, dec'd—accounts with estates to be settled with execs, Philip, Stephen and Gertruyd Schuyler (12/6)

Schuyler, Adoniah, dec'd—farm at Elizabeth Town Point, N.J., for sale; execs, Gertrude and John Schuyler (12/6)

Cannon, John, late of NYC, dec'd—accounts with estate to be settled with execs, John and Le Grand Cannon of Norwalk and Stratford, Conn. (12/13)

Draper, John, publisher of the Boston News-Letter—died Nov. 30 in Boston in his 61st year (2/13)

Jones, Thomas, Esq., of NYC, son of the Hon. David Jones, Esq., of Fort Neck, L.I.—married Dec. 9 in NYC to Miss Suckey De Lancey, daughter of the late Hon. James De Lancey, Esq. (12/13)

Bogert, Cornelius, dec'd—house and lot on north side of Beaver St. in NYC for sale; apply to Catharine Bogert, admin. (12/13)

Smith, John, an Irishman, age c. 35—broke out of Morris Co., N.J., jail on Nov. 25 (12/20)

Williams, Capt. Philemon, master of brigantine *Industry*—died Nov. 19 on passage home from Curacao (12/20)

Lightin, Emanuel, servant, age c. 19 or 20—runaway Dec. 14 from John Roberts, miller (12/20)

Fanny, part Indian and part Negro, age c. 15—runaway from Adrian Van Brents of Eutricht (12/20)

Prince, Negro slave, who has been a mariner, age c. 28—runaway Dec. 19 from Michael Devoe of Esopus, Ulster Co. (12/27)

Barnes, Capt. Thomas, of NYC—died there Dec. 23 in his 65th year (12/27)

White, John, indented servant, shoemaker, age c. 21—runaway Nov. 18, 1762, from Jirrard Saxton of Albany (1/3)

Smith, John, age 23—deserted Dec. 25, 1762, from H.M.'s 35th Regt. of Foot at NYC (1/3)

Champlin, Oliver, late master of the sloop *Fair Lady*—died 13 days after leaving Cork; sloop arrived Dec. 29, 1762, at Newport, R.I., after voyage of 68 days from Cork (1/3)

Read (or Reid), Col. (John) of the 42nd or Royal Highland Regt.—married Dec. 28, 1762, in NYC to Miss Susannah Alexander, sister of the Earl of Sterling (1/3)

Palding, Abraham, late of NYC, dec'd—accounts with estate to be settled with execs., Joseph Palding, Joseph Palding, Jr., and William Ogilvie (1/3)

Prince, Negro slave, age c. 28—runaway Dec. 19, 1762, from Michael Devoe of Esopus, Ulster Co. (1/3)

Van Ranst, Cornelius, dec'd—house next to the house and lot of Robert Crommeline in NYC for sale; apply to execs., Luke Van Ranst and Lawrence Kortwright (1/3)

Anderson, James, apprentice, tanner, age 19—runaway Oct. 31, 1762, from Moses Ogden of Elizabeth-Town, N.J. (1/3)

Woodruff, Uzal, cordwainer, age 18—same as above

Ross, Isaiah, late of Dutchess Co.—accounts with estate to be settled with execs., Margaret Ross, Bartholomew Crannel, and William Kennedy (1/3)

Waddell, John dec's—accounts with estate to be settled with Ann Waddell in Dock St., NYC (1/3)

Bowley, Richard, dec'd—accounts with estate to be settled with admin., Verdine Elsworth (1/3)

Fanny, Negro slave, age c. 15, bought last Oct. from Jaques De Nise of Eutricht—runaway from Adrian Van Brents of Eutricht (1/3)

Smith, John, an Irishman, age c. 35—on Nov. 25, 1762, broke out of jail of Morris Co., N.J. (1/3)

Wilson, Archibald, young man—drowned Dec. 11, 1762, at Phila. while stepping from a sloop into a boat (1/10)

Pratt, Benjamin, Chief Justice of NY and member of Council—died Jan. 6 in NYC (1/10)

Martin, Isaac, 5-year old son of—fell from second story of a house on "Canon's Dock" in NYC but survived the fall (1/10)

Kennedy, Ann, servant, born in Ireland, age c. 22—runaway Dec. 27, 1762, from Alexander Magee and Thomas Lloyd in Phila. (1/17)

Lee, Mary, servant, born in North Country, England, age c. 30—same as above

Carty, Catharine, indented servant, born in Ireland, age c. 18—runaway night of Jan. 15, probably with a soldier, from her mistress, Margaret Long, living on Cruger's Wharf, NYC (1/17)

Smith, John, age 23—deserted Dec. 25, 1762, at NYC from a recruiting party of H.M.'s 35th Regt. of Foot (1/17)

Lawrence, Mary, late of Flushing, dec'd—all her moveable estate to be sold Jan. 27 by order of her execs, John and Mehatabel Hylton (1/24)

Crawford, William, dec'd—land near the Scotch meeting house in Monmouth Co., N.J., for sale (1/24)

Johnston, Andrew, Esq., dec'd—real estate for sale; apply to execs, John Barberie, John Johnston and Stephen Skinner (1/31)

Deserted Sept. 14, 1762, from Lt. Col. Eyre's company of H.M.'s 44th Regt. now at Montreal (1/31):

  Brown, Edward, born County of Cavan, Ireland, laborer, age 26

  Collins, Matthew, born County of Cork, Ireland, laborer, age 16

  Williams, Thomas, born County of Maidenhead, East Jersey, weaver, age 23

Rice, John, born in Germany, laborer, age 30—deserted Nov. 25, 1762, from Lt. Col. Eyre's company of H.M.'s 44th Regt. (1/31)

Deserted Oct. 11, 1762, from Capt. Dunbar's company of H.M.'s 44th Regt. (1/31):

  Frost, (*alias* Kettinger), Joshua, born in Boston, sailor, age 25

  Ralston, Joseph, born at Newcastle, Pa., laborer, age 28

  Farrel, Thomas, born in Georgetown, Md., laborer, age 23

Vickers, William, born at Talbot, Md., laborer, age 31—deserted Oct. 11, 1762, from Capt. Ault's company of H.M.'s 44th Regt. (1/31)

Thomas, Joseph, born in Phila., hatter, age 27—deserted Nov. 9, 1762, from Capt. Treby's company of H.M.'s 44th Regt. (1/31)

Lawrence, Thomas, who lately went from NY to reside at Is. of Martinico—died there Dec. last (2/7)

Partridge, Mrs. Perez, of East Greenwich (in Kent)—hanged herself "last Sunday" according to New Haven, Conn., dispatch of Dec. 28, 1762 (2/14)

Thorn, Richard, "of Flushing Bay-Side," L.I.—"drop'd down dead last Thursday Week, just as he had lifted up his Gun to fire at some Wild Ducks" (2/14)

Baker, Samuel, dec'd—plantation on Delaware River in Upper Makefield, Bucks Co., Pa., for sale; apply to execs, Joseph Baker and John Burroughs (2/14)

De Groot, Peter, dec'd—house on north side of lower end of Division St., NYC, for sale (2/14)

Philips, Mr., passenger on privateer snow *Monckton*, bound from Phila. to Martinico—drowned Dec. 14, 1762, in wreck of the snow (2/21)

Byrne, Capt., master of the *Monckton*, together with the first lieutenant, master, doctor and first prize master—same as above

Read, William, young man from Phila.—murdered in his store (in Havana?) about Feb. 1 (2/21)

Boyd, Mr. H, young man from Phila.—same as above

Lott, Hendrick, late of the Nine Partners, dec'd—plantation on Wappin Creek, 6 miles from Poughkeepsie, for sale; accounts with estate to be settled with the widow, Hester Lott, living on the plantation, or Abraham Lott in NYC (2/21)

Lindsay, John, Esq., dec'd—lots of his estate in Cherry Valley, Albany Co., for sale; apply to James De Lancey or Thomas Jones in NYC (2/21)

Clarkson, Devinus, of NYC—married Feb. 21 in NYC to Miss Polly Van Horne, daughter of David Van Horne of NYC, merchant (2/28)

Price, Samuel, dec'd—house in Elizabeth-Town, N.J., for sale by execs, Mathias Ogden and Robert Ogden, Jr. (2/28)

Rue, Rev. Lewis, dec'd—house in Bayard St., NYC, for sale; apply to Gerard William Beekman and Gerardus Duyckinck (2/28)

Hall, Samuel, of Newark, N.J.—drowned last Thursday week while crossing Hackinsack River on the ice in his sleigh (3/7)

Ilslee, Benjamin, dec'd—his plantation on the Country Road in Raway, adjoining the plantation of James Marshall, for sale (3/7)

Godfrey, William, sailor on schooner of Capt. Topham from Boston—fell to deck in NYC and was killed (3/14)

Schuyler, Adoniah, dec'd—land at Elizabeth-Town Point for sale (3/14)

Tappen, Mary, wife of Asher Tappen of Staten Island—husband will not be responsible for debts she may contract in future (3/21)

Fenwick, William, of Boston, merchant—died there Tuesday last of apoplexy at age of 47 (3/28)

Barnes, Thomas, dec'd—accounts with estate to be settled with execs, Phebe and Mary Barnes in NYC (3/28)

Breested, Andrew and Ann, dec'd—estate on William St. in NYC for sale (3/28)

Walker, Dr.—killed March 30 by a fall from his horse at Jamaica, L.I. (4/4)

M'knight, John, chapman,—accounts with his estate to be settled with James M'Connell at Mr. Neal Shaw's store at the Great Dock, two doors from the Royal Exchange (4/4 and 6/6)

Meyer, Mrs. John, residing near Orangeburg, S.C., and her daughter aged about 6 and an infant—murdered, about beginning of February, while her husband was in Charleston, by one of their Negro slaves (4/11)

Butler, John, an elderly man—drowned Feb. 25 when coming in a pettiauger from a vessel lying in the mouth of Port Tobacco Creek in Md. (4/11)

Tims, Mr.—same as above

Woodford, two men of that name, belonging to a New England schooner at Great Cloptank—drowned a few weeks ago when a small boat overset near Barker Landing in Md. (4/11)

Haynes, Joseph, an "eminent" merchant of NYC—died there April 9 (4/11)

Bancker, Christopher, Esq., of NYC, merchant—died Wed., April 13, in NYC, after a tedious illness, in his 68th year (4/18)

Duffie, Duncan, dec'd—accounts with his estate to be settled with Ennis Graham, an exec. (4/18)

May, Edward, a servant, born in England, bricklayer, age c. 24—runaway April 12 from John Halstead of Shrewsbury, N.J. (4/18)

MacCoy, Mr., a porter—drowned at Boston the night of April 12 (4/25)

The following were drowned Dec. 14, 1762, when the privateer snow *Monckton* overset [see also 2/21 entries above]:

Byrn, John, captain	Riely, Michael, seaman
Jeffreys, Richard, prize-master	Brown, Thomas, seaman
Allison, Thomas. master	Hanaway, Thomas, seaman
Walker, John, master's mate	Colester, Henry, seaman
Russel, David, doctor	Lawrell, George, seaman
Geary, Daniel, quartermaster	Morris, Daniel, seaman
Todd, Thomas, quartermaster	Dickey, Matthew, seaman
Robinson, Timothy, quartermaster	Buckin, William, seaman
Banks, Thomas, boatswain's mate	Roberts, William, seaman
Folk, John, carpenter	Jones, Robert, seaman
M'Laughlin, Edward, master at arms	Lewtagee, Lewis, landsman
Gonigall, Edward, armorer	M'Mullen, Samuel, landsman
Gold, George, gunner's mate	Magee, Hugh, landsman
Brookbanks, H., gunner's yeoman	Higgins, Dominick, landsman
Murray, John, ship's steward	Worrel, John, landsman
Collins, John, captain's steward	Smith, Robert, landsman
Lewis, William, sailmaker	Connor, Stephen, landsman
Magee, James, seaman	Clark, Lawrence, landsman
Davidson, Thomas, seaman	Crawford, Charles, landsman
Guster, John, seaman	Johnson, Johnes, cook
Carney, John, seaman	Davis, Peter, boy
Laws, Frederick, seaman	Hill, Dirck, boy
Tasker, Elias, seaman	Philips, John Mandevill, passenger (4/25)

Cannon, John, dec'd—two houses on Cannon's Wharf for sale (5/2)

Ross, Capt. James Josiah, dec'd—his farm of 620 acres at Roelef Janse's Kill in the Nine Partners in Dutchess Co., about 13 miles from Col. Hoffman's Landing on Hudson River, for sale, as also other property; apply to widow, Margaret Ross (5/2)

George, Negro slave, lately come from the Havannah, where he belonged to Lt. Pierce of the Royal Artillery, born in Antigua—runaway April 24 in NYC from Edward Agar in Broad St. (5/2)

Amelia, Negro slave, born in West Indies, age c. 22—runaway April 18 from Philip Kissick (5/2)

Eliot, Rev. Dr. Jared, of Killingsworth, Conn.—died there "last Friday se'nnight" according to a Boston item of May 2 (5/9)

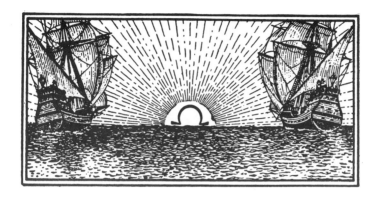

GENEALOGICAL DATA FROM THE NEW-YORK MERCURY

1763

Cory, William, Esq., lawyer in Albany—died there Sunday, April 24, after a short illness, in his 53rd year; survived by widow and children (5/16)

Hodgson, Sergt. Alvery, of Col. John Darby's company of H.M.'s 17th Regt. of Foot, born at Woolverhampton, Staffordshire, England, wigmaker—deserted May 8 (5/16)

Campbell, the Rt. Hon. Lord William, son of the Duke of Argyle—married Sunday, April 17, in Charleston, S.C., to Miss Sarah Izard, daughter of Ralph Izard, Esq., dec'd (5/23)

Murray, Capt. William, dec'd—accounts with estate to be settled with execs, Malcolm Campbell and Peter Pra Vanzant (5/30)

Daniell, John, Esq., captain in Col. Burton's Regt., who was on the last expedition against the Cherokees—married Feb. last at Litchfield to Miss Fenton, granddaughter of William Wedgood, of Haracles, Staffordshire, England (6/6)

Vanderwater, Henry, gunsmith, dec'd—his house in Maiden Lane, next door to Jacobus Rosevelt, Jr., is now occupied by Jonas Phillips (6/6)

Schuyler, Adoniah, dec'd—accounts with estate to be settled with John or Getrude Schuyler, execs (6/13)

Clapham, Col., and family—murdered in May at sawmill near Ft. Pitt, Pa. (6/13)

M'Cormick, Mr.—same as above

Frost, Capt. George, of Newport, R.I.—killed Nov., 1762, in River Gaboone, Africa, when slaves on his sloop rose against him (6/13)

Grant, William, of Newport, R.I., mate of Capt. Frost's sloop—same as above

Dunn, Patrick—killed in May by Indians at Beaver Creek, Pa. (6/20)

Kennedy, Hon. Archibald, Esq., Receiver General and Collector of Customs of NY, for many years member of Council—died June 14 in NYC, aged c. 78 (6/20)

Roberts, Mr. of N.J.—drowned June 15 near the dock at Whitehall in NYC (6/20)

Wendell, Evert and John—killed in June by Indians about 40 miles above Niagara (6/20)

Keckleman, Thomas, of NYC—accidentally shot and killed himself while hunting pigeons in the woods near the Glass House on Saturday, June 18 (6/20)

John, Negro slave, age c. 50—runaway June 17 from Theodore Godet (6/20)

Champaign, Negro slave, age c. 30—same as above

Priscilla, Negro slave, late property of Samuel Hodge, age c. 16—runaway from Rensselaer and Shipboy (6/20)

Sampson, James, age c. 40—runaway from ship *Boreas* of New-Providence, now in Bay of Honduras (6/20)

Brown, Thomas, "a young Lad"—same as above.

Jones, Richard, born in Wales, age c. 16—same as above

Clark, James—killed in June by Indians about 12 miles from Ft. Bedford, Pa. (7/4)

Williams, Anne, wife of Thomas Williams of Oysterbay—eloped from her husband (7/4)

Sleight, Matthew, dec'd—accounts with estate to be settled with Elizabeth Sleight, executrix, or execs, Evert Bancker and Francis and Isaac Marschalk (7/4)

Jacob, Negro slave, who speaks English, French and Spanish, age c. 23—runaway June 27 from George Wray of Albany (7/4)

Cox, Joseph, apprentice, age c. 14—runaway June 28 from Elisha Bell, master of the ship *Brotherly Love* (7/4)

Maddin, John, indented servant, age c. 22—runaway June 30 from William Moore, captain of the snow *Lamb* (7/4)

Ellis, Charles, indented servant, age c. 19—runaway in May from Frederick Jackert at the Dover Iron Works (7/4)

Woodbury, Ebenezer, master of the brig *Polly*, bound from South Carolina to Rhode Island—washed overboard in a gale and drowned Feb. 13 (7/11)

Stoddard, William (son of William Stoddard, Esq., of Boston), passenger on brig *Polly*, on way home after having served in H.M.'s navy most of the last war—same as above

Shadwell, a Negro, late of NYC—hanged himself July 5 in the house of William Kennedy in the East Ward of NYC (7/11)

Lane, Henry, late of Flatbush, L.I., dec'd—house for sale; apply to exec., Mrs. Rachel Lane (1/18)

Jackson, Thomas, born in America, age c, 14 (mulatto slave of Isaac Johnson, formerly of NYC, shopkeeper, but lately of Navisincks, dec'd)—manumitted by Johnson in his will (7/18)

Killfoy, Dennis, servant, age c. 19—runaway July 14 from Broughton Raynolds of Elizabeth Town, N.J. (7/18)

Lee, Elizabeth, Irish servant, age c. 22—runaway from Thomas Tredwell of NYC (7/18)

Bowen, William, tailor, speaks Dutch, French and Irish, age c. 28—runaway July 14 from his bail; reward for his capture offered by William Thorne at Old Slip Market in NYC (7/18)

Joe, Negro slave, born in Virginia, age c. 20—runaway June 12 from the brig *Catharine*, John Waterman, commander (7/18)

Anderson, William—murdered July 10 by Indians about 5 or 6 miles up Tuscorara and about 28 or 30 miles from Carlisle, Pa. (7/25)

Graham, John—killed in July by Indians about 1 or 2 miles "this side" of Tuscorara Mt. and about 18 or 20 miles from Carlisle (7/25)

Robinson, William—same as above

Welder, Samuel Stansbury—killed July 5 by Indians near Cumberland in Frederick Co., Md. (8/1 and 8/8)

Wade, Mr.—same as above

Logan, Alexander, and son—killed in July by Indians in Shearman's Valley, Pa. (8/1)

Pummeroy, Mr., and wife—killed July 22 by Indians about 3 miles from Shippensburgh, Pa. (8/1)

Johnston, Mrs.—same as above

M'Kean, Thomas, Esq., of New Castle, one of the representatives for New Castle Co., was married July 28 at Bordenton to Miss Borden of that place (8/1)

Danvers, Sir Robert—killed in May by Indians near mouth of Lake Huron (8/8)

Beekman, Catharine, dec'd—two houses (now in possession of Hugh Ryder and Mrs. Sarah White) at Beekman's Slip for sale; apply to execs, David and Effie Beekman and Magdelen Lynsen (8/8)

Holmes, Lt., commander at the Miamis—killed in June or July by Indians (8/8 and 8/15)

Jennet, Lt.—killed in July by Indians at Ft. Misselamackanac (8/8)

Tracey, Warrant, a trader—same as above (8/15)

Campbell, Capt.—same as above

Robertson, Capt.—apparently killed by Indians (8/8)

Turnbell, Mrs., and two sons—killed May 8 by Indians about one mile from fort at Detroit (8/15)

Fisher, James, and wife—same as above

Cameron, Evan, late of Norwalk, Conn., dec'd—house there for sale; apply to execs, Magdalen Cameron of Norwalk or John Provoost of NYC (8/15)

M'Knight, John, dec'd—admin., Agnes M'Knight, will make distribution to creditors of estate (8/15)

Moncrieffe, Mrs. Margaret (wife of Thomas Moncrieffe, Esq., Captain in H.M.'s 55th Regt of Foot and one of the majors of brigade to Sir Jeffery Amherst)—died Aug. 17 in NYC in her 23rd year; buried Aug. 18 at Trinity Church (8/22)

Drowned Aug. 17 when Mr. Watson's ferry overset near Robin's Reef, about 3 miles from Staten Island (8/22):

    Kennedy, Robert, a "Scotch gentleman," lately from Surinam; buried at Richmond Church, S.I. (8/29)

    De Loge, Mr., lately from Surinam—buried on Constable Point, N.J. (8/29)

    Anderson, James, a Scotch gentleman, lately from Madeira—buried at Richmond Church on S.I. (8/29)

    Gammel, David, a Scotch gentleman, long a resident of NYC—buried on Constable Point, N.J. (8/29)

    Morrison, Mr., a Scotch gentleman, who had been only a few months in NYC—buried on Constable Point, N.J. (8/29); his mahogany furniture imported from London for sale (11/21)

    Henderton, Mrs.

    Reynolds, Mrs. (wife of Capt. Reynolds now at sea)—buried at Trinity Church in NYC (8/29)

Tom, Negro slave, born at St. John's in Antigua, age c. 30—runaway Aug. 12 from Peter Benedict of Salem in Westchester Co. (8/29)

Graham, Capt. Lt. of the Highlanders—killed Aug. 5 or 6 by Indians not far from Pittsburg (8/29)

York, Negro slave, age c. 19—runaway Aug. 20 from Samuel Bridge of NYC (8/22)

Campbell Lt.—killed Aug. 5 or 6 by Indians not far from Pittsburgh (8/29)

Stanton, Capt., of the Virginia Militia—killed Aug. 9 by Indians at a fort above Pearsall's on the South Branch near Ft. Cumberland (8/29)

M'Intosh, Lt., of the Highlanders—killed Aug. 6 by Indians in engagement at Bushy Run (8/29)

Wall, Negro slave, born at Oyster-bay, age c. 40—runaway from John Leake of NYC (8/29)

Whitlow, Negro slave, blacksmith, age c. 30—runaway Aug. 20 from Adam Dobbs of Shrewsbury, N.J.; reward if brought back to master or to Charles Dobbs in NYC (8/29)

Dalyell, Capt.—killed July 31 in engagement with Indians near Sandusky (9/5)

Vanderhoof, Eleanor, wife of John Vanderhoof of Morris Co., N.J.—has eloped from her husband and "is strolling about with a base collier" (9/5)

Buglis, Francis, Irish servant, age 14—runaway Sept. 1 from Leonard Yeates, living at the sign of the Royal Hester (9/5)

Baptist, French Negro slave, belonging to estate of Robert Kennedy, age c. 40—runaway Aug. 22; reward will be paid by George Traile if slave is brought to Mrs. Fararo's (9/5)

Killed Sept. 2 by Indians at Munsey Creek Hill, Pa. (9/12):
  Clemons, John
  Scott, Alexander
  Chambers, James
  M'Lanachan, James

Kate, Negro slave, born in Westchester Co.—runaway Sept. 8 with child aged c. 15 months; reward if she is brought to the printer (9/12)

McCew, Mary, wife of William McCew of Albany—has eloped from her husband (9/12)

Killed Sept. 8 by Indians (9/19):
  Fincher, John (a Quaker), living near Reading, Berks Co., Pa., his wife, and two sons
  Miller, Nicholas, two children of
  Hubler, Frantz, of Bern Twp., about 18 miles from Reading, two children of

Johnson, Andrew, Esq., dec'd—accounts with estate to be settled with execs, John Barbarie, John Johnston, Stephen and Catharine Skinner (9/19)

Hoogeland, Christopher, merchant, late of Windsor, near Cranberry, East New Jersey, dec'd—accounts with estate to be settled with execs, Peter Schenck and Jacob Hoogeland (9/19)

Bancker, Christopher, decd—accounts with estate to be settled with William Bancker (9/26)

Borland, Francis, Esq.—died Sept. 1 in Boston in his 72nd year (9/26)

Greene, Thomas, Esq., late of Boston, dec'd—his heirs have offered £500 to Trinity Church of Boston for an assistant minister (9/26)

Sam, Negro slave, French born, a good cook, lately bought of Capt. James Delancy, age c. 30—runaway Sept. 5 from George Burns at the Province Arms in NYC (9/26)

Joe, Negro slave, born in Virginia, age c. 20—runaway June 12 in Phila. from the brig *Catharine*, John Waterman commander (9/26)

Godfrey, Thomas, late of Phila. son of the "famous" mathematician, Thomas Godfrey—died near Wilmington, N.C., on July 25 (10/3)

Johnston, Capt.—killed Sept. 13 or 14 by Indians near Niagara (10/3)

Minot, Peter, of Boston, and his wife—drowned in Sept. in the wreck of a sloop commanded by Capt. Freeman which was going from Halifax up the Bay of Fundy and St. John's River (10/10)

Horsy, Mr., master of a schooner coming up the Niagara with provisions—killed Sept. 4 by Indians about 9 miles from the fort at Detroit (10/10)

Bradey, Sarah, mulatto, born in Albany, age 25—runaway Aug. 10 from John Farrell in NYC; reward for her capture will be paid by Farrell in Albany or Benjamin Williams in New York City (10/10)

Hull, Joseph, Esq., Collector of Customs for Port of New London, Conn.—died there Sept. 30 (10/17)

Green, Timothy, printer, age 60—died Oct. 3 in New London, Conn., after a short illness with a violent fever (10/17)

Stinton, John, living about 8 miles from Bethlehem, Pa.—killed there early in October by Indians (10/17)

Wetherholt, Capt.—same as above

Killed Oct. 8 by Indians (10/17):
  Mekly, Jacob, of Whitehall Twp., Pa.—his son and daughter

Snider, Hance, of Whitehall Twp., Pa., his wife and three children

Allmong, Mrs. Jacob, of Whitehall Twp., Pa., and child

Aberdeen, Negro slave, age between 50 and 60—accounts due estate to be settled with admins, William Craig and Robert Ewing, merchants, in Hanover Sq., NYC (10/17)

Richards, Lt., of the Provincials—killed by Indians about 5 miles from Ft. Bedford and buried at the fort Oct. 8 (10/24)

Powel, William, late of Millford, Conn., dec'd—claims of his creditors to be received and examined at house of Lewis Mallet, innholder at Millford, by Nathaniel Farrand, Lewis Mallet, and Garret V.H. De Witt (10/24)

Mitchell, Andrew, apprentice, cordwainer, age 16—runaway from Hendrick Barr, living in Gold St., NYC (10/31)

Turner, Mr. Carpenter, at north end of Boston, four-year-old child of—died in Boston Oct. 19 (10/31)

Killed by Indians Oct. 15 while crossing from Pa. to the Jerseys (10/31):

Brink, Stephen

Brink, Garret

Vangada, Peter

Racer, Benjamin

Bennet, Abraham, sentenced to be hanged for horsestealing, age c. 35—broke out of jail of Essex Co., N.J.; reward for his capture offered by Sheriff Uzal Ogden (11/7)

Collins, William, Irish servant, age c. 25—runaway Nov. 7 from John Jamison of Middletown, Conn. (11/14)

Hawkins, John, Esq., Commissary and Paymaster of the Royal Artillery in North America—died Nov. 7 in NYC in 33rd. year after lingering illness of asthma; buried Nov. 10 in Trinity Church Yard (11/14)

Bostick, Rev. Daniel, Minister of Presbyterian Church in NYC—died Nov. 12 in NYC, leaving widow and several small children (11/14)

Benson, Robert, of NYC, brewer, dec'd—farm in the Bowery Lane for sale; apply to the widow, Catharine Benson (11/14)

Baily, Frantz, of Albany Twp., Berks Co., Pa., son of—killed Nov. 8 by Indians (11/21)

Schisler, Mrs. George and son, of Albany Twp., Pa.—same as above

Shober, Mr., of Albany Twp., Pa.—killed Nov. 8 by Indians at house of Jacob Tree (11/21)

Runaway from the shallop between Gloucester Point and Chester, Pa., all lately imported from Leith in ship *Boyd,* Capt. Dunlap; reward for their capture will be paid by Robert Ritchey in Phila. or Wm. Malcolm in NYC (11/21):

Mc Kay, John, servant, seaman, age 19

McQueen,—servant, seaman, age c. 21

Weigner, Christopher, servant, seaman, born in Sweden or Denmark, age 26

Dawson, John, seaman, age c. 22

Mc Donald, David, tinman or pewterer, age c. 26

Graham, David, tinman or pewterer, age c. 28

Keyes, Lucy, daughter of Robert Keyes of Watchusets Hill, Worcester Co., Mass.—wandered from home in April, 1755, at age of 4; never found; may have been captive in Canada; father offers reward of fifty dollars for information that leads to her recovery (11/21)

Liken, Phaebe, wife of Michael Liken, of Morris Co., N.J.—has aloped from her husband (11/28)

Williamson, James, living about 16 miles "up the County," near the foot of the North Mt. in Pa., and his two younger children—killed Nov. 7 by Indians (11/28)

Reed, William—killed Nov. 11 by Indians at Denning's Creek, about 3 miles beyond Bedford, Pa. (11/28)

Glass, David—same as above

GENEALOGICAL DATA FROM THE NEW-YORK MERCURY

1763

Hamilton, Henry—killed Nov. 22 by a footpad on Wissahicon Road, about 3 miles from Phila. (11/28)

M'Daniel, Mr.—drowned Nov. 21 in North River in NYC when knocked overboard by the boom (11/28)

Dunnin (or Dunham), Samuel, apprentice, age 18—runaway Nov. 20 from Benjamin Conn of Bernard's Twp., Somerset Co., N.J. (11/28)

Magee, James, Irish servant, age 10 or 20—runaway Nov. 3 from James Williams of NYC (11/28)

Killed Nov. 17 by Indians in Pa., across from N.J. (12/5 and 12/12):
  Westbrook, Capt.
  Cartwright, William
  Decker, Andrew
  Carter, Nathaniel
  Dunkin, William

Johnson, Lt., late of Gorham's—killed Nov. 28 by Indians at east end of Lake Erie (12/5)

Hayes, Catharine, age 53, wife of Patrick Hayes of New Branford, Conn.—husband offers reward to anyone who will seize her and have her jailed (12/5)

Stevenson, James, servant, born in Yorkshire, England—runaway Thursday night last from Thomas Oughton at the London Coffee-House in NYC (12/5)

Amelia, Negro slave, age c. 23—runaway Nov. 21 from Philip Kissick (12/5)

Gorman, Henry, Irish, tailor—runaway from Thomas Calhoun of Perth Amboy, N.J. (12/12)

Liggett, William, of Borough Town of Westchester, dec'd—accounts with estate to be settled with execs, Abraham Liggett or Richard Lawrence (12/9)

Drowned Dec. 7 when boat foundered in Lake Erie (12/9)

Davidson, Lt., of the Train

Paynter, Lt., of the 80th Regt.

Williams, Dr., of the 80th Regt.

McVicker, apprentice lad—runaway Dec. 16 from the snow *Lord Dunluce,* John Monford master; reward for capture of McVicker will be paid by Waddell Cunningham, merchant, in NYC (12/19)

McKillip, Hugh, apprentice lad—same as above

Layn, Edmund, born in New England, carpenter, age 24, enlisted in 1761 in Nova Scotia —deserted Dec. 11, 1763, in NYC, from H.M.'s 2nd Battalion of the Royal Regt. of Artillery, commanded by Col. George Williamson (12/19)

Chrystie, Dr. John, of Perth Amboy, N.J., dec'd—accounts with estate to be settled with Elias Boudinot, attorney, at Elizabeth Town; attendance will be given at house of James Callender, tavernkeeper, in Perth Amboy, on Jan. 18 to settle accounts; James Murray, admin. (12/19)

A gang of villains arrested Dec. 6 in a house in Roxbury, Mass., and jailed in Boston (12/26):

Robinson, William, age c. 35

Cassady, John, age c. 40

Willson, John, age c. 21

Sears, George, who says he served 3 years to an attorney in England

1764

Welsh, Mr.,—killed in May, 1763, by Wyondots (1/2)

Levy, Mr.—killed in May, 1763, by the Chippawas (1/2)

Smallman, Mr.—killed in May, 1763, by the Shawanese (1/2)

Bryan, James, born in London, England, age 34—deserted from Capt. Holland's Company of H.M.'s 60th Regt. (1/2)

Fisher, Elizabeth—her husband, Jeremiah Fisher of Philipsburg, warns he will not pay debts she may contract (1/2)

Livingston, James, Esq., dec'd—houses and lots belonging to his estate for sale (1/2)

Andariese, Hannah, wife of Nicholas Andariese of NYC—has eloped from her husband (1/9)

Aspeck, John Christian, late of NYC, dec'd—accounts with estate to be settled with execs, Casper Reisner and John Meyer (1/9)

Nixon, Thomas, late of Schenectady, dec'd—accounts with estate to be settled with Nathaniel Hazard of NYC (1/16)

Moses, David—accounts with his estate to be settled with Christopher Smith or John Ernest (1/16)

Honey, Thomas, son of Thomas Honey, late of Redruth, County of Cornwall, England —if alive, is requested to communicate with John Halse, master of the ship *Royal Exchange* at Halifax or Lawrence Kavanah, merchant, at Louisbourg (1/23)

Cyrus, Negro slave, age 28—runaway early in January from Jeremiah Stanton of Staten Island (1/23)

Tostbinder, Jacob, born in Somerset Co., N.J., cooper by trade—has escaped from Sheriff George Remer of that county (1/23)

Eldrington, Miss Mary, of Elizabeth Town, N.J., born at Eldrington Hall, Northumberland, England—died Jan. 27 at Elizabeth Town in her 109th year and was buried Jan. 28 in St. John's Churchyard (1/30)

North, Thomas, born in Ireland, stone cutter and mason by trade—suspected of having stolen money from chest of James Gelston in house of Mrs. Barhalt in Chappel St., NYC (1/30)

Young, John, apprentice cordwainer, age c. 18—runaway Jan. 30 from William Mariner of NYC (2/6)

Ellison, Gabriel, an Englishman, who has relatives in Bucks Co., Pa.—captured by Indians in Nov., 1762, but released in Jan., 1764 (2/6)

Eise, Hans, a German—captured by Indians near Ft. Cumberland but released some two years ago to Sir William Johnson (2/6)

Morris, Robert Hunter, Esq., Chief Justice and member of Council of N.J. and late gov. of Pa.—died Jan. 27 and buried at Morissania, N.Y. (2/6)

Goodwin, Capt. Richard, dec'd—accounts with estate to be settled with Sarah Goodwin, executrix (2/6)

Benson, Robert, of NYC, brewer, dec'd—estate in Bowery Lane for sale; apply to Catherine Benson (2/13)

Johnston, Andrew. Esq., dec'd—real estate belonging to estate for sale (2/13)

Ogden, Col. Josiah, dec'd—residence in Newark, N.J., for sale; apply to David and Jacob Ogden and Isaac Longworth (2/20)

Livingston, Philip, dec'd—land in Albany Co. for sale; apply to Philip Livingston (2/20)

Van Ranst, Capt., master of sloop *Mary* bound from NYC to South Carolina—washed overboard and drowned (2/20)

Fine, Mr., one of crew of the sloop *Mary*—same as above

Leguiere, Abraham, late of Bushwick, Kings Co., dec'd—land in Bushwick to be sold (2/20)

Duke, Negro slave, age 35—runaway Feb. 13 from Thomas Hamersley, of NYC, goldsmith (2/20)

Jacob, Negro slave, age c. 24—runaway from George Wray in Albany (2/27)

Hutchinson, Miss, of the North Parish of Danvers, Mass., daughter of Widow Mrs. Hannah Hutchinson, age 23—murdered Feb. 2, presumably by her brother, a lad of 17 (2/27)

Fraser, George, the elder, dec'd—property in Elizabeth Town, N.J., for sale (3/5)

Camoran, John, born in the Highlands of Scotland, age 32—deserted from Capt. John De Garmo's company (3/12)

Groesbeck, John, dec'd—accounts with estate to be settled with Thomas Lynch, exec. (3/12)

Stewart, Daniel, a blacksmith—last week fell into the dock near the ferry stairs at the Fly Market in NYC and was drowned (3/12)

Beek, John, dec'd—his tavern, on the public road on Staten Island between Elizabeth Town and the ferries, for sale; his execs. are Joseph Rolph and Joshua Mercereau (3/12)

Corsen, Daniel, dec'd—administratrix is Mary Corsen (3/12)

Mange, Jemima—arrested in Boston last week (Boston dispatch of March 12) on suspicion of murdering her new-born infant (3/19)

Secord, Abigal, wife of Daniel Secord of New Rochelle, N.Y.—has eloped from her husband (3/19)

Smith, Mary, wife of James Smith of NYC—has eloped from her husband (3/19)

Riley, Elizabeth, wife of Patrick Riley—has eloped from her husband (3/19)

Van Horne, Abraham, dec'd—real estate in Outward of NYC, along the East River, for sale (3/26)

Farrand, Dr. Daniel, of NYC, dec'd—accounts with estate to be settled with widow, Margaret Farrand (3/26)

Smith, John, Irish servant, butcher by trade, age 20—runaway March 20 from John Cornell of Long Island (3/26)

Ross, Capt. James J., dec'd—property in the Great and Little Nine Partners in Dutchess Co., for sale (4/2)

Black, John, servant, who says he is an Irishman but talks more like a German—runaway March 27 from David Graham of NYC (4/2)

Degrey, Mary, wife of Thomas Degrey, of New German Town, Hunterdon Co., N.J.—eloped from her husband in Dec., 1763 (4/2)

Douglass, Sarah, wife of James Douglass of Crown Point—husband will not pay debts contracted by her in the future (4/2)

Davidson, James, late of Milford, Conn., dec'd—claims of creditors will be examined by Lewis Mallet and John Harpin, Jr., at house of Mr. Mallet, innholder, at Milford (4/2)

Cooper, William, born in London, England, coach-harness maker and trimmer by trade, age 32—runaway from his bail; reward for his capture will be paid by Josiah Winants and Jonathan Hampton of Elizabeth Town, N.J. (4/2)

Field, Patrick, Irish servant, age c. 23 or 24—runaway from Myles Cooper, of King's College, NYC (4/9)

Marsh, Peter, servant, who says he came from Lancashire, England, age c. 30—runaway from Ralph Norton of Trenton, N.J. (4/9)

Poel, John, late of NYC, dec'd—house in Queen's St. or Smith's Fly near Burling's Slip in NYC for sale (4/9)

Hunt, Richard, English servant, age c. 30—runaway April 1 from Robert Lewis & Son (4/9)

Wright, Capt. Richard, late of NYC, dec'd—accounts with estate to be settled with Anne Wright, executrix (4/9)

Crage, James, apprentice, age c. 17—runaway about 4 weeks ago from James Campbell of Springfield Borough of Elizabeth Town, N.J. (4/9)

Bugles, Francis, servant, age 14—runaway from William Alberspe of NYC (4/9)

Annelly, William, born in Ireland, tailor by trade—deserted March 20 from Capt. Alexander White's company of NY troops in Albany (4/9)

Singleton, Thomas, from Long Island, shoemaker by trade—same as above

Voorhees, John, dec'd—land in Upper Freehold, Monmouth Co., N.J., for sale (4/9)

Ilslee, Benjamin, dec'd—plantation in Raway, N.J., for sale; apply to John Marshall (4/16)

Chambers, John, Esq., later member of Council of NY and formerly Chief Justice of Supreme Court of NY—died April 10 at his house in NY (4/16)

Hodgkins, Ebenezer, born at Grotton in New England, shoemaker by trade, age 32—deserted in March from Lt. Col. John Darby's company of the 17th Regt. (4/16)

Stevens, Peleg, born at Newport, R.I., wigmaker by trade, a private soldier, age 30—same as above

Sheron, Joseph, born in Lancashire, England, a silk troster by trade, a private soldier, age 27—deserted from Capt. Richard Montgomery's company of the 17th Regt. (4/16)

Kennison, Nicholas, born in Hampshire, New England, shoemaker by trade, age 22—same as above

Benger, Elliot and wife, Dorothea—requested to communicate with Hugh Gaine, printer (4/16)

Williams, John, carpenter by trade—runaway from his bail in NYC on April 21 (4/23)

Emmott, William, son of John Emmot, late of Dublin, Ireland, merchant—will learn something to his advantage by communicating with his brother, John Emmott, care of William Dunlap in Phila. (4/30)

Church, Capt. Edward, of Newport, R.I., 5 or 6-year old son of—run over April 20 by a pair of trucks on Thames St. and died of injuries the next day (4/30)

Cebra, James, late of Jamaica, Queens Co., merchant, dec'd—accounts with estate to be settled with Mary Cebra, administratrix, and James and John Cebra, admins. (4/30)

Charles, indented Indian apprentice, born on Long Island, age 18—runaway April 13 from Simon Fleet of Huntington, L.I. (4/30)

Cloyd, David, wealthy planter, living on James River, not far from Looney's Ferry, in Virginia, son of—killed by Indians March 20 (5/7)

Grinay, Susannah, wife of Jonathan Grinay of NYC—husband will not pay debts contracted by her in the future (5/7)

Thompson, John, apprentice, born in Ireland, age c. 17—runaway from Richard Deane (5/7)

Deserted from Capt. Richard Rea's company of NY troops commanded by Major William W. Hogan, at Schenectady (5/14):
Suthard, Abraham, born in N.J., age 30
Haslip, William born in England
Stewart, John, born in Ireland
Quin, Felix, born in New England

Deserted from Capt. Grant's company (5/14):
Thorn, Peter, born in Dutchess Co., NY
Norton, Thomas, born in England, mariner

Deserted from Capt. Dawson's company (5/14):
Falkner, John, born in Ireland, age 25
Welsh, John, born in NY, age 23
Palmer, John, born in England, age 30
Taylor, John, born in Ireland, age 40
Giddons, Roger, born in New Jersey

Deserted from Capt. White's company (5/14):
Vardee, George, born in England, age 25
Jorden, Thomas, born in Ireland, ropemaker by trade, age 37
McCain, Adam, born in NY
White, Joseph, born in France
Curle, Nicholas, born in France
Dennison, Peter, born in Ireland, laborer
Westover, Oliver, born in New Jersey, blacksmith
Thompson, James, born in England

Deserted from Capt. Degarmo's company (5/14):
Grixin, John, born in England, age 26
Annen, James, born in NY, cooper by trade, age 19
McEntire, Peter, born in Scotland, laborer, age 20
Hazard, Henry, born in Ireland, mariner
Chandler, John, born in England

Harry (or Traso), Negro slave, brought up in America, age 25 or 26—runaway from Samuel Cock of Township of Mansfield Wood House, Sussex Co., West Jersey (5/14)

Wageman, Elizabeth, wife of Michael Wageman of NYC, "Sweep-Chimney"—has eloped from her husband (5/14)

Jack, Negro slave, born at Hackinsack, late the property of Mr. Hallet at Hell Gate—runaway about May 4 from Edward Agar of NYC (5/14)

Autenreith, William—executed May 12 in Phila. for robbing houses of Mr. Clifford and Mr. McCall (5/21)

Williams, John—same as above

Denniston, John, late of Middlesex Co., N.J., dec'd—lands for sale by execs., Arthur Denniston and Andrew McDowel (5/21)

M'Intosh, George, a Scotsman, laborer, working on a new house of Mr. Apthorp at Blomendal—killed in a quarrel by another workman, Frederick Loudon, a Dutchman (5/21)

Emanuel, Negro slave, born in the Havannah, age c. 22—runaway May 14 from Thomas Ivers of NYC (5/28)

Cornell, Thomas, Esq., late of Rockway, Queens Co., dec'd—accounts with estate to be settled with execs., Valentine H. Peters and Jacob Mott (6/4)

Dey, Dirick, Esq., dec'd—accounts with estate to be settled with David Shaw (next door to Alderman Livingston's in NYC); the execs. are Theunis Dey and Mary Shaw (6/4)

Dickenson, Catharine, wife of Benjamin Dickenson of NYC—has eloped from her husband (6/4)

Brown, Mr.—lately killed by Indians at the mouth of the Aughwick in Pa. (6/11)

Velentine, John, late a soldier in the Provincial service—killed June 2 in NYC in a quarrel with a shoemaker named Doyle (6/11)

Arthur, Catharine, wife of George Arthur, of NYC, mariner—has eloped from her husband (6/11)

Brewin, George, born in county of Roscommon, Ireland, sawyer by trade, private in Capt. Thomas Falconer's company of H.M.'s 44th Regt. of Foot—deserted May 8 at Albany (6/11)

Farrel, John, born in County of Derry, Ireland, laborer—same as above

Seabury, Rev. Samuel—died June 15 at his seat at Hampstead, L.I. (6/18)

Kingston, John, dec'd—accounts with estate to be settled with Daniel Phenix (6/18)

Haulbeet, Ebenezer, servant, carpenter by trade, age c. 25—runaway a few days ago from Joseph King of Morris Town, East New Jersey (6/18)

Washbourn, Ebenezer, of Newport, R.I., mate of brig commanded by Capt. Rhodes of Piscataqua—died about end of Dec., 1763, at Cape Malpas on coast of Africa (6/25)

Donnaldson, Ronald, a redemptioner, age 23—runaway, together with a servant named Hugh Daniel, on June 17 from the snow *Prince of Wales,* Robert Wilson master (6/25)

Primus, Negro slave, age c. 25—runaway June 2 from John Miller of New London, Conn. (6/25)

Baily, Daniel, servant, born on Long Island, age 19 years and 6 mos.—runaway in company of a carpenter named John Grannis from Daniel Campbell of Schenectady (6/25)

Forbes, John, Jr., late of Long Island, dec'd—accounts with estate to be settled with one of administrators, William Butler, Thomas Pearsall, and Thomas Franklin, Jr. (6/25)

Smith, John, private and "musicianer," age 24—deserted from Lt. Col. William Eyer's company of H.M.'s 44th Regt. of Foot at Crown Point (7/2)

Lyons, John, late of NYC, bricklayer—accounts with estate to be settled with William Moore in Chappel St. (7/2)

Johnson, Guy, son-in-law of Sir William Johnson—set out June 17 for Niagara in company with John Duncan, Esq., of Schenectady (7/2)

Hodges, James, indented servant, born at Bristol, England, age c. 13—runaway June 25 from Sterling Iron Works; reward for his apprehension offered by William Hawxhurst (7/9)

Darby, Benjamin, apprentice, cordwainer and tanner, age c. 20—runaway July 4 from Moses Ogden of Elizabeth Town, N.J. (7/9)

Woodruff, Mary, wife of Samuel Woodruff—has eloped from her husband (7/23)

Phillips, Joshua, of Cambridge, Mass., cordwainer—died July 14 in Cambridge soon after drinking a large glass of rum and then a pint of milk (7/30)

Jack, Negro slave, age c. 35—runaway July 3 from Jacob Platneer of Livingston's Manor, Albany Co. (7/30)

Dunavan, James, indented servant, age c. 18 or 19—runaway July 26 from brigantine *Neptune,* William Cochran commander (7/30)

Elberson, Elbert. of NYC, age 76—last week fell out of a canoe off the Battery and was drowned (7/30)

Lawrence, John, Esq., Alderman of the Dock Ward of NYC—died Aug. 5 at his house in NYC (8/6)

Tennent, Rev. Gilbert, pastor of Second Presbyterian Church in Phila., Pa.—died there July 21 (8/6)

Lewis, Deborah, of Newport, R.I., age c. 32—always supposed to be a woman but has put on male clothes and is about to marry a widow (8/6)

Pidgeon, Mary, of NYC—found dead of natural causes on Aug. 4 in Mott St. in the Out Ward (8/6)

Sands, Mrs. James—has eloped from her husband (8/6)

Hancock, Thomas, Esq. of Boston, merchant and member of Mass. Council—died about 3 P.M. on Aug. 1 at his seat in the Council Chamber (8/13)

Cunningham, Mrs.—killed by Indians July 25 about 2 miles below Loudon, Pa. (8/13)

Brown, Mr., schoolmaster on Conecocheague Creek, about 12 or 15 miles from Ft. Loudon—killed, along with nine of his pupils, by Indians on July 26 (8/13)

Mumford, Elisha, son of Capt. William Mumford of Newport, R.I.—drowned in his 17th year on July 31 when boat overturned near the lighthouse in Newport Harbor (8/13)

Gould, Capt., master of Messieurs Forley's (or Forsey's?) brig of New London, Conn.—killed by slaves on board on May 13 as brig was weighing anchor at Senegal, bound to Goree (8/13)

Tillinghast, Charles, distiller, dec'd—accounts with estate to be settled with admins., Jonathan Holmes and William Wiley (8/13)

Watson, Peter, from Scotland, who has studied at Universities of Edinburgh and St. Andrews, now lodging at Mr. Wilson's house at the corner of the Fly Market in NYC—intends to open a school (8/20)

Littlefield, Mary, daughter of Moses and Mary Littlefield of the third parish in Braintree, Mass.—bitten Aug. 1 by a rattlesnake but recovered through medicine administered by Abel Puffer of Stoughton (8/27)

Barclay, Rev. Henry, Rector of Trinity Church, NYC—died in NYC on morning of Aug. 20 in his 53rd year (8/27)

Hays, Judah, eminent merchant of NYC—died there Aug. 19 (8/27)

Seymour, John, High Dutch servant, age 36—runaway Aug. 21 from John M'Clean of NYC (8/27)

North, Thomas, from London—has opened a school in NYC in Horse and Cart St., facing the Moravian Church St.; Elizabeth North will teach needlework (8/27)

Hill, William, servant, coopersmith by trade, age 28—runaway, in company with another servant named Richard Robinson, hatter by trade, from Francis Sanderson of Lancaster, Pa. (8/27)

Dysert, Miss, daughter of James Dysert—killed Aug. 24 by Indians near Big Spring in Pa. (9/3)

Kingsbury, John, Esq., late colonel in provincial service in Mass. and justice of the peace for Lincoln Co.—died Aug. 22 of apoplectic fit in Boston (9/3)

The following captives have been recovered from the Indians by Sir William Johnson:
Shepherd, Mr., of Conn.

Chapman, Abigail, of N.E but taken at Cushietunk, Pa., together with infant child

Carter, Sarah, taken in Pa., together with sister Elizabeth

Duncan, John, a boy, and sister, Sarah, taken at Leckawecksein, Pa.,

Trim, Ezra, a boy taken at the same place

Up de Graave, Peter, and sister, Catharine, taken at Cushietunk

Otter, Sarah, and sister, Joannah, taken at Cushietunk

Barnet, Sarah, Lena and Hose, taken 7 years ago at Goblintown, Carolina (9/3)

Martin, Edward, indented servant, born in Greenwich, near London, England, blacksmith and farrier by trade, age c. 32—runaway Aug. 27 from William Wood of NYC (9/3)

Sleght, Matthew, dec'd—accounts with estate to be settled with Elizabeth Sleght (9/10)

Stimble, Isaac—killed in August by Indians on the road near Ourry Bridge (9/10)

Baldwin, Daniel, and wife Jane—taken by Indians at Wyoming, Pa.; Daniel was burned to death and Jane died of hunger last winter (9/10)

Howell, John—taken by Indians at Wyoming, Pa., and found dead in the woods (9/10)

Baldwin, Abraham, a boy, born in New England but taken by Indians at Wyoming and murdered (9/10)

Caesar, Negro slave, age c. 32—runaway Aug. 24 from Johannes Veeder of Coknawaga on Mohawk's River; reward for his capture will be paid by Johannes Veeder or by Simon J. Veeder, merchant, at Albany (9/10)

Jacob, a slave, calling himself James Start or James Pratt (his mother was Negro, his father Indian)—runaway Aug. 17 from Gilbert Smith of Upper Freehold, Monmouth Co., N.J. (9/10)

Miller, Capt. Joseph, of NYC—killed in Africa by Negroes (9/10)

Ryneck, Andrew, indented servant, journeyman baker, age c. 21 or 22—runaway Sept. 8 from John Shoults of NYC, baker (9/10)

Miller, John, living within a mile of George Bowman's and about 12 miles from Winchester, Pa.—killed, along with three of his family, by Indians (9/10)

Thompson, Malege, Mulatto servant, age 30—runaway Sept. 8 from Michael Montgomery at the Cross Roads in New London Township, Chester Co., Pa. (9/24)

Frank, *alias* Francisco, Negro slave, who has lived among the Spaniards, age c. 25—runaway Sept. 9 from Thomas Pryor of Philadelphia (9/24)

Tracy, Elisha, master of schooner *Delight,* who sailed Jan. 18 from New London, Conn., bound for the West Indies—washed overboard March 24 and drowned (9/24)

Gibbons, Mrs.—killed Aug. 25 by Indians (9/24)

Leake, Robert, Esq., Commissary General—married Sept. 18 in NYC to Anne Bancker, widow of Christopher Bancker, late of N.Y., merchant (9/24)

Pompey, Negro slave, age c. 36—runaway Sept. 14 from Ephraim Nichols of Stratford, Conn. (9/24)

Lawrence, John, Esq., dec'd—accounts with estate to be settled with execs, Thomas, Jonathan and Daniel Lawrence (10/1)

Elberson, Abraham, dec'd—accounts with estate to be settled with Rachel Elberson, executrix, and Jonathan Morrel, exec. (10/1)

Ross, Capt. James J., dec'd—property in Little Nine Partners, Dutchess Co., for sale (10/1)

Loyse, Susannah, wife of Simon Loyse of NYC, bricklayer—her husband will pay no debts she may contract in the future (10/8)

Mount, Negro slave, age c. 20—runaway from Robert Barkley of Lamington, Somerset Co., N.J. (10/15)

Klinehoff, Paul, late of Elizabeth Town, N.J., dec'd—house and lot there, adjoining land of St. John's Church, next door to Mr. John West, on Golden Hill, for sale (10/15)

Campbell, Mary, who on May 21, 1758, at age of 10, was captured by Indians in Cumberland Co., Pa.—her father and mother ask that she be helped to return to them from Albany (10/15)

Ellis, Alice, wife of John Ellis, of NYC, painter—has eloped from her husband (10/15)

Boweren, Elizabeth, wife of Martin Boweren, of Newtown, L.I.—has eloped from her husband (10/15)

Campble, Capt. Laughlen, dec'd—meeting of trustees of the Scotch Patent to be held at house of his widow, Sarah Campble in Ann St., Montgomery Ward, NYC (10/15)

GENEALOGICAL DATA FROM THE NEW-YORK MERCURY

1764

Pelton, William, apprentice boy, born in Conn.—runaway Sept. 23 from William Goforth of NYC, cordwainer (10/15)

M'Daniel, Daniel, Scotch boy—runaway Oct. 7; reqard for his capture will be paid by Franklin and Underhill, at Cannon's Dock, NYC (10/22)

Robb, Mr., of Boston, sugar baker—buried Oct. 10 in Boston (10/22)

Young, Mr., son of, of Boston—same as above

Ben, Mulatto slave, age c. 18—taken up by Phineas Rumsey of Goshen, Orange Co., NY (10/22)

Housler, Christopher, a German—has absconded, with wife and five children, from Burlington Co., N.J.; reward of £10 for his capture offered by William Foster, Robert Powell, Asher Woolman, Benjamin Thomas, Daniel Earnest and Caleb Austin (10/29)

Campbell, Edward, who says he was born in Scotland but is supposed born in Ireland, sadler by trade, age 21—deserted Oct. 23 from Lt. Col. Elliot's company of H.M.'s 55th Regt. in Albany (10/29)

Powell, George, English servant, who came from Cork in the ship *Pitt*, James Baily master, age c. 20—runaway Oct. 28 from Francis Harris, living in Second St., Philadelphia (11/5)

Hide, Benjamin, of Attleborough, Mass.—murdered Oct. 23 by Jonathan Sheppardson of the same town (11/5)

Jones, Margaret—on Oct. 29, while intoxicated, fell from main deck into the hold of the man of war *Coventry*, lying in NY harbor, and was killed (11/5)

Nevill, Samuel, Esq., Second Judge of Supreme Court of N.J., former Mayor of Perth Amboy and Speaker of the N. J. Assembly—died Oct. 27 at Perth Amboy in his 67th year (11/5)

Marsh, Samuel, of Woodbridge, N.J., 12-year-old son of—on Oct. 24 crushed to death by a wagon (11/5)

Hanna, John, Irishman, in jail for counterfeiting—broke out of jail in Borough of Elizabeth, N.J.; reward offered by Sheriff Moses Ogden (11/5)

Matthews, Julius (or Justus?), Irishman—same as above

Peterkop, William, skinner by trade, living in Wood St., Phila., together with wife and two children—on Nov. 7 suffocated to death by fumes from a pot of charcoal in their room (11/12)

Fortune, Negro slave, age 17—runaway Nov. 6, together with a slave named Tom, from William Bates of NYC (11/12)

Bounce, Mrs., of second parish in Hingham, Mass.—on Nov. 5 delivered of three male children (11/19)

McMillan, Anthony and wife Martha—are suing James Lynch (12/3)

Gormon, John, apprentice, age c. 19—runaway from George Tucker, blacksmith (12/3)

Carroll, Thomas, from Newry, North of Ireland—will open school in NYC; his wife will also teach (12/3)

Noon, Thomas, Irish servant. age c. 18—runaway from William Holly of Goshen, NY (12/3)

Waters, Daniel, dec'd—brick house and lot at Brookland Ferry, Kings Co., NY, for sale by execs., Sarah Waters and William Thorne (12/24)

Richards, Capt. William, dec'd—accounts with estate to be settled with Henry Cruger and John Provoost (12/24)

Dinon, Nancy, Irish indented servant, age c. 29—runaway Dec. 27 from the Widow Richards on Rotton-Row in NYC (12/31)

Oliphant, William, apprentice, tailor by trade, age between 17 and 18—runaway from John Pool of Middlebrook, Somerset Co., N.J. (12/31)

1765

John, a Portuguese—runaway from his bail in NYC (1/14)

Duvell, Nicholas, a Frenchman —same as above

Kennedy, Francis, from Loudoun—condemned to death for murder at Williamsburg, Va., in Dec. 1764 (1/14)

Bridgman, Hezekiah, from Henrico—condemned to death for felony at Williamsburg, Va., in Dec. 1764 (1/14)

Leves, Richard, from Cumberland—same as above

M'Donagh, Henry, servant, shoemaker by trade, age 30—runaway Jan. 5 from Greg, Cunningham & Co. in NYC (1/14)

Sculthorp, John, late of NYC, dec'd—accounts with estate to be settled with James Wilmot, admin. (1/14)

Jin, Negro wench, age 20, who formerly belonged to Thomas Franklin of NYC—runaway Jan. 1 from James Horton of Maroneck, Westchester Co., NY (1/14)

Arenbergo, Frederick, master of schooner *Lunenburg-Packet*—drowned Nov. 5, together with his brother, when the ship was cast away in Mahon Bay (1/21)

Morrell, William, apprentice, born at Newtown, L.I., shoemaker by trade, age 11—runaway Dec. 24, 1764, from John Cree (1/21)

Clay, Mary, wife of Christian Clay of NYC—has eloped from her husband (1/21)

Arden, James, dec'd—house and various goods in William St., NYC, for sale; accounts with estate to be settled with Thomas Arden, exec. (1/28)

Bamper, Mr., of NYC, six-year-old son of—on Jan. 23 run over by a sleigh and killed (1/28)

Magee, Michael—fell through the ice near Jamaica South on Long Island and was drowned (1/28)

Douglass, Mr.—same as above

Hall, Dennis—sentenced in NYC to be hanged Feb. 8 for picking pockets (1/28)

Yates, Mary—same as above

Blake, James, Esq.—died Jan. 19 at Wrentham (Providence dispatch), age c. 80 (2/11)

Pratt, Joseph—died Jan. 13 at Bridgewater, aged 99 years and 11 months (Providence dispatch) (2/11)

Simons, Mr., of Springfield, Mass.—frozen to death there last Saturday se'nnight (Hartford, Conn. dispatch of Jan. 28), leaving a widow and several small children (2/11)

Lightly (or Pretty),* Joseph (both names probably false), age c. 30—jailed in Hartford, Conn., on suspicion of murder (2-11)

Morris, Lewis, dec'd—tracts of land in Orange, Albany and Westchester Counties belonging to his estate for sale; apply to Richard Morris in NYC (2/11)

---

* Joseph seems to have taken the matter of surnames pretty lightly. ED.

Drowned Nov. 13, 1764, in Barnstable Bay: (2/18)
  Green, John, master of the ship *Beulah*
  Eyre, Col.
  Kennedy, Lt.
Clowes, Samuel, dec'd—house and land that formerly belonged to him in Jamaica, Queens Co., offered for sale by Thomas Braine of Jamaica (2/25)
Brady, Thomas, indented servant, age 19—runaway Feb. 17 from James Armstrong of NYC (2/25)
Barnebey, Mrs. Ruth, born at Marblehead, Mass., for some 40 years midwife in Boston, who last August completed her 100th year—died Feb. 12 in Boston (3/4)
March, William, dec'd—administrator of estate was Jacob March (3/4)
Brown, Samuel, dec'd—house and land of his estate in Bernards Town, Somerset Co., East New Jersey, for sale by execs., John Ayers and John Rey (3/4)
Riker, Andrew—plantation at Newtown, L.I., for sale by John B., Abraham, and Samuel Riker (3/4)
Miller, John, Irish servant, who attended the bar at the ferry, age 24—runaway from Francis Koffler (3/4)
Kennedy, Abraham, Esq., late of NYC, dec'd—notice about farm in Bergen inserted in paper by Archibald and Catharine Kennedy (3/11)
English, Robert, Irish servant, age c. 15—runaway March 2 from Robert Pilson (3/11)
Livingston, Robert, dec'd, and Livingston, Robert, Jr., dec'd—5 lots of estate for sale; enquire of Philip Schuyler, Esq., at Albany, or Philip Livingston, William Bayard and William Smith, Jr., at NYC (3/11)
Shaw, John, late of NYC, currier, dec'd—because of his death, partnership with George Shaw of NYC, tanner, dissolved; accounts with partnership to be settled with James and George Shaw, execs. (3/11)
Holyorn, Mr.—fell from wharf near the King's Yard in Boston and was drowned (3/25)
Oge (*alias* Sunderland), James, age c. 22—made off with a horse and reward for his capture is offered by Thomas Leonard of Princeton (3/25)
Smith, John, late of NYC, carman, dec'd—accounts with estate to be settled with Christopher Bensen, exec. (4/1)
Bradburn, Alexander, indented Irish servant, barber by trade, age c. 17 or 18—runaway April 29 from Robert Orr, perukemaker in King St., NYC (4/1)
Cato, Negro slave, age 26—runaway from James Wharry of East Nottingham Township, Chester Co., Pa. (4/8)
Crawford, John. dec'd—his farm on Rye Neck for sale by execs., Charles Theall and Maurice Smith (4/8)
Knight, Robert, age 25—April 3 broke out of Salem jail in N.J.; reward offered by Sheriff John Budd (4/15)
Catts, Michael, a Dutchman, age c. 25—broke out of Salem jail in company of Robert Knight and an ex-soldier, Thomas Dicker (4/15)
Runaway April 19 from Leonard Lispenard: (4/22)
  Sullivan, Timothy, indented servant, native of Ireland, about 5 months in NY, a callenderer by trade, age c. 30
  M'Carty, Timothy, indented servant, native of Ireland, woolen-weaver by trade, age c. 22
  M'Cardell, Philip, indented servant, native of Ireland, brewer and distiller by trade, age c. 24
Riggs, Edward, lately come from Ireland, educated in Dublin, who for past 12 months has taught languages at Marble Town, Ulster Co., NY—has opened a school in Kingston and teaches Latin and Greek (4/22)
Boutchiar, John—separated April 23 by mutual consent from wife Anne (4/29)

Hendrickson, William, born in Somerset Co., N.J., formerly soldier in the N.J. Regt., age c. 24—broke out of Somerset jail April 15; reward offered by William Millan, sub-sheriff (4/29)

Cozzens, Capt. Joseph, late of Newport, dec'd—accounts with estate to be settled with Thomas Franklin, Jr. (4/29)

Crane, Susannah, wife of Jeremiah Crane of Newark, N.J.—husband will not pay debts contracted by her in future (4/29)

Jones, Dr. Evan, dec'd—tract of land called the Hermitage about 3 miles from New Windsor in Ulster Co., NY, was recently purchased from his execs. by George Falls (4/29)

Swaaner, Mr., of NYC, tailor—May 3 murdered his 3-month-old child (5/6)

M'Ellroy, Edward, indented servant, joiner by trade, age c. 20—runaway March 19 from John Keating (5/6)

Clancy, Mary, indented Irish servant, age c. 24—runaway April 29 with Thomas Brown (who has been for 2 months past in workhouse and is servant to Messers Greg, Cunningham, and Co.) from James Morrison, wigmaker, on the New Dock in NYC (5/6)

Irwen, George, soldier, age c. 20—deserted Feb. 16 from H.M.'s 27th or Inneskellen Regt. at Montreal (5/6)

Pye, Joseph, born at Birmingham, England, saddletree-riveter, age c. 24—runaway April 26 from his bail; reward for his capture offered by John Craig of Elizabeth Town, N.J. (5/6)

Van Horne, Garret, of NYC, merchant—died May 6 in NYC of a painful illness, leaving widow and many small children (5/13); accounts with his estate to be settled with executrix, Anna Van Horne, and execs., Lawrence and Joseph Reade, Jr. (6/10)

Fisher, George, servant, bookbinder by trade, age between 25 and 26—runaway in April from printing office of Jo. Royce of Williamsburgh (5/13)

Cato, Negro slave, age c. 28—runaway Oct. 28 from Benjamin Westervelt of Poughkeepsie (5/13)

King, Ary, late of NYC, dec'd—accounts with estate to be settled with execs., John and Ary King (5/13)

Murray, Joseph, Esq.—action in Court of Chancery by his execs., Charles Williams and Thomas Jones, agt. William Cosby, Jr. (5/13)

Lattouch, Isaac—accounts with estate to be settled with assignees, Henry Cuyler, Jr., and John Alsop, who lives in Wall St. in house where Adrian Banker lived (5/20)

Clark, John, apprentice, of Scotch parents, age 19—runaway May 11 from Jonathan Cowdery of NYC (5/20)

Shees, Matthew, indented Irish servant, tailor by trade, age c. 19—runaway May 20 from Matthew Watson of Albany (5/27)

Ross, Capt. James J., dec'd—farm in Little-Nine-Partners, Dutchess Co., for sale; apply to Bartholomew Crannel at Poughkeepsie, or Margaret Ross and William Kennedy in NYC (6/3)

Ribble, Barbary, age c. 7—May 27 in Philadelphia thrown from a cart drawn by runaway horse and killed (6/3)

Hart, Christian, age c. 15—May 28 in Philadelphia thrown from a cart and killed (6/3)

Thompson, ——, young Scotch lad—drowned May 28 in North River in NYC (6/3)

Hepborn, John, apprentice lad, hatter by trade—runaway May 21 from William Hammell in Princeton, N.J. (6/3)

Haley, Michael, Irish servant—runaway May 27 from John M'Kinney of NYC, tailor (6/3)

Bokels, Henry, Irish servant, age c. 18—runaway from Joseph Valentine, living on the north side of Hempstead, Long Island (6/3)

Lechmere, Thomas, Esq., formerly Surveyor General of Customs for Northern District of North America—died May 30 in Boston in 82nd year (6/10)

Fosdick, Mrs., living in north part of Boston—fell down stairs May 30 and broke her neck (6/10)

Dobbins, Anthony, of NYC, dec'd—accounts with estate to be settled with Mary Dobbins, executrix (6/10)

Ben, Negro slave, born in Barbadoes, age c. 35—runaway from Augustine Reid of Morris Co., N.J. (6/10)

Tone, Negro slave, a Spaniard—runaway from Hendrick Hoghtaling of Coxsahkie, Albany Co. (6/17)

Joe, Negro slave, age c. 20—runaway from Augustine Reid of Morris Co., N.J. (6/10)

Joice, Edward, Irish servant, age c. 23—runaway June 5 from Daniel Amos, living near Greenwich (7/17)

M'Alieff, Henry, Irish servant, shoemaker by trade, age c. 35—runaway about June 13 from Cornelius Bryan, living on Raccoon Creek in Greenwich Township, Gloucester Co., N.J. (6/24)

Welch, Catharine, Irish servant—runaway June 12 from William Gilliland of NYC (6/24)

Carmer, James, late master of brig belonging to Philadelphia—died at sea; command of brig taken over by mate, Jonathan Carmer (6/24)

Sparling, Philip, indented servant, born in Ireland, age c. 15—runaway June 7 from Charles Miller, of NYC, baker (6/24)

Luter, Catarine, indented servant, age c. 14—runaway June 7 from George Horner of NYC (7/1)

Davis, William, cooper, living in Water St., Philadelphia—killed June 25 by lightning (7/1).

Dannefelder, George, indented servant, who speaks no English and bad German, butcher by trade—runaway in June from Peter Hasenclever of Ringwood (7/1)

Christophers, John, indented servant, a Dane—same as above

Prince, Negro slave, age c. 18—runaway June 28 from Isaac Gomez of NYC (7/8)

Forbes, Alexander, of Brooklyn. L.I.—accounts with estate to be settled with John Rapalje (7/15)

Daws, John, servant, an Englishman, age c. 40—runaway July 14 from Jonathan Huntting of Morris Co., N.J. (7/22)

Bright, Mrs., living in north part of Boston—fell downstairs July 8 and broke her neck (7/22)

Sherlock, Oliver—drowned July 16 in NY harbor (7/22)

Quackenbos, Cornelius, late of NYC, dec'd—accounts with estate to be settled with Annatje Quackenbos, executrix, and William Wovnat,* exec. (7/22)

Toby, Negro slave, this country born, age c. 21—runaway July 9 from Augustus Vanhorne (7/22)

Hector, Negro slave, age c. 30—runaway July 22 from John Pell, miller, living at Tappan, Orange Co., NY (7/29)

Laverty, Edward, indented Irish servant, claiming to be a maltster, age c. 28—runaway from Philip Livingston's distillery on Long Island (7/29)

M'Knight, John, dec'd—dividend on his estate will be paid to creditors at Henderson and Ewing's store (7/29)

Jack, a Mulatto, country born, age c. 40—escaped about May 20 from William Prew, who had taken him out of the Philadelphia Workhouse (8/5)

Harris, Abraham and Sarah, who lived in Boston about 20 years ago—friend desires news of them or their children (8/5)

Cons, Jacabina, wife of Leonard Cons—has left her husband (8/5)

---

*Wynant. Ed.

Dublin, Negro slave, age c. 55—runaway in July from James Barnard, innholder in Philipsborough, Westchester Co. (8/5)

Somerendick, Egbert, of Fish-Kills, NY, dec'd—accounts with estate to be settled with Tunis Somerendick in NYC or Zacharias Van Vorhis at Fish-Kills (8/12)

M'Neill, David, apprentice, cooper by trade, age c. 18—runaway Aug. 6 from William Riddel, living in Bound Brook, N.J. (8/12)

Hunter, Anthony, of NYC—drowned Aug. 10, together with Negro lad, when skiff over-set about 100 yards from shore of Johnston's Ferry at Staten Island (8/12)

Erwin, Robert (by some called William), battoeman (who calls himself a carpenter by trade), age c. 30—has stolen servant girl, Catharine M'Gra, "tayloris by trade," age c. 26, from her master, William M'Cew of Albany (8/12)

Nicholson, George, apprentice, born near Leith, Scotland, ship carpenter by trade, age c. 19—runaway July 19 from George M'Alin of Philadelphia, ship carpenter (8/12)

Haynes, Joseph, dec'd—his farm (now in possession of Caleb Hyat), at Great Kills, be-tween 3 or 4 miles from NYC on road leading to Bloomendale, for sale (8/12)

Lawrence, John, late of Newtown, L.I., dec'd—accounts with estate to be settled with execs., Richard, Thomas, Jonathan and Danile Lawrence (8/12)

Sket, Richard Barnsley, mattross, born in Parish of Muchwinlock, County of Shropshire, who enlisted July 10, 1765, in NYC, in Royal Regt. of Artillery and who had served in H.M.'s 43 Regt. of Foot at siege of Louisbourg and in General Elliot's Light Horse in Germany—deserted Aug. 9 in NYC (8/12)

Bliss, Mr., wagoner of the Bordentown stage—thrown from wagon and crushed to death July 30 while returning from Amboy Ferry (8/19)

Nealson, Mary Anne, wife of Duncan Nealson, of NYC, ship carpenter—her husband will not pay debts contracted by her henceforth (8/19)

Plumsted, William, Esq., alderman of Philadelphia—died there Aug. 11 and buried next day in St. Peter's Church Burying Ground (8/19)

Truxton, Thomas, Esq., dec'd—Negroes once owned by him have arrived in NYC from Jamaica and are for sale (8/26)

Mersereau, Mrs., of Staten Island—Aug. 31 thrown from a wagon and killed when one of the wheels ran over her (8/26)

Langly, Joseph, indented servant, age c. 18—runaway Aug. 6 from Anthony Woodward of Upper Freehold, Monmouth Co., N.J. (8/26)

Roberts, John, indented servant age c. 18—same as above

Turned over by Indians to Sir William Johnston: (8/26)

   Hout, Elizabeth, taken by Indians 9 years ago near Easton, Pa., age c. 22

   Huffer, Jacob, son of, age c. 18 or 20

   Chapman, Mr., of Cushietunk, Pa., two daughters of, ages c. 9 and 7

Nesbet, Jonathan, dec'd—accounts with estate to be settled with John Anderson, admin. (9/2)

Anderson, James (son of Jonathan Anderson, dec'd), born in Monmouth Co., N.J., tailor by trade, age 22—runaway Aug. 1 from his bail in Freehold Township, Mon-mouth Co., N.J.; reward for his capture offered by Aaron Mallison (9/2)

Cook, Mr., of Bay of Honduras—murdered by his Negroes (9/2 and 9/16)

Spencer, Lucy, wife of Nehemiah Spencer of Spencer Town, Albany Co., N.Y.—has eloped from her husband (9/2)

Delancy, Mary, servant girl, age 18 or 19—runaway Sept. 3 from Richard Harris, living in Scotch St. (9/9)

Teeple, James, apprentice, shoemaker by trade, age 19—runaway from Benjamin Harris of Bound Brook, Somerset Co., N.J. (9/9)

Sanders, Robert, late of Albany, merchant, dec'd—accounts with estate to be settled with John Sanders of Schenectady (9/16)

Charles, Negro slave, age c. 38, taken from Dr. Blair of the artillery on the day General Braddock was defeated; then carried to Canada and there was in possession of M. De Va Driel until Montreal was taken; next returned to his former master, who presently sold him to Walter Rutherfurd, Esq., in NYC—runaway Sept. 2 from John Duncan, Esq., of Schenectady (9/16)

Donivan, Ricket, indented servant, born in Ireland, age c. 20—runaway Sept. 4 from John Macomb of Albany (9/16)

Clark, Thomas, of Elizabeth Town, N.J., a judge of the county court—died there Sept. 11 (9/23)

Bray, James, born in County of "Tippararry," Ireland, who came to North America about 17 years ago and lived with a gentleman named Kearney in N.Y. or N.J.—asked to apply to Hugh Wallace, merchant, in NYC (9/30)

Joseph, Mulatto slave, a Spaniard, age c. 25—runaway Sept. 18, in company with a Spanish Negro belonging to Mr. Bayard of NYC by whom he was sent to Albany to be sold, from Barent Ten Eyck of Albany (9/30)

Gale, Samuel, Esq., of Goshen, Orange Co., NY, dec'd—some of his real estate to be sold (9/30)

Baylis, Col. John, of Dumfries, Va.—early in Sept. killed in a duel (9/30)

Oyl, Alexander, apprentice, tailor by trade, age c. 14—runaway from William Thorne of NYC (9/30)

Dublin, Negro slave, age c. 21—runaway Oct. 6 from William Graham, living on Rotton-Row, NYC (10/7)

McManus, Philip, Irish servant, age c. 17 or 18—runaway Oct. 7 from Smith Ramadge of NYC (10/14)

Boquet, Brig. General—report of his death arrived from Pensacola (10/21)

Wynkop, Lucas, of Fish-Kills, Dutchess Co., NY—married there Oct. 10 to Margaret Van Tessel of the same place (10/21)

Robbin, Negro slave, born in America, age c. 27—runaway Oct. 10; reward for his capture will be paid by Dr. Thomas Wright of Eastchester or Daniel Wright, lately moved to Peck's Slip in NYC (10/21)

Rose, Negro slave, born in America, age c. 30—same as above

Ball, John, late of NYC, dec'd—accounts with estate to be settled with execs., Isaac Ball and Abraham Van Dyck (10/28)

Drowned Dec. 3 when ship overset on way from Philadelphia to Mount Holly: (12/9)
    Mullin, Edward, and wife
    Hoffman, Elizabeth
    Ewing, Juliana
    M'Cullough, Mary

Anderson, Susannah, wife of Jacob Anderson—has eloped from her husband (12/16)

Nick, Mulatto slave, age c. 22—runaway Dec. 15 from Lewis Morris (12/23)

Langdale, John, Jr.—Dec. 23 knocked overboard by the boom of the sloop *Squirrel* of Philadelphia, Capt. John Taylor, bound from Philadelphia to Antigua, and drowned (12/30)

GENEALOGICAL DATA FROM THE NEW-YORK MERCURY

1766

Killed early October, 1765, by Creek Indians (1/6):
    Hogg, James
    Payne, William, and his brother, a boy
Anderson, Susannah, wife of Jacob Anderson—has eloped from her husband (1/6)
Harrison, William, native of Nottingham, England, mariner—made a deposition Sept. 1, 1764, in Boston (1/6)
Nick, mulatto slave, age c. 20—runaway Dec. 15, 1765, from Lewis Morris in NYC (1/6)
Ramsey, James, who came 10 or 12 years ago from County of Armagh in North of Ireland and settled at Little Britain, Lancaster Co., Pa., whence he removed to the Jerseys—will learn something to his advantage if he applies to William Gilliland, merchant in NYC (1/20)
Baldwin, Nehemiah, Esq., late of Newark, dec'd—accounts with estate to be settled with Stephen Baldwin, exec. (1/20)
White, Joseph, late merchant of Albany, dec'd—creditors of the estate to send accounts to Albany to Volckert P. Douw, Martin van Bergen and George Wray (1/27)
Berry, Mr., Chief Justice of North Carolina—committed suicide in Dec. in Newbern by shooting himself (2/3)

Drowned Jan. 17 at Fish Kills falling through ice while crossing the river (2/3):
  Darling, Joseph
  Kilburn, Mr.
Tingley, Samuel, late of NYC, ship chandler, dec'd—accounts with estate to be settled
  with Agniss Tingley, exec. (2/3)
Toney, Negro slave, age c. 40—runaway from Jacob Snediker at the New Lots on Long
  Island (2/17)
Abrahams, James, late of Perth Amboy, dec'd—two plantations of estate to be sold at
  auction by execs., John Combs and Nicholas Eversen (2/17)
Berton, Peter, of Oyster Bay, L.I., who made his will in 1704 or 1705 and left it in
  hands of some of the old French inhabitants of Staten Island or New Jersey—his son,
  Capt. Peter Berton offers a reward of £10 for the will (2/24)
Robbins, John, late of NYC, dec'd—tanyard at Fresh Water in NYC for sale (2/24)
M'Kim, William and wife Mary—signed on Feb. 21 an agreement to separate (2/24)
Smith, Michael—burned to death Feb. 22 in cabin of a wood flatt at Arch St. Wharf in
  Phila. (3/3)
Haynes, Joseph, dec'd—household effects and farm at Great Kills to be sold (3/10)
Smedley, William, of Chester Co., Pa.—drowned March 6 when a flatt bringing staves
  from Chester to Phila. was caught by a storm (3/17)
Hampton, Mary—found March 18 hanged in an outhouse near the college in NYC (3/24)
Voorhees, Hendrick, late of Monmouth Co., N.J., dec'd—estate—except for 50 acres given
  to son William and about 60 acres in law with the Craigs, to be sold by the execs.,
  Peter Voorhees, David Williamson and Dirick Zutphin (3/31)
Bayard, Major Robert, of NYC—married evening of March 16 in Boston to Miss Rebec-
  cah Apthorp, youngest daughter of the late Charles Apthorp, Esq., of Boston (3/31)
Miller, John, indented servant, born in Switzerland, age c. 40—runaway about 4 weeks
  ago from J.M. Prevost (4/7)
Hukel, Eve, German servant—runaway April 12 from L. Garrison (4/14)
Betts, Capt. Daniel, late of Newton, L.I., dec'd—farm in Newton for sale; enquire of
  Waters Smith of Jamaica or Jacob Fieldon on the premises (4/14)
O'Neal, Owen, weaver by trade, age c. 22—runaway from Andrew Lycan of Penepack,
  Lower Dublin Twp., Philadelphia Co., Pa. (4/14)
Drowned March 5 in wreck of the snow *Nancy* at Hereford Bar about 17 miles north
  of Cape May (4/21):
  Kerr, Capt. Walter, master of the snow
  Oliver, John, mate of the *Nancy*
  Fortescue, ———, apprentice on the *Nancy*
  Jones, John, master of the sloop *Ann*, earlier taken up at sea by the *Nancy*—
  Mason, Andrew, mate of the *Ann*
  Brown, John, one of crew of the *Ann*
  Muttony, David, one of crew of the *Ann*
  Wood, Peleg, one of crew of the *Ann*
  Wilson, Capt., William, and wife and child, of Phila.
  Corser, Capt. John, of Phila.
  Smith, Robert, a young lad, brother of Rev. Dr. Smith of Phila.
  Willson, Rev. Mr., of NY
  Giles, Rev. Mr., of NY
  Mott, Mr., of Conn., a tanner
Colvin, William, late midshipman on H.M.S. *Coventry* and formerly mate of the mer-
  chant ship *Aletto*, age c. 30—deserted from the *Coventry*, apparently at NYC (4/21)
Gavin, Francis, servant, a laborer, age c. 28—runaway April 17 from Jacamiah Smith at
  Springfield, near Elizabeth Town, N.J. (4/28)

Fry, Christian and wife Margarita, both German indented servants—runaway April 13 from Moses Clements in the Broad-Way, opposite the New Church in NYC (4/28)

Burch, Sarah, born Sarah Wheeler at Flushing, L.I., wife of David Burch of Sodack, Albany Co.—eloped from her husband in company of John Spencer, who says he was born in North Carolina (4/28)

Darsee, William, late of Tiverton, R.I., dec'd—a reference to two oxen raised by him (5/12)

Cato, Negro slave, age c. 34—runaway in April from Charles Doughty of Westchester (5/12)

Thomson, William, late of Millstone, Somerset Co., N.J., attorney at law, dec'd—accounts with estate to be settled with execs., Benjamin Thomson, Peter Schenk and Edmund Leslie (5/12)

Gerbeaux, Henry, dec'd—his exec., Peter Vallade of New Rochelle, desires demands against him, on his own account or as executor, to be presented to Lewis Pintard, merchant (5/12)

Leonard, Zephaniah, Esq.—died at Boston, Mass. April 23 in his 63rd year; his wife died the same day in her 62nd year (5/19)

McCormack, Alexander, Irish servant, age c. 40—runaway May 20 from Timothy Day of Morristown, N.J.; McCormack has a wife Mary and a son c. 18 months old (5/26)

Ward (*alias* Murray or Morgan), Luke, Irish servant, age c. 14 or 15—runaway June 13, 1765, from John Crawford, of Warrington, Bucks Co., Pa. (6/2)

Raft, John, apprentice—runaway from Andrew Burn (carpenter or joiner) (6/2)

Bill, Negro slave, formerly belonging to Cornelius Clopper of Rariton Landing, N.J., age c. 20 or 22—runaway April 1 from John Klein, of NYC (6/9)

Youngs, Joseph, apprentice, house carpenter by trade—runaway from James Whippo, of Oyster Bay, L.I. (6/9)

Runaway May 29 from Ringwood Iron Works in East Jersey, German miners (6/9):
Schaeffer, Henry, age 38
Langwieder, Joseph, age c. 36
Ortindn, Mathias, age c. 24
Denck, Simon, age c. 25

Deserted at NYC from Major Bayard's Company of H.M.'s 60th or Royal American Regt. (6/9):
Caventish, John (*alias* John Miller), born Dublin, Ireland, weaver by trade, who worked on L.I. before he enlisted as drummer and fifer, age c. 19
Cochran, David, born in North of Ireland, laborer, age c. 20
Cochran, William, born in North of Ireland, age c. 21

MacManus, Philip, Irish servant, age 19—runaway May 26 from John Heating, of NYC (6/16)

Randell, Dr. Annenias, born on L.I., age c. 25—escaped from jail of Somerset, Co., N.J. (6/16)

Ashton, Edward, a "young Man" tailor—runaway from his bail June 12; had served his time with William Large in Bristol, Pa.; reward for his capture offered by William Ashton, of Bristol, Pa. (6/16)

Pritchel, Walter and Winford, servants, lately come from Ireland—runaway June 12 from Henry Neill of Phila. (6/16)

Clatworthy, George, late of NYC, pedlar—accounts with estate to be settled with Alexander Robertson, admin. (6/23)

Charles, Negro slave, born on Island of Jamaica, marked "P. Le Count" under his left breast—runaway beginning of June from Andrew Myer, living in Dock St., NYC (6/30)

Drowned May 25 in wreck of Capt. Gwin's ship off the Isle of Sables (6/30):
Blackman, Benjamin, of Boston
Cohoun, Capt.
Gwin, Capt., nephew of

Perry, Joseph, of Northampton, Co., Pa.—killed June 16 by lightning which struck a barn there (6/30)

Sears, Capt. Isaac, of NYC, 7-year-old son of—drowned "Sunday week last" near Beekman's Slip (6/30)

Cooper, Mr., of NYC, butcher—fell from his horse between Hampstead and Jamaica and died of injuries June 27 (6/30)

Pain, George, of NYC, mariner—during his absence his wife Sarah has married again and goes by name of Sarah Neil (7/7)

Joe, Mulatto slave, age c. 29—runaway from Ephraim Logue, of Bohemia Manor, Caecil Co., Md. (7/7)

Allanby, Capt. Robert, master of the *Peggy* of Bristol—drowned mid-June in James River upon falling from scaffold while painting the vessel's stern (7/7)

Haynes, Godfrey, who followed business of lobster catching for the NYC market and who had a family in Rye—drowned July 1 while swimming near Burling's Slip (7/7)

Turner, Thomas, apprentice, cooper, age.c. 18—runaway July 2 from James Neavin, cooper in French Church St., NYC (7/7)

Pridey, William, dec'd—garden and lot in Bowery Lane, about one mile from NYC, for sale; apply to John Tabor Kempe, Esq., of NYC, or Ann Pridey, of NYC (7/7)

Brooks, David, late of Stratford, dec'd—accounts with estate to be settled with execs., John and David Brooks (7/7)

Munro, Barnabas, apprentice, age c. 19—runaway July 14 from Samuel Wickham, of Goshen, Orange Co., NY (7/21)

Dean, Capt., from S.C., bound to Holland—drowned while trying to get Capt. Lindsey, of Piscataqua, off wreck of latter's ship (7/21)

Mayhew, Rev. Dr. Jonathan, age 46—died July 9 in Boston (7/21)

Epps, Mrs., son of, of Chesterfield Co., Va.—died June 12 from beating at hands of a Negro girl (7/21)

Boone, Capt. Humphrey, living in plantation on north side of Severn in Md.—died in June of cancer (7/21)

Storrs, Lemuel, a "New- England Renagado," who has kept school in N.J.—escaped July 16 from Sheriff John Moores in Perth Amboy (7/21)

Runaway June 28 from Ringwood Iron Works, East Jersey, German miners (7/28):
Geyes, Peter, age 35

Hahsmidt, Jacob, age 25

Schneyder, Philip, age c. 30

Hoever, Anthony

Thompson, Patrick, Irish servant, tallow chandler—runaway July 7 from Archibald Gardner, of Phila. (7/28)

Norris, Isaac, Esq., Quaker, Alderman of Phila. and for c. 20 years Speaker of Pa. Assembly—died at Fair Hill July 13 in his 65th year (7/28)

Finley, Rev. Dr. Samuel, President of the College of New Jersey—died July 10 in Phila. in his 51st. year (7/28)

Nugent, Capt. Richard, dec'd —distribution from his estate will be made to creditors by James Duane (8/4)

Stevens, Capt. James, late of Newport, R.I., master of sloop *Rising Sun*—drowned at sea in July on way from New Providence to Newport (8/11)

Executed at Burlington, N.J., Aug. 1, for murder of two Indian women, Hannah and Catharine (8/11):
Annin, James, age 54

M'Kinzy, James, age 19

Godden, William, matross of the Royal Regt. of Artillery—drowned in Aug. at Turtle Bay, NYC, while bathing in the river (8/11)

Parsels, Thomas, who lived on and owned part of Parsels's Island—drowned Aug. 9 while trying to swim on horseback across river to his house; his body was found floating at Hell-Gate (8/11)

Nichols, Mrs. Mary Magdalen, of NYC, dec'd—household goods and furniture to be sold at her late residence in French Church St. (8/11)

Clossen, Peter, German servant, baker, age c. 25—runaway July 18 from Jacobus Montanye & Co., at Burling's Slip, NYC (8/11)

Brockholst, Henry, late of Pompton, N.J., dec'd—accounts with estate to be settled with execs., Beverly Robinson, David V. Horne, David Clarkson, William Livingston, Frederick Philipse (8/11)

Brockholst, Mary, late of NYC, dec'd—same as above

Rutlidge, Robert, merchant of Prince Edward Co., Va.—killed June 3, in Benjamin Mosby's tavern at Cumberland Courthouse, by Col. John Chiswell (8/18)

Welch, Mr., an Indian trader, and grandchild—killed by Indians early in May while going from Fort Prince George to the Sugartown in the Lower Cherokee country (8/18)

Murdered near Broad River on the road from the Upper Cherokee country to Virginia (8/18):

  Boyd, Mr., a trader from Virginia

  Field, Mr.

  Bourke, Mr.

Watson, Capt., master of brig from Virginia—killed by slaves in the River Gambia on coast of Africa (8/18)

Cutts, Samuel, apprentice boy of Charles Town near Boston, age 15—runaway Aug. from master, Benjamin Mecom, printer, of New Haven, Conn. (8/18)

Runaway July 20 from masters, John Ledyard and William Stanly of Hartford, Conn., Negro slaves (8/18):

  London, age c. 34

  Dige, age c. 23

  Tack, age c. 35

Gruber, Henry, Dutch servant, age c. 19, formerly apprentice to Daniel Mylander—runaway end of June from Charles Gemberling, shoemaker, at upper end of Market St., Phila. (8/18)

Pendergast, William—found guilty of high treason in Dutchess Co., NY, and sentenced to death (8/18 and 8/25); reprieved Sept. 1 (9/15)

Gordon, John, Scotch servant, age c. 18—runaway Aug. 10 from Samuel Sharp, living near the Head of Elk, Caecil Co., Md. (8/25)

Bray, James, who left Irleland about 16 years ago at age of 26 and lived for a time with Mr. Carney, of NYC, merchant; brother, now in NYC, desires news of James (9/1)

Ben, Negro slave, age 28, who formerly belonged to Thomas Budde at Morris Town, N.J., and then to a widow, Elizabeth Finn, at Prakenas, Bergen Co., N.J.—runaway Aug. 23 from Nathaniel Richards, of Newark, N.J. (9/1)

Jim, Negro slave, age c. 36—runaway Aug. 16 from Dr. William Bush, of Horse-Neck, Conn.; reward for his capture offered by Dr. Bush or will be paid by Dr. James Murray, of NYC (9/1)

Howlin, Eleanor, wife of Oliver Howlin, of NYC, laborer—has eloped from her husband (9/15)

Dolson, Tunis, first male born in NYC after it was ceded to the English by the Dutch—died Aug. 30 at Goshen, NY, in his 102nd year (9/15)

Runaway Aug. 31 from David Thompson, shipbuilder, of Phila. (9/15):

  Stell, Peter, Scotch apprentice, age c. 19

  Shank, James, English apprentice, age c. 20

Martin, Sarah, wife of Thomas Martin, of NYC—has eloped from her husband (9/15)

Stevenson, Mrs. Jane, dec'd—household furniture to be sold at her house, nearly opposite the Presbyterian Meeting House in NYC (9/15)

Tom, Negro boy, part Indian, age c. 16—runaway Sept. 3 from Robert Hallett in NYC (9/15)

Verplank, Mr., of NYC, merchant, little daughter of, age c. 3—killed Sept. 15 at Oswego Market in NYC by blows from feet of horse (9/22)

Thompson, William, attorney at law, late of Millstone, Somerset Co., N.J., dec'd—property to be sold by execs., Benjamin Thompson, Peter Schenck and Edmund Leslie (9/22)

Van Norestrant, Albert, late of NYC, dec'd—property in Montgomerie Ward to be sold by execs., Jacob Duryee, Garret V. Norestrant and Isaac Mead (9/22)

Moore, John, Irish servant, age 22—runaway Sept. 12 from Samuel Henry of Trenton, N.J. (9/22)

Armstrong, Capt. Thomas, master of sloop *Polly*, from Pensacola—drowned Sept. 13 when he fell overboard while coming up the river at Phila. (9/29)

M'Vicker, Capt., master of ship *Antrim*—died 8 days after ship left our capes on voyage to Barbados (9/29)

Hacket, Col. John, of Andover, Sussex Co., N.J.—died there Sept. 20 (9/29)

Runaway Sept. 14 from John Overing and Samuel Whitehorn, of Newport, R.I. (9/29):
  Fox, John, native of Ireland, indented servant lad
  Harrington, Darby, native of Ireland, indented servant

Artsen, Albert, dec'd—house and lot in William St., NYC, for sale; apply to Daniel Dunscomb (10/6)

Clark, Tally, late master of sloop *Prosperous*—Sept. 23, off George's Banks, seized by whale he was trying to lance and carried under water (10/6)

Matthews, John, cabin boy on ship of Capt. Brynen, from Newry—fell Sept. 24 from mizen yard and was drowned (10/6)

Hyer, Peter, of NYC—died in apoplectic fit Sept. 30 (10/6)

Bradley, Richard, Esq., dec'd—tracts of land in Ulster Co., property of his children, for sale (10/6)

Mowrey, Joshua, of Newport, R.I.—accidentally killed Sept. 30 on Taylor's Wharf by blow from bar of a capstan; he leaves widow and several children (10/13)

Charles, a sailor, supposed to have been murdered on high seas by William Cearon (10/13)

Sullivan, John, laborer, of Phila.—found dead in Sept. in hold of a new ship at wharf in Phila. (10/13)

Nicholson, Mary, young girl, of Society Hill in Phila.—Oct. 6 murdered her infant son (10/13)

Tingley, Capt. Samuel, dec'd—house in NYC, now occupied by widow, Agness Tingley, for sale (10/20)

Cyrus, Negro slave, who has learned some Latin and knows the Greek characters, age c. 30—runaway Oct. 1 from Henry Holland, on north side of Staten Island (10/20)

Morse, Benjamin, of Southboro—Oct. 19 found dead in trough of a horse shed at Little Cambridge, Mass.; he leaves widow and 6 children (10/27)

Scanlan, Dennis—executed Oct. 18 at Phila. for highway robbery (10/27)

Ryall, Abraham—executed Oct. 18 at Phila. for burglary (10/27)

Crist, John, age c. 80—reprieved at Phila. Oct. 18 when under sentence of death for burglary (10/27)

Sentenced to death by court at Newark, N.J., for horse stealing (10/27):
  M'Carthy, James, native of Ireland, age c. 21, who says his mother lives in Phila.
  Morris, John, native of Ireland, age 49

Roney, James, Irish servant, age c. 19—runaway from John Provoost, of NYC (10/27)

De La Somet, John, banished from France in 1684 for his religion—died early October in Fauquier Co., Va., aged upwards of 130 years (11/3)

Chiswell, Col. John, of Williamsburg, Va.—died there Oct. 15 (11/3)

Molton, William, of Phila.—killed Oct. 5 when struck by lightning on board brig *Greyhound*, bound from Barbados to Portsmouth (11/3)

Mitchell, Capt., master of ship bound from London to Quebec—drowned when ship was cast away near Island of Antecosta (11/3)

Runaway Oct. 27 from Timothy Ogden, of Elizabeth Town, N.J. (11/3):

Lambert, Abner, apprentice shoemaker, age c. 20

Allan, Zachariah, apprentice shoemaker, age 15

Runaway from snow *James and Mary,* John Moor master (11/10)

Cook, William, apprentice, age c. 20

Cook, John, apprentice, age c. 19

Coulter, James, apprentice, age c. 19, who had served part of his time to a barber

Smith, Perro, mulatto slave, born and bred near Boston, age c. 35—runaway Nov. 3 from George Armstrong of Morris Co., N.J. (11/10)

Brimingham, James, Irishman—reward for his capture offered by Dr. Joseph Munsell, of Smith's Clove, Orange Co., NY, from whom he stole a horse (11/17)

Colters, James, Irishman—same as above

Ford, Philip, Esq., Sheriff of Chester Co., Pa.—died Oct. 24 in his 34th year, leaving widow and five small babes (11/17)

Cashaw, Abraham, living near the ferry on Long Island—fell from an apple tree and died Nov. 15 (11/17)

Barkeloe, Harmanus, the late—farm on Long Island at the Narrows for sale; apply to Harmanus Barkeloe, near the premises, or Engelbert Lott, at Flat Bush (11/24)

M'Cormick, Alexander, ditcher by trade, age c. 40—escaped from jail of Morris Co., N.J. (11/24)

Prince, Negro slave, age c. 20—runaway from Isaac Gomez of NYC (12/1)

Gowing, Joshua, servant, age c. 26, who came to America last spring—runaway from Major James in NYC (12/1)

Baldwin, Timothy, of Parish of Amity, New Haven, Conn.—died there Nov. 23 (12/8)

Miller, Peter, Irishman, mason by trade—runaway Oct. 30 from his bail, living in West Nantmill Twp., Chester Co., Pa.; reward offered by William and Alexander Gould (12/8)

Pepperrell, Hannah, wife of Isaac Pepperrell, of NYC, mariner—has eloped from her husband (12/8)

Newman, Sarah, wife of Jonathan Newman, of Norwalk, Conn., but late of Long Island—husband will not pay debts contracted by her in future (12/8)

Oliphant, William, apprentice tailor, age c. 20—runaway Dec. 1 from John Pool, of Middlebrook, Somerset Co., East New Jersey (12/8)

M'Mullen, Michael, Irish servant, skinner and breeches-maker, age 28—runaway Dec. 1 from Cornelius Ryan, living opposite the Coffee House in NYC (12/8)

Ter Bush, Henry, dec'd—lots in Twp. of Fishkills, Dutchess Co., NY, for sale; apply to Simon Ter Bush, living near the premises (12/8)

Van Veghten, Naltie, late of Albany, dec'd—accounts with estate to be settled with Val. and Ephraim Van Veghten (12/15)

Beck, Anne, wife of Joseph Beck—has eloped from her husband (12/15)

Bond, Jacob, late of NYC. cooper, dec'd—accounts with estate to be settled with execs., Christopher Benson and Sarah Bond (12/15)

Cuyler, Henry, Esq., said to be eldest inhabitant of NYC, merchant—died there Dec. 14 (12/22)

Skinner, Elizabeth, dec'd—property in Manor of Cortlandt for sale; apply to Cortlandt Skinner, Stephen Skinner or James Parker (12/22)

Simmons, Anne, young woman, who left her parents in Charlestown, S.C., about five years ago and came to NYC—news of her sought (12/22)

Tucker, Morris, of Cumberland, R.I., and three children—perished Dec. 6 when his house caught fire (12/29)

Fitz Patrick, Barnaby, seaman—drowned Dec. 24 near Peck's Slip, NYC (12/29)

1767

Halsey, James, noted mathematical instrument maker—died Dec. 15, 1766, in Boston, with apoplectic fit (1/5)

Wallis, Abigail, wife of Gamaliel Wallis of Boston—same as above

Seamor, Robert—convicted in Sussex Co., N.J., of murder of an Indian and executed Dec. 20, 1766 (1/12)

Robinson, Septimus, Esq., born in Phila, former representative in Assembly, High Sheriff of the County and Justice of the Court of Common Pleas—died in Phila. Tuesday sennight in his 74th year (1/19)

Weed, Esther, for near seven years past Matron of the Pennsylvania Hospital—died Jan. 7 in Phila. (1/19)

M'Nalley, Mary, wife of Arthur M'Nalley, in the Northern Liberties, near the Barracks, in Phila.—Jan. 9 found dead in bed from wound in back of her head (1/19)

Romer, Henry, a German tailor, who lived with family in small house on the Commons, about 4 miles from NYC—died in snowstorm near his home on New Year's Day (1/19)

Clap, Rev. Thomas, late President of Yale College—died in New Haven, Conn., and was buried there Jan. 8 (1/19)

Peters, Dr. Charles, dec'd—plantation on north side of Hempstead Plains, Queens Co., for sale by execs., Valentine H. Peters and Benjamin Hewlett (1/19)

Waite, John, of Chelsea, Mass.—frozen to death last Saturday sennight while returning home from Lynn, where he had been catching eels (1/26)

Bird, Mr., of Dorchester, Mass.—frozen to death the same night while returning home from Boston (1/26)

Mayhew, Dr. Jonathan, late of Boston, dec'd—his widow, Elizabeth, was sent £100 Sterling by Thomas Hollis of London, in grateful memory of her husband (1/26)

Thomas, Michael, of Ulster Co., NY, age c. 40—runaway from his bail Jan. 19 in NYC, together with his wife (1/26)

Stewart, Duncan, Esq., Collector of Customs for the Port of New London, Conn.—married evening of Jan. 8 in Boston to Miss Nancy Erving, youngest daughter of Hon. John Erving, Esq., of Boston (2/2)

Manwaring, David—married Jan. 15 in New London, Conn., to Miss Patty Saltonstal, daughter of Col. Gurdon Saltonstal (2/2)

Breese, Mrs. Rebecca, wife of Samuel Breese of NYC and daughter of late Rev. Dr. Finley—died Jan. 27 in NYC in her 19th year of consumption (2/2)

Arnold, Hezekiah, tailor, dec'd—accounts with estate to be settled with Thomas Brown (2/2)

Cuyler, Henry, late of NYC, dec'd—accounts with estate to be settled with execs., Henry and Teleman Cuyler (2/2)

Runaway Jan. 31 from John Keating of NYC (2/2):
  McManus, Philip, indented servant, born in Ireland, chimney sweeper, age c. 19
  Dublin, Negro slave, chimney sweeper, age c. 18

Grover, Hon. William, Esq., Chief Justice of East Florida—died from exposure after wreck of sloop *Mary,* James Sheffield master, off coast of Florida, southward of the Matanzas (2/9)

Temple, Hon. John, Esq., Surveyor General of North America—married Jan. 20 in Boston to Miss Bowdoin, daughter of Hon. James Bowdoin, Esq., of Boston (2/9)

Banyar, Goldsbrow, Esq., of NYC—married Feb. 5 in NYC to the Widow Appy (2/9)

Kerr (or Kert?), David, laborer—killed Jan. 28 at Sterling Iron Works when run over by wagon (2/9)

Ford, Elizabeth, of NYC—murdered Feb. 4 in NYC near house of Mary Williams, *alias* M'Guire (2/9)

Wilder, Thomas, from England—died in NYC Feb. 6 (2/9)

Woodward, William, age c. 15, son of Francis Woodward, of Rock-Creek, Frederick Co., Md.—Jan. 4 accidentally killed when he slipped, fell and was crushed by log he was carrying (2/16)

Morris, Mrs. Elizabeth, a Quaker, of Phila.—died there Feb. 2 in her 94th year (2/16)

Ashley, Edward, of Groton, New London Co., Conn.—lately died there in his 108th year (2/16)

Spencer, Mrs. Ruth, of Hartford, Conn.—died there Jan. 24 in her 98th year (2/16)

Robertson, William, master of sloop *Bee*—reported drowned Dec. 1, 1766, at Anguilla but may have been murdered (2/16)

Executed Feb. 9 in NYC (2/16):
  Williams, Mary
  Crawford,——
  McCarroll,——
  Venus, Negro slave

Morris, Matthew, late of NYC, innholder, dec'd—goods to be sold (2/16)

Johnston, William, of Phila.—hanged himself Feb. 15 in his house at corner of Front and Race Sts. in Phila. (2/23)

Peter, Negro slave, age c. 22—runaway Feb. 10 from Richard Mercer, living in King St., NYC (2/23)

Livingston, James, Esq., dec'd—property in patent of Wallomscot, Albany Co., NY, for sale; apply to Robert James Livingston or Peter R. Livingston, Esq. (2/23)

Stevenson, Mrs. Jane, dec'd—accounts with estate to be settled with James Ramsay (2/23)

Parker, Sarah, wife of mate of vessel now at sea—Feb. 21 found dead in bed in her house in Pearl St., NYC (3/2)

Heurtin, Susanah, widow, of Newark, N.J.—goods to be auctioned at her house (3/2)

Stymes, Benjamin, of Long Island, dec'd—lot at foot of Battoe St., NYC, for sale; apply to Christopher Stymes, near Oyster Bay, L.I. (3/2)

Lyle, Abraham, dec'd—accounts with late partnership of Kennedy and Lyle to be settled with execs., James Lyle, John Van Allen and David Edgar (supplement to 3/2)

Thomas, Michael, of Ulster Co., NY, a German, age c. 40—runaway, together with his wife, from his bail; reward for his capture offered by Joseph Wharry, of Ulster Co. (supplement to 3/2)

Glasgow, Negro slave, age c. 18—runaway from Alexander Moore, living at Cohansey Bridge, Cumberland Co., West N.J. (supplement to 3/2)

Cuyler, Henry, late of NYC, dec'd—accounts with estate to be settled with exec. (supplement to 3/2)

Haynes, Joseph, dec'd—farm on the Great Kills for sale by execs. (supplement to 3/2)

Arnold, Hezekiah, tailor, dec'd—accounts with estate to be settled with Thomas Brown, exec. (supplement to 3/2)

Drowned at sea (3/16):
  Lowther, Capt., son of
  Alexander, James, mate
  Caldwell, Archibald, sailor
  Casswell, James, sailor

Dalbo, Peter, who set out in a wood flat from Racoon Creek to Phila.—drowned March 4 (3/16)

Kerr, an "antient Woman"—same as above

Johnston, Andrew, Esq., dec'd—real estate in N.J. for sale; apply to Lewis Johnston, Esq. (3/16)

Williamson, David, 19-year-old son of—killed March 1 at Providence, R.I., by accident in launching of a vessel about the Great Bridge in Providence (3/23)

Mendes, Abraham Perarer, late of Jamaica, merchant—March 4 married in Newport, R.I., to Miss Sally Lopez, daughter of Aaron Lopez, of Newport, merchant (3/23)

Cary, William, of Windham, Conn.—about last week in Jan. his wife gave birth to three children, two boys and a girl, of whom two are still alive (3/23)

Flint, Silas, of Windham, Conn.—March 4 his wife gave birth to four girls, all of whom died (3/23)

Clatworthy, George, late of NYC, dec'd—accounts with estate to be settled with admins., Alexander Robertson, Thomas Crabb, and Archibald M'Vicker (3/23)

Nold, Philip, Dutch indented servant, age c. 30—runaway March 8, with one John George Herman; reward for capture will be paid by Benjamin Kendall in Phila. or Samuel Bowne in NYC (3/23)

Fergus, Robert, of Amelia Co., Va., age 83—married March 3 to Anne Jones, age between 14 and 15 (3/30)

Draper, Samuel, of Boston, co-partner with Richard Draper, publisher of the *Massachusetts Gazette*—died March 21 in Boston in his 30th year (3/30)

Rodman, Thomas, of Newport, R.I., master of brig *Dolphin*—drowned when brig foundered on passage from Bay of Honduras to Jamaica (3/30)

Warder, Mrs. Lydia, widow of late John Warder of Phila.; she was born 1680 in London and came to Phila. with her father, John Goodson, at about the time Phila. was founded; she was a Quaker—died March 16 in Phila. in her 87th year (3/30)

Moore, Henry, of Cranbury, N.J., formerly a schoolmaster in NYC—about March 20, when returning home from Spotswood, fell from horse and died the next day (3/30)

Abel, Lodwick, a German servant, age c. 24—runaway March 1 from Jacob Speira, gardiner, of NYC (3/30)

Dickenson, William, age c. 17, apprentice to Timothy Phelps, of Hartford, Conn.—accidentally killed March 16 at East Hartford when gun of ferryman went off (4/6)

Dunn, John, of NYC, an elderly man, who went with 14-year-old son in a small schooner to fetch oysters—drowned April 1 in Rockaway Bay (4/6)

Porter, Stephen, age c. 34, born in Bristol, England, murderer of Capt. Wescot of Liverpool—supposed to have arrived about nine months ago in NYC (4/6)

Williams, Richard, a free Negro—April 8 drowned off Merick Beach, about 3 miles from Hempstead Church, L.I., while trying to reach shore from the wreck of ship *Britannia*, Capt. Richards master (4/13)

Wright, Richard, late of NYC, mariner, dec'd—house opposite the French Church for sale (4/13)

Williams, Patrick, "elderly" indented servant, breeches maker—runaway from James Caldwell, of Phila. (4/20)

Green, Jonas, Esq., printer to the Province of Maryland and for upwards of 21 years past publisher of the *Maryland Gazette*—died April 10 in Annapolis; his son succeeds him in the business (4/27)

Helme, Mrs. Agnes, wife of Benjamin Helme, Esq. of NYC—died there Aug. 22 in her 27th year (4/27)

Rice, Samuel, Irish servant, age c. 50—runaway April 16 from James Popham, living at Newark, Newcastle Co., Pa. (4/27)

Schenck, Hendrick, late of Millstone, Somerset Co., N.J., merchant, dec'd—accounts with estate to be settled with Peter Schenck, exec. (4/27)

Izard, Ralph, Esq.—married May 1 to Miss Alice De Lancey, second daughter of Peter De Lancey, Esq., of Westchester (5/4)

McDonagh, James, servant, age 19—runaway April 24 from Darby Doyle, living at Canoe Brook, Essex Co., N.J. (5/4)

Jeffery, John, late of Red Hook, Dutchess Co., NY, merchant—debtors to his estate to pay Mary Jeffery or Anthony Jeffery, of Red Hook (5/4)

Joe, Negro slave, age c. 30—runaway March 24 from William Hendrickson, living at Middletown Point, N.J. (5/11)

Sharp, Elizabeth, age c. 17, born in Hampshire, England, and brought to America last fall by Capt. Clark—runaway from Jacob Bright of Phila. (5/11)

Talbot, St. George—died May 7 at his seat near NYC at an advanced age (5/11)

Walton, Mrs. Mary, wife of William Walton of NYC and daughter of late Hon. James De Lancey, Esq.—died May 9 in NYC in her 31st year (5/11)

Forbes, John, Jr., dec'd—dividend to be paid to his creditors (5/11)

Primus, Negro slave, age c. 23—runaway a few days ago from John Combes of Jamaica, L.I. (5/11)

King, Charity, wife of Aury King, of Orange Town, Orange Co., wheelwright—has eloped from her husband (5/18)

Escaped May 11 from jail of Elizabeth, N.J. (5/18):
  Hardy, John, born in America, fuller, age c. 26
  Gordon, Thomas, born in Scotland, former schoolmaster, age c. 40

Van Nordstrant, Albert, late of NYC, dec'd—accounts with estate to be settled with execs., Garret Van Norstrant, Jacob Durye and Isaac Mead (5/18)

Godfrey, Edward, age c. 19—absconded May 8 from house of Jacob Martin at Piscataqua, N.J. (5/18)

Runaway May 19 from William Johnson and John Beldin, Jr., of Norwalk (5/25):
  Dover, Negro slave, age c. 18, country born
  Siscat, Samuel, Indian mulatto, age c. 19

Cuyler, Henry, dec'd—real estate for sale by execs., Abraham, Henry, John and Tilaman Cuyler (5/25, 7/6)

Feke, Capt., of ship *Peggy*, of Newport, R.I.—drowned when ship was wrecked on way to London (5/25)

Duryee, Capt., of NYC—murdered by Mr. Andrews on voyage from NYC to Antigua (5/25)

Otway, Joseph, Esq., Capt. in the 29th Regt. and Superintendent at the Shore—died in the Gulf May 11 on board sloop of Capt. Gibbs; he left a wife and child (5/25)

Sylvia, Negro slave, age c. 28, formerly slave of Ralph Furman—runaway May 7 from William Stewart, living in King St., NYC (5/25)

Tony, Negro slave, bred with John Middlesworth at Rariton, age c. 35—runaway April 30 from Anthony Tate of Newtown, Bucks Co., Pa. (5/25)

Lyle, Abraham, dec'd—demands on estate to be sent to Waldron Blaw, near the Exchange; those indebted to estate to pay John Van Allen, exec. (5/25)

Perkins, Joseph, late of North Castle, fuller, dec'd—demands on estate to be brought to Charles Green at North Castle; debts to be paid to Charles Green or to James Perkins (now of full age), son of the deceased (6/1)

Breese, Sidney, of NYC, merchant—died there June 10 (6/15)

Kelly, John, Esq., for many years a lawyer in NYC—died there June 9 (6/15) execs. Robert Crommelin and Aug. V. Cortlandt (6/29, 7/6)

Runaway from Daniel Broadhead, living in Macongie Twp., Northampton Co. (6/15):
  Sawny, mulatto slave, age c. 23
  Reed, Joseph, English servant

Vanhall, mulatto servant, age c. 40—runaway June 2 from Abraham Davenport, Esq., of Stanford (6/15)

Unker, Philip, of Phila., carter—died there June 11 after drinking too much cold water when he was overheated (6/22)

Moore, Mrs., wife of Lambert Moore, Esq., Comptroller of Customs, NYC, and daughter of late worshipful Edward Holland, Esq.—died June 14 in NYC in her 37th year and was buried June 15 in family vault in Trinity Churchyard (6/22)

Steymets, Peter, dec'd—accounts with estate to be settled with execs., Christopher and Benjamin Steymets (6/22)

GENEALOGICAL DATA FROM THE NEW-YORK MERCURY

1767

Boone, William, late commander of brig *Mansfield*, bound from Martinico to Phila.—fell overboard June 15 off Cape Hatteras and was drowned (6/29)

Cannon, John, late of NYC, dec'd—accounts with estate to be settled with William Cannon of Phila., brother of the deceased (6/29, 7/6)

Justis, William—June 30 struck dead by lightning at Trenton, N.J. (7/6)

Haynes, Mrs. Joseph, of NYC, widow—died July 2 in NYC and was buried next day in family vault in Trinity Church (7/6)

Vanhall, mulatto man-servant, age c. 40—runaway June 2 from Abraham Hait of Stanford, Conn. (7/6)

Muchmore, Ebenezer, dec'd—estate in upper part of Piscataway, Middlesex Co., N.J., for sale by Lucy Muchmore, Micaiah Dunn and Joseph Fitzrandolph, execs. (7/13)

Roberts, Thomas, dec'd—real estate in NYC and in Great or Hardenburgh Patent for sale; apply to Jane Durham and Thomas Hunt, Jr. (7/13)

Brodrick, John, servant, tailor, age c. 27—runaway May 24, in company with Rose O'Brien, also servant of the subscriber, from Jacob Keiser of Phila. (7/20)

Cato, Negro slave, age c. 40—runaway from Jacob Arden of Kakiat, Orange Co., NY (7/27)

Darby, Samuel, of Canterbury, Conn., age c. 40—killed May 15 by lightning while sitting near chimney in his brother's house in Canterbury (7/27)

Cahoon, George, Jr., of Cumberland Co., Va., age 15 or 16—carried off, with three brothers and three sisters, at about age of 6, by the Iriquois and purchased by a French officer, has just arrived from New Orleans (7/27)

M'Cormick, Alexander, Irishman, age c. 40—escaped July 24 from jail of Morris Co.; reward offered by Sheriff Daniel Cooper (7/27)

Smith, Abraham, Negro, age c. 30, who says he formerly belonged to Benjamin Smith of Rhode Island—now in jail in Orange Town, Orange Co., NY; apply to Ebenezer Wood, undersheriff (7/27)

Nickson, Ashel, servant, age c. 25—runaway July 7 from James Stickney of Newburgh, Ulster Co., NY (7/27)

Fell, Christopher, late of NYC, merchant, dec'd—house and ground between Burling's and Beekman's Slips, on north side of Queen St. and south side of Orange St., for sale; apply to Simon Johnson, one of the execs. (7/27)

Eckenhait [Ekenhout], Maria, late widow of Abraham Tak but formerly widow of Cornelius Vander Heyden—died March 18, 1766, at Middleburg in Zeeland, leaving legacy to legitimate child or children of her son Hendrick Vander Heyden, who lived at Lunenburg, Nova Scotia, and is supposed to have died there in 1761; apply to Messers Herman and John Berens, merchants in London (6/8, 7/27)

Drowned July 21 when a vessel going out of Cow Harbor, L.I., was overset about three miles from shore (8/3):

Weeks, Jonas, boatman

Abbot, John, boatman

Tyron, Ellis, late soldier in the 46th Regt.—July 27 found drowned near the Ferry Stairs in NYC (8/3)

M'Fadden, ——, a woman lately arrived in NYC from Phila.—died July 27 in a fit (8/3)

Gobourn, Henry, of Island of Jamaica, who died in NYC about two years ago—marble monument is now erected to his memory in Trinity Church (8/3)

124

Brass, Adolph, late of NYC, ship chandler, dec'd—accounts with estate to be settled with Mary Brass, admin. (8/3)

Leroy, Grace, wife of John Leroy, of NYC, laborer—has eloped from her husband (8/3)

Regilar, Leonard, dec'd—lot in Montgomery Ward, forming the corner of William and Frankfort Sts., near the High Dutch Lutheran Church, for sale by execs., Phillip Lydig and Peter Grim (8/3)

Tom, Negro slave, baker, age c. 24—runaway July 29 from Matthew Hyer of NYC (8/3)

Lynsen, Abraham, late of NYC, merchant, dec'd—real estate to be sold by Catharine Lynsen, Abraham Lynsen, Thomas Smith and Cary Ludlow (4/13, 8/3)

Depuy, Samuel, dec'd—tracts of land in Smithfield Twp., Northampton Co., Pa., for sale by Nicholas Depuy (8/3)

Johnson, William (*alias* William Herring)—convicted of stealing books out of St. Paul's Church in NYC and sentenced to be executed Aug. 17 (8/10)

Waters, Anthony, daughter of, living on north side of Staten Island—killed Aug. 8 by lightning in her father's house (8/10)

Rogers, Simon, apprentice, age 19—runaway Aug. 4 from Jacob Taylor, shoemaker, of Princetown, N.J. (8/10)

Wilson, Elizabeth Louisa, English servant, age c. 25—runaway Aug. 4 with Simon Rogers, in company of Isaiah, age 21, an apprentice of John Denton (8/10)

Quite, Charles, mulatto slave, half Indian, age c. 28—runaway July 22 from Richard James of Upper Freehold, Monmouth Co., N.J., near Imlay's Town (8/10)

Scanet, Patrick, sailor—died suddenly in Boston on Aug. 3 (8/17)

Smith, ——, of East Haddam, Conn., a young man—found dead there Aug. 6; death supposed to be caused by falling from a log (8/17)

Robinson, ——, sailor—drowned Aug. 11 when he fell from a canoe in Hay Creek, Pa. (8/17)

Hoogland, John, dec'd—on July 20 Abraham Vanness was elected representative from Somerset Co., N.J., in his place (8/17 and 31)

Caron, Capt., very old commander of Island of Bermuda, who made many voyages from NYC—died recently at Turk's Island (8/17)

Bevons, Charles, of Brooklyn, NY—died there Aug. 20 in his 88th year (8/17)

Ferrer, Erasmus, servant, age c. 18—runaway Aug. 18 from John Cree of NYC (8/17)

Kelly, David, Irish servant, barber, age c. 22—runaway June 21 from Joseph Deniston of Nantucket (8/24)

Webster, Martha—Francis Webster will not pay debts she may contract (8/31)

Trench, William, mariner, age c. 24—ran away with stolen goods on Aug. 28 from lodgings on Golden Hill in NYC; reward offered by Daniel Bane (8/31)

Nicoll, Benjamin, Esq., dec'd—debts to estate to be paid to James Duane (8/31)

Coughren, Elenor—her husband, Mathew Coughren, warns all persons to give her no credit (8/31)

Stewart, Robert, of Warwick Twp., Bucks Co., Pa., age c. 50, his son John, age 24, another son Benjamin, age 21, and another son Joseph, age between 13 and 14—died Aug. 24 when overpowered by fumes at the bottom of a well; Robert's brother-in-law was Benjamin Snodgrass; Robert left a wife, a son, and five daughters (9/7)

Clark, Miss, daughter of Capt. Thomas Clark of NYC—arrived first week of September from Bristol as passenger on the *Grace*, Capt. Chambers (9/7)

Keith, William, soldier of the 16th Regt.—found drowned Sept. 6 near the end of Pearl St., NYC (9/7)

Stillwell, Samuel, late of NYC, merchant, dec'd—accounts with estate to be settled with Mrs. Ann Devisme (9/7)

Bigger, James, servant, born in Pa.—runaway Aug. 12 from James Elliot of Bloody Run, Cumberland Co., Pa. (9/7)

Sam, Negro slave, age 22—runaway near end of August from Johannis Hoghtaling of Poughkeepsie Precinct (9/7)

Crommelin, Charles, dec'd—lands in Orange Co. belonging to his estate for sale (9/7)

Bidder, Richard, late of NYC, dec'd—house and lot facing St. Paul's Chapel for sale by Syntyche Bidder, executrix, and Daniel Bidder and William Weaver, execs. (9/14)

Burne, George, age c. 28 or 30—19 of Aug. broke out of jail in Kingston, Ulster Co., NY; reward offered by Sheriff Daniel Graham (9/14)

Hudson, Dr. Seth, noted counterfeiter—lately died of smallpox in Albany (9/21)

Van Ness, Henry, of NYC, painter—killed last week from recoil of musket which he fired (9/21)

De Peyster, Abraham, Esq., Treasurer of NY—died second week in Sept. in his house in NYC in his 74th year and was buried Sept. 19 in vault in Trinity Church (9/21)

Thompson, Adam, of NYC, physician—died Sept. 18 in NYC (9/21)

Agar, Edward, of NYC, chemist, and wife Margaret—Richard Speaight, apprentice to Dr. William Stewart of NYC, admits he spread false and scandalous reports about the Agars (9/21)

Bonnet, Daniel, dec'd—house at upper end of Chapel St. in NYC for sale; apply to Daniel Bonnet, Pener Ricker or Edward Laight, execs. (9/21)

Drowned Aug. 8 in latitude 25 (9/28):

Tabry, Anthony, master of brig *Sally*, bound from Phila. to Hispaniola

Mars, Humphry, mate of brig *Sally*

Sherver, Joseph, mariner on brig *Sally*

Bess, Samuel, mariner on brig *Sally*

Burns, John, mariner on brig *Sally*

Johnson, Sir John, son of Sir William Johnson—arrived Sept. 27 in NYC a passenger on ship *New Edward*, Capt. Thomas Miller, from London (9/28)

Murray, James, of NYC—died there Sept. 23 (9/28)

Provoost, John, of NYC, merchant—died Sept. 24 in his 55th year (9/28)

Livingston, Mrs. Mary, of NYC, wife of Peter Van Brough Livingston and sister of John Provoost—died Sept. 24 in NYC and was buried with her brother Sept. 26 in family vault in Trinity Church (9/28)

Vanderbelt, Cornelius, of Staten Island—Sept. 23 found dead on road leading from courthouse to his dwelling (9/28)

Towrs, Lawrence, laborer—murdered Sept. 12 at house in Hackinsack, N.J., by a Negro (9/28)

Devoore, Mary, wife of David Devoore, of Turtle Bay—husband will not pay debts she may contract (9/28)

Standall, John, dec'd—farm and mills at Grigstown, Somerset Co., West N.J., on Millstone River, about half a mile below Rocky Hill Mines, to be let (9/28)

Hadley, Anthony, of Stoneham, Mass., age 90—perished Sept. 23 in storm while returning home from Boston; leaves a widow and three children (10/5)

Hadley, Mr., of Stoneham, Mass., son of Anthony Hadley, age 52—perished Aug. 23 in storm; leaves a widow and eight children (10/5)

Rumbold, Thomas, late of Long-Alley, near Moorfields, Middlesex Co., Eng., and his brother William, of the same place (sons of Thomas Rumbold, of the same place, stocking trimmer, dec'd, who was son of William Rumbold, heretofore of King's Clere, County of Southampton, yeoman, dec'd.) supposed to have gone to North America about 50 years ago, then about 16 or 17 years of age—if alive, they, or otherwise their heirs are to apply to Capt. Thomas Miller in NYC, Messers Bristow and Winterbottom in London, or James Gwyn in London (10/5)

Havens, Capt. Rhodes, master of ship *Dolphin*, just arrived in Newport, R.I., from NYC —drowned at Newport Oct. 3 (10/12)

Shaw, John, late of NYC, currier, partner of George Shaw, tanner—John is dead and debtors to partnership are to settle accounts with James Shaw (10/12)

Hull, John, age c. 34 or 35—probably impostor, claiming to be son of Col. Hull of Maryland (10/19)

Byrne, Robert, Irish servant, young fellow—runaway Oct. 6 from Charles Ramadge of NYC (10/19)

Lefferts, Abraham, of NYC—died Oct. 22 in his house in NYC in his 75th year, leaving three older brothers (10/26)

M'Kean, Rev. Robert, Rector of Perth Amboy—died there Oct. 17 in his 35th year (10/26)

Hart, Daniel, of Hunterdon Co., N.J.—murdered Oct. 12 by his Negro slave (10/26)

Abraham, Indian slave, age c. 23—runaway Oct. 21 from John Thomas, Esq., of Westchester Co. NY (10/26)

Ritchey, Jude, wife of Alexander Ritchey—has eloped from her husband (10/26)

Stevens (or Stephens), James, Esq., captain in the Royal Train of Artillery—died Oct. 31 in NYC in his 43rd year (11/2 and 11/9)

M'Namar, Daniel, Irish servant, perukemaker and haircutter, formerly servant of Capt. Wilson of the 59th Regt., age c. 16—runaway Oct. 31 from Alexander Leslie of NYC (11/9)

Bache, Richard, of Phila., merchant—Oct. 29 married Miss Sally Franklin, only daughter of Benjamin Franklin of Phila. (11/9)

Branson, Catharine (*alias* Hannah Harding), an Irishwoman—convicted of grand larceny and hanged Nov. 23 in NYC (11/9 and 11/30)

Miller, John, Irish servant, age c. 26—runaway Nov. 1 from Francis Kofeler of Brooklyn Ferry (11/9)

Carpenter, John J., merchant, dec'd—house and farm in New Windsor for sale by execs., Hezekiah Howell, Jr., and Jane Carpenter (11/9)

Runaway Nov. 7 from John and Isaac Holloway of Reckless Town, Burlington Co., N.J. (11/16):

  Barker, Peter, apprentice, tailor, age c. 20

  Jones, John, apprentice, shoemaker, age c. 17 or 18

Drowned in wreck of ship at Cape Cod (11/16):

  Babcock, Jonathan, passenger on a vessel belonging to Stonington, Conn.

  Minor, Mr., passenger on vessel from Stonington

  Griffin, Mr., passenger on vessel from Stonington

Muirson, Mrs. Mary, wife of George Muirson, Esq., of Brookhaven, Suffolk Co., NY—died there Oct. 23 of a lingering illness and was buried Oct. 25 in family burying-place on Manor of St. Georges (11/16)

Evans, Edward, of Barrington, N.H.—lately died there at age of 100 (11/30)

St. Clair, Hon. Col. Sir John—died in Elizabeth Town, N.J., last Thursday week and was buried following Saturday (12/7)

Runaway Nov. 28 from Conrad Kotts and Richard Borden of Trentown, N.J. (12/7):

  Simons, Henry, Irish servant, tailor

  Gillgruse, James, Irish servant, shoemaker

Morris, Mrs., belonging to the Play-House—drowned, together with her maid, last week when scow was overturned as they were crossing the Kill Vankull (12/14)

Disseau, John Babtist, servant, born in Canada, age c. 14—runaway Nov. 10, in company with Joseph Fletcher, age c. 17, son of Joseph Fletcher of NYC, from John Lilburn (12/14)

Neilson, James, dec'd—woodland in South Ward of Perth Amboy for sale (12/14)

Buckly, Mr., a pilot, of NYC—fell overboard Dec. 21 in the Narrows and died of exposure (12/21)

Pratt, Mrs. Margaret, of Boston—died there in the Alms House at age of 100 (12/28)

Fitch, Capt., of Windham, Conn., four-year-old son of—died Nov. 24 from having a pea lodged in his throat (12/28)

Bowman, Christian, a German, age c. 60, who was captured about 10 years ago by Indians, who killed his wife and children—lately escaped and came to NYC (12/28)

Gage, General—last Tuesday twins, a boy and a girl born to him (12/28)

Hunter, Mr., an artilleryman—died Dec. 26 in NYC from wound from a cutlass in a fray with a barber named Lysler (12/28)

Reilley, Dennis, servant, age 30—runaway Dec. 12 from ship *Three Brothers*, John Gwinn captain, lying in NY harbor (12/28)

1768

Wessels, Francis Van Dyck, who appparenely had stolen a schooner—drowned at New Haven, Conn., in Nov., 1767 (1/4)

Ormes, Dr. Samuel, of Phila., dec'd—goods to be sold (1/11)

Van Vleck, Catharine, dec'd—house and lot in Broad St., near City Hall in NYC, for sale; apply to John Van Vleck, Luke John Kiersted and Isaac Ryckman, execs (1/11)

Wilson, John, late of Flushing, dec'd—estate for sale; apply to execs., Mary Wilson on the premises, or John Thorn or John Field, Jr., of Flushing (1/11)

Hamilton, Andrew—Jan. 6 in Phila. married Miss Abigail Franks, daughter of David Franks, Esq., of Phila. (1/18)

Marston, John, of NYC, merchant—Jan. 7 in Phila. married Miss Rachel Lawrence, daughter of Thomas Lawrence, Esq., late Mayor of Phila. (1/18)

Breese, Samuel, NYC, merchant—Jan. 7 in Phila. married Miss Anderson of Phila. (1/18)

Drowned middle of last week while crossing North River from Great Wapping's Kill in a sleigh (1/18):

Polhemus, Daniel

Mills, Mr., merchant

Brigs, James

Houston, Mr.

Brockhurst, Mrs., late of NYC, dec'd—two houses and lots in Stone St. for sale (1/25)

De Bevoeise, Jacobus, late of Gowanus, dec'd—farm for sale; apply to Johannis De Bevoeise in Brooklyn or Jacobus De Bevoeise, execs., or Nancy De Bevoeise, executrix (1/25)

Tingley, Capt. Samuel, dec'd—house, storehouse and water lot, near Beekman's Slip, for sale (1/25)

Philips, Alexander, an Irishman, weaver, age c. 20—absconded Jan. 18 from house of Peter Reade at Cakeat, Orange Co. NY (1/25)

Leake, Andrew, dec'd—property adjoining his mill and lands in Bedminster Twp., Somerset Co., N.J., for sale (1/25)

The New-York Mercury ceased publication as such on 25 January 1768. Beginning with the issue of 1 February 1768, the paper was known as *The New-York Gazette; and The Weekly Mercury,* and so continued until 10 November 1783. Dr. Scott's abstracts of genealogical data from the combined newspaper will be carried in alternate issues of THE RECORD, starting in October. In July and January issues a new series of genealogical abstracts from an unusual source will be printed.

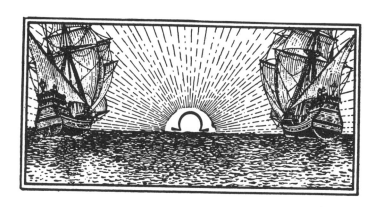

GENEALOGICAL DATA FROM THE NEW-YORK GAZETTE
AND THE WEEKLY MERCURY

1768

Mease, John, of Philadelphia, merchant—died there Jan. 11, 1768, and was buried Jan. 13 in the burial ground of the First Presbyterian Church (2/1)

Stoops, Nicholas, seaman on board brig *Friendship*, Capt. Gilbert, bound from Philadelphia to Bristol—washed overboard and drowned Nov. 12, 1767 (2/1)

Neville, Francis, Irish servant, age c. 20—runaway from Samuel Sykes of Chesterfield, Burlington Co., West New Jersey (2/1)

Bydder, Richard, late of NYC, dec'd—house and lot adjoining the Five-Alley in NYC for sale by execs., Syntyche Bydder, William Weaver and Daniel Bydder (2.1)

Talbot, St. George, dec'd—real estate for sale by execs., John Livingston and Jeremiah Leaming (2/1)

Tingley, Capt. Samuel, dec'd—house, storehouse and water lot near Beekman's Slip in NYC for sale by William Malcolm (2/1)

Philips, Alexander, Irish lad, age c. 20—absconded Jan. 18, 1768, from house of Peter Reade at Cakeat, Orange Co., NY (2/1)

Reading, Hon. John, Esq., late President of the Council of New Jersey—died at Amwell, N.J., Nov. 5, 1767, at an advanced age (2/8)

Imlay, Peter, son of John Imlay, Esq., of Bordentown, N.J.,—died there on his twentieth birthday (2/8)

Died of exposure in wreck of Staten Island ferry Jan. 28 (2/8):

George, William Cornelius, said to belong to Rhode Island

Bury, William, lad belonging to the ferry

Groen, Jacob Marius, dec'd—houses belonging to his estate in Pearl St., NYC, for sale; apply to Silvester Marius Groen (2/8)

Provoost, John, Esq., dec'd—accounts with estate to be settled with execs., Eve and Samuel Provoost (supplement of 2/8)

De Bevoeise, Jacobus, late of Gowanus, dec'd—farm for sale; apply to Johannis, Jacobus or Nancy De Bevoeise, execs. (supplement of 2/8)

Kipp, Capt.—died in wreck of his schooner near Member Rock (2/15)

Arnold, Capt. Henry, dec'd—house within half a mile of the church in Shrewsbury, N.J., for sale by execs., Sarah Arnold and James Sackett (2/15)

Buise, John, late of the Outward of NYC, dec'd—accounts with estate to be settled with execs., John Hardenbrook and Matthew Buise (2/15)

Thomas, Sarah, widow, of Elizabeth Town, N.J.—house for rent; apply to Edward Thomas (2/15)

Cox, Lt. George, of the Artillery—died in July, 1767, on board ship *Good Intent*, Capt. William Bett master, bound from Senegal to Teneriffe (2/22)

Johnson, Hezekiah, dec'd—one half of his house and lot situated about two miles from Newark on the main road to Elizabeth Town, N.J., for sale; apply to Moses Scott (2/22)

Dobbins, Mrs., dec'd—accounts with estate to be settled with William M'Kinly (2/22)

Ketteltas, John, of NYC, merchant—died there Feb. 28 in his 29th year (2/29)

Bratt, Catharine, dec'd—house on west side of Smith St., in NYC, for sale by execs., William Heyer, Jeremiah Wood, and Lawrence Wessels, Jr., (2/29)

De Peyster, Abraham, Esq., dec'd, late Treasurer of NY—his execs. by act of Assembly are ordered to make certain payments to present treasurer, Abraham Lott (2/29)

Palmer, Silas, indented servant, born in New England, age c. 25—runaway about Jan. 6 from Mary Moore of Morris-Town, East New Jersey (2/29)

Studden, John, mate of ship commanded by Capt. Farrell—accidentally killed Feb. 12 on ship off Carolina (3/7)

Drowned March 4 when boat belonging to Daniel Marlin of Marlin's Cove, Manor of Philipsborough, overset while going up the North River about 14 miles from NYC (3/7):

Barnard, James

Marlin, Abraham, of NYC, blacksmith

Van Tassal, William

Zuriker, John, son of Mr. Zuriker, of NYC, stonecutter

Drowned Dec. 15, 1767, when ferryboat, crossing from Connecticut to Narraganset, was overset (3/14):

Greene, Russell, of East Greenwich, merchant

Perry, Mr., who had just returned home from having been two years at sea

Shearman, Mr., of Narraganset

Sheffield, Mr., the ferryman

Burger, Deborah, dec'd—brick house opposite Peck's Slip, NYC, late her property, for sale (3/14)

Kast, Johan Jurgh—land in Albany County granted in 1724 to him, his wife

Anna, his children, Ludwick, Sarah, Dorothy, Margaret, Elizabeth, Mary and Anna Mary, and to Gertruy (wife of Johan Jurgh Kast, Jr.) and to Sarah and Dorothy (daughters of Johan Jurgh Kast, Jr.) (3/14)

Armstrong, Mr., from Dublin, merchant—washed overboard and drowned about Feb. 15 while a passenger on Capt. Eaton's schooner, bound from Dublin to NY (3/21)

Taylor, Mary, late of Chiseldon, Wilts, England, who came to NY some years since—if living she is to apply to Eleazer M'Comb at house of John Morton, merchant, NYC (3/21)

Bahanna, Thomas, dec'd—property on Bahanna's Island for sale by Widow Bahanna (3/21)

Frokinger, Johannis, servant, from Germany—runaway from John Slidell, of NYC, soapboiler and tallow chandler (3/21)

Moore, Augustine, Esq., attorney, of Morris Town, N.J., dec'd—accounts with estate to be settled with executrix, Mary Moore (3/28)

Stoughton, John, Esq., late of the Landing Place at Ticonderoga—accounts with estate to be settled with executrix, Ruth Stoughton (3/28)

Blair, Gilbert, mate of the brig *Diamond,* Capt. Craw master—murdered Dec. 31, 1767, by one of the crew (4/4)

Brinckerhoff, Jacob, dec'd—farm on the north side of the Fishkills, Dutchess Co., where the widow lives, for sale; apply to the execs., John and Isaac Brinckerhoff (4/4)

Waters, Benjamin, of Newtown, L.I., dec'd—house for sale (4/11)

Hoy, Hugh K., late of NYC, dec'd—accounts with estate to be settled with Anne Hoy, admin. (4/18)

Hambach, Frederick, a German, an Indian trader, who served as an officer in the provincial forces of Pa.—murdered Jan. 9 by Indians in an Indian village on the Miamis River (5/2)

Rogers, Mr., an Indian trader, a relative of Major Rogers—murdered by Indians about the beginning of February at St. Joseph's (5/2)

Stephens, Francis, storekeeper and paymaster of H.M.'s Ordinance in NYC—married April 28 to Miss Polly Reade, daughter of Hon. Joseph Reade, Esq., of NYC (5/2)

Conyn, Tryntie, wife of Casparus Conyn, Jr., of Claverack—has eloped from her husband and taken his child with her (5/2)

Renaudet, James, dec'd—house and lot, now in possession of Samuel Cowdery, hatter, between Burling's Slip and Beekman's Slip, for sale; apply to Adrian Renaudet, exec. (5/2)

Frasier, Isaac, convicted of burglary and of setting fire to the Fairfield, Conn., jail—sentenced to be hanged (5/9)

Walter, John, dec'd—house and lot in Hanover Sq., NYC, seized and to be sold (5/9)

Schuyler, Anne Elizabeth, dec'd—accounts with estate to be settled with Abraham Lott (5/9)

Brett, Sarah, wife of Francis Brett, Jr., of Fishkills—has eloped from her husband (5/9)

Wilson, Godfrey, who left Yorkshire about 40 years ago and resided some time at the Yallows, Island of Jamaica, carpenter, painter and glazier—if alive, is requested to apply to John Wilson, agent to Mr. Robinson, in London (5/9)

Sparker, Henry, of Newport, R.I., shoemaker—run through and killed with a sword on May 3 in a brawl with officers from H.M.'s sloop *Senegal* at Newport (5/16)

Phillipse, Philip, Esq., of NYC— died May 9 at his house in King St., NYC, in his 44th year (5/16)

Stearndall, John, of Rockey-Hill, dec'd—accounts with estate to be settled with Richard Curson, admin., or Jacob Bergen, Esq., of Rockey-Hill (5/16)

Harre, Negro slave, who has lived with Mr. Dingman of Kinderhook, age 30 or 35—runaway from Philip Schuyler (5/16)

Haynes, Joseph, merchant, dec'd—country house and stables, about three miles from NYC, on road to Bloomindale, for sale by John Dyckman (5/16)

Stephen, Capt. Alexander, late an officer in H.M.'s Royal American Regt.—died May 8 in Frederick County, Va. (5/23)

Myer, John, late of Haerlem, dec'd—real estate at Haerlem formerly belonging to Adolph Myer, dec'd and now in possession of the Widow Myer, for sale by John Roberts, sheriff (5/23)

Bealie, Thomas, an Englishman—escaped from jail of Sussex Co. (5/23)

Runaway April 6 from Chang Water Forge in Sussex Co. (5/23):
  Newton, Jacob, born in New England, blacksmith and collier, age c. 37
  Morris, William, age c. 35

Murphy, Thomas, Irish servant, shoemaker, age c. 20—taken away by runaways from Chang Water Forge in Sussex Co. (5/23)

King, Matthew, Irish servant, age c. 17—runaway about Sept. 1, 1767, from Marcus King, living near Pluckhimin in Somerset Co., N.J. (5/30)

Adams, George, Irish servant, age c. 18—runaway May 26 from Daniel Remsen, of Jamaica, L.I. (5/30)

Perkins, Lt., of the Royal Irish Regt.—fell overboard and was drowned May 26 while coming in stage boat from Burlington, N.J. (6/6)

Hadden, Bartholomew, of Westchester, "a poor old blind man"—his Negro slave Hannable ran away from him on April 23 (6/6)

Thompson, Alexander, dec'd—land in Perth Amboy, N.J., for sale by executrix, Barshaba Thompson (6/6)

Brunce, Negro slave, age c. 30—runaway May 18 from Charles Erersole of Reading Twp., Hunterdon Co., East New Jersey (6/6)

Bensen, Robert, dec'd—dwelling, brewhouse and malthouse for sale by Widow Catharine Bensen (6/6)

Hugont, Peter, dec'd—property in Scotch St., NYC, for sale (6/13)

Runaway Feb. 29 from John Jones and Phineas Lockwood, of NYC (6/13):
  Davis, Squire, apprentice shoemaker, age c. 18
  Street, Nathaniel, apprentice shoemaker, age c. 18

Peter, Negro slave, shoemaker and baker, age c. 35—runaway June 1 from Adam Simmons, of Rye, Westchester Co., NY (suppl. to 6/13)

Jonas, Negro slave, age c. 24—runaway June 6 from Stephen Ward of East Chester, Westchester Co., NY (suppl. to 6/13)

Dowell, Capt. William, of Phila.—died there June 8 in his 49th year (6/20)

Willett, Thomas, late of NYC, dec'd—accounts with estate to be settled with execs., Elizabeth and Christopher Willett (6/20)

Harry, Negro slave, age 40—runaway June 4 from John Acton, of Pumpton, N.J. (6/20)

Shier, Negro slave, caulker, age c. 40—runaway from Caleb Cornwell, of Hempstead, Queens Co., L.I. (6/ 20)

Wright, John, late of Flushing, dec'd—house for sale; apply to execs., James Buvelot and John Field, Jr. (6/27)

Richardson, Thomas, of Annapolis, Md., merchant, a "young" man—killed by lightning June 16 in a room at Mr. Adair's in Baltimore (7/4)

Wiley, William, a native of NY, an "eminent" distiller—died May 30 at Middletown, N.J., in his 28th year (7/4)

M'Kinzie, James, Irish servant, age c. 25—runaway from John Macomb of Hosack, near Albany (7/4)

M'Donald, Catharine, wife of Collin M'Donald, of the Manor of Livingston, Albany Co., NY—has eloped from her husband (7/4)

Ryall, Capt. Joseph, late of NYC, dec'd—household effects to be auctioned off at his house near the Merchant's Coffee-House (7/11)

Kip, Isaac, dec'd—farm at Rynbeck, Dutchess Co., for sale (7/11)

Lawler, James, born in Ireland, age c. 23 or 24—taken up by Benjamin Blagge, Esq., and committed to Bridewell; says he belongs to Cornelius Ten Broek, Esq., of Albany (7/11)

Walton, Hon. William, Esq., member of Council and eminent merchant of NYC—died there July 11 in his 63rd year and was buried July 13 in the family vault in Trinity Church (7/18); accounts with estate to be settled with execs., William and Jacob Walton (7/25)

Seal, Thomas, born in west of England, a matross, age 27; has a wife, born in Ireland, age c. 32, who was a nurse in Phila. and was formerly married to a Mr. McClone—has deserted from Capt. David Hay's company of the Royal Regt. of Artillery (7/18)

Ladley, Rev. Archibald, minister of the Dutch Church in NYC—married July 11 in NYC to Miss Polly Hoffman, daughter of Col. Martin Hoffman (7/25)

Bush, John, apprentice to a mason, age c. 19—while working on the Dutch Church in NYC on July 20 fell 40 ft. to the ground and died within two hours (7/25)

Smith, Mr., a young man lately from Boston—on June 30, at New Haven, Conn., diving from a scow at East River Ferry, dislocated his neck and died the next day (7/825)

Kidd, Francis, Irish servant, weaver by trade—runaway July 14 from Samuel Rowland, of Charlotte Precinct, Dutchess Co., NY (7/25)

Whyte, Alexander, born in Ireland, late clerk of the markets in NYC, a former captain in the NY Provincials, who had been with Col. Bradstreet in 1763 and 1764—runaway from his special bail (7/25)

Vanberentlau, John Henry, a Dutchman, age c. 45—accused by John Little, living on Schuylerkill, of stealing horses (7/25)

Sullivan, Daniel, servant who came from Ireland about a year ago, tailor by trade —runaway July 6 from John Galloway (7/25)

Weyman, William, noted printer of NYC—died July 27 in NYC (8/1)

Norway, Negro slave, who once lived with William Ralston, innholder in Phila., age c. 33—runaway July 29 from William Provoost in NYC (8/1)

Barker, Samuel, late of NYC, dec'd—house on Cowfoot Hill, opposite to Mrs. Walton's, in NYC, now in the possession of Richard Barker, to be sold at auction (8/1)

Walters, William, Welch servant, mason by trade, who came to NYC in the ship *New-Hope* from Bristol and who has as wife a Welch woman, age c.45—runaway from John Gifford, of NYC (8/1)

Van Tine, Mary, wife of John Van Tine—has eloped from her husband (8/1)

Brown, John, hired servant, born in Switzerland—left home of Christopher Heysham, in Flushing, on July 26 and is urged to return (8/8)

Provoost, John, Esq., dec'd—accounts with estate to be settled with Eve Provoost, executrix (8/8)

Moore, Miss Fanny, youngest daughter of William Moore, Esq., of Morehall, Chester Co., Pa.—died there Aug. 1 in her 23rd year (8/8)

Meader, George, who came to NYC from England four years ago and taught school in NYC—found dead in his chamber in NYC on Aug. 4 (8/8); accounts with his estate to be settled with Henry Grigg, admin. (8/22)

Woodruff, Hon. Samuel, Esq., member of Council of N.J.—died Aug. 11 in Elizabeth Town, N.J. (8/22); his goods to be sold by admins., Elizabeth, Benjamin, Joseph, Jr., and Isaac Woodruff (9/5)

Harber, Thomas, an Irishman—stole items from Matthias Burnet of Hanover in Morristown, N.J., and ran away July 12; reward for his capture offered by Matthias Burnet and James Wilkinson (8/22)

Furman, Mrs. Ezekiel, of Newtown, L.I.—last Sunday took ill in meeting-house and died at house of Mr. Fish of that place (8/22)

Eckerman, Jacob J., of Orange Co., NY—in jumping over a fence wounded himself with an axe and bled to death (8/22)

Abbet, Mr., of NYC, undertaker—injured Aug. 26 by rafter falling from house of Mr. Quackenboss of NYC and died (8/29)

Runaway Aug. 20 from Henry A. Frankin and Peter Remsen (8/29):

Garrick, Negro slave, born in St. Kitts, age 20

Quash, Negro slave, born in Island of Jamaica, who has been in NY two years, age c. 18

Poillion, Abraham, dec'd—farm on south side of Staten Island, near the Great Kill, for sale by Peter Poillion (8/29)

Stephen, sometimes called Pompey, "young" Indian servant—runaway Aug. 15 from William Mott, of Great Neck, L.I. (8/29)

Foster, John, apprentice "lad," born in the Jersies—runaway from Robert Andrews (9/5)

Vincent, Charles, servant, age c. 25—runaway May 1 from Ezra Kirttand, of Stratford, Conn. (9/5)

Burger, Widow, dec'd—her Negro slave named Kate has run away; Joseph Burger warns against harboring the runaway (9/5)

Lawson, James, Irish servant, age c. 21—runaway Sept. 11 from Abraham Lawrence, of Flushing, L.I. (9/12)

Brinkerhoft, Joris, of NYC—died there Sept. 3 at a very advanced age (9/12); accounts with estate to be settled with execs., Dirck, Abraham and Dirck Brinckerhoof, Jr., and Abraham Van Deursen (10/10)

Walton, Madam, of NYC—died there Sept. 3 in her 90th year (9/12)

M'Evers, James, of NYC, merchant—died Sept. 8 in his 40th year and was buried Sept. 10th in family vault in Trinity Churchyard (9/12); accounts with estate to be settled with execs., Eilzabeth and Charles M'Evers and Charles W. Apthorp (9/19)

Schermerhorn, Capt. John, of NYC—died there Sept. 10 (9/12)

Watson, John, late of Perth Amboy, N.J., merchant, dec'd—accounts with estate to be settled (9/19)

Stevenson, Thomas, late of NYC, mariner, dec'd—accounts with estate to be settled with adminis., Daniel Stevenson and James Stewart (9/19)

Clarke, James Hill, an Indian trader at Myamic River—shot and killed by John Myers, his interpreter, a Frenchman (9/19)

Caesar, Negro slave of Garret Middagh—executed Sept. 16 at Flatbush, L.I., for robbery of house of Widow Rapalje at Brooklyn Ferry (9/19)

Lefferts, Jacobus, of Bedford, L.I.—died there Sept. 8 in his 83rd year and was buried Sept. 10 in the family vault; he leaves three older brothers (9/19)

Van Horne, Mrs. Catharine, dec'd—house next to house of Mr. John Dalley in NYC for sale (9/19)

Grumbley, Christopher, late of NYC, Irish servant, age c. 22—runaway from Patrick Smyth (9/19)

Davidson, David, late of NYC, cabinetmaker, dec'd—affairs of his partnership with James Strachan to be settled (9/26)

Lawrence, Thomas, merchant, son of Thomas Lawrence, Esq.—married Sept. 22 in Phila. to Miss Rebecca Bond, daughter of Dr. Thomas Bond (10/3)

Bagley, Josiah, dec'd—house in Broad St., near the City Hall in NYC, for sale by Martha Bagley (10/3)

Vanderbelt, John, dec'd—farm at Cow-Neck, L.I., for sale by execs., John and Garret

Vanderbelt and Petrus and Hend. Onderdonck (10/10)

Harford, John, an Irishman, tailor by trade, living in Strawberry Ally, Phila., who formerly worked for Mr. Ennis Graham, tailor, near the Coffee House in Phila. —absconded from his bail; reward for his capture offered by Thomas Harrison (10/10)

Moore, John, born in Ireland, wagon- and chairmaker, who formerly worked at the Fishkills—escaped from Jeremiah Colmon, Undersheriff for Orange Co., NY, on north side of the Highlands (10/10)

Smith, Henry, dec'd—property in hands of executrix, Ann Wickham, has been seized and is to be sold by Sheriff Daniel Graham (10/10)

Mullin, Thomas, Irish servant, age c. 26—runaway Sept. 18 from George Reirson, living at Foster's Meadow, Hempstead, L.I. (10/10)

M'Cowen, Thomas, apprentice tanner and currier, age c. 19—runaway last Thursday from James M'Cartney, in Bayard St., NYC (10/10)

Escaped a few days ago from jail of Morris Co., N.J. (10/17):

Smith, John, born in Ireland, age 45

Harbor, Thomas, born in Ireland, a "young" fellow

Temple, Grenville, son of Hon. John Temple, Esq.—born last week and baptized Oct. 23 in Trinity Church, Boston, with General Gage and Robert Temple, Esq., as godfathers (10/31)

Reading, Capt. Daniel, of Amwell, N.J., son of the Hon. John Reading, dec'd—accidentally shot while hunting and died Oct. 15 (10/31)

Brown, William, Irish servant, age 17—runaway Oct. 29 from Henry Grigg, of NYC, innkeeper (10/31)

Marton, Rebecca, wife of John Marton, of Phillipsburgh—has eloped from her husband (11/7)

Therlo, John, master of a sloop belonging to Mr. Weight, of Casco Bay—shot and killed Sept. 4, off St. Pierre, Martinique, by the mate of the Guarda Coasta there (11/2)

Morgan, Lawrence—was washed overboard Oct. 16 from ship of Capt. Blewer, bound from Pensacola to Phila., and drowned (11/3)

Noke, Negro slave, age c. 16—runaway from estate of John Schermerhorne, dec'd reward for his capture offered by execs., Luke Van Ranst, Isaac Sears, Jeremiah Brower and Lawrence Kortright (11/21)

Lewis, John, of the Out-Ward of NYC—on Nov. 22 his daughter, aged 4, died from accidental burns (11/28)

Van Duehren, Rev. J. Bernardus, dec'd—property at Stone Arabia, Albany Co., NY, belonging to his heirs, for sale (11/28)

Brower, Nicholas, Jr.—is separated from his wife Mary (12/5)

Nicoll, William, Esq., member for Suffolk Co. of the House of Representatives of NY—Dec. 3, on way from his lodgings on north side of Hempstead Plains to NYC, was taken ill and died at house of Capt. Timothy Smith, on Hempstead Plains (12/5)

Willet, Thomas, dec'd—houses, one in Dock St. and the other in Bayard St., NYC, for sale by Elizabeth Willet (12/12)

Cuff, Negro slave, age c. 25—runaway from Elbert Herring, of NYC (12/19)

Boyd, Adam, who lately arrived in Phila. from Barbados, son of William Boyd, Esq., late of Drumawolling, and grandson of Col. Boyd, late of Ballycastle, County of Antrim, Ireland—died Dec. 1 in Phila. at age of 20 (12/19)

French, John, Esq., late of NYC, dec'd—demands on his estate are to be settled with the widow or with Abraham Schank, Esq., exec. (12/19)

Billie, Negro slave of Hon. John Taylor, Esq., age c. 30—runaway about Oct. 10 from Neabsco Iron Works in Va. (12/19)

GENEALOGICAL DATA FROM THE NEW-YORK GAZETTE; AND THE WEEKLY MERCURY

1768

Scipio, Negro slave of John M'Millian, of Prince William Co., Va., age c. 30—runaway together with Billie (12/19)

Patterson, Capt., master of sloop in coasting business from Boston to Kennebeck—drowned Dec. 4 in wreck of sloop, with two of crew, Mr. Rogers and Mr. Kinney, and the following passengers from Pownalborough

Allen, Capt. Thomas Holberton

Chapman, Ralph (who had a wife and five children)

Barker, John

Perry, Mr.

Pierce, John

Hersey, Mr.

Fitch, Mrs., wife of Jonas Fitch and mother of five children

Mrs. Stilsen, a Dutch woman. (12/26)

O'Reiley, Rev. F. Luke, of St. Croix—died Dec. 13 in Phila. (12/26)

Sawn, Richard, of Phila., hatter—died there Dec. 18 (12/26)

Abbot, Abijah, late of NYC, carpenter, dec'd—accounts with estate to be settled with executrix, Mary Abbot (12/26)

1769

Partridge, Capt. Samuel—married Dec. 13, 1768, in Boston to Miss Elizabeth Hubbart (1/2)

Franklin, Mrs. Elizabeth, widow of John Franklin, of Boston, dec'd (brother of Benjamin Franklin of Phila.)—died Dec. 16, 1768, in Boston at age of 71 (1/2)

Deane, Capt. Le Chevalier, of NYC—died on his passage from Jamaica to the Bay and was buried at Rattan (1/2)

Ogden, Moses, late of Elizabeth Town, N.J., dec'd—accounts with estate to be settled with execs., Mary, Robert, Jr., and John Cousens Ogden (1/2)

Bagley, Josiah, dec'd—house in Broad St., near City Hall, NYC, for sale; accounts with estate to be settled with Martha Bagley (1/2)

Troup, Capt. Robert—died Dec. 28, 1768, at his seat in Morris Co., N.J., aged 60 (1/9)

Johnson, James, servant, born at Holyhead, Wales—runaway Jan. 15 from William Dobbs and James Taylor (1/16)

Franks, Jacob, eminent merchant of NYC—died there Jan. 16 and was buried Jan. 17 in the Jews Burying Place (1/23); the home in which the family of the late Mr. Franks lives is to be let; enquire of Anne Chambers (1/30)

Jim, Negro slave, age c. 30—runaway in November, 1768, from William Hyer, living at Middletown Point, East New Jersey (1/23)

Gregory, Richard Fletcher, confined for debt in jail of Amherst County, Va.—died Dec. 5, 1768, in burning of the jail (1/30)

Strachan, James, of NYC, cabinetmaker—Jan. 25, walking along dock near Burling's Slip, he tripped on a rope, fell into the river, and was drowned (1/30); accounts with estate to be settled with widow, Catharine Strachan, admin. (2/6)

M'Daniel, James, who came to America from Ireland "about last June Twelvemonth," age c. 20—is asked to communicate with Edes and Gill at Boston (1/30)

Graham, Robert, convict, age c. 40—broke out of Kingston jail at latter end of Nov., 1768; reward for his capture offered by Daniel Graham, sheriff (2/6)

Marshall, William, son of Henry Marshall, of Manor Cunningham, County Danne-
gall, Ireland—is asked to apply to Capt. George Marshal in NYC or to Thompson and Alexander (2/6)

De Foreest, Henry, dec'd—printing press and types for sale; enquire of widow,
Susanna De Foreest in NYC (2/13)

Stevenson, James, Esq., who resided upwards of 40 years in Albany—died there
Feb. 2 in his 72nd year (2/13)

Tucker, Dr. James, late physician in Surinam—died Feb. 15 in NYC (2/20)

Seaman, David, late of Oyster Bay, Queens Co., NY, dec'd—farm for sale by execs.,
Zebulon, William and David Seaman and Richard Willets (2/20)

Rea, Capt. Richard, dec'd—accounts with estate to be settled with George Brewerton,
Jr., exec. (2/27)

Reuter, Valentine, German servant, age c. 15—runaway Feb. 23 from John W.
Polleman (2/27)

Braine, Thomas, dec'd—property near Schenectady for sale; apply to Jacob Banks,
of Jamaica, Queens Co., L.I. (2/27)

Kass, Mr., a German—murdered by a Cayuga Indian a few days ago at German
Flats, NY (3/6)

Dido, Negro slave, age c. 17 or 18—runaway March 2 from her mistress, Mrs.
Horsmanden, of NYC (3/6)

Brinckerhoff, Joris, dec'd—accounts with estate to be settled with execs., Dirck,
Abraham and Dirck Brinckerhoff, Jr., and Abraham Van Duersen (3/6)

Robbins, Samuel, an Indian boy, age c. 18, who, at St. Croix, entered the brigantine
Minerva, Adam Babcock owner and William Sherman master—will be paid five
dollars by Phineas Stanton, Jr., if he will appear at Superior Court to be held
at Norwich, Conn., the fourth Tuesday of March next (3/13)

Leonard, Henry, dec'd—farm at Canoe Brook, N.J., late his property, for sale; enquire of David Ogden, Esq., of Newark (3/13)

Deserted March 9 at NYC from H.M.'s 16th Regt. of Foot (3/13):
 Bullfinch, John, born in Cloness, North of Ireland, laborer
 Claire, Robert, born in Dublin, Ireland, stocking-weaver, age 23
 Broome, James, born in Birmingham, England, cutler, age 29

Forbes, Gilbert, of NYC, ironmonger—died March 7, in NYC, of inflammation of the
lungs, leaving a widow and numerous children (3/13)

Van Tuyl, Otto, dec'd—farm and ferry to be let by his execs., Jacob and Cornelius
Corsen and Benjamin Seaman (3/13)

Brockols, Mary, dec'd—farm at Rye, Westchester Co., NY, estate of John Crawford,
to be sold at suit of her execs., David Van Horne, Beverly Robinson, William
Livingston and David Clarkson (3/20)

Ned, Negro slave, age c. 20—runaway March 13 from Samuel Smith, of Reading,
Conn. (3/20)

Burchill, Capt., dec'd—house in NYC for sale (3/20)

Templer, Capt., of the 26th Regt.—married March 14 in Elizabeth Town, N.J., to Lady
Sinclair, widow of Sir John Sinclair (3/20)

Rivington, James, of NYC, bookseller—married March 16 in NYC to Elizabeth Van
Horne, widow of Cornelius Van Horne (3/20)

Van Alstyne, Matthew, late of NYC, merchant, dec'd—accounts with estate to be
settled with Sarah Van Alstyne, executrix (3/20)

Pugsley, John, dec'd—real estate in Manor of Pelham, Westchester Co., NY, for sale
by execs., James and William Pugsley (3/20)

King, Matthew, Irish servant—runaway March 15 from Marcus King, living near
Pluckimin (3/27)

Brady, Michael, Irish servant, age c. 19—runaway March 18 from William Tucker, of Trenton, West New Jersey (3/27)

McPherson, James, apprentice lad—runaway March 30 from Bartholomew Coxetter, of NYC (4/3)

Sparling, Philip, servant boy—runaway from Charles Miller, living on Golden Hill, NYC (4/10)

Myer, Gertje, of NYC, shopkeeper, and Myer, James, of NYC, baker, dec'd—accounts with their estates to be settled with Andrew Myer, admin. (4/10); furniture and shop goods of Gertje Myer, dec'd, to be sold at her house in Smith St. (4/24)

Murphy, Thomas, Irish servant, shoemaker, age c. 19—runaway in March, 1768, from Jacob Starn, living on Change Water Iron Works, Sussex Co., West New Jersey (4/10)

Cherry, Rueben, of Connecticut Farms, Essex Co., N.J.— will not be responsible for debts contracted by his wife Hannah, widow of Isaac Willis (4/17)

King, John, dec'd—farm at Bronck's River Bridge, Tuckeyhoe, for sale by execs., Linus and John King, of NYC (4/17)

Ogilvie, Rev. John—married April 17 at Trinity Church, NYC, to Mrs. Margaret Philips, widow of the late Philip Philips and daughter of Nathaniel Marston, of NYC, merchant (4/24)

Graham, Robert, age 40, committed to jail of Kingston, Ulster Co., NY, on charge of murder—broke jail; reward for his capture offered by Daniel Graham, sheriff (4/24)

Ernest, John, dec'd—house in Dock St., near Coentjes Market, NYC, where he lived, is to be let (4/24)

Kennedy, Capt. Archibald, Esq.—married April 27 in NYC to Miss Nancy Watts, daughter of Hon. John Watts, Esq., of NYC (5/1)

Raline, Jacob, High Dutch servant, age 30—runaway April 26 from James Varian, of Scaresdeal, Westchester Co., NY (5/1)

Roosevelt, Nicholas, Esq., dec'd—house at North River for sale (5/1)

Wright, Samuel, of NYC, mariner—will not pay debts contracted by wife Rebeckah (5/8)

Aymar, John, dec'd—house and two lots in Fair or Nassau Streets, near the Moravian Meeting, NYC, for sale by John Aymar, exec. (5/8)

Panton, Lt., of the man-of-war *Rose*—killed with a harpoon by a sailor on the brig *Pitt-Packet*, bound from Cadiz to Marblehead, as he was trying to press the seamen of the brig (5/8)

Murray, Cornelius, servant, born in England, age c. 19—runaway from Broughton Reynolds, of Elizabeth Town, N.J. (5/8)

Runaway from Jacob Brangle and Christian School in Freederick Town, Md. (5/8):
Humes, Thomas, an Englishman, gardener, age c. 25 or 26
Weply, Henry, an Englishman, bricklayer

Coon, Elizabeth, dec'd—house in NYC, opposite to John Harris Cruger's to be sold; accounts with her estate to be settled with Thomas Randel or George Brewerton, Jr. (5/15)

Burbige, Mr., living near Ligonier—killed in April by an Indian (5/22)

Duryee, Capt., master of the sloop *Polly*, of NYC—murdered in Sept., 1766, together with his mate, Mr. Demilt, two passengers (a father and son) and the cabin boys, by Joseph Andrews, a seaman; Andrews is to be executed May 23 in NYC (5/22)

Porter, Stephen, accused of murdering Capt. Westcot of the sloop *Sally*, of Bristol, in 1766—hanged himself May 18 in his cell in jail in NYC (5/22)

M'Laughlin, Mr.—on May 17, while scraping side of a vessel in NYC, fell into water near the Ferry Stairs and was drowned (5/22)

Carpenter, John J., merchant, dec'd—mills near the road from New Windsor to
   Goshen, Orange Co., 7 miles from Hudson River, for sale (5/22)
Drowned at sea—seamen on Capt. Russel's ship:
   Innis, William
   Elder, James
   Montgomery, Thomas
   Semple, William
   Welch, Mr. (6/12)
Brown, Thomas, late of NYC, ironmonger—died in London some months since
   (6/12)
Cuyler, Henry, dec'd—real estate for sale; accounts with estate to be settled with
   Abraham Cuyler at the house of Jane Cuyler in King St., NYC, or with Henry
   Cuyler (6/19)
Leonard, Rev. Silas, dec'd—land about two miles below New Windsor, Orange Co.,
   adjoining Hudson River, for sale by execs., Elizabeth and Silas Leonard (6/19)
Wyer, Deacon, of New Braintree, Mass.—his son killed by lightning June 11 (6/26)
Sowers, Thomas, Esq., H.M.'s chief engineer in America—married June 24 in NYC
   to Miss Nancy Myer, oldest daughter of John Myer, of NYC, merchant (6/26)
Gale, Col. Samuel, late of Goshen, NY, dec'd—land in that town for sale by Samuel
   Gale, Esq. (7/3)
Forbes, Gilbert, dec'd—accounts with estate to be settled with Philander Forbes,
   executrix, and Gilbert Forbes and John Young, execs. (7/3)
French, John, Esq., late of NYC, dec'd—his creditors to meet at house of Mrs.
   Brock in NYC (7/10)
Brunce, Negro slave, age c. 30—runaway from Jacobus Van Derveer, of Reading
   Town, Hunterdon Co. (7/10)
Frank, Negro slave, age c. 24—runaway June 3 from Daniel Van Mater, of Free-
   hold, Monmouth Co., N.J. (7/10)
Milner, Hannah, wife of Edward Milner, Sr., aged 100 years and 10 months, born
   in America, mother of 14 children, grandmother of 82, and greatgrandmother
   of 110, of whom there are living 7 children, 65 grandchildren and 91 great-
   grandchildren—died June 23 at Montgomery, Philadelphia Co., Pa. (7/17)
Van Horne, Andrew, dec'd—farm at Piscataway, N.J., for sale (7/17)
Tull, Thomas, joiner, age c. 21 or 22—absconded from his bail in Phila. (7/24)
Runaway from Edmund Milne, of Phila. (7/24):
   Gordon, James Samuel, servant, born in England, age 24
   Logan, James, servant, born in County of Antrim, Ireland, age 16
Coejemans, Andries, dec'd—lands are offered for sale by Thomas Smith but are
   claimed by the Coejemans heirs (9/24)
Fairbanks, Mrs., of Bristol, R.I., aged 92—keeps a school of 20 children and spins
   a fifteen-knotted skein of linen every day (7/24)
Nichol, William, of Grub St., Cripplegate Parish, London, boatswain of ship *Edward*,
   lately arrived—on July 19 found accidentally drowned in NYC (7/24)
Jack, Negro slave of Isaac Ketcham, of Huntington, L.I.—escaped from custody and
   supposed to have been taken away by Samuel Titus, a cooper (7/24)
Reese, Andrew, son of—killed July 17 by lightning while reaping on plantation of
   George Mason at Kennet, Chester Co., Pa. (7/31)
Cushing, Col., of Falmouth, son of—killed by a whale off Cape Elizabeth (7/31)
Mumford, Samuel, formerly post rider between Newport and Boston—died July 16
   at Newport, R.I., (7/31)
Detmus, Lawrence—died last Friday week at Flatbush, L.I., age 92 (7/31)
Hennesey, John, convicted of stealing satin covering of cushions in St. Paul's Church,
   NYC—sentenced to be executed Aug. 23 (7/31)

Jubeart, John, convicted of counterfeiting (7/31) and executed at NYC Sept. 6 (9/11)

De Lancey, Miss Matty, age 19—died July 30 in NYC (8/7)

Brady, Michael, Irish servant, age c. 20—runaway July 23 from William Tucker, of Trenton, West Jersey (8/7)

Hazard, Hon. George, of Newport, R.I.—married last "Friday Se'nnight" (Newport dispatch of Aug. 7) in South Kingstown to Miss Jenny Tweedy, of Newport (8/14)

Dunn, Robert Joseph, Esq., of Jamaica—married Aug. 6 in Newport, R.I., to Miss Amy Tweedy, daughter of Dr. John Tweedy of Newport, sister of Jenny Tweedy (8/14)

Lefferts, Mr., of Flatbush, L.I., aged 92—has a wife aged 81, whose maiden name was also Lefferts; she said she had six sisters at present alive and aged 81, 79, 75, 73, 68, 64 and 63; her parents exceeded the age of 80 before they died. Mr. Lefferts says that he has two brothers still alive, aged 91 and 86; another of his brothers, who died within the past three years, married at age of 100 and lived to age of 106 (8/14)

Low, Widow, dec'd—her house in Stone St., NYC, for sale by execs., Peter and Cornelius P. Low (8/21)

Runaway Aug. 13 from Samuel Henry of Trentown, N.J. (8/21):
  Fitz Gerald, Nicholas, Irish servant
  Murphy, Andrew, Irish servant

Steuart, Andrew, of Wilmington, N.C., printer—accidentally drowned in river early in July (8/28)

M'Crea, Rev. James, dec'd—land in Somerset Co., N.J., to be sold by Catharine M'Crea, executrix, and James M'Crea, executor (8/28)

Bartholomew, Mrs., of North Haven, Conn., who for some time had been under a deep melancholy because of loss of a son—on Aug. 8 committed suicide by cutting her throat with a razor (8/28)

Cosine, Garret, late of NYC, dec'd—accounts with estate to be settled with execs., Walter Cosine and William W. Gilbert (8/28)

Hanns, Christopher, English servant, painter, age c. 26—runaway Aug. 15 from William Tod, of Phila. (9/4)

Collyson, Francis, for several years past post rider between NYC and Albany—on Aug. 28 accidentally fell down stairs and died from injuries, leaving a widow and two young children (9/4)

Belding, Henry, apprentice, age c. 17—runaway Aug. 20 from Abner Osburn, of Stanford, New England (9/4)

Worrall, Isaac—drowned Sept. 8 while returning from Frankford to Phila., leaving a widow and five children (9/18)

M'Laughlin, Daniel—drowned Sept. 8 while trying to cross Tacony Creek on Bristol Road (9/18)

Moore, Sir Henry, Gov. of NY—died Sept. 11 at Fort George in NYC (9/18); accounts with his estate to be settled with admins., Alexander and Susanna Jane Dickson and Ph. Livingston, Jr. (9/25)

Harris, George, Esq., of the Island of St. Croix—died Sept. 21 in NYC and was buried Sept. 23 in St. George's Chapel (9/25)

George, Negro, age c. 30, slave of Capt. Provost of Perhamus, N.J.—broke out of workhouse in NYC on Sept. 9 (9/25)

Lowey, James, dec'd—lot with two houses, adjoining property of Casper Wister, in Montgomery Ward of NYC, near the shipyards, for sale by execs., Jane and Michael Lowey and Joseph Totten (9/25)

Andrews, Joshua, dec'd—accounts with estate to be settled with Thomas Gardner, admin. (9/25)

Robinson, Mrs. Lydia, midwife, age 70—died Sept. 17 in New London, Conn. (10/2)

Mares, Joseph, aged c. 24, who sailed from Bordeaux to Santo Domingo about ten years ago—is asked to apply to Messers Read and Yates in NYC (10/2)

Walker, John, an Englishman, lately arrived in the *Dutchess of Gordon,* bricklayer, age c. 23—runaway Sept. 24 from John Bessonet (10/2)

Pitcher, William, a former soldier, age c. 38, who has a wife in Shrewsbury—ran away with the above-mentioned John Walker (10/2)

Ben, Negro slave, age c. 30—runaway Sept. 17 from Nathaniel Richards, of Newark, N.J. (10/2)

Gomez, David, dec'd—house in Green St., NYC, for sale by execs., Daniel, Isaac and Benjamin Gomez (10/2)

Pitkin, Hon. William, Esq., Gov. of Conn.—died Oct. 1 at his house in East Hartford (10/9)

Clap, Mrs. Mary, widow of the late Rev. President Clap—died Sept. 23 in New Haven, Conn., in her 66th year (10/9)

Benthousen, Jacob, of Poughkeepsie, a skipper—fell into river Oct. 4 and was drowned (10/9)

Ackland, James, dec'd—48-year lease on place at Corlear's Hook, where Mr. Van Den Ham now lives, for sale by James Ackland, admin. (10/9)

Jim, Negro, born in Guinea, slave of Daniel Hughs, of Frederick's Town County, Md., at iron works on Antetum Creek—now in jail at Westchester (10/9)

Henderson, Mr.—killed by Capt. Cavenaugh, who was convicted of manslaughter (Boston dispatch) (10/16)

Robinson, Hon. John, Esq., one of commissioners of H.M.'s Customs—married Oct. 6 in Boston to Miss Nancy Boutineau, second daughter of James Boutineau, Esq., of Boston (10/16)

Hedges, James, a laborer—on Oct. 8 at Kensington, Pa., murdered his wife (10/16)

Du Bois, Mathew, dec'd—real estate at the Fish-Kills, Dutchess Co., NY, upon Hudson River, for sale by Mathew and Peter Du Bois (10/16)

Vanderbelt, Jacob, late of Staten Island, dec'd—accounts with estate to be settled with Mary Vanderbelt, executrix (10/16)

Holmes, John, of NYC, oysterman—last Saturday week went to bed very drunk and later in night was found dead on the floor by his wife (10/23)

Hannan, Mr., a mason, who some time ago worked in NYC—executed at St. Augustine for murder of his wife and child (10/23)

Abbot, Abijah, late of NYC, dec'd—real estate to be sold by Mary Abbot, executrix (10/23)

Runaway from Jonathan Squire and John Williams at Canoebrook, Essex Co., N.J. (10/23):

Cato, Negro slave, age 30

Scipio, Negro slave, age c. 25

Savage, John, son of Henry Savage, Esq., of Saintfield, County of Down, Ireland—is asked to apply to John Nixon, attorney, in Charlestown, S.C., or to Templeton and Stewart in NYC (10/23)

Weyman, Widow Hester, dec'd, who lately lived in Smith St., opposite to Mr. Grove Bend's—accounts with her estate to be settled with execs., Peter Goelet and Gabriel H. Ludlow (10/23)

Collyson, Francis, dec'd—accounts with estate to be settled with Mary Collyson at Albany or with William Malcolm in NYC (10/23)

Foy, Capt. Richard, master of the sloop *Live Oak,* of NYC, inward bound from Santo Domingo—drowned Oct. 20 when ship ran aground on Squan Beach, a little to the westward of Shrewsbury Inlet, together with:

Campbell, John, supercargo, nephew of the owner of the vessel, Jacobus Van Zandt

Williams, Henry, seaman

Haynes, Joseph, seaman

Sample, John, seaman

Lahay, John, seaman

Abbit, John, passenger

Sands, James, passenger (10/30)

Groves, Capt., master of the ship *Tyger,* bound from Jamaica to Bristol—died aboard ship early in Oct. (10/30)

Died on voyage of Capt. Cline's ship, bound from Turks Island to NYC, seamen:

Mitchell, Robert

Froth, Henry

Burns, Robert (10/30)

Marlow, Samuel, of Prince George's County, Md.—drowned Oct. 24 while trying to cross South River to see a race (11/6)

Cumerford, Mrs., of Annapolis, Md.—stabbed to death Oct. 24 at Annapolis (11/6)

Lowder, Jonathan, post rider between Boston and Hartford, age 55—killed Oct. 27 when his horse took fright and threw Lowder's head against a wheel (11/6)

Thody, Col. Michael, of NYC, many years a military man—died Oct. 29 in NYC and was buried Oct. 31 in Trinity Churchyard (11/6)

Marsh, Elizabeth, wife of Joshua Marsh, of Elizabeth Town, N.J.—has eloped from her husband (11/6)

Wentworth, John, Gov. of New Hampshire—married Nov. 11 in Portsmouth, N.H., to Mrs. Frances Atkinson, widow of Theodore Atkinson, Jr., Esq., of Portsmouth (11/820)

Tweedy, Nathaniel, eldest son of Dr. John Tweedy, of Newport, R.I.—died in Phila. last Monday Se'nnight (Newport dispatch of Nov. 13) (11/20)

Lane, Henry, late of NYC, dec'd—house at the North River for sale (11/20)

Abrell, John, late of NYC, pilot, dec'd—house in New St., near Brock's Tavern, for sale (11/20)

Andress, John, an Indian, born at Point Judith, close by R.I., age c. 20, formerly servant of Capt. Giles at North River, then of Mr. Palmer—runaway last Wednesday from James Prince, of NYC (11/20)

M'Coy, Daniel, a Highlander born, tailor, age c. 30—runaway Sept. 20 from James Richey, at Kingston, Ulster Co., NY (11/20)

Runaway from Elijah Williams, of Stockbridge, Berkshire Co., Mass. (11/20):

Gains, Jude, indented servant, age c. 25

Harrington, Jabez, indented servant, age c. 25

Robinson, Capt., master of the brig *Wolfe,* of London—died on passage from Teneriffe to NYC (11/27)

Smith, Hon. William, Esq., justice of the Supreme Court of NY and late a member of Council of NY, born in England and arrived in NYC in 1715—died Nov. 22 in NYC in his 73rd year and was buried in the Presbyterian Meeting (11/27)

Campbell, Mr., convicted of robbery—to be executed in NYC Dec. 22 (12/4)

Harrison, Morley, youngest son of George Harrison, of NYC, merchant—died Dec. 1 in NYC in his 20th year (12/4)

Young, David, late of NYC, dec'd—house in Cart and Horse St., NYC, two doors from the New Dutch Church, to be let by the Widow Young, living near Mrs. Barclay's (12/4)

GENEALOGICAL DATA FROM THE NEW-YORK GAZETTE; AND THE WEEKLY MERCURY

1769

Drake, Joshua, apprentice, age c. 19—runaway last Wednesday from Samuel Carpenter, of Goshen, Orange Co., NY (12/11)

Prince, Hezekiah son of Capt. John Prince of Boston—died while mate of Capt. Frazier's schooner on voyage from Cape Nichola Mole to Boston (12/18)

Montjoy, Benjamin, late of Boston, one of crew of ship of Capt. Seymore, of NYC—died on voyage (2/18)

Kneeland, Samuel, late an eminent printer of Boston—died there Dec. 14, having nearly completed his 73rd year (12/25)

Wheelwright, Nathaniel, Esq., late of Boston, dec'd—a trial in Boston over part of his estate; Dr. Joseph Warren, administrator, was plaintiff (12/25)

Shoals, John, European born, a Swede, Dane or Dutchman, a pirate, one of the men who carried off the ship *Black Prince*, of Bristol—has escaped from Newbury (12/25)

1770

English, Capt., master of a brig belonging to Boston—Nov. 10 died at sea (1/8)

Daley, Mr., a pedlar—murdered about 3 years ago, probably by a certain Mowry, in R.I. (1/8)

Engle, Paul, of Germantown, Pa., age c. 80—died when his home burned on Dec. 30, 1769 (1/8)

Runaway Jan. 4 from the ship *Henry*, Capt. Hunter master, in NYC: (1/8)
  Gannon, Barney, apprentice, age c. 18
  McElvey, Patrick, apprentice, age c. 18

Rodgers, Joseph, redemptioner, blockmaker by trade, age c. 21—runaway in NYC on Jan. 4 from the brig *Free-Mason*, Capt. John Sample master, from Newry (1/8)

Foster, Josiah—buried on the 11th instant in the Quaker burial place in Eversham, Burlington Co., N.J., who died there two days before in his 88th year (1/22)

M'Donald, William, living near Bound Brook, N.J.—so mishandled about ten days ago by three men, Harris, Buskirk and Howell, also of Bound Brook, that he died (1/22)

Ryan, Thomas, tried in Supreme Court in NYC and found guilty of burglary—sentenced to be executed Feb. 16 (1/22)

West, Hannah, tried in Supreme Court in NYC and convicted of picking pockets—same as above

Pell, Samuel, of NYC, a "noted Tobacconist"—died last Tuesday week in NYC in his 80th year (1/22)

Murphey, Alexander, dec'd—his effects to be sold in NYC and accounts with his estate to be settled with John Van Der Bilt, admin. (1/22)

Ackerman, Nicholas, dec'd—farm at Clark's Town, Precinct of Haverstraw, Orange Co., NY, for sale; title will be given by John Ackerman, heir at law (1/22); accounts with estate to be settled with John Harring, exec. (8/6)

Denton, Nehemiah, dec'd—plantation in Newborough, adjoining the river, for sale; apply to Nehemiah Denton, living on the premises, or to Samuel Denton, living in Jamaica, L.I. (1/22)

Farnum, David, of Andover, Mass.—died Jan. 14, together with his two sisters, when his house burned; all three were elderly (1/29)

Francis, Catharine, wife of John Francis, of NYC—has eloped from her husband (1/29)

Cregier, Simon, dec'd—real estate in NYC for sale by his execs., Cornelius Cregier and Luke Keirsted (1/29)

Myer, Ide, dec'd—real estate in Bridge St., commonly called Wynkoope St., in NYC, for sale by execs., John Ide Myer, Gerardus Myer and Jacobus Turk (2/5)

Murray, James, dec'd—property at corner of the Fly Market in NYC for sale (2/5)

Lucas, Charles in jail of Monmouth Co., N.J., for debt, with wife Margaret (2/12)

Eatton, John, dec'd—farm at Shrewsbury, N.J., for sale (2/12)

Reynolds, Michael, dec'd—mills at Cranberry Brook, Middlesex Co., N.J., for sale by execs., Grace and John Reynolds (2/19)

Woodruff, Joseph, Jr., dec'd—house in Elizabeth Town, N.J., for sale by William P. Smith, Isaac Woodruff and Elias Boudinot (2/26)

Smith, Mary, wife of Hugh Smith, of Precinct of New Windsor, Ulster Co., NY—has eloped from her husband (2/26)

Pugsley, John, late of Manor of Pelham, Westchester Co., NY, dec'd—farm for sale by execs., James and William Pugsley (2/26)

Gore, Capt. John, of Boston, son of, age c. 19—wounded by shot fired by Ebenezer Richardson in Feb., 1770 (3/12)

Snider, Christopher, age c. 11, who lived at the house of Madam Apthorp in Boston— same as above

Young, David, dec'd—house in Cart and Horse St., NYC, within two doors of the New Dutch Church, for sale; apply to Widow Young, living at corner of John's St., next door to the Widow Barclay's (3/12)

Emmerns, Jacob, Jr., and son Thomas—in jail of Monmouth Co., N.J. for debt (3/12)

Abbot, Abijah, dec'd—real estate in Out Ward of NYC for sale (3/12)

Killed by British soldiers at Boston on March 5: (3/19)

  Gray, Samuel, of Boston, ropemaker

  Attucks, Crispus, a mulatto, born in Framingham, Mass., but lately belonging to New Providence (3/19 and 3/26)

  Caldwell, mate of Capt. Morton's vessel

  Maverick, Samuel, age 17, son of the Widow Maverick, apprentice to Mr. Greenwood, joiner

  Monk, Christopher, age c. 17, apprentice to Mr. Walker, shipwright

  Clark, John, age c. 17, whose parents live at Medford, apprentice to Capt. Samuel Howard, of Boston

  Parker, David, apprentice to Mr. Eddy, wheelwright

Cole (later given as Carr), Patrick, age c. 30, who worked with Mr. Field, leather breechesmaker in Queen St—wounded in Boston March 5 by British soldiers and died March 14 (3/19 and 3/26)

Colgan, Capt. Fleming, for many years commander of a vessel out of the port of NY— died March 16 in NYC in his 48th year (3/19)

Livingston, Thomas, dec'd—real estate on Hudson River for sale (3/19)

Tilyou, Peter, Sr., of NYC, chairmaker—report that he has been ill used by son Vincent Tilyou and Vincent's wife Ann is denied by Vincent and wife (3/19)

Low, Peter, dec'd—house at Rariton Landing, N.J., for sale by Cornelius Low on the premises or by his son, Isaac Low, in NYC (3/26)

Tom, Negro slave, age c. 20—runaway March 23 from Nicholas Anthony, tanner, in Broad St., NYC (3/26)

Simonson, Isaac, dec'd—farm and ferry at the Narrows on Staten Island for sale by Garret Rapalje in NYC or Frederick and Jeremiah Simonson on the premises (3/26)

Glen, John, Esq., of Albany, merchant—died there March 24 in his 65th year and was buried there March 29 in the Dutch Church (4/2); accounts with estate to be settled with execs., Henry and Cornelius Glen and Jacob Cuyler (5/21)

Mercer, Dr. William, late of New Brunswick, N.J., dec'd—accounts with estate to be settled with execs., Lucy Mercer, Anthony White and George Harrison (4/2)

Coejeman, Andries, dec'd—reference to his heirs in connection with property west of Hudson River, between Albany and Esopus (4/2); apply to Abraham Lott, Samuel Staats Coejemans, Esq., at Rariton, N.J., or Joachim Staats and Rutger Bleecker, Esqrs., in Albany (4/16)

Guyon, Nicholas, native of Island of Rhe, near Rochelle, France—he lodges at Mr. Joseph Colley's, at the Edinburgh Castle, on the New Dock, NYC, where he acts as broker in French, Dutch and English and sells jewellery (4/2)

Ismael, Negro slave, born in America—runaway April 2 from Capt. Samuel Richards, of Norwalk, Fairfield Co., Conn. (4/9)

Sweeny, Lawrence, late of NYC—died there April 10 (4/16)

Vassal, Richard, Esq., of Island of Jamaica, an English gentleman of large fortune—married March 29 to Miss Polly Clarke, daughter of Thomas Clarke, Esq. (4/16)

Strachan, Widow, dec'd—partnership with John Faulkner dissolved (4/16)

Knott, Peter, late of Shrewsbury, N.J., dec'd—accounts with estate to be settled with execs., Gavine Drummond, of Shrewsbury, and Coenradt Hendricks, of Middletown Point (4/23)

Jim, Negro slave, born in Guinea, age c. 20—runaway April 14 from Tappan, Orange Co., NY (4/30)

Casey, Samuel, from London, silk dyer and scowerer—has removed from house at corner of Maiden Lane, NYC, to house a few doors higher up in New Dutch St., next door to Capt. Stiles's (4/30)

Lacy, Cadey—executed last Saturday at Gloucester; Phila. dispatch (4/30)

Beekman, Dr. William, of NYC—died there April 26 in his 86th year and was buried April 28 in the family vault in the New Dutch Churchyard (4/30)

Clay, Thomas—convicted of burglary by Supreme Court of NY and sentenced to be hanged May 18 (4/30)

Osburn, Jacob—same as above

Low, Cornelius, Jr., late of New Brunswick, N.J., attorney at law, dec'd—accounts with estate to be settled with execs., Isaac Low, of NYC, merchant, or James Hude, Esq., attorney at law, New Brunswick (5/7)

Greenfield, Michael, indented servant, nailer by trade, age c. 40—runaway April 14 from Hermon Hoffman, of Red Hook, Dutchess Co., NY (5/7)

Williams, Thomas, and his son John—are insolvent debtors in jail of Monmouth Co., N.J. (5/7)

Bellow, Negro wench, born in Barbados, age c. 23—runaway April 28 from Richard Harris, living in Broad St., NYC (5/7)

Peter, mulatto, age c. 35—runaway from Henry Allen, of Great Neck, L.I.; reward for his capture will be paid by Henry Allen or by Jacamiah Allen, gunsmith, in NYC (5/7)

Van Der Veer, John, weaver by trade, age 42—went away on April 25; is not in his right senses; reward for his return offered by his mother, Belitje Van Der Veer, of Flatbush, L.I. (5/14)

Sutton, Joseph, of New Castle, Westchester Co., NY—henceforth will not pay debts contracted by his wife Martha (5/14); farm on King St., Greenwich, Conn., and Rye, NY, where Joseph Sutton lately deceased lived, for sale by Richardson Sutton (11/26)

Neer, Zachariah, a German—runaway from his bail in Albany with Angle, a Dutch woman born in Albany, another man's wife (5/28)

Robinson, Thomas, Jr., age between 40 and 50, jailed for debt—broke out of jail of Suffolk Co., NY, on May 29 (6/4)

Davis, Benjamin, born at Smith Town, Suffolk Co., NY, a young man, in jail for horse stealing—same as above

Denniston, Elizabeth, wife of William Denniston, of Raway—has eloped from her husband (6/4)

Vandeburgh, William, late of Poughkeepsie, dec'd—house there for sale by Henry Vandeburgh and Richard Davis (6/11)

Cato, Negro slave, born in Guinea, age c. 12, a "Sweep-Chimney," formerly belonging to Capt. Goodridge of the packet—runaway June 2 from Capt. Nicholas Fletcher, living near the New Goal, NYC (6/11)

Provoost, Miss Katharine, of NYC, only daughter of late John Provoost, Esq.—died June 12 in her 16th year (6/18)

Bolton, Richard, Irish servant—runaway from Abigail Lord, of Fairfield, Conn. (6/18)

Davis, Benjamin, sailor—will not pay debts contracted in future by his wife Christian (6/25)

Fitzgerald, Nicholas, Irish servant, age 25 or 26—runaway from Samuel Henry (6/25)

James, mulatto slave, age c. 26—runaway from Benjamin Stevenson, of New Rochel, Westchester Co., NY (6/25)

Waldron, William, of Hornshook, dec'd—land for sale by Ann Waldron, exec., and David Waldron, exec. (7/2)

Elson, William, overseer for Mr. Stephen West, of Prince George Co., Md.—murdered June 14 by three of his Negroes (7/9)

Stanton, Daniel, of Germantown, Pa., a zealous preacher—died there June 26 and was buried June 27 in the Friends Burying Ground (7/9)

Parker, James, Esq., late of NYC, printer, comptroller and secretary of the Post Office for the northern district of the British colonies, who till of late usually resided at his house in Woodbridge, N.J., where he was a magistrate and captain of a troop of horse—died July 2, at the house of Mr. Hollingshead in Burlington, N.J., in his 56th year and was buried July 3 near his parents in the Meeting House Yard at Woodbridge (7/9); accounts with estate to be settled with Mary Parker, executrix (7/23)

Collins (*alias* Hamilton), Anthony, recently come to NYC from Middletown, Conn.—murdered July 2 in NYC, allegedly by a seaman named George Seymour, born in Ireland (7/9)

GENEALOGICAL DATA FROM THE NEW-YORK GAZETTE; AND THE WEEKLY MERCURY

1770

Cato, Negro slave, age c. 25—runaway July 8 from Nicholas Wickhoff, of Newtown, L.I. (7/16)

Beekman, Col. Henry, dec'd—real estate, acquired by him long ago, for sale (7/16)

Dick, Negro slave (who sometimes calls himself Richard Camp), age c. 60—runaway June 29 from Ebenezer White, of Danbury, Conn. (7/16)

Savage, Capt. Joseph, master of sloop belonging to Wethersfield, Conn.—thrown overboard by mate and one of his crew and drowned while on voyage from St. Eustatia to Leeward (7/16)

Dunn, Hannah, wife of Thomas Dunn, of NYC, combmaker—has eloped from her husband (7/23)

Freeman, Gilman, of Morristown, N.J.—will not pay debts contracted in future by his wife Mary (7/23)

Dickenson, John, Esq.—married July 19 in Phila. to Miss Mary Norris (7/30)

Smith, Hon. Benjamin, Esq., of Charlestown, S.C.—died July 28 at Newport, R.I., in his 53rd year (8/6)

Lunan, Alexander, of Phila., merchant—died there July 24 and was buried in burying ground of St. Peter's Church (8/6)

Forrest, Arthur, Esq., commodore—died June 25 at Kingston, Island of Jamaica (8/6)

Mincer, Negro slave, born in Guinea, age c. 23—runaway July 21 from Samuel Bradley, Jr., of Fairfield, Conn. (8/6)

Case, John, Esq., Deputy-Postmaster—died first week of August at Tower Hill, South Kingston, R.I. (8/13)

Mitchell, Jacamiah, late of Flushing, L.I, dec'd—house at town landing of Flushing to be sold by Sarah Mitchell, executrix, and execs., John Carl and John Field, Jr. (8/20)

Long, Martin, Dutch servant, born in Poland, age c. 38—runaway from Daniel M'Farland, of Mountholly (8/20)

Barbarie, John, Esq., Collector of Port of Perth Amboy, N.J.—died a few days since at his house in Perth Amboy (8/20)

Smith, Rev. Charles Jeffery—died Aug. 10 at Brookhaven, Suffolk Co., NY (8/20)

Haynes, Joseph, late of NYC, dec'd—real estate for sale (8/20)

Ackerman, Abraham, of Hackinsack, N.J.—Aug. 21 found dead, shot in head, in field near his house; he had gone out to shoot pigeons (8/27)

Antill, Edward, late of Piscataqua, N.J., dec'd—accounts with estate to be settled with Ann Antill, executrix, and Lewis Antill, exec. (8/27)

Smith, Gilbert, who with wife and family about three years ago removed from Lancaster Co., Pa., to NY—his son, Malcolm, requests that news of father and family be sent to him at Mr. Glover Hunt's in Phila., in Race St., between Third and Fourth Sts., opposite the Dutch Church (9/3)

Ishmael, Negro slave, age c. 30, formerly belonging to Capt. Samuel Richards, of Norwalk, Conn.—runaway Aug. 26 from Eliphalet Kellog, living in Ball-Town, Queen's Borough, Albany Co., NY (9/3)

Dudley, William—will not in future pay debts contracted by wife Mary (9/3)

Ashfield, Hon. Lewis Morris, Esq., dec'd—library of his law books to be sold at Perth Amboy, N.J., by V. Pearse Ashfield, admin. (9/3)

Carryl, Patrick, of NYC, druggist, dec'd—shop he kept near 30 years in Hanover Sq., now kept by Benjamin Jones, is removed to Hunter's Quay (9/10)

Lippincott, Mr., of Haddonfield, N.J., nine-year-old daughter of—on Aug. 25 ravished and murdered by a Dutch servant, age c. 16 (9/10)

York, Negro slave, born in Guinea, age between 40 and 50—runaway in June from Joseph Holman, of Monmouth, N.J. (9/10)

Duff, Roger, Irish servant, age c. 30—runaway Sept. 2 from Adam Hoops, of "Summerseat," Bucks Co., Pa. (9/17)

Baxter, Isaac, Irish servant, age c. 20—same as above

Long, Henry, weaver, age c. 45 or 50—runaway from John Scott, of Morris Town, N.J. (9/17)

Calderwood, Capt. James, of H. M.'s 26th Regt. of Foot—died Sept. 10 at his lodgings in Broad St., NYC, in his 22nd year (9/17)

Pierson, Rev. John, for many years minister at Woodbridge, N.J.—died Aug. 23 at Hanover, N.J. (9/17)

Dudley, William, of NYC, carpenter—has accused his wife Mary and his apprentice, Daniel McEuen, of having had unlawful relations, which they deny (9/17)

Cuyler, Henry, late of NYC—died Sept. 17 at Amboy and was buried Sep. 18 in the New Dutch Churchyard in NYC (9/24)

McClean, John, of Orange Co., NY, who had been a drummer in King William's army in Ireland—died lately in Orange Co., NY, in his 109th year (9/24)

Vanderspiegel, John, late of NYC, dec'd—accounts with estate to be settled with Peter V.B. and William Livingston and Jeremiah Platt, execs. (9/24)

Phoenix, Alexander, Sr., lately dec'd—accounts with estate to be settled with execs., Mary Exceen, Catharine Waldron and Daniel Phoenix (9/24)

Livingston, Robert, Esq., eldest son of Hon. Robert R. Livingston—married Sept. 9 Miss Stevens, only daughter of Hon. John Stevens, Esq., at his country seat in Hunterdon, N.J. (10/1)

Graham, Mrs. Elizabeth, wife of Rev. Chauncey Graham, of Fishkill, NY—died there Sept. 17 (10/1)

Harding, Vall., of Middletown, N.J., currier—about two months ago his wife Anne ran away with another man (10/1)

Eastwood, Habbacock, who had served his time with a weaver near Burlington, age 25 —runaway from Robert M'Ghee, of Cranberry, East New Jersey (10/1)

Nickles, John, age 25, born in Ireland, who served his time near Delaware—same as above

Whitefield, George, chaplain to Countess of Huntingdon—died Sept. 30 at Newbury Port (10/8)

Blavelt, David, late of Orange Co., NY, dec'd—notice about a bond by his execs., Peter Harring, John Perry and Johannes D. Blavelt (10/8)

Johnson, Mrs., formerly Mrs. Chetwood—keeps a public house next to courthouse in Elizabeth Town, N.J. (10/8)

Thurston, Peleg, of Newport, R.I., dec'd—John Thurston is exec. of estate (10/8)

Keen, Mounce, of Pilesgrove, West New Jersey, born of Swedish parents at Chester, Pa. —died at beginning of last August at Pilesgrove at age of 105 years and 8 months (10/15)

Will, Negro slave, born at Bermuda, the property of Paul Bascome, of that island— runaway Oct. 10 from sloop *Speedwell*, lately arrived at NYC from Boston; reward offered by Paschal N. Smith (10/15)

Gomez, Isaac, dec'd—accounts with estate to be settled with Matthias Gomez, exec. (10/15)

Arch, Negro slave, age 30—runaway from Reolof Van Dike, of Somerset Co., East New Jersey (10/15)

Draper, Sir William—married Oct. 13 in NYC to Miss Susanna De Lancey, daughter of Hon. Oliver De Lancey (10/22)

Lee, William, Esq., Capt. Lt. in the Royal Regt. of Artillery—died Oct. 15 in NYC and was buried Oct. 18 at Hempstead, L.I. (10/22)

De Lancey, Peter, Esq.—died Oct. 17 at his house in Westchester in his 62nd year (10/22); accounts with estate to be settled with execs., Elizabeth, Stephen, John, and James De Lancey (11/12)

Saloue, Cherokee chief—died early in Sept. of a fever near Salisbury, N.C. (10/29)

Platt, Obadiah, Esq., of Huntington, L.I.—died there Sept. 28 (10/29)

Hungerford, Mrs. Samuel, of New Fairfield, Conn., now in her 43rd year—has 12 children and 5 grandchildren; account is given of her ability in spinning (10/29)

Townley, Richard, of Elizabeth Town, N.J., ten-year-old son of—accidentally wounded with a scythe and bled to death on Sept. 13 (10/29)

De Botetourt, Baron Norborne—died Oct. 15 at Williamsburg, Va. (11/5)

Lill, Negro wench, age c. 17, born on L.I., late the property of Mr. Jecamiah Mitchell, of Flushing, boatman—runaway Oct. 27 from Edward Agar, of NYC (11/5)

Dick, Negro slave, age c. 22—runaway Oct. 27 from Joseph Drake, of Goshen, Orange Co., NY (11/5)

Miller, Sarah, wife of Johannis Miller, of Wallkill, Ulster Co., NY—has eloped from her husband (11/12)

Schuyler, Brandt, dec'd—property at New Windsor and in Perth Amboy to be sold by Samuel Schuyler (11/12)

Hall, Miss Debry, only daughter of Mr. David Hall, of Phila., printer—died there Nov. 2, aged 16 years, and was buried Nov. 4 in Christ Church Burying Ground (11/12)

Sturgeon, Rev. William, curate of Christ Church Parish and afterwards of the united Churches of Christ Church and St. Peter's in Phila. from 1747 to July 1766—died there Nov. 3 and was buried Nov. 5 in Christ Church Burying Ground (11/12)

De Lancey, Oliver, son of Peter De Lancey, lately dec'd—came passenger to NYC in the packet (11/12)

Ames, William, born in Deal, in Kent, about 1727, who about 1750, in Deal, married Thomasine Frithers, or Frivers, by whom he had one daughter, Elizabeth, who lived with her aunt, Mrs. Sanderson, at Yarmouth, in Norfolk, till the death of the latter, and the daughter is since dead; about 1758 William Ames went on a voyage; he is lately reported in England to be living in NYC and employed in trading from NYC to the West Indies in partnership with one Ward, master of a schooner belonging to NY—if living, he is desired to apply to Messers Geldard and Gimingham, in Staple Inn, Holborn, London; or, if Ames is dead, anyone with knowledge of his death is asked to give information to Charles Mc Evers in NYC or to Messers Geldard and Gimingham (11/12)

Clarkson, Freeman, dec'd—farm at Flatbush, L.I., and remainder of a lease of ground in Cart and Horse St., NYC, for sale by execs., David, Matthew or Levinus Clarkson (11/12)

Abraham, Negro slave, age c. 24—runaway from Peter Huggeford, of White Plains, Westchester Co., NY (11/19)

John, young Negro slave—runaway from W.P. Smith at Elizabeth Town, N.J. (11/19)

Pomp, Negro slave, age c. 23—runaway Oct. 11 from Aaron Wait, living at Salem, Mass. (11/19)

Holmes, Stanley, dec'd—two houses and lots of estate in Montgomery Ward, NYC, fronting William St., commonly known as Cart and Horse St., nearly opposite to New Dutch North Church, for sale (11/19)

Morrell, Salyer, late of Newtown, L.I., dec'd—creditors are to present accounts to Richard Alsop (11/19)

Warren, Sir Peter, dec'd—house and lot in the Broadway, NYC, adjoining his house and that of Garit Vangelder, for sale; enquire of Elizabeth or John Slidell (11/26)

Van Kleeck, Lawrence, late of Poughkeepsie, dec'd—accounts with estate to be settled with and farm in Poughkeepsie to be sold by execs., Baltus Van Kleeck, merchant, living in NYC, or Leonard Van Kleeck, Esq., living at Poughkeepsie (11/26)

Bevan, Thomas, indented servant, age c. 25—runaway Nov. 15 from James Miller, living in Bladensburgh, Prince George Co., Md. (12/3)

Sands, Gideon, dec'd—farm at bottom of Cow-Neck, L.I., for sale by execs., Richard and Benjamin Sands (12/3)

Stymes, Christopher, late of NYC, house carpenter, dec'd—accounts with estate to be settled with William Elsworth, Jr., admin. (12/3)

Kane, mulatto, age c. 28—runaway from Jacob Schermerhorn, living at Rynbeck, NY (12/3)

Dobbs, Charles, late of NYC, dec'd—accounts with estate to be settled with William Dobbs, exec. (12/3)

Kennedy, William, indented servant, formerly soldier in Yorkshire, England—runaway from the snow *James and Mary*; reward for his capture offered by Archibald M'Vicker (12/3)

James, servant, part Negro, part Indian—runaway Nov. 23 from Jacob Balding, of Fish Kills, Dutchess Co., NY (12/10)

Hall, Elihu, Esq., of Md.—about Nov. 20 his son was baptized George Whitefield Hall (12/10)

Mesier, Peter, of NYC—died Dec. 8 in NYC in his 74th year (12/10)

Beekman, John, of NYC, merchant—married in Phila. to Miss Elizabeth Renaudet, of Phila. (12/17)

Bullock, Joseph, of Phila., merchant—married in Phila. to Miss Baynton (12/17)

Potts, Isaac, of Chester Co., Pa.—married to Miss Patty Bolton, of Plymouth, Philadelphia Co., Pa. (12/17)

Jeffery, Indian boy, born on L.I., age 18—runaway from Zacheus Newcomb, of Charlotte Precinct, Dutchess Co., NY (12/17)

Montross, John, Esq., late of Fishkills, Dutchess Co., NY, dec'd—plantation for sale by execs., William Van Wyck, Theodorus Van Wyck, Jr., and Jacob Dubois (12/17)

White, John, an Irishman, age c. 35—on Dec. 13 he robbed the sloop *Phoebe*, of Horse-Neck, Greenwich, Conn.—reward for his arrest offered by John Addington (12/24)

Hatier, John, of NYC—died there last Sunday week in his 79th year (12/24)

Shaw, William—executed Dec. 13 at Springfield, Mass., for murder of Edward East (12/31)

1771

De Lancey, Peter, Esq., Deputy-Postmaster General for the Southern district of North America—married Oct. 8 in Charleston, S.C., to Miss Elizabeth Beresford, daughter of Richard Beresford, Esq. (1/7)

Haynes, Joseph, dec'd—his farm at Great-Kilns on Bloomingdale Road for sale (1/7)

Bradshaw, Hannah, commonly called "Man of War Nance," age c. 30—burned to death in her room in Division St., NYC, on Dec. 31, 1770 (1/7)

Phoenix, Alexander, late of NYC, dec'd—real estate in NYC to be sold by execs., Mary Exceen, Catharine Waldron and Daniel Phoenix (1/7)

Montros, John, Esq., late of Fishkills, Dutchess Co., NY, dec'd—plantation for sale by execs., William Van Wyck, Theodorus Van Wyck, Jr., and Jacob Dubois, Jr. (1/7)

De Lancey, Peter, Esq., dec'd—lots in Borough of Westchester for sale by his execs. (1/14)

Stewart, John, dec'd—grist mill and 170 acres of land on Otter Kill, Ulster Co., 12 miles from New Windsor, for sale by John Bradner or John Stewart, both of Goshen (1/14)

Stark, Abraham, servant, age c. 18—runaway Dec. 29, 1770, from Robert Culver, living in Roxbury, Morris Co. (1/14)

Cuyler, Henry, dec'd—house in Dock St., NYC, for sale by execs. (1/14)

Garrison, Capt. Lambert, of NYC, master of sloop *Success*—died Nov. 21, 1770, after shipwreck, on island of Moyognano (1/21)

White, Capt. Henry, late of NYC, dec'd—accounts with estate to be settled with Margaret White, executrix (1/21)

Close, Samuel, late of Greenwich, Fairfield Co., Conn., dec'd—accounts with estate to be settled with execs., Amos and Abraham Mead (1/21)

Prickett, Richard—will not pay debts contracted in future by his wife Mary (1/21)

Will, Negro slave, age c. 50—runaway Dec. 30, 1770, from John Vanlieu, of Flushing, L.I. (1/21)

Barclay, Alexander, Esq., Comptroller of H.M.'s Customs for Port of Phila.—died Jan. 12 in Phila.; he was son of late David Barclay, merchant, of London, and grandson of "the celebrated Apologist," Robert Barclay of Urie (1/28)

Field, Robert, living upon Rotten-Row, NYC, a barber—found dead in his bed on Jan. 23 (1/28)

Livingston, Robert James, late of NYC, merchant—died Jan. 25 in his house in NYC in his 44th year (1/28)

Wallace, William, of NYC—had caused the town crier on Jan. 13 to notify public not to trust his wife Anne; he now clears her good name and states that she had not deserted him and their three children (1/28)

Roosevelt, Nicholas, dec'd—reference to his dock in NYC (1/28)

Smith, Ephraim, dec'd—farm in Flushing, L.I., for sale by execs., Samuel Skidmore, of Flushing, and Samuel Denton, of Jamaica, L.I. (2/4)

Stewart, James, Irish servant, age c. 22—runaway from John Little, living at the sign of the Indian Queen, in Market St., Phila. (2/4)

Heavener, Barbara, wife of George Heavener, of NYC—has eloped from her husband (2/4)

Burger, Alderman, dec'd—house in Peck's Slip, NYC, for sale; enquire of Helena Cormick, on premises, or David Dickson (2/4)

Whiston, Mr., a young man whose parents live at Bethpage, L.I.—on Jan. 21, when racing with three other young men near Mr. Water's tavern on Hempstead Plains, L.I., fell from his horse and died (2/4)

Ustick, Stephen, late of NYC, dec'd—accounts with estate to be settled with Jane Ustick, executrix, and William Ustick, exec.; the house of the deceased in Ann St., near the North Church, to be sold (2/4)

Ogden, Capt. Nathan—shot dead early in Jan. at Wyoming by one Stewart (2/11)

Wilson, Alexander, shopkeeper, dec'd—accounts with estate to be settled with Jane Wilson, executrix (2/11)

Butler, Major, of the 29th Regt.—lately married at Charles Town, S.C., to Miss Middleton, daughter of Colonel Middleton (2/18)

Kelly, Susanna, wife of William Kelly, of NYC, merchant—died Feb. 11 in NYC and was buried Feb. 13 in chancel of Trinity Church (2/18)

Welch, Patrick, of NYC, age c. 12—on Feb. 15, while skating at Fresh Water, fell through a hole in the ice and was drowned (2/18)

Druer, Timothy, of Essex Co., N.J.—will not pay debts henceforth contracted by his wife Sarah (2/18)

Bates, John, late of NYC, dec'd—accounts with estate to be settled with widow, Rachel Bates (2/18)

Clawson, Thomas, dec'd—farm in Piscataway, N.J., for sale by Tobias Van Norden at Bound Brook (2/18)

Bayard, Mrs. Rebecca, wife of Major Robert Bayard, daughter of late Hon. Charles Apthorp, Esq., of Boston, sister of Rev. Apthorp of London, sister-in-law of Hon. Barlow Trecothick, late Lord Mayor of London—died Feb. 22 in Flushing, L.I., in her 25th year (2/25)

Colgan, Capt. Fleming, late of NYC, dec'd—accounts with estate to be settled with execs., Christopher Smith and Wyn. Van Zandt (2/25)

Humphreys, Humphrey, born in Horsham Twp., Phila Co., Pa.,who at age of 22 or 23 enlisted in the king's service in 1756, a shoemaker by trade—is asked to apply to printer of the newspaper (2/25)

Townsend, John, late of Mamaroneck, Treasurer of Westchester Co., NY, dec'd—accounts with estate to be settled with execs., Isaac Gedney and Samuel Townsend (2/25)

M'Kenzie, Donald, servant, age c. 12—runaway Feb. 4 from John McArthur, living in Fredericksburgh, Dutchess Co., NY (2/25)

De Peyster, Abraham, Esq., dec'd—houses and lots in NYC for sale (3/4)

Lee, Mrs. Rhoda, wife of Jared Lee, of Southington, a parish in Farmington, Conn.—accidentally burned to death on Feb. 12 (3/4)

Reade, Joseph, Esq., of NYC, merchant and member of Council for NY—died in NYC March 2 in his 79th year (3/4)

Smith, Hon. William, Esq., dec'd—accounts with estate to be settled with John W. Smith (3/4)

Hastier, John, dec'd—possessions for sale at his house in Hanover Sq., NYC; apply to Marguerite Hastier at the house; execs. are Mary Basset, Elizabeth Luce, Marguerite and Catharine Hastier (3/4)

Hamilton, Elizabeth, dec'd—lands near Anthony's Nose on the Mohawk's River for sale (3/4)

Johnson, Nicholas, late of NYC, dec'd—accounts with estate to be settled with execs., John Burt Lyng and William Sherer; house at Whitehall is still kept by his widow (3/4)

Jeffery, Capt. Richard, dec'd—house in Princes St., where his widow lives, for sale by his widow, Mary Jeffery (3/4)

Mills, Susannah, belonging to the 14th Regt.—fell through the ice on Feb. 16 while crossing the ice at the south end of Boston and died of exposure (3/11)

Jacquith, Widow Sarah, of Wilmington—died there Feb. 6 in her 90th year; she had been mother of 16 children (10 survive her, 5 sons and 5 daughters), 68 grandchildren, 166 great-grandchildren and 4 great-great-grandchildren, in all 248 living offspring (3/11)

Emens, Christopher, dec'd—lot and two dwellings at Brooklyn Ferry for sale; apply to Jane Emens, executrix, living on the premises, or Joachim Gulick, executor, near Ten Mile Run, N.J. (3/11); name is given as Jocham Gulet, exec. (4/8)

Sands, Gideon, dec'd—farm on bottom of Cow-Neck, Twp. of Hemstead, Queens Co., NY, for sale by execs., Simon, Richard and Benjamin Sands (3/11)

Hill, James, Tide-Surveyor for the Port of Boston, lately dec'd—William Sheppard, Esq., has been appointed in his place (3/11)

Sy, or Cyrus, Negro slave, age 16—runaway about 8 weeks ago from Isaac Coats, bricklayer, of Vine St., Phila. (3/18)

Mitchell, Jacamiah, late of Flushing, dec'd—house at Flushing Town Landing for sale by execs., Sarah Mitchell, John Carle and John Field, Jr. (3/18)

Dean, Joseph, born in Dublin, a son of William Dean (formerly a soldier in the XXIX Regt. and who since lived near Gorey, County of Wexford, Ireland)—legacy awaits him; he is asked to apply to Messers Hugh and .'Alexander Wallace, merchants, in NYC (3/18)

Dean, William, born at Gibraltar, a sergeant in the Young Buffs, who married at Warrington in Great Britain, a son of the aforementioned William Dean—same as above

Syme, or Symon, a mulatto, half Negro and half Indian, a chimney sweeper, age c. 24—runaway March 7 from Peter Low, living at upper end of Maiden Lane near Broadway, NYC (3/18)

Ludlow, Gabriel H., of NYC, merchant—married March 14 in NYC to Miss Nancy Williams, second daughter of Charles Williams, Esq., of H.M.'s Customs (3/18)

Woodruff, Joseph, dec'd—house and lot near the landing in Elizabeth Town, N.J. for sale; apply to William P. Smith or Elias Boudenot, Esq. (3/25)

Chancellor, Capt. Samuel, master of the brig *Queen of the May*, of Phila., lying at anchor at Cape Henlopen—died of the cold on March 9 (3/25)

Byrne, Capt. Barnaby—died March 23 when taken with a fit while on way with Mrs. Byrne from NYC to Jamaica, L.I. (3/25)

Willson, John, late of Flushing, dec'd—dwelling for sale by execs., Mary Willson, John Field, Jr., and John Thorne (3/25)

Brit, Negro slave, age c. 30—runaway 18 months ago from Jacamiah Smith, living at Springfield, near Elizabeth Town, N.J. (3/25)

Lee, Mary, wife of Seth Lee, of Goshen, Orange Co., NY—has eloped from her husband (4/1)

Tom, Negro slave, age c. 30—runaway March 24 from John Haring, of Orange Town, NY (4/1)

Gordon, James Samuel, indented servant, born in London, jeweller by trade, age c. 26—runaway March 24 from Edmond Milne, of Phila., goldsmith; the runaway calls the woman gone with him Mary Gordon, alias Mary Dill (4/1)

Lynott (or Lynett), Thomas, Esq., dec'd—stock cattle, utensils and Negroes on premises at Katt's Kill, where widow Elizabeth lives, for sale by widow or by Joseph Greswold, exec., in NYC (4/1)

Green, William, dec'd—farm in Nine Partners, Dutchess Co., NY, for sale by execs., Peter and James Germond (4/8)

Hennion, Johannis, dec'd—stock, furniture, utensils, Negroes for sale at house of the deceased at Preakness, Bergen Co., N.J., by execs., Theunis Day and Johannis Van Houstan (4/8)

Stephenson, Henry, late of Trafford-Hill, near Yarm, North Riding of County of York, England, who embarked at London in July, 1770, for NYC but is supposed to have arrived in Va. or Md. in Sept.—is asked to apply to printer of the newspaper (4/8)

Rodgers, Thomas, living in Front St., near Market St. Corner, Phila.—died April 6 when his house burned; also died in the fire a Mrs. Baxter, apparently his son-in-law's mother (4/15)

Shirley, William, Esq., Lt. General in H.M.'s army—died March 24 in Boston in his 77th year (4/15)

Harsin, Garret, dec'd—house and lot in upper end of Smith St., NYC, now in possession of Mr. Norris, a barber, for sale by Garret Harsin in French Church St. (4/15)

Livingston, Peter Van Brug, Esq., of NYC, merchant—married April 9 at Elizabeth Town, N.J., to Mrs. Ricketts, widow of late William Ricketts, Esq. (4/15)

Lawrence, Mrs. Elizabeth, wife of Robert Lawrence, Esq.—died March 28 at Upper Freehold, N.J., in her 74th year and was buried in Quakers Burying Ground (4/15)

Richards, Elizabeth, dec'd—house and lot near the New Goal, NYC, for sale by exec., Jacob Sharpe (4/22)

Barklay, Alexander, late Comptroller of Customs for Port of Phila., dec'd—Philip Loring, Esq., has been appointed in his place (4/22)

Ishmael, Negro slave, age c. 30—runaway Aug. 26 last from Eliphalet Kellog, living in Ball Town, Patent of Kayaderosseros, alias Queensborough, Albany Co., NY (4/29)

Dailey, Mary, convicted as pickpocket—to be executed in NYC May 10 (4/29); executed (5/12)

Harper, Martha, wife of Anthony Harper, of NYC, gunsmith—found dead in her bed on April 17 (4/29)

Kelso, Anthony, indented servant, age c. 30—runaway early in April from John M'Donald, of Charlestown, Cecil Co., Md. (4/29)

Cary, Mary, widow of Samuel Cary—her brother, Joseph Cary, states that he lately lived at Schenectady with Mr. John Farrel but now lives in Albany, where he may be found if one enquires at house of Capt. William Pemberton (4/29)

Brasier, Capt. Henry, of NYC—lately died at St. Augustine (5/6)

Floyd, Hon. Richard, Esq., colonel of Suffolk Co., NY, militia, first judge of the Inferior Court of Common Pleas—died April 21 at his house a few miles from Town of Brookhaven, in his 68th year (5/6)

M'Cartney, James, late of NYC, dec'd—accounts with estate to be settled with execs., Alexander Stewart and Daniel M'Cormick (5/6)

Smith, Widow Sarah, of Herrick's Twp., in Hampstead, Nassau Island—offers reward for a stolen horse (5/6)

Magin, Widow Sarah—farm known as Peesten Bowery, formerly property of Peter Van Brughen, in Albany Co., on east side of Hudson River, about 5 miles north of Albany, for sale by Sarah Magin and William Magin (5/13)

Jack, Indian slave, age c. 18—runaway from William Brownejohn, Jr. (5/13)

Brutus, slave, age c. 18, who lately belonged to Dr. Chovet—same as above

St. John, Buckingham, of Norwalk, Conn., one of tutors in Yale College—drowned May 5 when small sloop, commanded by Jabez Cables, age c. 16, overset on voyage from New Haven to NYC (5/20)

Henry, David, indented English servant, age 19 or 20—runaway May 12 from William M. Barnet, of Elizabeth Town, N.J. (5/20)

Baker, Hester, age 11, who was born deaf and dumb—her father, Jacob Baker, of Elizabeth Town, N.J., states that she is beginning to hear and speak through help from Dr. Graham (5/20)

Snow, Henry, who was born at Torbay in 1674 and who in 1688 served under William of Orange—died last week in upper parish of Littery, aged 97—Boston dispatch dated May 16 (5/27)

Thompson, John—executed May 23 in Phila. (5/27)

Blakey, William, a ship carpenter—killed May 12 by William Casey, master of a Phila. sloop, in a quarrel that began at the house of Mrs. Dunn in the Fields, NYC (5/27)

Jack, Negro slave, age c. 35—runaway May 28 from John Hulet, of Oysterbay, Queens Co., NY (6/3)

Howard, Ensign, of the 18th Regt.—lately found drowned in Chartrie's Creek (6/3)

Roberts, Mrs., Wife of John Roberts, Esq., High Constable of NYC—died May 27 in NYC (6/3)

Tom, Negro slave, age c. 23—runaway from David Clarkson, of NYC (6/3)

Hervey, George, of NYC, broker, dec'd—house opposite City Hall for sale by John Crawley, admin. (6/3)

Richards, Elizabeth, dec'd—house and lot near New Goal in NYC for sale by Jacob Sharp, exec. (6/10)

Afer, mulatto slave, age c. 18—runaway Wednesday night last from George Weeks, of Oyster Bay, Queens Co. NY (6/10)

GENEALOGICAL DATA FROM THE NEW-YORK GAZETTE; AND THE WEEKLY MERCURY

Long, Samuel, boatswain—murdered by his captain, Zachary Day, on high seas near Cuba (6/10)

Day, Capt. Zachary Day—executed March 25 for the abovementioned crime (6/10)

Bell, Thomas, chief mate of a sloop belonging to Montego Bay—executed April 1 at NYC for piracy (6/10)

Wolff, Jenny, wife of Conradt Wolff, of NYC, butcher—her husband will not pay debts contracted by her in the future (6/17 and 6/24)

Johnston, Samuel, Irishman, age 22 or 23—runaway with goods he stole from Isaac Guion at New Rochelle, NY (6/24)

Kruse, Abraham, dec'd—plantation on Staten Island for sale by Johannis Simenson and Anthony Stoutenburgh (6/24)

Smith, Richard, indented servant, age c. 24, born in west of England, who came to America in Capt. Holmes from Bristol—runaway June 18 from potash works at Fresh-water, NYC; reward for his capture offered by James Cargill (6/24)

Morrell, Thomas, late of Newtown, L.I., dec'd—estate for sale by execs., Jonathan, Jacob and Samuel Morrell (6/24)

Lynott, Thomas, late of Cat's Kill, dec'd—land there for sale by Joseph Griswold, exec. (6/24)

Isaac, Negro slave, age c. 35—runaway from Daniel and Israel Lewis, of Charlotte Precinct, Dutchess Co., NY (7/1)

Camp, John D., Jr., of Elizabeth Town, N.J.—on June 27 was compelled by David Brant to marry his daughter, Catharine Brant; Camp will not pay debts contracted by her (7/1)

Conner, Barney, indented servant, born in Ireland, age c. 25—runaway June 23 from Matthias Heyer, baker, in NYC (7/1)

Hinds, Michael—executed May 29 in Charleston, S.C. (7/8)

Hammond, Mrs., of Newtown, Mass., wife of Ephraim Hammond—died June 28 of apoplexy (7/8)

Charles, mulatto, age c. 40—runaway about June 14 from William Bayard, living on farm at Hoobock, opposite NYC (7/8)

Kelly, George, seaman—on July 8 fell into harbor at NYC and was drowned (7/15)

Townsend, John, late dec'd—house at Mamaroneck, Westchester Co., NY, to be let by Elizabeth Townsend (7/15); accounts with estate to be settled with execs., Isaac Gedney and Samuel Townsend (9/2)

Horton, Caleb, of White Plains, Westchester Co., NY—has died and his young son, Underhill Horton, who had left his father, is requested to apply to James Horton, Jr., exec. (7/22)

King, William, Irish servant, age c. 30, who came last June with Capt. Robert Miller—runaway May 27 from John Glen and Andrew Hollmes, of Carlisle, Pa. (7/22)

Stewart, Michael, Irish servant, age c. 35, who came last June with Capt. Robert Miller—same as above

Parker, Charles, Irish servant, age c. 20—same as above

Davis, Henry, Irish servant, age c. 30—runaway June 27 from Glen and Hollmes (7/22)

Ogden, Nathan—shot Jan. 21 at fort at Wyoming by Lazarus Stewart (7/22)

Christey, John, apprentice "boy," baker by trade—runaway July 16 in NYC from Walter Quakenbos, David Barclay and John Seger (7/22)

Fisher, Christopher, apprentice, barber by trade, age 15—same as above

Christey, Daniel, apprentice "lad," blacksmith by trade—same as above

Wadsworth, Benjamin, of Duxboro, Mass., five children of—have died of putrid fever (7/29)

Farnsworth, Samuel, of Hartford, Conn., supercargo of sloop *Fancy*, owned by Richard Alsop of Middletown, Conn.—on Dec. 25, 1770, was washed overboard and drowned on voyage from New London, Conn., to West Indies (7/29)

Hubbard, Capt. Richard, master of sloop *Fancy*—same as above

Gilbert, Mr., of East Haddam, Conn., one of crew of the *Fancy*—drowned Jan. 1 (7/29)

Taylor, Justus, of East Haddam, Conn., one of crew of the *Fancy*—drowned Jan. 2 (7/29)

Birch, Mr., native of England, age between 60 and 70—hanged himself at Newtown, L.I. (7/29)

Tryon, Mrs., mother of Gov. Wm. Tryon of NY and of Miss Tryon, a maid of honor to the queen—died May 17 in London (7/29)

Burt, John, Esq., of Stratfield, Conn.—killed by lightning July 28 when church in that town was struck (8/5)

Sherman, David, of Stratfield, Conn.—same as above

Remsen, Peter, dec'd—accounts with estate to be settled with execs., Janetje, Simon, Jacob and Henry Remsen (8/5)

Fil, Negro slave, age c. 16—runaway about May 1 from Samuel Treadwell, of Eastchester, Westchester Co., NY (8/5)

Gordon, James, born in Enniskillen, Ireland, laborer, age 21—deserted from H.M.'s 29th Regt. of Foot (8/5)

Lovell, John, laborer, age 27—same as above

Tom, Negro slave, age c. 30—runaway July 27 from Frederick Haring, of Orange Town, NY (8/5)

Oram, Sergeant William, born in north of Ireland, shoemaker by trade, age 36—deserted from H.M.'s 26th Regt. quartered in NYC (8/5)

Roosevelt, Jacobus, of NYC, a batchelor—drank cold water from well in yard of his sugar house, became ill and died Aug. 7 (8/12)

Deforrest, Susannah, wife of Abraham Deforrest—husband will not pay debts contracted by her in future (8/12)

Child, Jonathan Friend, apprentice, age 17—runaway Aug. 4 from sloop *Speedwell* at Beekman's Slip, NYC; reward for his capture offered by Paschal N. Smith (8/12)

O'Niel, Michael, servant, age c. 16—runaway from Martha Vernon (8/12)

Clark, James, of Stony Brook, N.J., one of first settlers there—died there Aug. 10, aged 77, and was buried Aug. 11 in Friends Burying Ground (8/19)

Thatcher, Mrs. Elizabeth, widow of Bartholomew Thatcher, late of Kingwood, West New Jersey—died July 29 in Kingwood, aged 87; she had 17 children, 118 grandchildren, 133 great-grandchildren and 1 great-great-grandchild (8/19)

German, Hugh, Welch servant, tailor by trade, age 30—runaway Aug. 8, 1770, from Hugh Fraser, tailor, in Baltimore Town; he left in company of a Dutchman named Ollis, a tailor, age c. 30 (8/19)

Debow, Frederick, dec'd—plantation in Lower Freehold, N.J., about 5 miles from Monmouth Court House, for sale by Matthias Mount, exec. (8/19)

Boyle, Solomon, dec'd—plantation in Morris Twp., N.J., for sale by execs., Isaac Woodruff, John Chetwood and Solomon Boyle (8/19)

Dunster, Daniel Donaldson, dec'd—lands in eastern division of N.J. for sale (8/26)

Hurry, Cornelius, servant, born in or near Bristol, England, age c. 25—runaway Aug. 16 from Broughton Reynolds, of Elizabeth Town Point, Essex Co., N.J. (8/26)

Aris (or Arison), George, servant, born in England, age c. 27 or 28—same as above

De Lancey, James, Esq., a representative of NYC in the Assembly and a son of Hon.

James De Lancey (late Lt. Gov. of NY)—married Aug. 19 at Shrewsbury, N.J., to Miss Allen, daughter of Hon. William Allen, Esq., Chief Justice of Pa. (8/26)

Aitkin, Charles, Esq., of Island of St. Croix—married Aug. 22 at seat of Jacob Le Roy, Esq., to Miss Cornelia Beekman, daughter of the late Cornelius Beekman, of NYC, merchant (8/26)

Brown, Mary, wife of Thomas Brown—her husband will not pay debts contracted by her in future (9/2)

Cato, Negro slave, age c. 45—runaway July 30 from Jacob Arden, of NYC (9/2)

Little, Nathaniel, apprentice, weaver by trade, age 18—runaway from James Black and Daniel Pearson, of Springfield, near Elizabeth Town, N.J. (9/2)

Foster, Ichabod, tailor by trade, age 18—same as above

Cosine, Cornelius, dec'd—decree in chancery between his execs. and Wm. Hutton, James Henry and others (9/9)

Plumstead, Nathaniel, apprentice, age 18—runaway from John Strickland, of NYC, cordwainer (9/9)

Prickett, Mary, wife of Richard Prickett—has eloped from her husband (9/9)

Gibbons, John, carver and gilder, age 27—deserted July 22 from H.M.'s 29th Regt. (9/9)

Jones, Thomas, cabinetmaker, born in Buvissakane, County of Tipperary, Ireland, age 21—deserted Aug. 30 from H.M.'s 29th Regt. (9/9)

Hart, John, born in city of Limerick, Ireland, age 22—same as above

Frank, Negro slave, age 20—runaway Sept. 2 from Jeremiah Brower, of Kings County, L.I. (9/9)

Verwy, Lawrence, apprentice, gunsmith by trade, age c. 18—runaway July 26 from Collin Van Gelder (9/9)

Waters, Anthony Whitehead, dec'd—personal estate on Staten Island to be sold by execs., Jabez Johnson and Tolman Waters (9/16)

Ben, Negro slave, age 17 or 18—runaway from Wessel Van Schaick, of Albany (9/16)

Lewis, Jacob, servant, age c. 19—runaway Sept. 13 from Daniel Coleman, of Blooming Grove (9/23)

Van Dam, Rip, dec'd—13th of Kayaderasseras Patent to be sold by exec., Robert Livingston, Jr. (9/23)

Stanton, Jeremiah, Esq., formerly captain in 60th Regt.—died Sept. 23 at his house on Staten Island (9/30)

Redmond, Andrew, turner and spinning wheel maker, age c. 30—runaway Aug. 31 from Legh Master, living at Legh Furnace, Little-pipe Creek, Frederick Co., Md. (9/30)

O'Brien, John, weaver by trade, age c. 26—same as above

Will, Negro slave, age c. 30—runaway Sept. 21 from Capt. Stoffel Probasco and Hendrick Probasco, of Millstone, near Somerset Court House, N.J. (9/30)

Prym, Negro slave, age c. 25—same as above

Kessler, Francis, late of Kings Co., dec'd—accounts with estate to be settled with David Matthews, Esq., by order of Sarah Joyce, exec. (10/7)

Thomas, Rev. John, Pastor of the Independent Church of Charles-Town, S.C.—died Sept. 29 (10/7)

Cooke, Mrs., wife of Rev. Mr. Cooke, missionary at Shrewsbury, N.J.—died Sept. 23 in Shrewsbury (10/7)

Lyle, Abraham, dec'd—persons owing debts to estate to pay same to Gerard William Beekman, George Folliot & Co., and Greg, Cunningham & Co. (10/7)

Spragge, Joseph, age c. 35—Sept. 6 broke out of jail of Dutchess Co. (10/14)

Kennedy, Hugh, age c. 30, confined for debt—same as above

Sherlock, William, late of Jamaica, L.I., dec'd—estate to be sold by execs., Samuel Doughty and Henry Dawson (10/21)

John Baptist, Negro slave, age between 40 and 50—runaway from William Darlington (10/21)

Gustan, Catharine Araway, High Dutch girl, age c. 16—runaway Oct. 14 from George
Campbell, living in Irish St., NYC (10/21)

Plenderleith, Lt. John, of the Royal Artillery—married Oct. 21 in NYC to Miss Jennet
Smith, daughter of Hon. William Smith, Esq. (11/4)

Alway, John, a boy belonging to Capt. Clark of ship *Ellin*, from Bristol, age 11 on Dec.
3, 1770—disappeared on that day from ship lying at NYC (11/4)

Downes, Rev. Jonathan, late fellow of St. John's College, U. of Cambridge, and Rector
of St. Peter's Parish, Island of Barbados—died at Bristol Oct. 14 and was buried
Oct. 15 in St. Mary's Church, Burlington, N.J. (11/11)

Holland, Elizabeth, daughter of William Holland, heretofore of James River, Va., shipwright, and Agnes, his wife—Elizabeth or her offspring to apply to Alexander
Colden, Postmaster at NYC, or to James Dixon, Postmaster at Williamsburg, Va.
(11/11)

Messers Bradley, Derby and Vanderlip, of NYC, oystermen—overset and drowned Nov.
5 (11/11)

Davis, John, age c. 22—on Oct. 22 stole a horse from Joseph Tomlinson, of Stratford,
Conn. (11/11)

Miller, Paul, dec'd—house in New Brunswick, N.J., to be sold by Thomas, Paul and
Christopher Miller (11/18)

George, Negro slave, age c. 25—runaway from Jacob Moses, living in Pearl St., NYC
(11/18)

Kettletas, Garret, of NYC, merchant—married last Tuesday se'nnight at Islip, L.I., to
Miss Charity Nicoll, daughter of William Nicoll, Esq., a representative of Suffolk
Co. NY (11/18)

Humphreys, Henry, merchant—married Nov. 9 at house of Mr. Treasurer Lott in NYC
to Miss Gardener, sister of Capt. Valentine Gardener of H.M.'s 55th Regt. (11/18)

M'Cartney, James, dec'd—house on north side of Bayard St., NYC, to be sold by execs.,
Alexander Stewart and Daniel M'Cormick (11/18)

De Laplaine, Joshua, late of NYC, merchant, dec'd—accounts with estate to be settled
with execs., Mary De Laplaine, Samuel Bowne and Thomas Pearsall (11/25)

Peckin, William, born at Eccleshall, County of Stafford, England, who was a soldier in
the 17th Regt. of Foot at Ft. Stanwix in Oct., 1763—is requested to apply to Noel
and Hazard, booksellers, in NYC (12/2)

Flack, Conradt, of Newport, R.I.—last Friday in a quarrel murdered his wife—Newport
dispatch of Nov. 25 (12/2)

Randle, Capt. Thomas, Jr., of NYC—on Nov. 27 was knocked overboard by boom near
Sandy Hook and was drowned (12/2)

Cunningham, Loudon, of Talbot Co., Md.—accidentally shot and killed while hunting
by Mr. John Johnson (12/9)

Mills, James, of NYC, for many years Deputy Sheriff of NYC and for the last 36 years
goaler in NYC—died there Dec. 1 in his 61st year (12/9)

Middleton, Mrs. Susannah, wife of Dr. Middleton, of NYC—died there Dec. 6 in her 43rd
year (12/9)

Waddell, Capt. John, master of sloop *John*, inward bound from West Indies—on Dec. 3
slipped, fell overboard near Sandy Hook and was drowned (12/9)

Schuyler, Arent, formerly of New Barbadoes Neck, Bergen Co., N.J., dec'd—his will is
sought by John Schuyler of New Barbadoes Neck (12/9)

Schuyler, Philip, late of Pompton, Bergen Co., N.J., eldest son of the abovementioned
Arent Schuyler—a deed by him to his brothers, John, Peter and Adonijah Schuyler
is sought by John Schuyler (12/9)

Smedley, Col. James, late of Fairfield, Conn., dec'd—accounts with estate to be settled
with execs., David Suer and John Smedley (12/9)

Crosley, George, smith and farrier, working near Waterman's livery stables in the Broadway, NYC—has formed a partnership with his son-in-law, Nathaniel Wheeler (12/9)

Woolsey, Benjamin, Esq., dec'd—farm in Oyster Bay, Queens Co., L.I., for sale by execs., Jacob Carpenter and James Townsend (12/9)

De Camp, Hendrick, dec'd—farm 1½ miles from Raway Landing, N.J., for sale by executor, John D. Camp (12/9)

Henderson, Mrs. Tiese—real estate in NYC for sale by John Imlay, Alexander Moore and Peter Corne (12/9)

Scull, John—died Dec. 4 at Reading, Pa. (12/16)

Hopkins, Stephen, Esq., dec'd—farm in Nine Partners, Dutchess Co., NY, for sale by Roswell Hopkins (12/16)

Reed, James and Ezra, brothers, of Nine Partners, Dutchess Co.—about 4 weeks ago their storehouse burned down (12/16)

Blair, Rev. John, of Wall-Kill, NY—died there Dec. 8 in his 51st year (12/23)

Hubbard, William, Esq., late of Southold, Suffolk Co., NY—accounts with estate to be settled with Daniel Phenix (12/23)

Lyle, Abraham, late of Albany, dec'd—accounts with estate to be settled with Gerard William Beekman, Hamilton Young and John Moore, trustees appointed to manage the estate (12/23)

Keefe, John, late of Flushing, dec'd—farm for sale; apply to David Bowne (12/23)

Duilap, Capt., master of sloop *Paoli*, belonging to Mr. Gerrish of Halifax—drowned Dec. 3 in wreck of sloop at Nantucket (12/30)

Otis, Amos, mate of sloop *Paoli*—same as above

1772

Casey, Michael, age 17—frozen to death Dec. 5, 1771, in wreck, near Oyster Ponds at east end of Long Island, of schooner *Hannah*, Captain Jabez Perkins, of Swanzey, bound to Norwich, Conn. (1/6)

Mortier, Abraham, Esq., Paymaster General to H.M.'s forces in North America—died Dec. 29, 1771, in his house in NYC in his 60th year and was buried Dec. 31 in Trinity Churchyard (1/6)

Johnston, Dick, Negro, age c. 36—taken up in NYC; owner may have him by applying to William Shearer at the Sign of the Fighting Cocks in NYC (1/6)

Bowers, Henry, Jr., of Swansey in New England—married Jan. 6 in NYC to Miss Mary Myer, youngest daughter of John R. Myer, of Wall St., NYC (1/13)

Kilby, Christopher, Esq., formerly a contractor for North America, well-known in NYC—died lately in England (1/13)

Guest, Mrs. Ann, wife of Henry Guest—died of cancer Jan. 4 in Brunswick, N.J. (1/13)

Will, Negro slave, age c. 24—runaway Nov. 14, 1771, from Samuel Banks, of New Castle, Middle Patent, Westchester Co., NY (1/13)

Johnson, Rev. Samuel, D.D., missionary from the Society for Propagating the Gospel in Foreign Parts and late President of New York College—died Jan. 14 in Stratford, Conn., in his 76th year (1/20)

Miller, Capt. Robert, master of brig *Conolly*, bound from Dublin to Phila. drowned, with all on board, when ship was cast away on Welsh coast (1/20)

Hawkins, Richard, seaman on ship of Capt. John Marshall, bound from St. Kitts to NYC —on Jan. 5 fell from maintop to deck and was killed (1/20)

Antill, Dr. Lewis—married last week in Ulster Co., NY, to Miss Alice Colden, daughter of Col. Cadwallader Colden, of Ulster Co. (1/20)

Taylor, Peter, master of brig belonging to Boston, bound from Gouldsborough— drowned, with all his crew, when brig was cast away on Barnstable bar (1/27)

Smith, James, son of Hon. John Smith, Esq., dec'd—was married Jan. 13 in Burlington to Miss Hetty Hewlings. Phila. dispatch. (1/27)

Tracy. Ensign, of the 18th Regt.—killed by Lt. Robert Hamilton, of the same regt., who was acquitted of charge of manslaughter (1/27)

Longfield, Henry, dec'd—real estate on Rariton River, almost contiguous to New Brunswick, N.J., for sale by Anthony White (1/27)

Allin, Samuel, of Sandisfield (Hartford dispatch of Jan. 21), two small children of—burned to death in conflagration of house about end of Dec., 1771 (2/3)

Odel, Capt. Smith, of Stratford, Conn., for many years a coaster from Stratford to Boston and NYC—on Jan. 27, when opposite to Hempstead, was knocked overboard by boom and drowned (2/3)

Frank, Negro slave, age c. 20—runaway from Jeremiah Brower (2/3)

Permentor, Mrs. Mary, wife of Elias Permentor, of Borough of Westchester—her husband will not pay debts contracted by her in future (2/10)

Willcocks, Timothy, of Stratford, Conn.—desires his son, Timothy Willcocks, Jr., to appear at house of Joseph Tomlinson, of Stratford, where he will be kindly received by his father (2/10)

Blair, Rev. John, Minister of Wall Kill, who died there Dec. 8, 1771—elegy on his death is printed (2/10)

Banks, Capt., of New York City, who was passenger on board Capt. Burr—died on passage from St. Eustatia (2/17)

Ashfield, Lewis Morris, dec'd—notice concerning goods in hands of his administrator, Vincent Pearce Ashfield (2/17)

Moore, Samuel, of Newburgh, Ulster Co., NY—killed a few days ago in a quarrel by David Horton (2/17)

Beekman, Gerard G., Jr., of NYC, merchant, son of Gerard G. Beekman, of NYC, merchant—was married week before last to Miss Cornelia Van Cortlandt, second daughter of Pierre Van Cortlandt, Esq., Representative for the Manor of Cortlandt in Westchester Co. (2/17)

Verplanck, Philip, late of Manor of Cortlandt, dec'd—accounts with estate to be settled with execs., James and Philip Verplanck (2/17)

Mills, James, dec'd—three lots near the sugar house on top of the hill that leads to Fresh Water, NYC, for sale by J. Roberts, sheriff (2/17)

Cary, Samuel, dec'd—two tracts of land in East New Jersey, within a quarter of a mile of Prince-Town, for sale by Sarah Cary, executrix, and Samuel Cary and David Twining, execs. (2/17)

Robinson, Capt., lately a passenger—died at Antigua (2/24)

Warren, Widow, widow of Sir Peter Warren and sister of Oliver De Lancey, Esq., of NYC—died about middle of November, 1771, in England (2/24)

Cuyler, Barent, of NYC, merchant, who went to Barbados for his health—died a few days after his arrival in Barbados (2/24)

Rutgers, Robert, dec'd—dwelling, and brewery to be let by widow, Elizabeth Rutgers (2/24)

Robbins, John, dec'd—real estate at Fresh Water, NYC, for sale by Abraham Mesier (2/24)

Harris, Capt. Richard, dec'd—farm on Staten Island, about one mile from Blazing Star Ferry and three miles from the English Church, for sale by execs., John Alstyne and Abraham and Richard Harris (2/24)

Hughes, John, Esq., late collector of Port of Phila. and late Stamp Master for Pennsylvania—died Feb. 1 (3/2)

Williams, John, late of Jericho, Oysterbay, Queens Co., NY, yeoman, dec'd—Zebulon Williams, second son of Temperance, a daughter of the said John Williams, and Robert Williams, second son of Hannah, a daughter of said John Williams, are confirmed in use of name Williams which they have assumed, having previously been called Zebulon and Robert Seaman (3/2)

Crawford, George—drowned last Saturday week when canoe overset as he was bringing wheat from Rodman's Island, opposite New Rochelle (3/2)

Anderson, John—same as above

Rea, John, a seafaring man belonging to ship *Lucy*, Capt. Anderson master, of Liverpool—drowned Feb. 28 when he fell into New York harbor (3/2)

Richardson, Mr., who used to sell oysters in NYC—drowned last week in New York harbor (3/2)

Remsen, Peter, dec'd—accounts with estate to be settled with execs., Janatje, Simon, Jacob and Henry Remsen (3/2)

Carpenter, John J., merchant, dec'd—mills by side of the great road leading from Goshen to New Windsor on Hudson River for sale by Hezekiah Howell, Jr., near the premises (3/9)

Cuyler, Henry, dec'd—real estate in NYC for sale (3/9)

Edmonds, Jacob, servant, this country born, age c. 21—runaway March 3, in company of a certain John Smith, from Thomas Stephens and Nicholas Everett, of Maidenhead Twp., Hunterdon Co., N.J. (3/9)

Swigard, Peter, late of NYC, tobacconist and chocolate maker, dec'd—accounts with estate to be settled with John Anderson, exec. (3/9)

Cartay, Mary, Irish servant, age c. 20—runaway March 8 from John Miford, living on Pot-bakers Hill, NYC (3/16)

Lansingh, Isaac, of Albany—died there Feb. 10, aged 93 years and 7 months; he had two brothers, one of whom died Dec. 6, 1767, aged 86 years and 7 months and the other on June 30, 1771, aged 97 years, 6 months and 19 days (3/16)

Johnson, Simon, Esq., for many years alderman of NYC—died there March 9 in his 70th year (3/16)

Pintard, Mrs. Susannah, wife of Lewis Pintard, of NYC, merchant—died March 11 in NYC in her 29th year (3/16)

Kyson, Catharine, of NYC, aged 72—her eyes were touched a few days since by Dr. Stephen Little, of Portsmouth, N.H., and her sight was restored (3/16)

Jarvis, Isaac, apprentice, age c. 16—runaway Dec. 13, 1771, from Hezekiah Nichols (3/16)

Woodruff, Samuel, dec'd—property in Elizabeth Town, N.J., to be sold by Matthias Williamson, sheriff (3/16)

Woodruff, Joseph, dec'd—house in Elizabeth Town for sale by William P. Smith, Isaac Woodruff and Elias Boudinot (3/16)

Lashly, Mary, dec'd—house at corner of Flattenbarack Hill, near the Old City Hall in Broad St., NYC, for sale by execs., Charles Philips and Isaac Marschalk (3/16)

Chilcott, Mrs. Christian, wife of Charles O. Chilcott, of NYC, mariner—husband will not pay debts contracted by her in future (3/23)

Ben, Negro slave, age c. 18—runaway from Joseph Lewis, of Huntington, L.I. (3/23)

Livingston, Henry, Esq., merchant, a native of NY—died on Island of Jamaica (3/23)

Ogden, Mrs. Mary, wife of Isaac Ogden, Esq., of Newark, N.J.—died there March 15 (3/23)

De Peyster, Pierre, dec'd—house in Queen St., NYC, for sale by James Desbrosses, the present tenant (3/23)

Roosevelt, Cornelius, dec'd—accounts with estate to be settled with Margaret Roosevelt, executrix, and execs., Jacobus Roosevelt, Jr., Abraham Duryee and John De Peyster, Jr. (3/23); house opposite the Teawater Pump and other real estate for sale by same (7/20)

Richards, Elizabeth, dec'd—house near the New Gaol for sale by Jacob Sharp, exec. (3/23)

GENEALOGICAL DATA FROM THE NEW-YORK GAZETTE; AND THE WEEKLY MERCURY

1772

Hunt, Elvin, dec'd—farm in borough town of Westchester for sale by execs., John Ferris, Daniel White and William Honeywell (3/30)

Myer, Gertryde, dec'd—house in Smith St., NYC, for sale; enquire of Capt. Alexander M'Donald in King St. (3/30)

Smith, John, late of NYC, brazier, dec'd—accounts with estate to be settled with Edward Laight, admin. (3/30)

De Hart, Dr. Matthias, dec'd—house in Elizabeth Town, N.J., for sale; apply to William D'Hart at Morris-Town or Jacob D'Hart, Esq., at Elizabeth Town (4/6)

Stanton, Jeremiah, Esq., dec'd—plantation about a mile from Doyles's Ferry on Staten Island for sale (4/6)

Boelen, Widow Catharine—died April 2, in NYC, aged 82 years and 7 months; she was youngest of six sisters, whose maiden names were Waldron ("a reputable Dutch Family of this Province"); three of them lived to a great age, Judith to 85, Anne to 84, Mary to 80; and two are still living, Sarah and Cornelia, the one of whom is 89, the other 84 years and 5 months; the mother of these truly venerable matrons died in the 95th year of her age of a scratch in her arm which mortified (4/6)

M'Guire, Patrick, carpenter's apprentice, age c. 23—runaway from Joshua Mills, of Newburgh, Ulster Co., NY (4/13)

Patraway, James—killed by hogsheads shifting in storm on March 21 in hold of sloop *Ranger,* Capt. G. Sage master, belonging to Middletown, Conn., northward of Cape Hatteras, on voyage from Jamaica to NYC (4/20)

Roosevelt, Jacobus, lately dec'd—his brother Isaac has moved to house of deceased brother on northwest side of Queen St., NYC (4/20)

Wilkison, Mary, wife of Edward Wilkison, of Woodbridge, N.J.—has left her husband and gone to live with family of her father, William Flat, of Woodbridge (4/27)

Rumbold, Thomas, late of Long Alley, near Moorfields, Middlesex Co., and his brother, William Rumbold, of same place, who were sons of Thomas Rumbold, of the same place, stocking trimmer, dec'd who was the son of William Rumbold, late of King's Clere, County of Southampton, yeoman, dec'd—the heirs of Thomas and William Rumbold, namely William Rumbold, Mary the wife of Alexander Laing, both of Maryland, Mary the wife of Garret Blackford, of New Jersey, Rumbold of Cashel in Ireland, Rodolphus Rumbold of Tipperary in Ireland, William Rumbold of Jamaica, and William Rumbold of the Bay of Honduras are to enter proof of their claims as heirs before John Eames, one of the masters of High Court of Chancery in England (5/4)

English, Capt., master of sloop from Jamaica bound to NYC—died about four weeks ago when his ship was cast away some 40 leagues from the Havannah (5/4)

Schick, Catharina Margarita, otherwise Lisch, wife of Christian Schick, of John's-Town, Albany Co., NY, blacksmith—husband will not pay debts contracted by her in future (5/4)

Waldron, Samuel, dec'd—accounts with estate to be settled with execs., Peter and Catharine Bogert and Francis Basset (5/4)

Harry, Negro slave, age c. 25—runaway April 21 from Elisha Benedict, of Albany (5/4)

Ackland, James, dec'd—Corlear's Hook Tavern, lately occupied by him, in Out-ward of NYC, is now in occupation of John Brandon (5/4)

Decamp, Hendrick, dec'd—farm within two miles of Raway Landing, N.J., for sale by John Decamp and William Smith, execs. (5/11)

Charles, Indian, age c. 20—runaway May 11 from William Field, of Phillips's Manor, Westchester Co., NY (5/18)

Peet, Negro slave, age c. 26, formerly property of Joseph Scudder, of Ash Swamp—runaway May 8 from Abraham Tucker, of Elizabeth Town, N.J. (5/18)

M'Masters, Andrew, an Irishman, who came to America about a year ago with Capt. M'Cutchon, blacksmith, age c. 30—runaway May 9 from his bail in Phila. (5/25)

Van Horne, Garret, dec'd—real estate in NYC for sale by James De Peyster and Joseph Reade (5/25)

Walton, Thomas, of NYC, merchant, "a Gentleman much esteemed by all who knew him"—died May 23 in NYC in his 37th year (5/25)

Johnson, Widow Mary, late of NYC, tavernkeeper, dec'd—accounts with estate to be settled with admins., Jacob Remsen, John Sylvester and Charles Nicoll (6/1)

Snedeker, Johanna, wife of Gerret Snedeker, of NYC—husband will not pay debts contracted by her in future (6/1)

Penn, Richard, Governor of Pa.—married May 21 in Phila. to Miss Polly Masters (6/1)

Hicks, William, Esq., Prothonotary of Bucks Co. and member of Governor's Council of Pa.—died May 25 (6/1)

Budd, John, dec'd—land in Hanover Twp., Morris Co., N.J., for sale; title will be given by Matthew Lum and Joseph Wood, auditors to William Budd (6/1)

Downman, Capt., of H.M.'s Royal Regt. of Artillery—married May 28 in NYC to Miss Jane Day, niece of Col. James (6/1)

Betts, Benjamin, dec'd—house in entrance of Bowery Lane, opposite to the Widow Ricker's, NYC, for sale (6/1)

Manuel, Negro slave, age c. 30—runaway May 31 from John Sandford and John Northrop, of Fairfield Co., Conn. (6/1 and 6/15)

Robin, Negro slave, age c. 25—same as above

Everson, John, dec'd—accounts with estate to be settled with widow, Elsey Everson, living at house of Robert Ray, in Smith's St., NYC (6/1 supplement)

Berkins, David, apprentice, age c. 16—runaway May 11 from Stephen Bates, of Fishkills, Dutchess Co., NY (6/8)

Dick, Negro slave, age c. 24—runaway May 25 from Joseph Drake, of Goshen, NY (6/8)

Seabury, Mrs. Elizabeth, dec'd. widow of late Rev. Samuel Seabury, dec'd—dividend to be paid by trustees of estates, Richard Hewlet and S. Clowes (6/8)

Leach, Clement, of New London, Conn., age 74—found dead in bed on May 24 (6/8)

Swane, Mr., sailor—drowned May 4 when sloop *Sally*, Capt. Jesse Hunt master, bound from NYC to Charlestown, S.C., was cast away on Cape Look-out Shoals (6/8)

Trigleth, Miss, a young woman—same as above

Lipseed, James, grenadier of the 26th Regt.—fell May 24 from gunwale of sloop *Beggars-Benison*, on voyage from NYC to Albany, and was drowned (6/15)

Gilliland, Mrs. Elizabeth, of Wilesborough, near Lake Champlain—died there May 19, aged 32, leaving a husband and five children (6/15)

Brown, Capt. John, of H.M.'s Royal American Regt.—married June 11 in NYC by the Rev. Dr. Rodgers to Miss Molly Livingston, daughter of Peter Van Brugh Livingston, Esq., of NYC (6/15)

Homfray, Jeston, Esq., of Spotswood, N.J., a native of Ols Swinford in Worcestershire—died June 3 in his 45th year and was buried June 5 in Parish Church of Spotswood (6/15)

Trainer, Peter, dec'd—house in Princes St., adjoining Mr. Bull, near the tanyards, NYC, for sale (6/15)

Van Horne, Mrs. Anne, dec'd—house in Chapel St., NYC, for sale; enquire of Augustus Van Horne or John Reade (6/15)

Frederick, Hannah, wife of Michael Frederick, of Fish Kills, NY—eloped June 3 from her husband (6/15)

Eagles, William, dec'd—two houses in Broadway, NYC, for sale by William Eagles (6/22)

Mercer, William, dec'd—real estate in Brunswick, N.J., for sale by execs., Lucy Mercer, Anthony White and G. Harrison (6/22)

Abel, Negro slave, age c. 30—runaway June 8 from Zephaniah Platt, of Poughkeepsie, NY (6/22)

Morehouse, John, apprentice, age 18—runaway May 23 from Caleb Stagg, of Danbury, Fairfield Co., Conn. (6/29)

Runyon, Mr., of Hopewell Twp., Hunterdon Co., N.J.—on June 13 run over by his wagon near Pennington and killed (6/29)

Brewster, Samuel, Esq., of South Haven, Suffolk Co., L.I.—struck by one of his Negroes on June 22 and died the next day (6/29)

Ray, Miss Hannah, daughter of John Ray, of NYC, merchant—died June 27 in NYC in her 22nd year of consumption (6/29)

Costekin, Anthony, indented servant, native of Ireland—runaway June 24 from Michael Ganter, of NYC, gunsmith (6/29)

Cato, Negro slave, age c. 17—runaway May 23 from Philip Van Petta, of Schenectady (6/29)

M'Daniel, Daniel, born in Scotland, who lived for a time in Port Penn, New-Castle County—stole a watch and other articles on June 24 from shallop of John Tracy at falls of Trentown (7/6)

Pinkney, Philip, age c. 28 or 30—June 22 broke out of Westchester Co. jail (7/6)

Killock, Oliver, shoemaker and cooper, age 23 or 24—same as above

Purdie, Nathan, cooper, age c. 60—same as above

Harris, Mr., a merchant's clerk at Ft. Bute in the river—killed recently by the superintendent in a quarrel (7/13)

Davies, Capt.—died on Island of Rattan and was buried there (7/13)

Farrel, James, of Greenwich, N.J.—lately murdered at Stockbridge in New England, supposedly by a certain Harvey; he left a wife and several children (7/13)

Taylor, Thomas, Irish servant, age c. 23—runaway from John Bull, of Norrington Twp., Philadelphia Co., Pa. (7/13)

McCan, William, Irish servant, age c. 33—same as above

Harding, Charles, mulatto slave, age c. 30, carpenter and joiner who learned his trade from Lewis Allmorn, of Nansemond Co., Va., who sold him to Edward Voss, bricklayer, of Va.—runaway from Samuel Owings, Jr., and Alexander Wells, living near Soldiers Delight, Baltimore Co., Md. (7/20)

Maitland, Col. Richard, Deputy Adjutant General of H.M.'s troops in America, fourth son of Charles, Earl of Lauderdale, and his wife, Lady Ann Ogilvie, daughter of James Ogilvie, Earl of Findlater, etc.—died July 13 in NYC in his 48th year and on July 14 was buried in Trinity Church Yard (7/20)

Bryant, Capt. William, of Perth Amboy, for upwards of 30 years a navigator between NYC and London—died July 14 in Perth Amboy, N.J., in his 78th year (7/20)

Tom, mulatto slave, age c. 30—runaway July 11 from Charles Broadhead, of the Wallkill, Ulster Co., NY (7/20)

Walker, Hon. Robert, Esq., a judge of the Superior Court and member of the Council of Conn.—died July 13 at his home in Stratfield, Conn., of an apoplectic fit (7/27)

Johnson, Isaiah, age c. 21—escaped June 27 from Newark, N.J., jail, where he was committed on suspicion of burglary (7/27)

Plato, Negro slave, age c. 28—runaway July 19 from Nathan Field, of Harrison's Purchase, Rye, Westchester Co., NY (7/27)

Nichols, Mrs. Margaret, wife of Richard Nichols, Esq., of NYC—died July 20 in NYC in her 73rd year and was buried in family vault in Trinity Church Yard (8/3)

Thompson, William Esq.—died July 30 at Goshen, Orange Co., NY, in his 52nd year (8/3)

Foy, Capt.—married July 16 to Miss Hannah Van Horne, daughter of John Van Horne, Esq., of Kills Hall (8/3)

Markland, John, apprentice, age between 16 and 17—runaway July 28 from Hugh Gaine, of NYC, printer (8/3)

Bartram, Mrs. Eleanor, of Front St., Southwark, "an old gentlewoman," the mother of Alexander and George Bartram, merchants of Phila.—Aug. 4 was struck down by Philip Hines and her life is despaired of (8/10)

Gomez, Benjamin, of NYC, merchant—died Aug. 8 in NYC in his 62nd year, leaving an only daughter (8/10)

Tittle, John, of Baltimore, Md., age between 30 and 40—absconded with money from sale of tinware at Charlestown, Md.; reward for his arrest is offered by William Bowen, of Baltimore, Md., tinman, and Thomas Russell, blacksmith, of Princetown, N.J. (8/10)

Freyer, George Paul, Dutch servant, who has been in America almost two years, age c. 21—runaway April 26 from Jesse Bonsall and John Pearson, of Darby Co., Pa. (8/10)

Bedine, Mr. and Mrs. Francis, of Wall Kill, Ulster Co., NY—both died at same time a few days ago (8/17)

Hams, Ezekiel, indented servant, blacksmith, age c. 30—runaway Aug. 2 from Jesse Fairchild, of Albany (8/17)

Moore, Augustine, Esq., late of Morris-Town, N.J., dec'd—house at Morris-Town for sale by widow, Mary Moore (8/24)

Cato, Negro slave, age c. 22, who about three months ago belonged to Charles Tooker, of Borough of Elizabeth, Essex Co., N.J.—runaway Aug. 8 from John De Peyster, Jr., of NYC (8/24, 11/30)

Cornwell, Joseph, dec'd—estate joining Success Pond, Flushing, Queens Co., NY, for sale by execs., Daniel Thorne and Henry Woolley (8/31)

Norwood, Cornelius, late of NYC, shopkeeper, dec'd—real estate for sale; also accounts with estate to be settled with execs., Andrew and Richard Norwood and Samuel Broadhurst (8/31)

Stephens, Michael, servant, Frenchman, age c. 22—runaway Aug. 23 from Thomas Harrison, living in Strawberry Alley, Phila. (8/31)

Kelly, Thomas, Irish servant, age c. 17—same as above

Pryor, William, painter, apprentice boy—runaway Aug. 23 from Thomas and James Barrow, painters, in Broad St., NYC (8/31)

Gorman, Hugh, apprentice, age c. 20—runaway Aug. 20 from Alexander Stewart, of NYC (9/7)

Harding, Rev. Robert, for 23 years pastor of Roman Catholic Congregation in Phila.— died there Sept. 1 in his 70th year (9/7)

Hoffman, Col. Martin—died Aug. 29 in NYC in his 66th year (9/7); accounts with estate to be settled with Anthony and Martin Hoffman in Red Hook or with execs., in NYC, Alida and Nicholas Hoffman and Isaac Roosevelt (11/16)

Lambert, John, of NYC, merchant—died Sept. 2 in NYC and was buried at the New Brick Meeting (9/7)

O'Brien, Charles, age c. 11, son of Mr. O'Brien, of NYC, schoolmaster—was drowned Sept. 5 when boat in Second River, near Newark, overset (9/7)

Gojion, Lawrence, *alias* John Johnston, indented servant, born in Phila., carpenter, who has two brothers living at the Wallkill in Ulster Co., NY—runaway Aug. 28 from Jacob Lawrence, living at Nine Partners, Dutchess Co., NY (9/7)

Verplanck, Isaac, of Albany—as one of the great-grandchildren of Abraham Verplanck, dec'd., lays claim to lots in Wall St., NY (9/7)

Paul, Moses, murderer of Mr. Cook—executed Sept. 2 about a mile from New Haven, Conn.; Rev. Mr. Occom preached a sermon, previous to the execution, in the Brick Meeting House (9/14)

Graeme, Dr., dec'd.—Richard Hockley, Esq., is appointed Naval Officer of Port of Phila. in his place (9/14)

Beatty, Rev. Charles, many years minister at Neshaminey, Pa.—died Aug. 13 in Barbados, where he had gone to sollicit benefactions for the College of New Jersey (9/14)

Elliot, Solomon, well-known in Phila. as a Carolina trader—murdered in South Carolina by a Mr. and Mrs. Kelly, at whose house he lodged (9/14)

Claus, Negro slave, age c. 18—runaway from Isaac Leggett, of Westchester, NY (9/14)

Boel, Mrs. Elizabeth, widow of late Rev. Henry Boel, minister of Dutch Reformed Churches in NYC—died Sept. 9 in NYC in her 69th year; she was daughter of late Garret Van Horne, of NYC, merchant; she was buried Sept. 11 in family vault (9/14)

De Lemontonie, John, dec'd—accounts with estate to be settled with exec., Catharine De Lemontonie (9/21)

Clarkson, Matthew, of Flatbush, L.I., merchant, formerly of NYC—died Sept. 18 (9/28)

Thompson, William, who says he was born in New Jersey, age c. 24 or 25—on Sept. 22 stole goods from house of Sampson Benson, of Harlem, Out-ward, NYC (10/5); executed in NYC on Nov. 13 (11/2 and 11/23)

Jelf, Joseph, of Elizabeth Town, N.J., merchant—died there Sept. 30 (10/5)

Hoghland, Adrian, dec'd—farm in Bloomingdale, Out-ward of NYC, for sale by execs., Richard Fletcher and Benjamin and William Hoghland (10/12)

Low, Mrs. Ann, wife of Cornelius P. Low, of NYC, merchant—died Oct. 4 in NYC in her 51st year and was buried in family vault in New Dutch Church Yard (10/12)

Burdon, William, of Great Farrington, County of Devon, mercer, who in 1755 went to NYC as a factor and lived for a time with Mr. Johnscourt at the Meal Market, age c. 36—news of him is desired by Charles Burdon, near Hatherly Devon (10/12)

Deserted from First Battalion of Royal American Regt. (10/12):

Jordon, James, born in Ireland, wheelwright, age 25

Mill, John, born in Pa., tinker, age 23

St. Clair, Alexander, born in Scotland, laborer, age 24

Hands, John, born at Goshen, NY, shoemaker, age 23

Collins, Dennis, born in Ireland, laborer, age 20

Sheilds (or Sheets), James, age c. 30—supposed to have murdered James Johnson, whose corpse was found in a grove near Saybrook Ferry, New London Co., Conn. (10/26)

Atsatt, Thomas was arrested and jailed at Newport, R.I., on suspicion of having murdered a man near Saybrook Ferry (11/2)

Conklin, Elias, late of Precinct of Newburgh, dec'd—Stephen Case has bought land in Newburgh from Nicholas Conklin, heir at law of Elias (11/2)

Hoogland, John, dec'd—farm at Flushing, L.I., for sale by Elbert Hoogland in Flushing or Stephen Rapalje in NYC (11/2)

Bennet, Wynant, dec'd—personal estate to be sold at his house at Gawaanis, Twp. of Brooklyn, Kings Co., NY, by his execs., Johannis Bergen, Simon Boerum and John Rapalje (11/2)

Stevenson, Capt. John, of NYC, mariner, dec'd—goods to be sold (11/2)

Sambo, Negro slave, age c. 25—taken away Oct. 18 from Caleb Morgan, of Eastchester, NY, by a white man supposed to be John Norris, age c. 30, who often goes to the Jerseys (11/2)

Montanye, Jacobus, late of NYC, dec'd—accounts with estate to be settled with John
Felthausen, of NYC (11/9)

Sheerer, Mary, wife of John Sheerer, Jr., of Nine Partners, Dutchess Co., NY—has eloped
from her husband (11/9)

Gomez, Benjamin, dec'd—accounts with estate to be settled with execs., Rachel and
Mattathias Gomez; persons indebted to late partnership of Benjamin and Mattathias
Gomez are to pay debts to Mattathias (11/9)

Chadwick, Capt., of the 16th Regt. in Pensacola—lately married to Miss Chester, the
governor's daughter (11/16)

Wigneron, Dr. Charles Anthony, who arrived in NYC some 15 days before from Newport, R.I.—died Nov. 10 at home of Mrs. Pine in NYC from smallpox, which he
took by innoculation, in his 56th year (11/16)

Berragar, Henry, High Dutch servant, age c. 27—runaway Oct. 2 from William and Isaac
Clarke, living near Princetown, N.J. (11/16)

Yerry, *alias* George Wortman, High Dutch servant, age c. 20—same as above

————, Nicholas, High Dutch servant, age c. 21—same as above

De Bevoeise, Jacob, late of Gowaanus, dec'd—unsold lands about 2 miles from New
York Ferry for sale by execs., Johannes and Jacobus De Bevoeise (11/23)

Warren, John, servant, age c. 21—runaway Oct. 15 from George Norris, of Princeton,
N.J. (11/23)

McDonald, Collin, redemptioner, born in Highlands of Scotland, tailor, age c. 36—runaway in Phila. from ship *Wolfe*, Richard Hunter master, from Londonderry
(11/23)

Hubbard, William, formerly of Southold, dec'd—accounts with estate to be settled with
Ezra Lehommedieu in Suffolk Co. or with Daniel Phaenix, admin. (11/23)

Schuyler, Myndert, late of NYC, dec'd—accounts with estate to be settled with Elizabeth
Schuyler, admin. (11/23)

Jack, Negro slave, age c. 28—runaway from Lewis Morris of Morrissania, Westchester
Co., NY (11/23)

Mingo (or Tim), Negro slave, age c. 30—runaway Oct. 18 from Samuel Ogden, of Boon-
town, Morris Co., N.J. (11/30)

Nickerson, Thomas, master of a schooner which sailed Nov. 14 from Boston, bound
to Chatham—boarded at sea, according to Ameli or Ansell Nickerson, and killed;
he was a "cousin german" of the captain, and was arrested on suspicion; they were
both from Barnstable, Mass. (11/30)

Newcomb, Elisha, of Barnstable, who married a sister of the Nickersons—killed on
the schooner (11/30)

Kent, William, Jr., of Barnstable, age c. 13—killed on the schooner (11/30)

Thorp, Mrs., wife of John Thorp, of Jew's Alley, NYC—murdered Nov. 26 by her husband (11/30)

Edwards, John, age c. 17—runaway from the snow *Freeholder*, John Ton master (11/30)

Quill, Thomas, age c. 24, barber and peruke-maker, who had served his time with
Robert Graves, peruke-maker in Phila. and with George Myers in Lancaster—runaway Nov. 25 from John James, of Lecock Twp., Lancaster Co., Pa. (12/7)

Grayham, Alexander, Scotch or Irish born, age, 37 or 38—stole money and goods from
store of John M'Lean, of Danbury, Conn. (12/7)

Nicol, Mrs. Joanna, wife of William Nicol, Esq., of Islip, L.I., one of the representatives
of Suffolk Co.—died Dec. 3 in NYC in her 42nd year (12/7)

Warren, Sir Peter and Lady Susan—accounts with their estates to be settled with Oliver
De Lancey (12/7)

Sharpas, William, late of NYC, dec'd and his daughter, Elizabeth Sharpas, dec'd—all
persons with claims on estates to apply to Zephaniah Bond, living at David Grigg's,
at the Sign of the Philadelphia Arms, in Oswego St., NYC, who is impowered to

sue for and to receive share of Mary Parnham, of Md., widow (once married to Philip Briowe), and her children (12/7)

D. L. Montanie, John, painter and glazier, dec'd—accounts with estate to be settled with Catharine D. L. Montanie, executrix (12/14)

Rand, Joshua, late of Detroit, dec'd—accounts with estate to be settled with John Backhouse, admin. (12/14)

Merritt, George, dec'd—farm joining the Jews Creek in New Marlborough Precinct, Ulster Co., NY, for sale by Gabriel or David Merritt, living on premises (12/14; 12/28)

Remington, Israel, born (1758) and living in Hingham, Mass.—is a young giant, weighing about 200 lbs. and is 5ft. in height (12/21)

Wallace, Alexander, late of NYC, tallow-chandler, dec'd—accounts with estate to be settled with widow, Jane Wallace, executrix (12/28)

Bezley, Oliver, dec'd—farm in New Rochelle for sale (12/28)

Henderson, Tiesie, dec'd—real estate for sale (12/28)

Broke out of Morris Co., N.J., jail on Dec. 7 (12/28):

Norris, John, age c. 28, charged with stealing a Negro from one Morgan, of Eastchester

Hall, George, a West-countryman, age c. 25

Campbell, George, Irishman, age c. 24

M'Curdy, Daniel, age c. 24, brought up in Suckersunny, Morris Co., N.J.

Douglas, James, age c. 23

GENEALOGICAL DATA FROM THE NEW-YORK GAZETTE; AND THE WEEKLY MERCURY

1773

Hall, David, of Phila., printer—died there Dec. 24 in his 58th year and was buried Dec. 27 in Christ's Church burying ground (1/4)

Parker, James, late of NYC, printer, dec'd—two houses and lots in Beaver St., NYC, for sale by Daniel Marsh at Roosevelt's Dock, NYC, or Mary Parker at Woodbridge (1/4)

Horsfield, Israel, dec'd—real estate at Brooklyn Ferry for sale by Henry Van Vleck, acting executor, or Thomas Horsfield near the premises (1/4)

Singo, Negro slave, age c. 30—runaway from Archibald M'Curdy, living near Goshen and the Precinct of Wall-Kill (1/11)

Roberts, Ichabud, apprentice, shoemaker and tanner, age c. 19—runaway from Isaac Plume, of Newark, N.J. (1/11)

Robinson, Thomas, native of Ireland, hostler—runaway Jan. 6 from William Graham, living at the Sign of the Unicorn, Elizabeth Town, N.J. (1/11)

Warrin, John, servant, age c. 18—runaway from George Norris, near Princeton, N.J. (1/11)

Jack, Negro slave, age c. 30, purchased from Hendrick Emons, of Rocky Hill, N.J.—runaway Dec. 27, 1772, from Peter Keteltas (1/11)

Dick, Negro slave, age 19—runaway from Charles Inglis, living in Hanover Square, NYC (1/11)

Johnston, Boulter, Esq., of H. M.'s 70th Regt., brother of Sir Richard Johnston—married Jan. 12 at Greenwich, Conn., to Miss Alida Bayard, eldest daughter of Col. William Bayard (1/18)

Gourlay, Mr., of partnership of Gray and Gourlay, dec'd—Hugh Gray gives notice that partnership is dissolved by death of Gourlay (1/18)

Chester, Capt., late commander of brig *Norwich Packet,* which sailed from New London, Conn., on Aug. 21—drowned in gale on Sept. 16, 1772, as related by Douglas Woodworth, chief mate (1/25)

Buzzy, John, a single man, hired in NYC, one of crew of oyster boat owned by James Thompson, of NYC—drowned Jan. 21 in wreck of boat on east end of Rockaway Bar (1/25)

Riley, Thomas, who lived near Horse Neck, where he left a wife and three children, one of crew of oyster boat—same as above

Waddel, Mrs. Geesie, wife of William Waddel, of NYC, merchant, and daughter of Francis Filkin, Esq.—died Jan. 19 in NYC in her 33rd year and was buried Jan. 21 in Trinity Church Yard (1/25)

Bockee, Rebeccah, dec'd—house in Maiden Lane, NYC, for sale; enquire of William Bockee or Frederick Roorbach (1/25)

Harris, Capt. Richard, dec'd—farm on Staten Island for sale by execs., John Alstyne and Abraham and Richard Harris (1/25)

Rout, Simeon—buried and killed Dec. 24, 1772, by collapse of earth while digging a well in Piermont, N.H. (2/1)

Welsh, Mr., from Canada, a well-digger by trade—same as above

Stone, John—accidentally wounded with a knife on Dec. 21, 1772 in Scarborough, Mass., and died in less than 48 hours, leaving a widow and several small children (2/1)

Ten Broeck, Cornelius, Esq., of Albany, merchant—died there Jan. 9 in his 67th year and was buried Jan. 12 in the Dutch Church (2/1)

Roos (or Roose), Gerrit, dec'd—two houses in Division St., in NYC, for sale by Anthony Rutgers, admin. (2/1)

M'Fall, Robert, Scotch servant—runaway about Dec. 10, 1772, from Peter Stuyvesant, living in the Bowery, NYC (2/1)

Carskaden, Robert, dec'd—farm in Little Britain, Ulster Co., for sale by Patrick and James McClaghry (2/8)

Everson, John, dec'd—land in Great Nine Partners Patent, Dutchess Co., NY, for sale by George Everson (2/8)

Sam, Negro slave, age c. 26—runaway Aug. 29, 1772, from John Bryan, of Manor of Cortlandt (2/8)

Mullock, Joshua, dec'd—his creditors to meet at house of Samuel Francis, at the Exchange, NYC (2/8)

Seaman, Davis, dec'd—farm in Twp. of Oysterbay, Queens Co., NY, for sale by execs., Zebulon Williams, Richard Willits, William and David Seaman; apply to Zebulon Williams (late Zebulon Seaman), Richard Willits or William Seaman at Jericho, or to David Seaman, at the head of New Slip in NYC (2/15)

Jelf, Joseph, dec'd—farm in Mendom, Morris Co., N.J., and houses in Elizabeth Town for sale by execs., William B. Jelf and John Chetwood (2/15)

Cowan, Samuel, servant, a joiner, who was born in America and learned his trade in Phila., age c. 25—runaway from Samuel Owings, Jr., of Baltimore, Md. (2/15)

Quinn, Patrick, Irish servant, age c. 40—same as above

Wallace, Alexander, tallow-chandler, dec'd—accounts to be settled with Jane Wallace, exec. (2/15)

Waldron, Samuel, dec'd—farm at New Harlem, at the nine mile stone from NYC, on the road leading to King's Bridge, for sale; apply to Teunis Ryer on the premises or to Lawrence Myer at Harlem (2/22)

Wright, John, dec'd—two small houses, opposite Capt. Normond Tolmie's, in NYC, for sale by Samuel Loudon, exec. (2/22)

Whitman, Joseph, born on Long Island, tailor and weaver—runaway from Josiah Hunt, of North Castle, Westchester Co., NY (2/22)

Smith, John, dec'd—house opopsite the Coffee-House Bridge, where Messers Thompson and Selby live, for sale (2/22)

Way, Isaac, age c. 40, who says he was born in Pa. and was brought up in Phila.,—on Sunday evening, Jan. 24, came to house of Nathan Burril, Jr., in Norwalk, Conn., and, being deranged, tried to commit suicide (3/1)

Rogers, Capt. Robert, of first battalion of the Royal Regt. of Artillery, son of the late Capt. Rogers of the 8th or Queens Regt. of Foot—died the 23rd ultimo in NYC in his 32nd. year, leaving a widow and three children (3/1)

Dawson, Richard, late of NYC, butcher, dec'd—accounts with estate to be settled with Elizabeth Dawson, admin. (3/1)

Van Tuyl, Otto, dec'd—farm on Staten Island, where James Arnot now lives, for rent; apply to Col. Benjamin Seaman, Cornelius Cruse on Staten Island, or Andrew Van Tuyl, at Mr. Garret Rapalje's in NYC (3/1)

Pugsley, John, dec'd—Appleby's Island, adjoining Manor of Pelham, for sale by James, William, Gilbert and David Pugsley (3/1)

Frost, Zebulon, dec'd—farm in Twp. of Oysterbay, L.I., for sale by Benjamin Townsend, living in Jericho, Benjamin Coles at Musqueto Cove, or Penn. Frost at Metenicock (3/1 suppl.)

Van Dyck, John, late of Twp. of New Utrecht, Kings Co., NY, dec'd—plantation for sale by exec., Adolphus Bensen, living at Harlem, in Out-ward of NYC (3/8)

Comes, John, dec'd—house in town of Jamaica, L.I., where his widow now lives, for sale by Kiziah Comes, executrix, and Henry Dawson, exec. (3/8, see also 12/13)

Remsen, Peter, dec'd—accounts with estate to be settled with Janetie Remsen, executrix, and Simon, Jacob and Henry Remsen, execs. (3/8)

Waldron, Peter, dec'd—farm at Harlem, in Out-ward of NYC, for sale by execs., Elizabeth, Cornelia, Peter and John P. Waldron (3/15)

Smedes, Benjamin P., of Poughkeepsie Precinct, Dutchess Co., NY, miller, dec'd—lands in hands of the administrator, Jacob Smedes, are to be sold by order of sheriff (3/15)

Willis, John, servant, born in Boston, tailor—runaway March 1 from John Bainbridge (3/22)

Schenk, Johannis—two farms in Reading Town, Hunterdon Co., N.J., late his property, for sale by Peter Schenk, at Mill-stone, Sommerset Co., (3/22)

Weseneer, Christian—killed by Indians about Dec. 15, 1772, at Detroit (3/22)

Robins, John, dec'd—tanyard at the Fresh Water, NYC, to be let (3/22)

Riel, Abraham, late of Out-ward of NYC, dec'd—furniture and other items for sale by Robert Sinclair, admin. (3/22)

Mills, Capt. Treat, late of Stratford, Conn.—estate is insolvent and creditors are to meet at inn of Elisha Mills in Stratford by order of commissioners, Samuel Adams and Augur Judson (3/22)

Ned, Negro slave, age c. 31—runaway Jan. 5 from Simon Mabee, of Cortlandt's Manor, Westchester Co., NY (3/22)

Cornell, John, late of Flushing, dec'd—farm at Whitestone, adjoining the Sound, for sale by Thomas Cornell (3/29)

Du Bois, Gualtharus, dec'd—accounts with estate to be settled with execs., Walter and Margaret Dubois (4/5)

Pinkard, Jonathan, indented English servant, watchmaker, age c. 25—runaway March 25 from Samuel Jefferys, of Phila., watchmaker (4/5)

Wright, Jonas, dec'd—house in Cherry St., to east of Walter Franklin's and nearly opposite Capt. Tolmie's, in NYC, for sale (4/5)

Ricketts, Jacob, son of late Col. Ricketts—married March 30 in NYC to Miss Polly Thompson, daughter of James Thompson, formerly of NYC; farm of Col. Ricketts in Elizabeth Town, N.J., for sale (4/5)

Alberton, Richard, dec'd—farm at Newbury, Ulster Co., NY, for sale (4/5)

Scotland, Negro, who says he is free and came from the West Indies to Phila., age c. 22—taken up in January by Benjamin Hopkins and James Tripp, of North Castle, Westchester Co., NY (4/12)

Haynes, Joseph, dec'd—real estate for sale by Taylor and De Lancey (4/12)

Genter, John, dec'd—accounts with estate to be settled with execs., Humphrey Jones and James Van Varck (4/12)

Smith, Thomas, age c. 25—broke out of jail of Westchester Co. on April 15; reward for his capture offered by James De Lancey, Jr., sheriff (4/19)

Hobbs (or Hubbs), Zephaniah, age c. 30—same as above

James, Negro slave, age c. 30—runaway from Joshua Carman, Jr., of the Fishkills, Dutchess Co., NY (4/19)

Cush, Negro slave, age between 28 and 30—runaway about three months ago from John Foster, living at Southampton, L.I. (4/19)

Wilson, Alexander, of NYC, who arrived in the East Indies in 1752—any relations are to apply to Hugh Gaine to hear something to their advantage (4/26)

Harrison, George, Esq., of NYC, son of the Hon. Francis Harrison, formerly member of H. M.'s Council for NY, descended from an ancient family in Berkshire—died April 18 in NYC and was buried April 20 in the family vault in Trinity Church Yard (2/26)

Levine, John, of NYC, occulist—died April 19 in NYC in his 35th year and was
buried April 21 in Trinity Church Yard (4/26)

Dewit, John, a "young" man—died April 19 in a house on Cowfoot Hill, NYC, and
was buried April 22 (4/26)

Hamilton, Rev. John, of Charles-Town, Md., both a clergyman and physician—died
there April 12 (5/3)

Burns, John (*alias* Thomas Watson)—executed April 28 in NYC for robbing house
of Samson Benson (5/3 and 5/31)

Thompson, John, servant, age c. 30—runaway April 4 from Samuel Yarley, of Falls
Twp., Bucks Co., Pa. (5/3)

GENEALOGICAL DATA FROM THE NEW-YORK GAZETTE; AND THE WEEKLY MERCURY

De Peyster, Pierre, dec'd—lot on Golden Hill, NYC, for sale by Anthony Bleecker (5/3)

Fisher (or Fitched), Abraham, born on Long Island, of English descent, age c. 34— runaway April 12 from John Van Etten, living in Fork's Twp., Northampton Co. (5/10)

Schuyler, Myndert, dec'd—accounts with estate to be settled with Elizabeth Schuyler, executrix (5/10)

Vanhorne, Cornelius C., dec'd—house in Little Dock St., NYC, lately tenented by Mr. Speaight, chemist, and also a house in rear of the same, tenented by Mr. Myers, carpenter, between houses of Col. William Bayard and David Provoost, for sale (5/10)

Valentine, Capt. Mark, commander of a private ship of war, native of England, whence he came some 36 years ago—died last week in NYC (5/10)

Wilson, Joseph, of NYC, who for many years commanded a ship out of Port of NY, son of a former mayor of NYC—died May 6 in NYC in his 76th year (5/10)

Jauncey, Capt. John, Jr., dec'd—all with claims against his estate are to meet at Mr. Hull's tavern, near the City Hall, NYC (5/10); accounts with estate to be settled with Philip Kissick, admin. (6/14)

Bret, Negro slave, age c. 33. whom the Salmons have had at Weyoming for three years past—runaway March 13 from Jecamiah Smith, living at Connecticut Farms, near Elizabeth Town, N.J. (5/10)

Byington, Abraham, of Parish of Farmingbury, in Waterbury, Conn., apprentice, age c. 18—accidentally shot and killed May 23, at a general muster of the militia, by another apprentice, a certain Harrison, age c. 18 (5/17)

Greaton, Rev., Episcopal minister of Huntington, L.I.—died there April 17 (5/17)

Yoeman, James, of NYC, watchmaker—died May 13 in NYC (5/17)

Crawford, William, late of NYC, cooper, dec'd—accounts with estate to be settled with Sidney Crawford, executrix (5/17)

Hager, Negro wench, age c. 20—runaway May 9 from Jacob Morrell, of Morris Co., N.J. (5/24)

Austin, Mr., late in charge of grammar school at Albany, dec'd—teacher is sought in his place (5/24)

Tankard, William, indented servant, native of Ireland, age c. 20—runaway from D. Dulany, of Annapolis, Md. (5/24)

Barry, Bernard, indented servant, native of Ireland, age c. 28—runaway from James Mawe, of Annapolis; Upton Scott, of Annapolis, will pay reward for recovery of bay horse taken by Barry (5/24)

Lee (or Grove), William, age c. 28 or 30—on May 17 broke out of jail of Orange Co., in Goshen, NY (5/31)

Bennit, Justice, country born, age c. 21 or 22 same as above

Flaningham, Alexander, a young man, born at Goshen—same as above

Pero, Negro slave, age c. 18—runaway March 20 from Elijah Clark, living at Great-Egg-Harbor, Gloucester Co., N.J. (5/31)

Furman, ———, woman of Princeton, N.J.—died there May 21 (5/31)

Richey, William—died at Princeton, N.J., on May 22, before house of Capt. Stanford (5/31)

Waddel, Mrs. Anne, relict of John Waddel, late of NYC, merchant—died May 26 at her seat in Harlem in her 57th year and was buried May 28 in family vault in Trinity Church Yard (5/31)

Reddon (or Redmon), Mr., age between 25 and 30, who said he came from Pa.—passed a counterfeit bill on May 28 or 29 to Samuel Harris, of Morris Town, N.J. (6/7)

Harman, Mrs. Catharine Maria, one of American Company of Commedians and granddaughter of Colley Cibber, Esq.—died May 27 in NYC in her 43rd year and was buried May 28 in Trinity Church Yard (6/7)

Ingles, Rev. Charles, of NYC—married May 31 to Miss Margaret Crook, daughter of John Crook, Esq., late of Kingston, Ulster Co., NY, dec'd (6/7)

Leonard, William, Irish servant, tailor, age c. 25—runaway June 1 from James M'Kenney, living in Princes St., NYC (6/14)

Duncan, Thomas, of NYC, merchant, son of George Duncan, of Great George St.—married June 8 to Miss Peggy Beverhudt, of Hanover Square (6/14)

Crook, Mr., of NYC, pilot—drowned June 9 near Governor's Island when coming up from the Narrows (6/14)

Wallis, Mrs. Jane, wife of Thomas Wallis, barrack master at Niagara—died June 9 in her 28th year and was buried June 10 in the Old Presbyterian Meeting Yard (6/14)

Bant, Richard, who left England about 13 years ago and is supposed to sail in a merchant ship from Boston or NYC—is asked to apply to Speakman and Carter, chemists, in Phila., to learn something to his advantage (6/14)

Bond, Dr. Phineas—died June 11 in Phila. in his 56th year (6/21)

De Lancey, Stephen, Esq., eldest son of Hon. Oliver De Lancey, Esq., of NYC—married June 16 in NYC to Miss Kitty Barclay, eldest daughter of the late Rev. Dr. Barclay, of NYC (6/21)

Adolphus, Mrs., wife of Isaac Adolphus, of NYC, merchant—died June 18 in NYC of apoplexy (6/21)

Forester, Joseph, Irish servant, age c. 24—runaway from the brig *Peter and John,* John Simons master (6/21)

Harry, mulatto slave, age c. 20—runaway from Thomas Brown, of Newark, N.J. (6/21)

Rice, Abraham, late of NYC, dec'd—accounts with estate to be settled with Capt. Robert Sinclair, admin. (6/21)

Harker, Richard, late of New Marlborough, Ulster Co., NY, dec'd—accounts with estate to be settled with Joseph Morey, exec. (6/28)

Dubois, Peter, of Fish-Kills, Dutchess Co., NY—died June 20 as result of fall from horse (6/28)

White, Robert, Esq.—knocked down and killed about 6 weeks ago in street near St. Paul's Church by one Francis Personel, *alias* Parsells (6/28)

Goelet, Mrs. Mary, wife of Peter Goelet, of NYC, merchant, and daughter of Henry Ludlow, of NYC—died June 26 in NYC in her 39th year, leaving husband and 8 children; she was buried June 27 in family vault in Trinity Church Yard (6/28)

Ward, William, and wife, of Salem, Mass.—drowned June 17 when boat overset in squall off Marblehead (7/5)

Diggadon, Mr. and wife, of Salem—same as above

Kimball, John, and wife, of Salem—same as above

Giles, Eleazer, widow of, of Salem—same as above

Fairfield, Dr., daughter of, of Salem—same as above

Becket, John, of Salem, boatbuilder, wife of—same as above

Ludlow, John, Jr.—died last week from injuries when horse ran away and was buried in Flushing, L.I. (7/5)

Personel, Francis Burdett, native of Ireland, gunsmith, who came to America about 6 years ago and who married on April 4 Mary Burtin, whose father lived in Newtown, L.I.—reference to him as murderer of Robert White; executed Sept. 10 (7/5, 8/2, and 9/13)

Johnson, Sir John, son of Sir William Johnson—married June 30 to Miss Polly Watts, daughter of Hon. John Watts, Esq., of H.M.'s Council (7/5)

Williams, Charles, Esq., Naval Officer of H.M.'s Customs of Port of New York—died July 2 in NYC in his 74th year and was buried July 3 in Trinity Church Yard (7/5)

Bell, Adam, of NYC, young man—drowned July 2 while bathing in North River (7/5)

Emery, ———, woman—drowned May 7 when sloop *Industry*, John Gleen master, bound from Bay of Honduras to NYC, was cast away on the Northern Triangles (7/5)

Cook, Dr., of Poughkeepsie, Dutchess Co., NY, two sons of, ages 8 and 12—drowned June 29 in Kearny's Mill Dam (7/5)

Pratt, Mica—married at Abington, Mass., to Miss Mary Parkman, whose grandmother, aged 100, mounted on horseback behind a gentleman of 80, rode to Abington to attend the wedding (7/12)

Thompson, William, who had nearly completed his 21st year, son of Capt. Joseph Thompson, of New Haven, Conn.—was drowned July 3 while bathing in the West River near the bridge (7/12)

England, Thomas, of Phila., tallow chandler—murdered about 12 years ago in Phila. (7/12)

Costigin, Francis, Esq., of New Brunswick, N.J., attorney—died there last Thursday week (7/12)

Roosevelt, Mrs. Hannah, wife of Jacobus Roosevelt, of NYC, merchant—died July 9 in NYC in her 45th year and was buried July 10 in the Dutch Church Yard (7/12)

Ludlow, Elizabeth, of Nassau Island, late Elizabeth Salmon, of Huntington, L.I., wife of Daniel Ludlow, of Greenwich, Conn.—her husband will not pay debts contracted by her in future (7/19)

Pfotzer, George, Dutch servant, age c. 20—runaway July 4 from Christopher Marshall, living in Chestnut St., Phila. (7/19)

Kelly, Mr., in jail in Phila. for counterfeiting Maryland eight dollar bills—died last week of a fever (7/19)

Hendersen, Richard, indented servant, age 25, lately arrived from Ireland in ship *Robert,* Matthew Russell master—runaway from Robert Davis (7/19)

Oliver, James, dec'd—accounts with estate to be settled with John Davan, admin. (7/19)

Ford, Samuel, age c. 30, accused of counterfeiting—broke out of jail of Morris Co., N.J. (7/19)

Cobb, Mrs., of Williamsburgh, Va., age 66—cataracts successfully removed from her eyes by Dr. Graham (7/26)

Baker, John, son of Charles Baker, late of Cove Lane, Cork, Ireland, who arrived in America about 10 years ago—is asked to apply to Mrs. Anne Baker, at Mrs.

Smith's in Broad St., NYC; a letter concerning John Baker may be directed to Godfrey Baker, Esq., Cork (7/26)

Grant, James, late of NYC, trader, dec'd—accounts with estate to be settled with Henry Ustick, admin. (8/2)

Letteridge, John, servant, born in Ireland, age c. 20—runaway July 26 from Joseph Riggs, living near Cranberry, Middlesex Co., N.J. (8/2)

M'Cuw, James, age c. 25, indented servant, lately arrived from Newry in ship *Robert,* Capt. Russel—runaway from master, John Stephenson (8/2)

Bassett, Stephen, of Wessel, N.J.—Peter Simmons was left Stephen's executor but Anne Bassett, executrix, warns all persons not to pay debts owing estate to Simmons (8/2)

Black, Robert, redemptioner, age c. 30—runaway July 25 from ship *Robert*, Matthew Russell master (8/2)

Montgomery, Richard, Esq., brother of the Countess of Ranelagh—married last Thursday sevennight at the Manor of Livingston to Miss Livingston, eldest daughter of Hon. Robert R. Livingston, Esq., one of the judges of the Supreme Court of NY (8/2)

Duyckinck, John, dec'd—persons with claims on partnership of late John Duyckinck and Gerardus De Peyster, merchants at Coracoa, are to apply to Widow Affe Duyckinck and Gerardus De Peyster at Coracoa (8/9)

Ducharm, Mr.—murdered on the River Mississippi (8/9)

Connell, Daniel, age 20 or 25, lately arrived in the brigantine *Galway Packet*, Hugh Fallon master—runaway Aug. 1 from Mrs. Lynch, in Broad St., NYC (8/9)

Kempe, John Tabor, of NYC, Attorney General for NY son of—died Aug. 4 in NYC (8/9)

Tuder, John, of NYC, merchant—died Aug. 6 in NYC in his 73rd year and was buried Aug. 7 in Trinity Church Yard (8/9)

M'Farlane, Walter, son of Andrew M'Farlane, of Glenfroun in North Britain—will hear something to his advantage if he applies to Joseph Scott in Phila., Walter and Thomas Buchanan & Co. in NYC or William Duegued in Boston (8/16)

Day, William, servant, age 35 or 40—runaway Aug. 8 from Jonathan I. Dayton, William Parsons and Jonathan Skinner, living in Elizabeth Town, N.J. (8/16)

Conine, Cornelius, servant, age c. 20—runaway Aug. 9 from Jonathan I. Dayton, of Elizabeth Town, N.J. (8/16)

Carthy, James, Irish servant, age c. 16—runaway Aug. 13 from Samuel Auchmuty (8/16)

Barney, William, of Baltimore, Md.—wounded by pistol accidentally discharged by his three-year-old son and died 48 hours later (8/30)

Montanye, Vincent, dec'd—three houses in Queens St., NYC, for sale by execs., Peter and Mary Montanye and Alexander Hosack (8/30)

Close, Jabez, apprentice tailor, age c. 19—runaway April last from Baxter, of Salem, Westchester Co., NY (8/30)

Smith, Phineas, age c. 6½, fourth son of Rev. Dr. Smith, of Phila.—drowned Aug. 16 near one of the wharfs of Phila. and was buried in Christ Church Burying-ground (8/30)

Armstrong, John, formerly of NYC—about two months ago died in Bay of Honduras of wounds received in a scuffle at hands of Hugh Murtry (8/30)

Lamson, Rev. Joseph, of Fairfield, Conn.—died there Aug. 13 in his 56th year and was buried there the next day (8/30)

GENEALOGICAL DATA FROM THE NEW-YORK GAZETTE; AND THE WEEKLY MERCURY

[1773]

Finley, Miss Susannah, daughter of Rev. Dr. Finley, President of New Jersey College —died Aug. 27 in her 23rd year and was buried Aug. 28 in the Old Presbyterian Church in NYC (8/30)

Hutchinson, John, apprentice, age c. 18—runaway Aug. 20 from ship *Needham*, Capt. Cheevers master (8/30)

Mason, Sebastian, English servant, who arrived in Phila. at end of May from Bristol, age 23—runaway from John Dunlap, of Phila. (8/30)

Lindsey, David, apprentice hatter, age c. 17—runaway Aug. 28 from Caleb Hewes, living in Lombard St., near New Market, Phila. (9/6)

Depeyster, Frederick, Esq.—died Sept. 1 at John Philip Livingston's, Esq., at Strawberry Hill, Dutchess Co., NY (9/6)

Simson, Samson, an Israelite—died Aug. 29 in NYC in his 51st year (9/6)

Rind, William, of Williamsburgh, Va., printer—recently died there (9/6)

Gauladet, Thomas, of NYC, tobacconist and distiller—died Sept. 6 in NYC in his 52nd year (9/13)

Leinbeck, Mr., of New Moravian Settlement in Sussex Co., N.J., ten-month-old son of—died about three weeks ago when accidentally scalded (9/20)

Bristol, Negro slave, age c. 25—runaway Sept. 13 from John Richards, living at Barbados-Neck, N.J. (9/27)

Reynolds, David, native of Pa., age c. 32—executed Sept. 17 at Morris Town, N.J., for counterfeiting (9/27)

Lynn, Moses, of NYC, tavernkeeper on Moor's Dock near Peck's Slip, two-and-one half-year-old son of—drowned Saturday se'nnight (9/27)

Grogan, Hugh, age c. 22, who arrived in NYC from Liverpool about 6 months ago and was servant to Mr. Cocks, tailor, on Dock St.—drowned this day se'nnight (9/27)

Douglass, Mrs., wife of Mr. Douglass, manager of the American Company of Commedians, mother of Mr. Lewis Hallam and of Mrs. Mattocks, of Covent Garden Theatre and aunt of Miss Hallam—died last week in Phila. (9/27)

Floyd, Charles, of Smith Town, L.I.—died there Sept. 16 of a fever (9/27)

Tennent, Rev. William Macky, of Greenfield in Conn.—married Sept. 21 to Miss Rodgers, daughter of Rev. Dr. Rodgers of NYC (9/27)

Aigins, James, seaman—found hanged from beam in his house in NYC on Sept. 27 (10/4)

Forbes, Miss Sally, daughter of Mrs. Abigail Forbes, of NYC—died Sept. 29 in NYC and was buried Oct. 1 in Friends Meeting House Yard (10/4)

Durkin, Matthew, native of Ireland, apprentice weaver, age c. 15—runaway Sept. 28 from Cornelius Ryan (10/4)

Hickling, William, country born, apprentice, age c. 12—same as above

Pitchford, Negro slave, age c. 14—runaway Sept. 17 from Samuel Willis, of Middletown, Conn. (10/11)

Wriesberg, Daniel, Esq., formerly lieutenant in the Royal American Regt.—died Oct. 4 at Mount Hope, N.J. (10/11)

Crawford, William, dec'd—furniture to be sold at dwelling in Little Dock St., NYC (10/11)

Boice, Jeremiah, age c. 25—runaway June 6 from Alexander White, High Sheriff of Tryon Co., NY (10/18)

Agan, Joshua, apprentice—runaway June 6 from master, Gilbert Tice, of Johnstown, NY (10/18)

Morris, Patrick, Irish servant, age c. 22—runaway from Mt. Holly Iron Work in N.J.; reward offered by Thomas Mayberry (10/18)

House, Thomas, age c. 22, apprentice to James Gregory—same as above

Fanning, Col. Edmund, Secretary to H.E. Gov. Tryon—lately married at Newbern, N.C., to Miss Sukey Cornell, daughter of Hon. Samuel Cornell, Esq., member of H.M.'s Council for N.C. (10/18); report of marriage designated as premature (11/22)

Barber, Mrs., wife of Francis Barber, master of Grammar School in Elizabeth Town, N.J.—died there Oct. 14 (10/18)

Marston, Mrs. Mary, wife of Nathaniel Marston, of NYC, merchant—died Oct. 14 in NYC in her 68th year and was buried Oct. 17 in family vault in Trinity Church Yard (10/18)

Le Lancey, Mrs. Dorathy, wife of John De Lancey, of NYC, merchant—died Oct. 15 in NYC in her 31st year and was buried Oct. 17 in family vault in Trinity Church (10/18)

Lane, Henry, dec'd—house at North River, NYC, in rear of Peter Mesier's, for sale by Elizabeth Lane (10/18)

Thomson, William, Esq., attorney, dec'd—house on Millstone River, about 8 miles from New Brunswick, 14 from Princeton and 6 from Bound Brook, for sale by Margaret Thomson (10/25)

Crane, Miss, of Elizabeth Town, N.J.,—on Oct. 20, when going to visit her sister at Fresh Kills, Staten Island, fell from skiff and was drowned (10/25)

Smith, Mrs., relict of John Smith, an eminent leather dresser, at corner of Queen St., NYC—died Oct. 24 in Chapel St., NYC (10/25)

Elvendrop, Capt. John, of Esopus—married Oct. 24 at Hackinsack, N.J., to Miss Zobriski, daughter of Peter Zobriski, Esq. (10/25)

Gage, General—daughter lately born to general and wife (10/25)

Ward, Moses, young man—run over last week by a cart and killed when returning from Peek's Kill Landing to Cortland's Manor (10/25)

Closs, Miss, daughter of Col. Closs, of Tryon Co., NY, and granddaughter of Sir William Johnson—died Oct. 23 in NYC in her 11th year (10/25)

Darby, William, apprentice blacksmith, age c. 19—runaway Oct. 19 from James Butler and Richard Baylis, of Goshen, NY (11/1)

Evens, Samuel, country born, shoemaker and carpenter, age 28—escaped from his bail Oct. 19; reward for capture offered by James Butler and Richard Baylis (11/1)

Ames, Levi, age 21, born at Groton, Mass., son of Jacob Ames, who died when Levi was two years old—executed Oct. 21 at Boston for burglary (11/1)

Gordon, Mr., a young gentleman lately arrived in NYC in ship *Pearl*, Capt. Tucker master, from Highlands of Scotland—died Oct. 27 in NYC of putrid inflamatory fever (11/1)

Moore, John, Esq., of NYC—married Oct. 26 to Miss Livingston, daughter of James Livingston, Esq., of Dutchess Co., NY (11/1)

Seymour, Capt. James, for many years commander of ship out of NYC—died Oct. 22 in NYC and was buried Oct. 23 in Trinity Church Yard (11/1)

Kingsland, Col. William—died Oct. 24 at his house on New Barbados Neck in his 69th year (11/1)

Rosebottom, James, Irish servant, weaver—runaway Nov. 1 from John Beck (11/8)

Bloomfield, Mrs. Sarah, wife of Dr. Moses Bloomfield, of Woodbridge, N.J.—died Oct. 25 in her 40th year (11/8)

White, Miss Fanney, daughter of Hon. Henry White, of NYC, merchant—died Nov. 5 in NYC (11/8)

Smith, John, servant, born in Staffordshire, England, formerly in service of Mrs. Marston, of NYC—runaway Oct. 19 from William Paxon and Patrick Colvin, at Trenton Ferry, Pa. (11/15)

Quin, John, indented Irish servant, age c. 21 or 22, who had been employed at Marblehead—runaway Nov. 1 from James Der Kinderen, living in Strawberry Alley, Phila. (11/15)

Mercer, Dr. William, dec'd—grist mill and dwelling, about one half mile from New Brunswick on River Rariton, for sale by execs., Lucy Mercer, Anthony White, Esq., and Peter Schenk, Esq. (11/22)

Easton, Samuel, of Newport, R.I.—died there Nov. 10 in his 90th year (11/22)

Miller, Richard, Esq., of Brookhaven—died there Nov. 4 in his 58th year (11/22)

Jay, Frederick, of NYC, merchant—married in NYC on Nov. 17 to Miss Barclay, daughter of Andrew Barclay, merchant, in Wall St. (11/22)

Peck, Capt., coasting captain, of Guilford, Conn., bound for North Carolina—fell overboard in NY Harbor on Nov. 16 and was drowned (11/22)

Armstrong, Miss, young woman—on Nov. 9 was attacked and beaten in Wall St., NYC, so that she died Nov. 20 (11/22)

Saunders, Tom, indented mulatto servant, born on Staten Island, age c. 22—runaway Nov. 19 from Capt. Henry Wendell's Sloop (11/22)

Hamilton, Mr., of Maryland—married last Saturday se'nnight in Phila. to Mary Richardson, late one of the American Company of Commedians (11/29)

Clinton, Charles, Esq., father of George Clinton, Esq., one of the members for Ulster Co., NY—died Nov. 18 at his seat, at Little Britain, in his 83rd year; he arrived from the North of Ireland in 1732, was lt.-col. of a regt. of Ulster Co., had the first seat on bench of that county, and, when nearly 70, commanded a regt. under General Bradstreet in the reduction of Ft. Frontenac (11/29)

Jauncey, James, Jr., Esq., son of James Jauncey, Esq., member in General Assembly for NYC and NY County—married Nov. 23 at Minto, seat of Andrew Elliot, Esq., Collector of H.M.'s Customs and Receiver General of Province of New York, to Miss Elliot, daughter of Andrew Elliot and niece of Sir Gilbert Elliot, Treasurer of the Navy (11/29)

Bonticout, Mr., a French gentleman for many years an inhabitant of NYC—died there a few days ago, aged 92 (11/29)

Johnston, Dr. Lewis—died Nov. 22 at Perth Amboy, N.J., at an advanced age (11/29)

Bowne, Robert, of NYC, merchant—was married last Thursday week at the Friends Meeting in Shrewsbury, N.J., to Miss Betsey Hartshorne, daughter of Robert Hartshorne, Esq. (11/29)

Richardson, Joseph, man of middle age—reward offered for his capture as a counterfeiter (12/6)

Smith, John, perhaps born at Falls Twp., Bucks Co., Pa., age c. 23 or 24—runaway Nov. 20 from Thomas Temple, of Pennsbury Twp., Chester Co., Pa. (12/6)

Terry, William, of Penryn, Cornwall, merchant, who died about 50 years ago, left two sons, Richard and William; one of these lived at or near Bristol and had two sons called Arthur, or Richard and William Terry; one of these sons, a barber and peruke maker, was at Penryn about 18 or 20 years ago and told an

aunt, Joice Terry, of Penryn, since dead, that he was going to live in America—
if he can give proofs he will inherit a house in Penryn (12/6)

Garrison, Mrs. Mary, wife of Benjamin Garrison, of NYC, merchant—died Dec. 2 in
NYC in her 32nd year and was buried Dec. 5 in Trinity Church Yard (12/6)

Crane, Mrs., aged 74—died last week in Elizabeth Town, N.J. (12/6)

Price, Mr., aged 97—same as above

Garthwait, Mrs., aged 73—same as above

Herring, Elbert—died Dec. 3 at his house in the Bowery, Out-Ward of NYC, in his
68th year (12/6); furniture and goods for sale by execs., Elizabeth and John
Haring and Petrus Bogert, Samuel Jones and John De Peyster, Jr. (12/20)

Comes, John, dec'd—house and farm where widow now lives in Jamaica, L.I., for
sale by Kezia Comes, executrix, and Henry Dawson, exec. (12/13; see also
3/8)

M'Kain, Hugh, Irish servant, tailor, of middle age—runaway Nov. 1 from Conrod
Boner, living in Taronytown, Frederick Co., Md. (12/13)

Kelly, Mary, lately from Ireland, age c. 18 or 20, who has lived 14 years in London—
runaway Sept. 8 from G. Barnes, at the Sign of the Harp and Crown, in
Wilmington (12/13)

Guion, Ammon, lately deceased—division will be made to creditors by Sarah Guion,
widow (12/13)

De Lancey, Mrs., wife of James De Lancey, Esq., one of the Representatives to
General Assembly for NYC and NY County—a few days ago in Phila. delivered
of a son at residence of Hon. William Allen, Chief Justice of Pa. (12/13)

Morgan, Mrs. Anne, wife of Benjamin Morgan, Esq., and sister of William Hicks,
Esq., late Prothonotary of Bucks Co., Pa.—died Dec. 1 at Middlebrook, Somerset
Co., N.J. (12/13)

Valentine, Thomas, native of Ireland, surveyor, for some years resident of NYC—
died Dec. 3 in NYC in his 31st year (12/13)

Williams, Thomas, age c. 25, who had been one of a band of counterfeiters in Conn.—
committed to Bridewell last week (12/13)

Maxson, John, of New London, Conn., child, a grandson of—fell into water on Dec.
5, seemed dead but recovered (12/20)

Hopkins, Capt. Michael, of Amenia Precinct, Dutchess Co., NY—drowned last week
in a river (12/20)

Ludlow, Gabriel, formerly eminent merchant of NYC—died Sunday se'nnight at an
advanced age in his house in King St., NYC, and was buried Tuesday following
in family vault in Trinity Church Yard (12/20)

Babcock, Mrs. Abigail, wife of Adam Babcock, of New Haven, Conn., merchant —
died Dec. 16 in New Haven in her 31st year (12/20)

Strickland, John, Esq., ensign in second battalion of the Royal Americans—died
Saturday se'nnight in NYC (12/20)

Gardner, Alida, aged between 2 and 3, daughter of James and Margaret Gardner, of
Goshen, Orange Co., NY—killed Nov. 19 when her throat was cut either by Mrs.
Gardner (who was deranged) or by a Negro (as Mrs. Gardner said) (12/20)

Harden, Mary, age between 2 and 3, daughter of Abraham Harden, of Goshen, a
neighbor of the Gardners—same as above

Moorhead, Rev. John, Pastor of Presbyterian Church in Boston—died there Dec. 2
in his 70th year; born North of Ireland, graduated from U. of Edinburgh and
came to Boston in 1727 (12/27)

Powell, Morgan, apprentice lad—runaway from ship *Experiment,* George Robson master (12/27)

Walker, James, Scotch apprentice lad—same as above

Holmes, Jonathan, of NYC, merchant on Beekman's Slip—died Dec. 19 in NYC (12/27)

Rutgers, Mrs. Helena, relict of Capt. Anthony Rutgers, late of NYC—died Dec. 21 in her house in NYC in her 72nd year (12/27)

GENEALOGICAL DATA FROM THE NEW-YORK GAZETTE; AND THE WEEKLY MERCURY

1774

Leake, Robert, Esq., Commissary General of North America—died Dec. 28 at his seat in the Bowery in the Out-Ward of NYC in his 54th year and was buried Jan. 2 in the family vault in Trinity Church Yard (1/3); accounts with estate to be settled with execs., Ann Leake and Robert Ross (1/31)

Townsend, Jacob, of NYC, merchant—died Dec. 28 in NYC in his 55th year (1/3)

Smith, William, of Ash Swamp, Essex Co., N.J., two sons of, aged c. 18 and 15—died Dec. 25 of asphixiation (1/3)

Chardavoyne, Isaac, dec'd—house, now in possession of William Chardavoyne, for sale by execs., Anne Wessels and Elias, Isaac and William Chardavoyne (1/3)

Buchanon, Alexander—sentenced to death on Dec. 17 at Court of Oyer and Terminer in Easton, Northampton Co., Pa. (1/10)

Wilson, Thomas, who on Oct. 19, 1768, murdered William Hewit—was sentenced to death on Dec. 17 at Court of Oyer and Terminer in Easton (1/10)

Rutgers, Petrus, dec'd—three houses at North River to be sold by Adrian Rutgers, Richard Sharpe, John Morin Scott and Benjamin Kissam (1/10)

Crooker, Robert, late of Rye, dec'd—farm in Twp. of Oyster-Bay, Queens Co., NY, for sale by John Monfort at Whately or Timothy Titus or William Crooker at Rye (1/10)

Bornschier, Justus, Dutch servant, shoemaker—runaway Oct. 24, 1773, from John Roop and George Leiz, of Phila. (1/10)

Mum, Catharine, Dutch servant—same as above

Kortright, John, late of the Out-Ward of NYC, dec'd—accounts with estate to be settled with John Kortright (1/17)

Moncrieffe, Mrs., wife of Major Moncrieffe and youngest daughter of James Livingston, Esq., dec'd—died Jan. 11 in NYC in her 34th year, leaving her husband and an only daughter, and was buried Jan. 14 in the Old Presbyterian Church (1/17)

Judah, Barruck—died Jan. 12 in NYC in his 95th year, leaving a numerous offspring (1/17)

Plat, Epinetus, of Huntington, L.I., son of—accidentally wounded last Christmas while hunting deer and his life is despaired of (1/17)

Denie, Robert, of NYC, merchant—married Jan. 19 in NYC to Mrs. Lambert, relict of John Lambert, late of NYC (1/24)

Blackwell, Jacob, son of Jacob Blackwell, Esq., of Kings Co., L.I.—married Jan. 22 to Miss Polly Hazard, daughter of late Nathaniel Hazard, of NYC, merchant (1/24)

Tiffany, Timothy—married Jan. 6 at Lyme, Conn., to Miss Parthenia Colt (1/31)

Reener, Jesse, of St. George's Manor, Suffolk Co., L.I.—house burned Jan. 24 and wife and three children burned to death (1/31)

Holmes, Jonathan, late of NYC, merchant, dec'd—accounts with estate to be settled with Sarah Holmes, admin. (1/31)

Kirk, John, apprentice, age c. 18—runaway Jan. 27 from Christian Schultz, of NYC, baker (1/31)

Johnston, Dr. Lewis, late of Perth Amboy, N.J., dec'd—land for sale by execs., James Parker, John Smyth and Heathcoat Johnston (2/7)

Stevenson, Edmund, Esq.—died Jan. 29 at his seat at Frog's Neck, Westchester Co., NY, in his 66th year (2/7)

Waddell, John, dec'd—houses in NYC for sale by William Waddell, Henry Waddell, Eleazer Miller, Jr., and John Taylor (2/7)

Cameron, Elizabeth, wife of Hugh Cameron, of Somerset Co., N.J.—husband will not pay debts contracted by her in future (2/7)

Woodhull, Richard, Jr., dec'd—¼ part of his share in schooner *Whaler* and other items will be sold at his house in Brookhaven by Sarah Woodhull, admin. (2/7)

Gardiner, Johannes Meyer, late of NYC, dec'd—accounts with estate to be settled with execs., Henry Will and Johannes Zuricher (2/7)

Carpenter, Mrs., widow of Thorn Carpenter, dec'd—injured Jan. 29 when horses took fright while she was returning in a sleigh from NYC to L.I. with Jordan Cole and Dr. William Lawrence, of Musqueto Cove (2/14)

Berry, Lancelot Grave, Esq., Collector of Port of Newbern, N.C., and only son of the late Hon. Charles Berry, Esq., Chief Justice of North Carolina—married Jan. 1 at Newbern to Miss Sally Outerbridge, only daughter of the late Capt. Outerbridge (2/14)

Beardsley, Mrs. Catharine, wife of Rev. John Beardsley, Missionary of the Society at Poughkeepsie, Dutchess Co., NY, and oldest daughter of David Brooks, of Stratford, Conn.—died Feb. 5 in Poughkeepsie (2/14)

Lyon, Thomas, late of Philipsborough, Westchester Co., NY, boatman, age c. 27 or 28—absconded from his bail; reward for his capture offered by William Coley (2/14)

Devereux, Elizabeth, wife of William Dereveux—husband will not pay debts contracted by her in future (2/14)

Totten, Peter, Sr., dec'd—farm, now in tenure of Daniel Totten, on King St., which runs from the Saw-Pit landing direct to North Castle, about 4 miles from the Saw-Pit landing, in the Twp. of Rye, Westchester Co., NY, for sale; apply to Peter Totten and Robert Dickinson in North Castle, execs. to Gilbert Totten's estate, or to Joseph Totten, in NYC (2/14)

Mooney, James, native of Ireland, age c. 38 or 40, blacksmith, who has worked in Liverpool and Bristol and who arrived in NYC last fall from Belfast in ship *Friendship*, William M'Cullough master—runaway from William Cliffton, of Phila. (2/21)

Townsend, John, dec'd—house in Mamaroneck, Westchester Co., NY, for sale by Samuel Townsend, exec. (2/21)

Magee, James, seaman—fell Feb. 17 and was crushed and killed in NYC by a hogshead of rum (2/21)

Dyckman, Jacob—fell from horse Feb. 17 while returning home to Harlem from NYC at bottom of hill below Mrs. Mac Gowin's, fractured his scull, and his life is despaired of (2/21)

White, Mr., and his whole family—murdered Dec. 25, 1773, at Ogeechee, Georgia, by Creek Indians, as it is supposed (2/28)

M'Donough, Capt. Terence, of H.M.'s packet *Domet*—drowned Jan. 21 at Charles-Town, S.C. (2/28)

Smith, Paschal Nelson, partner with James Aspinwall, Esq.—married Feb. 22 in NYC by Rev. Dr. Auchmuty to Miss Hester Sears, daughter of Isaac Sears, eminent merchant of NYC (2/28)

Warren, Samuel—injured Feb. 17 at Wapping's Creek, when sleigh overset, and died the next day (2/28)

Perry, Thomas, late of NYC, watchmaker, dec'd—accounts with estate to be settled with widow and executrix, Ruth Perry (2/28)

Thompson, Jonathan, Jr., late of NYC, merchant, dec'd—accounts with estate to be settled with John Hosmer, on Cromline's Wharf, by order of exec., Jonathan Thompson (2/28)

Doty, Isaac, dec'd—his Negro slave is for sale by execs., Margaret and Samuel Doty (2/28)

Grant, Lt—killed, along with members of the Sherral family, by Indians on Jan. 23 in Georgia (3/7)

Burton, William, Esq., nephew of Bartholomew Burton, Esq., late Governor of the Bank of England—married March 1 in NYC by the Rev. Dr. Cooper, President of King's College, to Miss Isabella Auchmuty, daughter of the Rev. Dr. Auchmuty, Rector of NYC (3/7)

Goold, Edward, merchant in company with Messers Beekman and Son—married March 2 in NYC by the Rev. Dr. Ogilvie to Miss Huggins, niece of the lady of David Beekman, a West India merchant of NYC (3/7)

Colden, Mrs. Elizabeth, wife of Alexander Colden, Esq., Surveyor General of NY, and second daughter of Richard Nicolls, Esq., of NYC—died March 4 at the family seat on Long Island in her 49th year and was buried March 5 in the family vault in Trinity Church Yard (3/7)

Seaman, Mrs. Elizabeth, wife of Edmund Seaman, Esq., Clerk to the General Assembly of NY, and daughter of John Zabriskie, Esq., of Hackinsack, N.J.—died March 4 at her house in NYC in her 30th year (3/7)

Dickson, Capt. Samuel, master of a sloop—drowned Jan. 8 when ship was lost near Island of Madeira (3/7)

Saunders, Capt. Abraham, master of brig *Tryon*, of NY—same as above

Englar, Adam, master of sloop *Garland*, of NY—same as above

Stevenson, Edward, Esq., dec'd—farm at Ammewalk, Cortlandt's Manor, Westchester Co., NY, for sale by execs., Edward and Gloryanna Stevenson, living at Westchester, or Benjamin Stevenson, at New Rochelle (3/7)

Waddle, Mrs., the late—house and garden lately occupied by her in Haerlem for sale; inquire of Samuel Judah or Thomas Randall (3/7)

Brandt, Christina, wife of John Brandt, of NYC, baker—has eloped from her husband (3/7)

Brett, Matthew, dec'd—farm at Fish-Kills, Dutchess Co., NY, for sale (3/7)

Reade, Lawrence, of NYC, merchant—died Dec. 4, 1773, on road from London to Bath, in his 52nd year (3/14)

Sowers, Capt. Thomas, H.M.'s principal engineer in America—died March 9 at his house in NYC in his 40th year and was buried March 11 in the Presbyterian Church (3/14)

Oliver, Lt. Gov.—died March 3 in Boston in his 68th year (3/14)

Watson, Mrs., wife of Alexander Watson, Esq., of Perth Amboy, N.J.—died at beginning of March at the Blazing Star (ferry) on her way to NYC (3/14)

Dickinson, Samuel, master of sloop *Harriot*, of South Carolina—perished Jan. 8 in wreck of the sloop at Madeira as it was about to sail for South Carolina (3/14)

Henrigues, Capt. Ano. J.G., master of Portuguese schooner *No. So. do Monte de St. Antonio*—perished Jan. 8 in wreck of ship at Madeira (3/14)

Terry, William, dec'd—house adjoining courthouse in Poughkeepsie, NY, for sale by execs., Edmund Terry, James Livingston and Myndert Van Kleeck (3/21)

Horton, Elijah, late of Mamaroneck, dec'd—accounts with estate to be settled with Gil. Budd Horton, admin. (3/21)

Mills, Rev. William, Minister of Presbyterian Church at Jamaica, L.I.—died March 18 in NYC in his 36th year (3/21)

Smith, John, late of NYC, cartman, dec'd—named as execs. his wife, Catharine Smith, and Christopher Benson (3/21)

Peters, Edward, mulatto servant, age c. 35—runaway June 7 last from Ezekiel Root, of Pittsfield, Berkshire Co. (3/28)

Cooper, Rufus, mulatto servant, age c. 21—same as above

Bradberry, Mrs. Elizabeth, dec'd—farm adjoining Passaick River, near Third River, in N.J., for sale; apply to Nicholas Van Dyck, of NYC, or Francis Van Dyck, of New Brunswick, N.J. (4/4)

Smith, Capt. Josias, Land and Tide-Waiter and Clerk to the Wardens of the Port of New York—died March 31 at his house in NYC in his 77th year (4/4)

De Lancey, Mrs., wife of Stephen De Lancey, Esq. (son of the Hon. Oliver De Lancey, Esq., of NYC)—on April 2 was delivered of a son and daughter (4/4)

Grumly, John, Clerk of Surrogate Office in NYC—died April 2 at his lodgings in NYC (4/4)

Swan, William, dec'd—4,000 acres of land for sale (4/4)

Lawrence, William, young indented servant, native of Ireland—runaway from Samuel Fraunces, of NYC (4/4)

Hyer, Walter, dec'd—accounts with estate to be settled with William Hyer in Smith St., NYC, or Cornelius Hyer, in New St., NYC (4/4)

Jack, servant, age c. 32—runaway March 22 from Isaac Tappen, living in Woodbridge, N.J. (4/11)

Kneller, William, indented servant, born in London, age 22—runaway about March 18 from Micajah James, of Baltimore Town (4/11)

Fullanton, John, servant, born in Scotland or North of Ireland—runaway March 28 from Samuel Webb, living in Westchester (4/11)

Pintard, Lewis, of NYC, merchant—married April 3 at New Rochelle, NY, to Mrs. Vallard, of New Rochelle (4/11)

Reade, John, son of the late Hon. Joseph Reade, Esq.—married April 6 in NYC by Rev. Dr. Livingston to Miss Kitty Livingston, daughter of Robert Gilbert Livingston, Esq. (4/11)

Magra, Dr. James, of NYC—died there April 13 at "a very advanced Age" (4/18)

Chambers, Mrs. Ann, widow of Hon. John Chambers, Esq., late one of the judges and member of H.M.'s Council for NY—died April 14 in NYC in her 74th year and was buried April 16 in vault of the Cortlandt family on the estate of Col. Cortlandt in Yonkers (4/18); accounts to be settled with execs., Aug. Van Cortlandt & John Jay (5/2)

Bogert, Capt. John, son of John Bogert, Esq., of NYC, merchant—died March 5 at Surinham (4/18)

Mc Cann, Hugh, age c. 19 or 20, born in County of Armagh, Ireland, who has been about four years in America—ran away with a large sum of money from John Watson, of NYC (4/18)

Caesar, Negro slave, age c. 30—runaway Sunday night last from Lewis M'Daniel, living at Bedford, Westchester Co., NY (4/18)

Cuff, Negro slave, age c. 29—same as above

Seaman, Mrs., wife of William Seaman, Esq.—died during week of April 25–May 2 as a result of injuries received when house near Jericho, L.I., burned the previous week (4/25 and 5/2)

De Peyster, Abraham, Esq., dec'd, late Treasurer of NY—persons in debt to his estate are requested to pay trustees of estate (5/2)

Han, George, Dutch servant, shoemaker—runaway April 3 from John Rup, living in Second St., near Race St., in Phila. (5/2)

Broner, Frederick, Dutch servant, shoemaker—same as above

Chamberlin, Lewis, Esq., late of Amwell, Hunterdon Co., N.J., dec'd—accounts with estate to be settled with Dirick Sutphen, exec. (5/2)

Jay, John, Esq., of NYC, barrister—married week before last to Miss Sally Livingston, third daughter of William Livingston, Esq., at her father's home near Elizabeth Town, N.J. (5/9)

Cartwright, Henry, son of Richard Cartwright, of Albany—fell from on board the snow *Sir William Johnson,* Capt. Dean master, on passage from London, March 17, and was drowned (5/9)

Dudley, Francis, dec'd—accounts with estate to be settled with William Dudley (5/9)

Skidmore, Jeremiah—murdered at his plantation in Virginia last Jan.; person who has his will is requested to deliver it to John or Samuel Skidmore at Jamaica or to Hugh Gaine in NYC (5/9)

Harrison, Richard, Esq.—married May 3 by Rev. Mr. Sayre to Miss Jones, eldest sister of Dr. Jones, of NYC; ceremony was performed at Matthews-Field, seat of Vincent Matthews, Esq., in Orange Co., NY (5/16)

Franklin, Walter, of NYC, merchant—married May 12 to Miss Mary Bowne, daughter of Daniel Bowne, of Flushing, L.I. (5/16)

Cuyler, Mrs. Catharine, wife of Henry Cuyler, of NYC, merchant—died May 15 in NYC in her 28th year (5/16)

Jack, elderly Negro, "Guinea mark'd," who formerly lived on Staten Island—runaway April 27 from I.G. Tetard, living at King's-Bridge (5/16)

GENEALOGICAL DATA FROM THE NEW-YORK GAZETTE; AND THE WEEKLY MERCURY

1774

Livingston, Henry, Jr., son of Henry Livingston, Esq., of Poughkeepsie—married May 18 to Miss Welles, daughter of Rev. N. Welles, of Stanford (5/23)

Brewster, Mary, wife of James Brewster, of NYC. shipwright—husband will not pay debts contracted by her in future (5/23)

Orsburn, Abraham, apprentice, age c. 19, born in Morris Town, N.J.—runaway May 15 from Moses Carman, of Hanover, Morris Co., N.J. (5/30)

Depeyster, Isaac, for many years Chamberlain of NYC—died May 26 in NYC at an advanced age (5/30)

Stewart, Mrs. Susanna, wife of Alexander Stewart, of NYC, wine merchant—died May 27 in NYC in her 56th year (5/30)

Bogart, Henry C., of NYC—died May 27 at his house in Smith St., aged 41 and was buried May 29 in family vault in the New Dutch Church Yard (5/30); accounts with estate to be settled with execs., Cornelius and Nicholas C. Bogart (6/6)

M'Entire, John, late of New Brunswick, dec'd—accounts with estate to be settled with execs., John and James Beard (5/30)

Mc Durcan, Patrick, indented Irish servant, age c. 15—runaway May 26 from John C. Knapp, living in Broad St., NYC (5/30)

Vicetur, Adam, indented servant, age c. 40—runaway April 5 from Martinus Nestell, living in Palatine District, County of Tryon. NY; reward for his capture offered by owner or Jasper Nestell, in NYC (6/6)

M'Larnan, John, indented servant, born in North of Ireland, age 23 or 24—runaway May 24 from James De Lancey, living in Westchester Co., NY (6/6)

Pulby, John David, born in Dantzick—runaway from his bail, living in NYC; reward for his capture offered by Peter Hall (6/6)

Beard, Victor, born in France, who has been several years in America—same as above

Richards, Stephen, late of Albany, dec'd—accounts with estate to be settled with execs., Philip Livingston, John Van Rensselaer and Abraham Ten Broeck (6/6)

Templeton, Oliver, of NYC, merchant—married last week in NYC by Rev. Dr. Cooper, President of King's College, to Miss Kitty Brownejohn, daughter of William Brownejohn, eminent druggist of NYC (6/13)

Sleight, Matthew, son of the late Matthew Sleight, of NYC, merchant—died June 4 at his mother's house in NYC in his 19th year and was buried June 5 in the family vault in the New Dutch Church Yard (6/13)

Simson, Sampson, late of NYC, merchant, dec'd—accounts with estate to be settled with Solomon Simson, exec. (6/13)

Winter, William, apprentice, age c. 16—runaway June 11 from Jeremiah Wool (6/20)

Moncrieffe, Thomas, Esq., Major of Brigade upon the American Establishment—married June 15 by Rev. Charles Inglis to Miss Helena Barclay, fifth daughter of Andrew Barclay, eminent merchant of NYC, at her fathers' house in Wall St. (6/20)

Speir (or Spear), William (or Benjamin), living on Duncard Creek, near Ft. Pitt—murdered June 4, together with his wife and four children (6/27)

Ropes, Nathaniel, Esq., dec'd—Hon. William Brown is appointed a justice of the Superior Court of Mass. in place of Ropes (6/27)

Wall, Henry, living near Muddy Creek—killed June 6 by Indians (6/27)

Keener, Mr., living near Muddy Creek—same as above

Proctor, Mr., living near Grave Creek—same as above

Campbell, Mr., lately from Lancaster Co., Pa.—killed by the Mingoes at Necommer's Town (6/27)

Griffiths, John, Esq., of Kingsbury, Assistant Judge—died June 21 at house of Patrick Smyth, Esq., of Smythfield, near Ft. Edward, and was buried June 23 at Kingsbury (6/27)

Reeve, Mary, wife of Daniel Reeve, of Southold, Suffolk Co., NY—husband will not pay debts contracted by her in future (6/27)

Main, William, indented Scotch servant, who says he lived four years in Glasgow and arrived in NYC in brig *Commerce*, Capt. Nicholls, from Glasgow—runaway June 22 (6/27)

Prince, Negro slave, age c. 40—runaway May 1 from Andrew John Hopper, living at Paramus, Bergen Co., N.J. (6/27)

Rice, Abraham, late of NYC, dec'd—dividend will be paid to creditors by Robert Sinclair, admin. (6/27)

Gouverneur, Herman, dec'd—land in Albany Co. for sale by execs., Mary and Nicholas Gouverneur and Hugh Wallace (6/27)

M'Clure, Francis, who formerly lived at Weilin Creek—killed in June by Indians at Ten Mile Creek, above Red-stone (7/4)

Reade, Lawrence, late of NYC, merchant, dec'd—real estate in Town of Jamaica, L.I., for sale by Joseph and John Reade and Richard Yates (7/4)

Murphy, Peter, servant, age c. 19—runaway from Jonathan Baldwin, living at Princeton, N.J. (7/4)

M'Goun, Jeremiah, "apprentice boy," barber—runaway from James Thompson, living at the corner of Beekman's Slip, NYC (7/4)

Mills, Rev. William, late dec'd—farms in N.J. for sale by execs., Mary Mills at Jamaica, James Caldwell at Elizabeth Town, Jonathan Dayton at Springfield, and Ebenezer Hazard at New York (7/4)

Yeomans, Mr., heir to a large estate on Island of Antigua—died in his 20th year on board *Earl of Halifax Packet*, Capt. Bolderson master, on voyage from Falmouth to NYC (7/11)

Smith, John, late of Island of St. Croix, brass founder and coppersmith, dec'd—accounts with estate to be settled with Edward Laight, admin. (7/11)

Gray, Hugh, dec'd—accounts with co-partnership of Hugh Gray and Alexander Cruckshank to be settled with survivor; accounts with estate of Hugh Gray to be settled with Alexander Robertson and Thomas Galbreath, admins. (7/11)

Griffing, George, dec'd—house in Wall St., NYC, to be sold and accounts to be settled with Elizabeth Brown, admin., William Griffing and John Brown (7/11)

Gamble, Samuel, native of Ireland, tailor, age c. 33—runaway from his bail June 26; reward offered by Ruth Perry, living near the Coffee House, NYC (7/11)

Griffy, Edward, indented Irish servant, age c. 24, who came to Phila. last spring in ship *Narrow*, Capt. Hill—runaway July 10 from Simon Addes, living in Middlesex Co., N.J. (7/18)

Hack, Negro slave, age c. 40—runaway July 10 from Lawrence Van Buskirk, living at Ramapough, Orange Co., NY (7/18)

Aspinwall, John, Esq., of NYC, merchant—died July 15 at his house in NYC in his 69th year (7/18)

Johnson, Sir William—died July 11 at Johnson Hall in his 60th year and was buried July 13 at church in Johnstown (7/18 and 7/25)

Tuthill, Jemiah, wife of James Tuthill, of Cornwall Precinct, Orange Co., NY—husband will not pay debts contracted by her in future (7/18)

Johnson, Lady, wife of Sir John Johnson—lately delivered of a daughter at Ft. Johnson (7/25)

Brown, Capt. William, late of Smith St., NYC—died at Hispaniola, leaving a widow and numerous children (7/25)

Simpson, John, indented servant, born in Ireland, age between 25 and 30—runaway July 6 from John Jacob Faesh, of Mount Hope, Morris Co., N.J. (8/1)

Fitch, Thomas, Esq., late Governor of Connecticut—died July 18 at Norwalk, Conn. in his 75th year (8/1)

Wipey, Joseph, friendly Indian, lately assassinated in County of West-Moreland—Gov. Penn has offered a reward of £100 for conviction of the murderer (8/8)

Thorp, Joseph, native of England, age c. 35, who has lived some time in Boston and Quebec and was in trade in New-Castle, Va., where he has a brother—has run away with money entrusted to him (8/8)

Dihm, Lorenz, Dutch servant, age c. 35—runaway June 19 from George Wither, living in Earl Twp., Lancaster Co., Pa. (8/15)

Beekman, John, of NYC, merchant—died Aug. 11 at his house in Maiden Lane, NYC, in his 53rd year and was buried Aug. 12 in family vault in Trinity Church Yard (8/15); accounts with estate to be settled with execs., James J., John, Jr., and Theophilus Beekman (8/29)

Duane, James, Esq., of NYC, five-year-old son of—drowned Aug. 9 when he fell from wharf at Manor of Livingston (8/15)

Connely, Thomas, Irish servant lad, barber and hairdresser, who formerly lived in NYC, later became valet to Col. Richard Tilghman, of Queen Ann's County, Md. and later was indented to Robert Wilson, at the head of Wye River, in Md., from whom he ran away and was put in jail in Phila.; there William Brobson, living at Wilmington, Newcastle Co., acquired him and brought him home—he ran away July 27 from Mr. Brobson (8/15)

Moore, Lambert, Esq., Comptroller of H.M.'s Customs for the Port of New York—married Aug. 14 to Miss Onderdonk, daughter of Henry Onderdonk, of Hempstead Harbour, L.I. (8/22)

Spence, James, servant, lately arrived from Scotland, carpenter, age between 30 and 40—runaway from Abraham Schenk, of New Rochelle (8/22)

Franks, Miss Polly, second daughter of David Franks, Esq., of Phila.—died Sunday evening last in Phila. in her prime of life and was buried Monday forenoon in Christ Church burying ground (Phila. dispatch, dated Aug. 21) (8/29)

Morgan, John, Irish servant, age c. 20—runaway Aug. 10 from Jeremiah Manning, living in Woodbridge, N.J. (8/29)

Welch, Enoch, apprentice, age c. 19—runaway Aug. 17 from James Starr, of Phila. (9/5)

Madison, Samuel, Irish servant, age c. 20—same as above

M'Cready, John, age c. 30, blacksmith and currier, lately arrived on board the *Golden Rule,* Capt. Cragg master, from Isle of Whitehorn—runaway from his bail; reward for his capture offered by Patrick M'Miking (9/5)

Young, John, indented servant, who speaks the Northumberland dialect, age c. 21—runaway Sept. 8 from the *John and Jane,* Abel Chapman master, just arrived from London (9/12)

Ross, Alexander, indented servant, age c. 19, who speaks the Scotch dialect—same as above

Snaith, Thomas, indented servant, age c. 14—same as above

Adolphus, Isaac—died Sept. 7 at his house in NYC (9/12); Philip Adolphus, his brother will soon depart for Europe; accounts will be settled with execs., Hayman Levy, Myer Myers, Isaac Moses, and Philip Adolphus (10/3)

M'Kee, Peter, of Morris Town, N.J., merchant—was married Sept. 4 to Miss Elizabeth Ogden, daughter of Dr. Jacob Ogden, of Jamaica, L.I. (9/12)

Ducket, Valentine, who deserted from H.M.'s 65th Regt.—executed in Boston on Sept. 2 (9/19)

Treville, Sir John, Knight of Malta, Capt. of Cavalry—married Aug. 28 at Hampton to Mrs. Abigail Stoneman, of Newport, R.I. (9/19)

Keteltas, Mrs. Jane—died last Sunday week in her 76th year at Mt. Pleasant, seat of James Beekman, Esq. (9/19)

Richards, Mrs. Elizabeth, widow of Paul Richards, Esq.—died Sept. 12 in her 75th year and was buried Sept. 14 in Trinity Church (9/19)

Zabriski, John, Esq.—died Tuesday se'nnight at Hackinsack (9/19)

Farquhar, Capt. James, of NYC—married Sept. 15 in NYC to Miss Elizabeth Curson, second daughter of Richard Curson, of NYC, merchant (9/19)

Will, Negro slave, age c. 27—runaway Aug. 26 from James Banks, living in Middle-Patent, North Castle, Westchester Co., NY (9/19)

Clark, James, indented Scotch servant, age c. 25—runaway Sept. 10 from Tiddeman Hull, of NYC (9/19)

Hill, Samuel, apprentice hatter, age c. 16—runaway Sept. 12 from the papermill at Hampstead Harbour on Long Island; reward for his capture will be paid by Henry Onderdonk, Henry Remsen, or Hugh Gaine (9/26)

Jurney, Daniel, apprentice, age c. 18—runaway from Hartshorne Fitz Randolph, living in Morris Co., N.J. (9/26); taken up by John Chappenois, of Philipsburgh (10/17)

Bradstreet, Major General John—died of dropsy Sept. 25 in NYC in his 63rd year; he came to America upwards of 30 years ago (9/26 and 10/3)

Thomas, Nathan, age c. 20—on Aug. 11 hired a bay mare from Samuel Bartholomew, living in Goshen, Conn., but has never returned (10/3)

Brower, Jeremiah, Jr., merchant in Charlestown, S.C.—married Sept. 6 to Miss Christina Miller, daughter of Major Stephen Miller, Esq. (10/3)

Brown, Benjamin, dec'd—his son, William Brown, of Rye, Westchester Co., NY, is confined in jail for debt at White Plains (10/10)

Robinson, John, indented Scotch servant, carpenter—runaway from James V. Cortlandt (10/10)

M'Lintock, John, indented Scotch servant, gardner—same as above

Miller, William, indented servant, age c. 30—runaway Sept. 19 from Daniel and Samuel Hughes, at the Antietam Forge, Frederick Co., Md. (10/10)

Wilcox, John, convict servant from England, age c. 27—same as above

Lodge, Miss Catharine, daughter of Abraham Lodge, Esq., dec'd—died Oct. 7 in NYC of a fever (10/10)

Seybring, Cornelius, of NYC, merchant—died Aug. 2 at Tortola (10/10)

Grumly, John, dec'd—accounts with estate to be settled with admins., John Shaw and Hercules Mulligan (10/17)

Caldwell, David, age c. 40, who lately resided in Princeton and who was born in Pa., served his time in Phila., and is a shoemaker—runaway from his bail Oct. 18; reward for his capture is to be paid by Thomas Irwin, merchant, in Second St., Phila., or by Thomas Patterson, of Princeton, N.J. (10/17)

Van Deursen, Henderick, dec'd—real estate in New Brunswick, N.J., for sale by execs., Wm. V. Deursen and Matthew Sleight (10/17)

Stevenson, Robert, son of John and Mary Stevenson, born in the town land of Cottown, Parish of Banger, County of Down, Ireland, who went from Ireland to America some years ago—is requested to apply to Messers Greg, Cunningham & Co., merchants, in NYC, or to Thomas Ewing, merchant, in Baltimore (10/17)

Simonson, Aaron, formerly of NYC—lately died at Charlestown, S.C. (10/17)

Cullen, James, indented servant, born in Ireland, age c. 21—runaway from ship *Liberty*; reward for his capture is offered by Templeton and Stewart (10/17)

De Peyster, Mrs. Ann, late of NYC, dec'd—real estate for sale by execs., Pierre Van Cortlandt and Cornelius De Peyster (10/24)

Ogden, Capt. Amos, late of Roxbury, Morris Co., N.J., dec'd—accounts with estate to be settled with John Blagge (10/24)

De La Montagnie, Abraham, dec'd—accounts with estate to be settled with Mery De La Montagnie, admin. (10/24)

Cockie, John, of NYC—died Oct. 17 (10/24)

Lott, Abraham E., of NYC, merchant—married Oct. 20 on Long Island to Miss Rebecca Duryee (10/24)

Gale, Col. James, of Goshen, NY, dec'd—real estate in Goshen for sale (10/31)

Molineaux, William, of Boston, merchant—died there Oct. 22 in his 58th year (10/31)

Gautier, Andrew, Esq.—married Oct. 23 by Rev. Dr. Chandler, at Elizabeth Town, N.J., to Miss Margaret Hastier (10/31)

Garland, Mrs., native of England, midwife—died Oct. 26 in NYC in her 88th year (10/31)

Travers, William, English convict servant, age 22 or 23, who has been three months in America—runaway Oct. 11 from Nicholas Merryman, Jr., living near the Falls of Gun-Powder in Baltimore Co., Md. (11/7)

Ute, Andrew, Scots servant man—runaway Oct. 30 from Robert Aitken, bookseller, opposite the London Coffee House, Front St., Phila. (11/7)

Costant, Negro slave, age c. 26—runaway from John Williams Sanders, living near Princeton, N.J. (11/7)

Jarvis, James, of NYC, hatter—died Nov. 4 in NYC in his 42nd year and was buried Nov. 5 in Trinity Church Yard (11/7) [See also 12/6.]

Diamond, Negro slave, age c. 18—runaway from Daniel Ensley, butcher, in the Fly Market, NYC (11/7)

Emery, James, age 22, born in Paisley, Scotland, weaver—runaway Nov. 1 from Alexander Robertson, of NYC (11/7)

Peet, Negro slave, age c. 27—runaway Sept. 19 from Aaron Longstreet, Jr., of Princeton, N.J. (11/14 & 11/21)

Dubois, Matthew, boatman from Sagarties on North River—found dead on Nov. 11 in his bed on his boat (11/14)

Cookson, Capt. Joseph, of ship *Exeter,* of Port of Bristol—died Nov. 11 in NYC in his 55th year (11/14)

Livingston, Philip, Esq., son of Philip Livingston, Esq., of NYC, merchant—arrived Nov. 11 in NYC from Jamaica by way of Phila. (11/14)

Killed Oct. 12 in battle with Indians at mouth of the Kanwaha (11/21):

Lewis, Col. Charles, of Va.

Field, Major John, of Va.

Murray, Capt. John, of Va.

M'Clenachan, Capt. Ro., of Va.

Wilson, Capt. Samuel, of Va.

Ward, Capt. James, of Va.

Allen, Lt. Hugh, of Va.

Cundiff, Ensign, of Va. (11/21 and 12/5)

Bracken, Ensign, of Va. (11/21 and 12/5)

Children of Daniel Bliss of Rehoboth, Mass., died there of fever and flux (11/21):

Daniel, age 22, eldest son

Hezekiah, age 20, second son

Sarah, age 15

Comfort, age 10

Ester, age 16 months

Hammond, Rev. Noah, Pastor of Baptist Church at Coram, Nassau Island—died Nov. 4 in his 56th year (11/21)

Fristole, Rev. Daniel, Pastor of Baptist Church in Va. and of a sister church in Md.—died about Nov. 4, leaving a widow and seven children (11/21)

Nero, Negro slave, age c. 20, who formerly belonged to Capt. Nathaniel Underhill, of Westchester Co.—runaway Nov. 14 from Amos Pine, of Beekman's Precinct, Dutchess Co., NY (11/21)

Ogilvie, Rev. John, Assistant Minister of Trinity Church, NYC—died Nov. 26 in NYC in his 51st year and was buried Nov. 27 in family vault in Trinity Church Yard (11/28); he descended from a North Britain family, was educated at Yale, in 1750 was appointed missionary to Albany and the Mohawk Indians, and was called to Trinity Church in 1764 (12/5)

M'Bride, James, servant, age between 20 and 30, a dish turner by trade—runaway Nov. 19 from Dirck Barcalow, of Upper Freehold, Monmouth Co., N.J. (11/28)

Simpson, Catharine, dec'd—mortgage was executed by her to Jane Forbes, who will sell real estate in NYC (12/5)

Coe, Capt. William, of New-Hempstead, Orange Co. Precinct, Town of Haverstraw—was drowned Nov. 25 in North River near Dobbs Ferry; reward for recovery of his body will be paid by Judge John Coe or Peter Vandervoort, living at Kakiate (12/5)

Drowned Nov. 25 in oversetting of boat of Mr. Kearse, belonging to Haverstraw (12/5):

Blauvelt, Capt. Peter, wife and son of

Blauvelt, Isaac

Blauvelt, Jacob, son of Isaac

Blauvelt, Jacob A.

Coe, John, Esq., daughter of

Crum, Peter, Esq., wife of

Robinson, Andrew, born at Belinure, North of Ireland—same as above (12/5 and 12/12)

Everit, Daniel—killed Dec. 1 about one mile from Brooklyn Ferry on L.I. in accident involving wagon of Luke Eldert (12/5)

Anthony, Halder, of Shrewsbury, N.J., master of sloop bound from NYC to Barnegat—died Nov. 21 of hunger and grief five days after sloop was wrecked (12/5)

Port-Yoyal, Negro slave, age 41—runaway from Robert Furniss, of New-Castle (12/12)

Stephen, Negro slave, age c. 23—runaway Oct. 10 from Abraham Slinlang, living two miles below Albany (12/12)

Hurd, Mrs. Elizabeth, wife of Ebenezer Hurd, Jr., post rider of Stratford, Conn., and daughter of Rev. Christopher Newton, of Stratford—died Nov. 28 at Stratford at age of 24 years and 3 months (12/12)

Lee, William, indented English servant, shoemaker, age c. 27—runaway Oct. 8 from ship *Hill*, George Marshall master, lying at New York; reward offered by Thomas Harris, living near the Draw-Bridge, Water St., Phila. (12/12)

Colden, Alexander, Esq. (eldest son of Lt. Gov. Colden), Postmaster and Surveyor General of Province of NY—died Dec. 12 in NYC and was buried Dec. 14 in family vault in Trinity Church Yard (12/19)

Tharp, James Murphy, of Island of Jamaica, age 19—died Dec. 15 at his lodgings in NYC (12/19)

Gage, William, second son of General Gage—died in London about two months ago (12/19)

Van Horne, John, Esq., of Rockey-Hill, N.J.—died lately (12/19)

Brooks, George, of Island of Jamaica, age 22—died Dec. 21 in his lodgings in NYC (12/26)

Hamilton, Henry—executed Dec. 21 in NYC for highway robbery (12/26)

Adams, John—same as above

Coleman, Patrick, indented Irish servant, tailor—runaway Dec. 18 from brig *Julian*, Capt. Burke master; reward offered by Greg, Cunningham and Co. (12/26)

Jarvis, James, dec'd—accounts with estate to be settled with execs., Mary and Arthur Jarvis and Isaac Stoutenburgh (12/26)

GENEALOGICAL DATA FROM THE NEW-YORK GAZETTE; AND THE WEEKLY MERCURY

1775

Man, Isaac, dec'd—accounts with estate to be settled with Elias Desbrosses, Henry White and Richard Yates (1/2)

Cary, Edward, age 70—was murdered last Sunday evening about two miles from Phila. on the Germantown road (Phila. dispatch of Dec. 28) (1/2)

Gallwey, Hon. Stephen Payne, member of H.M.'s Council for Island of Antigua—married Dec. 29, 1774, by Rev. Dr. Auchmuty, to Miss Phila De Lancey, third daughter of Hon. Oliver De Lancey, Esq., of NYC, at Mr. De Lancey's seat at Greenwich (1/2)

Prime, Benjamin Young, M.D.—married last Sunday se'nnight at Huntington, L.I., to Mrs. Greaton, widow of late Rev. James Greaton, late Episcopal Minister in Huntington (1/2)

Stag, Mr., a baker, of NYC, son of—drowned Dec. 30, 1774, when he fell off a wharf near the Bear Market (1/2)

Jackson, John, Esq., ensign in H.M.'s 64th Regt. of Foot, stationed at Castle William—died last Friday se'nnight (1/2)

Mesier, Abraham, merchant in Cortlandt St., NYC—died Monday morning (1/2)

Maturin, Gabriel, Esq., Capt. in H.M.'s 31st Regt. of Foot—died Dec. 15 in Boston (1/2)

M'Creddie, Jane, Scotch servant, age 25, who came Sept. last from Greenock—runaway Jan. 1 from John Myford, living in Little Dock St., near the Coenties Market, NYC (1/2)

Ogilvie, Rev. John, dec'd—accounts with estate to be settled with Nathaniel Marston, one of the execs. (1/9)

Governeur, Herman, dec'd—6,086 acres of land in Albany Co. for sale by execs., Mary Governeur, Hugh Wallace and Nicholas Gouverneur (1/9)

Miller, James—drowned Dec. 27, 1774, when schooner *Elizabeth*, Capt. Jenkins master, bound from the West Indies to NYC, was cast away in a snow storm off the point of Sandy Hook (1/9)

Ramsey, Daniel—same as above

De Grote, Samuel, of New Marlborough, Ulster Co., NY, joiner, two children of—died when house burned on Jan. 1 (1/9)

Waldron, Richard, of NYC—died Jan. 4 in NYC (1/9)

Robinson, Thomas, late of NYC, dec'd—real estate in NYC for sale by execs., Robert and John Hartshorne (1/9)

Garrison, John, dec'd—farm near Prince's Bay, Richmond Co., NY, for sale; apply to Hannah Garrison, living on the premises, or Henry Perine (1/16)

Reade, Lawrence, late of NYC, dec'd—property in Jamaica, L.I., for sale by execs., Joseph and John Reade and Richard Yates (1/16)

Bodin, Rev. John, of NYC—married Jan. 8 to Miss Polly Jarvis, daughter of late James Jarvis, of NYC, dec'd (1/16)

Dillon, Joseph (son of Capt. Dillon, Commander of H.M.'s packet *the Mercury*) married Jan. 10, by the Rev. Dr. Auchmuty, to Miss Joanna Van Horne, daughter of Garret Van Horne, late an eminent merchant of NYC (1/16)

Duane, Mrs. Margaret, widow of Anthony Duane, late of NYC, merchant—died Sunday se'nnight in NYC in her 90th year (1/16)

De Noyelles, John, Esq., member of Assembly for Orange Co., NY—died Jan. 12 at his seat at Haverstraw (1/16)

Russel, James, age c. 19, apprentice, weaver by trade—runaway Jan. 5 from James Black, of Springfield (1/23)

Winterbottom, James, a sweep, age 16—runaway from H. Zedtwitz (1/23)

Samond, William, servant, age c. 18—runaway from ship *Monimia*, Capt. Morrison master (1/23)

Lawrence, Thomas, vendue master, alderman and sometime mayor of Phila.—died Jan. 21 in Phila. in his 54th year (1/30)

Frelinghuysen, Frederick, professor in Queens College—married Jan. 10 at Millstone, Somerset Co., N.J., to Miss Gitty Schenk, daughter of Hendrick Schenk, late merchant at Millstone, dec'd (1/30)

Hogland, Adrian, dec'd—farm on east bank of Hudson River, at Bloomingdale, for sale by execs., Richard Fletcher and Benjamin and William Hogland (1/30)

De La Montagnie, Abraham, late of NYC, innholder, dec'd—accounts with estate to be settled with Mary De La Montagnie, admin. (2/6)

Noonan, Robert, servant, age c. 14, lately imported in the *Needham,* Capt. Cheevers master, from Cork—runaway Jan. 30 from Daniel M'Cormick, of NYC (2/6)

Ridley, Mrs. Sarah, wife of Nicholas Ridley, Esq., of Kingston, Island of Jamaica—died Jan. 31 in NYC and was buried Feb. 2 in Trinity Church Yard (2/6)

Seaman, Edmund, Esq., of NYC, merchant—was married Feb. 2 in NYC to Miss Hester Van Ranst, daughter of Peter Van Ranst, late of NYC, dec'd (2/6)

Ogden, Samuel, Esq., of Morris Co., N.J.—was married Feb. 5 at Morrissania to Miss Euphemia Morris, daughter of the late Col. Lewis Morris, of Westchester Co., NY (2/6)

Field, John, late of Flushing, dec'd—farm of 160 acres, adjoining the bay, for sale by John Field (2/13)

Burwell, Joseph, apprentice, carpenter by trade, age c. 19—runaway Jan. 23 from James Campbell, of Springfield, East New Jersey (2/13)

Watts, Robert, Esq., son of Hon. John Watts—married Feb. 4 at Baskenridge, seat of the Earl of Stirling, to Lady Mary Alexander, his lordship's eldest daughter (2/13)

Hodsden, John, Esq., of Charlestown, S.C.—was married Tuesday evening last, by the Rev. Dr. Rodgers, to Miss Grant, of NYC (2/13)

Ross, Alexander, Esq., of Middlesex Co., N.J.—was married Sunday night last to Miss Sally Farmer, sister to Christopher Billopp, Esq., member of the Assembly for Richmond Co., NY (2/13)

Caesar, Negro slave, age c. 40—runaway from John Barnes, at his grist mills near Poughkeepsie (2/20)

Carr, James, late of NYC, carman, dec'd—accounts with estate to be settled with execs., Charles Nicholl and Joseph Allicocke (2/20)

Elliston, Mrs. Mary, widow of Robert Elliston, Esq., late Comptroller of H.M.'s Customs for Port of New York—died Feb. 14 at her farm near Kingsbridge in her 88th year and was buried Feb. 17 in family vault in Trinity Church Yard (2/20)

Tryon, William, Lt. Gov. of NY—on Feb. 18 entered into the 88th year of his age (2/20)

Brown, James, servant, shoemaker by trade, age 23, who arrived last fall with Capt. Moore from Ireland—runaway Feb. 20 from William Hudson, of Mendem, Morris Co., N.J. (2/27)

Goetcheus, Rev. Johannes Henricus, of Hackinsack and Scrallenburgh, Bergen Co., N.J., dec'd—accounts with estate to be settled with and real estate to be sold by Albert Banta, David B. Damarest and Hendrick Kuyper (2/27)

Bateman, William, servant, age c. 25, jeweller and lapidary, born in England, who came from London to Phila. in ship *Minerva*, Arthur Hill master, and who worked in NYC with Charles Oliver Bruff—reward for taking him is offered by Peter Berton, of NYC (2/27)

Edwards, Isaac, Esq., Auditor General of North Carolina and Representative of Newbern in the Assembly—died Friday last at Newbern (Newbern dispatch of Jan. 27) (2/27)

Martin, H. E., Gov. of North Carolina, four-year-old son of—died at Newbern Monday last (Newbern dispatch of Jan. 27) (2/27)

Hamilton, ———, a lad of c. 16—run over by wagon and killed Feb. 24 at Newtown, L.I. (2/27)

Roberts, ———, lad of c. 12—same as above

Troup, John, Esq., of Jamaica, L.I.—died Feb. 21 at Jamaica in his 70th year (2/27)

Livingston, Thomas, dec'd—land in Saratoga Patent for sale by Philip Schuyler (3/6)

M'Diarmed, Hugh, servant, native of Highlands of Scotland, tailor, age c. 25—runaway Feb 15 from James Moore, of Schenectady, Albany Co., NY (3/6)

Furman, Jane, dec'd—real estate in Somerset Co., N.J., for sale by execs., Hendrick Berrien and John Scott (3/6)

Nevius, Susannah, widow, dec'd—plantation in Somerset Co., N.J., adjoining Rariton River, opposite the town landing, near the new bridge, a mile and a half from New Brunswick, for sale by David Nevius and Lucas Schenk, execs. (3/6)

Lawrence, Elisha, Esq., Sheriff of Monmouth Co., N.J.—married Feb. 27, by Rev. Mr. Cooke, at Shrewsbury, to Miss Mary Ashfield, eldest daughter of the late Hon. Lewis Morris Ashfield, Esq. (3/6)

Garman, Catharine, wife of Christopher Garman—has left her husband's bed and board and he will not pay debts contracted by her in future (3/6)

M'Bride, Mrs. Phebe, wife of James M'Bride—died March 1 at Morris Town, N.J., leaving husband and three small children (3/13)

Willett, John, dec'd—farm about ¼ mile from Mr. Underhill's mills in Flushing, L.I., for sale; apply to execs., David Colden or Thomas Willett (3/13)

Beekman, John, dec'd—accounts with estate to be settled with execs., J. J., John and Theo. Beekman (3/13)

Woster, Capt. John, late of Stanford, Fairfield Co., Conn., dec'd—John Holly, administrator, advises that Woster, for about 12 years before his death, resided principally at Barbadoes (3/13)

Ogden, Col. Josiah, dec'd—house near town wharf in Newark, N.J., for sale by David and Jacob Ogden and Isaac Longworth (3/30)

Whaley, William, English servant, age 30—runaway March 12 from Abraham Kentzing, of Phila. (3/20)

Whitehead, William, English servant, a combmaker, age c. 25—runaway from William Haselwood, combmaker, living in Fourth St., Phila. (3/20)

Kortwright, Cornelius, formerly of NYC, merchant—died lately on Island of St. Croix (3/27)

Turvey, Daniel, apprentice, age c. 19—runaway from Hartshorne B. Randolph, of Morris Co., East New Jersey (3/27)

Van Houten, Margaret, wife of Roillof Van Houten—husband will not pay debts contracted by her in future (4/3)

Winslow, Joshua, of Boston, merchant—died there March 20 in his 39th year, leaving widow and six children (4/3)

Span, Catharine, wife of Richard Span—has left her husband's bed and board and he will not pay debts contracted by her in future (4/3)

Heyliger, Col. John, of Island of St. Croix—married last Wednesday week, in NYC, by Rev. Mr. Inglis, to Miss Sally Kortwright, eldest daughter of Lawrence Kortwright, Esq., of NYC (4/3)

Colden, Alexander, Esq., dec'd—accounts with estate to be settled with Richard Nicholls Colden, acting executor (4/10)

Stevenson, Edward, Esq., dec'd—farm on Frogg's Neck, in Borough of Westchester, for sale by Glory Anna, Edward and Benjamin Stevenson (4/10)

M'Calay, Daniel, Highland boy, age 17—runaway from William Wear, of Newborough, Ulster Co., NY (4/10)

Allen, John, of Phila.—married April 6 in NYC, by Rev. Dr. Auchmuty, to Miss Johnston, daughter of David Johnston, Esq., of NYC (4/10)

Van Horne, Cornelius, dec'd—real estate will be sold at house of Widow Van Voorhies in New Brunswick, Somerset Co., N.J. (4/24)

Oliver, Negro slave, age c. 22, belonging to Samuel Smith, living on north side of Staten Island—runaway March 18 from Abraham Lawrence, of Flushing, L.I. (4/24)

Maxwell, George, servant, born in north of England—runaway from Hugh Wallace (4/24)

Banker, Richard, of Hanover Square, NYC, merchant—died April 18 in NYC, of a putrid fever, in his 48th year (4/24); accounts with estate to be settled with Sarah Bancker, executrix (5/29)

Thompson, Humfrey, age 25, who has taught school for 12 months past at Ramapoh, Orange Co., NY—absconded April 22 from his bail; reward offered by Lewis Conklin, Jr. (5/1)

Brovort, John, late of NYC, dec'd—accounts with estate to be settled with Whitehead Hicks, admin. (5/8)

Bogart, Henry C., dec'd—articles for sale in house lately occupied by him (5/8)

Hait, Mary, wife of Daniel Hait, of Bedford, Westchester Co., NY—has eloped from her husband (5/8)

Forman, William, Esq., Paymaster of H.M.'s Royal Artillery—died last Friday se'nnight (5/8)

Livingston, John, of NYC, merchant—married April 11 in NYC to Miss Leroy, daughter of Jacob Leroy, of NYC (5/15)

Isaac, Solomon (*alias* Isaac Jones), servant, age 36, born in London, who came 10 years ago to America, served 7 years in Va. or Md., came to NYC, where he was jailed, then went to Phila., where he was again jailed—runaway from Hartshorne Fitz Randolph, of Morris Co., N.J. (5/22)

Meek, William, servant, age c. 40—runaway May 7 from John Elder, of Paxton, Lancaster

Alexander, John, servant, born in Scotland, age c. 22—same as above

Warren, William, English servant, tailor, age c. 24—runaway May 22 from Thomas Harrison, living in Strawberry Alley, Phila. (5/29)

McDaniel, Hugh, servant, born in America, age c. 30—same as above

Joe, Negro slave, age 21—runaway about 14 days ago from Isaac Van Blarcum, living at Paramus, Bergen Co., N.J. (5/29)

De Peyster, Capt. Joseph Reade, son of James De Peyster, of NYC, merchant—married May 22 to Miss Nancy Betts, at seat of her father, Thomas Betts, in Kings Co., L.I. (5/29)

Cooper, Anne, servant, age c. 23, who was born in Scotland and came from there 13 months ago—runaway May 27 from Thomas Steele, living in Beekman St., NYC (5/29)

Ricket, William, servant, age c. 24, son of John Ricket, late of Brookland Ferry, L.I.—runaway from John Harriman, living at Paquanack, Morris Co., N.J. (6/5)

Butler, William, late of NYC, merchant, dec'd—accounts with estate to be settled with execs., James Desbrosses, Jr., and Sarah Butler (6/5)

Holmes, Thomas, indented servant, age c. 37, who has taught school at Haerlem—runaway June 4 from John Myers and Isaac Day (6/12)

Frapwell, John, English servant, age c. 32—runaway June 4 from George Brown, of Falls Twp., Bucks Co., Pa. (6/12)

Greer, James, Irish servant, age c. 23—runaway June 4 from Samuel Bunting, Jr., of Falls Twp., Bucks Co., Pa. (6/12)

Smith, Joseph, Esq., of Burlington, Treasurer of West New Jersey—married June 13 to Miss James, daughter of Abel James, Esq., of NYC (6/19)

Cleverly, Thomas—died June 9 at Morris Town, N.J. (6/19)

Neat, William, eminent American merchant—died lately in London (6/19)

Bauscher, Peter, blacksmith, dec'd—accounts with estate to be settled with execs., George Janeway and John Walter (6/19)

America, Negro slave, age 20—runaway from sloop *Seaflower;* reward offered by John Sebring (6/19)

Hendricks, Mrs. Hester, wife of Uriah Hendricks, of NYC, merchant—died June 24 in NYC in her 32nd year, leaving husband and eight small children (6/26)

Durant, Benjamin, indented English servant, age c. 22 or 23—runaway night of June 20 from Samuel Deabury (6/26)

Todd, James and William, late of Minemore, County of Derry, Ireland—are informed that their father and mother have arrived in NYC (7/3)

Brag, John, English servant—runaway May 27 from Joseph Pemberton, grazier, living in Third St., Phila. (7/3)

Bill, Negro slave, age c. 23—runaway June 1 from Abraham Kintzing, of Phila. (7/3)

Livingston, Robert, Esq.—died June 27 at Claremont, Manor of Livingston, in his 88th year (7/3)

Brovort, Elias, of NYC—died June 29 at his house in Maiden Lane in his 57th year (7/3)

Watts, Mrs., wife of Hon. John Watts, Esq., and sister of Hon. Oliver De Lancey, Esq., member of H.M.'s Council—died July 3 in NYC (7/10)

Lawrence, Thomas, of Phila., merchant—married last week to Miss Morris, daughter of Col. Lewis Morris, of Morrissania, Westchester Co., NY (7/10)

Cato, Negro slave, age c. 25 or 26—runaway June 4 from Frances Holland, of City of Albany (7/10)

Gardner, Col. Thomas, of Cambridge, Mass.—died last Monday of wounds received in battle on June 17 (7/17)

Boerum, Simon, Esq., Clerk of Kings Co., Representative in General Assembly and Delegate to Continental Congress in Phila.—died July 11 at his house on L.I. (7/17)

Tom, Negro slave, age c. 22, this country born—runaway July 2 from Jacob Holcomb, living near Coryell's Ferry, Amwell Twp., Hunterdon Co., N.J. (7/24)

Litchfield, John, Esq., late of H.M.'s 16th Regt., son of John Litchfield, Esq., of Northampton in Great Britain, married to daughter of John Morin Scot, Esq.—died last Friday se'nnight at his father-in-law's seat at Greenwich, from which his body was removed to vault in Trinity Church Yard (7/24)

Van Varick, James, dec'd—in his lifetime he assigned all his estate to his creditors (7/24)

Collings, Joseph, apprentice, tailor, age between 19 and 20—runaway July 20 from Alexander Meharg, of Newtown, L.I. (7/31)

Jackson, Josiah, living at Butternut, Tryon Co., NY—murdered June 10 (7/31)

Livingston, Miss Polly, eldest daughter of Peter R. Livingston, Esq.—died July 11 at the Manor of Livingston (7/31)

Killbrun, Lawrence, late of NYC, dec'd—accounts with estate to be settled with Judith Killbrun or Abraham H. Van Vleck, merchant (7/31)

Kearney, Phillip, Esq., of Amboy, N.J., attorney—died there July 31 at an advanced age (8/7); accounts with estate to be settled with executrix, Isabella Kearney (9/25)

Ross, Rachel, wife of Nathaniel Ross, at Connecticut Farms, near Elizabeth Town, N.J. —husband will not pay debts contracted by her in future (8/14)

Wallar, Capt. Peter, of NYC—died Aug. 2 in his 38th year at the seat of Richard Lawrence on Staten Island and was buried Aug. 4 in Trinity Church Yard (8/14)

Lisk, Benjamin, born in NY, blacksmith, prisoner for debt—broke gaol in Newark, N.J. on Aug. 6 in company of another prisoner, Nathan Parant, committed on suspicion of robbery (8/14)

Nicholls, Richard, Esq., attorney, resident of NYC for 60 years—died Aug. 19 in NYC (8/21)

Murry, Lewis, indented Irish servant—runaway July 19 from William Stacy, of Baltimore Town (8/21)

Smith, Dr. William Drewet—married Aug. 14 in Phila. to Miss Peggy Stedman, daughter of Alexander Stedman, Esq., of this city (8/28)

Hancock, John, Esq., President of the Continental Congress—married Aug. 28, by the Rev. Mr. Eliot, at the seat of Thaddeus Burr, Esq., to Miss Dorothy Quincy, daughter of Edmund Quincy, Esq., of Boston—Fairfield, Conn. dispatch (9/4)

Habersham, Hon. James, Esq., President of H.M.'s Council of Georgia—died Aug. 28 at Brunswick, N.J., in his 63rd year while on his way to NYC and was buried Aug. 31 in family vault of Nathaniel Marston, Esq., in Trinity Church Yard (9/4)

Cheever, Ezekiel, late of Morris Town, N.J., dec'd—accounts with estate to be settled with execs., Jacob Morrell, Nathan Reeve, Jon. Cheever (9/4)

Duryee, Jorst, late of Jamaica South, Queens Co., L.I., dec'd—real estate for sale by execs., Jacob Duryee and Albert Terhuner (9/11)

Sturdevant, Eliphalet, age c. 28, former sailor (who enlisted under name of Eli Betts)— deserted Aug. 23 from 8th company of 7th Conn. Regt. commanded by Col. Charles Webb; reward offered by William G. Hubbell, Capt. of the 8th Company (9/11)

Titus, Negro slave, age c. 25—runaway Sept. 5 from Henry Van Dyck (9/11)

Simpson, Mr., of Pa., who was wounded at Plowed Hill—has died (9/18)

Vaugtan, James, pedlar—murdered Sept. 9 in Ewchland Twp., Chester Co., Pa., by a certain Elliot (9/25)

Ben, Negro slave, age 18—runaway from John Concklin (9/25)

Stewart, Arthur, servant, born in Ireland, age c. 22—runaway Sept. 9 from Richard Runyon, living at Long Hill, Morris Co., N.J. (9/25)

Baxter, Augustine, dec'd—farm on Frog's Neck, Westchester Co., NY, for sale by execs., Daniel Quinby and Augustine Drack (10/2)

Watts, John, Jr., Recorder of NYC—married Oct. 2 at Union Hill, Borough of Westchester, to Miss Jane De Lancey, daughter of the late Peter De Lancey, Esq. (10/9)

Barclay, Thomas H., Esq.—married Oct. 25 at Union Hill, Borough of Westchester, to Miss Susanna De Lancey, daughter of the late Peter De Lancey, Esq. (10/9)

Witter, Mrs. Catharine, wife of Thomas Witter, of NYC, merchant—died Oct. 7 in NYC in her 53rd year (10/9)

Seton, Mrs., wife of William Seton, merchant, of NYC—died Oct. 4 in NYC in her 27th year (10/9)

Jones, David, Esq., Speaker of the General Assembly and one of the judges of the Supreme Court of NY for many years—died last week at his seat in Suffolk Co., Long Island, at an advanced age (10/16)

Jelf, Joseph, dec'd—house and shop in Elizabeth Town, N.J., to be let by Mrs. Jelf (10/16)

Horsen, John, lately dec'd—farm at Bloomingdale, about 5 miles from NYC, for sale by execs., Jacob Horsen and Martinus Schoonmaker (10/16)

Sagers, Benjamin, convict English servant, blacksmith and gunsmith—runaway from Aweray Richardson (10/16)

Cressop, Capt. Michael (eldest son of Col. Thomas Cressop, of Potowmack, Va.), who arrived in NYC Oct. 12 from camp at Cambridge, Mass.—died in NYC Oct. 18 of a fever in his 28th year, leaving a widow and four children (10/23)

Perry, John, Irish servant lad—runaway Aug. 12 from Richard Tettermary, of Phila. (10/23)

Ogden, Nicholas, son of Hon. Judge Ogden—married last Thursday week at Newark, N.J., to Miss Hannah Cuyler, sister of Henry Cuyler, Esq., of NYC (10/23)

Platt, Mrs., wife of Jeremiah Platt, of NYC, merchant—died recently at New Haven, Conn., and on Oct. 18 her remains were brought to NYC and buried in the family vault at the New Dutch Church (10/23)

Randolph, Hon. Peyton, of Va., late President of the Continental Congress—died Oct. 22 in Phila. of an apoplectic stroke in his 53rd year (10/30)

Row, Isaac, age c. 30—apparently died about Oct. 5 on a raft; his body was found by Capt. Thomas Tworbirdge of the sloop *Union* (10/30)

Ward, William, born in town of Fairfield, Conn.—died Oct. 26 at Manor of Philipsburg, Westchester Co., aged 105 years, 4 months, 20 days (11/6)

Bayard, Mrs. Catharine, wife of Nicholas Bayard, Esq., of NYC—died Nov. 2 in NYC in her 32nd year, leaving husband and five small children (11/6)

Ming, Negro slave, age 20—runaway from Benjamin Hutchinson, of Southold, Suffolk Co., L.I. (11/6)

Van Horne, David, of NYC, merchant—died Nov. 10 in NYC in his 63rd year (11/13)

Bogart, John, of NYC—died Nov. 8 in his 79th year at his house at corner of Cortlandt St., Broad-Way, NYC (11/13)

Fairchild, Caleb, late of Kinderhook, dec'd—accounts with estate to be settled with widow, Nancy Fairchild, living at Kinderhook (11/13)

Murray, James, servant, nailmaker, age c. 20—runaway Nov. 12 from Henry Ustick (11/20)

Murray, James Jeffray, servant, nailmaker, age between 19 and 20—same as above

Livingston, Rev. Dr. John, one of the ministers of the Dutch Churches in NYC—married Monday evening in NYC to Miss Sally Livingston, youngest daughter of Philip Livingston, Esq., a delegate from NY to the Continental Congress (12/4)

Duyckinck, Gerardus, Jr., of NYC, merchant—married Monday evening to Miss Suckey Livingston, daughter of Henry Livingston, Esq., at his seat in Dutchess Co. (12/4)

Verplanck, Mrs. Effe, wife of Philip Verplanck, Esq., of Fish Kills, Dutchess Co., NY—died there Nov. 15 in her 39th year, leaving husband and five small children (12/4)

Brinckerhoff, Dirck, late of NYC, merchant, dec'd—accounts with estate to be settled with Dirck Brinkherhoff, Jr., acting exec. (12/11)

Livingston, Hon. Mr. Justice—died Dec. 9 at Claremont in Manor of Livingston in his 58th year; his eldest son is a member of the Continental Congress; General Montgomery's lady is his eldest daughter; his second son is serving with rank of major in Canada (12/18)

De Lancey, Miss Elizabeth, third daughter of the late Peter De Lancey, of Westchester—died Dec. 17 at Union Hill in her 26th year (12/25)

Fowler, Elijah, dec'd—land (whereon Capt. Joseph Drake now lives) in Eastchester, Westchester Co., NY, for sale by Joshua Pell, Jr., and Solomon Fowler, Jr. (12/25)

GENEALOGICAL DATA FROM THE NEW-YORK GAZETTE; AND THE WEEKLY MERCURY

1776

Leverage, John, apprentice lad, shoemaker—runaway 19 Dec. from Daniel Sickles, next door to the Coffee-House, NYC (1/1)

Moncrieffe, Helena, wife of Thomas Moncrieffe, Esq.—died Dec. 22, 1775, in NYC (1/1)

Long, Miss, of NYC—accidentally burned to death on Dec. 28, 1775 (1/1)

Van Horne, John, Esq., of Rockey-Hill, N.J.—married Jan. 1 to Miss Heard, daughter of Nathaniel Heard, of Woodbridge, N.J. (1/8)

Sinclair, Robert, late of NYC, merchant, dec'd—accounts with estate to be settled with Jannett Sinclair, exec. (1/15)

Ogden, Mrs., wife of Hon. David Ogden, Esq.—died Dec. 30, 1775, in Newark, N.J., in her 60th year (1/15)

Loxford, William Newman, English servant—runaway from Robert Wright, living near Allen's Town (1/15)

Sam, Negro slave, born in N.J., age c. 21, who formerly lived in Dr. Mercer's family—runaway Jan. 10 from Col. John Reid, living near the fort (1/15)

Caesar, Negro slave, age c. 40—runaway Nov., 1775, from James Morrison, of Montreal, merchant (1/15)

Platt, Jonas, late of NYC, merchant—died last Nov. in Savannah, Ga. (1/22)

Price, Samuel, age c. 35, lately master and owner of a coasting schooner in Ga.—on Oct. 31, 1775, with 8 other men, made off with a schooner owned by Patrick Mackay, Esq., of the island of Sappello, Ga. (1/22)

Wells, Samuel, born in R.I., age c. 25—same as above

Jamson, James Lee, son of Capt. John Jamson, of Bucks Co., Pa.—baptized last Thursday —Phila. dispatch of Jan. 24 (1/29)

Howard, Martin, Esq., of Newport, R.I., for many years justice of the peace of Newport— died there Jan. 4 in his 74th year (1/29)

Clepham, George, Esq., purser of H.M.'s ship *Asia*, in NY harbor—died Jan. 24 of apoplectic fit and was buried Jan. 25 in Trinity Church Yard (1/29)

Bixton, James, English servant lad—runaway about a fortnight ago from Donald M'Lean, of NYC (1/29)

Lott, Andrew, Esq. (son of Abraham Lott, Esq., Treasurer of Province of NY)—married Feb. 1 to Miss Alice Goelet, daughter of Peter Goelet, of NYC, merchant (2/5)

Mc Clean, John, who left Dublin some years ago and resided, with his wife Susannah, for a while at house of Capt. Hyson—will hear something to his advantage if he will go to Chatham, Morris Co., N.J. (2/12)

Beekman, Col. Henry, formerly Sheriff of City and County of NY, for above thirty years representative of Dutchess Co. in the Assembly, whose only daughter married the late Mr. Livingston—died Jan. 3 at his seat in Dutchess Co. the day after he completed his 88th year; he was descended from the lieutenant governor on the west side of Delaware (2/12)

Bockee, Abraham, Esq.—died Jan. 22 at the Nine Partners in his 58th year (2/12)

Bockee, Mrs. Abraham—died Jan. 28 at the Nine Partners in her 60th year (2/12)

Wolfes, Frederick, late of NYC, painter and glazier, dec'd—accounts with estate to be settled with F. Muhlenberg, exec. (2/12)

Hodsden, John, Esq., of NYC, for many years a merchant in Charles Town, S.C.—died last Saturday se'nnight in NYC (2/19)

Johnson, Samuel, apprentice, age c. 19, skinner and Breeches maker—runaway Feb. 13 from Rachel Getfield, living in NYC (2/19)

Saunders, John, young fellow, who escaped from a constable in Princetown, N.J., in Dec., 1775—reward for his capture offered by Howten Mershon, deputy constable (2/26)

Lee, Mary, wife of Seth Lee, of Hampenborough—has eloped from her husband (2/26)

Mulligan, Cook, young merchant of NYC—died there Feb. 21 (3/4)

Gilliot, Mary Elizabeth, dec'd—accounts with estate to be settled with exec., George Cornwell, of New Rochelle (3/4)

Johnston, Dr. Lewis, late of Perth Amboy, N.J., dec'd—property for sale by execs., James Parker, John Smyth and Heathcote Johnston (3/4)

Ross, Alexander, Esq., late of Ross Hall, near New Brunswick, N.J., dec'd—accounts with estate to be settled (3/4)

Post, David, blacksmith, dec'd—accounts with estate to be settled with John Byvanck, admin. (3/4)

Tom, Negro slave, age c. 23, late property of John Beck, of NYC, butcher—runaway March 5 from John Carpenter, living near the Brooklyn Ferry (3/11)

Ben, Negro slave, age 18 or 19—runaway March 7 from Casparus Conyn, of Claverack, Albany Co. (3/18)

Hanks, George, servant lad, born in England, shoemaker—runaway March 10 from William Ross, of Lancaster, Pa. (3/18)

Smith, Miss Johanna, only daughter of Christopher Smith, of NYC, merchant—died March 12 in NYC, aged 17 years and 6 months (3/18)

Creighton, James, Sr., of NYC—died there March 18, aged 77 (3/25)

Ward, Hon. Samuel, Esq., late member of the Continental Congress—died March 26 in Phila. and was buried March 27 in Baptist Church (4/1)

Syrus, mulatto, age 25—runaway March 8 from Joshua Powers, of Black Point, Lyme, Conn. (4/1)

Van Deursen, Henry, dec'd—house in New Brunswick, N.J., for sale by execs., William Van Deursen and Matthew Sleight (4/1)

Stewart, Alexander, of NYC, wine merchant—died April 9 in NYC in his 61st year (4/15)

Wakeman, Peter, of Greenfield, Conn.—his son was baptized Charles Lee Wakeman on March 3 (4/15)

Dimon, Capt. Jonathan, in the Continental service—his son was baptized Richard Montgomery Dimon on March 24 (4/15)

Goodsel, James—his son was baptized John McPherson Goodsel (4/15)

Lawrence, Uriah, Jr., late of Dutchess Co., dec'd—accounts with estate to be settled with Uriah Lawrence (4/15)

Bartlet, John, age 20—deserted March 27 from company of Capt. Nathan Pearce, Jr., in the Continental service (4/15)

Seymour, Sinclair, master of the *Cabot*—killed in action (4/22)

Wilson, Lt., of the *Cabot*—same as above

Fitzpatrick, Lt., of the *Alfred*—same as above

Simon, mulatto slave, age c. 30, born at Rariton, N.J.—runaway April 14 from Thomas Palmer, of New-Burgh, Ulster Co., NY (4/22)

Carpenter, Mrs. Elizabeth, of NYC—died there April 16 in her 85th year (4/22)

Colgen, Mrs. Mary, widow of late Rev. Mr. Colgen, for many years Rector of the Parish at Jamaica, L.I.—died April 17 at Jamaica, L.I., aged 67 (4/22)

Waldron, William, dec'd—real estate in Albany for sale (4/22)

Pamela, Negro slave, age c. 22—runaway from Gerard G. Beekman, at Beekman's Slip (4/22)

Marston, Miss Mary, of NYC—died there April 22 in her 84th year and was buried April 25 in family vault at Trinity Church (4/29)

Ryan, Polly, wife of Lewis Ryan, of NYC—has eloped from her husband (4/29)

Tom, Negro slave, age 21—runaway April 23 from Daniel Enslee, butcher in the Fly Market, NYC (4/29)

Brower, Jeremiah, of NYC, merchant—died last Sunday week at Hackensack in his 48th year and was buried the next day in family vault at the New Dutch Church (5/6)

Anderson, Alexander, of NYC—last Sunday week his twins were baptized, by Rev. Mr. Treat, George Washington Anderson and Martha Dandridge Anderson (5/6)

Marsh, Mary, wife of Isaac Marsh, of Elizabeth Town, Raway—has eloped from her husband (5/6)

Prentice, Edward, resident of Cambridge, age c. 30—deserted April 19 from Capt. Oliver's Co. in Col. James Reed's Regt., while on march from Winter Hill (5/6)

Welch, Thomas, native of Ireland, age 25—deserted, in company with an Irishman named John Berry, from Capt. James Wilson's Co. of Col. Irwin's Regt. (5/6)

Gooch, Joseph, native of Braintree, Mass.—deserted, in company with Nedediah Olney, from Capt. Thomas Pierce's Co. of artillery in Col. Knox's Regt. (5/6)

Stewart, Alexander—partnership of Stewart and Nicoll dissolved because of Stewart's death (5/6)

Forsythe, Robert, private soldier, age c. 24—deserted from Capt. Samuel Hay's Co. in 6th
Battalion of Pa. Regulars (5/6)

Roosevelt, Jacobus, of NYC, merchant—died there May 5 in his 85th year (5/13)

Tuder, Mrs. Mary, widow of Capt. John Tuder, late of NYC, merchant—died May 10 in
NYC (5/13)

Oaks, Capt. George, late of Marblehead in New England—murdered about April 1 near
Roanoke Island, N.C., by Joseph Evans, late of Salem Co., N.J.; Oaks left a widow
and seven children (5/20)

Ross, John, Esq., long an attorney of Phila.—died there May 5, aged 61, and was buried in
St. Paul's Church (5/20)

Kirkland, Col. Moses, belonging to South Carolina, age between 50 and 60—escaped May
8 from jail of Phila., where he was confined by order of the Continental Congress
(5/20)

Horsmanden, Mrs. Anne, wife of Hon. Daniel Horsmanden, Chief Justice of Supreme
Court of NY—died last Sunday week in her 60th year (5/27)

Avery, Mrs., wife of Rev. Mr. Avery, Rector of Parish at Rye—died there May 13 in her
39th year (5/27)

Peyton, Thomas, Esq., of Gloucester, Va.—married last Saturday to Miss Nancy Washington, of the same county—Gloucester Co. dispatch of May 13 (6/10)

Watson, Mr. young schoolmaster in Schenectady—found May 20, murdered on road between Schenectady and Albany   (6/10)

Cobham, James, late tavernkeeper in NYC—died June 4 in NYC and was buried June 9
in Presbyterian Church Yard (6/10)

Lynch, John, born in Ireland, age 40—deserted from Capt. Henry O'Hara's Co., stationed
at Ft. George, above Albany (6/10)

Duly, Joshua, born in Essex, Morris Co., N.J.—same as above

Post, Adrian, born in Essex, Morris Co., N.J.—same as above

Groves, Thomas, Irishman, age c. 25—deserted from Capt. Nathaniel Tuttele's Co. in
Col. Webb's Regt. (6/10)

Shay, John, age c. 28—deserted from Capt. Dimond Morton's Co. of artillery in Col.
Henry Knox's Regt. (6/10)

Farlow, William, an old countryman, age c. 28—deserted from Lt. Henry Burbeck's Co. of
artillery (6/10)

Mels, James, apprentice lad, shoemaker—runaway May 27 from Timothy Ogden, of
Elizabeth Town, N.J. (6/10)

Burn, Arthur, native of Ireland, weaver, who married a wife in New Fairfield in New
England—deserted from Capt. John Wiley's Co. in Col. M'Dougel's N.Y. Regt. (6/10)

Jones, Daniel, native of Morris Co., age 18, weaver—same as above

Moor, Hezekiah, of Salisbury, Middlesex Co., Mass., age 22—deserted from General
Washington's guard; reward for his capture offered by Capt. Caleb Gibbs (6/17)

Boyd, William—his son baptized Robert Washington Boyd on June 2 at Presbyterian
Church at Pequea (6/24)

Wilson, William—his son baptized Richard Montgomery Wilson on June 9 at Presbyterian Church at Pequea (6/24)

De Forest, Benjamin, merchant—his son baptized John Hancock De Forest on June 2
at Ripton, in Stratford, Conn. (6/24)

Jack, Negro slave, age c. 25, Guiney born, brass founder—runaway June 20 from Jacob
Wilkins, of Newark, N.J. (6/24)

Gill, William, age between 40 and 50—stole a horse on June 16 from Jacob Comly, living
at Smithfield, Manor of Moreland, Phila. Co., Pa. (6/24)

Smith, Mrs. Elizabeth, widow of Hon. William Smith, Esq., one of the judges of Supreme
Court of NY—died a few days ago in Wethersfield, Conn., in her 68th year (7/1)

Berrara, Francis, Spanish servant, age c. 30—runaway, with one Francis Rodrigo, on June
23 from Basto Furnace; reward for capture will be paid by master, John Cox, of

Burlington, N.J., or by Joseph Ball at the Basto Furnace at the Forks of Little Egg Harbor (7/1)

Mains, Thomas, born in Parish of Cumberland, County of Down, Ireland, brother of Matthew Mains—will hear something to his advantage on applying to H. Gaine (7/1)

Dunscomb, Mrs. Margaret, wife of John Dunscomb, wine merchant—died July 1 (7/8)

Nathaniel, Negro slave, who was born at Newtown, Queens Co., and lived at Flatbush, age 24—runaway, together with his brother Jacob, a slave of Jeromus Remsen, from Henry Wyckoff, living in Kings Co., L.I. (7/8)

Prince, Negro slave, age c. 21, butcher—runaway July 1 from Goodheart Siegler, living in Rosevelt's Street, near the Tea Water Pump, NYC (7/15)

Peters, Rev. Dr.—died July 10 in Phila. at an advanced age (7/22)

Smith, Samuel, Esq.—died July 13 at Burlington, N.J., in his 56th year (7/22)

Lawrence, Mrs. Mary, wife of Thomas Lawrence, Esq.—died last Sunday se'nnight at Morrissania and was buried the following Tuesday in family vault (7/22)

Ball, George, of NYC, merchant—died July 17 in NYC (7/22)

Cato, Negro slave, age c. 24—runaway July 20 from John Smith, living at Frog's Neck in Westchester (7/29)

Taylor, George, born in Germany—deserted July 9 at Bergen, N.J., from William Kelly's Co. of riflemen (7/29)

Sarly, Capt. Jacob, of NYC—died July 31 in NYC in his 86th year (8/5)

Conyne, Jemima, wife of Casparus Conyne, of District of Manor of Livingston—her husband will not pay debts contracted by her in future (8/5)

Clark, Abijah, apprentice lad, blacksmith—runaway July 27 from James Odell, of Poughkeepsie (8/12)

Owens, William, native of Ireland, age c. 23 or 24, schoolmaster at Blooming Grove—is sought as a Tory (8/12)

Prince, Negro slave, age c. 25—runaway June 16 from William Conray, Jr., of Dover, Dutchess Co., NY (8/12)

Thomas, Capt. of U.S. Army—fell on a tender in the North River and is supposed to have died (8/19)

Caster, Negro slave, age c. 35—runaway July 30 from Philip Kissick, of NYC (8/19)

Potts, Isaac, brought up near Sussex Co. Court House, N.J., age c. 21—deserted from Capt. William Bond's Co. of Col. Ephraim Martin's Regt. (8/19)

Weaver, John, brought up near Sussex Court House, N.J., age c. 21—same as above

Westlick, John, brought up near Sussex Court House, N.J.—same as above; has a wife near Spotswood Forge, N.J.

Langden, John, age 16—runaway from Daniel Green, shoemaker, near the Fly Market, NYC (8/19)

Van Wyck, Capt., together with Lieutenants Versereau and Depeyster—killed Aug. 21 by lightning in General M'Dougall's camp near the Bull's Head in the Bowery, NYC (8/26)

Bartlett, Ephraim, a soldier—killed Aug. 21 by lightning at house of Joseph Hallet, in Hanover Square, NYC (8/26)

Kingsbury, Asa, recently discharged as a surgeon's mate from the Continental Army—died Aug. 20 in NYC (8/26)

Baker, Sergt. Sherebirh, of Upton, Worcester Co., Mass.—deserted from Capt. James Foster's Co. in Col. Jonathan Smith's Regt. (8/26)

Wood, John, age c. 20, of Upton, Worcester Co., Mass.—same as above

Burney, Fortune, a Negro, of Grafton, Worcester Co., Mass., age c. 20—same as above

GENEALOGICAL DATA FROM THE NEW-YORK GAZETTE; AND THE WEEKLY MERCURY

1776

—NEWARK SERIES—

Batt, Capt., late of the 18th Regt.—had married a daughter of Mr. M'Calay, of Phila. (9/2)

Tom, Negro slave, age c. 50—runaway from John Vail (9/2)

Marschalk, Francis, of NYC—died Sept. 6 in NYC at an advanced age (9/9)

Eddy, Joseph, soldier, age c. 32 or 33—deserted from Capt. Oliver Root's Co. in Col. Smith's Regt. (9/9)

Noel, Garret, for many years a bookseller of NYC—died Sept. 22 in Elizabeth Town, N.J., in his 70th year (9/28)

Hake, Miss Katey, eldest daughter of Samuel Hake, late of NYC, merchant—died Sept. 22 at Newark, N.J., in her 7th year (9/28)

Deserted Sept. 16 from Capt. Robert Johnston's Co. of the 1st Battalion York Forces (9/28):

Babcock, David, age c. 23
Oddle, Thomkin, age 26
Finch, Charles, age 21
Ferguson, Thomas, age 27
Parcels, Mathias, age 24
Egbert, John, age 30

Blackman, John, age 30

Wily, Edward, age 23

Wilmot, Henry, merchant, late of Tarry Town, near King's Bridge, NY—died there about 10 days ago (10/15)

Boyd, Jonathan, born in England, age c. 45—deserted from Capt. Simon Smith's Co. in Col. Bradley's Regt. (10/5)

Gautier, Andrew, for many years Alderman for the Dock Ward of NYC—died Oct. 14 at Aquacanock Bridge (10/19)

Cuyle, Henry, late of NYC, merchant—died week before last in Newark, N.J. (10/19)

Cato, Negro slave, age c. 23 or 25—runaway Oct. 8 from Mattathias Gomez; reward offered if brought to Mrs. Deborah Gomez, in Second St., near Walnut St., Phila., or to Francis Basset, at house of Dr. Burnet, in Newark (10/19)

Dwight, Joseph, late of NYC—lately died in River Delaware when returning from the West Indies to Phila.; widow is asked to apply to William Hadden, of Newark, N.J., to hear something to her advantage (10/26)

Tite, Negro slave, age c. 40—runaway Oct. 30 from James Stewart; reward will be paid by Stewart at Ezekiel Ball's near Springfield (11/2)

END OF NEWARK SERIES

York, Negro slave, age c. 19—runaway Oct. 3 from William Maxwell, living in Wall St., NYC (10/14)

York, young Negro slave—runaway from Charles Arding, of Jamaica, L.I. (10/14)

Bourne, Capt., of the Guards—died Oct. 20 in NYC (10/21)

Hoeysfinger, Capt., Hessian officer—died Oct. 16 in NYC and was buried Oct. 17 in Trinity Church Yard (10/21)

Wilmot, Henry, merchant, late chairman to the General Committee in NYC—died a few days ago in New Jersey (10/21)

Feonce, Negro slave, age 17—runaway Oct. 2 from John Rapalje, living at Brooklyn Ferry (10/21)

Sinclair, Hon. William, lieutenant in H.M.'s 71st Regt. of Foot—died Oct. 22 in NYC (10/28)

Willett, Mrs. Elizabeth, widow—buried Oct. 26 in family vault in Trinity Church Yard; she died in her 66th year (10/28)

Ned, Spanish Negro, age c. 40—runaway from Philip Skeene, Esq., of Skeensborough (10/28)

M'Kenzie, Charles, lately dec'd—accounts with estate to be settled with John M'Kenzie or Walter Urquhart, in Wall St., NYC (10/28)

Will, Creole Negro, age 19—runaway from Finnly Nicholson, at Mr. Thomas Hepborn's store in Mr. Bogart's house in Dock St., NYC (11/11)

Reiffarth, John Christopher, late Suttler to the Hessian Grenadier Battalion of Minnigerode, dec'd—accounts with estate to be settled with Ungar, auditor, at camp at Dobb's Ferry (10/28)

Joe, Negro slave, age c. 30—runaway from Samuel Sackett, living near the Fly Market, NYC (12/2)

Jack, Negro slave, age c. 30—runaway from Waters Smith, of Newton, L.I. (12/23)

Duffe, James, a Loyalist—died Dec. 24 at his seat on Staten Island in his 40th year (12/30)

Caesar, Negro slave, age c. 30—runaway Dec. 22 from William Wood (12/30)

GENEALOGICAL DATA FROM THE NEW-YORK GAZETTE; AND THE WEEKLY MERCURY

1777

Betty, Negro, age c. 22, lately purchased from Cornelius Van der Vear—runaway from William Tongue, in Hanover Square, NYC (1/6)

Prince, Negro slave, age c. 21 or 22, who formerly lived with Mr. Lashel or Lasher, in the Broadway, NYC—runaway Jan. 1 from the ship *Union*, William Hamilton master (1/6)

Daniel, Negro slave. age c. 9—runaway from Richard Harris, living in Little Queen St., NYC (1/20)

Frank, Negro slave, age c. 19—runaway from George Bevoise, living near Brooklyn Ferry (2/17)

Marshal, James, age c. 22—deserted from ship *Lord North*, George Ross master (2/17)

Fralich, Christian, sugar baker, of NYC, dec'd—accounts with estate to be settled, on order of Benigne Fralich, executrix, and John Bonn and Timothy Horsfield, execs., with Abraham Wilson, merchant, at No. 333 Dock St., NYC (2/24)

Cyrus, Negro slave, age c. 14—runaway from P. M'Davitt, of NYC (2/24)

Coghlar, Lt. John, of the 7th or English Fusiliers—was married Feb. 24, by the Rev. Dr. Auchmuty, to Miss Margaret Moncrieffe, only daughter of Thomas Moncrieffe, Esq. (3/3)

Loui, Negro slave, age c. 20, who lately came from St. Vincent's with the 6th Regt.—runaway Feb. 16 (3/3)

Auchmuty, Rev. Dr. Samuel, born in Boston, educated at Harvard, who became Assistant Minister of Trinity Church, NYC, in 1748 and Rector in 1764, upon death of Dr. Barclay—died March 4 in NYC in his 55th year and was buried March 6 in chancel of St. Paul's Church (3/10); accounts with estate to be settled with Robert N. Auchmuty, admin. (3/17)

Watson, Isaac, born either in Cumberland or Westmoreland, England, age c. 21, apprentice to Robert Waters, Esq., in White Haven—deserted March 7 from the brigantine *Watters*, Joseph Jackson master, lying near Peck's Slip (3/10)

Deall, Mrs. Elizabeth, wife of Samuel Deall, of NYC, merchant—died March 12 in NYC in her 49th year (3/17)

Hurd, James, age c. 23, servant to the lieutenant of marines—deserted from H.M.'s ship Brane (3/17)

Thompson, Joseph, Negro slave, age c. 50—runaway March 9 from Jacob Bennet, Jr., at Bushwyck (3/17)

Winslow, Isaac, Esq., late of Roxbury, near Boston—died March 23 in NYC (3/24)

Jepson, Lt. William, of the 28th Regt.—married in NYC to Miss Appe, of NYC (3/24)

Phillipse, Frederick, of NYC—married in NYC to Miss Polly Marston, daughter of the late Nathaniel Marston, of NYC (3/24)

Hayes, Margaret, wife of William Hayes, sawyer, of NYC—has eloped from her husband (3/24)

Slocum, Charles, of North Kingston, R.I.—shot and killed Thursday by George Babcock —Newport dispatch of April 5 (4/14)

Kniffin, Jonathan, of Rye, in Conn., young daughter of—killed some days ago by a party of rebels (4/14)

Emmitt, James. Esq., for many years attorney in NYC—died lately at Newtown, L.I. (4/14)

Lowe, Cornelius, Esq.—died last week at Rariton Landing, N.J. (4/14)

Davis, Capt. Halkith, of ship *Britannia*—accounts with dec'd Capt Davis's estate to be settled with Philip Millan on board ship (4/14)

Flories, Antonio, Spaniard, born in Mallaga, age 14—runaway from brigantine *William*, James M'Ewen master; reward offered by Archibald Wilson, in Queen St., NYC (4/14)

Sandwich, James, apprentice, age 16—runaway April 3 from the snow *Rum Adventure*, Peter Lesebeater master, lying at Peck's Slip, NYC (4/14)

Doutherts, George, indented servant, age c. 18—runaway from brigantine *Venus*, Richard Thirsby master (4/14)

Osborn, Negro slave, age 27—runaway from Powles Hook (4/21)

Taylor, Capt. John, of NYC—died April 23 in his house in NYC (4/28)

Wright, Dr. Thomas, late of East Chester, dec'd—accounts with estate to be settled with execs., Benjamin Hildreth, Sr., and Thomas Greswold (4/28)

Archer, John, servant, age c. 21—runaway from transport *Nancy*, lying in harbor of Newport, R.I., William Brown master (4/28)

Turvey, Nathaniel, apprentice, age c. 15—runaway from the *Grand Duke*, victualler, lying at Brownjohn's wharf (4/28)

Miller, William, apprentice, age c. 16—runaway from *Argo* transport, lying in North River, George Tate master (4/28)

Day, Thomas, apprentice, age 16—runaway from the *Thomas and Betsey*, victualler, Charles Edward master (5/5)

Wetmore, Gurdon, of Hartford—lately hanged by the rebels (5/5)

Smithies, Mr., surgeon—married last week, by Rev. Mr. Inglis, to Miss Burgess, of NYC (5/12)

Brown, Lt., of the 14th Regt.—married last week in NYC to Miss Polly French, daughter of Joseph French, Esq., of Jamaica, L.I. (5/12)

Bailey, Mrs., wife of Dr. Richard Bailey, of NYC—lately died at Newtown, L.I. (5/12)

Hildreth, Joseph, for about 40 years Clerk of Trinity Church—died last week at his house in NYC (5/12)

Low, Cornelius, dec'd—property to be sold at house of John Taylor, near the Fly Market, NYC, where Judge Hicks lately lived (5/12)

Shaw, George, apprentice, age c. 22—deserted May 9 from the victualler, *Prince of Wales*, lying at Moore's Wharf, Henry Denton master (5/12)

Fairfield, David, apprentice, age c. 20—same as above.

York, Negro slave, age c. 20—runaway from Thomas Greswold, distiller, living at No. 19 Ferry St., NYC, and later at No. 10 Ferry St., near Peck's Slip (5/12 and 6/2)

Dougel, Robert, apprentice boy—runaway from John Barrow, baker, at No. 13 King St., NYC.(5/12)

Sam, Negro slave, age c. 28, property of the heirs of the late Hester Weyman—runaway; reward offered by execs. of Mrs. Weyman's estate, Peter Goelet and Gabriel H. Ludlow (5/19)

Chess, Negro slave, age c. 20—runaway May 15 from Stephen Skinner, living at Corlear's Hook (5/26)

Runaway from the transport *Christie*, A. Bodfield master, lying in the North River (5/26):

Williams, John, Irishman, age c. 18, sailor

M'Vicker, Archibald, a Scotchman, age c. 25, sailor

Rankin, George, native American, age c. 28, sailor

Nicol, James, Scotchman, age c. 21, sailor

Banks, Alexander, Scotchman, age c. 20, sailor

Wilkes, Negro slave, age c. 19 or 20—runaway from Thomas Harriot, living at Jamaica South, L.I. (5/26)

Hicks, Thomas, Esq., late of Flushing, Queens Co., dec'd—accounts with estate to be settled with Whitehead Hicks, admin. (6/2)

Pompey, Negro slave, age c. 17—runaway May 30 from John Mowatt, cabinet and chair maker, in William St., NYC (6/2)

Peter, Negro slave, age c. 25—runaway May 24 from Jacob Hicks, living at Brooklyn Ferry (6/2)

Rose, Capt., of Marbletown—arrested by rebels on way to NYC, tried and executed about a month ago (6/9)

Middagh, Lt., of Marbletown—same as above

Patten, Abraham, rebel spy—executed at Brunswick on June 30, leaving a wife and 4 children at Baltimore, Md. (6/9)

Kingston, Francis, native of Devonshire, age c. 30, who came to N.J. a few years ago— came June 29 into NYC with a flag and has disappeared (6/9)

Stone, William—executed May 27 in Hartford, Conn., for recruiting for the King's service (6/16)

Abraham, part Negro and part Indian, age c. 45—runaway, together with wife and 2 children, from Thomas Pell, Manor of Pelham (6/30)

Deserted from the transport *Pacifick,* James Dunn master (6/30):

   Graham, Archibald, sailor, age c. 27, a north countryman

   Burn, Michael, born in Dublin, sailor, age c. 24

   Baxter, William, born at Aberdeen, Scotland, sailor, age c. 21

Charity, Negro, age c. 19—runaway, together with her two-year-old child named Peter, from Samuel Pearce, living in Chapel St., NYC (6/30)

Butler, Richard, born in Phila.—deserted June 28 from ordnance ship *Nancy,* William Brown master (6/30)

Sylvester, Daniel, born in Portugal—same as above

Davison, John, servant, age c. 20—runaway June 25 from victualler the *Two Friends,* Thomas Jones master (6/30)

Andrew, mulatto, born in Honduras, a lad—runaway June 15 from transport *Swan,* Jonathan Deal master (6/30)

Plymouth, Negro slave, age c. 26—runaway from Terence Kerin (6/30; 7/21)

Orridge, James, born in Parish of Bolton, County of Lancaster, England—deserted from H.M.'s 17th Regt. of Infantry (6/30)

Kerin, Edward, Esq., of NYC, volunteer in 22nd Light Co., son of Terence Kerin, Esq., of NYC—died July 6 in NYC in his 17th year of a wound received in the late action in N.J. (7/14)

Frank, Negro slave, age c. 18 or 19—runaway July 8 from George Debevoise (7/14)

Duke, Negro slave, age c. 20—runaway July 5 from Nicholas Ogden, living on Long Island (7/21)

Jessemy, Negro slave, age c. 25—runaway from Richard Bayler, of NYC (7/28)

Tar, William, apprentice, age c. 19—runaway from *Britannia,* victualler, Thomas Hayman master, at NYC (7/28)

Dick, Negro slave, baker, born on St. Kitts—runaway March 26 from Francis Conihane, living at 909 Peck's Slip (7/28)

Franklin, Mrs., wife of William Franklin, Gov. of N.J.—died July 28 in NYC in her 43rd year and was buried in chancel of St. Paul's Church the next evening (8/4)

Van Veghten, Lt.—killed in July at Ft. Edward (8/11)

M'Crea, Janey, of Ft. Edward—killed and scalped by enemy in July (8/11)

Joe, Negro slave, age c. 18—runaway Aug. 2 from Isaac Valentine, living at Westchester (8/11)

Jauncey, James, Jr., Esq., Master of the Rolls and Member of H.M.'s Council for NY—died Aug. 8 in NYC in his 30th year (8/11)

Martin, John, son of Major Martin of the Royal Artillery—died Aug. 7 in NYC in his 14th year (8/11)

Storey, John, seaman, born at Newcastel in Northumberland—deserted from ship *Perseus*, George Keith Elphinstone commander (8/11)

Murray, James, seaman, born in London—same as above

Colden, Richard, Esq., Surveyor and Searcher of H.M.'s Customs for Port of New York—died Aug. 15 at his house in NYC (8/18)

Brown, Mrs. Frances, wife of William Brown, Esq., of Maroneck, Westchester Co., NY, and daughter of Peter Barbarie, Esq., long an eminent merchant of NYC—died Aug. 22 in NYC in her 67th year (8/25)

Mallet, Mrs. Catharine, wife of Dr. Jonathan Mallett, Chief Surgeon and Purveyor of H.M.'s Hospital in NYC—died Sept. 3 at her nouse in NYC (9/8)

Kortright, Mrs. Hannah, wife of Lawrence Kortright—died Sept. 6 in NYC in her 39th year (9/8)

Willington, Lt. of the 28th Regt.—married to Miss Roberts, youngest daughter of John Roberts, Esq., High Sheriff of NYC and NY County (9/22)

McNiel, Ensign Hector, of the King's American Regt.—died Sept. 5, at the camp at King's Bridge, in his 27th year, and was buried the next day (9/22)

Stuyvesant, Peter, Esq.—died Sept. 18 at his house in the Bowery in his 87th year (9/22)

Pontenner, Mary—on May 12 married Richard Watkins but has now eloped from him (9/22)

Taylor, Capt. John, dec'd—accounts with estate to be settled with execs., Charles Nicoll, Willett Taylor and Evert Bancker, Jr. (9/22)

Tom, Negro slave, age c. 14–runaway Sept. 14 from Dr. Donald M'Lane (9/22)

Harman, Negro slave, age c. 25—runaway from farm at Bloomingdale of Brigadier General De Lancey (9/22)

Dick, Negro slave, age c. 35, born in Bermuda—runaway in Feb. from Abraham Lent, living at Newtown, L.I. (9/22)

Vathiest, John, born in Rochelle, France, age 18—deserted Sept. 2 from Capt. John Collett's company of Prince of Wales American Regt. in camp at Kingsbridge (9/22)

Rainhalt, Mathias, born in Mentz, Holland, age 17—same as above

Bristol, Negro slave, age 17—runaway Aug. 26 from Peter Houseman, of Staten Island (9/22)

Fork, Negro slave, age c. 25—runaway Sept. 6 from Thomas Brookman (9/22)

Ware, Negro slave, country born, age 24—runaway Sept. 14 from Abraham Lent, of Newtown, L.I. (9/22)

Roosevelt, Jacobus, late of NYC, merchant, dec'd—accounts with estate to be settled with Augustus Van Cortlandt, only acting executor in NYC (9/22)

Talmash, Hon. J. (brother of Earl Dysert), commander of the *Zebra*—killed in duel, fought at Hull's in NYC, the evening after the arrival of the fleet, by Capt. Pennington of the Guards (brother of Sir Ralph Pennington); his body was buried in Trinity Church Yard (9/29)

Jones, Thomas Shatford, of NYC, merchant—married since our last in NYC to Miss Adriana Zeegers, of Island of St. Johns in West Indies (9/29)

Anthony, Negro slave, age 28—runaway from Sangrey Warrey (9/29)

Charlton, Rev. Richard, born in Ireland, appointed in 1747 as missionary from the Society for Propagating the Gospel—died Oct. 7 at his house on Staten Island in his

72nd year (10/13)

Campbell, Mrs. Jane, age 70, widow of Robert Campbell, of Fresh Ponds, N.J., daughter of Andrew Gillaspie, of Enniskillen, Ireland, and sister of John Gillaspie, of Charlestown, S.C.—was buried Oct. 9 in Trinity Church Yard in NYC (10/13)

Banks, Francis, Esq., commander of H.M.'s ship *Renown*—died at Newport on Sept. 8 (10/13)

Runaway from P. Stuyvesant, of Petersfield, near NYC (10/13)

Primus, Negro slave, age c. 22

Syphax, Negro slave, age c. 34

Scipio, Negro slave, age c. 18

Thompson, William, boy, apprentice to George Brown, Esq., merchant, in Stockton, owner of ship *Diana,* army victualler, William Brown master—runaway Oct. 18 from the *Diana* (10/20)

Bet, Negro wench, born at Flatbush, L.I.—runaway Oct. 14 from Philip Lenzi, confectioner, at No. 517 Hanover Square, NYC (10/20)

M'Gillis, Gillis, apprentice lad, breeches maker—runaway In August from William Bell (10/27)

Fountain, Negro, age c. 25—runaway about Oct. 16 from George Walgrove, of NYC (10/27)

Thorne, Dr. Joseph, late of NYC, dec'd—accounts with estate to be settled with Stephen Thorne, admin., at the house of Stephen Thorne, Jr., merchant, in the Fly Market, NYC (10/27)

Hake, Mrs. Helena, wife of Samuel Hake, formerly merchant in NYC and sometime since returned to his native England—died about a fortnight ago at Rynbeck, NY (11/3)

Hegeman, Elbert, Esq.—died Oct. 23 at New Lots, Twp. of Flatbush, Kings Co., L.I., in his 91st year and was buried Oct. 25 at New Lots (11/10)

Stephens, Mrs. Mary, wife of Francis Stephens, Esq., Storekeeper to the Board of Ordnance, and daughter of the late Joseph Reade, Esq., member of H.M.'s Council—died Nov. 5 in NYC (11/10)

Duncan, Charles, Esq., of Maroneck, formerly a lieutenant in the Royal American Regt.—died Oct. 29 at his lodgings at the Hermitage (11/10)

Allen, John, of Bloom's-grove, Worcestershire, wire drawer, who about 7 years ago embarked for America with his son John, resided for some years with Mr. Wells, a painter, in NYC, then became an Anabaptist preacher in eastern part of Mass. and was last heard of from Kennebec—his father, John Allen, of Bury St., St. James's, Esq., has died, leaving him £500; he is asked to apply to the only surviving executor, Mathew Yetman, of Percy St. London, apothecary (11/10)

Colden, Nicholls, Esq., dec'd—accounts with estate to be settled with widow, Henrietta Colden, admin. (11/10)

Simpson, Miss Margaret, daughter of late John Simpson, Esq., of Boston—died Nov. 14 in NYC and is to be buried Nov. 17 from house of John Winslow (11/17)

Simpson, John, son of late John Simpson, Esq., of Boston—died Nov. 16 in NYC and is to be buried Nov. 17 from house of John Winslow (11/17)

Betts, Thomas, Esq., dec'd—part of moveable estate to be sold at house of widow, Ann Betts, admin., on road to Jamaica, L.I., about eight miles from the ferry (11/17)

Nat, Negro slave, age c. 24—runaway Nov. 16 from Henry Wickoff, living at New Lots, Kings Co., L.I. (11/24)

Davies, John, age c. 20—deserted from the Portsmouth Division of marines on board H.M.'s ship *Brune* (11/24)

Moss, William, age 22—same as above

Donop, Count—died of wounds received in late attack on Red Bank and was buried at

212

Red Bank (12/1)

Cleaveland, Mrs., wife of Capt. Cleaveland, of H.M.'s 16th Regt.—died Nov. 25 in NYC (12/1)

Cotton, Mrs., wife of Capt. Cotton, of H.M.'s 27th Regt. of Foot, stationed at Phila.— died since our last (12/1)

GENEALOGICAL DATA FROM THE NEW-YORK GAZETTE; AND THE WEEKLY MERCURY

1778

Adam, Walter, apprentice, age c, 18—deserted from on board the *Susannah*, Matthew Woodhouse captain (1/19)

Colvil, Miss Sally, daughter of the widow Colvil, of NYC—died last Sunday week at Newtown, L.I. (1/19)

Brooks, Thomas, of Leeds, Yorkshire—was carried Jan. 14 in NYC to Miss Elizabeth Sarley, of NYC (1/19)

Barton, John, age 15 and Barton, Joseph, age 6, sons of Col. Barton, now a prisoner in Conn.—died since our last (1/26)

Robinson, Beverly, Jr., Esq., Lt. Col. of the Loyal American Regt.—married Jan. 21, at Flushing, L.I., to Miss Nancy Barclay, youngest daughter of Rev. Dr. Barclay, formerly Rector of Trinity Church in NYC (1/26)

Turnbull, Col. George, of the New York Volunteers—married Jan. 24 in NYC to Miss Catharine Clopper, only daughter of Cornelius Clopper, of NYC (1/26)

Henner, Mary Barbara, bound servant girl, age c. 24—runaway from Bernard Michael Houseal, living at No. 10 Little Queen St., NYC (2/9)

Ackland, Lady Harriet, wife of Major Ackland and sister of Earl of Ilchester—delivered of a son on Feb. 2 in NYC (2/9)

Richards, John, of New Barbados Neck—his murderer, a certain Brower, has been apprehended (2/9)

De Heister, Lt. General—died Nov. 19 at Cassell (2/9)

Nash, General, who died Oct. 4 at Battle of Germantown—Congress has ordered a monument to be erected to him in North Carolina (2/16)

Cornell, Mrs. Susannah, wife of Hon. Samuel Cornell, Esq.—died Feb. 10 at Flushing, L.I., in her 47th year and was buried Feb. 12 at the Parish Church of Flushing (2/16)

Iliff, William—lately executed as a Tory at Morris Town, N.J. (3/2)

Mee, John—same as above

Gilcrist, Adam, formerly a tailor in Broad St., NYC—died some time ago in N.J.; one of his sons was killed in the rebel army (3/2)

Hamilton, Lt. Alexander James, of the 45th Regt. of Infantry—married Feb. 11 to Miss Mary Deane, daughter of Richard Deane, of NYC, distiller (3/2)

Kettletas, Wynant, eldest son of Peter Kettletas, of NYC—died March 11 in NYC and was buried March 12 in family vault in the New Dutch Church Yard (3/2)

Deal, Samuel, native of England, who resided some 20 years in NYC as a merchant—died March 24 at his house in NYC in his 64th year (3/30); accounts with his estate to be settled with execs., Charles Ingles and Francis Panton (4/13)

M'Adam, John, Jr., of NYC, merchant—married a few days since to Miss Glorianna Margaretta Nicoll, daughter of William Nicoll, Esq., of Suffolk Co., L.I. (3/30)

Barrington, Hon. Capt. William, of the 7th Regt.—was married a few days ago at Greenwich, near NYC, to Miss Teresa Clarke, daughter of the late Thomas Clarke, Esq. (4/6)

Desbrosses, Elias, Esq., merchant, of NYC—died March 26 in his 60th year and was buried March 28 in family vault in Trinity Church Yard (4/6)

Fish, Mrs. Elizabeth, wife of Jonathan Fish, Esq., late of NYC—died April 9, at Newtown, L.I., in her 47th year (4/13)

213

Elphinston, Mrs. Dorothea, wife of William Elphinston, Invalided Conductor of Royal Artillery—died April 9 in NYC (4/13)

Hutchinson, Margery, wife of late Capt. Hutchinson, of NYC, and her sister, Catharine (also given as Anne) Haly (who came to America in 1745)—are requested to apply to Hugh Gaine, since a sister of theirs wishes to see them (4/20 and 4/27)

Hester, Negro slave, age c. 34—runaway April 7 from Waters Smith, of Newtown, L.I. (4/20)

Wilson, Mrs., wife of Abraham Wilson, of NYC—on April 16 was safely delivered of three children (4/20)

Wallace, James, Esq., one of Commissioners of H.M.'s Victualling Office—died upwards of 80 years in age, leaving a large estate to his son, Sir James Wallace, Commander of H.M.'s ship *Experiment* (4/27)

Floyd, Mrs. Elizabeth, widow of Col. Richard Floyd—died April 9 at her seat in Suffolk Co., L.I., aged 70, and was buried April 12 at family burying ground at Brook-Haven (4/27)

Moore, Rev. Benjamin—married April 20 in NYC to Miss Charity Clarke, eldest daughter of late Major Clarke (4/27)

Deserted from H.M.'s shop *Perseus,* George Keith Elphinstone commander (4/27):

Savage, James, a Negro, born in Charlestown, age c. 29

Beesden, David, born at Bermuda, age 34

Newborne, Samuel, born at Bermuda, age c. 24

Young, Joseph, born at Bermuda, age c. 14

Leggett, Martha, wife of Gabriel Leggett, of West Farms—has eloped from her husband (4/27)

Moll, Negro wench, age c. 40—runaway from Joseph Totten, of 169 Queen St., NYC (5/4)

Diana, Negro wench, age 18—same as above

Bayard, Capt., of the King's Orange Rangers—married April 26 in NYC to Miss Catharine Van Horne, of NYC (5/4)

Gilpin, Thomas—died March 2 at Winchester, Va. (5/11)

Helme, Mrs. Rachael, wife of Benjamin Helme, Esq., late of NYC—died April 11 at Burlington, N.J., in her 29th year and was buried April 13 in the Friends burying ground in Burlington (5/11)

Thomas, Ensign Lewis, of H.M.'s 52nd Regt.—died May 4 in NYC and was buried May 6 in St. Paul's Church Yard (5/11)

Peter, a young Negro who formerly belonged to John Carpender but was lately purchased of Benjamin Williams—runaway May 10 from Joseph Allicocke (5/11)

To be executed April 24 at Poughkeepsie (5/18):

Smith, William

Akely, Daniel

Jenkins, Samuel

Harris, Myndert

Cornel, Daniel

Simpkins, Mr.

Morgan, Mr.

Carpenter, Daniel, of Fishkill Landing, son of—was baptized on April 19, by Rev. Mr. Freleigh, by name of George Washington (5/18)

Couwenhoven, John—lately died at Brooklyn Twp. on L.I. (5/18)

Van Dyke, John—same as above

Remsen, Arris—same as above

Poole, Dr. William, Chief Physician of the Naval Hospital on Long Island—died last Friday se'nnight (5/25)

Halstead, W. Anthony, Esq., Commander of the *Jersey* hospital ship, stationed at NYC—died Sunday se'nnight (5/25)

Schaak, Mrs. Elizabeth, wife of Peter Van Schaak, Esq., late of NYC, and second daughter of Henry Cruger, Esq.—died at Kinderhook (5/25)

Brown, Ensign, of Col. Greaton's Regt.—sentenced to be shot May 28 (6/1)

Woollsey, Francis, of Island of Granada, merchant—died June 28 in NYC in his 35th year and was buried June 30 in Trinity Church Yard (6/1)

Blyth, William, age c. 27—deserted from ordnance store ship *Lord Townshend*, Hugh Spence captain (6/8)

Shanks, Mr., a spy—was executed June 4 in N.J. (6/22)

Bayley, Richard, of NYC, surgeon—was married June 16, by Rev. Dr. Inglis, at Flatbush, to Miss Charlotte Barclay, youngest daughter of the late Andrew Barclay, merchant (6/22)

Zabriskie, George—shot some days since in the road near Paramus (6/29)

Monckton, Lt. Col., of the 5th Regt.—killed (7/6)

Gore, Capt. John, of the 5th Regt.—killed (7/6)

Grant, Mrs. Anne, wife of John Grant, Esq., Commissary of the Royal Artillery, and daughter of Dr. John Campbell, so celebrated in the literary world for his writings—died July 2 in NYC in her 37th year and was buried in chancel of St. Paul's Church (7/6)

Bonner, Lt. Col., of Pa.—killed in battle (7/13)

Dickenson, Major, of Va.—killed in battle (7/13)

Livingston, Philip, Esq., for many years merchant and alderman of East Ward of NYC—died recently (7/13)

Brown, Lt., of the 21st Regt. British—shot dead in June by a sentinel of the guard at Prospect Hill (7/20)

Joe, Negro slave, age c. 12—runaway from Jacob Wilkins, near the Albany Pier (7/20)

Nolte, John Henry, age 21, Hessian by birth, tailor, servant—runaway July 23 from Anthon George Kysch, Hessian Deputy Commissary, at No. 38 King St., NYC (7/27)

Atwood, Mrs. Anne Lewis, wife of Dr. Atwood, of NYC—died July 27 in her 40th year (8/3)

Schlemmer, Lt. Col. Arnold, native of Hershfeld, Hesse—died July 29 in NYC in his 52nd year, leaving a widow and infant son (8/3)

Schuyler, Dirick—died Aug. 5 at his house in NYC in his 78th year (8/10)

Wagener, Capt. John, dec'd, of battalion of Grenadiers commanded by Lt. Col. De Minnigerode—claims on estate to be presented at encampment of the battalion (8/31)

Hille, Lt. George William, of company Regt. De Losberg, who was killed Oct. 22 before Red Bank—same as above

De Offenbech, Lt. Charles Werner, of company of Prince Hereditaire's Regt., who was killed Oct. 22 before Red Bank—same as above

Cockeraft, Mrs., wife of William Cockeraft, of NYC—died Aug. 24 in NYC in her 58th year (8/31)

Sentenced by court martial to be executed for deserting to the enemy (9/7):

    Lyons, Samuel, late Lt. of the *Dickinson* galley

    Ford, Samuel, Lt. of the *Effingham* galley

    Wilson, John, Lt. of the *Ranger* galley

    Lawrence, John, gunner of the *Dickinson* galley

Daniel, Negro slave, age c. 16, who was purchased from Mr. Fisher, of NYC, merchant, and who formerly lived with Dr. Steward and often went to Jamaica, L.I., to see his sister—runaway from Philip Kissick about 5 weeks ago (9/7)

Tom, Negro boy—taken June 11 at Phila. from Edward Fitz Randolph (9/7)

Lamb, James, Esq., Lt. and Adjutant in H.H.'s 35th Regt.—married Aug. 31 at Flatbush to Miss Mathews, eldest daughter of David Mathews, Esq., Mayor of NYC (9/14)

Eden, Mrs., wife of His Excellency, William Eden, Esq., one of the Royal Commissioners— Sunday week she was safely delivered of a daughter in NYC (9/28)

Horsmanden, Hon. Daniel, Esq., President of H.M.'s Council and Chief Justice of NY —died Sept. 23 at Flatbush, L.I., in his 88th year (9/28)

Allan, James, Esq., son of Hon. William Allan, Esq., of Phila.—died a few days ago in Phila. (9/28)

Susan, Negro wench, age 22—runaway Sept. 26 from William Sackett, of Newtown, L.I. (10/5)

Brownejohn, Samuel, youngest son of Dr. Brownejohn—was married Sept. 19 to Miss Talmon, eldest daughter of Dr. Talmon (10/5)

Martin, Mrs. Elizabeth, wife of Hon. Josiah Martin, Esq., Gov. of North Carolina—died Oct. 4 at Brooklyn, L.I. (10/5)

Lee, Alexander, apprentice—deserted last Friday from the navy victualler ship *Grand Duke* (10/12)

Fagan, Jacob, leader of a band of villians in Monmouth Co., N.J.—was shot and killed about 10 days ago—Trenton dispatch of Oct. 10 (10/19)

Marston, Nathaniel, of NYC, merchant—died Oct. 21 in NYC in his 75th year and was buried Oct. 22 in family vault in Trinity Church Yard (10/26)

Woods, Mrs., wife of John Woods, Esq., attorney, of NYC—died in NYC since our last (11/2)

Abeel, John—died since our last in NYC in his 51st year (11/2)

Jones, Humphrey, of NYC—died there since our last in his 70th year (11/2)

Reade, Mrs. Anne, widow of Hon. Joseph Reade, Esq. late member of H.M.'s Council for NY—died Nov. 3 in NYC in her 77th year (11/9)

Shaw, Mrs. Sarah, wife of Charles Shaw, of NYC, merchant—died a few days ago in NYC (11/16)

Martin, Hon. Josiah, Esq.—died Nov. 21 at his seat at Rockaway, L.I., in his 79th year (11/23)

De Lancey, Mrs., widow of Hon. James De Lancey, Esq., late Gov. of NY—died 8 weeks ago at Crompond in Manor of Cortland (11/30)

Carter, Capt. William, late of H.M.'s 65th Regt. and Assistant Barrack Master for N.Y. Island—died Nov. 25 in NYC (11/30)

Chamier, Daniel, Esq., born in London, came to America in 1753 and settled in Maryland, Auditor and Comptroller of Accounts—died Nov. 27 in NYC in his 58th year (11/30)

Hunter, John, late merchant of Norfolk, Va.—died Nov. 23 in NYC (11/30)

Cornell, Cornelius, late of Flatbush, Kings Co., dec'd—accounts with estate to be settled with Gilliam Cornell (12/7)

Graham, Francis, Esq., Capt. of Grenadiers in H.M.'s 37th Regt.—died Dec. 2 of apoplexy at Jamaica, L.I. (12/7)

Martin, John, late of Aberdeen, journeyman printer—died Dec. 12 in NYC in his 30th year (12/14)

Bache, Miss Helena, a daughter of Theophilact Bache, Esq., of NYC—died a few days ago and was buried in family vault at Trinity Church Yard (12/21)

Dick, Negro slave, age c. 11—enticed away from victualler ship *Jane,* lying at Burling's Slip; reward offered by Conelly M'Causland (12/21)

Draper, Lady, wife of Lt. General Sir William Draper and second daughter of Brig. General De Lancey, of NYC—lately died in England (12/28)

GENEALOGICAL DATA FROM THE NEW-YORK GAZETTE;
AND THE WEEKLY MERCURY

1779

The following prisoners were sentenced to death for high treason at a Court of Oyer and
Terminer in Gloucester, West Jersey—Phila. dispatch of Sept 9 (1/4):

Wells, Harrison	Fennemore, Abraham
Hammet, William	Birch, James
Dilkes, John	Fusman, Daniel
Cook, Patterson	Stringe, Charles
Nightingale, Thomas	Cox, Laurance
Lord, Isaac	Franklin, John
Lloyd, David	Dill, Joseph
Urine, Gideon	Pratt, Joseph

for burglary: Benjamin Bartholomew

Willard, Habijah, eldest son of Abijah Willard, Esq., one of H.M.'s Councillors for Mass.
—died Dec. 26, 1778, in NYC (1/4)

Byvanck, Mrs., wife of John Byvanck, of NYC—died lately in NYC (1/11)

Vredenburgh, William, of NYC, hatter—has died (1/11)

Deserted from transport *Lively*, Thomas Hall master (2/8):

Steel, Joseph, age c. 20

Peters, James, age c. 20

Rushton, Catharine, wife of Peter Rushton—has eloped from her husband (2/8)

Chamier, Daniel, Esq., Auditor General, lately dec'd—claims against estate to be brought in and a Negro woman for sale by Achsah Chamier, administratrix (2/15)

Hornbrook, Mrs. Anne, wife of Capt. Theophilus Hornbrook, of NYC—died Feb. 17 in NYC in her 78th year and was buried the next day in the Old Dutch Church Yard (2/22)

Deserted from transport *Clibborn*, William Thomas master (2/22):

Rogers, William, seaman, age 25

Clemons, John, seaman, age c. 25

Croning, John, seaman, age c. 18

Wetmore, Charles, apprentice, age c. 17

Van Nander, Hendrick, of Bushwick, Kings Co., dec'd—farm for sale by Gabriel Duryea, exec. (2/22)

Stanton, Capt. Jeremiah, late of Staten Island, dec'd—property for sale by Richard Conner and Aaron Cortelyou, trustees for Stanton's children (2/22)

Covenhoven, John, dec'd—brick house in Montgomery Ward, NYC, for sale by execs., Rem, Nicholas and John Covenhoven (3/1)

Supinye, Peggy, wife of Joseph Blansieur—husband will not pay debts contracted by her in future (3/1)

Tom, Negro slave, age c. 21—runaway from Benjamin Smith, living at Jamaica, L.I. (3/1)

Rook, Philemon, apprentice, age c. 18—deserted from armed victualler *Admiral Keppel*, Thomas Hammond commander (3/1)

Martin, John, dec'd—two lots at lower end of Broadway, opposite the battery, for sale; apply to Valentine Nutter, stationer, opposite the Coffee-house (3/15)

Gardiner, Mr—stabbed to death last week at Sussex by his brother-in-law, Mr. Tharp, in a dispute about two dogs—Chatham dispatch of March 23 (3/29)

Murray, James, Esq., Representative in General Assembly of South Carolina—killed Jan. 12 at Edisto, S.C., when a gun burst (4/5)

Isabella, mulatto girl, age c. 18—runaway April 3 from service of Jacobus Lent, of Newtown, L.I. (4/12)

Jack, Negro boy, who formerly lived with Christopher Blundle, now Port Master of NY —runaway April 5 from Robert Thompson, 908 Water St., NYC (4/12)

Farrel, Barbery, wife of Martin Farrel—husband will not pay debts contracted by her in future (4/12)

Straw, Mr., a Loyalist—executed as a spy on April 16 at Hackinsack, N.J. (4/19)

Coal, Mr., a Loyalist—same as above

Cathcart, Right Hon. Lord—married April 17 at NYC to Miss Elliot, daughter of Andrew Elliot, Superintendent General of Police of the Province of NY (4/19)

Lawrence, Mrs. Mary, wife of Lt. Col. Elisha Lawrence, of General Skinner's Brigade, and daughter of Hon. Lewis Ashfield, Esq., of Monmouth Co., N.J.—died April 14 in NYC in her 27th year and was buried April 15 in family burying ground in Trinity Church Yard (4/19)

Campbell, Capt., of the *Congress* galley—killed March 21 in action near Yawmasee Bluff in Georgia (4/26)

Winthrop, Francis B., of NYC, merchant—married April 22 in NYC to Miss Marston, eldest daughter of Thomas Marston, Esq. (4/26)

Harris, Thomas, seaman, age c. 27—runaway from transport ship *John*, Edward Phillips master, at Turtle Bay, NYC (4/26)

Jordan, Capt.—died April 29 at NYC (5/3)

Laird, David, Esq., Captain of H.M.'s ship *Jersey*—married April 24 at NYC, by the Rev. Dr. Seabury, to Miss Butler, daughter of William Butler, Esq, Assistant Commissary General (5/3)

Furnival, Lt. William, Commander of H.M.'s sloop *Haerlam*—was married Sunday se'nnight at NYC to Miss Scandret, only daughter of the late Timothy Scandret (5/3)

Boothe, Robert, formerly of Trenton, butcher, who some years ago lived in NYC, and his wife Agnes—are desired to apply to William Backhouse in NYC to learn something advantageous (5/3)

Groesbeck, Mrs. Anne, widow of late John Groesbeck, of NYC, merchant—died May 4 in NYC in her 67th year and was buried next day in family vault in Trinity Church (5/10); real estate for sale by Anne Drummond, sole executrix (7/12)

Hadden, William, native of town of Holt, Norfolk Co., England, long a resident of America, who up to the time of the rebellion was in charge of the Academy at Newark, N.J., and who about two years ago fled to NYC—died May 7 in NYC in his 58th year and was buried May 9 in Trinity Church Yard (5/10)

Dick, an Indian boy—runaway from Hamilton Young (5/10)

Jane, or Gin, Negro wench, age c. 30—runaway from John Dyckman, in the Bowery Lane, NYC (5/17)

Fitz Simons, Francis, attorney, who was in NYC about 3 years ago, son of John Fitz Simons, of Kavat, Crossdown, County of Caven, Ireland—is asked to apply to Robert Hargrave, distiller, in Smith St., NYC, to hear something to his advantage (5/24)

Fenwick, Robert, Esq., Capt. in the Royal Regt. of Artillery and Bridge Master to the Army in America—died May 23 in NYC and was buried May 24 in a vault in Trinity Church Yard (5/31)

Runaway from James Smith, at Herricks, L.I. (5/31):

Caesar, Negro slave, age 20

Jack, Negro slave, age 19

Dashwood, Francis, Esq., Secretary to the Post Office—was married May 26 at Judge Ludlow's house at Hampstead, L.I., to Miss Anne Ludlow, sister of the judge (6/7)

Murray, Nathaniel, age c. 50—runaway June 2 from ship *Mars*, Thomas Kentish commander (6/14)

Long, James, son of John Long, of NYC—died June 19 is NYC in his 28th year (6/21)

Nicoll, Henry, Esq.—married June 17 at Spring Hill to Miss —— cie Willet, granddaughter of the late Cadwallader Colden, Esq., Lt. Gov. of NY, and daughter of —— Willet, Esq., of Queens Co., L.I. (6/21)

Johnston, Rachel, wife of John Johnston—husband will not pay debts contracted by her in future (6/21)

Skinner, Capt., of troop of American Light Horse—killed June 26 in a tavern at Woodbridge, N.J., by soldiers of H.M.'s 37th Regt. (7/5)

Executed June 8 at Goshen (7/12):

Flueling, James

Smith, James, son of the noted Claudius Smith

M'Cormick, James

Keith, Daniel, one of Burgoyne's soldiers

Gault, Robert, merchant—married July 5 in NYC to Miss Elizabeth Hallet, daughter of Joseph Hallet, of NYC (7/12)

Dick, Negro boy—runaway July 19 from Thomas M'Kie (7/19)

Bina, Negro wench, age 20—runaway Thursday morning last from James Dun, living at the sign of the *Recruiting Serjeant* in the Bowery, NYC (7/26)

Sam, Negro slave, age c. 38—runaway from Capt. George Lovie, of the sloop *Hope* (8/2)

Jack, Negro slave, age 12—runaway from James Ardin, living in Water St., NYC (8/2)

Coffin, Col. William, of a leading family of Boston, who had removed to NYC—died July 29 in NYC (8/2)

Esther, Negro wench, age c. 38—runaway Aug. 6 from Joseph Allicocke (8/9)

Kebble, Stephen, native of England, Assistant to the Commissary's Dept.—died Aug. 8 in NYC in his 41st year (8/16)

Deal, Mrs., wife of Robert Deal, of NYC, merchant—died Aug. 9 in NYC (8/16)

Cornick, Hugh, indented servant, age 16—runaway from ship *Nancy*, William Marshal master, lying at Cruger's Dock, NYC (8/30)

Frank, Indian slave, age c. 35—deserted from ship *Minerva*, William Dunloss master, lying in the North River (8/30)

Gregg, John, eldest son of Thomas Gregg, Esq., of Belfast, merchant—died Aug. 24 in NYC in his 30th year (8/30)

Moore, Miss Grace, second daughter of Capt. Thomas William Moore, of General De Lancey's Brigade—died Aug. 31 in NYC in her 17th year and was buried Sept. 1 in Trinity Church Yard (9/6)

Myers, William, Esq., Capt. of Grenadiers in the 26th Regt.—was married last week in NYC to Miss M'Evers, eldest daughter of James M'Evers, of NYC (9/6)

Smythe, Hon. Lionel, son and heir of the Right Hon. Lord Viscount Strangford and Captain of Light Infantry in the Regt. of Royal Welsh Fusileers—was married Sept. 5 in NYC, by the Rev. Dr. Inglis, to Miss Philips, eldest daughter of Frederick Philips, Esq. (9/13)

Brewerton, Col. George, of the Second Battalion of General De Lancey's Brigade—died Sept. 11 at Jamaica, L.I., in his 40th year (9/13)

Sam, Negro slave, age c. 20—runaway Sept. 6 from Henry Dawson, at No. 200 Queen St., NYC (9/13)

Mason, Catharine, formerly known by the name of Widow Frazer, of Broad St., NYC, wife of Thomas Mason, of NYC, tavernkeeper—husband has separated from her and will not pay debts contracted by her in future (9/20)

M'Donald, Ann, servant, age 17—runaway from Thomas Harrison, No. 321 corner of Dock St., NYC (9/20)

Vosburgh, Col. Peter, of Kinderhook, Albany Co., Loyalist—died Sept. 17 at Gewanas, L.I., in his 57th year (9/27)

Peter, Negro slave, age 16—runaway Sept. 23 from Long Island; reward offered by John Beck, No. 26 Fly Market St., NYC (9/27)

Bacchus, Negro slave, age c. 15—runaway (9△27)

Lester, Negro slave, age c. 15—runaway (9/27)

Norton, Peirce George Cope, now aged c. 22, who arrived at Phila. about seven years ago in a vessel commanded by Capt. Duncan—is asked to apply to Hugh Gaine to learn something to his advantage (9/27)

M'Adam, William, of NYC, merchant—died Oct. 1 in NYC in his 54th year (10/4); accounts with estate to be settled with Adam Steuart and John Loudon M'Adam (10/13)

Apthorpe, William, late of Boston—died Oct. 8 at the seat of the Hon. Charles Ward Apthorpe, Esq., at Bloomingdale (10/11)

Grim, Mrs., wife of David Grim, of William St., NYC—died Oct. 6 in NYC in her 44th year (10/11)

Cuyler, John, son of the late Henry Cuyler, of NYC, merchant—died Oct. 6 of a fever at Jamaica, L.I. (10/11)

Chandine, Charles—died recently at Staten Island in his 83rd year (10/11)

Kettletas, Capt. John, many years a resident of NYC—recently died at Staten Island (10/11)

Philips, Mrs., wife of Frederick Philips, Jr., Esq., and daughter of the late Nathaniel Marston, Jr., Esq.—died Oct. 14 in child-bed, in NYC, in her 19th year (10/18)

De Minnigerode, Col. Baron, Commandant of the 3rd Battalion of Hessian Grenadiers—died Oct. 16 in NYC in his 49th year and was buried in the Lutheran Church in NYC (10/25)

M'Kenzie, Alexander, dec'd—two new houses for sale by Fegan and Dean; enquire of Charles Mathewson on the premises (10/25)

Breen, Richard, apprentice boy—runaway from the snow *Newcastle Jane* (11/1)

Isabella, Negro woman, age 28, born on Long Island, formerly belonged to Capt. Whitehead, of Jamaica, L.I.—runaway Nov. 6 from Edward Barden (11/8)

Stephen, Negro slave, age c. 22—runaway Sunday last from Obadiah Whiston (11/8)

Bruce, William, Esq., Physician to the Hospital on expedition that sailed from NYC last fall to St. Lucia, under General Grant—recently died in the West Indies (11/15)

Smith, Capt. Jesse, of NYC of apoplectic fit (11/22)

Hamilton, John—married Nov. 15 in NYC to Miss Polly Harvie (11/22)

Hilton, Benjamin, Esq., late of Albany—married Nov. 18 at Hampstead Plains, L.I., to Miss Susannah Grisswold (11/22)

Cunningham, Lt., of the Legion—married Nov. 10 to Miss Hill, daughter of John Hill, Inspector, at Brooklyn (11/22)

Rogers, Henry, Lt. in H.M.'s Royal Regt. of Artillery—married Nov. 16 to Miss Isabella Kearny, daughter of Philip Kearny, Esq., late of Perth Amboy, N.J. (11/22)

Guddle, Edward, indented servant, age c. 15—deserted Nov. 17 from the brig *Thompson*, army victualler, Henry Hunt master (11/29)

Condemned to death at Court of Oyer and Terminer held in Oct. at York-Town, York Co., Pa., for counterfeiting (12/6):

Patton, Nathaniel

Trout, Henry

Fletzer, George—condemned to death at same court for murder of Christian Baughman (12/6)

Boyd, James—condemned to death at same court for robbing Thomas Stevenson on the highway (12/6)

Pedly, Thomas—condemned to death at same court for burglary of house of John Folan in York-Town (12/6)

Orchard, Elizabeth, wife of John Orchard—her husband will not pay debts contracted by her in future (12/6)

Maitland, Hon. Lt. Col. of the 71st Regt., brother of the Earl of Lauderdale— died last Monday in Savannah, Georgia, and was buried in family vault of the Hon. John Graham, Esq.—Savannah dispatch of Oct. 28 (12/13)

Simpson, Capt. John, of the Georgia Loyalists—killed Oct. 8 in Georgia (12/13)

M'Intosh, Capt. Aeneas, Captain and Paymaster of the 71st Regt.—lately died at Savannah, Ga. (12/13)

De Visme, Peter—washed overboard and drowned on passage from NYC to Ga. (12/13)

Duffee, Capt., in General De Lancey's Brigade, together with his lieutenant both died in Ga. (12/13)

Tony, mulatto, age 21—runaway Dec. 10 from Thomas Skinner, of No. 256 Broad St., NYC (12/13)

George, Negro slave, born in Virginia, age c. 14—runaway Dec. 17 from Hugh Wallace (12/20)

Parker, Samuel Franklin, printer—died Dec. 6 at Woodbridge, N.J., in his 35th year (12/27)

Madan, Lt. Col., of the Guards—died Dec. 25 in NYC in his 36th year (12/27)

Crew, Capt. James, lately commander of the privateer sloop *Lady Dunmore*, of Port of NY—died Dec. 19 in NYC in his 29th year (12/27)

GENEALOGICAL DATA FROM THE NEW-YORK GAZETTE; AND THE WEEKLY MERCURY

1780

Rachel, Negro slave, age 30—runaway; reward if returned to 919 Water St., NYC (1/10)

Kebble, Stephen, dec'd—accounts with estate to be settled with James Dole, exec. (1/17)

Napier, Hon. Mrs., wife of the Hon. Capt. Napier, of the 80th Grenadiers, sixth son of the late Right Hon. Lord Napier—died Jan. 10, aged 23, at Mr. Vanderbelt's house in Flushing, L.I., and was buried Jan. 12 in the family vault of the late Lt. Gov. Colden, at Springfield; she leaves two daughters, aged 2 and 3, under protection of Col. Archibald Hamilton, a relative of her husband (1/17)

Amiel, Mrs. Elizabeth, wife of John Amiel, of NYC, merchant—died Jan. 15 in NYC in her 30th year (1/17)

Ganter, Michael, of NYC, gunsmith, dec'd—accounts with estate to be settled with execs., Mary Magdalen Ganter, Samuel Magee and Jacob Resler (1/17)

Haynes, Thomas, laborer, age c. 25, born in Province of Munster, Ireland—deserted from H.M.'s 82nd Regt. of Foot at Yellow Hook (1/17)

Conner, Bryan, age c. 18, born in Province of Leister, Ireland—same as above

Traile, George, of NYC, tobacconist—lately died in NYC (1/24)

Marschalk, Andrew, of NYC, surveyor—lately died in NYC (1/24)

Saunders, Christianna, late Longstreet—act passed in Dec., 1779, by Assembly of New Jersey to divorce her from her husband, John Saunders (1/31)

Gifford, William—act passed Dec., 1779, by New Jersey Assembly to dissolve his marriage with his wife Elizabeth (1/31)

Cathcart, the Right Hon. Lady—on Jan. 25 was safely delivered of a daughter at his lordship's house in NYC (1/31)

Hartshorne, Lawrence, of Monmouth Co., N.J.—married Jan 20, by the Rev. Mr. Cook, to Miss Betsey Ustick, daughter of William Ustick, of NYC, merchant (1/31)

Waters, Talman. Esq., late of Flushing, dec'd—farm for sale by Samuel Doughty and William and John Waters (2/7)

Duke, Negro slave, age c. 47—runaway from James Tweed (2/7)

Turk, Jacobus, dec'd—two houses in Broadway, NYC, for sale by execs., Henry Roome and Elizabeth Campbell (2/7)

Gillespie, Mrs. Elizabeth, wife of John Gillespie, of NYC, shopkeeper—died Feb. 6 in child-bed and was buried Feb. 8 in St. Paul's Church-yard (2/14)

Badger, Mrs. Susannah, widow of Capt. Barnard Badger, late from Phila.—died Feb. 6 in NYC in her 45th year and was buried in NYC (2/14)

Hick, Mrs., wife of Mr. Hick, of Great George St., NYC—died Feb. 10 in NYC (2/14)

Fisher, Jabez, of Phila.—died lately in London (2/21)

Jones, Major General, who had been 38 years in the army—died Nov., 1779, at Llanidloes, Montgomeryshire, aged 53 (3/6)

Fish, Jonathan, late of Newtown, L.I., dec'd—accounts with estate to be settled with Sarah Fish, administratrix (3/20)

Kate, Negro slave, age c. 25—runaway, with her two-year-old son Jacob, from James Rodgers, of Huntington Bay (3/27)

Nicoll, William, Esq., formerly member of General Assembly for Suffolk Co., NY—died March 1 at his seat at Islip, L.I., in his 65th year (3/27)

Graves, Rev. Matthew, for 32 years missionary at New London, Conn., Loyalist—died March 29 in NYC and was buried March 30 in chancel of St. George's Chapel (4/3)

Bastow, Catharine, dec'd—accounts with estate to be settled with Thomas De J'Alton and John Fegan at No. 948 Water St., NYC (4/10)

Vandewater, Peter, of Flushing, L.I., dec'd—property to be sold by execs., John Rodman and John Field (4/17)

Ballendine, Col. Hamilton—hanged March 5 at Charlestown, S.C., for making drawing of the town and fortifications (4/24)

Norris, John, peruke maker—died last week at his house in NYC (4/24)

Kelso, Negro slave, age c. 30—runaway early in Jan. (4/24)

Linford, James (son of Rebecca Linford, late of city of Bristol, dec'd), who left England about 1755, was a sailor, and, according to his brother William, married Christian Van Riper, daughter of a farmer at Aquackanunc, N.J., lived in N.J., and, as a boatman, carried timber in his sloop to NYC—if he will apply to the printer he will learn something to his advantage (5/1)

Carrol, William, apprentice lad—deserted April 27 from the armed sloop *Neptune,* Stewart Ross captain, lying at the Kills at Staten Island (5/1)

Underhill, Benjamin, dec'd—land and buildings on East River, near Cromelin's Wharf, between Peck and Beekman's Slips, for sale by execs., Isaac, Amos and David Underhill (5/8)

Bowman, Jonathan, born at Hull, in Yorkshire, age c. 18—runaway May 5 from victualler ship *Williamson,* John Wray master (5/8)

Camp, John, born at Hull, in Yorkshire, age 16—runaway from victualler ship *Grand Duke,* Thomas Harman master (5/8)

Bogart, John J., late of NYC, peruke maker, dec'd—accounts with estate to be settled with Thomas Greswold, No. 168 Queen St., NYC (5/22)

Runaway from the Cork victualler brigantine *John and Mary,* John Sherrard master (5/22):

Gilly, John, born in Cork, age c. 18

Denhany, Daniel, born in Cork, age c. 20

Ross, Wiliam, born in Cork, age c. 20

M'Coy, John, deserter from the Continental Army found guilty of burglary—executed May 16 at Newtown, Sussex Co., N.J. (5/29)

Beaumont, Mrs., wife of Hammond Beaumont, Esq., one of surgeons of H.M.'s Hospital—died April 21 (5/29)

Attwood, Thomas, of H.M.'s Hospital, son of Thomas Bridgen Attwood—died April 20 and was buried in Trinity Church Yard (5/29)

Barton, Rev. Thomas, the Society's missionary for Lancaster, Pa., where he resided 21 years—died May 25 in NYC, aged 50 years, and was buried May 26 in chancel of St. George's Chapel (5/29)

Martin, Capt., of the Hessian Engineers, Deputy Quartermaster General to the Hessian troops in America—died last Saturday week in NYC and was buried the next day (6/5)

Barclay, Rev. Dr. Henry, dec'd—real estate in NYC for sale by widow, living near Hell Gate, on Long Island, by Major Thomas Barclay, of the Loyal American Regt. at Bloomingdale, Island of New York, or John Kelly, Notary Public, 843 Hanover Square, NYC (6/5)

Chambers, Robert, Jr.—said to have been killed by Indians on Yellow Creek, near Bedford (6/12)

Cruger, Henry, Esq., of NYC, merchant—died at Bristol on Feb. 5 in his 76th year (6/12)

Killed by Indians (6/19):
Fisher, Col., two brothers of
Hansen, Capt.

Meredith, Capt., of the 70th Regt—married June 18 at Jamaica, L.I., to Miss Gertrude Skinner, third daughter of Brigadier General Skinner (6/19)

Clifton, Lt. Col. Alfred, of the Roman Catholic Volunteers—died June 16 in NYC at an advanced age (6/19)

Devoore, David, dec'd—at house near the five mile stone on road leading to Kingsbridge, will be sold al, furniture and other goods (6/26); farm to be let by execs., Samuel Brownejohn and Thomas Walker (7/24)

M'Lane, Donald, Esq., surgeon to H.M.'s 77th Regt.—married June 29 in NYC, by the Rev. M'Laglan, to Miss Henrietta M'Donald, of Invernessshire, North Britain, daughter of Capt. Allan M'Donald, of the 84th Regt. (7/3)

Lately executed at Washington's camp (7/3):
Clawson, John, formerly of Woodbridge
Hutchinson, Mr., a young man from Morris Town
Lacy, Ludovic, of Sussex

Fitz Randolph, Nathaniel, noted partisan in rebel service—died a few days ago of wounds received in skirmish at Springfield (7/3)

Moore, Capt. Daniel, of the brig *Admiral Rodney*—wounded July 8 in engagement with rebel brig, supposed to be the *Holker*, of Phila., and died July 10 of wounds; was buried the same day in family vault in Trinity Church Yard (7/17)

Runaway from ship *Albion*, Peter Lawson commander (7/17)
Reid, John, boatswain's mate, age c. 30
Kelly, Robert, age c. 18

Ben, Negro slave, age c. 25—runaway from John Carpenter, of Brooklyn Ferry (7/17)

Trumbull, Madam, wife of Gov. Trumbull of Conn.—died Monday of last week at her seat in Lebanon, Conn., aged 61 years and 5 months—New London dispatch of June 9 (7/24)

Henderson, James, Esq., one of the field surgeons to the Royal Artillery in North America—died July 10 in NYC in his 30th year (7/24)

Killed July 21 at Col. Cuyler's Refugee Post, near Ft. Lee, about 8 miles from NYC (7/24):
Philips, Thomas, of the Artillery
M'Murdy, John

De Hayne, Major General, in service of Landgrave of Hesse Cassel—died July 25 in NYC in his 60th year and was buried July 26 (7/31)

Van Cortlandt, Mrs. Francis, widow of the late Col. Frederick Van Cortlandt, of Lower Yonkers, Westchester Co.—died July 2 in her 79th year (8/7)

Tom, Negro slave, age c. 16—runaway Aug. 1 from Dr. M'Lean, 6 Water St., NYC (8/7)

Squire, Negro slave, age 26—runaway Dec. 13, 1779, from Linus King (8/7)

Franklin, Walter, old inhabitant and eminent merchant and underwriter of NYC—died Aug. 6 in NYC of apoplexy (8/14); his house in Montgomery Ward for sale (11/27)

Elphinstone, Mr., formerly officer in Cameronian Regt. and of late in civil department of the Ordnance—died Aug. 7 in NYC (8/14)

Wanton, Hon. Joseph, Jr., Superintendent General of the Police of Rhode Island—died Aug. 10 in NYC (8/14)

De Velernaais, First Lt. of the frigate *Hermione*—died last Monday at Newport, R.I., of wounds received in engagement with a British frigate—Newport dispatch of July 22 (8/14)

Lefferts, Jacobus L., of NYC, merchant—married Aug. 7 to Miss Maria Lott, daughter of the late Mr. Lott, of L.I. (8/14)

Booth, William, native of England—died Aug. 7 in NYC in his 74th year (8/14)

Devoor, David, of Out Ward of NYC—died Aug. 9 in his 97th year (8/14)

Brower, Peter, of NYC—died Aug. 10 in his 81st year (8/14)

Folly, John, apprentice, age c. 17—runaway from ship *Father's Desire*, lying in North River, Richard Morsom master (8/14)

Jack, Negro slave, age 20, who formerly belonged to Capt. Benson—runaway from Richard Jenkins, No. 24 John St., NYC (8/14)

Schiflin, Jacob, Esq., First Lt. of the Detroit Volunteers—married Aug. 13 in NYC, by the Rev. Mr. Waltars, to Hannah Lawrence, eldest daughter of John Lawrence, of NYC, merchant (8/21)

Crosby, William, Esq., Lt. of the Royal Navy, late of the *Sea Horse* Indiaman—died Aug. 14 in NYC (8/21)

Amory, John, native of NYC, who resided some years in Albany before the rebellion—died Aug. 11 in NYC in his 30th year (8/21)

Wade, Capt., of H.M.'s 38th Regt.—married Aug. 1 to Miss Deane, junior daughter of Richard Deane, Esq. (8/21)

Crawford, Miss Peggy, from Boston—died Aug. 14 in NYC in her 18th year (8/21)

Boyd, James, of NYC, commander of a vessel—died Aug. 17 in NYC in his 46th year of a disorder he contracted on the Island of Jamaica (8/21)

Livingston, Miss Elizabeth, daughter of the late James Livingston, of NYC, merchant—died Aug. 18 in NYC in her 52nd year (8/21)

Sweeten, John, Deputy Commissary of Forrage—died Aug. 19 at Newtown, L.I., in his 45th year (8/21)

Freeman, Lt., of the 54th Regt.—died and was buried in NYC on Aug. 21 (8/28)

Rudolph, Conrad, Esq., Grand Apothecary of the Hessian Army—died Aug. 20 in NYC in his 32nd year and was buried Aug. 21 in the Reformed German Church Burial Ground (8/28)

Gosling, George—lately died at Charlestown, S.C., in his 50th year (8/28)

Lawrence (or Launce), Negro slave, age c. 14 or 15—runaway from Dennis Dennis, at the Narrows, L.I. (8/28)

Corne, Mrs. Elizabeth, late wife of Capt. Corne, of NYC—died Aug. 30 at Bushwick, L.I., and was buried the next day (9/4)

Pownall, Capt., of H.M.'s frigate *Apollo*—killed last June in engament with a French frigate (9/4)

Jarvis, Samuel, a Loyalist, long Recorder of the Town of Stanford, Conn.—died Sept. 1 in NYC in his 60th year (9/11)

Ogden, Dr. Jacob—died Sept. 3 at Jamaica, L.I., in his 59th year (9/11); accounts with estate to be settled with Elizabeth Ogden, exec. (12/4)

Cargey, Robert—married Aug. 29 in NYC, by the Rev. Mr. Bisset, Rector of Trinity Church in Rhode Island, to Miss Hermione Harrison, eldest daughter of the late Peter Harrison, Esq., Collector of H.M.'s Customs for the Port of New Haven (9/11)

Whitehead, Capt. Benjamin, of Jamaica South, L.I.—died June 6 in his 75th year (9/11)

Jack, Negro slave, age 20, who formerly belonged to Capt. Benson—runaway from John Cornell, of Brooklyn Ferry (9/11)

Paris, Negro slave, age c. 21—runaway from Lawrence Kortwright, of NYC (9/11)

Minto, Negro slave, age c. 23—runaway from John Dikeman, living in the Bowery Lane, NYC (9/18)

Hutchinson, Francis, Esq., late captain in H.M.'s Royal American Regt.—died Sept. 22 in NYC (9/25)

Mash, Mrs., of Jamaica, L.I.—died there last week at an advanced age (9/25)

M'Isaac, Malcolm, late steward to Gov. Tryon—died Sept. 19 in NYC (10/2)

Stuyvesant, Nicholas W., Esq.—died Sept. 28 in NYC of a fever in his 58th year at his seat in the Bowery; he was eldest son of Col. Stuyvesant and great-grandson of the Dutch governor; his brother is Peter Stuyvesant; he was buried in family vault on patrimonial estate (10/2)

Bale, Richard, Esq., surgeon's mate to the General Hospital—died Sept. 25 in NYC (10/2)

Vardill, Mrs., wife of Capt. Thomas Vardill, of NYC—died week before last (10/2)

Sacket, Samuel, late of NYC—died last Saturday, Sept. 30, at his seat near Jamaica, L.I. (10/2); accounts with estate to be settled with execs., Christopher Smith and Cary Ludlow (10/23)

Crowe, Jonathan, Loyalist refugee from Mass.—died Sept. 30 in NYC and was buried Oct. 1 in Trinity Church Burying Ground (10/9)

Striker, James—married Sept. 28 to Miss Polly Hopper, only daughter of John Hopper, of Bloomingdale (10/9)

Hicks, Whitehead, Esq., one of the judges of the Supreme Court of NY—died Oct. 3 at Flushing Bay, L.I. (10/9)

Nicoll, Mrs. Elice, wife of Henry Nicoll, of NYC, grand-daughter of the late Gov. Cadwallader Colden of NY and daughter of Col. Willet, late of L.I.—died Oct. 7 in her 24th year (10/9)

Hosmer, Capt. Joseph, a refugee from Conn.—died last week on Long Island (10/9)

Bonnel, Mrs. Grace, wife of Isaac Bonnel, Esq., of Amboy, formerly High Sheriff of Middlesex Co., N.J.—died Sept. 30 and was buried Oct. 1 in Trinity Church Yard (10/16)

Selkrig, Mrs. Grizzel, wife of James Selkrig, of NYC—died Oct. 10 in NYC in her 53rd year (10/16)

Lewis, Mrs., wife of John Lewis, Loyalist refugee from Boston—died Oct. 5 in NYC (10/16)

Beau, Miss Blanche, schoolmistress in NYC—died Oct. 12 in her 60th year (10/16); accounts with estate to be settled with execs., Elizabeth Beau, William Ustick, George Dominick and D. Seabury (12/11)

Seabury, Mrs. Mary, wife of Rev. Dr. Seabury, of NYC—died Oct. 12 in her 44th year (10/16)

Stewart, James, of NYC, merchant—died Oct. 13 in NYC in his 40th year (10/16); accounts with estate to be settled with administratrix, R. Stewart (1/15/1781)

Kissick, Mrs., wife of Philip Kissick, of NYC, merchant—died Oct. 13 in NYC (10/16)

Harris, Richard, of NYC—died Oct. 13 in NYC (10/16)

Pettit, Thomas, of NYC—died Oct. 13 in NYC (10/16)

Axtel, Mrs., wife of Hon. Col. Axtel, of Flatbush, L.I.—died Oct. 15 (10/23)

Cossing, Nathaniel, Sr., Esq., late Deputy Cashier to the Board of Commissioners in Boston—died a few days ago on the fleet at NYC (10/23)

James, Negro slave, age between 14 and 15—runaway from Andrew Zimmerman, in Warren St., NYC (10/23)

Mott, Richard, son of Capt. Jacob Mott of Hempstead—married Oct. 21 to Miss Martha Sutton, daughter of Lt. Robert Sutton of Hempstead (10/30)

Boel, Henry, for many years a clerk in the General Post Office, NYC—died in NYC last Tuesday se'nnight—item headed Oct. 25 (10/30)

Walter, John, Esq., Major of Brigade to Brigadier General De Lancey—died Oct. 22 of a fever in NYC (10/30)

Blackwell, Col.—died Oct. 24 at his house near Hallet's Cove (10/30)

Nicholls, Richard, Esq., dec'd—real estate for sale; enquire of Dr. Middleton in the Broadway, NYC, or Harrison and Auchmuty, attornies, at No. 22 Maiden Lane (10/30)

Franklin, Henry, of NYC, merchant, a Quaker—died Nov. 3 in NYC (11/6); accounts with estate to be settled with William Rhinelander, No. 188 Queen St., NYC, by order of execs., Mary Franklin, William Rhinelander and William Rickman (11/20)

Car, John, of NYC, printer—died Nov. 8 in NYC and was buried Nov. 10 in the Old Dutch Church Yard (11/13)

King, Mrs. Cornelia, wife of Capt. Linus King, of NYC—died Nov. 15 in NYC in her 57th year (11/20)

Dobs, Capt. Jarvis, of the sloop *Abigail*—married Nov. 19 at Flushing, L.I., by the Rev. Mr. Bloomer, to Miss Hetty Wortman (11/27)

Clarke, Capt. Heymen, of the *Industry*—married Nov. 19 at Flushing, L.I., by the Rev. Mr. Bloomer to Miss Annauchy Wortman (11/27)

Farrington, Capt. Matthew, of the *Nancy*—married Nov. 19 at Flushing, L.I., by the Rev. Mr. Bloomer, to Miss Phoebe M'Cullom (11/27)

Blackie, James, of NYC, merchant—died Oct. 17 in NYC in his 43rd year and was buried Oct. 19 in Trinity Church Burial Ground (11/27)

Rachel, Negro slave, age c. 30—runaway from James Baker, 181 Fair St., NYC (11/27)

Cockran, Mrs. Elizabeth, wife of Capt. Cockran and daughter of the first Englishman who ever kept a tavern in New York after it was conquered by the Dutch—died Nov. 25 in NYC in her 92nd year (11/27)

Nanny, Negro wench, age c. 40, formerly property of Capt. Montrisure, of NY, and was sent in 1773 to Charlestown, S.C., by Capt. Peter Schermerhorn, from whom she was purchased—runaway from Thomas Phepoe. of Charlestown, S.C. (12/4)

Bland, Ellias, who came to NYC a few weeks ago from his seat in N.J., with intention of returning to London, where for many years he had been an eminent American merchant—died Dec. 1 in NYC in his 60th year (12/4)

Cuff, Negro slave, age c. 30—runaway from John Hutchinson, living near the four mile-stone leading to Ft. Knyphausen (12/11)

Colvil, Mrs. Elizabeth, late of Newtown, L.I., dec'd—accounts with estate to be settled with Henry Roome or William Grigg, of NYC (12/11)

Cavenagh, Henry, who sailed upwards of 7 years ago from Dublin to NYC—if he will apply to Moore and Keir, of NYC, merchants, he will hear something to his advantage (12/18)

Nicoll, Charles, of NYC, merchant—died Dec. 12 in NYC in his 59th year (12/18)

Jack, Negro slave, age c. 15—runaway from Laghlan Mackintosh, at H.M.'s Issuing Store at Burling's Slip, NYC (12/18)

Chener, John, apprentice, age 16 or 17, born in Nancy in Lorrain—runaway from the navy victualler, the brig *Britannia*, R. Coart master (12/18)

GENEALOGICAL DATA FROM THE NEW-YORK GAZETTE; AND THE WEEKLY MERCURY

1781

Baremore, Major Mansfield, Commandant of the Loyal West Chester Refugees—died Dec. 26, 1780, in NYC of wounds (1/1)

Learmonth, John (son of Alexander Learmonth, of Edinburgh), who some years ago was a pilot from Phila. and resided in Lewis Town—is asked to apply to Dr. William Moore, No. 5 Wall St., NYC, to hear something to his advantage (1/8)

Sacket, John, apprentice, age 19—runaway about 14 days ago from Abel Hardenbrook, Jr., of NYC (1/8)

Isabella, Negro wench, age c. 22, born on L.I., at Mr. Van Nostreen's, near the Walla-bought, and by him sold to Mr. Skillman, at Bushwick—runaway (1/8)

Seaman, Samuel, late of Westbury, L.I., dec'd—accounts with estate to be settled with execs., John Williams, Samuel Way, and Henry Post (1/8)

Middleton, Dr. Peter, native of North Britain, physician for 30 years in NYC—died Jan. 9 in NYC (1/15); accounts with estate to be settled with Robert Nicholls Auchmuty, 226 Queen St., NYC, acting exec. (1/29)

Robinson, William T., of Rhode Island—married Jan. 10 at the Friends Meeting House in NYC to Miss Sally Franklin, daughter of Samuel Franklin, of NYC, merchant (1/15)

Hamilton, Alice, wife of Col. Archibald Hamilton, commander of the Queens County Militia, and granddaughter of the late Lt. Gov. Colden—died Jan. 9 in NYC, aged 37 (1/15)

Selkrig, James, of NYC, merchant—married Jan. 7 to Mrs. Gardner, formerly a resident of Newport, R.I. (1/15)

Heath, of NYC, silversmith, dec'd—reference to his house fronting Maiden Lane (1/22)

Stewart, James, late of NYC, dec'd—accounts with estate to be settled with R. Stewart, administratrix (1/29)

Ball, Stephen, a spy, who was active in the execution in N.J. in 1779 of Thomas Long, a refugee from Jersey—was executed Jan. 25 at Bird's-Point, Bergen Co., N.J. (1/29)

Dickenson, Nathaniel, Esq.—married Jan. 25 in NYC to Miss Hannah Cock, sister of William Cock, notary public in NYC (1/29)

Bogart, Mrs. Lena, wife of John Bogart, Esq., of NYC—died since our last in her 63rd year (1/29)

Pool, Sarah, widow—died since our last in NYC in her 77th year (1/29)

Marsh, Mrs., dec'd—lot in Jamaica, L.I., for sale by Rev. John Sayre, No. 33 Smith St., NYC (1/29)

Folliott, Andrew, dec'd—house in Jamaica, L.I., for sale (1/29)

Dudley, Francis, dec'd—real estate in Crown St., NYC, for sale (1/29)

Trail, George, dec'd—accounts with estate to be settled with Edward Agar and John Segar, administrators (1/29)

Franklin, Matthew, of Flushing, dec'd—farm in Flushing, about 1½ miles from the landing, on the road leading to Fresh Meadow, for sale by execs., John Farrington and James Browne (2/5)

Hamersley, Mrs. Margaret, wife of Andrew Hamersley, of NYC, merchant—died Jan 30 in NYC in her 44th year (2/5)

Waddington, Mr., Jr., eminent merchant of NYC—married Feb. 6 in NYC to Miss Mary Ann Desbrosses, sister of James Desbrosses, Esq., and niece of the late alderman of NYC, Elias Desbrosses, Esq. (2/12)

Hosmer, John, late of NYC, merchant, dec'd—accounts with estate to be settled with Mary Hosmer, administratrix (2/12)

Grant, John, Esq., late Commissary and Paymaster of H.M.'s Royal Artillery—the packet has brought an account of his death (2/19 and 3/12)

Nicoll, Charles, dec'd—accounts with estate to be settled with Edward Nicoll, Evert Bancker, Jr., and Charles N. Taylor, at the house of the deceased in Little Dock St., NYC (2/26)

Mott, John, dec'd—farm on east side of Cow Neck, Twp. of Hempstead, adjoining the harbor, for sale by Richard Sands and Adam Mott, execs. (2/26)

Menzies, Major Alexander, of General Delancey's 3d. Battalion, dec'd— accounts with estate to be settled with Sarah Menzies, admin., living at Hempstead, L.I. (2/26)

Duane, Cornelius—died March 8 in NYC and was buried March 9 in Trinity Church Yard (3/12)

Cameron, Capt. Allan, of the New York Volunteers—died March 3 in Charlestown, S.C., and was buried March 4 in St. Philip's Church (3/19)

Blunt, John Werril, Assistant Surgeon to H.M.'s General Hospital, dec'd— accounts with estate to be settled with John Buckler, 46 Great Dock St., NYC (3/19)

Barre, John, dec'd—farm at New Utrecht for sale by Isaac Cortelyou and Adrian Hageman (3/26)

Devoor, David, dec'd—farm, near five mile stone on road leading to King's Bridge, in Out Ward of NYC, to let; apply to Samuel Brownejohn (3/26)

Hastie, Mrs. Sarah, wife of James Hastie, of NYC, merchant—died April 3 in NYC (4/9)

Camaron, Capt., of the 37th Regt.—married April 3 to Miss Jouet, of NYC (4/9)

Van Cortlandt, James, Esq., of Yonkers, Westchester Co.—died April 2 in NYC in his 55th year (4/9)

Blank, Mrs. Mary—died April 9 in NYC in her 96th year (4/16)

Mann, Elias, Loyalist—killed in action on April 23 (4/30)

Burke, Miss Ann, of NYC—died April 30 in NYC in her 70th year (5/7)

Smith, Thomas, late of NYC, dec'd—accounts with estate to be settled with John Kingston, exec. (5/21)

Kippin, Mrs. Sarah, wife of William Kippin, of NYC—died May 19 in NYC in her 59th year (5/21)

Cupples, Moses, native of Clough, near Ballymena, County of Antrim, Ireland, who in 1775 lived near the Red Lyon on the great road leading from Phila. to Lancaster, in Whiteland Twp., Chester Co., Pa.—is asked to apply to Daniel M'Cormick to hear something to his advantage (5/28)

Kibble, Mrs. Catharine, widow of Stephen Kibble, dec'd—died June 11 in NYC, aged 39 years (6/18)

Cornell, Samuel, Esq., member of H.M.'s Council for North Carolina—died June 14 in NYC, leaving five daughters (6/18)

Tilton, Margaret, wife of William Tilton, of NYC, cordwainer—has left her husband and he will not pay debts contracted by her in future (6/25)

Lorentz, John George, Esq., Counsellor at War, Treasurer, and Commissary General to the Hessian Troops in America—died June 29 in NYC in his 68th year of an apoplectic fit (7/2)

Reddington, Michael, Esq., late of Ballivalane, near Corke, who left Ireland 2 or 3 years ago—a large property has been left to him by his father, Thomas Reddington, Esq. (7/9)

Rowning, Morris, apprentice, age c. 19—runaway from the victualler *Aurora*, Constable Saunders master, lying at the commissary's wharf (7/9)

Hector, Negro slave, age c. 40, formerly property of Col. Buskirk, of L.I.—runaway from John Andrew Simerman, milkman, in Water St., NYC (7/9)

Killed at Pensacola during the nine weeks siege: (7/9)

Carrol, Lt., of the 16th Regt.

Pinhorn, Lt., of the Loyal Foresters

Ussal, Ensign, of the Waldeckers

Martin, Isaac, of NYC, a Quaker—died July 12 in NYC (7/16)

Sawney, Negro slave, age c. 14—runaway (7/16)

Mitchell, Andrew, merchant—married in NYC to Miss Stites, daughter of John Stites, merchant (7/23)

Bouchier, James, Commander of the *Raynham Hall* Indiaman—married to Miss Allicocke, daughter of Joseph Allicocke, merchant (7/23)

M'Lean, Peter—married to Widow Anne Davies, sister of Charles Loosely, at Brooklyn Hall (7/23)

Boss, Mary, wife of Joseph Boss, of Newtown, L.I.—has lately been turned out of doors by her husband (7/23)

Armstrong, Capt., of the First Maryland Regt.—killed in action (7/30)

Howard, Mrs. Anne, wife of Sheffield Howard, Esq., formerly eminent merchant of NYC—died July 23 in NYC at age of 53 (7/30)

McLachan, Lt. Col.—killed in action in first week of July in S.C. (8/6)

Wright, a rebel officer—killed in July in S.C. by a force under Lt. Waugh (8/6)

Waugh, Lt., in command of the South Carolina Convalescents—killed in action in action in July (8/6)

Walton, Mrs. Mary, widow of Jacob Walton, formerly an eminent merchant of NYC—died Aug. 1 in NYC in her 78th year (8/6)

Prince, Negro slave, age c. 18, born in NYC with Capt. Harris and bred on Long Island, lived with one Fisher, a tobacco cutter, and since with Capt. Fletcher—runaway from Capt. Fletcher (8/6)

Hogen, Patrick, apprentice boy—runaway from Robert Campbell, cordwainer (8/6)

M'Kean, Capt.—died of wounds in July (8/13)

Appleby, Robert, of NYC, brewer—married last Wednesday se'nnight to Miss Peggy Moore (8/13)

Reilly, Mrs. Susannah, wife of Terrence Reilly, of NYC, merchant—died Aug. 10 in NYC in her 39th year (8/13)

Attwood, Dr. Thomas Bridgen, of NYC—married Aug. 12 in NYC to Miss Catharine Ten Eyck, from Albany (8/13)

Mulliner, Joseph, of Egg Harbor, N.J.—convicted lately of treason at a court in Burlington and sentenced to be hanged Aug. 8 (8/20)

White, Thomas, Esq.—died Aug. 6 in NYC in his 57th year (8/20)

Waynman, Mrs. Sarah, widow of Capt. William Waynman, of Newtown, L.I.—died Aug. 14, aged 63 (8/20)

Walton, Miss Polly, eldest daughter of Jacob Walton, Esq., of NYC—died Aug. 14 in NYC in her 18th year (8/20)

Cramond, Lt. James, of H.M.'s 42nd Regt., Aid de Camp to General Knyphausen—died Aug. 30 in NYC and was buried at St. Paul's (9/3)

Burk, Miss Mary, of NYC—died Sept. 1 in NYC, aged 68 (9/3)

Provost, Peter Prau, late of NYC, blacksmith, dec'd—accounts with estate to be settled with his son, David Provost, of L.I., gunsmith (9/3)

White, Thomas, Esq., late of NYC, dec'd—accounts with estate to be settled with Ann White, admin. (9/3)

Forbes, James, late of NYC, merchant, dec'd—accounts with estate to be settled with Richard Sause and John Thompson, execs. (9/3)

Beveridge, Margaret, wife of David Beveridge—her husband will not live with her nor will he pay debts contracted by her in future (9/3)

Seaman, Mrs. Elizabeth, wife of Benjamin Seaman, Esq.—died Aug. 31 in NYC in her 58th year (9/10)

Bailie, William, seaman from west of Scotland, on ship *Three Brothers*, William Sippens master—died on board Sept. 6 off Sandy Hook (9/10)

Robertson, Robert, a young man—drowned Sept. 6 out of a sloop in North River (9/10)

Zublee, Rev. Mr., formerly a member of Congress for Georgia—died lately in his 57th year (9/17)

Thompson, General, in service of Congress—died lately in Pa. (9/17)

(S)chrock, Christian, age 18, musketeer of the German Brunswick troops—deserted Sept. 11 out of the hospital on Golden Hill, NYC (9/17)

Clarke, Dr. William, of Monmouth Co., N.J.—died last Saturday week in his 68th year (9/24)

M'Cridie, James, late of Bedford, L.I., dec'd—his creditors are to meet Sept. 25 at house of Thomas Chitwynd in Bedford (9/24)

Lownsbury, William, one of a party of rebels seeking to plunder the house of Moses Jarvis, merchant, at Huntington, L.I.—killed there Sept. 23 by a shot fired by Mr. Jarvis (10/1)

Killed in action in Sept. in S.C. (10/1)
  Lloyd, Lt., of the 63rd Regt.
  Hickman, Lt., of the 19th Light Co.
  M'Clean, Capt., of the New York Volunteers
Kerr, Capt.—mortally wounded in Sept. in action in S.C. (10/1)
Pell, Mrs. Mary, widow of Samuel Pell, formerly of NYC, tobacconist—died Sept. 29 in
  NYC in her 89th year (10/1)
Sleight, Mrs., daughter of Mrs. Pell—died a few weeks before her mother in her ——
  year (10/1)
Winslow, John—died Sept. 28 in NYC in his 39th year (10/1)
Bristol, Negro slave, age c. 14—runaway from Major James Grant, of the King's American
  Regt. (10/8)
Barry, Lt. William, of the Royal Forresters—died a few days ago of a fever and was
  buried at Hallet's Cove, L.I. (10/15)
Killed Sept. 8 in action at Eutaw: (10/22)
  Dobson, Capt., of the Md. Brigade
  Edgerly, Capt., of the Md. Brigade
  Dewall, Lt., of the Md. Brigade
  Gould, Lt., of the Md. Brigade
  Campbell, Lt. Col., of the Va. Brigade
  Oldham, Capt., of the Va. Brigade
  Wilson, Lt., of the Va. Brigade
  Goodman, Capt., of the N.C. Brigade
  Goodwin, Capt., of the N.C. Brigade
  Porterfield, Capt., of the N.C. Brigade
  Dillon, Lt., of the N.C. Brigade
  Carlisle, Mr., volunteer in the cavalry
  Carson, Lt., of the artillery
  Rutherford, Major, state officer of S.C.
  Polk, Lt., state officer of S.C.
  Lusk, Adjutant, of S.C.
  Holmes, Lt., of the S.C. Militia
  Simons, Lt., of the S.C. Militia
Cobb, Capt. John, who was drowned Sept. 13 between Staten Island and Long Island—
  reward for recovery of his body will be paid by William Tomson, 28 Little Dock St.,
  NYC (10/22)
Scudder, Nathaniel, several years member of Continental Congress, member of N.J.
  Assembly — killed by Loyalist Refugees at Black Point, N.J. (10/22)
Prevost, David, Esq., of NYC—died a few days ago, aged upward of 90; accounts with
  estate to be settled with David Mathews (10/29)
Killed Sept. 8 in action between Lt. Col. Stewart, of the Old Buffs, and rebel General
  Greene: (11/5)
  Kelly, Capt. Dennis, of the 64th Regt.
  M'Lean, Capt., of the New York Volunteers
  Kerr, Capt., of Brig. Gen. Delancey's
  Lloyd, Lt., of the 63rd Regt.
White, Capt., of Col. Vose's Battalion of Infantry—killed in action Oct. 11 (11/12)
Hetfield, William, of Elizabeth Town, N.J.—shot dead Nov. 3 on return from Staten
  Island by Peter Terrat (11/12)
Sidell, John, tailor, native of Germany, upwards of 30 years a resident of NYC—died Nov.

10 in NYC (11/12); accounts with estate to be settled with execs., Magdalene and Augustus Sidell (11/19)

Walton, Mrs. Mary, dec'd—two houses, No. 185 Queen St. and No. 23 in Beekman or Chapel St., near corner of Gold St., NYC, for sale (11/12)

David, mulatto slave, age c. ₋₋ —runaway (17/12)

Jude, mulatto wench, age c. 30—runaway (11/12)

Sylvia, Negro wench, with child aged about 2—runaway (11/12)

Butler, Capt. Walter—killed in action in Tryon Co., about 14 miles above Ft. Dayton (11/12)

Wier, Daniel, Esq., Commissary General of H.M.'s Forces in North America—died Nov. 12 in NYC in his 47th year (11/19)

Moncrief, William, late Capt. of the Queen's Rangers and brother of Lt. Col. Moncrief of the Engineers—died Nov. 16 in NYC (11/19)

Douglass, Andrew Snape, Commander of H.M.'s ship *Chatham*—married Nov. 14 in NYC to Miss Burgess, of NYC (11/19)

Johnson, Mrs. Rebecca, wife of Rinoldo Johnson, Esq.—died Sept. 24 at Baltimore, Md., and was buried at Aquasco, Prince George Co. (11/19)

Ball, Isaac, house carpenter, Loyalist, former captain of the Fire Engine Company—died Nov. 15 in NYC, aged 54 (11/19)

Ashfield, Mrs. Sarah, wife of Vincent P. Ashfield, of NYC, merchant and daughter of the late Hon. Lewis Morris, Esq., Judge of the Admiralty for the Province of NY—died a few days ago (11/19)

Hill, Mrs., wife of Capt. Thomas Hill, of NYC—died Nov. 15 in NYC at a very advanced age (11/19)

Killed between 26 Sept. and 19 Oct.: (11/26)

Cochran, Major, acting Aid de Camp to Lord Cornwallis

Campbell, Lt., of the 74th Company of Light Infantry

Lyster, Lt., of the 63rd Company of Light Infantry

Dunn, Lt., of the 63rd Company of Light Infantry

Mair, Lt., of the 23rd

Guyon, Lt., of the 23rd

Kerr, Capt., of the 33rd

Frazer, Lt., of the 71st

Rall, Capt., of the 76th

Parkin, Commissary, of the 76th

Griffiths, Andrew, late surgeon to H.M.'s frigate *Guadeloupe*—died No. 23 in NYC and was buried in Trinity Church Yard (11/26)

Caldwell, Rev. Mr., Minister of the Dissenting Congregation at Elizabeth Town, N.J.— shot and killed Nov. 24 at the Point by a certain Morgan, a native of Ireland (12/3)

Johnston, Capt. Thomas, of the 3rd Battalion of Royal Artillery—died Nov. 24 in NYC and was buried in Trinity Church Yard (12/3)

Killed Nov. 13 at Hillsborough, N.C.: (12/3)

Litterel, Col.

M'Niel, Col.

Dawson, Roper, dec'd—farm on Staten Island for sale by Mrs. Dawson (12/10)

Williams, Nathaniel, Sr., late of Huntington, L.I., dec'd—accounts with estate to be settled with Seaman and Cock, Water St., NYC (12/10)

Gordon, Thomas (son of James Gordon), born at Lurgan, County of Armagh, who sailed from Belfast about 3 years ago—is to apply to printer to hear something to his advantage (12/10)

Cudjoe, Negro boy—runaway from on board the ship *Emanuel and Hercules,* Alexander M'Dougall commander (12/17)

Desbrosses, Miss Elizabeth—died Dec. 13 in NYC in her 65th year (12/17)

Nicoll, Capt. John, formerly Naval Officer of the Port of Rhode Island—died Dec. 13 in NYC in his 62nd year (12/17)

Duncan, Thomas, dec'd—creditors of him and his son, James Duncan, shoemakers, are asked to lodge copies of their accounts with William and James Douglass, 239 Queen St., NYC, or with James Dole, Broadway (12/24)

Campbell, Colin, Esq., son of the late Rector of Burlington, West Jersey—was married Dec. 26 in NYC to Miss A.M. Seabury, daughter of the Rev. Dr. Seabury, of NYC (12/31)

Murray, Mary, wife of Robert Murray, of NYC, merchant—died Dec. 24 in NYC (12/31)

Killed in action at Mr. Edgehill's plantation, within 15 miles of Ninety-Six: (12/31)
  Hayes, Col.
  Owens, Capt.
  Leonard, Capt.
  Williams, Capt.
  Hancock, Capt.

Turner, John, late of Virginia, merchant, dec'd—accounts with estate to be settled with George Moor, exec., at No. 65 Cherry St., NYC (12/31)

GENEALOGICAL DATA FROM THE NEW-YORK GAZETTE; AND THE WEEKLY MERCURY

1782

Yates, Mrs., and four children—killed in Dec., 1781, by husband, James Yates, who says he was born in Westchester Co. (1/7)

Wheeler, Mr.—sentenced to death on Dec. 15, 1781, for robbing the house of Cornelius Schermerhorn, of Schotock, about 12 miles from Albany (1/7)

Wood, Mr.—same as above

Moore, John, of NYC, merchant, in partnership with Mr. Kerr—died Dec. 31, 1781, in NYC (1/7)

Walker, James, a young lad—fell overboard Jan. 1 from brig *Adventure,* William Purvis master, and was drowned (1/7)

Smythies, William, surgeon, an English gentleman who came to NYC a few years ago with the British Guards—died Jan. 9 in NYC (1/14)

Harrison, Mrs. Mary, wife of Richard Harrison, Esq., of NYC—died Jan. 10 in NYC (1/14)

M'Lean, Donald, native of North Britain, druggist in NYC, who in the last war was surgeon to the 77th Regt.—died Jan. 10 in NYC (1/14)

Parcels, Abraham, late of NYC, dec'd—accounts with estate to be settled with execs., Hubert Van Wagenen, William Perse and Thomas Thorne (1/14)

Auchmuty, Richard, of H.M.'s General Hospital, second son of the late Rector of NYC—died Jan. 1 in Gloucester, Virginia (1/21)

Sprigg, Thomas, Esq.—died Dec. 29, 1781, at his seat on West River in Maryland in his 67th year (1/21)

Inglis, Charles, eldest son of the Rev. Dr. Inglis, Rector of Trinity Church in NYC—died Jan. 20 in NYC in his 8th year (1/21)

Johnston, Henry, Esq., Lt. Col. of the 17th Regt. of Foot, nephew of General Walsh—was married Jan. 24 to Miss Franks, youngest daughter of David Franks, Esq., at her father's house in the Broad-Way, NYC (1/28)

Forbes, Lt. Edward, of the marines on board the man-of-war *Lion*—died Jan. 22 of dysentery at Col. De Wurmb's quarters at Westbury, L.I., and was buried near the Quaker Meeting House at Westbury (1/28)

Stanton, Giles, late of Newport, R.I., for several years commander of a vessel belonging to Newport—died Jan. 24 in NYC (1/28)

Bell, John (son of Robert and Mary Bell, late of London, dec'd), who came to America about 10 years ago—is asked to apply to Samuel Franklin in NYC or to John Franklin in Phila. to hear something to his advantage (1/28)

Loring, Joshua, Esq., who in the last war was commander in chief of H.M.'s vessels on the Lakes in the Province of NY—his death is mentioned in the English papers (1/28)

Morgan, James—executed Jan. 29 at Westfield, N.J., for the murder of the Rev. James Caldwell (2/11)

Lissa, Negro wench, age c. 24, who formerly belonged to Parson Burnet, on L.I.—runaway Feb. 8 from John Carrow, living at No. 3 Fair St., NYC (2/18)

Waters, Talmon, dec'd—farm at Flushing Fly for sale by execs., John Waters, William Waters and Samuel Doughty (2/18)

Grete, age c. 30, a grenadier—deserted from Lt. Col. de Langerke's Battalion of Hessian Grenadiers (2/25)

Van Varick, Mrs. Effee, late of NYC, dec'd—accounts with estate to be settled with John Walter, acting executor, and John B. Stout, administrator (2/25)

Price, Mr., belonging to H.M.'s Hospital—was married Feb. 24, in NYC, by the Rev. Dr. Inglis, to Miss Brownejohn, youngest daughter of William Brownejohn, Esq. (3/4)

Dyckman, Abraham, a principal rebel guide—killed March 4 in action (3/11)

Barto, Lt. Col., late of New Jersey—was married Feb. 25, by the Rev. Dr. Inglis, in NYC, to Mrs. Elizabeth Sarly, daughter of Dr. William Brownejohn, of NYC (3/11)

Talbot, Capt., of H.M.'s 17th Regt. of Light Dragoons—died March 7 at his lodgings in NYC and was buried March 9 in St. Paul's Church Yard (3/11)

Boyd, Capt., of H.M.'s 38th Regt., who lately left for England in the packet—died a few days after his arrival at Falmouth (3/11)

Lindsay, Capt., born in Edinburgh, North Britain, who came to NYC about 1758—if he will apply to the printer he will hear something to his advantage (3/18)

Moore, Mrs. Frances, widow of the late Hon. Col. John Moore, of NYC—died March 23 in NYC in her 90th year (3/25)

Clepham, James, M.D., Physician to the North American Squadron—died April 1 in NYC (4/8)

Lawrence, Richard, late of Newtown, L.I., dec'd—accounts with estate to be settled with William or Thomas Lawrence, both of Newtown (4/8)

Jackson, Thomas—drowned April 6 from on board the navy victualler *Polly*, lying off Governor's Island (4/8)

Doughty, Elias, dec'd—farm in Twp. of Flushing, L.I., near the Great Plains, for sale by John and Charles Doughty (4/15)

Caesar, Negro slave, age c. 26—runaway from Richard Jenkins, No. 24 John St., NYC (4/22)

Williams, Nathaniel, dec'd—accounts with estate to be settled with Rachel Williams, executrix, at her house in Huntington (5/20)

Johnston, George, late of Kerrimore, Scotland—is asked to apply to the printer to hear something to his advantage (5/20)

Harriot, Mrs., wife of Capt. Thomas Harriot, of NYC—died May 29 at Bushwick, L.I., in her 44th year (6/3)

Pitcher, James, Esq., Commissary of Musters—died June 5 in NYC (6/10)

Jack, Negro slave, age c. 15—runaway June 2 from William Rhinelander, No. 198 Queen St., NYC (6/10)

Lee, Cesar, a Negro boy, age c. 14, chimney sweep—runaway from John Post, cooper, at Peck's Slip, NYC (6/10)

Balfour, Col. Andrew, formerly of Newport, R.I.—was killed March 12 by Tories in his house in Randolph Co., North Carolina (6/17)

Frank, Negro slave, age 19—runaway June 12 from Douwe Ditmars, of Jamaica, L.I. (6/17)

Clark, John—was convicted of piracy at court held in NYC and was sentenced to be hanged (6/24)

Williams, Thomas Charles, of NYC, merchant, who had been to Virginia to settle an account—died on board ship on return to NYC (6/24)

Thurston, Edward, Esq., of Newport, R.I.—died June 21 in NYC in his 51st year (6/24)

Canfield, Mr., native of Northampton, Mass., who deserted from the First New Hampshire Regt. and joined Major Roger's Rangers—is to be executed June 6 at Saratoga (7/8)

Williams, Rev. Stephen, of Parish of Long Meadow—buried June 12 in Mass. (7/8)

Pearss, William, member of the Reformed Church of Holland in NYC—died July 5 in NYC in his 63rd year (7/8); accounts with his estate to be settled with execs., Charles Philips, Hubert Van Wagenen and David Masterton (8/12)

Latham, Thomas—died July 9 at Bridgetown, N.J. (7/15)

Walton, Mrs. Mary, wife of Jacob Walton, Esq., for many years Representative in the General Assembly for NY City and County, and daughter of the late Hon. Henry Cruger, Esq.—died Aug. 1 at Flatbush, L.I., in her 38th year and was buried Aug. 3 in family vault in Trinity Church Yard (8/5)

Gray, Richard, born at Falmouth in Cornwall, England, shoemaker—if he will apply to printer he will hear something to his advantage (8/5)

Lynch, Major John, dec'd—farm in Southwood, L.I., leading on road from Hempstead Plains to Far Rockaway, for sale by Thomas Lynch, admin. (8/5)

Walton, Jacob, Esq., late member of the General Assembly of NY—died Aug. 9 at Flatbush (8/12)

Hilton, John, of NYC, descended from the Hiltons and Musgraves, ancient baronets in the County of Cumberland—died Aug. 12 in NYC (8/19); real estate and goods for sale by execs., Ralph Hylton and Thomas Braine, and Mary Hylton, executrix (8/26)

Horne, John, Surgeon to H.M.'s 17th Regt. of Infantry—died Aug. 12 at his quarters on Long Island (8/19)

Kissam, Daniel, Esq., Judge of Court of Common Pleas, Representative for many years in General Assembly—died, as result of a fall from his horse, on Aug. 4 at his seat at Cow Neck, Long Island (8/19)

Okerson, Samuel, formerly of Long Bridge, N.J.—died Aug. 10 on Long Island in his 53rd year (8/19)

Treadwell, Col. Benjamin—died Aug. 27 at his house at Great Neck, L.I., in his 80th year (9/2)

Gardiner, Abraham—died Aug. 21 at East Hampton, L.I., in his 61st year (9/2)

Ben, Negro boy—runaway Aug. 20 from Dr. David Brooks, of Cow Neck, L.I. (9/2)

Wanton, Mrs. Elizabeth, wife of William Wanton, Esq., late of Rhode Island—died Sept. 4 in NYC (9/9)

Campbell, Patrick, Esq., Major of the 71st Regt.—died last week on L.I. (9/9)

Price, Enoch, of Hanover, was accidentally scalded and killed Sept. 10 (9/16)

Upham, Mrs. Elizabeth, wife of Major Upham, of the King's American Dragoons—died Sept. 15 at her house in Fair St., NYC, in the prime of life and was buried Sept. 16 (9/16)

Van Dam, John, of NYC—died Sept. 18 in his 39th year (9/23)

Pearce, Mrs. Ann, wife of Capt. Samuel Pearce, of NYC—died Sept. 19 in NYC, aged 24 years (9/23)

Williams, Thomas C., dec'd—auction to be held at his house, 53 King St., NYC, by the execs., Sarah and John Williams (9/23)

Earl, Capt., master of the schooner *Harlequin*—was killed Sept. 18 in an engagement near Reedy Island in the Delaware (9/30)

Denyse, Mrs., wife of Denyse Denyse—died Sept. 29 at the Narrows on Long Island (9/30)

Burns, George Walters, a volunteer in the 54th Regt. and son of Capt. George Burns of the Royal Fencible Americans—died Sept. 28 in NYC and was buried Sept. 30 in Trinity Church Yard (10/7)

Smith, Edward, native of England, of NYC, tinman—died Sept. 28 in NYC (10/7); his goods for sale by execs., Prier Lynch and Benjamin Stout, Jr. (10/7) and Jan. 6, 1783)

Smith, William, eminent merchant of Charlestown, S.C.—lately died there (10/7)

M'Donald, Donald, printer—died Sept. 28 at Newtown, L.I. (10/7); accounts with estate to be settled with Alexander Cameron, admin. (10/14)

Brevoort, Henry, merchant—died Oct. 2 in NYC and was buried Oct. 3 in family vault in Old Dutch Church Yard (10/7); accounts with estate to be settled with Mary Brevoort, executrix, and Theophilus Anthony, executor (11/11)

Richardson, Mrs. Elizabeth, wife of Capt. William Richardson, of NYC—died Oct. 3 in NYC in her 50th year (10/7)

Cooke, Hon. Nicholas, Esq., late Gov. of State of Rhode Island—lately died at Providence (10/14)

Nordbergh, John, a native of Sweden, formerly of the Royal American Regt. and Commandant of Ft. George—died Oct. 10 in NYC, aged 70 (10/14)

Hamilton, Capt., of the 54th Regt.—was married Oct. 26 in NYC to Miss Bardin, late of Rhode Island (10/28)

Stewart, Patrick, Esq., Captain in the British Legion—died Oct. 25 in NYC and was buried Oct. 27 in St. Paul's Church Yard (10/28)

Burr, James, living near Cow Neck, L.I.—killed there Oct. 24 by a force of rebels (10/28)

Martin, Capt., of Mass.—killed Oct. 24 in attack on Burr and Burtis near Cow Neck (10/28)

Kissam, Benjamin, Esq., of NYC, attorney—died Oct. 25 in NYC and was buried Oct. 26 in the family vault in the New Dutch Church Yard (10/28)

Brower, Samuel—accidentally killed Oct. 30 near Denyse's Ferry on L.I. when a gun went off in his canoe (11/4)

Tomlinson, John, convicted of high treason at a court of oyer and terminer at Newtown, Bucks Co.—was executed Oct. 27 (11/4)

Nixon, Robert, who lived at Plattin, near Drogheda, Ireland, house carpenter, and who left Ireland 6 or 7 years ago—if he will apply to the printer he will hear something to his advantage (11/4)

Dick, James, native of Scotland, who resided above 40 years in Maryland—died Sept. 24 at Lewis Town, Md., in his 76th year (11/11)

Corby, William, late of NYC, innholder, dec'd—accounts with estate to be settled with Anne Corby, executrix and execs., Richard Jenkins and Jasper Ruckel (11/11) and 1/20, 1783)

Rutherford, John, Esq.—was married Oct. 30 at Society Hall, near Princetown, N.J., by the Rev. William Frazer, to Miss Helana Morris, daughter of Lewis Morris, Esq., of Morrissania (11/18)

Clarkson, David, Esq.—died Nov. 14 in NYC (11/18)

Hedges, William, late belonging to H.M.'s Naval Yard—died Nov. 12 in NYC (11/18)

Le Grange, Mrs. Frances, wife of Bernardus Le Grange, Esq., late of Brunswick, N.J.—died Nov. 18 in NYC (11/25)

De Pertuis, Teresia, wife of Eslienne De Pertuis—husband will pay no debts contracted by her in future (11/25)

De Rabenau, Capt., of the Regt. Dietfort—died Nov. 30 in NYC (12/2)

Drinker, John, a native of Phila.—died there Nov. 17, aged 103 (12/2)

Taylor, Morford,—shot and killed Dec. 4 when passing Sandy Hook (12/9)

Bogert, John, Esq., formerly a magistrate of NYC—died Dec. 5 in NYC and was buried in family vault in the New Dutch Church Yard (12/9)

Vining, Michael, shipwright, having returned to NYC after a long absence, desires to locate his daughters. Mary, aged 16, and Betsey, aged 13 (12/9)

Peacock, William, Esq., formerly commander of the *Carysfort* and lately appointed commander of H.M.'s ship *L'Aigel*—died Dec. 13 in NYC (12/16)

Wheate, Sir Jacob, commander of H.M.'s ship *Cerberus*—was married Dec. 12 in NYC, by the Rev. Mr. Moore, to Miss Maria Shaw, of NYC (12/16)

Ball, Peter, of NYC—was married Dec. 21 at Jamaica, L.I., by the Rev. Mr. Bloomer, to Miss Charity Lott (12/23)

Brasher, Col. Abraham, formerly of NYC—died Dec. 6 at Morristown, N.J., aged 48 years (12/30)
Smith, Isaac, of Brookhaven, L.I., officer of marines on the privateer *Virginia*—killed Dec. 5 in boarding the ship *Rennet* (12/30)
Billy, age c. 20, born in Guinea, lately from the Island of Jamaica—runaway from Daniel McCormick (12/30)

GENEALOGICAL DATA FROM THE NEW-YORK GAZETTE; AND THE WEEKLY MERCURY

1783

Hastey, James, born at Matching Green, Essex, England (son of James Hastey), who enlisted in the 7th Regt. of Guards in 1774, was at St. Vincent's in 1775 and was ordered thence to Boston—if he will apply to Capt. Normand Tolmie at the shipyards he will hear something to his advantage (1/6)
Morgan, Lt. Nicholas, of the (N.J.) State Regt.—was mortally wounded Dec. 9, 1782 (1/13)
Hoop, James, late of NYC, dec'd—accounts with estate to be settled with Jane Robertson, executrix, and William Robertson, executor (1/13)
Meredith, Charles—died Jan. 3 in Phila. in his 64th year and was buried Jan. 5 in Christ Church Burying Ground in Phila. (1/20)
Warder, Jeremiah, formerly eminent merchant of Phila.—died there Jan. 4 (1/20)
Thornhill, John, celebrated mechanic—died Jan. 7 in Phila. (1/20)
Bonsall, Mrs., wife of Richard Bonsall, of NYC, late of Phila.—died Jan. 12 in NYC and was buried Jan. 14 in St. Paul's Church Yard (1/20)

Ten Eyck, Mrs. Izyntie, of NYC—Jan. 14 in NYC in her 82nd year (1/20)

Cowenhoven, Rem, eminent bolter of Brooklyn—died Jan. 15 at his seat at Brooklyn, L.I., in his 59th year (1/20)

Deane, Alkanah, of NYC—died Jan. 16 in NYC in his 76th year (1/20)

Lewis, John, of NYC, peruke-maker—died Jan. 24 in NYC in his 45th year (1/27)

Drowned Jan. 21 when his pettiauger sank in a snow storm off Governor's Island: (1/27)
Warner, Mr., a carpenter
Canon, a boy apprenticed to Mr. Warner
M'Fee, Capt.

Alexander, William, Earl of Stirling, Viscount of Canada, Major General in the service of the United States and Commander of the American Forces in the Northern Department—died Jan. 14 in Albany in his 57th year and was buried Jan. 16 in the Low Dutch Church of Albany (2/10)

Thomas, Mrs., and her daughter—perished Jan. 12 in burning down of their house in Middletown, Conn. (2/10)

Chappel, Andrew, of Chesterfield Society, Conn., child of—died Jan. 23 of burns in fire which consumed Mr. Chappel's house (2/10)

Lenox, Miss Catharine, late of Phila.—died Feb. 1 in NYC (2/10)

Beekman, John (son of the late John Beekman, of NYC, merchant)—died on night of Sunday se'nnight in his 37th year (2/10)

Fullerton, Capt. William, a native of North Britain, who sailed master out of NYC near 20 years—died Feb. 5 in NYC in his 50th year and was buried Feb. 6 in Trinity Church Yard (2/10); accounts with estate to be settled with John Bridgewater, admin. (2/17)

Fisher, Joshua, Loyalist and eminent merchant of Phila.—died Jan. 31 in Phila. (2/10)

Purviance, Andrew, of Phila., merchant—died Jan. 27 at his farm in Salem Co., West Jersey (2/17)

Van Vleck, Mrs. Margaret, wife of Isaac Van Vleck, of Phila., merchant—died Jan. 31 in Phila. in her 27th year and was buried on Sunday in the Second Presbyterian Church Burying Ground (2/17)

Rosbrugh, Robert, of Somerset Co., N.J.—died Jan. 21 in Trenton, N.J., in his 80th year (2/17)

Henry, David, son-in-law of Robert Rosbrugh—died Jan. 23 at Lamberton, Somerset Co., N.J., in his 56th year (2/17)

Simmons, Capt., master of the sloop *Revenge,* bound from Port-au-Prince to Boston—killed Nov. 6, 1782, when ship was captured by a privateer out of St. Augustine (2/24)

Wood, Isaac, of Poughkeepsie—killed a few days ago by falling out of a sleigh (2/24)

Roney, Lt. John, of General De Lancey's 1st Battalian—accounts with estate to be settled with Hugh Wallace, admin (2/24)

Marston, Mrs., wife of John Marston, Esq., of NYC—died Feb. 17 in NYC (2/24)

Hays, Mrs. Prudence, wife of Barrack Hays, of NYC, merchant—died Feb. 20 in NYC (2/24)

Gerresen, Jane, dec'd—accounts with estate to be settled with Frances Norris, executrix (3/3)

Weyman, Mrs. Anne, wife of William Weyman, of Newtown, L.I.—died last of Feb. at Newtown in her 26th year (3/3)

Sacket, John, formerly a merchant of NYC—died March 4 in NYC, aged 67 (3/10)

Lynch, Daniel, dec'd—house opposite the Brooklyn Fort for sale (3/17)

Dunscomb, John, many years an eminent wine merchant of NYC—died March 24 in NYC in his 74th year (3/31); accounts with estate to be settled with Daniel Dunscomb, No. 10 Nassau St., NYC (5/12)

Ward, Moses, of No. 10 Peck's Slip, NYC, five-year-old daughter of—drowned March 28 in Hell-Gate (3/31)

Sutherland, Ebenezer, Lt. of Marines—died April 6 at the house of John Vanderbelt, Esq., at Flatbush, and was buried April 8 in the churchyard at Flatbush (4/14)

Duff, Negro boy—runaway from Mathew Daniel, living at 34 Duke St., NYC (4/21)

Gibson, James, age c. 21—convicted of rape by a court at Hartford, Conn., and was sentenced to be executed the fourth Wednesday in June (4/28)

Stuart, Col., of the Maryland line—on returning Saturday from Col. Washington's, dislocated his neck, when his horse fell down near Sandy Hill, and died Sunday—Charlestown, S.C., dispatch of March 25 (4/28)

Berwick, Simon, Esq., a member of the Senate—Wednesday night, on way home, at the crossroads at the Cyprus, about 36 miles from town, was shot and killed by highwaymen—Charlestown, S.C., dispatch of March 19 (4/28)

Lefferts, Leffert, Esq., of Bedford, L.I., daughter of—accidentally killed April 24 when pistol she was removing went off (4/28)

Morrison, Mrs., wife of Major John Morrison, Deputy Commissary General to the army, and eldest daughter of the Hon. Joseph Wanton, Esq., Jr., late of Rhode Island—died May 6 in NYC (5/12)

Roberts, Joseph, who became an inhabitant of NYC in 1735 and was many years High Sheriff of NYC—died May 7 in NYC, aged nearly 90 (5/12)

Jack, Negro slave, age c. 23—runaway May 6 from Valentine Nutter (5/12)

Bennet, James, late of NYC, jeweller, dec'd—accounts with estate to be settled (5/12)

Bell, Robert, who came from County Down, Ireland, and kept a public house at Brooklyn Ferry in 1780—if he will apply to Hugh and Alexander Wallace, of NYC, merchants, he will hear something to his advantage (5/19)

Du Bois, Zachariah, late of Precinct of Cornwal, Orange Co., NY, dec'd—farm for sale; apply to Anne Du Bois, executrix, and Jesse Woodhull, Seth Macom and Thomas Moffatt, execs. (5/19)

Van Horne, Mrs. Mary, wife of Capt. Cornelius Van Horne, of NYC—died May 23 in NYC in her 26th year (5/26)

Monach, John, late of NYC, merchant, dec'd—accounts with estate to be settled with John Gray and James Colquhoun, administrators (5/26)

Wright, James, of Charlestown, S.C.—killed in duel by a Mr. Fitzpatrick (6/2)

Laight, Benjamin, youngest son of Edward Laight, of NYC—died in NYC, aged 19, and was buried June 3 in Trinity Church Yard (9/9)

Blundell, Christopher, of NYC—died June 14 in NYC at an advanced age (6/16); goods in house on the Battery for sale by execs., Peter B. Livingston and Anthony Belton (6/30)

Feldhouse, John, of NYC, dec'd—accounts with estate to be settled with Gustavus Shewkirk, acting executor and administrator (6/16)

Luce, Negro wench, age c. 30, who formerly lived with Edward Price, the pilot, at Cruger's Wharf—runaway; reward will be paid if slave is returned to master at No. 49, the corner next to the Exchange (6/30)

Stewart, Mrs. Mary, wife of Capt. Alexander Stewart and only sister of Major General M'Doogall—died June 10 in her 42nd year and was buried in the Presbyterian Church Burying Ground in Newark, N.J. (7/14)

Van Zant, Miss Katharine, daughter of Wynant Van Zant, of Wall St., NYC—died July 9 in NYC and was buried July 11 in the family vault at the New Dutch Church (7/14)

Morton, John, dec'd—accounts with estate to be settled with John Shaw at No. 214 Water St., NYC (7/14)

Lutwyche, Mrs. Jane, wife of Edward G. Lutwyche, Esq., and only daughter of John Rapalje, Esq., of Brooklyn—died July 18 in her 23rd year (7/21)

Bogert, Henry, of NYC, youngest son of John Bogert , Esq., lately dec'd—died Sept. 17 in NYC, aged 14 (9/22)

Inglis, Mrs. Margaret, wife of the Rev. Dr. Inglis, of NYC—died Sept. 21 in NYC in her 35th year (9/22)

Wood, Dr. John, dec'd—persons with claims against the estate are to present them at No. 23 Wall St., NYC (9/22)

Abbot, Mrs., and child, passengers in ship *Tonyn*, bound for Liverpool—drowned in wreck of ship near St. Augustine (9/29)

Hazard, Ebenezer, Postmaster General—married Sept. 11 at Shrewsbury, N.J., to Miss Arthur, of Shrewsbury (9/29)

Lynsen, Mrs. Magdalen, widow of Abraham Lynsen, merchant—died Sept. 20 at Verplank's Point, Westchester Co., NY (9/29)

Farmer, Mrs. Mary, wife of Jasper Farmer, of N.J., and daughter of late Ebenezer Grant, of NYC, merchant—died Sept. 25 in her 44th year (9/29)

Tytler, Capt. Peter, of the 80th Regt.—married to Miss Isabella Erskine, youngest daughter of the Hon. David Erskine, Esq., of Alva (10/6)

Ramsay, Lt. Col, of the Scots Fusileers—has died (10/6)

Dick, Negro slave, age 32—runaway from Jonathan Ford, of Morris Co., N.J. (10/6)

Hocklin, Eleanor, aged c. 60, whose maiden name was Eleanor Nicholas, born in the Parish of Constenton, Co. of Cornwall, who about 9 or 10 years ago went from Parish of Camborne to N. America and resided in NYC—is to apply to printer to hear something to her advantage (10/6)

Pickles, Capt. William—murdered by some Genoese sailors, of whom three, Francisco Messcar, Pedro Giacabo and Marten Bruselli, were convicted at a court in Phila. (10/6)

Torrey, Lt. Col., of Brigadier Hazen's Regt.—died Sept. 20 in Boston and was buried Sept. 22 (10/13)

Gordon, Col. James, of the 80th Regt.—died Oct. 17 in NYC and was buried the next day (10/20)

Kreamer, Elias, a German—died Aug. 7 at Coventry, Conn., from having eaten toadstools, which he thought to be mushrooms (10/27)

Bebee, Jonathan, in his 87th year—was married Oct. 7 at East Haddam, Conn., to Mrs. Remember Nye, aged 85 (10/27)

Ray, Richard, formerly of NYC—died Sept. 25 at Albany in his 29th year (11/3)

Jenkins, David, age c. 14, tailor—runaway from his master, Matthew Parker, of Phila. (11/3)

Anthony, Negro slave, age c. 35—runaway from S. Clowes, of Hampstead, Queens Co., L.I. (11/3)

Brooks, Philip, bookbinder, native of Dublin, who came to Phila. in 1773 and left NYC in 1780—information concerning him is desired (11/3)

Jack, Negro slave, age c. 11—runaway from his master; reward is offered if slave is returned to No. 201 Water St., near the Coffee House, NYC (11/3)

Griffith, Capt. John, native of Haverford West in Wales, nearly 50 years a citizen of NYC and for many years commander in the London, Amsterdam and Carolina trade—died Nov. 5 at his house in Smith St., NYC, aged 74 (11/10)

Dina, Negro wench, age c. 15—runaway from Frederick Weissenfels, living at No. 2 Fair St., NYC (11/10)

Rapalje, Abel, late of NYC, merchant, dec'd—accounts with estate to be settled with Rem Rapalje, at No. 28, opposite the Fly Market, NYC (11/10)

Brownejohn, William, native of England and long an inhabitant of NYC—died July 25 in NYC in his 78th year (7/28)

Sharwin, Richard, eminent saddler, who left England many years ago and settled in Boston, whence he removed with the British troops to NYC—died July 25 in NYC in his 45th year (7/28)

Deakin, John, who about six years ago sailed from Portsmouth in man-of-war *Experiment* and was in her at the attack on Sullivan's Island, S.C., and after that on the *Phoenix* and in hospital in NYC, and who married a farmer's daughter on L.I.—if he will apply to the printer he will hear something to his advantage (7/28)

Smith, Major John, of the 42nd or Royal Highland Regt.—died July 25 at Paulus Hook and was buried there (7/28)

Davis, Salomon, formerly commander of a vessel in the London trade—on July 31, when returning from NYC to his home at Satauket, L.I., was shot dead by highwaymen (8/4)

Hewston, Brinsley, Esq., of H.M.'s 71st Regt. and Town Major of the garrison—died Aug. 1 at his house in NYC (8/4)

De Gironcourt, Baron, Lt. of Artillery and Deputy Quartermaster General to the Hessian troops—married Aug. 17 in NYC to Miss Elizabeth Corne, daughter of Capt. Peter Corne, of NYC (8/18)

Hartert, Theodore Hartman, Capt. of the Hessian Regt. Prince Charles—accidentally ridden over and killed Aug. 7 by persons unknown while he was walking near his quarters on Greenwich road; he was buried Aug. 9 in St. Paul's Church Yard (8/18)

Dunbar, Capt., of the Royal Artillery—died Aug. 10 in NYC and was buried Aug. 11 in St. Paul's Church Yard (8/18)

Vandenham, John—died Aug. 17 in his house at Corlear's Hook in his 76th year (8/18)

Runaway from David Hasbrouck, Nathaniel Lefaver and Andries Lefever, Jr., of New Paltz, Ulster Co., NY: (8/25)
William, Negro slave, age 27
Harry, Negro slave, age c. 30
John, Negro slave, age c. 19

Vanderveer, Cornelius, of Monmouth Co., N.J., dec'd—accounts with estate to be settled with John Smock, Cornelius Vanderveer, Jr., and Joseph Throckmorton (8/25)

Jackel, John, dec'd—accounts with estate to be settled with Ann Sharwin, administratrix (8/25)

De Hackenberg, Baron Frederic, Major General in the service of the Landgrave of Hesse—died Aug. 27 in NYC, aged 61, and was buried Aug. 28 in the Lutheran Church Vault, Frankfort St., NYC (9/1)

Mac Lean, Donald, druggist, dec'd—accounts to be settled with Donald Mac Lean, No. 205 Water St., NYC (9/1)

Murray, George—died Sept. 3 in his house in NYC at an advanced age (9/8)

Rapalje, Abraham, son of Rem Rapalje, of NYC—died Sept. 3 in NYC (9/8)

Miller, Mrs. Sarah, wife of Capt. Christopher Miller, of NYC—died Sept. 10 in NYC in her 43rd year (9/15)

Mesnard, Daniel, of NYC—died Sept. 10 in NYC in his 76th year (9/15)

M'Lane, John, of Chesterfield, N.H., age c. 30—on Sept. 2, at a public house about 3 miles from Salem, on the Boston road, he tendered several counterfeit coins but escaped when Timothy Davis, of Gloucester, sought to have him arrested (9/22)

Fisk, Mrs. Ephraim, of Killingworth, Conn.—on Aug. 27 was delivered of four children, two sons and two daughters (9/22)

Ustick, Mrs. Susannah, wife of William Ustick, of NYC, merchant—died Sept. 14 in NYC and was buried Sept. 15 in Trinity Church Yard (9/22)

Abbet, - Mr. 134
Abbit, John 142
Abbot, - Mrs. 242; Abi-
jah 136,141,144; John
124; Mary 136,141
Abeel/Abel, John 81,216;
Lodwick 122
Abercrombie, - Major
General 47
Abrahams, James 114
Abramse, Andrew 66
Abrell, John 142
Ackerman, Abraham 147;
John 143; Nicholas 143
Ackland, - Major 213;
Lady Harriet 213; James
141,162
Ackley/Akely, Daniel 214;
Mary 19; William 19
Acton, John 132
Adair, - Mr. 132
Adam, Walter 213
Adams, Eliphalet 32;
George 132; John 1,192;
Samuel 171; Thomas 62
Addes, Simon 188
Addington, John 150
Adogan, Dennis 11
Adolphus, - Mrs. 174;
Isaac 174,189; Philip
189
Adriance, Abraham 71;
Joris 71
Agan, Joshua 178
Agar, Edward 82,92,102
126,149,229; Margaret
126
Aigins, James 177
Airs, Abraham 9
Aitkin/Aitken, Charles
157; Cornelia 157;
Robert 190
Alagon, Richard 54
Albee, - /Mr./ 38; Oba-
diah 38
Alberspe/Albrespy, Wil-
liam 59,101
Alberton, Richard 171
Alexander, Thompson &
137; - Lt. 44; James
2,45,72,121; John 52,
196; Mary 72,84; Lady
Mary 194; Robert 10,
55; Susannah 90; Wil-
liam 240
Allanby, Robert 116
Allen/Allan/Allin, - Lt.
36; Miss 157; Alice
19; Henry 47,145; Hugh
191; Jacamiah 145;
James 67,216; John 196,
211; Joseph 38,79; Mar-
garet 73; Ralph 19;
Robert 85; Samuel 160;
Sarah 51; Thomas Hol-
berton 136; William
73,76,157,180,216;
Zachariah 119
Allicocke, - Miss 230;
Joseph 194,214,219,
230
Allison, John 34; Thomas
92
Allman, Thomas (alias of
Thomas Vernon) 25
Allmong, - Mrs. Jacob 97
Allmorn, Lewis 164
Alsop, John 44,79,86,109;

Richard 150,156
Alston, - Capt. 44
Alstyne, John 160,169
Alvay, John 58
Alway, John 158
Amery, Jane 66; Joseph 66
Ames, Elizabeth 149; Ja-
cob 62,178; Mrs. John
86; Levi 178; Thomas-
ine 149; William 149
Amherst, Jeffery Sir 82,
95
Amiel, Elizabeth 222;
John 222
Amory, John 64,225; Mary
64
Amos, Daniel 110
Andariese, Hannah 99;
Nicholas 99
Anders, Gotlieb 41
Anderson, - Capt. 161;
Miss 128; Alexander
202; David 84; George
Washington 202; Jacob
112,113; James 41,88,
90,95,111; John 8,13,
17,41,53,55,84,111,161;
Jonathan 111; Martha
Dandridge 202; Susannah
112,113; William 94
Andress, John 142
Andrew, John 4
Andrews, - Mr. 123; Jo-
seph 138; Joshua 141;
Robert 134
Andrise, Elias 20
Andrisen, Marytje 20
Angel, Jeremiah 65
Annelly, William 101
Annen/Annin, James 102,
116
Annow, John 53
Anstruther, - Major Gen-
eral 70
Answorth, Lawrence 81
Anthony, Abraham 19;
Hendrick 17; Nicholas
144; Theophilus 238
Antill, Alice 159; Ann
147; Edward 147; Lewis
147,159
Antonides, Vincencius 25
Antony, Elizabeth 17
Appe, - Miss 207
Appleby, Peggy 231; Ro-
bert 231
Appy, - Widow 120; John
82
Apthorp/Apthorpe, - Mad-
am 144; Mr. 102; Rev.
152; Charles 63,114,
152; Charles Ward/
Charles W. 134, 220;
Rebeccah 114,152; Wil-
liam 220
Apty, Thomas 8
Archer, Elizabeth 49;
James 49; John 208
Arden/Ardin, Jacob 124,
157; James 107,219;
Thomas 107
Arding, Charles 13,55,56,
59,206
Arenbergo, Frederick 107
Argyle, Duke of 93
Aris (or Arison), George
156
Armstrong, - Capt. 230;

Miss 179; Mr. 131;
George 119; James 108;
John 25,176; Nehemiah
82; Thomas 118
Arnold, Benedict 67; Henry
130; Hezekiah 120,121;
Sarah 130
Arnot, James 170
Arrowsmith, Michael 31
Arthur, - Miss 242; Cath-
arine 103; George 103
Artsen, Albert 118
Ascough/Ayscough, Rich-
ard 73,82,86
Ashcraft, Jacob 47
Ashfield, Lewis 218; Lew-
is Morris 147,160,195;
Mary 195; Sarah 233;
Vincent Pearse/V. Pearse
147,160,233
Ashley, - Major 40; Ed-
ward 121; John 2
Ashton, Edward 115; Hes-
ter 73; John 53; Philip
52; William 52,115
Aske/Ask, Benjamin 11,21
Askwith, - Capt. 44
Aspeck, John Christian 99
Aspinwall, John 188
Atkins, John 59
Atkinson, Benjamin 63;
Frances 142; Theodore,
Jr. 142
Atsatt, Thomas 166
Attucks, Crispus 144
Attwood/Atwood, - Dr. 215;
Anne Lewis 215; Catha-
rine 231; Thomas 224;
Thomas Bridgen 224,231
Auboyneau, Frances 72
Auchmuty, Harrison & 227;
Rev. 183,184,193,194,
196,207; Isabella 184;
Richard 235; Robert Ni-
cholls/Robert N. 207,
228; Samuel 176,207
Ault, - Capt. 91
Austin, - Mr. 173; Caleb
106
Autenreith, William 102
Avery, - 19; Capt. 19; Mrs.
203; Rev. 203; Robert 50
Axtel, - Col. 227; Mrs.227
Aymar, John 138
Ayres, Charles 55; John
108; Joseph 9,18

Babcock, Abigail 180;
Adam 137,180; David
205; George 207; Jona-
than 127
Babrien, Margaret Barbery
84
Bache, Helena 216; Nancy
75; Richard 127; Sally
127; Theophilact 49,65,
70,75,79,216
Backhouse, John 168; Wil-
liam 219
Bacon, John 45
Badger, Barnard 223; Jo-
seph 52; Susannah 223
Bagley, Josiah 134,136;
Martha 134,136
Bagnall, Anna 10; Benja-
min 10; Benjamin, Jr.
10;

245

Bagnall (cont'd), Eliza-
  beth 10
Bahanna, - Widow 131;
  Thomas 131
Bailey/Bayley/Bailie/
  Baily/Bayly/Bale/Balie,
  - Capt. 59; Lt. 60;
  Mrs. 208; Charlotte
  215; Daniel 103; Frantz
  97; James 50,106; Jane
  50; John, Jr. 12; Rich-
  ard 36,208,215,226;
  Samuel 51; William 231
Bainbridge, John 171
Bainsley, - Capt. 54
Baird, Thomas 58
Baker, - Mr. 71; Anne
  175; Charles 175; God-
  frey 176; Hester 154;
  Jacob 87,154; James
  62,227; Jesse 71; John
  175,176; Joseph 84,91;
  Richard 20; Samuel 91;
  Sherebirh 204
Balden, William 16
Balding, Jacob 150
Baldridge, Daniel 88
Baldwin, Abraham 105;
  Daniel 105; Jane 105;
  Jonathan 187; Nehemiah
  113; Stephen 113; Timo-
  thy 119
Balfour, Andrew 236
Ball, - Mr. 15; Charity
  238; Ezekiel 206;
  George 204; Isaac 112,
  233; John 112; Joseph
  204; Peter 238; Ste-
  phen 229
Ballendine, Hamilton 223
Bamper, - Mr. 107
Bancker/Banker, Adrian
  50,109; Anne 83,105;
  Christopher 57,92,96,
  105; Christopher, Jr.
  83; Evert 84,87,94;
  Evert, Jr. 210,229;
  Flores 88; Richard 196;
  Sarah 196; William 96
Bane, Daniel 125
Banks, - Capt. 160;
  Alexander 209; David
  18; Francis 211; Jacob
  137; James 15,189;
  Samuel 159; Thomas 92
Bannister, Annesley 16;
  Thomas 10
Bant, Richard 174
Banta, Albert 195
Banton, Edmond 46
Banyar, Goldsbrow 120
Barber, - Mrs. 178; Fran-
  cis 178
Barbarie/Barberie, Fran-
  ces 210; John 3,88,90,
  96,147; Peter 2,210
Barbour, William 12
Barclay/Barklay/Barkley,
  - Miss 179; Mrs. 142;
  Rev./Dr. 174,207,213;
  Widow 144; Alexander
  151,153; Andrew 49,75,
  179,187,215; Charlotte
  215; David 151,155;
  Helena 187; Henry 73,
  104,224; John 88; Kitty
  174; Nancy 75,213;
  Robert 84,105,151;

Susanna 198; Thomas
  224; Thomas H. 198
Barden/Bardin, - Miss
  238; Edward 221
Baremore, Mansfield 228
Barhalt, - Mrs. 99
Barkeloe/Barcalow, Har-
  manus 119; Dirck 191
Barker, John 136; Peter
  127; Richard 133; Sam-
  uel 40,133
Barnard, Elizabeth 25;
  James 72,111,130
Barnebey, Ruth 108
Barnes/Barns, G. 180;
  John 194; John (alias
  John Greenwood, alias
  John Thompson, alias
  George Brown) 11; Mary
  91; Phebe 91; Roger
  73; Samuel 39; Thomas
  89,91
Barnet, Hose 104; Lena
  104; Sarah 104; Wil-
  liam M. 154
Barney, William 176
Barr, Hendrick 97
Barre, John 229
Barrington, Eunice 79;
  Nicholas 79; Teresa
  213; William 213
Barrot, John 32
Barrow, James 165; John
  208; Thomas 165
Barruk, Judah 182
Barry, Bernard 173;
  David 69; William 232
Bartholomew, - Mrs. 140;
  Benjamin 217; Samuel
  189
Bartlett/Bartlet, Eph-
  raim 204; John 202
Barto, - Lt. Col. 236;
  Elizabeth 236
Barton, - Col. 213; John
  213; Thomas 224; Wil-
  liam 77
Bartow, Anthony 65; Bazel
  71; Thomas 41
Bartram, Alexander 165;
  Eleanor 165; George
  165; John 82
Bascome, Paul 148
Bassett/Basset, Anne 176;
  Efey 78; Francis 69,78,
  162,206; John 78; Jo-
  siah 71; Mary 152;
  Nancy 10; Stephen 176;
  Thomas 10
Bastow, Catherine 223
Bateman, William 195
Bates/Baites, Alexander
  18; Ester 17,18; John
  151; Rachel 151; So-
  lomon 3,4; Stephen
  163; William 17,18,
  106
Batt, - Capt. 205
Batterson, Joseph 69
Baughman, Christian 221
Bauscher, Peter 197
Baxter, - Mrs. 153;
  /Mr./ 176; Augustine
  198; Isaac 148; Wil-
  liam 209
Bayard, - Capt. 214;
  Major 115; Mr. 112;
  Alida 169; Catharine

199,214; Elizabeth 39;
  Nicholas 35,39,199;
  Nicholas, Jr. 85; Re-
  beccah/Rebecca 114,152;
  Robert 114,152; Samuel
  23,50,60,68; William
  59; (and Co.) 84,108,
  155,169,173
Bayeux, John 13; Thomas
  76
Bayler, Richard 209
Baylis, John 112; Richard
  178
Baynton, - Miss 150
Beach, - Mrs. 80
Beaks, Stephen 1
Bealie, Thomas 132
Bear, John 55
Beard, James 186; John
  186; Victor 186
Beardsley, Catherine 183;
  John 183
Bearman, Catharine 78;
  Johannis 78
Beasley, William 33,77
Beatson, Richard 18
Beatty, - Mr. 53; Charles
  166
Beau, Blanche 226; Eliza-
  beth 226
Beaumont, - Mrs. 224;
  Hammond 224
Bebee, Jonathan 242; Re-
  member 242
Beck, Anne 119; John 179,
  201,220; Joseph 119
Becker, Conrad 23;
  Michael 85
Becket, John 175
Beckman, David 85
Bedford, Catharine 50
Bedine, Francis 165; Mrs.
  Francis 165
Bedlow, William 77
Beeck/Beek, Epenetus 88;
  Johannes 21; John 100
Beekman,& Son, Messrs
  184; Catharine 95;
  Cornelia 157,160; Cor-
  nelius 35,50,157;
  David 95,184; Effie 95;
  Elizabeth 150; Gerard
  25; Gerardus 33; Gerard
  G. 160,202; Gerard G.,
  Jr. 160; Gerard Wil-
  liam 91,157,159; Henry
  147,201; James 73,189;
  James J. 188; John 150,
  188,195,240; John, Jr.
  188; J.J. 195; Theo-
  philus/Theo. 188,195;
  William 145
Beesden, David 214
Belchelsderfer, Frederick
  43
Belcher, - Gov. 20,27;
  John 58; Jonathan 53,
  55
Belden/Beldin, John 19;
  John, Jr. 123; Samuel
  19
Belding, Henry 140;
  Jonathan 63
Belford (or Belfore),
  Ensign 57
Belknap, Caleb 63
Bell, - Mr. 5; Adam 175;
  Elisha 94; John 3,7,10,

246

Bell (cont'd.), John 61, 235; Mary 235; Robert 235,241; Thomas 6,15, 155; Walter 62; William 211
Bellamy, John 69
Bellarow, - Widow 7
Bellew/Bellow, - Capt. 47,50
Belton, Anthony 241
Bemper, - Capt. 43
Bend, Grove 141
Benedict, Elisha 162; Matthew 13; Peter 95; Thomas 13
Benger, Dorothea 101; Elliot 101
Bennet/Bennit, Abraham 97; Jacob, Jr. 207; James 241; Justice 173; Peter 68; Richard 41; Wyant 166
Benson/Bensen, & Turner 71; Alderman 30; Capt. 225,226; Adolphus 170; Catharine/Catherine 97,100,132; Christopher 108,119,184; Robert 35, 97,100,132; Sampson/ Samson 166,172
Benthousen, Jacob 141
Berens, John, Messrs Herman & 124
Beresford, Elizabeth 150; Richard 150
Bergen, Jacob 132; Johannis 166
Berkins, David 163
Berogain, Peter 15
Berragar, Henry 167
Berrara, Francis 203
Berrien/Berrian, Cornelius 56; Hendrick 195; John 78,79
Berry, - 37; Chief Justice 113; Col. 17; Charles 183; John 202; Lancelot Grave 183; Sally 183
Berryhill, Andrew 48; William 41
Berton, Peter 114,195
Berwick, Simon 241
Beslinger, - Mr. 41
Bess, Samuel 126
Bessonet, John 141
Bethel, Benjamin 51
Bethune, Henry 31
Betts/Bett, Ann 211; Benjamin 163; Daniel 114; Eli (alias of Eliphalet Sturdevant) 198; Nancy 196; Thomas 196,211; William 130
Beven/Bevan, Thomas 19, 150
Beverhudt, Peggy 174
Beveridge, David 231; John 46; Margaret 231
Bevoise, George 207
Bevons, Charles 125
Beynton, - Mr. 8
Bezley, Oliver 168
Bickers, - Capt. 47
Bickford, - Mr. 8
Bidder/Bydder, Daniel 126,129; Richard 126,

129; Syntche/Syntyche 126,129
Biddle, James 81
Bielman, Mrs. David 45
Bigelow, Isaac 55
Bigger, James 125
Billinger, - Capt. 18
Billopp, Christopher 194
Birch, - Mr. 156; James 217
Bird, - Mr. 48,120; (or Boyde), James 48
Birdsall, Samuel 77
Bishop, Richard 34; Robert 76
Bisset, - Capt. 15; Rev. 226; Widow 15; Andrew 17; Mary 17
Bixton, James 201
Blaau, Cornelia 78; Uriah 78
Black, James 157,194; John 101; Michael 59; Robert 176
Blackford, Garret 162; Mary 162
Blackie, James 227
Blackman, Benjamin 115; John 206
Blackwell, - Col. 227; Jacob 182; Polly 182
Blackwood, John 67
Blagge/Blage, Benjamin 40,133; John 190
Blair/Blaer, - Dr. 112; Lt. 46; Gilbert 131; James 9,45; John 16, 45,159,160
Blake, - Widow 17; James 107; Jane 12,15; John 15
Blakey, William 154
Bland, Elias 227
Blank, Casparus 37; Mary 230
Blansieur, Joseph 218
Blauvelt/Blavelt, David 148; Isaac 191; Jacob 191; Jacob A. 191; Johannes D. 148; Peter 191
Blaw, Waldron 123
Bleecker/Bleeker, Anthony 173; John R. 74; Rutger 145
Blewer, - Capt. 135
Bliss, - Mr. 111; Comfort 191; Daniel 191; Ester 191; Hezekiah 191; Samuel 28; Sarah 191
Bloodgood, Susanna 65; William 65
Bloomer, - Rev. 227,238
Bloomfield, Moses 179; Sarah 179
Blundell, Christopher 241
Blunt, John Werril 229
Blyth, James 16; William 215
Boar, Christopher 63
Bobin, Isack 14
Bockee, Abraham 201; Mrs. Abraham 201; Rebeccah 169; William 169
Bodfield, A. 208

Bodin, John 194; Polly 194
Bodkin, & Ferrall, Messers 76
Boel, Elizabeth 166; Hendricus 38; Henry 166, 227; Thomas 7
Boelen, Catharine 162
Boerum, Simon 166,197
Bogart/Bogert, - Mr. 206; Catharine 89,162; Cornelius 89,186; Henry 242; Henry C. 186,196; John 185,199,229,238, 242; John J. 223; Lena 229; Nicholas C. 186; Peter 162; Petrus 180; William 25
Boice, Jeremiah 178
Bokee, - Mr. 36
Bokels, Henry 109
Bolderson, - Capt. 187
Bollard, Robert 12
Bolles, Ebenezer 87
Bolton, Patty 150; Richard 146
Bond, Jacob 119; Phineas 174; Rebecca 134; Sarah 119; Thomas 134; Uriah 27; William 204; Zephamiah 167
Boner, Conrod 180
Bonn, John 207
Bonnel/Bunnil, David 63; Grace 226; Isaac 226
Bonner, - Lt. Col. 215
Bonnet, Daniel 126
Bonsall, - Mrs. 239; Jesse 165; Richard 239
Bonticout, - Mr. 179
Bookins, Henry 27
Bookman, John 22
Boone, Humphrey 116; William 124
Booth/Boothe, Agnes 219; Mingo 52; Robert 219; William 225
Boquet, - Brig. Gen. 112
Borden, - Miss 95; Richard 127
Borland, Francis 96
Bornschier, Justus 182
Bosch, Anne 12; Justus 12
Boss, Joseph 230; Mary 230
Bostick, Daniel 97
Bouchier, James 230
Boudinot/Boudenot, Elias 99,144,153,161
Bounce, - Mrs. 106
Bourdeaux, Thomas 7
Bourke, - Mr. 117
Bourn/Bourne, - Capt. 206; Peter 54
Boutchiar, Anne 108; John 108
Boutineau, James 141; Nancy 141
Bowdoin/Bodoin, - Miss 120; Francis 21; James 120
Bowen, John 43; William 94,165
Boweren, Elizabeth 105; Martin 105
Bowers, Henry, Jr. 159; Mary 159
Bowley, Cornelia 89; Richard 89,90

Bowman, Christian 128;
George 105; John 43;
Jonathan 223; Mary 7
Bowne, Betsey 179;
Daniel 186; David 159;
Joseph 71,78; Margaret
25; Mary 186; Peter 53;
Robert 25,179; Samuel
67,122,158
Boyd, - Capt. 236; Col.
135; Mr. 117; Adam 135;
Mr. H. 91; James 221,
225; Jonathan 206;
Robert Washington 203;
William 45,135,203
Boyle, Solomon 156
Boyles, James 29
Boynton/Boyntou /= Boyn-
ton?/, - Mr. 8,17
Brabner, Robert 85
Bracken, - Ensign 191
Bradberry, Elizabeth 185
Bradburn, Alexander 108
Braddick, Mary 31
Braddock/Bradock, - Capt.
14; General 112; Ed-
ward 36
Bradford, - Mrs. 58; Mr.
58; Andrew 2; Corne-
lius 29; William 4,7,9,
39,72
Bradley, - Col. 206;
/Mr./ 158; Richard 118;
Samuel, Jr. 147
Bradner, John 151
Bradshaw, Hannah (alias
Man of War Nance) 150
Bradstreet, - Col. 133;
Gen. 179; John 189
Brady/Bradey, Michael
138,140; Sarah 96;
Thomas 108
Brag, John 197
Braine, Mary 12; Thomas
12,108,137,237
Bramble, Sarah 32
Brandon, John 162
Brandt/Brant, Anthony
45; Catharine 155;
Christina 184; David
155; John 184; Samuel
24
Brangle, Jacob 138
Braning, John 59
Brannan, Christopher 87
Branson, Catharine (alias
Hannah Harding) 127
Brasher/Brasier, Abra-
ham 239; Henry 154
Brass, Adolph 125; Gerrit
21; Mary 125
Bratt/Brat, - Widow 24;
Abraham 27; Catharine
130; Johannes 24
Bray, James 112,117;
William 33
Breen, Richard 221
Breese, John 22,25; Re-
becca 120; Samuel 120,
128; Sidney 123
Breested/Bresteade,
Andrew 91; Ann 91;
Peter 15
Brerton, - Lt. 36
Bresier, - Mr. 34
Breton, John 33
Brett, Catharine 15;
Francis, Jr. 131;

Matthew 184; Sarah 131
Brevoort/Brovort, Elias
197; Henry 238; John
196; Mary 238
Brewerton, George, Jr.
137,138,220
Brewin, George 103
Brewster, Daniel 37;
James 186; Mary 186;
Samuel 164
Bridge, Samuel 95
Bridges, Timothy 65
Bridgewater, John 240
Bridgham, Joseph 24
Bridgman, Hezekiah 107
Briggs/Brigs, Isaac 80;
James 128
Bright, - Mrs. 110; Jacob
123
Brimingham, James 119
Brinckerhoff/Brinkerhoff/
Brinckerhoof/Brinker-
hoft, Abraham 134,137;
Dirck 46,72,134,137,199;
Dirck, Jr. 134,137,199;
Isaac 131; Jacob 131;
John 131; Joris 33,134,
137
Brink, Garret 97; Lambert
42; Peter 59; Petrus 51;
Stephen 97
Briowe, Mary 168; Philip
168
Bristow, & Winterbottom
126
Broadhead, - Mr. 52;
Charles 41,164; Daniel
41,123
Broadhurst, Samuel 165
Brobson, William 188
Brock, - Mrs. 139; /Mrs.
or Mr.?/ 142
Brockols, Mary 137
Brockholst, Henry 117;
Mary 117
Brockhurst, - Mrs. 128
Brodrick, John 124
Broner, Frederick 185
Brook, Henry 8
Brookbanks, H. 92
Brookman, Thomas 210
Brooks, Catharine 183;
David 116,183,237;
Elizabeth 213; George
192; John 116; Philip
242; Thomas 213
Broome, James 137
Brosius, Sebastian 41
Broughton, - Gov. 20;
Thomas 16
Brower, - /Mr./ 213;
Adolph 21,24; Christine
189; Jeremiah 135,157,
160,202; Jeremiah, Jr.
189; Mary 135; Nicholas,
Jr. 135; Peter 225;
Samuel 238
Brown/Browne, - Capt. 31;
Ensign 215; Lt. 208,
215; Mr. 103,104;
Arthur 53,54,56,81;
Benjamin 189; Betsy 81;
Edward 90; Elizabeth
188; Frances 210; George
48,197,211; George
(alias of John Barnes)
11; James 48,195,229;
John 31,58,59,114,133,

163,188; Lawrence 69;
Mary 157; (alias Ed-
wards), Mary 78; Molly
163; Obadiah 87; Polly
208; Samuel 108; Thomas
22,30,36,50,92,94,109,
120,121,139,157,174;
William 35,135,187,188,
189,208,209,210,211
Brownejohn/Brownjohn, -
Dr. 216; Miss 236;
/Mr./ 208; Elizabeth
236; Kitty 187; Samuel
216,224,230; William,
Jr. 154,187,236,243
Brownsnord, John 43
Bruce, William 221
Bruff, Charles Oliver 195
Bruit, - Mr. 21
Bruleman/Brulumman, John
75
Bruselli, Marten 242
Bryan/Brian, - Mrs. 18;
Cornelius 110; Dennis
24; Isabellah 74;
James 25,99; John 74,
170;
Bryant, Ebenezer 80;
Roger 88; William 32,
164
Brynen, - Capt. 118
Bryson, James 31
Buchanan, Alexander 182;
Thomas 176; Walter 176
Buck, Robert 57
Buckhout, Darkas (alias
Tabathy) 10; Peter 10
Buckin, William 92
Buckingham, St. John 154
Buckler, Andrew 9; John
229
Buckley/Buckly/Bulkley,
- Capt. 57; Mr. 127
Budd, - Widow 82; John
108,163; William 163
Budde, Thomas 117
Buglis/Bugles, Francis
96,101
Buise, John 130; Matthew
130
Bull, - Mr. 163; John 164
Bullege, Andrew 22
Bullfinch, John 137
Bullock, John 24; Joseph
150; William 24
Bundle, Christopher 218
Bunker, Peter 40
Bunting, Samuel, Jr. 197
Burbeck, Henry 203
Burbige, - Mr. 138
Burch, David 115; Sarah
115
Burchill, - Capt. 137
Burdine, Thomas 33
Burdon, Charles 166;
William 166
Burger, - Alderman 151;
Widow 134; Deborah 130;
Garret 50; Joseph 134
Burgess/Burges, - Miss
208,233; James 34;
John 30
Burgoyne, - /Gen./ 219
Burk/Burke, - Capt. 192;
Ann 230; Mary 231
Burling, James 40; John
40,54,55; Samuel 40,55
Burlingham, Thomas 60

Burn/Burne, Andrew 115;
Arthur 203; George 126;
Michael 209
Burnet, - Dr. 206; Gov.
21; Parson 235; Gilbert
2; John 12,33; Mathias
134; William 2
Burney, Fortune 204
Burnham, Elisha 70;
William 73
Burns, Barnaby 79;
George 78,96,237;
George Walters 237;
John 126; John (alias
Thomas Watson) 172;
Robert 142
Burr, - Capt. 160;
President 61; Aaron 54;
David 65; James 238;
John 11,19; Jonathan
86; Joseph 77; Thad-
deus 198
Burril, Nathan, Jr. 170
Burroughs/Burrough, John
91; William 33
Bursheau, - /Servant_7 39
Burt, John 156
Burtin, Mary 175
Burtis, - /Mr._7 238
Burton, - Col. 93; Bar-
tholomew 184; Isabella
184; William 184
Burwell, Joseph 194
Bury, William 130
Bush, Hans 41; Henry 77;
John 62,133; Justice
77; Lambert 41; Wil-
liam 117
Buskirk, - /Mr._7 143
Bussart, Philip 44
Bussey, - /Mr._7 21
Bussing, John 56
Butler, - Major 151;
Miss 83,218; James 178;
John 7,91; Richard 209;
Sarah 197; Thomas 37;
Walter 233; William 37,
103,197,218
Butterfield, William 11
Butts, Benjamin 19
Buvelot, James 132
Buzzy, John 169
Byerly, Thomas 1
Byfield, Nathaniel 5
Byington, Abraham 173
Byrne/Byrn, - Capt. 91;
Barnaby 153; Mrs.
Barnaby 153; Edward 2;
John 92; Robert 127
Byvanck, - Mrs. 217;
Anthony 24; Evert 49,
84; John 201,217

Cable/Cables, Ebenezer
69; Jabez 154
Cabot, Marston 45
Cahoon, George, Jr. 124
Calderwood, James 148
Caldwell, - Capt. 34,49;
/Mr._7 144; Rev. 233;
Archibald 121; David
190; James 122,187,235;
Katharine 28
Calhoun, Thomas 98
Calkins, Israel 62
Call, Mrs. Philip 38
Callender, James 99

Callichan, Dennis 50;
Mary 50
Cameron/Camaron/Camoran,
- Capt. 230; Alexander
237; Allan 229; Eliza-
beth 183; Evan 95; Hugh
183; John 100; Magda-
len 95
Camp, Catharine 155; John
223; John D., Jr. 155;
Richard (see Dick) 147
Campbell/Campbel/Campble/
Camble, - Capt. 95,218;
Capt. Lt. 60; Lt. 95,
233; Lt. (or Ensign?)
57; Lt. Col. 232; Major
61; Mr. 142,187; (alias
Hamilton, alias Johnson)
- /Mr._7 46; A.M. 234;
Anne 215; Archanle 4;
Archibald 8; Charles
31; Colin 234; Daniel
39,103; Duncan 74; Ed-
ward 106; Elizabeth
223; George 158,168;
James 64,101,194; Jane
211; John 51,78,142,
215; Laughlen 105; Mal-
colm 85,93; Mary 4,105;
Patrick 237; Robert 38,
211,231; Sarah 93,105;
William 18,69; Lord
William 93
Canada, - Mr. 28
Candel, Rudolph 41
Canfield, - Mr. 236
Cannon/Canon, - 240; John
61,89,92,124; Le Grand
89; William 124
Capen, Edward 63
Carahan, John 29
Carbonelle, - Ensign 60
Carey, Thomas 63
Cargey, Hermione 226; Ro-
bert 226
Cargill, James 155
Carill, Morris 7
Carl/Carle, John 147,152
Carlisle, - Mr. 232
Carman, Joshua, Jr. 171;
Moses 186
Carmer, Aeltye 39; James
110; Jonathan 110;
Nicholas 39
Carnan, Rowland 37
Carney, - Mr. 117; John
92
Caron, - Capt. 125
Carpenter, John 214
Carpenter, - Mrs. 183;
Daniel 214; Elizabeth
202; George Washington
214; Jacob 159; Jane
127; John 31,201,224;
John J. 127,139,161;
Nathaniel 64; Samuel
143; Thorn 183
Carr/Car, - Capt. 61;
Anne 10; James 194;
John 227; Mark 79; Pat-
rick (see Cole, Pat-
rick) 144; Wm. 10
Carree, Lewis, Jr. 21
Carroll/Carrol, - Lt. 230;
Thomas 107; William
223
Carrow, John 235
Carryl/Carril, Bryant

(called "Gilderoy") 72;
Patrick 148
Carskaden, Robert 170
Carson/Carsson, - Lt.
232; Archibald 18;
Hamilton 29; James 79
Cartay, Mary 161
Carter, Speakman & 174;
Elizabeth 104; Matthew
73; Nathaniel 98;
Sarah 104; Thomas 46;
William 216
Carthy, James 176
Cartwright, Henry 186;
Richard 186; William 98
Carty, Catharine 90
Carver, - Gov. 76; Wil-
liam 76
Cary, Edward 193; Henry
37; Jonathan 20; Jo-
seph 154; Mary 154;
Samuel 154,160; Sarah
160; William 122
Case, John 147
Cash, David 80
Cashaw, Abraham 119
Cassady, John 99
Casey/Cassey, John 28;
Michael 159; Samuel
145; William 154
Casswell, James 121
Castle, Robert 47
Castleton, Thomas 47
Cathcart, - Lady 222;
Lord 218
Cathern, Arthur 74
Catling, - Lt. 45
Catness, John 73
Catts, Michael 108
Cavenaugh/Cavenagh, -
Capt. 141; Henry 227;
Thomas 25
Cavendish, Joseph 76
Caventish (alias Miller),
John 115
Cearon, William 118
Cebbe, - Widow 75
Cebra, James 101; John
101; Mary 101
Cemp, Tinners 50
Chadwick, - Capt. 167
Challwell, Hannah 24
Chamberlain/Chamberlin,
- Ensign 87; Lewis 185
Chambers, - Capt. 80,125;
Anne/Ann 136,185; Ed-
ward 79; George 35;
Jame 3; James 96;
John 101,185; Robert,
Jr. 224; William 45;
Williams 24
Chamier, Achsah 218;
Daniel 216,218
Champion, Deborah 13,22
Champlin, Oliver 90
Chancellor, Samuel 153
Chandine, Charles 220
Chandler, - Rev. 190;
John 102; Thomas 79
Chapin, Elisha 47
Chapman, - Mr. 111;
Abel 189; Abigail 104;
Ralph 136
Chappel/Chapple, Andrew
240; William 71
Chappenois, John 189
Chardavoyne, Elias 182;
Isaac 182; William 182

249

Charles, William 59
Charlton, Richard 210
Chase, Jeremiah 36
Chauncey, - Rev. 9
Cheasman, William, Jr. 65
Cheever/Cheevers, - Capt.
177; Ezekiel 198; Jon.
198
Chener, John 227
Cheney, Thomas 2
Cherry, Hannah 138;
Reuben 138
Chester, - 37; Capt. 169;
Miss 167
Chetwood, - Mrs. 148;
Widow 65; John 156,170
Chew, Colby 57
Chicken, Cuthbert 31
Chidester, - Sergt. 47
Chilcott, Charles O. 161;
Christian 161
Child, Cephas 1; Francis
71; Jonathan Friend 156
Chism, William 34
Chiswell, John 19,117,118
Chitwynd, Thomas 231
Cholmsey, - Capt. 36
Cholwell, Thomas 37
Chovet, - Dr. 154
Christell, John 49
Christie/Christey/
Chrystie, Daniel 156;
John 40,43,44,99,155
Christophers, John 110;
Richard 8
Chrytie, George 78
Chubb, - /Mr./ 29
Church, - Capt. 83; Ed-
ward 101
Cibber, Colley 174
Cicere, Dorothy 52
Civil, Charles 79
Clague, Robert 80
Claire, Robert 137
Clancy, Mary 109
Clap, - President 141;
Mary 141; Thomas 120
Clapham/Clepham, - Col.
93; George 201; James
236
Clark/Clarke, - Capt.
123,158; Lt. 60; Major
214; Miss 125; /Mr./
28; Mr. 6,15; Widow 9;
Abijah 204; Annauchy
227; Benjamin 53;
Charity 214; Cornelius
80; David 48; Elijah
173; George 12,22; Mrs.
George 13,22; Heymen
227; Isaac 167; James
94,156,189; James Hill
134; John 73,109,144,
236; Lawrence 92;
Michael 48; Polly 145;
Richard 54; Tally 118;
Teresa 213; Thomas 112,
125,145,213; William
77,167,231
Clarkson, Anne Margaret
65; Betsey 58; David
50,58,65,66,68,117,137,
149,154,238; Devinus
91; Freeman 50,66,149;
Levinus 149; Matthew/
Mathew 22,24,37,50,58,
66,149,166; Polly 91
Classon, Nicholas 2

Clatworthy, George 115,
122
Clawson, John 224; Tho-
mas 152
Clay, Christian 107;
Mary 107; Thomas 145
Clayton, - Capt. 67
Cleeland, Andrew 9; Mary
9
Clements, Andrew 72;
Moses 115
Clemons, John 96,218
Clerk, - Mr. 61
Cleaveland/Cleveland, -
Capt. 31,212; Mrs. 212;
Rev. 31,53
Cleverly, Thomas 197
Clifford, - Mr. 102
Clifton/Cliffton, Alfred
224; William 183
Cline, - Capt. 142
Clinton, Charles 179;
George 179
Clizbe, Samuel 48
Clopper, Catherine 213;
Cornelius 115,213; John
73
Close, Jabez 176; Samuel
151
Closs, - Col. 178; Miss
178
Clossen, Peter 117
Clough/Cluff, Peter 34;
William 63
Clowes/Clowns/=Clowes7,
Samuel/S. 75,82,108,
163,242
Cloyd, David 102
Coal, - Mr. 218
Coart, Capt. R. 227
Coats, Isaac 152
Cobb, - Mrs. 175; Henry
69; John 232
Cobham, James 72,203
Cobhan, William 88
Cobley, John 77
Cock, Seaman & 233;
Hannah 229; Samuel 102;
William 229
Cockcraft, William 78
Cockeraft, - Mrs. 215;
William 215
Cockever/Cochever, Chari-
ty 22; John 22
Cockie, John 190
Cockram/Cockrem, Philip
3
Cockran/Cochran/Cockrain/
Coughren, - Capt. 87,
227; Major 233; David
115; Elenor 125; Eli-
zabeth 227; Hugh 73;
James 69; Mathew 125;
Robert 46; Samuel 22;
William 103,115
Cocks, - Mr. 177
Coddrington, Thomas 11,
20
Codimants, George 74
Codner, James 19
Coe, John 191; William 191
Coejemans/Coejeman,
Andries 23,139,145;
Geertruid 23; Samuel
Stoats 145
Coey, Robert 30
Coffin, Ephraim 6,15;
Jonathan 6,15; William

219
Coggeshall, Joshua 7
Coghlar, John 207; Mar-
garet 207
Cohen, Samuel Meyer 28
Cohoun, - Capt. 115
Coils, William 51
Cola, - Mrs. 41; Mr.
Cold, - Corp. 61
Colden, - Lt. Gov. 86,
222,229; Miss 66;
Alexander 158,184,192,
196; Alice 159; Cad-
wallader 66,72,84,159,
219,226; Mrs. Cadwa-
llader 84; Catharine
86; David 195; Eliza-
beth 184; Henrietta
211; Nicholls 211;
Richard 210; Richard
Nicholls 196
Cole/Coles, Benjamin 86,
170; Jacob 39,58;
Jordan 183; Nicholas
58,59; (or Carr),
Patrick 144; Samuel 1
Coleman, Daniel 157;
Patrick 192
Colester, Henry 92
Coletrust, Edward 46
Coley, William 183
Colgan/Colgen, - Rev.
65,202; Fleming 144,
152; Mary 65,202;
Thomas 41,72
Collett, John 210
Colley, Joseph 145
Collin, James 46
Collings, Joseph 197
Collins (alias Hamilton),
Anthony 146; Dennis
166; Giles 72; Henry
30; John 92; Margaret
74; Matthew 90; Wil-
liam 97
Collis, - Capt. 12
Collyson, Francis 140,141;
Mary 141
Colmon, Jeremiah 135
Colquhoon, Hugh 54;
James 241
Colskin, Nicholas 80
Colt, Parthenia 182
Colters, James 119
Coltis, - Sergt. 46
Colton, Catharine (alias
of Eleanor Debutcher)
84
Colvil, - Widow 213;
Elizabeth 227; Sally
213
Colvin, Patrick 179;
William 114
Combes/Combs/Comes/
Coombs, John 77,83,114,
123,171,180; Keziah/
Kiziah 171,180; Rich-
ard 12
Comly, Jacob 203
Conalley, William 1
Conde, Adam 27
Condick, George 1
Conihane, Francis 209
Conklin/Concklin, Ed-
mond 61; Elias 166;
John 198; Joseph 47;
Lewis, Jr. 196; Nicho-
las 166

Conn, Benjamin 98
Connar, Daniel 30
Connell/Connel, Daniel
176; William (alias
William Weaver) 61
Connely, Roger 58; Thomas
188
Connor/Conner, Barney
155; Barry 13; Bryan/
Brian 19,222; (alias
Smith), Catharine 19;
Hannah 82; Matthew 19;
Michael 64; Richard
218; Stephen 92; Ter-
ence 29; William 51
Conrad, Charlotte Maria
39
Conray, William, Jr. 204
Conro, Isaac 78
Cons, Jacabina 110; Leo-
nard 110
Consiglio, Francis 81
Conyn/Conyne/Conine/
Coneen, Casparus 202,
204; Casparus, Jr. 131;
(or Graham), Catharine
26; Cornelius 176;
Jemima 204; Tryntie 131
Cook/Cooke, - Dr. 175;
Mrs. 157; Mr. 17,111,
166; Rev. 157,195,223;
Cornelius 8; John 119;
Kathrine 4; Nicholas
238; Patterson 217;
Walter 48; William 119
Cookson, Joseph 191
Cooley, Isaac 61
Coon, - Capt. 30; Eliza-
beth 138
Coons, Adam 67
Cooper, - Mr. 11,116;
Rev. 184,187; Anne 197;
Daniel 124; Elianor 2;
Hugh 88; Lena 15; Mary
88; Myles 101; Rufus
184; William 101
Coppeler, Martin 47
Copson, John 3,6
Corby, Anne 238; William
238
Corey, David 4
Cormick, Helena 151
Corne, & VanDam 37; -
Capt. 225; Elizabeth
225,243; Peter 159,243
Cornell/Cornel, Corne-
lius 34,216; Daniel 214;
Ebenezer 81; Giliam 34,
216; John 100,171,226;
Richard 56; Samuel 82,
178,213,230; Sukey 178;
Susannah 213; Thomas
103,171
Cornick, Hugh 220
Cornwallis, - Lord 233
Cornwell, Caleb 132;
George 201; Joseph 165
Corsen, Cornelius 137;
Daniel 100; Jacob 137;
Mary 100
Corser, John 114
Cortelyou, Aaron 218;
Isaac 229
Cory, William 93
Cosby, Henry 32; Nancy 10;
William 8,17; William,
Jr. 109
Cosine, Cornelius 157;

Garret 140; Walter 140
Cosney, John 53
Cossing, Nathaniel, Sr.
227
Costekin, Anthony 164
Costigin, Francis 175
Cotton, - Capt. 212; Mrs.
212
Couch, Original 42
Coulter, James 119
Courtlandt/Courtland,
see also Van Cortlandt,
- Col. 7; Miss 7; Cath-
arina 16; Philip 16
Courtract, Bastian 59
Cousens, Barney 4; John 4
Covenhoven/Couwenhoven,
John 214,218; Nicholas
218; Rem 218,240
Coverly, - Capt. 26
Cowan, Samuel 54,170
Cowdery, Jonathan 109;
Samuel 131
Cox/Coxe, - Mr. 46;
Daniel 75; David 85;
George 130; James 31,
57; John 10,203; Jo-
seph 94; Laurance 217;
Matthew 44; Rebecca
10; William 2,6,75
Coxetter, Bartholomew
138
Cozzens, Joseph 109
Crabb, John 29; Thomas
122
Crackey, Sam 18
Craddock, - Mr. 76; Jo-
seph 79
Craig/Cragg/Crage, -
Capt. 189; Widow 53,56;
James 101; John 19,109;
Thomas 73; William 97
Cramond, - James 231
Crane, - Miss 178; Mrs.
180; Deborah 13,22;
James 27; Jeremiah 109;
Joshua 27; Susannah
109
Crannel, Bartholomew 89,
90,109; Robert, Sr.
14
Cranfurd, Joseph 3
Cranson, Samuel (alias
of James Crondel) 3
Cranston, Samuel 1
Craw, - Capt. 131
Crawford, - /Mr./ 121;
Alexander 86; Charles
92; George 160; John
108,115,137; Peggy 225;
Sidney 173; William 90,
173,177
Crawley, John 154
Creagh, - Mr. 37; Patrick
8
Creamer, Patrick 37
Cree, John 107,125
Cregier, Cornelius 144;
John 81; Martinus 37;
Simon 144; Thomas 81
Creighton, James 202
Cremmer, Timothy 24
Cressop/Cresap, - Col.
46,47; Michael 199;
Crew, - Capt. 47,61;
James 221
Crimble, - Lt. 36

Crist, John 118
Crofton, James 78
Croghan, - Capt. 44
Croker, Joseph 58
Crommeline/Crommelin,
Charles 126; Robert
90,123
Crondel, James (alias
Samuel Cranson) 3
Cronick, William 73
Croning, John 218
Crook/Crooke, - Mr. 174;
Charles 70; Gabriel
22; John 174; Margaret
174
Crooker, Robert 182;
William 182
Crookshanks/Crookshank/
Cruckshank, - Capt.
54,82; Alexander 188;
Thomas 69
Crosby, William 225
Crosley, George 158
Cross, Nathan 11
Croston, - Ensign 60
Crow/Crowe, John 37;
Jonathan 226
Crowshore, John 52
Croxton, - Capt. 54
Cruger, - /Mr./ 90,241;
Elizabeth 215; Henry
72,89,107,215,224,237;
Mrs. Henry 72; John 39,
89; John Harris 138;
Mary 237; Polly 72;
Sarah 39
Crum, Peter 191
Cruse, Cornelius 170
Cuer, - Mr. 16
Culbertson, Alexander 45;
John 49
Cullen, James 190; Wil-
liam 16
Culmore, Mrs. Philip 49
Culver, Robert 151
Cumerford, - Mrs. 142
Cuming, Robert 13
Cummins, Robert 3
Cundiff, - Ensign 191
Cunningham, - & Co.,
Greg 157,190,192; &
Nesbitt 47,86; - Col.
8; Lt. 221; Mrs. 104;
Widow 54; John 34,66;
Loudon 158; Samuel 66;
Waddel 55,72,99
Cupples, Moses 230
Curfey, Jo 6
Curle, Nicholas 102
Curry, Margery 58
Curson, Elizabeth 189;
Richard 132,189
Curtenius, Anthony 48
Curtis, - Capt. 38;
Samuel 61; William 37
Cushing, - Col. 86,139
Cutts, Samuel 117
Cuyle, Henry 206
Cuyler, - Col. 224;
Abraham 123,139; Ba-
rent 160; Catharine
186; Hannah 199; Henry
64,119,120,121,123,139,
148,151,161,186,199,
220; Henry, Jr. 109,
123; Jacob 144; Jane
139; John 123,220; Te-
leman/Tilaman 120,123

Daily/Dailey/Daley, - Mr.
143; John 19; Mary 154;
Sam 9
Dagg, John 23
Dagworthy, - Capt. 45
Daken, Samuel 61
Dalbo, Peter 121
Dalglish, Nathaniel 53
Dally/Dalley, Edward 46;
John 134
Dalrymple, John Sir 18;
Patrick 18
Dalyell, - Capt. 95
Damarest, David B. 195
Damsel, Andrew 50
Daniel/Daniell, Hugh 103;
John 93; Matthew 241
Daniels, Thomas 6
Dannefelder, George 110
Danolson, Archibald 69
Danvers, Robert Sir 95
Darby/Derby, - /Mr./ 158;
Benjamin 103; John 93,
101; Nathaniel 20;
Samuel 124; William 178
Darling, John 27; Joseph
114
Darlington/Darlinton,
Joseph 85; William 157
Darsee, William 115
Dashwood, Anne 219; Francis 219
Daugherty, Michael 28
Davan, John 175
Davenport, Abraham 73,
123; Samuel 6
David, Solomon 54
Davidson, - Lt. 99; David 134; James 101;
Lawrence 83; Thomas 92
Davies, - Capt. 164;
Anne 230; John 211;
Samuel 78; William 16
Davis, - Lt. 60; Benjamin 145,146; Christian
146; Daniel 61; David
44; Eleanor 29,30; Halkith 208; Henry 36,155;
Hugh 35; John 158;
Peter 92; Richard 146;
Robert 175; Solomon
243; Sarah 56; Squire
132; Thomas 13,21,34,
56; Timothy 243; William 110
Davison, John 209; John
(alias William Mackgee)
19
Daws, John 110
Dawson, - Capt. 102; Mrs.
233; Elizabeth 170;
Henry 157,171,180,220;
John 97; Jonas 75;
Richard 170; Roper 233;
Wolker 45
Day/Dey, Dirick 103;
Humphry 11; Isaac 197;
Jane 163; Theunis 103,
153; Thomas 208; Timothy 115; William 48,176;
Zachary 155
Dayton, Jonathan 187;
Jonathan I. 176
Deabury, Samuel 197
Deakin, John 243
Deal/Deall, Mrs. 220;
Elizabeth 207; Jonathan
209; Robert 220;

Samuel 207,213
Dean, Fegan & 221; -
Capt. 116,186; Jonathan 80; Joseph 152;
Joshua 11,20; Samuel
77; William 152,153
Deane, - Capt. Le Chevalier 136; Miss 225;
Alkanah 240; Mary 213;
Richard 102,213,225
Deaver, Patrick 35
Debevoise/Debevoeise/
Debvoeise/Debvoises,
George 209; Jacob 167;
Jacobus 66,128,130,
167; Johannis/Johannes
128,130,167; Nancy 128,
130
De Botetourt, Norbone
Baron 149
Debow, Frederick 156
Debutcher, Eleanor (alias
Catherine Colton) 84
De Camp/Decamp/D Camp,
Hendrick 159,163; John
159,163
Decheseau, Adam 21; Stephen 21
Decker, Andrew 98;
Charles 11; Johannes 24
Deering, - Mr. 27
Deffoe, Daniel 68
De Forest/Deforrest/De
Foreest/Deforrest,
Abraham 156; Benjamin
203; Henry 137; John
Hancock 203; Susanna/
Susannah 137,156
Defreest, Elizabeth 23
De Garmo/Degarmo, - Capt.
102; John 100
De Gironcourt, Elizabeth
Baroness 243; Baron
243
De Graf, Klas A. 27
De Grave, Garrit 24
Degrey, Mary 101; Thomas
101
De Groote/De Groot/De
Grote, - /Mr./ 74;
John 78; Peter 91;
Samuel 193
Degrushe, - /Mr./ /wharf/
89
De Hackenberg, Frederic
Baron 243
De Hart/Dehart/D'Hart/
De Haert, - Capt. 13;
Jacob 162; James 22;
Matthias 162; Mauritz
82; William 162
De Hayne, - Major General 225
De Heister, - Lt. Gen.
213
De Honneur, Samuel 13
De Jalton, Thomas 223
Dekey, Helena 63
De La Montagnie/De La
Montanie, Abraham 190,
194; Catharine 168;
John 168; Mary/Mery
190,194
De Lancey/Delancey/Delancy, Taylor & 171;
Capt. 71; Brig. Gen./
Gen. 210,216,220,221,
227,229,232,240; Miss

54,89; Mrs. 180,185,
216; /Mr./ 29; Alice
122; Anne 82; Dorothy
178; Elizabeth 149,150,
199; James 54,74,82,89,
91,96,123,149,156,157,
180,186,216; James, Jr.
171; Jane 198; John 149,
178; Kitty 174; Mary
111,123; Matty 140;
Oliver 34,73,89,149,
160,167,174,185,193,197;
Peter 122,149,150,151,
198,199; Phila 193;
Stephen 23,25,149,174,
185; Suckey 89; Susanna
149,198
De Langerke, - Lt. Col.
236
Delanoy, James 42; Jane
42
De Laplaine/Delaplaine/
Delaplain/Delaplane,
Joseph 82; Joshua 12,
69,158; Mary 158
De La Somet, John 118
De Lemontonie, Catharine
166; John 166
De Lo, John Hendrick 64
De Loge, - Mr. 95
De Marest, Guilliam 24
Demilt, - Mr. 138
Deming, - Mr. 28
De Minnigerode, - Baron
220
Denck, Simon 115
Denhany, Daniel 223
Denie, Robert 182
Dennis, John 53
Dennison/Denison, Peter
102; Timothy 20
Denniston/Deniston,
Arthur 102; Elizabeth
146; John 102; Joseph
125; William 146
Denny/Denne, Daniel 24;
Elizabeth 9; William
45
Denormandie, - Mr. 74
De Noyelles, John 194
Dent, Abigail 6,15
Denton, Henry 208; John
125; Nehemiah 143;
Samuel 143,151
Denune, James 2
Denyse/De Nise/Dennis, -
Mrs. 237; /Mr./ /Terry/
238; Denyse/Dennis 225,
237; Jaques 90
De Offenbech, Charles
Werner 215
De Pertuis, Eslienne 238;
Teresia 238
De Peyster/Depeyster, -
Lt. 204; Abraham 58,
126,130,152,185; Anne/
Ann 22,190; Betsey 58;
Catharine 88; Cornelia
3; Cornelius 3,190;
Frederick 177; Gerardus 176; Isaac 186;
James 60,163,196; John
22; John, Jr. 161,165,
180; Joseph Reade 196;
Nancy 196; Pierre 88,
161,173
Depuy, Nicholas 125;
Samuel 125

De Rabenau, - Capt. 238
Der Kinderen, James 179
Deronde, Lambertus 45;
  Nicholas 45
Derota, Maria 36
Desbrosses/Desbros, -
  Widow 15; Elias 67,72,
  193,213,229; Elizabeth
  234; James 161,229;
  James, Jr. 197; Mary
  Ann 229
Detmus, Lawrence 139
De Va Driel, M. 112
De Velernaais, - Lt. 225
Devereux, Elizabeth 183;
  William 183
Deverson, William 87
De Visme, Anne/Ann 76,88,
  125; Peter 221; Philip
  76,88
Devoe, Michael 89,90
Devoore/Devoor/Devore,
  David 80,126,224,225,
  230; Mary 126
Dewall, - Lt. 232
Dewing, Nathanael 18
Dewint, Andries A. 45
De Witt/Dewit, Garret V.
  H. 97; John 172
De Wurmb, - Col. 235
D'Harriette, Benjamin 3
Dick, James 238; William
  3,10; William Sir 20
Dickinson/Dickenson, -
  Major 215; Benjamin
  103; Catharine 103;
  Hannah 229; John 147;
  Mary 147; Nathaniel
  229; Robert 183; Sam-
  uel 184; William 122
Dicker, Brewer 43; Tho-
  mas 108
Dickey, Matthew 92
Dickson, Alexander 140;
  David 84,151; Samuel
  184; Susanna Jane 140
Diggadon, - Mr. 174
Diggs/Digges, Dudley 29;
  William 79
Dihm, Lorenz 188
Dilkes, John 217
Dill, Joseph 217; Mary
  (alias of Mary Gordon)
  153
Dillon, - Capt. 194; Lt.
  232; Joanna 194; Jo-
  seph 194
Dimon, Jonathan 202;
  Richard Montgomery 202
Dingman, - Mr. 132
Dinon, Nancy 107
Dinwiddie, - Mr. 47
Disseau, John Baptist
  127
Ditmars, Douwe 236
Dittond, Anthony Francis
  21
Diver, Edward 80
Dixon, - Capt. 61; Dan-
  iel (alias of Daniel
  Johnson) 29; James 158
Dobbins - Mrs. 130;
  Anthony 110; Mary 110
Dobbs/Dobs, Adam 95;
  Charles 95,150; Helty
  227; Jarvis 227; Mary
  9; William 73,136,150
Dobson, - Capt. 232;

Thomas 40
Dodd, - Widow 28
Dodge, Amos 71
Dogworth, Elizabeth 87
Dole, James 222,234
Dolson, Tunis 117
Dominick, George 226
Donahew, - Capt. 25
Donaldson, - Col. 60;
  Alexander 24
Donean, John 80
Dongan, Thomas 84; Wal-
  ter 1
Donivan, Ricket 112
Donnaldson, Ronald 103
Donolly, - Mr. 74
Donop, - Count 211
Dooly/Duly, Joshua 203;
  Michael 66
Doran, - /Mr./ 77; Bryan
  30
Dorlant, John 38
Dougel, Robert 208
Doughty/Doty, Charles
  115,236; Elias 236;
  Isaac 183; John 59,
  236; Margaret 183;
  Philip 67; Samuel 30,
  157,183,223,235; Tho-
  mas 66
Douglass/Douglas, - Mrs.
  177; Mr. 107,177;
  Andrew Snape 233; James
  101,168,234; John 55,
  81; Robert 31; Sarah
  101; Thomas 36; Wil-
  liam 234
Douthell, James 16
Doutherts, George 208
Douw, Volckert P. 113
Dow, Eliphas 34
Dowell, William 11,132
Dowers, - Capt. 28
Downes, - Miss 88; Jona-
  than 158
Downman, - Capt. 163;
  Jane 163
Doyle, - /Mr./ 103;
  Darby 122
Drack, Augustine 198
Drake, Joseph 149,163,
  199; Joshua 143
Draper, - Lady 216; John
  89; Richard 122; Sam-
  uel 122; Susanna Lady
  149; William Sir 149,
  216
Drasdale, - Major 1
Drinker, John 238
Drinkwater, John 59
Driscall, Dennis 26
Druer, Sarah 151; Timo-
  thy 151
Drummond, Anne 219; Evan
  9,18; Gavine 145;
  Joshua 59
Duane, Abraham 64; Antho-
  ny 64,194; Cornelius
  64,229; James 64,70,
  116,125,188; Margaret
  194; Polly 70
Du Bois/Dubois, Anne 241;
  Catharine 88; Elizabeth
  30; Gualtherius/Gual-
  tharus 30,171; Helena
  79; Jacob 150; Jacob,
  Jr. 150; Margaret 171;
  Mathew 141,191; Peter

88,141,174; Walter 171;
  Zachariah 241
Ducharm, - Mr. 176
Ducket, Martin 50; Val-
  entine 189
Dudley, Francis 186,229;
  Jonathan 53; Mary 147,
  148; William 147,148,
  186
Duegued, William 176
Duff, Hugh 73; Roger 148
Duffey/Duffee/Duffie, -
  Capt. 221; Cornelius
  54; Duncan 67,92; James
  206
Dugdale, - Lt. 66
Duilap, - Capt. 159
Dulany, D. 173; William 1
Dunavan, James 103
Dunbar, - Capt. 90,243;
  Patrick 64
Duncan, - Capt. 220;
  Charles 211; George 174;
  James 234; John 103,104,
  112; Peggy 174; Sarah
  104; Thomas 50,74,174,
  234
Duncason, James 63
Dunforth, John 81
Dunkin, William 98
Dunlap, - Capt. 97; James
  81; John 6,177; William
  101
Dunloss, William 220
Dunn/Dun, - Lt. 233; Mrs.
  154; Amy 140; Hannah
  147; James 209,219;
  John 3,122; Mary 3;
  Micaiah 124; Patrick
  93; Phineas 81; Robert
  Joseph 140; Thomas 147
Dunnin(or Dunham), Samuel
  98
Dunning, Lewis 53
Dunscomb, Daniel 56,64,
  118,240; Edward 47;
  John 204,240; Margaret
  204
Dunster/Dunstar, Charles
  1,22; Daniel Donaldson
  156
Duppell, Lawrence 46
Dupuy, - Dr. 38; Frances
  38
Duram, Samuel 21
Durant, Benjamin 197
Durham, - Widow 58; Jane
  124
Durkin, Matthew 177
Durrem, William 23
Duryee/Durye/Duryea/
  Durjee, - Capt. 123,
  138; Abraham 161; Gab-
  riel 218; Jacob 56,118,
  123,198; John 67; Jorst
  198; Rebecca 190
Dusseau, Joseph 53
Dusset, - /Mr./ 38
Duvell, Nicholas 107
Duyckinck/Duykinck, Affe
  176; Gerardus 91;
  Gerardus, Jr. 199; John
  176; Mary 21; Suckey
  199
Dwight, Catharine 65;
  Joseph 206; Stephen 65;
  Thomas 65
Dwyer, John 39

253

Dyckman/Dikeman, Abraham 236; George 46; Jacob 183; John 132,219,226; William 71
Dyer, - Mr. 67; Christopher 68
Dyke, Thomas 25
Dysert, - Miss 104; Earl 210; James 104

Eage, Jacob 70,71
Eagles, William 164
Eagon, John (alias of John Higgins) 22
Eames, Eben 61; John 162
Earl/Earle, - Capt. 237; Andrew 50; Jonathan 16; Joseph 16
East, Edward 150
Easton, Samuel 179
Eastwick, Thomas 70
Eastwood, Habbacock 148
Eaton/Eatton, - Capt. 131; John 144
Eckenhait /Eckenhout_7, Maria 124
Eckerman, Jacob J. 134
Eckinrod, - Mr. 52
Eden, - Mrs. 216; William 216
Eddy, - Mr. 144; James 86; Joseph 205
Edes & Gill 136
Edgar, David 121
Edgehill, - Mr. 234
Edgerly, - Capt. 232
Edmonds, - /Mr._7 41; Jacob 161; John 50
Edwards/Edward, - Rev. 57; Charles 208; Isaac 195; John 167; Jonathan 57; Mary (alias of Mary Brown) 78; William 70
Egbert, John 205
Eight, Mary 4
Eise, Hans 100
Elbersen/Elberson, Abraham 77,105; Elbert 104; John 77; Rachel 105
Elde, Agnes 32
Elder, James 139; John 196
Eldert, Hendrick 49; Lucas 49; Luke 192
Eldridge, Obediah 5
Eldrington, Mary 99
Elias, Benjamin 14
Eliston, Robert 44
Elliot/Eliot, - Col. 106; General 111; Miss 179, 218; Mr. 71,198; Rev. 198; Andrew 179,218; Gilbert Sir 179; James 125; Jared 92; Solomon 166
Ellis, - /Mr._7 72; Alice 105; Charles 94; Elias 68; John 31,105; William 25
Ellison, Gabriel 100
Elliston, Mary 194; Robert 194
Ellit, Francis 51; James 54; Nancy 51
Elphinston/Elphinstone, - Mr. 225; Dorothea

214; George Keith 210, 214; William 61,214
Elrington/Eldrington, - Ensign 78; Christina 3; Francis 7
Elson, William 146
Elsworth, Clement 17; Verdine 89,90; William, Jr. 150
Eltinge, Jan 88; Petrus 88; William 88
Elvendrop, John 178
Eman, Lawrence 72
Emens/Emons, Christopher 152; Hendrick 169; Jane 152
Emery, - /Miss or Mrs._7 175; James 190
Emmerns, Jacob, Jr. 144; Thomas 144
Emmitt, James 208
Emmot/Emmott, John 101; William 101
Emory, - Capt. 69; John 64
Engelbert, Anthony 12
England, - Lt. 58; Thomas 175
Englar, Adam 184
Engle, Paul 143
English, - Capt. 143,162; Widow 24; John 46; Robert 108
Ensley/Enslee, Daniel 190,202
Enslow, Andrew 53
Epps, - Mrs. 116
Erersole, Charles 132
Ernest/Earnest, Daniel 106; John 79,99,138
Erskine, David 242; Isabella 242
Erving, John 120; Nancy 120
Erwin/Erwine, Amos 89; Henry 34; John 30; Mary 89; Rachel 89; Robert (alias William) 111; Sarah 89; Susannah 89; Walter 64
Eustace, - Dr. 77; Catharine 59
Evans/Evens, - Mr. 21; Edward 127; Joseph 203; Lewis 46; Samuel 178; Seth 33
Evat, Ann 2
Everett/Everit, Daniel 192; Nicholas 161
Everson/Eversen, Elsey 163; George 170; John 163,170; Nicholas 114
Everts, Adam 27
Ewing, Henderson & 110; Juliana 112; Robert 97; Thomas 190
Exceen, Mary 148,150
Eyre/Eyer, - Col./Lt. Col. 90,108; George 78; Jehu 78; Manuel 78; Samuel 78; William 103
Eyres/Eirs, Phineas 25; William 4

Fabricius, Christian 41
Faesh, John Jacob 188

Fagan, Jacob 216
Fairbanks, - Mrs. 139
Fairchild, Caleb 199; Jesse 165; Nancy 199
Fairfield, - Dr. 175; David 208
Faitout, Aaron 9; Margarit 9
Falconer, Thomas 103
Fales, - Capt. 60
Fallon, Hugh 176
Falls, - Capt. 31; George 109
Fanning, Edmund 178; Sukey 178
Fararo, - Mrs. 96
Farlow, William 203
Farmer, Jasper 57,60,242; Mary 57,242; Sally 194; Thomas 50
Farnsworth, Samuel 156
Farnum, David 143
Farquarson, - Lt. 60
Farquhar, - Dr. 66,72; - Mrs. 72; Elizabeth 189; James 189
Farrand, Daniel 100; Margaret 100; Nathaniel 97
Farrant, John 3
Farrel/Farral, - Capt. 130; /Mr._7 96; Barbery 218; Elizabeth 17; James 164; John 78,82, 103,154; Martin 218; Roger 17; Thomas 90
Farren, Riging 80
Farrington, John 63,229; Matthew 227; Phoebe 227
Fatt, Michael 51
Fauconier, Peter 58
Faulkner/Falkner, John 102,145
Fausy, John 62
Faxon, William 79
Fegan, & Dean 221; John 223
Feke, - Capt. 123
Feldhouse, John 241
Fell, Christopher 124; Martin 49
Felthausen, John 167
Fennemore, Abraham 217
Fenton, - Miss 93; John 6
Fenual, Nicholas 25
Fenwick, Robert 219; William 91
Fergus, Anne 122; Robert 122
Ferguson, Thomas 205
Ferrall, Bodkin & 76; - Capt. 40
Ferrer, Erasmus 125
Ferris, John 162
Field, - Mr. 117,144; John 191,194,223; John, Jr. 128,132,147,152, 153; Nathan 164; Patrick 101; Robert 151; William 163
Fieldon, Jacob 114
Fielen, Cornelius, Jr. 27
Fifield, Joseph 81
Filkin, Francis 169; Geesie 169
Finch, Charles 205; John 25

Fincher, Henry 3; John
96
Findley, William 72
Fine, - Mr. 100
Finley, - Rev. 120,177;
John 53; Rebecca 120;
Samuel 116; Susannah
177
Finn, Elizabeth 117; Wil-
liam 17
Fish, - Mr. 87,134; Eli-
zabeth 213; Henry 84;
Jonathan 56,213,223;
Joseph 80; Sarah 223
Fisher, - Col. 224; Mr.
215,231; Abraham 173;
Archibald 66,70,75;
Christopher 156; Corne-
lius 70,75; Elizabeth
99; Garrit Van Horn/
Garrit V.H. 70,75;
George 109; Jabez 223;
James 95; Jeremiah 99;
John 66; Joshua 240;
Margaret 8; William 73
Fisk/Fiske, Mrs. Ephraim
243; Samuel 50; Sarah
20
Fitch, - Capt. 128; Mrs.
136; Jonas 136; Thomas
188
Fitz Gerald/Fitzgerald,
John 58; Nicholas 140,
146
Fitzherbert, William 72
Fitz Morris, Richard 31
Fitz Patrick/Fitzpatrick,
- Lt. 202; Mr. 241;
Barnaby 119; Stephen
62
Fitz Randolph/Fitzrand-
olph, Benjamin 49; Ed-
ward 215; Hartshorne
189,196; Joseph 124;
Nathaniel 224
Fitzroy, Lord Augustus 7;
Charles 7
Fitz Simons, Francis 219;
John 219
Flack, Conradt 158
Flamon, Cornelius 6
Flaningham, Alexander 173
Flanley, Patrick 38
Flat, Mary 162; William
162
Fleet, Simon 102; Thomas
60
Fletcher, - Capt. 231;
Major 51; Joseph 127;
Nicholas 146; Richard
166,194
Fletzer, George 221
Flierboom, SerVas 69
Fling, Daniel 44
Flingert, George 62
Flint, Silas 122
Flories, Antonio 208
Floyd, Charles 177;
Elizabeth 214; Richard
154,214
Flueling, James 219
Fly, William 1
Foerster, Jacob Christo-
pher 30
Foine, Thomas 55
Folan, John 221
Folk, John 92
Folks, Isaiah 3

Folliott, Andrew 229;
George & Co. 157
Folly, John 225
Fonck, Cornelius 39
Forbes, - Capt. 71; Capt.
Lt. 60; Gen. 67,68;
Abigail 177; Alexander
110; Edward 235; Gil-
bert 137,139; James
231; Jane 191; John 66;
John, Jr. 77,103,123;
Philander 139; Sally
177
Forbis, James 73
Forbush, John, Jr. 73
Force, Benjamin 6
Ford, Elizabeth 120;
Jonathan 242; Nathan-
iel 25; Philip 119;
Samuel 175,215
Forester, Joseph 174
Forguson, James 80
Forman, Aaron, Jr. 58;
Joseph 1; Lewis 78;
Samuel 78; William
196
Forrest, Arthur 147;
John 34
Forsythe, Robert 203
Fortescue, - /Mr./ 114
Fosdick, - Mrs. 110
Foster, Ichabod 157;
James 204; John 134,
171; Jonas 11; Joseph
24; Josiah 143; Ralph
62; Samuel 79; Stephen
61; William 106
Fowler, Caleb 64; David
18,77; Elijah 199;
Michael 39; Solomon,
Jr. 199
Fox, John 118
Foy, family 73; - Capt.
165; Hannah 165;
Richard 142
Foyle, Robert 33
Fralich, Benigne 207;
Christian 207
France, Henry 41
Francis, - Capt. 73;
/Mr./ 73; Catharine
143; John 143; Samuel
170
Franklin & Underhill 106;
Mrs. 209; Benjamin
127,136; Elizabeth 136;
Henry 227; Henry A.
134; James 85; John
43,136,217,235; Mary
186,227; Matthew 229;
Sally 229; Samuel 229,
235; Thomas 107; Tho-
mas, Jr. 103,109;
Walter 171,186,225;
William 88,209
Franks, - Miss 235; Abi-
gail 46,128; David 128,
189,235; Jacob 46,136;
Polly 189
Franois, Daniel 62
Frantz, Mrs. John 59
Frapwell, John 197
Frary, William 5
Fraser/Frazer/Frasier/
Frazier, - Capt. 143;
Lt. 233; Mrs. 6,15;
Widow, see Catharine
Mason 220; George, the

alder 100; Hugh 156;
Isaac 131; James 79;
John 88; Thomas 54;
William 238
Fraunces, Samuel 185
Frederick, Hannah 164;
Michael 164
Freeman, - Capt. 96; Lt.
225; Robert 23
Freidure, John Baptist 40
Freleigh, - Rev. 214
French, - Lt. 52; Hugh 10;
John 135,139; Joseph
208; Philip 23; Polly
208
Fresneau, Andrew 22
Freyer, George Paul 165
Frielinghuysen/Freling-
huysen, Frederick 194;
Gitty 194; Johannes 33;
Theodorus 33; Theodo-
rus Jacobus 33
Friend, John 38
Fristole, Daniel 191
Frithers (or Frivers),
Thomasine 149
Frokinger, Johannis 131
Fronheyser, Andrew 87
Frost, George 76,93;
(alias Kettinger),
Joshua 90; Penn. 170;
Zebulon 170;
Froth, Henry 142
Fry, Christian 115; Daniel
61; David 66; Elizabeth
61; John 25; Joshua 37;
Margarita 115
Fryar, John 81
Fullanton, John 185
Fullerd, Margaret 49;
Thomas 49
Fullerton, William 240
Furlong, - Capt. 39
Furman, - Widow 78; /Miss
or Mrs./ 173; Mrs.
Ezekiel 134; Jane 195;
Ralph 123
Furnam, Moore 75
Furniss, Robert 192
Furnival, William 219
Fusman, Daniel 217

Gabrielsund, - Capt. 34
Gaffe, Thomas 57
Gage, - General 128,135,
178,192; William 192
Gaine, Hugh/H. 51,61,72,
101,165,171,186,189,
204,220
Gains, Jude 142
Gainsberry, Elizabeth 32
Galbreath, Thomas 188
Gale, Elizabeth 50; James
190; Samuel 50,112,139
Gallacher, - Mr. 61
Gallagher, James 79
Galliday, Joseph 59
Galloway, Elizabeth 40;
John 133
Gallwey, Phila 193; Ste-
phen Payne 193
Gamble, Samuel 188
Gammel, David 95
Gannon, Barney 143
Gansey, Benjamin 87
Ganter, Helena 76; John
Henry 76; Mary Magdalen

Ganter (cont'd), Mary Magdalen 222; Michael 164,222

Garabrant, Francis 6

Garden, Benjamin 83; Mrs. Benjamin 83

Gardiner/Gardener, - Miss 158; Mr. 50,218; Abraham 237; Johannes Meyer 183; John 14; Valentine 158

Gardner, - Mrs. 229; Alida 180; Archibald 116; James 180; Margaret 180; Thomas 141, 197

Garland, - Mrs. 190; Sylvester 1

Garman, Catharine 195; Christopher 195

Garrison, Benjamin 180; Hannah 193; John 193; L. 114; Lambert 73,151; Mary 180

Garritson, Peter 24

Garthwait, - Mrs. 180

Gaston, Robert 42

Gatefield, William 51

Gatehouse, John 85; Richard 85

Gaub, George 78

Gauladet, Thomas 177

Gault, Elizabeth 219; Robert 219

Gautier, Andrew 190,206; Margaret 190

Gavin, Francis 114

Geary, Daniel 92

Geldard, & Gimingham 149

Gelen, Jacob, Jr. 27

Gemberling, Charles 117

Genter, John 171

George, Thomas 13; William Cornelius 130

Georges, John 11

Gerbeaux, Henry 115

German, Hugh 156

Germond, James 153; Peter 153

Gerresen, Jane 240

Gerrish, - Mr. 159

Getfield, Rachel 201

Gethins, - Capt. 36

Geyes, Peter 116

Giacabo, Pedro 242

Gibbons, - Mrs. 105; John 157

Gibbs, - Capt. 123; Caleb 203

Gibeons, David 2

Gibson, James 241; Joseph 35; Roger 81; William 53

Giddons, Roger 102

Gidney/Gedney, - Mr. 83; Isaac 152,155

Gieger, Nicholas 57

Giffins, Peter 45

Gifford, Elizabeth 222; John 133; William 222

Gilbert, - Capt. 129; Mr. 156; William W. 140

Gilcrist, Adam 213

Giles, - Capt. 142; Rev. 114; Charles 59; Eleazer 175; Susannah 46

Gill, Edes & 136; Joh/n/ 81; Samuel 70; William 203

Gillespie/Gillaspie, Andrew 211; Elizabeth 223; Jane 211; John 211,223; Robert 72

Gillet, - Mr. 85

Gillgruse, James 127

Gilleylen, John 43

Gilliland, Elizabeth 163; John 40; William 110, 113

Gilliot, Mary Elizabeth 201

Gilly, John 223

Gilman, Freeman 147; Mary 147

Gilmore, John 70; Phaebe 78; Robert 78

Gilpin, Thomas 214

Gilson, Henry 41

Gimingham, Geldard & 149

Giraud, Anne 71; Peter 71

Glass, David 97

Gleen, John 175

Glegg, - Capt. 75

Glen, Cornelius 144; George 51; Henry 144; John 144,155

Glentworth, Elizabeth 32; John 32

Gobourn, Henry 124

Goddard, Nicholas 71

Godden, William 116

Godet, Theodore 94

Godfrey, Edward 123; Simon 61; Thomas 96; William 91

Goelet, Alice 201; Catharine 20; Jacob 20; Jane 61; Mary 174; Peter 73,141,174,201, 208

Goetcheus, Johannes Henricus 195

Goforth, Aaron 6; William 106

Gojion, Lawrence (alias John Johnston) 165

Gold, George 17

Goldin, George 17

Golding, Justis 80

Goldwin, Peter 46

Gombauld, Moses 11

Gomez, Benjamin 141,165; 167; Daniel 72,141; David 141; Deborah 206; Isaac 110,119,141,148; Matthias 148,167,206; Mordecay 72

Gonigall, Edward 92

Gooch, Joseph 202

Good, Dorothy 82

Goodman, - Capt. 232

Goodrick, Charles 86

Goodridge, - Capt. 146

Goodsel, James 202; John McPherson 202

Goodson, John 122; Lydia 122

Goodwin, - Capt. 31,55, 232; /Mr./ 31; Joseph 62; Richard 100; Sarah 100

Goold, Edward 184

Gordon/Gorden/Goardon, - Capt. 15; Mr. 178; Widow 2; James 156, 233,242; James Samuel 139,153; John 19,117; Mary (alias Mary Dill) 153; Nathaniel 34; Patrick 9; Peter 32; Robert 5,7; Thomas 123, 233; William 2

Gore, John 144,215

Gorham, - Col. 26; William 26

Gorman/Gormon, Henry 98; Hugh 165; John 107

Gorton, - Mr. 83

Gosline, John 82

Gosling, George 225

Gott, John 11

Gould, - Capt. 104; Lt. 232; Alexander 119; William 58,119

Goulding, Piercewell 42

Gourlay, - Mr. 169

Gouverneur/Governeur, Herman 187,193; Maria 31; Mary 187,193; Nicholas 21,39,187,193; Sarah 39

Gowing, Joshua 119

Graeme, - Dr. 166; William 9,18

Graham/Grayham, - Capt. 95; Dr. 154,175; Alexander 167; Archibald 209; Chauncey 148; Daniel 126,135,136,138; David 97,101; Edward 38, 55,63; Elizabeth 148; Ennis 67,92,135; Francis 216; James 65; John 94,221; Robert 136,138; Sarah 77; William 112, 169

Grannis, John 103

Grant, - Capt. 48,102; Gen. 221; Lt. 184; Miss 194; Anne 215; Ebenezer 35,69,242; Elizabeth 51; James 46,176,232; John 32,36,215,229; Mary 242; William 93

Graves, Matthew 223; Robert 167

Gray, & Gourlay 169; - Capt. 51; Adam 15; Ennice /Eunice?/ 21; Hugh 169,188; John 241; Joseph 21; Richard 237; Samuel 144

Graydon, Alexander 81,87; Rachel 81

Greaton, - Col. 215; Rev. 173; Mrs. 193; James 193

Green, Caleb 64; Charles 123; Daniel 204; Godfrey 63; John 1,108; Jonas 122; Timothy 51, 96; William 56,153

Greene, - Gen. 232; Russell 130; Thomas 96

Greenfield, Michael 145

Greenland, James 75

Greenly, Elizabeth 18

Greenvil, Henry 1

Greenwood, - Mr. 144; John (alias of John Barnes) 11

Greer, James 197

Gregg/Greg, Cunningham & Co.

256

Gregg/Greg (cont'd),
Cunningham & Co. 107,
109,157,190,192; John
220; Robert 73; Thomas
220
Gregory, James 178; Richard Fletcher 136
Grete, - Grenadier 236
Greyless, James 12
Griffin, - Mr. 127; John
32,79; Jonathan 78
Griffing, George 188;
William 188
Griffith/Griffiths, -
Capt. 29; Mr. 52; Andrew 233; David (alias
of David Smith) 29;
James 82; John 187,242;
Paul 76; Rebecca 43;
Robert 69; Thomas 85;
William 43
Griffy, Edward 188
Grigg/Grig, - Capt. 48,
51; David 167; Henry
133,135; William 227
Grim, - Mrs. 220; David
220; Peter 125
Grimes, Hezekiah 28;
John 2,3
Grinay, Jonathan 102;
Susannah 102
Grislie, John 3
Griswold/Greswold/Grisswold, Joseph 82,153,
155; Susannah 221;
Thomas 208,223
Grixin, John 102
Groen, Jacob Marius 130;
Silvester Marius 130
Groenendeyk, Samuel 71
Groesbeck/Groesbeek/
Groosebeck, - Widow 34;
Anne 76,219; John 34,
100,219
Grogan, Hugh 177
Grommon, Ichabud 48
Grover, William 120
Groves, - Capt. 142;
Thomas 203
Gruber, Henry 117
Grumbley, Christopher
134
Grumly, John 185,190
Guddle, Edward 221
Guest, Ann 159; Henry
159; John 76
Guion/Guyon, - Lt. 233;
Ammon 180; Isaac 155;
Nicholas 145; Sarah 180
Gulick, Joachim (or Gulet, Jocham) 152
Gulusha, Daniel 47
Gunn, Samuel 27
Gunner, George 59
Gunnison, - Mr. 27
Gurney, Thomas 42
Gustan, Catharine Araway 158
Guster, John 92
Gutrdige, /Gutridge?/ -
Mr. 28
Gwin/Gwinn/Gwyn, - Capt.
115; Elizabeth 20;
James 126; John 128

Haber, Christian 4; Frederick 4

Habersham, James 198
Hacket, John 118
Hadden, Bartholomew 132;
Thomas 78; William 206,
219
Hadley, - Mr. 126; Anthony 126; Joseph 39
Haff, Lawrence 30,63
Haffy, Francis 55
Hager/Heger, Anna Margerieta 39; Harmanus
39; Jacob 39; Valentine 39
Hagge, Moses 61
Hahsmidt, Jacob 116
Hains, William 23
Hait, - Capt. 70; Abraham 124; Daniel 196;
Mary 196
Hake, Helena 211; Katey
205; Samuel 205,211
Halder, Anthony 192
Hale, Samuel 6,15
Halembeck, Hans 39
Haley/Haly, - Capt. 54;
Catharine (or Anne)
214; Margery 214;
Michael 109
Halkett/Halket, Peter
Sir 36
Hall, - Mr. 27,61; David 149,169; Debry
149; Dennis 107; Elihu 150; George 168;
George Whitefield 150;
Joseph 73; Peter 186;
Samuel 91; Thomas 5,23,
217; William 63
Hallam, - Miss 177; Lewis 177
Hallett/Hallet, - Mr.
102; Elizabeth 219;
Joseph 204,219; Richard, Jr. 51; Robert
117
Hallock, Jesse 52
Halsey/Halse, James 120;
John 99
Halstead/Halsted, Isaac
42; John 69,92; W.
Anthony 215
Ham, James 37
Hamanin, Maria Sharlotta
39
Hambach, Frederick 131
Hamersley, Andrew 229;
Lucretia 75; Margaret
229; Thomas 100
Hames, George 35
Hamilton/Hambleton, -
195; Capt. 238; Lt. 36,
56; Mr. 81,179; Abigail 128; Alexander 55;
Alexander James 213;
Alice 229; Andrew 128;
Anthony (alias of
Anthony Collins) 146;
Archibald 222,229;
Edward 10; Elizabeth
152; Henry 98,192;
James 73,77; John 59,
172, 221; Margaret 73;
Mary 179,213; Polly
221; Robert 159; William 68,88,207
Hammell, William 109
Hammett/Hammet, Thomas
4; William 217

Hammond, - Mrs. 155;
Ephraim 155; James 59;
Joseph 2; Noah 191;
Thomas 218
Hampton, Jonathan 101;
Mary 114
Hams, Ezekiel 165
Han, George 185
Hanaway, Thomas 92
Hance, John 39
Hancock, - Capt. 234;
/Mr./ 13; Dorothy 198;
John 198; Thomas 104
Hand, John 43
Handlin, John 41
Hands, John 166
Handy, Scot 77
Hanfard, - Lt. 36
Hanks, George 202
Hanna, John 106
Hannan, - Mr. 141
Hanns, Christopher 140
Hanson/Hansen, - Capt.
224; Alida 82; Henry
40
Harbard, John 35
Harber/Harbor, Thomas
134,135
Hardcastle, Henry 36
Harden, - Capt. 36; Abraham 61,180; Mary 180
Hardenbrook, Abel, Jr.
228; John 130
Harding, Amaziah 5; Anne
148; Charles 164;
Hannah (alias of Catharine Branson) 127;
James 7; Robert 165;
Vall. 148
Hardy/Hardie, John 87,123
Harford, John 135
Hargrave, - Capt. 87;
Robert 219
Harker, Richard 174
Harle, Ralph 19
Harmon/Harman - Capt. 9;
Catharine Maria 174;
Thomas 223
Harper, Anthony 154;
Martha 154
Harpin, John, Jr. 101
Harriman, John 197
Harrington, Darby 118;
Dennis 80; Jabez 142
Harriot, - Mrs. 236;
Thomas 209,236
Harris, - 143; Capt. 231;
Mr. 164; Abraham 110,
160,169; Benjamin 111;
Francis 106; George
140; Henry 2; Jacob 87;
John 56; Myndert 214;
Nathaniel 76; Newell 42;
Phebe 76; Richard 65,111,
145,160,169,207,226;
Samuel 174; Sarah 110;
Thomas 192,218
Harrison/Harison, & Co.
Auchmuty 227; - Mr.
173; Ensign 68; Francis
171; George/G. 142,145,
164,171; Hermione 226;
John 1; Mary 235; Morley 142; Peter 226;
Richard 186,235; Thomas 44,135,165,196,220;
William 10,19,113
Harsin, Garret 153

257

Hart, - Lt. 36; Christian 109; Daniel 127; John 37,157; William 57
Hartert, Theodore Hartman 243
Hartshorne, Betsey 179, 223; John 193; Lawrence 223; Richard 17; Robert 179,193
Harvey/Harvie, - /Mr./ 164; Polly 221
Hasbrouck, David 243
Haselwood, William 195
Hasenclever, Peter 110
Haskoll, John 2
Haslip, William 102
Hastie/Haste, James 230, 239; Sarah 230
Hastier, Catharine 152; John 75,152; Margaret 190; Marguerite 152
Hatfield/Hetfield, Matthias 8,232; William 232
Hatier, John 150
Haughwout, Joseph Arrowsmith 65
Haulbeet, Ebenezer 103
Havens, Rhodes 126
Haviland/Heaviland, - Col. 85; Ebenezer 56; Peter 24; Thomas 56
Hawden, Anna 10; James 10
Hawkins, Benjamin 74; Edward 79; John 97; Richard 159; Thomas 5, 86
Hawxhurst/Hauxhurt, Hannah 11; Sampson 11; William 77,85,103
Hay, Agnes 12; Andrew 12; David 79,88,133; Mary 79; Samuel 203; Sarah 79,88
Haydock, John 36
Hayer, - Capt. 77
Hayes/Hays, - Col. 234; Mr. 44; Barrack 240; Catharine 98; James 21; Judah 52,58,74,104; Margaret 207; Patrick 98; Prudence 240; William 207
Hayman, - Mr. 24; Charles Chasbar 2; Thomas 209
Haynes, Godfrey 116; Joseph 40,92,111,114,121, 132,142,147,150,171; Mrs. Joseph 124; Samuel 55; Thomas 222
Hayter, Catharine 56
Hazard, Noel & 158; Daniel 24; Ebenezer 187,242; George 12,140; Henry 102; Jenny 140; Jonathan 40; Mary 12; Nathaniel 14,24,99,182; Polly 182; Robert 12; Samuel 74
Hazellwood, - Lt. 60
Hazen, - Brigadier 242
Head, - Mr. 42
Healey, Francis 34
Heard, - Miss 200; John 8; Mrs. John 8; Nathaniel 200

Heath, - Mr. 229
Heathcote, Caleb 9; George 3; Martha 9
Heating, John 115
Heavener, Barbara 151; George 151
Hebon, Barnt 2
Heckie, Peter 19
Hedges, James 141; Stephen 6; William 238
Hedy, Arabella 69
Heffernan, Roger 43
Hegeman/Hageman, Adrian 229; Elbert 211
Heiss, George Caspar 41
Heldege, Peter 3
Helme, Agnes 122; Benjamin 122,214; Rachel 214
Henderson, & Ewing 110; - Mr. 141; Widow 37; Allen 53; James 18, 224; John 10; Richard 175; Tiese/Tiesie 159, 168
Henderton, - Mrs. 95
Hendricks/Hendrick, Abraham 7; Coenradt 145; Hester 197; Sarah 87; Uriah 197
Hendrickson, William 109, 122
Henner, Mary Barbara 213
Hennesey, John 139
Hennion, Johannis 153
Henrigues, Ano. J.G. 184
Henry, David 154,240; James 157; Samuel 118, 140,146
Hepburn/Hepborn, John 109; Patrick 23; Thomas 206
Herbert, David 79
Herin, - Capt. 32
Herman, Messers, & John Berens 124; John George 122
Hermensen, Nanneng 78
Herring/Haring/Harring, Elbert 135,180; Elizabeth 180; Frederick 156; John 143,153,180; Peter 148; William (alias of William Johnson) 125
Herrington, George 34
Herron, David 79
Hersey, - Mr. 136
Hervey, - Mr. 31; George 154; John 82; Thomas 82
Hesse/Hesse Cassel, Landgrave of 225,243
Hessee, Christophel 51
Heurtin, Susanah 121
Hewes, Caleb 177
Hewit, William 182
Hewlett/Hewlet/Hulet, Benjamin 120; John 154; Richard 163
Hewlings, Helty 159
Hews, Aaron 49; James 49; Malaciah 7
Hewston, Brinsley 243
Heyanan, Catharine 85
Heyer, Matthias 155; William 130
Heyliger, John 196;

Sally 196
Heyman, Moses 86
Heysham, - Capt. 51; Christopher 133
Hickey, John 12
Hickling, William 177
Hickman, - Lt. 232
Hicks/Hick, - Judge 208; Mrs. 223; Mr. 41,223; Anne 180; Edward 48; Jacob 209; Polly 48; Thomas 209; Whitehead 196,209,226; William 163, 180
Higgins, Dominick 92; John 84; (alias Eagon), John 22
Higly, - Capt. 70
Hildreth, Benjamin 19; Benjamin, Sr. 208; Joseph 208
Hill, - Capt. 19,188; Miss 221; Mrs. 233; Anthony 75; Arthur 195; Dirck 92; James 152; John 1,77,221; Nathaniel 32; Richard 2; Robert 14; Samuel 189; Thomas 74,233; William 104
Hille, George William 215
Hilyard, Joseph 62
Hinds/Hindes, Abraham 70; James 20; Michael 155
Hines, Philip 165
Hinson, John 49
Hobbs/Hubbs, Zephaniah 171
Hockley, Richard 166
Hocklin, Eleanor 242
Hodge, Isaac 69; Samuel 94
Hodges, - Capt. 48; James 103
Hodgkins, Ebenezer 101
Hodgson, Alvery 93
Hodsden, John 194,201
Hoeth, Frederick 41
Hoever, Anthony 116
Hoeysfinger, - Capt. 206
Hoff, Jacob, Jr. 60,65; Leonard 26; Peter 8; Rachel 8
Hoffman, - Col. 92; Alida 165; Anthony 165; Elizabeth 112; Hermon 145; Martin 135,165; Nicholas 165; Polly 133
Hogan/Hogen, Patrick 231; William W. 102
Hogeboom, Annatie 85; Jeremiah 85
Hogg, James 48,113; Rebecca 31; Robert 23
Hoghtaling/Hoeghtelen, Hendrick 81,110; Johannis 126
Holabord, Cornelius 71
Holbrook, Edward 20
Holcomb, Jacob 197
Hold, John 4
Hole, John 6
Holland, - Capt. 99; Mr. 65,67; Agnes 80,158; Edward 49,123; Elizabeth 80,158; Frances 65,197; Henry 65,78,80, 118; Richard 26; Thomas

Holland (cont'd), Thomas 5; William 80,158
Holliday, - Lt. 52
Hollingshead, - Mr. 146; Francis 79
Hollis, Thomas 120
Holloway, Isaac 127; John 127
Holly, Charles 82; John 195; William 107
Holman, Joseph 148; Stephen 82
Holmes/Hollmes/Holms, - Lt. 95,232; Andrew 155; John 54,141; Jonathan 104,181,182; Samuel 11; Sarah 182; Stanley 149; Thomas 197
Holt, - /Mr./ 15; John 85
Holton, - /Mr./ 4
Holyorn, - Mr. 108
Home, Charles 24; Elizabeth 23
Homfray, Jeston 163
Honey, Thomas 99
Honeywell, William 162
Hons, Catharine 77,82
Hood, - Mrs. 4
Hoogland/Hoghland/Hoogeland/Hogland, Adrian 166,194; Benjamin 166, 194; Christopher 96; Elbert 166; Jacob 96; John 125,166; William 166,194
Hooker, - Capt. 56
Hoop, James 239
Hooper, Robert Lettice/ Robert Letice 11,21
Hoops, Adam 148
Hope, Alexander 48
Hopkins, Benjamin 171; Mathew 66; Michael 87, 180; Roswell 159; Stephen 159
Hopper, Andrew John 187; John 226; Polly 226
Hopson, Samuel, Jr. 85; Samuel, Sr. 19,85
Hornbrook, Anne 218; Theophilus 218
Horne, John 237; Joseph 55
Horner, George 110
Horsen, Jacob 199; John 199
Horsfield, Israel 169; Thomas 169; Timothy 207
Horsmanden, - Mrs. 137; Anne 203; Daniel 74, 203,216; Mary 74
Horsy, - Mr. 96
Horton, - Capt. 52; Caleb 155; David 160; Elijah 184; Gilbert Budd 184; James 107; James, Jr. 155; Samuel 66; Underhill 155
Hosack, Alexander 176
Hoskins, Stephen 3
Hosmer, John 183,229; Joseph 226; Mary 229
House, Thomas 178
Houseal, Bernard Michael 213
Houseman, Peter 210

Housler, Christopher 106
Houston, - Mr. 128
Hout, Elizabeth 111
Houtvat, - Mrs. 48
Howard, - Ensign 154; Mrs. 28; Mr. 4; Anne 230; Beale 37; Charles 28; James 12; Jonathan 50; Martin 201; Samuel 144; Sheffield 230
Howe/How, - Capt. 28; Gen. Lord 60; Samuel 4
Howell, - /Mr./ 143; Hezekiah, Jr. 127,161; James 39; John 105; Mathew 7; Richard 31
Howey, John 15; Robert 80
Howlin, Eleanor 117; Oliver 117
Hoy, Anne 131; Hugh K. 131; Ralph 15
Hubbard, Benjamin 12; John 12; John, Jr. 12; Joseph 79; Richard 156; William 159,167
Hubbart, Elizabeth 136
Hubbell/Hubbel, Catharine 71; Ichabod 47; William G. 198
Huber, Martin 84
Hubler, Frantz 96
Hude, James 88
Hudson, Eleazer 17; Seth 126; William 195
Huffer, Jacob 111
Huffpouer, Catharine 76; Christean 76
Huggeford, Peter 149
Hughes/Hughs/Hues, Barnabas 88; Daniel 141, 190; John 160; Joseph 48; Malaky 2; Philip 47; Samuel 190; William 76
Huggins, - Miss 184
Hugont, Peter 132
Hukel, Eve 114
Hull, - Col. 127; Dr. 77; Mr. 173; John 127; Joseph 96; Tiddeman 189
Hulse, Anne 40; Ebenezer 40
Humastun, Caleb 87
Humes, Thomas 138
Humphreys, Henry 158; Humphrey 152; John 52
Hunckler, Daniel 41
Hungerford, Samuel 149
Hunt, Eliakim 26; Elvin 162; Glover 147; Henry 221; Jacob 65,69; James 69; Jesse 163; John 11,65,69; Jonathan 5; Josiah 170; Obadiah 8,17; Richard 101; Sampson 80; Thomas 23; Thomas, Jr. 124
Hunter, - Capt. 143; Major General 8,16; Mr. 128; Andrew 82; Anthony 78,111; John 216; Richard 167; Samuel 7,58; William 82
Huntingdon, Countess of

148
Huntting, Jonathan 110
Hurd, Ebenezer 192; Elizabeth 192; James 207
Hureen, Matthias 87
Hurley, Daniel 29
Hurry, Cornelius 156; Thomas 58
Huson, John 23
Hutchins, William 77
Hutchinson/Hutchenson, - Capt. 214; Miss 100; Mr. 224; Francis 226; Hannah 100; John 177, 227; Margery 214; Sally 77; Samuel 11
Hutton, Wm. 157
Huxly, - Capt. 30
Hyam, Uriah 23
Hyatt/Hyat, Abraham 53; Caleb 78,111; John 1
Hyde/Hide, - Mrs. 33; Mr. 33; Benjamin 106; Edward 13,22
Hyer, Cornelius 185; Matthew 125; Peter 118; Walter 185; William 136,185
Hylton/Hilton, Benjamin 221; John 90,237; Mahetabel 33,90; Mary 237; Ralph 30,237; Susannah 221
Hyson, - Capt. 201

Ilchester, Earl of 213
Iliff, William 213
Ilslee, Benjamin 91,101
Imlay, John 130,159; Peter 130
Inch, John 69
Ingersol, - Capt. 40
Inglis/Ingles, - Rev. 196,208,215,220,235, 236,242; Charles 169, 174,187,213,235; Margaret 174,242; Thomas 3
Ingraham, John 12
Innis, William 139
Ireland, William 86
Irwin/Irwen, - Col. 202; George 109; Thomas 190
Isaacs, Abraham 25; Hannah 25; Joshua 25; Ralph 65
Ivers, Thomas 103
Iverson, Richard 51
Ivey, John 4
Izard, Alice 122; Ralph 93,122; Sarah 93

Jackel, John 243
Jackert, Frederick 94
Jacklin, Robert 70,71
Jackson, - Mr. 86; Benjamin 47,68; Edward 52; Ephraim 84; Henry 46; James 5,41,43; John 23,193; Joseph 207; Josiah 197; Thomas 2, 94,236
Jacobs, Henry 32; Ralph 88; Sarah 88
Jacquith, Sarah 152

259

Jager, Balthazar 49
James, - Col. 163; Major
119; Miss 197; Abel
197; John 167; Micajah
185; Richard 125
Jamieson/Jamison, John
97; Robert 57
Jamson, James Lee 201;
John 201
Janeway/Janaway, George
197; William 2
Janney, Robert 84
Jansen/Janse, Johannes
15; Roelef 92
Jaquet, Joseph 58
Jarrat, Alane 16; Hannah
16
Jarvis, Arthur 192; Ben-
jamin 48,49,51,69;
Isaac 161; James 48,51,
190,192,194; Mary 192;
Moses 231; Polly 194;
Samuel 226
Jauncey, - Capt. 26;
James 79,179; James, Jr.
179,210; John, Jr. 173
Jay, Frederick 179; John
185; Sally 185
Jeffers, John 8; Mrs.
John 8; Thomas 17; Mrs.
Thomas 17
Jeffery/Jefferys, Antho-
ny 122; John 78,122;
Mary 122,152; Richard
92,152; Samuel 171
Jelf, - Mrs. 199; Joseph
166,170,199; William
B. 170
Jenkins, - Capt. 193;
/Mr./ 27; David 242;
John 43; Joseph 81;
Richard 225,236,238;
Samuel 214
Jennet, - Lt. 95
Jenney, Robert 12,22
Jepson, William 207
Jewell, James 85; Nathan-
iel 48
Jillet, William 29
Johnscourt, - Mr. 166
Johnson, - Gov. 20; Lady
188; Lt. 98; Mrs. 7,
148; Rev. Dr. 80;
Widow 84; Andrew 96;
Anthony 71; (alias
Dixon), Daniel 29;
David 11; Ebenezer 10;
George 86; Guy 103;
Hezekiah 130; Isaac 94;
Isaiah 164; Jabez 157;
James 136,166; John
34,74,96,158; John Sir
126,175,188; Johnes 92;
Jonathan 26; Margaret
85; Mary 11,163; Na-
thaniel 20; Nicholas
152; Polly 175; Rebe-
cca 233; Richard 26;
Rinoldo 233; Robert 16;
Samuel 159,201; Sarah
10; Simon 63,85,124,
161; William 27,40,123;
William (alias William
Herring) 125; William
Sir 100,103,104,111,
126,175,178,188
Johnston, - Capt. 73,96;
Col. 68; Miss 76,196;

Mrs. 94; /Mr./ 111;
Abraham 47; Alida 169;
Andrew 87,88,90,100,
121; Boulter 169; Da-
vid 31,196; Dick 159;
Elizabeth 75; George
236; Heathcoat/Heath-
cote 182,201; Helena
31; Henry 235; James
2; John 67,88,90,219;
John (alias of Law-
rence Gojion) 165;
Lewis 121,179,182,201;
Rachel 219; Richard
Sir 169; Robert 205;
Samuel 155; Simon 76;
Thomas 233; William
121
Jones, - Capt. 60,68;
Dr. 186; Major General
223; Miss 186; Adriana
210; Anne 122; Benja-
min 148; Betsey 74;
Daniel 203; David 89,
198; Deborah 13,22;
Eben 61; Evan 72,109;
Francis 23; George
Rice 20; Henry 45;
Humphry/Humphrey 74,
171,216; Isaac (alias
of Isaac Solomon) 196;
Jacob 45; James 10,19,
44; Jane 86; John 20,
59,72,80,83,87,114,
127,132; Jonathan 3;
Margaret 106; Rebecca
83; Richard 52,94;
Robert 92; Samuel 81,
180; Suckey 89; Thomas
59,66,72,89,91,109,157,
209; Thomas Shatford
210; William 67
Jordan/Jorden/Jordon, -
Capt. 218; James 166;
John 46; Thomas 102
Josephson, Manuel 88
Jouet, - Miss 230
Joyce/Joice, Edward 110;
Sarah 157
Jubeart, John 140
Judah, Samuel 184
Judd, - Ensign 44
Judson, Augur 171
Juel, Samuel 87
Jump, - Capt. 3; John
89; Valantine 59
June, Thomas 76
Jurianse, Hermon 50
Jurney, Daniel 189
Justee, John 55
Justis, William 124

Kannief, Jeremiah 69
Kanpschneider, John 69
Kantson (or Kanison),
Philip 21
Kar, Patrick 54
Kass, - Mr. 137
Kast, Anna 131; Anne Mary
131; Dorothy 131; Eli-
zabeth 131; Gertruy
131; Johan Jurgh 130;
Johan Jurgh, Jr. 131;
Ludwick 131; Margaret
131; Mary 131; Sarah
131
Katermeyer, Leonard 41

Kavanah, Lawrence 99
Kay, Robert 80
Kearney/Kearny, - /Mr./
112; Isabella 198,221;
Michael 2; Phillip/
Philip 198,221
Keating, John 109,120
Keats, Benjamin 75
Kebble, Stephen 220,222
Keckleman, Thomas 94
Keefe, John 159
Keen, Mounce 148
Keener, - Mr. 187
Keese, William 58
Keir, Moore & 227; Alex-
ander 10
Keirsted, Luke 144
Keiser, Jacob 124
Keith, Daniel 219; Wil-
liam 125
Kellog, Eliphalet 147,
154
Kelly/Kelley, - Mrs. 166;
Mr. 166,175; David 46,
125; Dennis 232; George
25,155; George (alias
William Welch) 32,37;
Henry 75; John 45,123,
224; Mary 180; Nugent
70; Robert 224; Susanna
151; Thomas 29,165;
William 32,48,77,87,
151,204
Kelsall, Johanna 15
Kelso, Anthony 154
Kelsy, James 71
Kemp, William 68
Kempe, John Tabor 116,
176
Kemptie, - Lt. 70
Kendall, Benjamin 122
Kendrick, Capt. E. 34
Keney, - Capt. 25
Kennedy, & Lyle 65,121;
- Lt. 50,108; Abraham
108; Ann 90; Archibald
75,93,108,138; Arthald
9; Catharine 108;
Francis 107; Hugh 157;
Nancy 138; Robert 95,
96; William 89,90,94,
109,150
Kenneway, - Capt. 33
Kennison, Nicholas 101
Kent, - Mr. 57; William,
Jr. 167
Kentish, Thomas 219
Kentzing, Abraham 195
Keriger, George Henry 12
Kerin, Edward 209; Terence
209
Kerr, - Capt. 232,233;
/Miss or Mrs./ 121; Mr.
235; (or Kert?), David
120; Robert 45; Walter
114; William 45
Kerrell, Hugh 49
Kerry, Margaret 23
Kersley, Samuel 20
Kessler, Francis 157
Ketcham, Isaac 139
Keteltas/Ketteltas/
Ketletas/Kettletas,
Abraham 13,40; Charity
158; Gerrit/Garret 13,
158; James 189; Jane
189; John 130,220;
Peter 169,213; Sarah 40;

Kettletas (cont'd),
  Wynant 213
Kettinger, Joshua (alias
  of Joshua Frost) 90
Keys/Keyes, Cornelius 62;
  George 80; James 13;
  Lucy 97; Robert 97
Kibble, Catharine 230;
  Stephen 230
Kidd, Francis 133
Kidder, Benjamin 62
Kidnee, Andries 45; John
  45
Kieff, Daniel 87
Kierstead/Kiersted, Ben-
  jamin 34; Elizabeth 77;
  Luke Benjamin 75; Luke
  John 128; Martha 75
Kilburn, - Mr. 114
Kilby, Christopher 54,
  159
Killbrun, Judith 198;
  Lawrence 198
Kilfoy/Killfoy, Dennis 94;
  Simon 50
Killet, Richard 81
Killock, Oliver 164
Kimball, - Mr. 174
King, Ary 109; Aury 123;
  Charity 123; Cornelia
  227; Edward 5; John
  5,7,88,109,138; Joseph
  103; Linus 138,225,227;
  Marcus 132,137; Matthew
  132,137; Thomas 34,57;
  William 155
Kingman, Elizabeth 33
Kingsbury, Asa 204;
  John 104
Kingsland, John 31; Wil-
  liam 178
Kingston, Francis 209;
  John 103,230
Kinloch, James 56
Kinney, - Mr. 136
Kinnyman, - Capt. 28
Kintzing, Abraham 197
Kipp/Kip, - Capt. 130;
  Benjamin 75; Isaac 133;
  Jacobus 51
Kippin, Sarah 230; Wil-
  liam 230
Kirk, John 182
Kirkindale, Mary 59
Kirkland, Moses 203
Kirkpatrick, John 53
Kirton, William 14
Kirttand, Ezra 134
Kissam, Benjamin 182,238;
  Daniel 237
Kissick, - Mrs. 226;
  Philip 92,98,173,204,
  215,226
Kitzmiller, Jacob 29;
  Martin 29
Klein, John 115
Klinehoff, Paul 105
Knapp, John C. 186
Kneeland, Samuel 143
Kneller, William 185
Kniffin, Jonathan 207
Knight, - Mr. 8; Robert
  108; Thomas 63
Knott, Peter 145
Knowland, - Mr. 44;
  James 31
Knowles, - Admiral 44
Knox, - Col. 202; Henry

  203; Peter 22
Knyphausen, - Gen. 231
Koch, John George 25
Koffer, - Capt. 52
Koffler/Kofeler, Francis
  108,127
Kortwright/Kortright,
  Cornelius 195; Hannah
  210; John 182; Law-
  rence 88,90,135,196,
  210,226; Sally 196
Koster, Joseph 23
Kotts, Conrad 127
Kout, Elizabeth 40
Kozyn, - Mr. 26
Kreamer, Elias 242
Kremer, Philip Barnet 35
Krousher, Mrs. John 44
Kruse, Abraham 155
Kuyper/Kuiper, Cornelius
  63; Hendrick 195
Kysch, Anthon George 215
Kyson, Catharine 161

Lackerman, Isaac 21
Lacy, Cadey 145; Ludovic
  224
Ladley, Archibald 133;
  Polly 133
Laforey, John 57
Lafyear, - Mr. 85
Lagrange, Anna 15
Lahay, John 142
Laight, Benjamin 241;
  Edward 35,40,75,126,
  162,188,241
Laing, Alexander 162;
  Mary 162
Laird, David 218
Lallhie, - Lt. 60
Lamb, James 216; Thomas
  3
Lambert, - Mrs. 182;
  Abner 119; John 165,
  182; Valentine 72
Lamson, Joseph 176
Land, Richard 10
Lander, - Mr. 5
Lane, - Capt. 35; Eliza-
  beth 178; Henry 47,94,
  142,178; Jacob 57;
  John 19; Rachel 94;
  William 1
Langaster, Christopher 62
Langdale, John, Jr. 112
Langdon/Langden, - Capt.
  21; Amos 11,20; John
  204
Langford, Edward 31
Langly, Joseph 111
Langwieder, Joseph 115
Lansingh, Isaac 161
La Portuga, Emanuel 50
Larby, Eliphalet 10,19
Large, Samuel 79; Wil-
  liam 115
Larking, Moses 67
Larrimore, - Mr. 52
Lasant, John 12
Lashel (or Lasher), -
  Mr. 207
Lashly, Mary 161
Latham, Samuel 64; Thom-
  as 237
Lattouch, - /Mr./ 47;
  Isaac 77,109
Lauder, Robert 70
Lauderdale, Earl of 221

Laverty, Edward 110
Lavolet, Anthony 32
Lawler, James 133
Lawrell, George 92
Lawrence/Lawrance, -
  Capt. 60; Mrs. 8; Mr.
  17,55; Abraham 56,89,
  134,196; Benjamin 35;
  Catharine 66; Daniel/
  Danile 56,89,105,111;
  Elisha 195,218; Eliza-
  beth 153; Hannah 225;
  Jacob 165; Job 82;
  John 66,82,104,105,111,
  215,225; Jonathan 105,
  111; Mary 90,195,204,
  218; Rachel 128; Re-
  becca 134; Richard 98,
  111,198,236; Robert 153;
  Susannah 35; Thomas 10,
  37,61,91,105,111,128,
  134,194,197,204,236;
  Uriah 202; Uriah, Jr.
  202; William 44,71,78,
  183,185,236,
Laws, Frederick 92
Lawson, James 134; Peter
  224
Layer, John 23
Layn, Edmund 99
Layson, John 45
Leach/Leech, Clement 163;
  Stephen 35,38,59,60,61
Leake, Andrew 128; Anne/
  Ann 105,182; John 35,66,
  77,85,95; Robert 105,182
Leaming, Jeremiah 129
Learmonth, Alexander 228;
  John 228
Leaton, James 43
Leavenworth, Edmund 68
Lechmere, Thomas 110
Le Count, John 45; P. 115
Ledby, John 87
Ledyard, John 117
Lee, Alexander 216; Cesar
  236; Elizabeth 94; Ja-
  cob 6,15; Jared 152;
  Mary 90,153,201; Rhoda
  152; Seth 153,201; Wil-
  liam 149,192; (or
  Grove), William 173
Lees, John 16
Lefever/Lefaver, Andries,
  Jr. 243; Nathaniel 243
Lefferts, - Mr. 140;
  Abraham 127; Dirck 84;
  Jacobus 134; Jacobus L.
  225; Leffert 241; Maria
  225
Leggett/Legget, Gabriel
  84,214; Isaac 166; Jo-
  shua 10; Martha 214;
  William 6,7
Legrand, Peter 21
Le Grange/Legrange, Ber-
  nardus 238; Frances
  238; Johannes 4
Leguiere, Abraham 100
Lehommedieu, Ezra 167
Lehunt, - Capt. 87
Leighton, John 17; Samuel
  17
Leinbeck, - Mr. 177
Leinberger, John 41
Leiz, George 182
Le Montet/Le Mountes (or
  Le Montes?), John 7,16

261

Lenox, Catharine 240
Lent, Abraham 210; Jaco-
  bus 218
Lentot, - Mr. 85
Lenzi, Philip 211
Leonard, - (a lad) 41;
  Capt. 234; Elizabeth
  139; Henry 137; John 1;
  Silas 139; Thomas 108;
  William 174; Zephaniah
  115
Le Roy/Leroy, - Miss 196;
  Grace 125; Jacob 157,
  196; John 125
Lesebeater, Peter 208
Lesher, John 38
Leslie/Lesley, Alexander
  127; C. Frederick 41;
  Edmund 115,118
Lester, John 8
Letteridge, John 176
Leverage, John 200
Leveredge, Samuel 33
Levergood, - Mrs. 57; Mr.
  57
Leves, Richard 107
Levine, John 172
Levit, William 4
Levy, - Mr. 99; Hayman
  189; Joshua 68; Nathan
  33
Lewis, - Capt. 39; Mrs.
  226; Charles 191;
  Daniel 31,155; Deborah
  104; Ellis 84; Israel
  155; Jacob 157; John
  75,135,226,240; Joseph
  161; Leonard 82; Robert
  & Son 101; William 92
Lewtagee, Lewis 92
Leycock, - Mrs. 41
Leyster, Jacob 5
Liddel/Liddle, - Dr. 81;
  (or Leddle), Joseph,
  Jr. 37
Liggett/Ligget, Abraham
  98; Gabriel 68; William
  14,98
Lightfoot, Alexander 47;
  Jean 52; Michael 34
Lightin, Emanuel 89
Lightly (or Pretty), Jo-
  seph 107
Liken, Michael 97; Phaebe
  97
Likens, John 84; Mary 84
Lilburn, John 127
Lilley, James 70
Lindsay/Lindsey, - Capt.
  116,236; David 177;
  John 91; William 11
Linford, Christian 223;
  James 223; Rebecca 223;
  William 223
Lippincott, - Mr. 148
Lipseed, James 163
Lisk, Benjamin 198
Lispenard/Lispenards, -
  Alderman 84; Anthony
  65; David 65; Ketty
  65; Leonard 65,66,73,
  108
Litchfield, John 197
Litterel, - Col. 233
Little, John 133,151;
  Nathaniel 157; Stephen
  161
Littlefield, Mary 104;

Moses 104
Livingston, Alderman 103;
  Justice 199; Miss 85,
  176,178; Mr. 59,201;
  Rev. 185; Catharine
  43,46,66; Cornelius
  84; Elizabeth 225;
  Henry 161,186,199;
  Henry, Jr. 186; James
  29,58,99,121,178,182,
  184,225; Jenney 29;
  John 46,129,177,196,
  199; Kitty 185; Mary
  126; Molly 163; Peggy
  58; Peter B. 241;
  Peter Robert/Peter R.
  58,121,198; Peter Van
  Brugh/Peter Van Brug/
  Peter Van Brough/
  Peter V.B. 82,85,126,
  148,153,163; Philip
  35,39,43,46,67,82,100,
  108,110,187,191,199,
  215; Ph., Jr. 140,191;
  Polly 70,198; Robert
  58,70,108,148,197;
  Robert, Jr. 108,157;
  Robert G. 35; Robert
  Gilbert 185; Robert
  James 121,151; R.R. 77;
  Robert R. 148,176;
  Sally 185,199; Suckey
  199; Thomas 144,195;
  William 117,137,148,
  186
Lloyd/Loyd/Loyde, - Lt.
  60,232; David 217; Ed-
  ward 37; Elianor 3;
  John 67,82; Joseph 63;
  Nathaniel 29; Thomas
  90
Lockwood, Joshua 69;
  Phineas 132
Lodge, Abraham 32,57,190;
  Catharine 190
Lodwick, - Col. 12
Logan, Alexander 94;
  James 139
Logue, Ephraim 116
London, John, Earl of 54
Long, - Capt. 11; Miss
  200; George 71; Henry
  148; James 219; John
  3,72,75,219; Leonard
  53; Margaret 90; Mar-
  tin 147; Samuel 155;
  Thomas 229
Longfield, Henry 160
Longstreet, Aaron, Jr.
  191; Christianna 222
Longworth, Isaac 100,195;
  Thomas 49
Loobey, Darby 82
Looney, - /Mr.7/Ferry7
  102
Loosely, Anne 230;
  Charles 230
Lopez, Aaron 121; Sally
  121
Lord, Abigail 146; Isaac
  217
Lorentz, John George 230
Loring, Joshua 235; Phi-
  lip 153
Lott, - Mr. 225; Mr.
  Treasurer 158; Abraham
  91,130,131,145,201;
  Abraham E. 190; Alice

201; Andrew 201; Chari-
  ty 238; Engelbert 119;
  Hendrick 91; Hester 91;
  Maria 225; Rebecca 190
Loudon, Frederick 102;
  Samuel 170
Louzada, Aaron 67
Lovell, John 156
Lovie, George 219
Low/Lowe, - Mr. 47; Wid-
  ow 140; Abraham 45;
  Ann 166; Cornelius 36,
  73,144,208; Cornelius,
  Jr. 145; Cornelius P.
  140,166; Isaac 144,145;
  Margaret 36; Peter 140,
  144,153; Sally 73
Lowder, James 45; Jona-
  than 142; Sanmuel /Sam-
  uel7 26
Lowey, James 140; Jane
  140; Michael 140
Lownsbury, William 231
Lowrey, James 52
Lowther, - Capt. 121;
  Mr. 44
Loxford, William Newman
  201
Loyse, Simon 105; Susan-
  nah 105
Lucas, Charles 144; El-
  dert 49; Frind 51
Luce, Elizabeth 152
Ludington, William 37
Ludlow, - Judge 219;
  Anne 219; Cary 125,226;
  Daniel 175; Elizabeth
  175; Gabriel 180;
  Gabriel, Jr. 75;
  Gabriel H. 141,153,208;
  Henry 68,174; John, Jr.
  175; Mary 174; Nancy
  75, 153; Sally 68
Lum, Matthew 163; Samuel
  44
Lunan, Alexander 147
Luney (or Lewney), Peter
  52
Lupardus, Christianus 34
Lurting, Robert 7,8;
  William 8
Lusk, - Adjutant 232
Luter, Catharine 110
Lutwyche/Lutwidge, -
  Capt. 79; Edward G. 241;
  Jane 241
Lutz, Simon 69
Lycan, Andrew 114
Lycorn, Mrs. St. Luke 85
Lyde, Mary Belcher 20
Lydig, Phillip 125
Lyell, Catherine/Catherin
  3,21; David 3; Fenwick
  3
Lyhin, Mary (alias Moll
  White) 83
Lyle, Kennedy & 65,121;
  Abraham 121,123,157,
  159; James 121
Lyman, - Col. 62; Elihu
  60
Lynch/Linch, - Mrs. 176;
  Cornelius 28; Daniel
  240; James 107; John
  203,237; Prier 237;
  Rebecca 28; Thomas 100,
  237
Lyng, John Burt 152

M'Neal/M'Niel/M'Neil/
M'Neill/M'Neel
(cont'd), - Col. 233;
Arthur 61,66; David 111;
Hector 210; James 32;
Samuel 67; Thomas 81
M'Neelage, Donald 67
MacNobb, John 16
Macomb/Macom, John 132;
Seth 241
M'Peak, Dennis 88
M'Pherson/MacPherson/
M'Farsen, - Lt. 60;
Andrew 65; James 138;
James, Jr. 83
M'Queen, - /Mr./ 97
McQuid, Barnaby 46
M'Quoid, Anthony 49;
Hugh 61
M'Vicker/McVicker, -
Capt. 118; /Mr./ 99;
Archibald 122,150,208

Mabee, Simon 171
Mabson, - Mr. 82
Machon, Samuel 19
Mack, Adam 27
Mackron, - Mr. 53
Madan, - Lt. Col. 221
Maddin, John 94
Madison, Samuel 189
Magin, Sarah 154; William
154
Maginis, Isabella 51;
Paul 51
Magwigin, Patrick 24
Mahane, James 12
Mahony, Dennis 73
Main, William 187
Mains, Matthew 204;
Thomas 204
Mair, - Lt. 233
Maitland, - Lt. Col. 221;
Ann Lady 164; Charles,
Earl of Lauderdale 164;
Richard 164
Malcolm, - Mrs. 32; Wil-
liam/Wm. 97,129,141
Mallbone, Godfrey 35
Mallet, - Mr. 101;
Catharine 210; Jonathan
210; Lewis 97,101
Mallison, Aaron 111
Mallone, Co 2 13
Maloan, Laughland 9
Maltby, John 85
Manchester, Joseph 67;
William 15
Mange, Jemima 100
Mann/Man, Elias 230;
Elizabeth 77; Isaac
66,77,193; Johannah 51
Manning, Jeremiah 189;
Peter 8; Thomas 62
Mansfield, - Capt. 25
Manwaring, David 120;
Patty 120
March, Jacob 108; John
12,21; William 108
Marduff, John 27
Mares, Joseph 141
Mariner, William 100
Markeshin, John 67
Markham, Joanna 1; John
12; Wm. 1
Markland, John 165
Marks, Joseph 81

Marlin, Abraham 130;
Daniel 130
Marlow, Samuel 142
Marr, William 19
Marrow, Martin 5
Mars, Humphry 126
Marschalk, Abraham 21;
Andrew 222; Andries
21; Francis 87,94,
205; Isaac 87,94,161
Marsden, - Capt. 71
Marsh, - Mrs. 229;
Daniel 169; Elizabeth
142; Isaac 202;
Joshua 142; Mary 202;
Peter 101; Samuel 106
Marshall/Marshal,
Christopher 175;
George 137,192; Henry
137; James 76,91,207;
John 28,101,159; Jo-
seph 63; William 137,
220
Marston, - Miss 218;
Mrs. 179,240; John
128,240; Ketty 65;
Margaret 138; Mary
178,202; Nancy 48;
Nathaniel 48,64,65,
70,138,178,193,198,
207,216; Nathaniel,
Jr. 220; Polly 207;
Rachel 128; Thomas
65,218
Martin, - Capt. 70,224,
238; Major 210; Ed-
ward 105; Elizabeth
216; Ephraim 204;
Isaac 90,230; Jacob
123; John 25,85,210,
216,218; Josiah 39,
216; Sarah 117; Thom-
as 117; William Thom-
as 39
Marton, John 135; Re-
becca 135
Mash, - Mrs. 226; Sam-
uel 46
Mason, Andrew 114;
Catharine 220; George
139; John 34; Sebast-
ian 177; Thomas 220
Master, Legh 157
Masterman, George 67
Masters, Polly 163
Masterton, David 237
Mather, John 10
Mathews/Matthews/Mat-
hew, - Lt. 63; Miss
216; David 157,216,
232,; Hugh 29; Isaac
15; Isaac, Jr. 15;
James 18; John 118;
Julius (or Justus?)
106; Moses 84; Vin-
cent 186
Mathewson, Charles 221
Matthisen, Nicholas 3
Mattysen, Cornelius 15
Mattocks, - Mrs. 177
Maturin, Gabriel 193
Maugridge, William 23
Mauritze, - Mrs. 57
Maverick, - Widow 144;
Samuel 144
Mawe, James 173
Maxson, John 180
Maxwell, George 196;

William 206
May, Edward 92
Maybury/Mayburry/May-
berry, Thomas 10,25,178
Mayfield, Joseph 86
Mayhew, Elizabeth 120;
Jonathan 116,120
Mead, Abraham 151; Amos
151; Isaac 118,123
Meader, George 133
Meaks, - Mr. 46
Meanderson, Joseph 80
Mears/Meares, Francis 34;
Lewis 30
Mease, John 129
Mecom, Benjamin 117
Medcalf, William 8
Mee, John 213
Meed, Andrew 2
Meek, William 196
Megoon, John 21
Meharg, Alexander 197
Mekay, Daniel 5
Mekly, Jacob 96
Mels, James 203
Melvin, Eleazer 34
Menagh, William 77
Mendes, Abraham Perarer
121; Sally 121
Menzies, Alexander 229;
John 2; Sarah 229
Mepherson, John 18
Mercer, - Col. 48; Dr.
201; James 54; John 45;
Lucy 145,164,179;
Richard 121; William
145,164,179
Mercereau/Mersereau, -
Mrs. 111; Joshua 100
Mercier, William 72
Meredith, - Capt. 224;
Charles 239; Gertrude
224
Merenes, Johannes 27
Merrick, - Rev. 86; Noah
86
Merritt/Merrit, David
168; Gabriel 168;
George 168; Mary 9;
Wm. 9
Merry, Sarah 14
Merryman, Nicholas, Jr.
190
Mershon, Howten 201
Mersyer, Andrew 42
Mesier, Abraham 160,193;
Peter 150,178
Mesnard, Daniel 19,243
Messcar, Francisco 242
Mestayer, Elias 9
Mesurvey, George 69
Meyer, Andrias 19; Fred-
erick 52; John 99; Mrs.
John 91
Middagh/Middah, - Lt. 209;
Garret 134; Jacobus 61
Middlesworth, John 123
Middleton, - Col. 151;
Dr. 158,227; Miss 151;
Aaron 4; Peter 228;
Susannah 158
Mier, Jacob 43; John 43
Mifflin, Elizabeth 10;
John 10
Miford, John 161
Mill, John 166
Millan, Philip 208; Wil-
liam 109

Lynn, - Mr. 44; Moses 177
Lynott, Elizabeth 153;
  (or Lynett), Thomas 153,
  155
Lynsen, Abraham 38,63,70,
  71,125,242; Catharine
  71,125; Elizabeth 63;
  Magdalen 95,242
Lyon/Lyons, John 103;
  Mary 60; Samuel 60,215;
  Thomas 183
Lysler, - /Mr./ 128
Lyster, - Lt. 233
Lystrum, Johannes 44

M'Adam, - Capt. 54;
  Glorianna Margaretta
  213; John, Jr. 213;
  John Steuart 220; Wil-
  liam 220
M'Alieff, Henry 110
M'Alin, George 111
McAllaster, James 52
M'Alpine, Daniel 74
McArthur, John 152
M'Atee, Hugh 51
Mackaowell, Alexander 2
M'Bride, James 191,195;
  Phebe 195; Rose 73
M'Cafferty, Bartholomew
  49
McCain, Adam 102
M'Calay, - Mr. 205;
  Daniel 196
McCall, - Mr. 102; John
  23
M'Camly, David 4
McCammel, Charles 19
McCann/McCan, Hugh 185;
  William 164
M'Cardell, Philip 108
McCarroll, - /Mr./ 121
M'Carthy, James 118
McCartney, James 77,83,
  135,154,158
M'Carty, John 45; Timo-
  thy 108
M'Causland, Connelly 216
M'Cew, Mary 96; William
  96,111
McClaghry, James 170;
  Patrick 170
M'Clean/McClean, - Capt.
  232; John 104,148,201;
  Mary 70,71; Susannah
  201; William 50
M'Clellan, David 41
M'Clenachan, Capt. Ro.
  191
M'Cleve, John 75
M'Clone, - Mr. 133
M'Clure, Francis 187
M'Comb/Macomb, Eleazer
  131; John 112
M'Connell/M'Connel,
  Esther 29; James 29,91
M'Cord, Mary 45
M'Cormick/McCormack, -
  Mr. 32,93; Alexander
  115,119,124; Daniel
  154,158,194,230,239;
  James 219; Mary 115
M'Cowen, Thomas 135
M'Coy/MacCoy/Macoy, -
  Mr. 92; Daniel 45,142;
  John 224; William 8
M'Crea, Catharine 140;

James 140; Janey 209
M'Cready/M'Creddie/M'Cri-
  die, James 231; Jane
  193; John 189
M'Cullom/M'Collum, Dun-
  can 51; Phoebe 227
M'Cullough, Mary 112;
  William 183
M'Curdy, Archibald 169;
  Daniel 168
M'Cutchon/M'Cutchin, -
  Capt. 163; Hugh 50
M'Cuw, James 176
McDaniel (or M'Donald)
  - Ensign 57; Mr. 98;
  Cornelius 70; Daniel
  106,164; Hugh 196;
  James 136; John 50,86;
  Lewis 185
M'Davitt, P. 207
M'Dermot/M'Deirmat, Mar-
  garet 29; Michael 17;
  Philip 29
M'Diarmed, Hugh 195
M'Donagh, Henry 107;
  James 122
McDonald, Alexander 18,
  162; Allan 224; Ann 220
  Catharine 133; Collin
  133,167; David 97;
  Donald 237; Henrietta
  224; James 49; John 154;
  William 49,143
M'Donel, - /Mr./ 6
M'Donough, Terence 183
M'Dougall/M'Doogall/M'
  Dougel, - Col. 203;
  Gen./Major General 204,
  241; Alexander 234;
  Mary
M'Dowell/McDowel, - /Mr./
  49; Mr. 45; Andrew 102
McDurcan, Patrick 186
M'Ellroy, Edward 109
McElvey, Patrick 143
M'Entire, John 186;
  Peter 102
McEuen/M'Ewen, Daniel
  148; James 208
M'Evers/M'Ever, - Miss
  220; Mr. 55; Charles
  76,85,134,149; Eilza-
  beth /Elizabeth/ 134;
  James 78,134,220; John
  38,67; Margaret 85;
  Mary 38; Patrick 67
M'Fadden, - /Miss or
  Mrs./ 124
M'Fall, Robert 170
M'Farland, Daniel 147
M'Farlane, Andrew 176;
  Walter 176
M'Farling, Richard 54
M'Fee, - Capt. 240
Magee/M'Ghee/Mackgee,
  Alexander 90; Brian
  46; Hugh 92; James 92,
  98,183; Michael 107;
  Robert 148; Samuel 222;
  William (alias of John
  Davison) 19
M'Gill, Michael 58
M'Gillis, Gillis 211
McGin, - Capt. 40
M'Glathay, Thomas 84
MacGowin/M'Goun, - Mrs.
  183; Jeremiah 187
M'Gra/Magrah/Magra,

Catharine 111; James
  185; Roger 31
McGrisor, Alexander 80
M'Guire, Mary (alias of
  Mary Williams) 120;
  Patrick 162
McHugh, James 28,70
M'Hurin, Otho 59
M'Illroy, William 55
McIntaylor (or Makist),
  John 12
M'Intosh/Mackintosh, -
  Lt. 95; Aeneas 221;
  George 102; John 72,76;
  Laghlan 227
McInvin, John 81
M'Isaac, Malcolm 226
M'Kain, Hugh 180
McKay/Mackay/M'Kee/M'Kie,
  Elizabeth 189; John 97;
  Patrick 201; Peter 189;
  Thomas 219
M'Kean/McKeen, - Capt.
  231; Adam 25; Robert
  127; Thomas 95
Mackeffee, Daniel 12
M'Kennet, John 54
M'Kenney, James 174
M'Kenzie/M'Kinzie/M'Kinze/
  M'Kinzy, - Capt. 54;
  Alexander 221; Charles
  206; Donald 152; James
  116,132; John 206
Mackey, James 53
McKillip, Hugh 99
M'Kim, Mary 114; William
  114
M'Kinley/M'Kinly, William
  51,130
M'Kinney, John 109; Thom-
  as 46
M'Knight, Agnes 95; John
  91,95,110
McLachan - Lt. Col. 230
M'Lanachan, James 96
M'Lane, Donald 210,224;
  Henrietta 224; John 243
M'Larnan, John 186
M'Laughlin/M'Laughlan/
  M'Lauglin, - Mr. 138;
  Daniel 140; Edward 92;
  James 10,19; John 85;
  William 35
M'Lean/MacLean, - Capt.
  232; Dr. 225; Anne 230;
  Donald 201,235,243,;
  John 167; Peter 230
M'Lintock, John 190
M'Mahan, Dennis 86
McManus/MacManus, Daniel
  66; Philip 112,115,120
M'Masters, Andrew 163
M'Michael/M'Michell, John
  65,68
M'Miking, Patrick 189
McMillan, Anthony 107;
  John 136; Martha 107
M'Muchan, Thomas 31;
  Michael, Michael 119;
  Samuel 92
M'Murdy, John 224
McNachten, Alexander 11;
  Neil 11
M'Nalley, Arthur 120;
  Mary 120
M'Namar, Daniel 127
M'Neal/M'Niel/M'Neil/
  M'Neill/M'Neel, - Col.

Miller, - /Mr./ 41; Abraham 52; Alexander 52; Charles 110,138; Christina 189; Christopher 158,243; Eleazer, Jr. 183; Henry 86; Henry (alias of Hendrick Right) 71; Jacob 16; James 150,193; Johannis 149; John 44,80,103, 105,108,114,127; John (alias of John Cavendish) 115; John Christophel 70; John Godfried 63; Joseph 105; Nicholas 96; Patty 48; Paul 158; Peter 119; Richard 179; Robert 155, 159; Samuel 63; Sarah 149,243; Stephen 189; Thomas 48,126,158; William 44,190,208
Mills, - Mrs. 58; Mr. 128; Alexander 5; Elisha 171; James 15,78, 158,160; Joshua 162; Mary 187; Susannah 152; Treat 171; William 184, 187
Milne, Edmund/Edmond, 139,153
Milner, Edward, Sr. 139; Hannah 139
Milwater, John 59
Mines, Joshua 89
Minor, - Mr. 127
Minors, Norton 76
Minot, Peter 96
Minser, George 44
Mitchell/Mitchel, - Capt. 119; Mr. 3,17; Alexander 57; Andrew 97, 230; Ebenezer 27; George 35; Jacamiah/ Jecamiah 147,149,152; James 53; John 46,63, 74; Joseph 53; Margaret 17; Robert 142; Sarah 147,152; William 53
Mitcheltree, Mrs. Hugh 43
Moffatt, Thomas 241
Molineaux, William 190
Moloy, William 52
Molton, William 118
Monach, John 241
Monckton, - Lt. Col. 215
Moncrieffe/Moncrief, - Lt. Col. 233; Major 182; Mrs. 182; Helena 187,200; Margaret 95, 207; Thomas 95,187,200, 207; William 233
Monford, John 99
Monfort, John 182
Monk, Christopher 144
Monkton, - General 73
Monroe/Monro, - Lt. 9; Hector 47; Hector Shirley 47; Hugh 17
Montanye, Jacobus & Co. 117; Jacobus 84,167; Mary 176; Peter 176; Vincent 176
Montgomery/Montgomerie, - General 199; Catharine 53; George 15; John 4; Michael 105;

Richard 101,176; Thomas 139
Montjoy, Benjamin 143
Montrisure, - Capt. 227
Montross/Montros, John 150
Moody, Henry 9
Moon/Moen, Christopher 83; Jacob 4,24
Moone, Elizabeth 47,50; Thomas 35,47,50
Mooney, James 183; John 36
Moore/Moor/More, & Keir 227; - Alderman 20; Capt. 58,195; Col. 71, 75,86; Lt. 57; Mr. 44; Rev. 238; Alexander 24, 121,159; Anne 82,86; Augustine 131,165; Barbara 39; Benjamin 214; Charity 214; Daniel 224; Deliverance 6; Fanny 133; Frances 71,236; Francis 57; George 234; Grace 220; Henry 122; Henry Sir 140; Hezekiah 203; Jacob 39; James 6,35,40,195; John 2,4,35,118,119, 135,159,178,235,236; Lambert 123,188; Mrs. Lambert 123; Mary 130, 131,165; Peggy 231; Quintane 26; Samuel 160; Susanna 86; Thomas William 82,86,220; William 35,94,103,133, 228
Moorehouse, John 69,164; Stephen 69
Moores, John 116
Moorhead, John 180
Moreton, - Mr. 37
Mcrey, Joseph 174
Morgan, - Mr. 168,214, 233; Anne 180; Benjamin 180; Caleb 85,166; James 235; John 189; Lawrence 63,135; Luke (alias of Luke Ward) 115; Nicholas 239; Owen 44
Morley, Thomas 75
Morphy, John 6
Morrell/Morrel/Morrill, Amos 74; Jacob 155, 173,198; Jonathan 105, 155; Levy 44; Phebe 79; Salyer 150; Samuel 79, 155; Thomas 155; William 107
Morris, - Capt. 88; Miss 197; Mrs. 127; Daniel 92; Elizabeth 121; Euphemia 194; Helana 238; John 118; Lewis 6,68,87,107,112,113, 167,194,197,233,238; Matthew 121; Nicholas 69; Patrick 178; Richard 68,107; Robert Hunter 100; Sally 68; Sarah 233; William 132
Morrison/Morison, - Capt. 74,194; Mrs. 241; Mr. 95; Donald 56;

James 60,109,201; John 241; Jonathan 63
Morse, Benjamin 118; Edward 14; Seth 31
Morsom, Richard 225
Mortier, Abraham 159
Morton, - Capt. 144; Dimond 203; John 131, 241
Mosby, Benjamin 117
Moses, David 99; Isaac 189; Jacob 158; Michael 23
Moss, William 211
Mott, - Mr. 114; Adam 229; Jacob 103,227; John 229; Martha 227; Patrick 32; Richard 227; William 47,134
Mount, Matthias 156
Mowatt, John 209
Mowrey, Joshua 118
Muchmore, Ebenezer 124; Lucy 124
Muckle, Robert 18
Mud, Francis 77
Muhlenberg, F. 201
Muir, - Capt. 80
Muirson, George 127; Mary 127
Mulharon (or M'Caron), Richard 86
Mulhaus, - Mr. 44
Mulligan, Cook 201; Hercules 190
Mullin, Edward 112; Thomas 135
Mulliner, Joseph 231
Mullock, Joshua 170
Mum, Catharine 182
Mumford, Elisha 104; Samuel 139; William 104
Munn, Jonathan 27
Munro, Barnabas 116; Pardon 79
Munsell/Monsell, Joseph 36,119
Munson, - Mrs. 5
Murphy/Murphey, Alexander 143; Andrew 140; Dominie 52; Edmund 58; Hannah 52; Peter 187; Reynolds 87; Thomas 132, 138
Murray/Murry, - Capt. Lt. 60; Cornelius 138; George 243; Grace 36; James 99,117,126,144, 199,210,218; James Jeffray 199; John 76, 92,191; Joseph 36,51, 66,76,109; Lewis 198; Luke (alias of Luke Ward) 115; Mary 234; Michael 46; Nathaniel 219; Robert 234; William 93
Murtry, Hugh 176
Muttony, David 114
Mutts, Johannes 54
Myer, - Widow 132; Adolph 132; Andrew 115,138; Gerardus 144; Gertje 138; Gertryde 162; Ide 144; James 138; John 132,139; John Ide 144; John R. 159; Lawrence 170; Margreta 40; Mary

Myer (cont'd), Mary 159; Nancy 139
Myers, - Mr. 173; George 167; John 134,197; Myer 30,38,189; William 220
Myford, John 193
Myrack, John 40; Mrs. John 40

Napier, - Capt. 222; Lord 222; Mrs. 222
Narbury, Peter 57
Narran, Thomas 62
Nartlow, - Lt. 36
Nash, - Gen. 213
Nasmus, William 34
Nealan, Bridget 66
Nealson, Duncan 111; Mary Anne 111
Neat, William 197
Neavin, James 116
Needham, - Capt. 60
Neer, Zachariah 145
Neil/Neill, Henry 115; Sarah (alias of Sarah Pain) 116
Neilson, James 127
Nelson, James 79; John 25,27
Nenegrare, Charles Augustus 7
Nesbitt/Nesbet, Cunningham & 47,86; Jonathan 111
Nestell, Jasper 186; Martinus 186
Nevil/Nevill/Neville, Francis 129; John 8,17; Samuel 8,106; Sarah 8,17
Nevison, Peter 8
Nevius, David 195; Susannah 195
Newbold, William 53
Newborne, Samuel 214
Newcomb, Elisha 167; Zacheus 150
Newell, - Mr. 34
Newkirk, William 89
Newlands, Alexander 19; James 19
Newling, - Mr. 76
Newman, Jonathan 119; Sarah 119
Newton, Christopher 192; Elizabeth 192; Jacob 132
Neyson, Mrs. Balsar 44
Nicholas, Eleanor 242; John 32
Nichol/Nicholl, Charles 194; William 139
Nichols/Nicholls, - Capt. 187; Ephraim 105; Hezekiah 161; Margaret 164; Mary Magdalen 117; Richard 164,198,227
Nicholson, Adam 43; Finnly 206; George 111; Mary 118
Nickels, - Mr. 57
Nickerson, Ameli or Ansell 167; Deborah 20; Nehemiah 20; Thomas 167
Nickles, John 148

Nickson, Ashel 124
Nicoll/Nicol, Stewart & 202; Benjamin 65,72, 125; Charity 158; Charles 163,210,227, 229; Edward 229; Elice 226; Glorianna Margaretta 213; Henry 219, 226; James 208; Joanna 167; John 234; William 4,135,158,167, 213,223
Nicolls/Nicols, John 25; Jonathan 24; Richard 184
Nightingale, Thomas 217
Nitchman, Martain 41
Nixon, John 141; Robert 238; Thomas 99
Noah, Frederick 48
Noel & Hazard 158; Garret 205
Nold, Philip 122
Nolte, John Henry 215
Noon, Thomas 107
Noonan, Robert 194
Nordbergh, John 238
Norman, Edward 66
Norris, - Mr. 153; Frances 240; George 34,167,169; Isaac 16, 116; John 6,166,168, 223; Mary 147
North, Elizabeth 104; John 104; Thomas 99
Northover, Elizabeth 25; Richard 25
Northrop, John 163
Northrup, Joseph 56
Norton, George 66; Peirce George Cope 220; Ralph 101; Thomas 102
Norwood, - /Mr./ 61; Andrew 165; Cornelius 165; Richard 165
Nugent, Richard 116
Nutter, Valentine 218, 241
Nutts, James 24
Nutty, John 20
Nye, Remember 242

Oakes/Oaks, George 203; Thomas 51
O'Brien/O'Brian, Charles 165; Darby 32,37; John 12,54,157; Mary 83; Rose 124
Occum, - Rev. 166
Oddle, Thomkin 205
Odell/Odel, James 204; Smith 160
Odiorne, - Mr. 56
Odwaller, - Mr. 40
Ogden, - Judge 199; Mrs. 200; Amos 190; David 100,137,195,200; Elizabeth 189,226; Euphemia 199; Hannah 199; Isaac 161; Jacob 100, 189,195,226; John Cousens 136; Jonathan 30; Josiah 100,195; Mary 136,161; Mathias 91; Moses 88,90,103, 106,136; Nathan 151, 155; Nicholas 199,209;

Robert, Jr. 91,136; Samuel 167,194; Timothy 119,203; Uzal 97
Oge (alias Sunderland), James 108
Ogilvie, - Capt. 75; Rev. 184; Ann Lady 164; James 81; James, Earl of Findlater 164; John 138,191,193; Margaret 138; William 90
O'Hara, Henry 203; John 78
Okerson, Samuel 237
Oldham, - Capt. 232
Oldman, Joseph 11
Oliphant/Olyphant, David 18; William 107,119
Oliver, - Capt. 202; Lt. Gov. 184; /Mr./ 41; James 175; John 114
Ollis, - /Mr./ 156
Olney, Nedediah 202
Onderdonk/Onderdonck, - Miss 188; Henderick/ Hend. 74,135; Henry 188,189; Petrus 135
O'Neal/O'Niel, Michael 156; Owen 114
Oneidon, Dennis 53
Onion, Stephen 2
Oram, William 156
Orchard, Elizabeth 221; John 221
Oreer, John 69
O'Reiley, F. Luke 136
Ormes, Samuel 128
Ormsby/Ormesby, - Capt. 58; John 6,15
PeirceOrr, Robert 108
Orridge, James 209
Orser, Johannis 64
Ortindn, Mathias 115
Orvis, David 2
Osborn/Osborne/Osburn, - Capt. 71; Abner 140; Abraham 186; Danvers Sir 32; Elizabeth 33; Jacob 145; John 33
Osgood, Silas 80
Otis, Amos 159
Otlay, Anthony 67
Otter, - Lt. 68; Joannah 104; Sarah 104
Otterson, William 66
Otway, - Lt. Gen. 47; Charles 51; Joseph 123
Oughton, - Col. 87; Thomas 98
Outerbridge, - Capt. 183; Sally 183
Outman, Samma (or Famma) 4
Overing, John 118
Overy, Peter 16
Owen/Owens, - Capt. 234; Charles 19; David 46; William 204
Owings, Samuel, Jr. 164, 170
Oxnard, Thomas 38
Oyl, Alexander 112

Pachal, Thomas 6
Page, - Ensign 50
Paine/Pain, Edward 6,15; George 116; John 31;

266

Paine/Pain (cont'd),
(alias Neil), Sarah 116
Painter, John 13,22
Palding, Abraham 90; Jo-
seph 90; Joseph, Jr. 90
Palmer, - Mr. 142;
Charles 6; Eliakim 28;
Isaac 34; John 102;
Silas 130; Thomas 28,
202; William 6
Pannil, - Sergt. 57
Panton, - Lt. 138; Fran-
cis 213
Parant, Nathan 198
Pardy, John 66
Park, Joseph 77; Thomas
77
Parker, Charles 155;
David 144; Jacob 16,
39; James 4,119,146,
169,182,201; Jesse 62;
Mary 146,169; Matthew
242; Samuel Franklin
221; Sarah 121
Parkin, - Commissary 233
Parkins, - Mr. 25
Parks, Samuel 74; William
3
Parmyter, Thomas 7,20
Parnham, Mary 168
Parris, Alexander 8
Parsells/Parcels/Parsels/
Parsell, Abraham 73,
235; Francis (alias of
Francis Personel) 174;
Mathias 205; Thomas 116
Parslow, Stephen 6
Parsons, William 176
Partridge, Mrs. Perez 91;
Elizabeth 136; Samuel
136
Patraway, James 162
Patrick, - /Capt./ 30;
William 10
Patter, John 87
Patterson, - Capt. 136;
Mr. 36; John 47; Thomas
190
Pattison, John 48
Patton/Patten, Abraham
209; James 39; Nathan-
iel 221
Paul, John 58; Moses 166
Pawling, Albert 26
Paxon, William 179
Paxton, Andrew 2; Roger
14
Payne, Benjamin 84; Wil-
liam 113
Paynter, - Lt. 99; Jacob
45
Payton/Peyton, - Capt.
13,22; Nancy 203; Sam-
uel 19; Thomas 203;
William 21
Peace, James 45
Peacock, William 238
Pearce, Ann 237; Nathan,
Jr. 202; Samuel 209,
237; Vincent 6
Pearles, Uriah 41
Pearsall, - /Mr./ 95;
Israel 64; Nathaniel 49,
64; Thomas 64,103,158
Pearse, Thomas 77
Pearson, Daniel 157;
Isaac 4; John 165
Pearss, William 237

Peck, - Capt. 179; Ben-
jamin 65; James 41
Peckin, William 158
Pedly, Thomas 221
Peek, John 15
Peeple, Mrs. Jacob 47
Peet, Thomas 76
Peggs, Richard 81
Peirson, Robert 5
Pell, Evert 49; John 52,
110; John, Sr. 52;
Joshua, Jr. 199; Mary
232; Samuel 143,232;
Thomas 209
Pelton, William 106
Peltreau, Abraham 25
Pemberton, - Rev. 67;
Israel, Sr. 33; James
34; Joseph 197; Wil-
liam 154
Pendergast, William 117
Penn, - Gov. 188; Polly
163; Richard 163;
Springet 3
Pennington, - Capt. 210;
Isaac 76; Ralph Sir 210
Penny, George 46; James
54
Pepperrell, Hannah 119;
Isaac 119; William Sir
68
Percy, Alexander 9
Perfect, John 11
Perine, Henry 193
Perkins, - Capt. 4; Lt.
132; Jabez 159; James
123; Joseph 123
Permentor, Elias 160;
Mary 160
Peronie, - Capt. 36
Perot, John 38
Perry, - Mr. 130,136;
John 148,199; Joseph
116; Ruth 183,188;
Samuel 49; Thomas 183
Perse, William 235
Personel (alias Parsells)
Francis/Francis Burdett
174,175; Mary 175
Peterkop, William 106
Peters, - family 67; -
Rev. 204; Charles 120;
Edward 184; George 75;
James 217; Valentine
103; Valentine H. 120
Peterson, Andrew 3;
Walter 30
Petterson, George 72
Pettit/Petit, Thomas 226;
William 5
Pew, Robert 41
Pfotzer, George 175
Pheasant, James 31
Phelps/Phalps, Timothy
122; William 53
Phepoe, Thomas 227
Philips/Phillips, - Miss
220; Mrs. 220; Mr. 91;
Alexander 128,130;
Charles 161,237; Edward
218; Elisha 19; Fred-
erick 220; Frederick,
Jr. 220; John 47; John
Mandeirll 92; Jonas 93;
Joshua 103; Margaret
138; Philip 138; Thomas
224
Philipse/Phillipse,

Catharina 16; Elizabeth
48; Frederick/Fred. 15,
48,117,207; Philip 131;
Polly 207
Phipps/Phips, Spencer 51;
Thomas 22
Phoenix/Phenix/Phaenix,
Alexander, Sr. 148,150;
Daniel 103,148,150,159,
167
Pickles, William 242
Picksley, Noah 26
Pidgeon, Mary 104; William
75
Pierce/Pierse, - Lt. 92;
Elizabeth 33; Isaac 13;
John 63,136; Joshua 33;
Thomas 82,202
Pierson, John 148
Pike, Benjamin 24
Pilson, Robert 108
Pine, - Mrs. 167; Amos
191
Pinhorn, - Lt. 230
Pinkard, Jonathan 171
Pinkney/Pinkny, Elizabeth
66; Israel 66; Philip
164
Pintard, Anthony 22; John
22; Lewis 115,161,185;
Samuel 12,22; Susannah
161
Pitcher, James 236; Wil-
liam 141
Pitkin, William 141
Pitman, Caleb 10
Pittomee, John 5
Pitts, John 40
Platt/Plat, - Mrs. 199;
Epinetus 182; Jeremiah
148,199; Jonas 201;
Obadiah 77,149; Zepha-
niah 164
Platneer, Jacob 103
Plenderleith, Jennet 158;
John 158
Plocknett, Andrew 22
Plume, Isaac 169
Plumer, Benjamin 6
Plumstead/Plumsted,
Nathaniel 157; William
111
Plunket, Anne 24
Plymton, Priscilla 20
Plymun, Margrietta 38
Poel, John 101
Poillion, Abraham 134;
Peter 134
Polhemus, Daniel 128
Polhill, Nathaniel 80
Polk, - Lt. 232
Polleman, John W. 137
Polly, Samuel 58
Polson, - Capt. 36
Pomfret, Richard 37
Pontenner, Mary 210
Poole/Pool, Anna Sophia
20; John 107,119; Peter
20; Sarah 229; Thomas 37;
William 214
Popham, James 122
Porter, John 54; Stephen
122,138; Thomas, Jr. 13
Porterfield, - Capt. 232
Post, Adrian 203; David
201; Henry 228; John
236
Potter, Thomas 58

Pottinger, - Lt. 57
Potts, Isaac 150,204; Patty 150; Thomas 6
Pow, George 53
Powell/Powel, George 106; Morgan 181; Robert 106; William 97
Powelse, Jacob 15
Power, Bernhard 78; Catharine 78; Mary 78
Powers, Joshua 202
Pownall, - Capt. 225
Poyer, Thomas 4
Pratt, Benjamin 90; James 105; Joseph 107, 217; Margaret 128; Mary 175; Mica 175; Sarah 83
Pratter, - Lt. 63
Prentice, - Rev. 26; Edward 202
Prescot, Jonathan 62; Solomon 63
Presser, C. E. 41
Pressler, John 59
Preston, Jonathan 62; Joseph 11,62
Prew, William 110
Price, - Lady 26; Mr. 180,236; Charles 26; Edward 82,241; Enoch 237; John 70,80; Samuel 91,201; Walter 3; William 55,79,87
Prickett, Mary 151,157; Richard 151,157
Prideaux, - General 68
Pridey, Ann 116; William 116
Priest, William 31
Prime, Benjamin Young 193
Primmer, Johan Jury 36
Prince, Hezekiah 143; James 142; John 143
Prior/Pryor, Hannah 74; Stephen 74; Thomas 105; William 165
Pritchel, Walter 115; Winford 115
Probasco, Hendrick 157; Stoffel 157
Proby, - Major 60
Proctor, - Mrs. 78; Mr. 187; Carden 32; John 63
Prout, Ebenezer 4
Provoost/Provost/Prevost, - Capt. 140; David 173,231,232; Eve 130,133; John 95, 107,118,126,130,133, 146; J. M. 114; Katharine 146; Mary 126; Peter Prau 231; Samuel 130; William 133
Puffer, Abel 104
Pugsley, David 170; Gilbert 170; James 137,144,170; John 28, 69,137,144,170; William 137,144,170
Pulby, John David 186
Pummeroy, - Mr. 94
Puntiner, William 71
Purcel, Michael 57
Purdie, Nathan 164
Purry, Charles 38

Purviance, Andrew 240
Purvis, William 235
Puter, - Capt. 40
Putland, Heron 11,21
Putnam, John 62
Pye, Joseph 109
Pygan, Lydia 6
Pyra, Mary 39

Quackenbush/Quackenbos/ Quakenbos/Quackenboss/ Quackenbusch/Quackinbush, - Mr. 134; Annatje 110; Benjamin 49; Cornelius 19,110; John 88; Mary 88; Walter 155
Qualls, John 63
Quane, Mark 76
Quick, Jacobus 69; Thomas 43
Quigg, Charles 32
Quill, - Capt. 65; Thomas 167
Quinn/Quin, Felix 102; Francis 88; John 179; Patrick 110
Quinby, Daniel 56,198
Quincy, Dorothy 198; Edmund 198
Quite, Charles 125

Race, William 35
Racer, Benjamin 97
Rae, William 73
Raft, John 115
Rainhalt, Mathias 210
Raline, Jacob 138
Rall, - Capt. 233
Ralston, Joseph 90; William 133
Ramadge, Charles 127
Ramond, Joshua 69
Ramsen, Jacob 56
Ramsay/Ramsey, - Lt. Col. 242; Daniel 193; James 113,121; Thomas 56
Rand, Joshua 168; Robert 64
Randall/Randell/Randel/ Randle, Amenias 115; Edward 79; Peter 62; Thomas 138,158,184
Randolph, Hartshorne B. 195; Peyton 199
Ranelagh, Countess of 176
Rankin, George 208
Rapalje/Rapalye, - Widow 134; Abel 242; Abraham 243; Garret 144, 170; Jane 241; John 110,166,206,241; Rem 242,243; Stephen 166; Teunis 83
Rasper, John 6
Rassett, John 60
Ratcliff, William 14
Ratsey, - Widow 37; Alice 73
Rattery, - Ensign 60
Ray, Francis 23; Hannah 164; John 164; Richard 20,242; Robert 163
Rea, John 161; Richard 102,137
Read/Reade, see also

Reed, & Yates 141; (or Reid), Col. (John) 90; Anne 216; John 13,163, 185,187,194; Joseph 4, 13,131,152,163,185,187, 194,211,216; Joseph, Jr. 109; Kitty 185; Lawrence 109,184,187, 194; Mary 211; Peter 128,130; Polly 131; Susannah 90; Thomas (alias Cuthbert) 69; William 31,91
Reader, Jacob 70
Reading, - Capt. 3; Daniel 135; James 15; John 130,135
Reardon, Thomas 1
Reddington, Michael 230; Thomas 230
Reddon (or Redmon) - Mr. 174
Redmond, Andrew 157
Redstrake, John 7
Reece, John 76
Reed/Reid, see also Read, Andrew 79; Augustine 110; Ezra 159; James 159,202; John 201,224; John, Jr. 55; Joseph 123; Thomas 76; William 97
Reener, Jesse 182
Reese, Andrew 139; Robert 69
Reeve, Daniel 187; Mary 187; Nathan 198; William 77
Regilar, Leonard 125
Reiffarth, John Christopher 206
Reilb, James 26
Reily/Reilley/Reilly, see also Riley, Dennis 128; (or Relay), John 30; Susannah 231; Terrence 231
Reirson, George 135
Reisner, Casper 99
Remer, George 99
Remington, Israel 168
Remsen, - Widow 66; Arris 214; Daniel 132; Hendrick 66; Henry 156, 161,171,189; Jacob 58, 156,161,163,171; Janetje/Janetie/Janatje 156,161,171; Jeromus 204; Peter 66,134,156, 161,171; Simon 156,161, 171
Renaudet, Adrian 65,131; Andrew 64; Elizabeth 150; & James 64,65,131
Rensselaer, & Shipboy 94
Rescarricks, George 3
Resler, Jacob 222
Reuter, Valentine 137
Rey, John 108
Reynolds, - Capt. 16,95; Mrs. 95; Broughton 94, 138,156; Catharine 31; David 177; Grace 144; John 45,70,144; Michael 144
Rhinelander, William 227, 236
Rhodes, - Capt. 103

Ribble, Barbary 109
Rice, Abraham 174,187;
James 29; John 90;
Nathaniel 30; Samuel
122
Richard, Elizabeth 49;
John 49; Paul 48,49,
65; Stephen 9,32,49
Richards, - Capt. 122;
Lt. 97; Widow 28,107;
Elizabeth 153,154,161,
189; John 177,213;
Nathaniel 117,141;
Paul 189; Samuel 13,
145,147; Stephen/Ste-
phens 28,187; William
107
Richardson, - Capt. 61;
Mr. 161; Aweray 199;
Ebenezer 144; Elizabeth
238; Henry 74; John 30;
Joseph 179; Mary 179;
Thomas 132; William 54,
238
Richey, James 142; Wil-
liam 174
Richman, William 5
Richmon, Harmon 12
Ricker, - Widow 163;
Pener 126
Ricket/Rickets/Ricketts,
- Capt. 12; Col. 171;
Mrs. 153; Jacob 171;
John 197; Polly 74,171;
William 74,153,197
Rickman, William 227
Ricky, - (lad) 41; Brice
41
Riddle/Riddel, John 62;
Thomas 10; William 67,
111
Ridgely, Henry 28
Ridgeway, Elizabeth 84
Ridley, Nicholas 194;
Sarah 194
Riel, Abraham 171
Rigar, John 83
Rigby, Thomas 15
Riggs, Edward 108; Jo-
seph 176; Thomas 34
Right, Hendrick (alias
Henry Miller) 71
Riker, Abraham 108;
Andrew 108; John B.
108; Samuel 108
Riley/Riely, see also
Reily, Elizabeth 100;
Michael 92; Patrick
100; Thomas 169
Rind, William 177
Ringe, John 23
Ripenbergh, Adam 49
Ritchey, Alexander 127;
Jude 127; Robert 97
Rivet/Rivets, Tunis 27,
33
Rivington, Elizabeth 137;
James 137
Roach, Timothy 73
Robb, - Mr. 106
Roberts, - (a lad) 195;
Miss 210; Mrs. 154;
Mr. 93; Amos 33; Antho-
ny 19; (or German),
Charles 85; George 80;
Ichabud 169; J. 160;
John 89,111,132,154,
210; Joseph 241; Ste-
phen 70; Thomas 124;
William 92
Robertson, - Capt. 95;
Alexander 115,122,188,
190; Jane 239; Robert
231; William 73,121,
239
Robins/Robbins, John 69,
114,160,171; Nathaniel
Jr. 65; Samuel 137;
Zachariah 26
Robinson, - Capt. 142,
160; Mr. 125,131;
Andrew 191; Beverly
117,137; Beverly, Jr.
213; James 45; John
77,141,190; Joseph 66;
Lydia 141; Margaret 77;
Nancy 141,213; Richard
104; Robert 7; Sally
229; Samuel 2,59;
Septimus 120; Thomas
169,193; Thomas, Jr.
145; Timothy 92; Wil-
liam 86,94,99; William
T. 229
Robson, George 181
Rochead, James 23; John
23
Rodgers, - Miss 177;
Rev. 163,177,194;
James 223; Joseph 143;
Thomas 153; William 32
Rodman, James 17; John
223; Thomas 122
Rodrigo, Francis 203
Rodwell, William 75
Rogers, - Capt. 50,63,
170; Major 131,236;
Mr. 4,131,136; Betsy
81; Henry 221; Hugh
80; Isabella 221;
Peter 79; Richard/
Richd. 50,82; Robert/
Robt. 50,81,170; Simon
125; William 63,218
Rolph, Joseph 84,100
Romer/Romur /both errors
for Roome/7, - Alder-
man 7; Henry 120
Roney, James 118; John
240
Rook, Philemon 218
Roome/Rome, Henry 223,
227; William 16,27
Roop, John 182
Roorbach, Frederick 169;
Johannes 68
Roos (or Roose), Gerrit
170
Roosevelt/Rosevelt, -
Mr. 45; Cornelius 161;
Hannah 175; Isaac 162,
165; Jacobus 156,162,
175,203,210; Jacobus,
Jr. 93,161; Margaret
161; Nicholas 138,151
Root, Ezekiel 184; Oli-
ver 205; Seth 63
Ropes, Nathaniel 187
Rosbrugh, Robert 240
Rose, - Capt. 209;
Israel 44
Rosebottom, James 179
Roseman, James 58
Ross, - Ensign 57; Alex-
ander 33,189,194,201;
Anne 33; Charles 47;
David 89; George 32,
207; Isaiah 90; James
Isaiah/James I. 68,89;
James Josiah/James J.
92,100,105,109; John
7,73,203; Margaret 89,
90,92,109; Nathaniel
198; Rachel 198; Ro-
bert 182; Sally 194;
Stewart 223; Thomas 34;
William 53,202,223
Rothenbuhler, Frederick
80
Rothwell, William 10
Rouf, John 38
Rouse, Robert 43
Rousevel, - Widow 25
Rout, Simeon 169
Row/Rowe, Isaac 199; John
80
Rowland, Elijah 67; Sam-
uel 133
Rowley, Edward 9
Rowning, Morris 230
Rows, James 63
Royal, - Col. 12
Royce, Jo. 109
Ruckel, Jasper 238
Rudolph, Conrad 225
Rudyard, John 1
Rue, Lewis 85,91; (or
Roe), Matthew 42
Rumbold, - /Mr./ 162;
Rodolphus 162; Thomas
126,162; William 126,
162
Rumsey, - Widow 9; Phin-
eas 106
Runyon, - Mr. 164; Rich-
ard 198
Rup, John 185
Rusco, Nathaniel 36
Rush, John 42
Rushton, Catharine 217;
John 16; Peter 217
Russell/Russel, - Capt.
139,176; Sergt. 61;
David 92; James 194;
Matthew 175,176; Thomas
165
Rust, Robert 53
Rutgers, - Widow 64,65;
Adrian 182; Anthony 48,
73,170,181; Catherine
18; Cornelia 73; Eli-
zabeth 48,160; Harma-
nus/Hermanus 9,18,32;
Helena 33,181; Hendrick
73; Petrus 33,182; Ro-
bert 160
Ruth, Thomas 32
Rutherford/Rutherfurd, -
Major 60,70,71,232;
Helana 238; John 238;
Walter 112
Rutledge/Rutlidge, Andrew
41; Robert 117
Ryall, Abraham 118; Jo-
seph 133
Ryan/Ryon, Cornelius 119,
177; John 69; Lewis
202; Peter 11; Polly
202; Thomas 143
Ryckman, - Mr. 80; Isaac
128; Jacobus 64; John
15
Ryder, Barnardus 72; Hugh
95; Robert 71

Ryer, Teunis 170
Ryerson, Dirick 82;
  George, Jr. 26; Marten
  23
Rynders, Jacob 10,19
Ryneck, Andrew 105
Rypel, Catharine 80;
  John 80

Sackett/Sacket, James
  40,63,130; John 40,
  228,240; Joseph 40;
  Samuel 40,206,226;
  William 40,216
Sage, Ebenezer 70; Capt.
  G. 162
Sagers, Benjamin 199
St. Clair, Alexander 166;
  John Sir 127
Salier, Thomas 33; Wil-
  liam 33
Salmon, Elizabeth 175
Saltonstall/Saltonstal,
  Gurdon 120; Patty 120;
  Richard 48
Saltur, - Dr. 57
Samond, William 194
Sample, Henry 88; John
  142,143
Sampson/Samson, George
  62; James 94
Sanders, John 111; John
  Williams 190; Robert
  111
Sanderson, - Mrs. 149;
  Francis 104
Sands, Benjamin 150,152;
  Gideon 150,152; James
  104,142; Jane 16;
  Nathaniel 16; Richard
  150,152,229; Simon
  152
Sandwell, - Capt. 24
Sandwich, James 208
Sanford/Sandford, Ben-
  jamin 5; John 163
Sansom, Samuel 39
Sarly/Sarley/Sarle,
  Anthony 48; Elizabeth
  213,236; Jacob 204;
  James 12; John 12
Satel, Abel 61
Saunders, Abraham 184;
  Christianna 222;
  Constable 230; John
  201,222; Tom 179;
  William 62
Sause, Richard 231
Savage, Henry 141; James
  214; John 80,141;
  Joseph 147
Sawn, Richard 136
Saxton, Jirrard 89
Sayre, - Rev. 186; John
  23,229
Scandret, - Miss 219;
  Timothy 219
Scanet, Patrick 125
Scanlan, Dennis 118
Schaeffer, Henry 115
Schaterly, - /Mr./ 57
Schenk/Schenck/Schank,
  Abraham 135,189; Gitty
  194; Hendrick 122,194;
  Johannis 171; Lucas
  195; Peter 96,115,118,
  122,171,179

Schermerhorn/Schermer-
  horne, Cornelius 235;
  Jacob 150; John 61,
  134; Peter 227
Scherp, Jacob 14
Schick, Catharina Mar-
  garita 162; Christian
  162
Schiflin, Hannah 225;
  Jacob 225
Schinkle, Hendrick 40
Schlemmer, Arnold 215
Schneyder/Snider, Christ-
  opher 144; Hance 97;
  Philip 116
School, Christian 138
Schoonmaker, Martinus
  199
Schrock, Christian 231
Schultz, Christian 182
Schuyler, - Col. the
  younger 26; Mrs.
  (Arent) 9; Adoniah/
  Adonijah 89,91,93,
  158; Anne Elizabeth
  131; Arent 9,158;
  Brandt 149; Cornelia
  89; Derick/Dirick
  37,215; Elizabeth 167,
  173; Gertruyd/Gertrude
  89,93; John 23,89,93,
  158; Myndert 167,173;
  Peter 36,84,158; Phil-
  ip 89,108,132,158,195;
  Samuel 149; Stephen
  89
Scott/Scot, Alexander
  96; Ely 27; Francis
  45; George 51; John 4,
  148,195; John Morin
  182,197; Joseph 176;
  Marianne 4; Moses 130;
  Thomas 47; Upton 173
Scribner, Sam 4
Scrol, Herman (or Carrol,
  Manus) 27
Scudder, Joseph 163;
  Nathaniel 232
Scull, John 20,159;
  Robert 75
Sculthorp, John 107
Seabring/Seybring,
  Aeltye 27; Cornelius
  190; Frederick 39;
  Isaac 66; John 197
Seabrook, - Capt. 22;
  Tho. 13
Seabury, - Rev. 48,218,
  226,234; Miss A. M.
  234; D. 226; Elizabeth
  163; Mary 226; Polly
  48; Samuel 48,103,163
Seal, Thomas 133
Seaman, & Cock 233; -
  Mrs. 185; Benjamin
  137,170,231; David 84,
  137,170; Davis 170;
  Edmund 184,194; Eliza-
  beth 184,231; Hester
  194; Robert 160; Sam-
  uel 228; William 84,
  137,170,185; Zebulon
  84,137,160,170
Searle, James 22; John
  5,22
Sears, - 37; Capt. 69;
  George 99; Hester 183;
  Isaac 116,135,183

Secler, Abraham 52
Secord, Abigal 100; Dan-
  iel 100
Sedon, Henry 85
Seger/Segar, John 155,
  229
Selby, Thompson & 170
Selkrig, Grizzel 226;
  James 226,229
Sellard, - Mr. 20
Semple, William 139
Senior, William 76
Senseman, Catharine 41;
  Joachum 41
Sergeant, David 66;
  Martha 66
Seton, - Mrs. 198; Wil-
  liam 198
Sewall, - Rev. 20; Mar-
  garet 17; Stephen 17
Seymour/Seymore/Seamor,
  - Capt. 57,143; George
  146; James 178; John
  38,104; Robert 120;
  Sinclair 202
Shae, Francis 25
Shank, James 117
Shanks, - Mr. 215
Shannon, Hugh 59; James
  68; Robert 61
Sharp/Sharpe, Elizabeth
  123; Henry 18; Jacob
  153,154,161; James 77;
  Richard 182; Samuel 117
Sharpas, Elizabeth 70,72,
  167; William 12,22,167
Sharwin, Ann 243; Richard
  243
Shate, - Sergt. 85
Shaw, Alexander 64; David
  69,103; Charles 216;
  George 108,127,208;
  James 108,127; John
  108,127,190,241; Maria
  238; Mary 103; Neal 91;
  Sarah 216; William 150
Shay, John 203
Shearer/Sheerer/Sherer,
  Gilbert 86; John, Jr.
  167; Mary 167; William
  31,152,159
Shedman, John 80
Sheeff, James 19
Sheels, Timothy 59
Sheerby, Thomas 81
Shees, Matthew 109
Sheffield, - Mr. 130;
  James 120
Shields (or Sheets),
  James 166
Sheldon/Shelden, Elisha
  63; Isaac 70; Joseph
  67
Shelly, William 79
Shennan, John 2
Shepherd/Shephard/Shepp-
  ard, - Capt. 47; Mr.
  104; Michael 81; Wil-
  liam 152
Sheppardson, Jonathan
  106
Sheridan, - Mr. 43
Sherlock, Oliver 110;
  William 157
Sherman/Shearman, - Mr.
  130; David 156; William
  137
Sheron, Joseph 101

270

Sherrard, Francis 9;
John 223
Sherver, Joseph 126
Shewkirk, Gustavus 241
Shilling, Barnet 35
Shipboy, Rensselaer & 94
Shippen, Joseph 28
Shirley, - Gen. 44,49;
William 36,153
Shoals, John 54,56,143
Shober, - Mr. 97
Short, William 51
Shoults, John 105
Shreve, Thomas 78
Shurmur, John 9; Samuel
9
Shute, - Lt. 83
Sickles, Daniel 200;
Jacobus 45
Sidell, Augustus 233;
John 232; Magdalene
233
Siegler, Goodheart 204
Sileway, John 62
Simerman /Zimerman?7,
John Andrew 230
Simes, David 2
Simeson, Rem 74
Simmons, - Capt. 240;
Adam 132; Anne 119;
Peter 176; William 54
Simons, - Lt. 232; Mr.
107; Henry 127; John
174
Simonson, Aaron 190;
Frederick 144; Isaac
144; Jeremiah 144;
Johannis 155
Simpkins, - Mr. 214
Simpson/Simson, - Mr.
198; Catharine 191;
John 188,211,221; Jo-
seph 62,88; Margaret
211; Sampson/Samson
42,177,187; Sarah 88;
Solomon 187
Sims, James 35; John 84;
William 12
Sinclair, - Lady 137;
Jannett 200; John 3;
John Sir 137; Robert
171,174,187,200; Wil-
liam 206
Sineau, Peter 24
Singleton, Thomas 101
Sipkins, Rebecca 43
Sippens, William 231
Siscat, Samuel 123
Sisirey, Dorothy 58
Sisluf, John George 43
Skaats, Bartholomew 61,
68; Jacoba 61,68;
Renier 72
Skeene, Philip 206
Sket, Richard Barnsley
111
Skidmore, Jeremiah 186;
John 186; Samuel 151,
186
Skillman, - Mr. 228
Skinner, - Capt. 219;
Gen./Brig.-Gen. 218,
224; Mr. 26; Catharine
96; Cortlandt 119;
Elizabeth 119; Gert-
rude 224; Jonathan 176;
Stephen 88,90,96,119,
208; Thomas 221

Sleight/Sleght, - Mrs.
232; Elizabeth 87,94,
105; Matthew 87,94,
105,187,190,202
Slidell, Elizabeth 150;
John 131,150
Slinlang, Abraham 192
Slocum, Charles 207
Smallman, - Mr. 99
Smallpiece, William 44
Smathers, William 23
Smedes, Benjamin P. 171;
Jacob 171
Smedley, James 158; John
158; William 114
Smidt, Eve Mary 35
Smith, - Capt. 17,57;
Capt. Lt. 36; Col. 205;
Mrs. 176,178; Mr. 17,
125,133; Rev. 114,176;
Abijah 47; Abraham
124; Amos 77,85; Ben-
jamin 65,124,147,218;
Catharine 184; Cathar-
ine (alias of Cathar-
ine Conner) 19;
Charles Jeffery 147;
Christian 67; Christ-
opher 99,152,202,226;
Claudius 219; Daniel
33; (alias Griffith),
David 29; Edward 237;
Elizabeth 23,63,71,
203; Ephraim 151;
Ezekiel 9; Geertruyd
13; Gilbert 105,147;
Hannah Elizabeth (alias
Doliane) 67; Henry 58,
135; Hester 183; Hetty
159; Hugh 144; Isaac
239; Jacamiah 114,153,
173; James 12,38,100,
159,219; Jennet 158;
Jenney 29; Jesse 221;
Joanna 60; Johanna
202; John 2,8,23,30,
40,52,60,64,81,89,90,
100,103,108,135,159,
161,162,170,178,179,
184,188,204,243; John,
see Young, John 65;
John Peterson 34;
John W. 152; Jonathan
204; Joseph 197; Jo-
sias 185; Juliana 58;
Malcolm 147; Margaret
86; Mary 62,100,144;
Maurice 108; Michael
114; Obadiah 12;
Paschal Nelson/Paschal
N. 148,156,183; Pat-
rick 62; Peggy 198;
Perro 119; Phineas
176; Richard 17,155;
Richard R. 60; Robert
65,79,92,114; Samuel
10,137,196,204; Sarah
40,154; Simon 206;
Susannah 9,12; Thomas
2,18,63,125,139,171,
230; Timothy 135;
Waters 114,206,214;
William 5,9,38,40,47,
63,67,70,84,142,152,
158,163,182,203,214,
237; William, Jr. 29,
108; William Drewet
198; William Peartree/

William P./W.P. 32,144,
149,153,161
Smock, John 243
Smyth/Smythe, John 86,
182,201; Lionel 220;
Patrick 134,187; Susan-
na 86
Smythies/Smithies, - Mr.
208; William 235
Snabely, Jacob 59
Snaith, Thomas 189
Snedeker/Snediker, Gerret
163; Jacob 114; Johanna
163
Snell, Adam 42; Hannah
52
Snodgrass, Benjamin 125
Snow, Henry 154
Solem, Cornelius 5
Solomon, Isaac (alias
Isaac Jones) 196
Somerendick/Somerindick,
Egbert 111; Tunis 73,
111
Sonmans, Peter 8,17;
Sarah 8,17
Souder, Michael 57
Soumain, - Lt. 36
Souther, James 23
Southerland/Sutherland,
- Lt. 60; Widow 26;
Ebenezer 241; John 18
Sowers, - Capt. 68;
Nancy 139; Thomas 139,
184
Soye, Joost 2
Spafford, Asa 62
Span, Catharine 196;
Richard 196
Sparhawk, John 35
Sparker, Henry 131
Sparling, Philip 110,138
Speaight, - Mr. 173;
Richard 126
Speakman, & Carter 174
Speir (or Spear), William
(or Benjamin) 187
Speira, Jacob 122
Spellen, James 72,76
Spelling, - Capt. 52,59
Spence, Hugh 215; James
189
Spencer, George 22; John
115; Lucy 111; Nehe-
miah 111; Ruth 121
Spendelow, - Lt. 36
Spikeman, - Capt. 50
Spinkle, Daniel 31
Splitdorff, - Lt. 37
Spotswood, Alexander 11,
20
Spragge, Joseph 157
Sprigg, Thomas 235
Spring, Caspar 41
Springer, Gideon 69
Sprong, Cornelius 45
Sprow, James 51
Squire, Anabella 78;
Jonathan 141; Zophar
78
Staats/States, - Dr. 4;
Adam 38; Joachim 145
Stackey, - Widow 24
Stacy, William 198
Stagg/Stag, - Mr. 193;
Caleb 164
Stahl, Daniel 41
Standall, John 126

271

Standard, Thomas 72
Stanford, - Capt. 174
Stanley/Stanly, John 12;
  William 117
Stanton, - Capt. 95; Dan-
  iel 146; Giles 235;
  Jeremiah 99,157,162,
  218; Phineas, Jr. 137
Stap, Thomas 39
Stark, Abraham 151
Starn, Jacob 138
Starr, - Mrs. 35; James
  189
Start, James 105
Stearndall, John 132
Stebbins, - Mr. 62
Stedman, Alexander 198;
  Peggy 198
Steed, Deborah 34; Smith
  34
Steel, - Mrs. 67; Joseph
  217; Thomas 77,197
Steenson, Robert 53
Steinbuchs, Jacob 49
Stelle/Stell, Gabriel 21;
  Peter 117
Stephens/Stephen, Alex-
  ander 132; Francis 131,
  211; Mary 211; Michael
  165; Polly 131; Thomas
  161
Stephenson, Henry 153;
  John 176
Sterland, James 18
Stevens, - Capt. 28,40;
  Miss 148; Campbell 11;
  Charles 59; George 31;
  James 3; (or Stephens),
  James 127; John 11,47,
  148; Joseph 50; Peleg
  101; Phinehas 44
Stevenson, Benjamin 146,
  184,196; Daniel 134;
  Edmund 182; Edward 184,
  196; Gloryanna/Glory
  Anna 184,196; James 98,
  137; Jane 117,121;
  John 166,190; Mary 190;
  Robert 190; Thomas 134,
  221
Steward, - Dr. 215
Stewart/Steuart, & Nicoll
  202; Templeton & 141,
  190; - Ensign 60; Lt.
  60; Lt. Col. 232; Mr.
  61,151; Adam 220;
  Alexander 154,158,165,
  186,202,241; Andrew
  140; Arthur 198; Ben-
  jamin 125; Daniel 100;
  Duncan 120; Henry 63;
  James 62,134,151,206,
  226,229; John 83,85,
  102,125,151; Joseph
  125; Lazarus 155; Mary
  241; Michael 155;
  Nancy 120; Patrick 238;
  R. 226,229; Robert 79,
  125; Susanna 186; Wil-
  liam 49,123,126
Steymets, Benjamin 123;
  Christopher 123; Peter
  123
Stickney, James 124
Stike, Nicholas 68
Stiles/Styles, - Capt.
  71,145; Daniel 35
Still, James 48; Michael
  11
Stillwell, Catharine 43;
  Dan 13; Richard 25,43;
  Samuel 125; Thomas 70
Stilsen, - Mrs. 136
Stimble, Isaac 105
Stimson, Abraham 62
Stinson, James 58; Marg-
  ery 58; Thomas 50
Stinton, John 96
Stirling/Sterling, Earl
  of 72,90,194; Alexander
  32
Stites, - Miss 230; John
  230
Stockholm, Aaron 78
Stockton, John 58; Rich-
  ard 78; Robert 53;
  William 40
Stoddard, - Mr. 57; Rob-
  ert 35; William 94
Stoddert, - Capt. 40
Stone, - Capt. 36; Mr.
  36; John 169; White 7;
  William 209
Stoneman, Abigail 189
Stoops, Nicholas 129
Storey, John 210; Joseph
  80
Stork/Storke, Edward 88;
  Samuel 32
Storm, Joris 60
Storrs, Lemuel 116
Stoughton, John 131;
  Ruth 131
Stout, Benjamin 71; Ben-
  jamin, Jr. 237; John
  B. 236; Zebulon 7
Stoutenburgh/Stouten-
  burg, Anthony 155;
  Isaac 192; Jacobus 60
Stow, Jonathan (alias
  "Johnsey") 15
Strachan, - Widow 145;
  Catharine 136; James
  134,136
Strangford, Lord Vis-
  count 220
Straw, - Mr. 218
Street, Nathaniel 132
Strickland, John 157,
  180
Striker, James 226;
  Polly 226
Stringe, Charles 217
Stringer, Robert 67
Stuart, - Col. 241;
  Elizabeth 78; William
  78
Studden, John 130
Sturdevant, Eliphalet
  (alias Eli Betts) 198
Sturgeon, William 149
Stuyvesant, - Alderman
  4; Col. 226; Nicholas
  W. 226; Peter/P. 170,
  210,211,226
Stymes, Benjamin 121;
  Christopher 121,150
Suddler, - Mr. 32
Suer, David 158
Sullivan, Daniel 133;
  John 5,118; Owen 46,
  80; Timothy 108
Summers, Sarah 87
Supinye, Peggy 218
Supple, Catharine 56;
  Daniel 56; Garrit 56
Suthard, Abraham 102
Sutton, - Capt. 19; Jo-
  seph 145; Martha 145,
  227; Richardson 145;
  Robert 227
Swaaner, - Mr. 109
Swales (or Swait), John
  30
Swan, - Capt. 33; James
  77,82; Timothy 63;
  William 185
Swane, - /Mr./ 163
Swartwout, - Mrs. 46
Sweeny, Lawrence 69,145
Sweet, Godf. 13
Sweeten, John 225
Sweigart/Swigard, George
  41; Peter 161
Sykes, Samuel 129
Sylvester, Daniel 209;
  John 163
Symes/Syms, Catherine 16;
  John 7; John Hendrick
  16; Mrs. William 18
Symonsen, Simon 84

Tabry, Anthony 126
Taggart, James 77
Tak, Abraham 124; Maria
  124
Talbot, - Capt. 236;
  Midsh. 36; George 17;
  St. George 123,129
Talmash, Hon. J. 210
Talmon, - Dr. 216; Miss
  216
Tankard, George 87; Wil-
  liam 173
Tappa, - Mrs. 67
Tappen, Aneke 7; Asher
  91; Isaac 185; Jurian
  7; Mary 91
Tar, William 209
Tasker, Elias 92
Tate, Anthony 123; George
  208
Tatton, - Capt. 36
Tayler, Daniel 12
Taylor, & De Lancey 171;
  - Mr. 44,79; Charles
  N. 229; Edward 81;
  Elizabeth 51; George
  204; Jacob 125; James
  28,136; Joab 54; Job
  49; John 78,86,102,112,
  135,183,208,210; Joseph
  59; Justus 156; Kitty
  86; Margaret 79; Mary
  44,131; Morford 238;
  Peter 159; Robert 51;
  Solomon 87; Thomas 164;
  Willett 210; William
  77
Teber, William 15
Teeple, James 111
Tell, Richard 39
Temple, Grenville 135;
  John 120,135; Robert
  37,135; Thomas 179
Templer, - Capt. 137
Templeton, & Stewart 141
  190; Kitty 187; Oliver
  187
Ten Broeck/Ten Brook/
  Ten Broek, Abraham 63,
  187; Cornelius 133,170;
  John 33,87

Ten Eyck/Ten Eych,
 Barent 112; Catharine
 231; Coenrad 35; Izyn-
 tie 240
Tennent, Gilbert 104;
 William Macky 177
Ter Bush, Henry 119;
 Simon 119
Terhuner, Albert 198
Terrat, Peter 232
Terry, Arthur 179; Edmund
 184; Joice 180; Richard
 179; William 179,184
Tetard, I. G. 186
Tettermary, Richard 199
Thayer/Thair, David, Jr.
 17; Elizabeth 33;
 Ephraim 33
Tharp, - Mr. 218; James
 Murphy 192
Thatcher, Bartholomew
 156; Elizabeth 156
Theall, Charles 108
Therlo, John 135
Thirsby, Richard 208
Thodey/Thody, Betsey 74;
 Elizabeth 50,58;
 Michael 50,58,65,74,
 142
Thomas, - Capt. 204; Mrs.
 240; Widow 33; Benja-
 min 106; Edward 130;
 Evan 6; John 8,29,30,
 127,157; Joseph 91;
 Lewis 214; Michael 120,
 121; Nathan 189; Sarah
 130; William 218
Thompson, & Alexander
 137; & Selby 170; -
 General 231; /Mr./ 109;
 Adam 126; Alexander
 132; Barshaba 132;
 Benjamin 118; Catharine
 30; David 117; Francis
 27; Humfrey 196; James
 30,81,102,169,171,187;
 John 5,22,73,80,102,
 154,172,231; John
 (alias of John Barnes)
 11; John, Jr. 39;
 Jonathan 183; Jonathan,
 Jr. 183; Joseph 175,
 207; Malege 105; Pat-
 rick 116; Polly 171;
 Robert 218; William
 52,117,165,175
Thomson/Tomson, Benjamin
 115; Margaret 178;
 William 115,166,178,
 211,232
Thorn/Thorne, Daniel 165;
 John 128,153; Joseph
 211; Peter 102; Stephen
 211; Stephen, Jr. 211;
 Richard 91; Thomas
 235; William 94,107,
 112
Thornhill, John 239
Thorp, - Mrs. 167; John
 167; Joseph 188;
 Michael 74; Peter 54
Throckmorton, Joseph
 243
Thurman, Francis 57,64,
 68; John 68; John, Jr.
 64,85
Thurmond, John, Jr. 57
Thurston, Edward 236;

John 148; Peleg 148;
 William 4
Tice, Gilbert 178
Tidd, Benjamin 42; John
 52
Tidmarsh, - Mr. 16
Tiebout/Tebout, Bartholo-
 mew 67; Cornelius 56,
 81; John 67
Tienhoven, Cornelius 19
Tiffany, Parthenia 182;
 Timothy 182
Tilghman, Richard 188
Tilldine, George 7
Tillinghast, Charles 104
Tilton, Margaret 230;
 William 230
Tilyou, Ann 144; Peter,
 Sr. 144; Vincent 144
Tims, - Mr. 92
Tingley, Agness/Agniss
 114,118; Samuel 114,
 118,128,129
Titcomb, - Col. 40
Tiffort, - /Mr./ 62
Titlefer, Mrs. Michal
 57
Tittle, John 165
Titus, Edward 56; Samuel
 139; Timothy 182
Tobler, Ulric 72
Todd/Tod, - Capt. 6,15;
 Mr. 6,15; James 197;
 Robert 5; Thomas 92;
 William 140,197
Tol, Daniel 27
Tollman, Stephen 49
Tolmie, - Capt. 171;
 Normand/Normond 170,
 239
Tolon, Barnabas 58
Tomlinson, John 238;
 Joseph 158,160; Nathan-
 iel 86
Toms, Simeon 47
Ton, John 167
Tongue, William 207
Tooker, Charles 165;
 Daniel 53
Toomer, John 37
Topham, - Capt. 91
Tork/Torke, John 7,16
Torrans, John 35
Torrey, - Lt. Col. 242
Torry, - Rev. 36
Tostbinder, Jacob 99
Totten, Daniel 183;
 Gilbert 183; Joseph
 140,183,214; Peter 183;
 Peter, Sr. 183
Towner, Deborah 13,22
Townley, George 23;
 Richard 149
Townsend/Townshend, -
 Col. 68; Lt. 36; Ben-
 jamin 65,76,170;
 Elizabeth 155; George
 82; Jacob 182; James
 159; John 152,155,183;
 Samuel 152,155,183
Towrs, Lawrence 126
Tracy/Tracey, - Ensign
 159; Elisha 105; John
 164; Warrant 95
Traile/Trail, George 96,
 222,229
Trainer, Peter 163
Travers, William 190

Treadwell/Tredwel, Ben-
 jamin 237; John 20;
 Samuel 156; Thomas 94
Treat, - Rev. 202
Treby, - Capt. 91
Trecothick, Barlow 152
Tree, Jacob 97
Treehill, - Dr. 85;
 Martha 85
Trench, William 125
Treville, Sir John 189
Trickey, William 59
Trigleth, - Miss 163
Trim, Ezra 104
Tripp, James 171
Trott, Benjamin 6
Troup, John 56,195; Rob-
 ert 27,136
Trout, Henry 221
Trubey, Andrew 65
Trumbull, - Gov. 224;
 Madam 224
Trump, - Mr. 52
Truxton, Thomas 81,82,
 111
Tryon, - Gov. 178,226;
 Miss 156; Mrs. 156;
 William/Wm. 156,195
Tucker, - Capt. 178;
 Abraham 163; George 107;
 James 65,69,71,137;
 John 84; Mary 71;
 Morris 119; Stephen 30;
 William 138,140
Tuder, John 176,203;
 Mary 203
Tull, Thomas 139
Tume, - Lt. 13
Tunis, Hannah 7; Peter
 7
Turk, Jacobus 144,223
Turnbull, - Mrs. 95;
 Catharine 213;
 George 213
Turner, Benson & 71;
 Carpenter 97; Enoch 20;
 John 32,33,234; Joshua
 4; Michael 71; Robert
 31; Thomas 116
Turvey, Daniel 195;
 Nathaniel 208
Tuthill, Daniel 34; James
 188; Jemiah 188
Tuttele, Nathaniel 203
Tweed, James 223
Tweedy, Amy 140; Jenny
 140; John 140,142;
 Nathaniel 142
Twells, Rachel 16
Twining, David 160
Tworbirdge, Thomas 199
Tyron, Ellis 124
Tytler, Isabella 242;
 Peter 242

Underhill, Franklin &
 106; - Mr. 195; Amos
 223; Benjamin 223;
 David 223; Isaac 223;
 John 76; Nathaniel 191
Ungar, - /Mr./ 206
Unker, Philip 123
Up De Graave, Catharine
 104; Peter 104
Upham, - Major 237; Eli-
 zabeth 237
Urine, Gideon 217

273

Urquhart, Walter 206
Ury, John 23
Ussal, - Ensign 230
Ustick, Betsey 223;
  Henry 176,199; Jane
  151; Stephen 151;
  Susannah 243; William
  151,223,226,243
Ute, Andrew 190

Vail, John 205
Valentine, Isaac 210;
  John 103; Joseph 109;
  Mark 173; Thomas 180
Valette, Peter 30
Vallade, Peter 115
Vallard, - Mrs. 185
Valleau, Peter 17
Van Aertsdalen, Dirck 24
Van Aken/Vanaken, Cor-
  nelius 42,43
Van Allen/Vanalen, Eli-
  zabeth 26; John 121,
  123; Lyckas 26
Vanalst, Andrew 35
Van Alstyne, Cathrine
  28; Matthew 137; Sarah
  137
Van Antwerpen, Daniel
  27; Johannes Peter 27
Vanberentlau, John Henry
  133
Van Bergen, Martin 113
Van Blarcum, Isaac 196
Van Brents, Adrian 89,
  90
Van Brughen, Peter 154
Van Buskerk/Van Buskirk,
  Lawrence Janse 40,188
Van Camp/Vancamp/Van
  Kamp/Van Kemp, Mrs.
  Gilbert 43; Guizebert
  42; Jacob 59; Jacobus
  51
Vance, John 53
Van Cliff (or Kliff),
  Geetie 5
Van Cortlandt/Cortlandt,
  see also Courtlandt, -
  Col. 185; Augustus/
  Aug. 123,185,210;
  Cornelia 160; Mrs.
  Francis 225; Frederick
  48,225; Geertruydt 5;
  James 190,230; Mary
  49; Nancy 48; Philip
  66; Pierre 66,160,190;
  Stephanis 5; Stephen
  49,58,66
Van Court, Elias 87
Van Dam, Corne & 37;
  John 237; Rip 18,35,
  157; Sarah 18
Vandeburgh, Henry 146;
  William 146
Van Den Bogart, Frans,
  Jr. 27
Van Den Ham/Vandenham,
  - Mr. 141; John 243
Vanderbilt/Vanderbelt,
  - Mr. 222; Cornelius
  126; Garret 134; Jacob
  141; John 134,143,241;
  Mary 141
Vander Heyden/Vanderhey-
  den, Cornelius 124;
  Hendrick 124; John 45;

Maria 124
Vanderhoff/Vanderhoof,
  - /Mr./ 54; Eleanor
  96; John 96
Vanderlip, - /Mr./ 158
Vander Pool, Malgert 24
Vanderspiegel, Anne/Anna
  9,18; John 9,18,148
Van Der Veer/Vanderveer/
  Van Der Vear, Belitje
  145; Cornelius 207,
  243; Cornelius, Jr.
  243; Dominicus 34;
  Jacobus 139; John 145
Vandervoort, Peter 191
Vandewater/Van Dewater/
  Vanderwater, Baffie
  24; Henry 93; Peter
  223
Vandeursen/Van Deursen/
  Van Duersen, Abraham
  87,134,137; Annaka 87;
  Hendrick 190; Henry
  202; Hester 87;
  William/Wm. 190,202
Van Duehren, J. Bernard-
  us 135
Van Dyck/Van Dyke/Van
  Dike, - Mrs. 5; Abra-
  ham 112; Francis 53,
  185; Henry 198; John
  170,214; Nicholas 185;
  Reolof 149; Rudolphus
  38
Van Etten, John 173
Vanfleara, Hans 42
Vangada, Peter 97
Van Gelder/Vangelder, -
  Mr. 5; Widow 37; Collin
  157; David 16; Garit
  150; Johannes 14;
  John 16,49
Van Gezan, Mary 84
Van Gordey, Peter 43
Van Hoesen, Rynier 27
Van Horne/Vanhorne/V.
  Horne/Van Horn, -
  Major 67; Abraham 50,
  100; Andrew 139; Anna/
  Anne 109,163; August-
  us 61,110,163; Cathar-
  ine 134,214; Cornelius
  29,61,137,196,241;
  Cornelius C. 173;
  Cornelius G. 14,57,74;
  David 68,91,117,137,
  199; Elizabeth 137,
  166; Garret 10,109,
  163,166,194; Garrit/
  Gerrit 19,57,61,74;
  Hannah 165; Helena 21;
  James 78; Joanna 194;
  John 65,165,192,200;
  Mary 241; Polly 91
Van Houstan, Johannis
  153
Van Houten, Elias 64;
  Margaret 196; Roillof
  196
Van Imburg/Van Inburgh,
  Gilbert 25,83
Van Ivere, Ide 73; Mynd-
  ert 73; Sarah 73
Van Kleeck/Van Kleck,
  Balshazer 66; Baltus
  150; Lawrence 150;
  Leonard 150; Myndert
  184

Vanlieu, John 151
Van Mater, Daniel 139
Van Nander, Hendrick 218
Van Ness/Vanness, Abra-
  ham 125; Henry 126
Van Nest, Jacob 30
Van Norden, Tobias 152
Van Nostreen, - Mr. 228
Van Nordstrant/Van
  Norstrant/Van Nore-
  strant/Van Nortshand,
  Albert 118,123; Garret
  118,123; Casparus 22
Van Pelt, John 27,84
Van Petta, Philip 164
Van Ranst/Van Rans, -
  Capt. 100; Cornelius
  24,88,90; Hester 194;
  Luke 88,90,135; Peter
  194
Van Rensselaer/Van
  Renslear, Elizabeth 63;
  John 187
Van Riper, Christian 223
Van Schaak/Van Schaick,
  Elizabeth 215; Jacob,
  Jr. 51; Peter 215;
  Wessel 157
Van Sickle, John, Jr. 75
Van Slyck, Adrian 27
Van Solingen, Godard 47,
  50
Van Tassal/Van Tessel,
  Margaret 112; William
  130
Van Tine, John 133; Mary
  133
Van Tuyl/Van Tyle, Andrew
  170; Dennis 44; Otto
  137,170
Van Varck, Andrew 75;
  Else 75; James 75,171
Van Varick, Effee 236;
  James 197
Van Veghten, - Lt. 209;
  Ephraim 119; Naltie
  119; Val. 119
Van Vleck, - Dr. 84;
  Abram 71; Abraham H.
  198; Catharine 128;
  Henry 169; Isaac 240;
  John 128; Margaret 240
Van Voorhies/Van Vorhis,
  - Widow 196; Zacharias
  111
Van Wagenen/Van Wagenan,
  Hubert 235,237; Jacob
  55,70
Van Wyck, - Capt. 204;
  Abraham, Jr. 46,52,72;
  Cornelius, Jr. 71;
  Mary 72; Richard 71;
  Theodorus 72,88; Theo-
  dorus, Jr. 150; Theo-
  dorus C. 44,46; William
  150
Van Wye, Lawrence 68
Van Zandt/Van Zant/Van-
  zant, Catharine 57;
  Jacobus 57,142; John
  35; Katharine 241;
  Peter Pra 93; Tobias
  57; Wynant/Wyn. 57,
  152,241
Vardee, George 102
Vardill, - Mrs. 226;
  Thomas 226
Varian, James 138

Vassal, Polly 145; Richard 145
Vatar, Thomas 38
Vathiest, John 210
Vaughan, Catharine 82; Mrs. Henshman 16
Vaughtan, James 198
Vaux, - Mr. 47
Veeder, Johannes 105; Simon J. 105
Vernon, Fortesque 34; Martha 156; Moses 11; (alias Allman), Thomas 25
Verplanck/Verplank, - Mrs. 72; Mr. 118; Abraham 166; Anne 51; Effe 199; Gulian 38,75; Isaac 166; James 160; Nancy 75; Philip 160, 199
Versereau, - Lt. 204
Verwy, Lawrence 157
Vesey, Mary 74; William 74
Vessels, - Widow 37
Vetch, Margaret 59
Vicetur, Adam 186
Vickers, William 91
Vielie, Cornelius 26
Vincent, Abraham 86; Charles 134; Francis 4; Judith 4; William 86
Vining, Benjamin 7; Betsey 238; Mary 238; Michael 238
Vinton, - Mr. 11
Viscoup, Daniel 38
Visger, Johannes 18
Vollweiller, Jacob Hendrick 16
Voorhees, see also Van Voorhies, Hendrick 114; John 101; Peter 114; William 114
Vosburgh, Peter 220
Vose, - Col. 232
Voss, Edward 164
Vought, John 71
Voughton, Michel 8
Vredenburgh, William 72, 217

Waddell/Waddel/Waddle, - Mrs. 184; Anne/Ann 86, 90,174; Geesie 169; Henry 183; Hugh 15; John 75,86,90,158,174, 183; William 169,183
Waddington, - Mr., Jr. 229; Mary Ann 229
Wade, - Capt. 225; Mr. 94
Wadsworth, Benjamin 156
Wageman, Elizabeth 102; Michael 102
Wagener/Waggoner, - Lt. 37; John 215
Wagstaff, Richard 51
Waite/Wait, Aaron 149; John 120
Wakeman, Charles Lee 202; Peter 202
Wald, John 62
Waldo, - Brigadier General 67
Waldron/Waldren, Ann/

Anne, 146,162; Catharine 148,150,162; Cornelia 162,171; Cornelius 46; Daniel 75; David 146; Elizabeth 171; Johanna 75; John P. 171; Judith 162; Mary 162; Peter 11, 171; Richard 78,193; Samuel 162,170; Sarah 162; William 146,202
Walgrave/Walgrove, George 18,211
Walker, - Dr. 91; Mr. 144; James 181,235; John 92,141; Robert 164; Thomas 18,86,224; William 51
Wall, - Mr. 32; Helena 76; Henry 187; Robert 31
Wallace/Wallis, Abigail 120; Alexander 153, 168,170,241; Anne 151; Gamaliel 120; Hugh 47, 73,112,153,193,196, 221,240,241; James 4, 86,214; James Sir 214; Jane 168,170,174; John 56; Sally 73; Thomas 174; William 151
Waller, Peter 198
Waller, John 51
Walsh, - General 235; Walter 51
Walter/Walters/Waltars, - Capt. 37; Rev. 225; Casper 47; John 68, 131,197,227,236; Robert 3; William 133
Walton, - Madam/Mrs. 133,134; Catharine 30; Helena 31; Jacob 30,31, 72,133,231,237; Mary 123,231,233,237; Polly 72,231; Thomas 163; William 16,54,123,133
Wanser, Thomas 80
Wanton, Elizabeth 237; John 22; Joseph, Jr. 225,241; William 237
Warburton, - /Col./ 54
Ward, - Capt. 149; James 191; Jonas 64; (alias Murray or Morgan), Luke 115; Moses 178, 241; Samuel 202; Stephen 72,132; Thomas 74; William 59,174, 199
Warder, Jeremiah 239; John 122; Lydia 122
Ware, Charles 32,38
Warne, Elizabeth 66; Joshua 66; Thomas 66
Warner, - Mr. 240; Edward 34; Elihu 62
Warrell/Warrel, Mr. J. 10; Joseph 79
Warren, - Lady 29; Mr. 19; Widow 160; John 167; Joseph 143; Peter Sir 34,150,160,167; Samuel 183; Stephen 80; Susan Lady 167; William 196
Warrey, Sangrey 210
Warrin, John 169

Warring, Jacobus 63
Washborn/Washbourn, Ebenezer 103; Thomas 62
Washington, - Col. 241; Gen. 203,224; Augustine 10; Nancy 203; William 71
Wasson, John 46
Watens, William 58
Waterman, - /Mr./ 158; John 94,96
Waters, - Mr. 151; Aeltye 39; Anthony 125; Anthony Whitehead 157; Benjamin 131; Daniel 107; Foster 4; James 1; John 39, 223,235; Robert 207; Sarah 107; Talman/ Talmon/Tolman 157,223, 235; William 1,223,235
Watkins, Mary 210; Richard 210
Watson, - Capt. 117; Mrs. 184; Mr. 95,203; Alexander 184; Isaac 207; James 53; John 17, 66,81,134,185; Matthew 109; Peter 104; Thomas (alias of John Burns) 172; Wallace 81
Watts/Watt, - Capt. 28; Lt. 67; Mrs. 197; Alexander 54; Jane 198; John 29,138,175,194, 197;; John, Jr. 198; Mary 194; Nancy 138; Polly 175; Robert 194; Thomas 33
Waugh, - Lt. 231
Way, Isaac 170; Samuel 228
Wayne, Robert 10
Waynman, Sarah 231; William 231
Wear, William 196
Weatherly, Benjamin 69
Weaver, John 204; Samuel 24; William 69,126,129; William (alias of William Connel) 61
Webb/Web, - Col. 203; Rev. 23; Charles 198; John 49; Joseph 62,79; Samuel 61,185
Webber/Webbers, Arnout 65; John 29; Jonathan 29; Wolfart 65
Webster, Francis 125; John 29
Wedgood, William 93
Webster, Martha 125
Weeks, George 154; Jonas 124
Weems, James 2
We?ein, Mary 9; William 9
Weight, - Mr. 135
Weigner, Christopher 97
Weissenburg, Catherine 21
Weissenfels, Frederick 242
Welch, - Mr. 117,139; Catharine 110; Enoch 189; James 69; Nicholas 39; Patrick 151; Richard 55; Thomas 202; William (alias of

Welch (cont'd), William
(alias of George Kelly)
32,37
Weld, Edmond 27
Welder, Samuel Stansbury
94
Wells/Welles, - Miss 186;
Mr. 211; Alexander 164;
Harrison 217; Rev. N.
186; Obadiah 32; Sam-
uel 201; Thomas 6
Welsh, - Mr. 99,169;
John 102; Robert 73
Wendell, Abraham 15;
Evert 93; Henry 179;
John 93
Wentworth, Frances 142;
Hugh 56; John 3,142
Weply, Henry 138
Wessels, Anne 182; Fran-
cis VanDyck 128; Law-
rence, Jr. 130; Wessel
83
Weseneer, Christian 171
West, Hannah 143; John
105
Westbrook, - Capt. 98;
Lt. 58; /Mr./ 58;
Abraham 59; Cornelius
59; Gideon 59
Westcot/Wescot, - Capt.
122,138
Westervelt, Benjamin 109
Westgate, Earl 87
Westlick, John 204
Westover, Oliver 102
Wetherholt, - Capt. 96
Wetmore, Charles 218;
Gurdon 208; James 73
Wetterstroom, - Capt. 47
Weyman, Anne 240; Hester
141,208; William 133
240
Wezer, - Mr. 47; Lenard
47
Whaley, William 195
Wharry, James 108; Jo-
seph 121
Whatnell, John 17
Wheate, Jacob Sir 238;
Maria 238
Wheeler, - Mr. 235;
Nathaniel 158; Sarah
115; Simon 61
Wheelwright, John 75;
Nathaniel 143
Wheeton, - Mr. 6
Whelpley, Joseph 61
Whichcotton, - Lt. 64
Whipple, Joseph 20
Whippo, James 115
Whiston, - Mr. 151; Oba-
diah 221
Whitcom, Joseph 27
White, - 37; Capt. 54,
102,232; Ensign 57; Mr.
183; Alexander 101,178;
Ann 231; Anthony 145,
160,164,179; Benjamin
54; Daniel 162; Ebene-
zer 147; Eleanor 7;
Fanney 179; Henry 77,
151,179,193; John 89,
150; Joseph 102,113;
Margaret 151; Mary 8;
Moll (alias of Mary
Lyhin) 83; Peter 1;
Robert 8,174,175; Sarah

95; Thomas 39,231; Tim-
othy 74
Whitefield, George 148
Whitehead, - Capt. 221;
Benjamin 226; William
195
Whitehorn, Samuel 118
Whiting, - Major 67
Whitman, Joseph 170
Whitmore, - Brigdier
General 83
Whitney, - Capt. 52
Whyte, Alexander 133
Wickham, Ann 135; Samuel
30,116
Wideman, - Lt. 36
Wier/Wieer, Daniel 233;
William 34
Wiel, Thomas 58
Wigg, John 76
Wiggins, William 11,20
Wigneron, Charles Antho-
ny 167
Wilcox/Wilcocks/Will-
cocks, John 190; Jo-
seph 50; Nancy 50;
Stillwell 50; Timothy
160; Timothy, Jr. 160
Wild, William, Jr. 35
Wilder, Josiah 13,22;
Thomas 120
Wileman, Henry 19
Wiley/Wily, Edward 206;
John 53,203; William
104,132
Wilkes/Wilks, James 36,
40,43; Sarah 36
Wilkie, - Mr. 83
Wilkins, - Major 88;
Jacob 203,215
Wilkinson, James 134
Wilkison, Edward 162;
Mary 162
Will, Henry 183
Willard, Abijah 217;
Habijah 217
Willett/Willet, - Col.
226; Mr. 219; Miss
-cie 219; Abraham 50;
Christopher 132; Elice
226; Elizabeth 132,
135,206; Frances 1;
John 78,89,195; John,
Jr. 26; Patty 48;
Thomas 48,50,65,69,
135,195; Richard 84,
137,170
Williams, - Capt. 18,74,
234; Col. 40; Dr. 99;
Mr. 18,36; Anne 94;
Benjamin 62,96,214;
Cathrine 28; Charles
48,66,67,76,86,109,
153,175; Daniel 42;
Dorothy 56; Eleazer 84;
Elijah 142; Elizabeth
48; Erasmus 73; Hannah
160; Henry 142; Honor
39; Isaac 53; James
98; John 1,7,39,59,
101,102,141,145,160,
208,228,237; Joseph
12; Lydia Mary Anne
38; Mark 66; Mary 121;
(alias M'Guire), Mary
120; Nancy 151; Nathan-
iel 236; Nathaniel, Sr.
233; Nicholas 85; Pat-

rick 122; Philemon 89;
Rachel 236; Rice 13,
56,60,66; Richard 122;
Robert 160; Sarah 237;
Stephen 236; Temperance
160; Thomas 4,90,94,
145,180; Thomas Charles/
Thomas C. 236,237;
William 84,86; Zebulon
160,170
Williamson, David 114,121;
George 99; James 97;
Margaret 7; Matthias
161; William 7
Willing, Charles 34;
Mary 59
Willington, - Lt. 210
Willis, Hannah 138;
Isaac 138; John 171;
Samuel 177
Willoc, William 43
Wilmot, Henry 206; James
107
Wilson/Willson, - Capt.
127; Lt. 202,232; Mrs.
214; Mr. 104; Rev. 114;
Abraham 207,214; Alex-
ander 151,171; Archi-
bald 90,208; Elizabeth
Louisa 125; Francis 30;
Godfrey 131; James 15,
56,65,69,74,78,202;
Jane 151; John 11,85,
99,128,131,153,215;
Joseph 173; Mary 128,
153; Richard Montgomery
203; Robert 85,103,188;
Samuel 53,54,191; Thom-
as 59,182; William 38,
114,203
Winant/Winants, Josiah
101; William 110
Winklepleigh, John 53
Winkler, Gertruid 16;
Herman 16
Winslow, - Col. 56; Ed-
ward 32; Isaac 21,207;
John 211,232; Joshua
196
Winter, William 187
Winterbottom, Bristow &
126; James 194
Winthrop, Francis B. 218
Wipey, Joseph 188
Wister, Casper 140
Wither/Withers, George
188; John 61
Witter, Catharine 198;
Thomas 198
Wolf/Wolfe/Wolff, Cathar-
ine 72; Conradt 155;
Elizabeth 68; Jacob 41;
Jenny 155; Matthew 72;
Patrick 68
Wolfes, Frederick 201
Wood, - Ensign 73; Mr.
35,235; David 79; Ebe-
nezer 124; Esther 120;
Isaac 240; Jeremiah
130,187; John 62,204,
242; Joseph 163; Peleg
114; Stephen 21; Thomas
6; W. 69; William 36,
69,105,206
Woodbridge, - Mrs. 86
Woodcock, Ebenezer 94
Woodcock, Ebenezer 62
Woodford, - /Mr./ 92

Woodhouse, Anthony 75; Matthew 213
Woodhull, Henry 49; Jesse 241; Martha 49; Richard, Jr. 183; Sarah 183
Woodlock, - Capt. 30
Woodruff, Benjamin 133; Elizabeth 133; Isaac 133,144,156,161; Jehiel 79; Joseph 88,153,161; Joseph, Jr. 133,144; Mary 103; Samuel 103, 133,161; Uzal 88,90
Woods, - Mrs. 216; John 49,216
Woodward, - Capt. 57; Anthony 111; Caleb 62; Francis 121; Joseph 7; William 121
Woodworth, Douglas 169
Woolcock, Lewis 73
Woolley, Henry 165
Woolman, Asher 106
Woolsey/Woollsey, Benjamin 48,159; Francis 215; Melancthon Taylor 70
Woolven, John 72
Worley, John 43
Worrel/Worrall, Isaac 140; John 92
Worth, Samuel 35,49
Worthington, James 6,15
Wortman, Annauchy 227; George (alias of Yerry) 167; Hetty 227
Woster, John 195
Wraxwall, Peter 68
Wray, George 94,100,113; John 223
Wriesberg, Daniel 177
Wright, - 231; Lt. 37; Mr. 22; Sergt. 61; Anne 101; Daniel 112; Elizabeth 88; James 241; John 38,79,132, 170; Jonas 171; Jonathan, Jr. 88; Jones 53; Joseph 26; Mary 32,39; Rebeckah 138; Richard 101,122; Robert 201; Samuel 138; Thomas 87, 112,208; William 38, 51
Wünsch, Felix 46
Wyckoff/Wickoff/Wickhoff, Henry 204,211; Nicholas 147
Wyer, - Deacon 139
Wynkoop/Wynkop, Cornelius 17; Lucas 112; Margaret 112
Wynne, - Capt. 60
Wyrick, Nicholas 27

Yager, Henry 27; Martin 52
Yarley, Samuel 172
Yates/Yeates, Read & 141; - Mrs. 235; James 235; Leonard 96; Mary 107; Richard 187,193,194
Yelverton, Gale 82; John 33
Yeth, William 44
Yetman, Mathew 211

Yeoman/Yeomans, - Mr. 187; James 173
York, Daniel 28; James 17
Young/Youngs, - Mr. 106; Widow 142,144; David 142,144; Hamilton 159, 219; John 62,100,139, 189; (or Smith), John 65; Joseph 115,214

Zeegers, Adriana 210
Zabriskie/Zabriski/Zobriski, - Miss 178; Elizabeth 184; George 215; John 184,189; Peter 178
Zedwitz, H. 194
Zeislof, George 44
Zenger, /Mr./ 18,25,26
Zepperly, Frederick 21
Zimmerman, Andrew 227
Zublee, - Rev. 231
Zuricher/Zuriker, - Mr. 130; Johannes 183; John 130
Zutphin/Sutphin, Dirick 114,185

Persons with No Surname (Indians,Kings, Slaves, etc.)

Abel 164
Aberdeen 97
Abraham 127,149,209
Aesop 40
Afer 154
Amelia 82,92,98
America 197
Andrew 209
Angle 145
Anthony 35,68,81,210,242
Arch 149

Bacchus 220
Baptist 96
Bellow 145
Ben 106,110,117,141,157, 161,198,202,224,237
Bet 66,211
Betty 207
Bill 115,197
Billie 135,136
Billy 239
Bina 219
Bohenah 70
Bret 173
Bristol 53,62,177,210, 232
Brit 153
Bromlow 74
Brunce 132,139
Brutus 154

Caesar 23,34,52,72,78, 86,105,134,185,194, 201,206,219,236
Castalio 81
Caster 204
Catharine 78,116
Cato 17,108,109,115,124, 141,146,147,157,164, 165,197,204,206
Cesar 73

Champaign 94
Charity 209
Charles 75,86,102,112, 115,118,155,163
Chess 208
Claus 4,23,166
Clause 3
Cockchick 72
Constant 190
Cuba 59
Cudjoe 234
Cuff 54,135,185,227
Cush 171
Cyrus 67,82,99,118,207

Daniel 207,215
David 233
Diamond 190
Diana 214
Dick 48,68,147,149,163, 169,209,210,216,219, 242
Dido 137
Dige 117
Dina 85,242
Dover 123
Dublin 111,112,120
Duff 241
Duke 100,209,223

Edward 21
Emanuel 103
Esther 219

Fanny 89,90
Feonce 206
Fil 156
Flora 68
Fork 210
Fortune 106
Fountain 211
Franck 49
Frank 51,75,139,157,160, 207,209,220,236
Frank (alias Francisco) 105

Garrick 134
George 92,140,158,221
Gin 78
Glasgow 72,121
Golloway 22

Hack 188
Hager 173
Hannable 132
Hannah 116
Hannibal (alias Sandy) 56
Harman 210
Harre 132
Harry 11,26,65,83,88,132, 162,174,243
Harry (or Traso) 102
Hector 48,110,230
Hester 214
Hezekiah 7
Hugh 31

Isaac 155
Isabella 218,221,228
Isaiah 125
Ishmael 147,154
Ismael 145

Jack 5,10,19,21,102,103, 110,139,154,167,169, 185,186,203,206,218,

Jack (cont'd), 219,225,
    226,227,236,241,242
Jack (alias John Johnson)
    77
Jack (or Selem) 81
Jacob 68,77,94,100,105,
    204,223
James 9,146,150,171,227
Jane (or Gin) 219
Jeffery 150
Jem 84
Jenny 10
Jeremy 35
Jerrey 69
Jerry 37
Jessemy 209
Jim 117,136,141,145
Jin 107
Job 6
Joe 5,32,47,81,94,96,
    110,116,122,196,206,
    210,215
John 94,107,149,243
John Baptist 157
Johnny 17
Jonas 132
Jordan 81
Joseph 112
Juba 86
Jude 233
Jupitor 22

Kane 150
Kate 58,96,134,223
Kelso 223
Kinsale 75

Lawrence (or Launce) 225
Lena 80
Lester 220
Licum 47
Lill 149
Lissa 235
London 68,84,117
Loo 82
Loui 207
Luce 241
Lucy 85
Lydia (aunt of Richard
    Tell) 39

Manuel 163
Martin (alias of Dick)
    68
Mincer 147
Ming 199
Mingo (or Tim) 167
Minto 226
Moll 214
Mount 105

Nanny 227
Nat 211
Nathaniel 204
Ned 137,171,206
Nero 86,191
Nicholas 167
Nick 112,113
Noke 135
Norway 133

Old Briton 29
Oliver 196
Osborn 208

Paddy 27
Pamela 202
Paris 226

Patience 6
Peet 163,191
Peggy 59
Pero 11,173
Peter 2,39,83,121,132,
    145,209,214,220
Phillis (or Phillida)
    38
Philip 41
Pitchford 177
Plato 164
Plymouth 209
Pollydore 82
Pomp 68,149
Pompey 105,209
Port-Yoyal /Port-Royal?/
    192
Primus 26,68,74,103,
    123,211
Prince 24,68,82,89,90,
    110,119,187,204,207,
    231
Princess 74
Priscilla 94
Prym 157

Quash 3,134

Rachel 222,227
Ralph 55,64
Rick 51
Robert 82
Robin/Robbin 23,60,74,
    77,87,112,163
Rose 112

Saloue 149
Sam 40,96,126,170,201,
    208,219,220
Sambo 166
Sarah 4
Sarah (alias Jenny) 73
Sawny/Sawney 123,230
Scipio 3,136,141,211
Scotland 171
Shadrack 47
Shadwell 94
Shier 132
Simon 66,202
Singo 169
Somerset 88
Squire 225
Stephen 192,221
Stephen (alias Pompey)
    134
Stoffil (or Stoffels) 4
Storde 26
Suck 78
Susan 216
Sy (or Cyrus) 152
Sylvester 82
Sylvia 123,233
Syme (or Symon) 153
Syphax 211
Syrus 202

Tack 117
Teer 5
Tite 206
Titus 198
Tobey/Toby 8,17,110
Tom 7,24,32,51,65,70,
    72,73,77,95,106,117,
    125,144,153,154,156,
    164,197,201,202,205,
    210,215,218,225
Tone (or Anthony) 68,110
Toney/Tony 38,55,114,123,

221

Vanhall 73,123,124
Venus 121

Wall 77,85,95
Wan 51
Ware 210
Wequalia 1
Whitlow 95
Wilkes 209
Will 74,82,148,151,157,
    159,189,206
William 148,154,243
Windsor (alias Jammy) 73
Wooster 8,17

Yaff 2
Yerry (alias George Wort-
    man) 167
York 26,58,83,95,148,206,
    208